Lecture Notes in Business Information Processing 583

LNBIP reports state-of-the-art results in areas related to business information systems and industrial application software development – timely, at a high level, and in both printed and electronic form.

The type of material published includes

- Proceedings (published in time for the respective event)
- Postproceedings (consisting of thoroughly revised and/or extended final papers)
- Other edited monographs (such as, for example, project reports or invited volumes)
- Tutorials (coherently integrated collections of lectures given at advanced courses, seminars, schools, etc.)
- Award-winning or exceptional theses

LNBIP is abstracted/indexed in DBLP, EI and Scopus. LNBIP volumes are also submitted for the inclusion in ISI Proceedings.

Massimo Marchiori · Francisco García Peñalvo ·
Karl Aberer
Editors

Web Information Systems and Technologies

20th International Conference, WEBIST 2024
Porto, Portugal, November 17–19, 2024
Revised Selected Papers

Springer

Editors
Massimo Marchiori
University of Padua
Padova, Italy

Francisco García Peñalvo
Salamanca University
Salamanca, Spain

Karl Aberer
EPFL
Lausanne, Switzerland

ISSN 1865-1348 ISSN 1865-1356 (electronic)
Lecture Notes in Business Information Processing
ISBN 978-3-032-25533-4 ISBN 978-3-032-25534-1 (eBook)
https://doi.org/10.1007/978-3-032-25534-1

This Springer imprint is published by the registered company Springer Nature Switzerland AG
The registered company address is: Gewerbestrasse 11, 6330 Cham, Switzerland

Preface

The present book includes extended and revised versions of selected papers from the 20th International Conference on Web Information Systems and Technologies (WEBIST 2024), held in Porto, Portugal, from 17 to 19 November.

The purpose of the International Conference on Web Information Systems and Technologies (WEBIST) is to bring together researchers, engineers and practitioners interested in the technological advances and business applications of web-based information systems, covering different aspects of Web Information Systems, namely Internet Technology, Web Intelligence and Semantic Web, Social Network Analytics, HCI in Mobile Systems and Web Interfaces.

WEBIST 2024 received 69 paper submissions from 20 countries, of which 17 (25%) were included in this book. The high quality of all the accepted papers was guaranteed by a strict double-blind review process in which submissions received three reviews each on average.

The best papers included were chosen by the event chairs and their selection was based on a comprehensive number of criteria that included the classifications and comments provided by the program committee members, the session chairs' assessment and also the program chairs' global view of all papers included in the technical program. The authors of selected papers were invited to submit revised and extended versions of their papers with at least 30% innovative material.

The papers selected to be included in this book contribute to the understanding of relevant trends of current research on Web Information Systems and Technologies, all covered by the ongoing WEBIST series. Being a broad field, WEBIST looks to be comprehensive in its coverage, and so the topics include Human-Computer Interaction, Generative AI Application Development and LLM Engineering, Natural Language Processing, New Trends in Internet Technology, Social Information Systems, Artificial Intelligence for the Web, Applications, Research Projects and Web Intelligence, Big Data and the Web, and last but not least Computational Intelligence on the Web and Decision Making.

We would like to thank all the authors for their contributions and also the reviewers who once again have helped ensure the high quality of this publication.

November 2024

Massimo Marchiori
Francisco García Peñalvo
Karl Aberer

Organization

Conference Chair

Massimo Marchiori	University of Padua, Italy

Program Co-chairs

Francisco García Peñalvo	Salamanca University, Spain
Karl Aberer	EPFL, Switzerland

Program Committee

Cesar Analide	University of Minho, Portugal
Demis Ballis	University of Udine, Italy
Jorge Barbosa	University of Vale do Rio dos Sinos, Brazil
Faiza Belala	Constantine 2 University, Algeria
Claudio Biancalana	Roma Tre University, Italy
Fernando Bobillo	University of Zaragoza, Spain
Roberto Boselli	University of Milano-Bicocca, Italy
Sabin Buraga	Alexandru Ioan Cuza University, Romania
Marut Buranarach	National Electronics and Computer Technology Center, Thailand
Pasquina Campanella	University of Bari "Aldo Moro", Italy
Allaoua Chaoui	University of Constantine 2 - Abdelhamid Mehri, Algeria
Pedro J. Clemente	University of Extremadura, Spain
Liviu-Adrian Cotfas	Bucharest University of Economic Studies, Romania
Christophe Cruz	Université Bourgogne Europe, France
Daniel Cunliffe	University of South Wales, UK
Guglielmo De Angelis	IASI-CNR, Italy
Flavio De Paoli	University of Milano-Bicocca, Italy
Toon De Pessemier	Ghent University - Imec, Belgium
Enrico Denti	Alma Mater Studiorum - Università di Bologna, Italy
Erdogan Dogdu	Angelo State University, USA

Martin Drlik	Constantine the Philosopher University in Nitra, Slovak Republic
Larbi Esmahi	Athabasca University, Canada
Przemyslaw Falkowski-Gilski	Gdańsk University of Technology, Poland
Giuseppe Fenza	University of Salerno, Italy
Luís Ferreira Pires	University of Twente, Netherlands
Flavius Frasincar	Erasmus University Rotterdam, Netherlands
Piero Fraternali	Politecnico di Milano, Italy
Xiang Fu	Hofstra University, USA
Massimiliano Garda	Università degli Studi di Brescia, Italy
John Garofalakis	University of Patras, Greece
Prashant Goswami	Blekinge Tekniska Högskola, Sweden
Gregor Grambow	Hochschule Aalen, Germany
Volker Gruhn	University of Duisburg-Essen, Germany
Carlos Guerrero	Universitat de les Illes Balears, Spain
Shanmugasundaram Hariharan	Vel Tech Rangarajan Dr. Sagunthala R&D Institute of Science and Technology, India
Ioannis Hatzilygeroudis	University of Patras, Greece
Sebastian Heil	Technische Universität Chemnitz, Germany
Sergio Ilarri	University of Zaragoza, Spain
Monique Janneck	Lübeck University of Applied Sciences, Germany
Karel Jezek	University of West Bohemia, Czech Republic
Christos K. Georgiadis	University of Macedonia, Greece
Mohsen Kahani	Ferdowsi University of Mashhad, Iran
Georgia Kapitsaki	University of Cyprus, Cyprus
Sokratis Katsikas	Norwegian University of Science and Technology, Norway
Dragutin Kermek	University of Zagreb, Croatia
Ilan Kirsh	ObjectDB Software, UK
Matthias Klusch	German Research Center for Artificial Intelligence (DFKI) GmbH, Germany
Fernando Koch	Independent Researcher, Brazil
Hiroshi Koide	Kyushu University, Japan
Fotios Kokkoras	University of Thessaly, Greece
Birgitta König-Ries	Independent Researcher, Germany
Petr Kremen	Cognizone, Belgium
Isaac Lera	Universitat de les Illes Balears, Spain
Martin Llamas-Nistal	University of Vigo, Spain
Angelica Lo Duca	IIT-CNR, Pisa, Italy
Francisco J. Lopez-Pellicer	Universidad de Zaragoza, Spain
Marco Manso	PARTICLE SUMMARY, Portugal
Andrea Maurino	Independent Researcher, Italy

Miroslaw Mazurek	Rzeszów University of Technology, Poland
Michele Melchiori	University of Brescia, Italy
Santiago Meliá	Universidad de Alicante, Spain
Walt Melo	Georgetown University, MITRE, USA
Owen Molloy	University of Galway, Ireland
Thomas Moser	St. Pölten University of Applied Sciences, Austria
Cédric Mouza	CNAM, France
Martin Musicante	Universidade Federal do Rio Grande do Norte, Brazil
Akiyo Nadamoto	Konan University, Japan
Akihito Nakamura	University of Aizu, Japan
Anand Nayyar	Duy Tan University, Vietnam
Artur Niewiadomski	University of Siedlce, Poland
Alex Norta	Tallinn University of Technology, Estonia
Daniel O'Leary	University of Southern California, USA
Marcin Paprzycki	Polish Academy of Sciences, Poland
Kalpdrum Passi	Laurentian University, Canada
David Paul	University of New England, Australia
Salvatore Flavio Pileggi	University of Technology Sydney, Australia
Bhanu Prasad	Florida A&M University, USA
Jim Prentzas	Democritus University of Thrace, Greece
Birgit Pröll	Johannes Kepler University Linz, Austria
Muhammad Asif Razzaq	Insight SFI Research Centre for Data Analytics, University of Galway, Ireland
Marina Ribaudo	Università di Genova, Italy
Thomas Risse	University Library Johann Christian Senckenberg, Germany
Davide Rossi	University of Bologna, Italy
Comai Sara	Politecnico di Milano, Italy
Georg Schneider	Trier University of Applied Sciences, Germany
Wieland Schwinger	Johannes Kepler University Linz, Austria
Leonardo Scommegna	University of Florence, Italy
Álvaro Sicilia	La Salle, Ramon Llull University, Spain
Selver Softic	CAMPUS 02 University of Applied Sciences, Austria
Christoph Stach	University of Stuttgart, Germany
Aleksandar Stanimirovic	University of Niš, Serbia
Eliza Stefanova	Sofia University, Bulgaria
Dragan Stojanovic	University of Niš, Serbia
Giorgio Terracina	University of Calabria, Italy
I-Hsien Ting	National University of Kaohsiung, Taiwan
Gianluca Torta	Università di Torino, Italy

Christos Troussas	University of West Attica, Greece
Liliana Patricia Valencia	King Juan Carlos University, Spain
Costas Vassilakis	University of the Peloponnese, Greece
Jari Veijalainen	University of Jyväskylä, Finland

Invited Speakers

Oscar Pastor	Universidad Politécnica de Valencia, Spain
Abraham Bernstein	University of Zurich, Switzerland
Mark Wilkinson	Universidad Politécnica de Madrid, Spain

Contents

Internet Technology

Web Intelligence and Semantic Web

Internet Technology

AI for Enhanced Public Services Gov.br

João Gabriel de Moraes Souza[1(✉)], Maísa Kely de Melo[2], Allan Victor Almeida Faria[1], Carlos David Castro de Souza Neto[1], Fause Carlos Mascarenhas Lustosa Junior[1], Li Weigang[1], Vinícius Di Oliveira[1], Pedro Carvalho Brom[1], Silvia Araújo dos Reis[1], Vérica Freitas[3], José Francisco Salm Junior[4], Herbert Kimura[1], Daniel Oliveira Cajueiro[1], Gladston Luiz da Silva[1], and Victor Rafael R. Celestino[1]

[1] University of Brasilia, Formiga, Brazil
jsouza@unb.br
[2] Federal Institute of Minas Gerais - Formiga, Formiga, Brazil
[3] Uberlandia Federal University, Santa Monica, Brazil
[4] Santa Catarina State University, Florianopolis, Brazil

Abstract. This paper presents an innovative methodology for integrating artificial intelligence (AI) into the Brazilian federal government's digital services, addressing the challenge of managing nearly 40 federal entities, 180 public agencies, and up to 5,000 public services. The proposed approach enhances efficiency, accessibility, and service quality by combining Lean Office, Design Sprint, Analytic Hierarchy Process (AHP), and advanced AI techniques, particularly Large Language Models (LLMs). Developed in collaboration with project management teams, public servants, and stakeholders, the methodology systematically identifies demands, selects AI projects, and prototypes solutions tailored to complex government environments. As a practical application, we implement a generative AI agent within the Gov.br portal, capable of interacting with citizens, answering inquiries, directing users to services, and facilitating human escalation when necessary. The results demonstrate how AI-driven solutions can optimize public service delivery, improve citizen participation, and streamline government operations. By providing a replicable framework, this research contributes valuable insights for governments worldwide, particularly in developing countries, seeking to leverage AI for digital transformation in public administration.

Keywords: Government AI · Public services innovation · Large Language Models (LLMs) · Digital government transformation

1 Introduction

The public sector increasingly adopts artificial intelligence (AI) to improve operations and service delivery [24], with at least 142 AI applications in federal administrations [12]. AI enhances government transparency, effectiveness, and efficiency [7,14,27], supporting both internal processes and citizen interactions through Information and Communication Technologies (ICTs) [17]. Key AI technologies, including machine learning (ML), natural language processing (NLP), and computer vision, enable automation, data analysis, and personalized services.

M. Marchiori et al. (Eds.): WEBIST 2024, LNBIP 583, pp. 3–17, 2026.
https://doi.org/10.1007/978-3-032-25534-1_1

AI applications in the public sector span diverse areas: facial recognition in policing [3], recidivism prediction [37], virtual agents for automation [34], social services forecasting [11], chatbots [6], healthcare [39], public transport [16], education [8], environmental management [13], and agribusiness [19]. These initiatives improve service accessibility and citizen engagement [33].

Despite its potential, AI integration in public administration requires clear strategies. The Brazilian federal government aims to define best practices for selecting AI projects. A methodology developed by [25] under the project "Artificial Intelligence Research Applied to the Prototyping of Solutions for the Federal Government's Artificial Intelligence Office" maps, prototypes, and documents AI solutions. Aligned with the Secretariat of Digital Government (SGD) [4], this approach supports AI governance, data models, and analytical tools to enhance public policy and service delivery. As digital transformation advances globally, this methodology provides a framework for AI adoption in government services.

It also details the step-by-step methodology for selecting and prototyping projects in AI Decision-Making in the Public Sector. This methodology was developed and applied in collaboration with AI and project management expert researchers, members of the SGD, and other bodies comprising the Brazilian Government's Artificial Intelligence Hub (NIA). Figure 1 illustrates NIA, highlighting partner institutions' diversity.

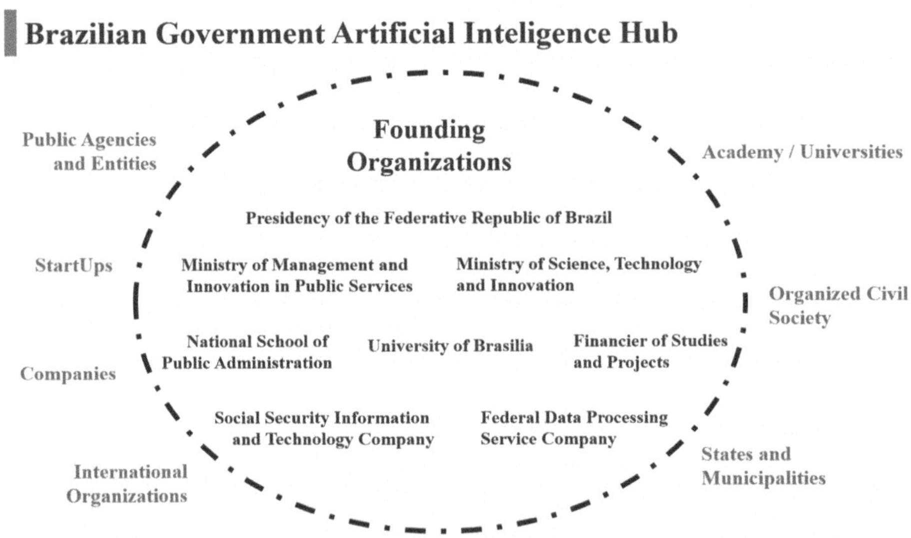

Fig. 1. Brazilian Government Artificial Intelligence Hub (NIA) [25].

This paper reports the results of the application of the methodology in federal government agencies , highlighting the recommended practices and the results obtained. The project selected for prototyping, resulting from the demands identified by the participating public agencies , was the Gov.br portal service [5]. This portal comprises pages from nearly 40 federal entities and 180 public agencies, integrating up to 5000 public services. More than 150 million Brazilians access it and record approximately four thousand accesses per second [15]. The prototyping involved the development of an Advanced Generative Agent to interact with citizens, assist them, clarify doubts, and direct them to the requested service pages, with human overflow in necessary cases.

The main contributions of this study are as follows:

- A structured methodology for selecting, prototyping, and deploying AI solutions in public administration, balancing technical feasibility with policy alignment.
- A novel approach combining Lean Office, Design Sprint, and AI-driven optimization to enhance public service efficiency and citizen accessibility.
- The application of Retrieval-Augmented Generation (RAG) techniques to improve interaction in government chatbots, ensuring contextual accuracy and responsiveness.
- A case study demonstrating the implementation of an Advanced Generative Agent for the Gov.br portal, highlighting practical challenges and lessons learned.
- Insights into AI governance and scalability in digital government transformation, offering a replicable framework for other public administrations.

These contributions provide a foundation for future AI-driven initiatives in public services, ensuring more efficient, scalable, and user-centered solutions in government operations.

2 Related Work

Implementing AI in the public sector requires addressing challenges such as explainability, data governance, and infrastructure. Although AI-human collaboration improves tasks and creates jobs, managing mistrust and resistance is crucial. A key question is whether engaging stakeholders – including citizens and suppliers – should be considered part of AI-human collaboration or a separate process supporting AI adoption. Stakeholder involvement promotes innovation, but requires clear regulations and governance [24]. If included within AI-human collaboration, this broadens the concept beyond workforce integration to external interactions with AI systems. However, treating it separately emphasizes the need for independent policy frameworks. With no unified legal framework for AI, most countries focus on process regulation rather than the legal status of AI-generated outputs [1]. This distinction is critical to shaping AI governance in public administration.

From a research perspective, gaps remain in understanding AI's impact on public values and governance challenges [7,17,24,26]. Government employees' perceptions of AI's role in governance and public administration require further study, as debates continue on whether AI will fundamentally transform the sector [17].

AI's growing relevance in government has drawn interest across disciplines, but this diversity often leads to fragmentation in theoretical and terminological approaches [35]. Technical research frequently overlooks real-world applications, and many AI typologies lack integration with existing frameworks. Despite the increasing discourse, AI adoption in the public sector lags behind the private sector [26]. Scholars agree that AI theory must provide tangible value to practitioners, as human oversight remains central in enforcing rules and public safety [2,7]. Governments face challenges in integrating social science insights with AI's technical aspects, making it difficult to establish clear priorities for AI governance [35]. Since AI in government is still in its early stages, current conceptualizations will shape future expectations [35]. The current AI in public services initiatives has been briefly examined by [25].

3 Empowering Services: AI Framework

A standardized methodology is essential for AI implementation in public services. To support the National Artificial Intelligence Strategy, [25] proposed a comprehensive approach for identifying demands, selecting projects, designing solutions, and prototyping AI applications in public administration. This methodology was developed through an extensive literature review, identifying key findings, limitations, and future potentials of AI in government. Additionally, the concept of Meta AI – learning to learn about AI – was applied through systematic applied research.

The methodology addresses the question: What is the best method for selecting AI projects in government when subjective judgment and numerous alternatives are involved? A literature review identified Multicriteria Decision Analysis (MCDA) methods, with the Analytic Hierarchy Process (AHP) [30] emerging as the preferred approach for project selection. To handle multiple alternatives efficiently, AHP Express [21] was selected.

Beyond project selection, Lean Office principles were integrated to enhance service efficiency and reduce bureaucratic overhead. A dual literature review on digitalization and Lean practices further refined the approach. The final methodology, developed in collaboration with AI researchers and the Secretariat of Digital Government (SGD), aligns with Brazil's unique public administration needs. The process steps are detailed in Fig. 2.

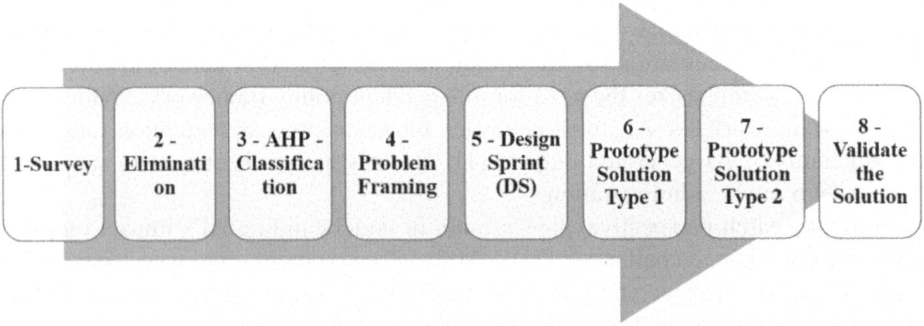

Fig. 2. Process for Project Selection and Prototyping [25].

4 Detailed Execution: Phase Guide

The development of the survey was based on the academic experience of the project team, as no specific survey was identified in the literature. The Design Sprint methodology was customized based on Design Sprint 3.0 [36]. At the grantor's request, a preamble to the survey was prepared, with guidelines for the application and use of AI models in public administration. The preamble contains content on premises for the preparation of guidelines, the definition of generative AI, applications of generative AI in government, and the limitations of generative AI and LLMs. From the survey, a list of possible projects and problems requiring solutions is obtained, which, after being selected and prioritized by the AHP Express multicriteria method, proceed to problem framing and, subsequently, to the design sprint phase. This survey was carefully designed to suit different levels of AI maturity in the agencies, aiming to collect specific knowledge about public sector processes associated with problems and needs that can be framed as strategic projects and addressed with AI-based solutions.

The selection of AI projects in the public service is a challenge that involves considering multiple criteria and stakeholders. AHP Express offers a systematic approach to handling such complex decisions, allowing the comparison of different projects based on a weighted criteria set. The Multiple-Criteria Decision Making Models, which include AHP Express, aim to establish a relationship of (subjective) preferences among the alternatives being evaluated/prioritized/ordered under the influence of various criteria in the decision-making process [28]. The Analytic Hierarchy Process (AHP) is a multi-criteria decision-making method that uses hierarchical or network structures to represent a decision problem and develops priorities for alternatives based on the decision makers' judgments [29]. It has been observed [30] that the formula for calculating the inconsistency of judgments and the maximum acceptable level usually shows low consistency when there are comparisons involving more than nine elements. Therefore, Step 2 - Elimination was devised by the authors of this work to resolve more than nine alternatives [31].

The step-by-step application of the AHP Express method is detailed in [21]. It follows the principles of traditional AHP, whose framework can be seen in [9,29]. The main difference is that, as the AHP Express method assumes judgment consistency, there is no need to calculate inconsistency. From the judgment of the preferred alternative, obtaining the values of the other pairwise comparisons through the relationship established in the initial judgment line is possible. The AHP Express method was chosen for being suitable for the agile project management model.

The Elimination phase (Step 2) was designed to achieve two main objectives: (i) eliminating AI project proposals deemed infeasible during the Survey phase and (ii) ranking the remaining proposals by maturity level in descending order. A structured set of criteria and sub-criteria was established to assess AI solutions. Initially formulated by AI specialists, including the authors of this study, these criteria were refined with input from stakeholders within the NIA. Table 1 presents the criteria and sub-criteria used to evaluate the feasibility of each AI project proposal. The detailed application of these criteria is described in [25].

These criteria encompass technical feasibility, data requirements, proposed solutions, societal impact, and strategic alignment. Responses to evaluation questions include: "YES," "NO," or "I DON'T KNOW." If any proposal receives a "NO" response for any sub-criterion, it is automatically eliminated. "YES" responses are scored as "1," while "I DON'T KNOW" responses are scored as "0." The final score for each proposal is obtained by summing all responses, and projects are ranked in descending order. Following this ranking, the top nine projects advance to the next phase, where they undergo further evaluation using the AHP Express method to determine priority and feasibility for prototyping.

In Step 3 - AHP Classification, the AHP-Express method, as detailed in [25], was utilized to classify and prioritize AI projects across various government sectors. The criteria, tailored for agile project management, were structured with sub-criteria and presented during stakeholder interviews:

1. **Urgency of Solution**: Estimated time required to solve the problem without AI, impact of inaction, and potential for increasing urgency.
2. **Availability of Data Sources**: Quality of internal data, cost and time required for acquiring external data.
3. **Broader Population Reach**: Number of affected individuals, geographical distribution, and accessibility across different income levels and digital skills.
4. **Greater User Value**: Expected user benefits, ease of use, and time savings.
5. **Projected Access Volume - Cost Estimate**: Estimated access volume per period, expected growth trends, and seasonality.
6. **Lower Technical Effort**: Problem complexity, availability of development tools, developer expertise, solution replicability, and maintenance difficulty.
7. **Ease of Implementation**: Integration with existing systems and regulatory compliance.
8. **Risks, Ethics, and LGPD (Brazilian Data Protection Law)**: Identified risks, ethical concerns, and compliance with LGPD.

Stakeholder meetings were essential for applying AHP Express. The process involved presenting up to nine project proposals from Step 2 (Elimination), the eight criteria, the Saaty Scoring Table, and an explanation of the methodology. Participants first ranked the importance of each criterion in relation to the core question, "Which AI project should be selected?" Then, they evaluated the importance of each project within each criterion. AHP Express was conducted using the [29] scale (1 to 9), where 1 indicates equal preference between factors, and 9 indicates an extreme preference for the first factor over the second.

Problem Framing (Step 4) involved a meeting with key stakeholders directly engaged with the identified and prioritized problem, including representatives from multiple areas due to its cross-functional nature. Participants were briefed in advance to analyze the causes and characteristics of the problem, ensuring a productive discussion and a shared understanding of its context and critical aspects. Given the project's objectives, data availability was a crucial factor. Relevant databases were examined to illustrate the problem, and the existing solution was analyzed to identify strengths and areas for improvement.

In Step 5 - Design Sprint, three of the five traditional Design Sprint steps were completed over two days with a multidisciplinary team (the Squad) composed of individuals directly involved in the problem [18]. The steps included: Understand/Map,

Table 1. Criteria and Subcriteria for Feasibility of AI Implementation in Public Services [25].

Criteria	Subcriteria
1- Technical Feasibility	– **Cost:** Development, implementation, and maintenance are economically viable. – **Time:** Implementation aligns with the PBIA timeline. – **Maintenance:** The AI solution is feasible to maintain and update. – **Operationalization:** Necessary resources (human, material, infrastructure) are available.
2- Data Availability	– **Patterns:** Data patterns can be learned to solve the problem. – **Quality:** Data is accurate, complete, and reliable post-preprocessing. – **Quantity:** Sufficient data exists for training and testing. – **Diversity:** Data represents the target population characteristics.
3- AI Contribution	– **Efficiency:** AI will improve process efficiency. – **Complexity:** The problem cannot be solved using simple rules. – **Prediction:** The problem requires classification or generative AI. – **Measurability:** The process outcome is measurable.
4- Societal Impact	– **Benefits:** AI will bring real benefits to society. – **Risks:** Negative impacts are considered and mitigated. – **Acceptance:** AI will be accepted by the public. – **Regulation:** The AI solution complies with legal regulations.
5- Strategic Alignment	– **Mission:** AI aligns with the organization's mission. – **Priorities:** AI contributes to strategic goals. – **Reputation:** The solution does not harm the organization's reputation. – **Governance:** AI advances public policy objectives.

Sketch, and Decide. In Understand/Map, long-term objectives were defined, key Sprint questions were addressed, a user map was created, expert interviews were conducted, and the target user was identified. During Sketch, the team split into two groups to analyze available information and generate solution proposals. In Decide, the entire team reviewed these proposals and finalized the solution definition.

Prototyping is accomplished in two separate steps. Step 6 - Prototype Solution Type I, involves mapping and developing prototypes using an agile approach in a demonstration environment, along with documenting the AI solutions identified in Step 5. Here, prototyping serves to assess the feasibility of an MVP solution, with requirements and specifications refined in collaboration with the requesting entity during the design sprint phase. The following Prototype Solution Type 2 (Step 7) is delivered as Python code within a controlled development environment, simulating the real-world problem. It includes a detailed technical report and a presentation for key stakeholders and interested parties.

Finally, in Step 8, to validate the AI solution in the public sector, a rigorous methodological approach is required to ensure effectiveness and efficiency. This study illustrates the validation of an MVP prototype for an interactive chatbot designed to provide information and virtual addresses for public services. The process begins by defining the chatbot's objectives and success criteria, measured by metrics such as response accuracy, interaction time, and user feedback.

Internal tests validate functionality, ensuring proper conversation flow and integration with public service databases. A controlled test phase follows, involving selected end users who provide qualitative and quantitative feedback to refine the solution. Based on this data, necessary adjustments are made before large-scale deployment. The chatbot is then released in a beta-testing phase, where real-world performance is continuously monitored through user feedback. Upon successful validation, full implementation occurs alongside an ongoing monitoring plan to adapt to evolving user needs and service updates.

A systematic validation process is essential for MVP prototypes in the public sector, combining functionality tests, controlled user evaluations, and real-world deployment. Robust testing and monitoring tools are critical to ensuring AI solutions effectively address user needs. Additionally, the prototype's user interface is designed for optimal evaluation, aligning with its specification process to meet technical and operational requirements, providing a solid foundation for large-scale implementation.

5 Results

This study proposes an innovative AI-driven methodology to enhance Brazilian public services, developed in collaboration with the SGD, AI researchers, and NIA members, as outlined in Sect. 3. The following presents the results obtained at each step of its application.

Initially, discussions between project executors and stakeholders determined that the Executive Secretaries of Ministries would define the agencies participating in the survey. A set of 16 open-ended questions was formulated to assess four key aspects: Service Context, Problem Characterization, AI Needs, and AI Solution Requirements. The survey was conducted in the Department of Digital Public Service Platforms (DESER) of SGD, identifying three project proposals. The elimination step was carried out by four members of the General Coordination of Automation and Service (CGATE), two AI professors, a facilitator professor, and SGD staff, with all three projects passing the filter and proceeding to AHP Express.

For AHP Express, three groups were interviewed: (i) AI-specialized professors, (ii) SGD public servants, and (iii) public servants from the originating proposal area. Each stakeholder's response was recorded following the criteria in Table 1. The projects analyzed in Step 2 included:

- Automated Recovery of Gov.br Account Access
- CGATE Citizen Support Channels
- Citizen Support Channel for Public Services on the Gov.BR Portal

Since these projects involve high citizen interaction through digital platforms, particularly the Gov.br Portal, classification results reflect their broad population impact. The final AHP Express evaluation, presented in Fig. 3, represents the geometric mean of the three assigned scores. The Citizen Support Channel for Public Services on the Gov.BR Portal was selected for prototyping.

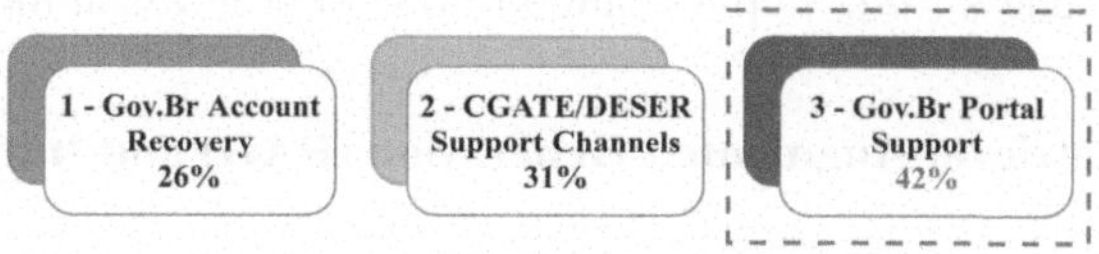

Fig. 3. AHP Express Result [25].

5.1 Problem Framing and Design Sprint

The problem framing and design sprint phases, as described in Sect. 4, established the key objectives and structure for the selected project. The primary goal is to increase public service participation through Gov.Br by 100% within one year. To achieve this, a generative AI chatbot was identified as the most suitable solution, designed to assist citizens by answering queries and directing them to relevant service pages. The project specifically addresses the challenge of improving service accessibility for users, ensuring that they can efficiently navigate the platform and find the information they need. The target audience consists of citizens who utilize Gov.br for public services, with the success of the initiative measured by a projected 25% reduction in support channel and ombudsman requests.

Following these definitions, the prototyping phase was structured to develop an Advanced Generative Agent that enhances user interaction on the Gov.br Portal, providing accurate assistance and guiding citizens to the appropriate services. This process is carried out in two distinct steps, as detailed in Sect. 4. The AI architecture and strategy, defined through collaboration between AI experts and key stakeholders, are outlined in the following sections.

AI Development Strategy

I. **Data Collection and Structuring:** Identify and organize available data, restructure additional information, and generate an FAQ document.
II. **Document Processing:** Extract text, topics, and keywords using document intelligence tools (Azure).
III. **Vector Database:** Generate semantic chunking, embeddings, and thematic organization with indexation.
IV. **Prompt Embedding:** Configure the generative agent for inclusive, accessible, and policy-compliant responses, defining restricted topics and enabling in-context learning.
V. **Advanced Semantic Search:** Improve response accuracy using a fine-tuned LLaMA model optimized with Retrieval-Augmented Generation with Fine-Tuning (RAFT) [40]. This technique integrates supervised fine-tuning with RAG [22] to improve document-based responses.

The proposed RAFT-based AI architecture [10] is a key innovation that enhances the accuracy of generative AI in citizen interactions. Validating an AI chatbot with an LLM involves testing functionality, performance, ethical considerations, and user experience, ensuring its effectiveness [38]. Step 8 (Validation) is in progress at the time of writing.

5.2 Chatbots: Retrieval-Augmented Generation (RAG) and Intelligent Agent Navigation

The chatbot is built on the Retrieval-Augmented Generation (RAG) framework [23], enabling it to retrieve relevant contexts and enhance responses generated by Large Language Models (LLMs). Its implementation follows a structured approach, beginning with data extraction, where FAQ content from the Gov.br website is captured, structured in JSON format, and converted into Markdown while retaining essential elements. To further refine search capabilities, image descriptions are generated using an LLM with vision capabilities, improving semantic search accuracy.

To optimize retrieval and enhance contextual understanding, the system applies text segmentation using the Parent Document Retriever [20]. This process first organizes content by headers into "parent" documents before applying a second segmentation step that further divides text into smaller "child" sections based on sentence structure or character limits. Following this, embedding generation is performed using OpenAI's text-embedding-3-small model, which encodes child documents into vector representations, linking them to corresponding parent documents in the database.

A semantic search mechanism based on cosine similarity retrieves the three most relevant documents, ensuring responses incorporate structured textual and visual content. The chatbot dynamically formats its responses in Markdown, integrating text, images, and links to provide a seamless user experience. These responses are rendered in an interface that converts Markdown into HTML, delivering enriched, well-structured outputs.

In parallel, an interactive virtual assistant was developed to facilitate navigation and information retrieval on the Gov.br portal. Implemented using the Streamlit framework, the system processes textual inputs in natural language, extracting relevant content and suggesting links to users. Web page extraction and analysis are performed using BeautifulSoup, allowing the identification of structural elements and the organization of available links in an accessible format, minimizing the need for manual navigation.

To improve search efficiency, the system integrates an advanced search model based on the Agente Zero framework, which converts the portal's database into a structured graph. This architecture enables more precise contextual searches by dynamically traversing the graph and identifying the most relevant links based on the user's navigation flow. Additionally, intelligent navigation dynamically constructs URLs for direct access to relevant content, reducing search time and improving the user experience.

To enhance usability, the chatbot maintains a history of user interactions, storing messages to preserve conversation context and ensure a fluid, efficient experience. This capability, combined with graph-based modeling and real-time semantic search, improves response precision and ensures a more intuitive user experience. The modular and expandable architecture allows for adaptation to other contexts, ensuring flexibility and scalability in various government applications.

The chatbot's effectiveness was validated through simulations, demonstrating its ability to provide clear, structured responses in natural language while maintaining an active, context-aware conversation. It also supplies official links, allowing users to access additional information as needed. Table 2 presents an example chatbot conversation, where all interactions were translated into English for clarity, while the knowledge base remains in Portuguese. Emojis used in responses were removed to maintain consistency in the structured output.

Table 2. Example of a conversation with Chatbot RAG.

User
Hello, I am Carlos.
Agent
Hello, Carlos! How can I help you?
User
I would like to know what account levels are available on gov.br.
Agent
The gov.br account has three levels of reliability: Bronze, Silver, and Gold. Each level offers a different degree of security and access to digital services. **Gov.br Account Levels** **1. Bronze** - Basic access to digital services. - Created with CPF and password. - Lowest level of security. **2. Silver** - More secure than Bronze. - Obtained through: • Facial validation via gov.br app (CNH). • Internet banking login from accredited banks. **3. Gold** - Highest security level and full digital service access. - Obtained through: • Facial validation via gov.br app (biometric data). • Digital certificate (ICP-Brasil). More information: gov.br account levels.

6 Discussion

This work presents a methodology for deploying AI in public services, integrating Lean Office principles to eliminate inefficiencies, optimize processes, and standardize workflows before automation. Once automated, a continuous improvement loop (kaizen) refines the NLP chatbot's workflow, further optimizing efficiency. Digitization enables process automation, reducing waste and creating opportunities to embed intelligence through advanced control algorithms. Key questions addressed in this approach include the relationship between operational excellence in public administration and AI-driven workflows, as well as the driving forces behind performance and efficiency improvements in public service delivery.

Beyond improving portal accessibility, the proposed generative agent provides additional benefits to the Brazilian government. Using Webometrics techniques [32], citizen interactions with the chatbot generate valuable data that can enhance public services. This data enables authorities to identify behavioral patterns, citizen needs, and service preferences, understand common complaints, develop data-driven policies, personalize services, improve operational efficiency, monitor service trends, and assess conversion rates where users successfully resolve their requests. These insights also contribute to refining usage metrics for the "Gov.br" portal.

A fundamental challenge in AI adoption for public administration is ensuring data privacy and security. The information collected spans multiple domains, including healthcare and smart cities, supporting public service improvements at different maturity levels. However, these applications raise concerns about safeguarding sensitive data, necessitating strict compliance with data protection regulations and ethical guidelines.

7 Final Remarks and Future Work

This paper proposed an innovative methodology for implementing artificial intelligence in Brazilian public services to enhance efficiency, accessibility, and service quality. Integrating Lean Office, Design Sprint, and advanced AI techniques, the methodology was designed to be both flexible and adaptable to diverse governmental needs. Collaboration among AI experts, public servants, and stakeholders was essential to ensure technical feasibility and alignment with public policies.

The methodology specifically addresses a demand from the Secretariat of Digital Government (SGD) within the National Digital Government Strategy. Given Brazil's extensive federal structure, it supports project selection and prototyping in a complex governmental system. Its comprehensiveness allows for application in other countries with large governmental infrastructures, fostering digital transformation across various contexts.

The development of an advanced generative agent for the Gov.br Portal not only meets the immediate demand but also transforms citizen interactions into a valuable data source. Analyzing this data enables service personalization and improved policymaking. We propose using LLaMA X, trained on Portuguese documentation, with RAFT to enhance accuracy. Future work includes developing a generative AI based on

ChatGPT for performance comparison and expanding applications to other sectors, such as integrating information from social welfare programs such as Bolsa Família, government systems for managing CPF (Social Security Number), CNPJ (National Registry of Legal Entities), SEI (Electronic System of Information), and payroll systems.

Acknowledgments. We extend our gratitude to the Ministry of Management and Innovation in Public Services, particularly the Secretariat of Digital Government (SGD), for financially supporting this project and facilitating the identification and prototyping of AI solutions.

References

1. Atabekov, A.: Artificial intelligence in contemporary societies: legal status and definition, implementation in public sector across various countries. Soc. Sci. **12**(3), 178 (2023). https://doi.org/10.3390/socsci12030178
2. Birhane, A., Kalluri, P., Card, D., Agnew, W., Dotan, R., Bao, M.: The values encoded in machine learning research. In: Proceedings of the 2022 ACM Conference on Fairness, Accountability, and Transparency, pp. 173–184 (2022). https://doi.org/10.1145/3531146.3533083
3. Blount, K.: Using artificial intelligence to prevent crime: implications for due process and criminal justice. AI Soc. **39**(1), 359–368 (2024). https://doi.org/10.1007/s00146-022-01513-z
4. BRASIL: Decreto N° 11.437, de 17 de março de 2023 (2023). https://www.planalto.gov.br/ccivil_03/_ato2023-2026/2023/decreto/D11437.htm#art5. Accessed 27 June 2024
5. BRASIL, M.d.G.e.I.e.S.P.: Serviços e informações do brasil (2024). https://www.gov.br/pt-br. Accessed 27 June 2024
6. Chen, T., Gascó-Hernandez, M., Esteve, M.: The adoption and implementation of artificial intelligence chatbots in public organizations: evidence from us state governments. Am. Rev. Public Adm. **54**(3), 255–270 (2024). https://doi.org/10.1177/02750740231200522
7. Chen, Y.C., Ahn, M.J., Wang, Y.F.: Artificial intelligence and public values: value impacts and governance in the public sector. Sustainability **15**(6), 4796 (2023). https://doi.org/10.3390/su15064796
8. Cohen, S., Manes Rossi, F., Brusca, I.: Debate: public sector accounting education and artificial intelligence. Public Money Manag. **43**(7), 725–726 (2023). https://doi.org/10.1080/09540962.2023.2209290
9. Colin, E.C.: Pesquisa operacional: 170 aplicações em estratégia, finanças, logística, produção, marketing e vendas. Livros Técnicos e Científicos (2007)
10. Di Oliveira, V., Bezerra, Y., Weigang, L., Brom, P., Celestino, V.: Slim-raft: a novel fine-tuning approach to improve cross-linguistic performance for mercosur common nomenclature. In: Proceedings of the 20th International Conference on Web Information Systems and Technologies, pp. 234–241. Porto (2024)
11. Dwivedi, Y.K., Sharma, A., Rana, N.P., Giannakis, M., Goel, P., Dutot, V.: Evolution of artificial intelligence research in technological forecasting and social change: Research topics, trends, and future directions. Technol. Forecast. Soc. Chang. **192**, 122579 (2023). https://doi.org/10.1016/j.techfore.2023.122579
12. Engstrom, D.F., Ho, D.E., Sharkey, C.M., Cuéllar, M.F.: Government by algorithm: artificial intelligence in federal administrative agencies. NYU School of Law, Public Law Research Paper (20-54) (2020). https://doi.org/10.2139/ssrn.3551505

13. Fan, Z., Yan, Z., Wen, S.: Deep learning and artificial intelligence in sustainability: a review of sdgs, renewable energy, and environmental health. Sustainability **15**(18), 13493 (2023). https://doi.org/10.3390/su151813493
14. Faria, A.V.A., de Melo, M.K., de Oliveira, F.A.R., Weigang, L., Celestino, V.R.R.: Automated SLR with a few labeled papers and a fair workload metric. In: Marchiori, M., Domínguez Mayo, F.J., Filipe, J. (eds.) Web Information Systems and Technologies. WEBIST 2022. LNBIP, vol. 494, pp. 1–23. Springer, Cham (2023). https://doi.org/10.1007/978-3-031-43088-6_1
15. Gov, A.: Gov.br é a página de governo mais acessada do mundo (2024). https://agenciagov.ebc.com.br/noticias/202403/gov-br-e-a-pagina-de-governo-mais-acessada-do-mundo. Accessed 27 June 2024
16. Jevinger, Å., Zhao, C., Persson, J.A., Davidsson, P.: Artificial intelligence for improving public transport: a mapping study. Public Transport **16**(1), 99–158 (2024). https://doi.org/10.1007/s12469-023-00334-7
17. Kitsios, F., Kamariotou, M., Mavromatis, A.: Drivers and outcomes of digital transformation: the case of public sector services. Information **14**(1), 43 (2023). https://doi.org/10.3390/info14010043
18. Knapp, J., Zeratsky, J., Kowitz, B.: Sprint: How to Solve Big Problems and Test New Ideas in Just Five Days. Simon & Schuster, New York (2016)
19. Kutyauripo, I., Rushambwa, M., Chiwazi, L.: Artificial intelligence applications in the agrifood sectors. J. Agric. Food Res. **11**, 100502 (2023). https://doi.org/10.1016/j.jafr.2023.100502
20. LangChain: How to use the parent document retriever (2024). https://python.langchain.com/docs/how_to/parent_document_retriever/
21. Leal, J.E.: AHP-express: a simplified version of the analytical hierarchy process method. MethodsX **7** (2020). https://doi.org/10.1016/j.mex.2019.11.021
22. Lewis, P., et al.: Retrieval-augmented generation for knowledge-intensive nlp tasks. Adv. Neural Inf. Process. Syst. **33**, 9459–9474 (2020)
23. Li, H., Su, Y., Cai, D., Wang, Y., Liu, L.: A survey on retrieval-augmented text generation (2022). https://arxiv.org/abs/2202.01110
24. Maragno, G., Tangi, L., Gastaldi, L., Benedetti, M.: Exploring the factors, affordances and constraints outlining the implementation of artificial intelligence in public sector organizations. Int. J. Inf. Manag. **73**, 102686 (2023). https://doi.org/10.1016/j.ijinfomgt.2023.102686
25. Kely de Melo, M., et al.: Implementing ai for enhanced public services gov.br: a methodology for the Brazilian federal government. In: Proceedings of the 20th International Conference on Web Information Systems and Technologies (WEBIST 2024), pp. 90–101. SCITEPRESS – Science and Technology Publications, Lda. (2024). https://doi.org/10.5220/0012997000003825, paper published under CC license (CC BY-NC-ND 4.0)
26. Neumann, O., Guirguis, K., Steiner, R.: Exploring artificial intelligence adoption in public organizations: a comparative case study. Public Manag. Rev. **26**(1), 114–141 (2024). https://doi.org/10.1080/14719037.2022.2048685
27. Rocha, C.A.A., et al.: Leveraging transfer learning for long text classification with limited data. In: Marchiori, M., Domínguez Mayo, F.J., Filipe, J. (eds.) Web Information Systems and Technologies. WEBIST 2022. LNBIP, vol. 494, pp. 98–120. Springer, Cham (2023). https://doi.org/10.1007/978-3-031-43088-6_6
28. Russo, R.D.F.S.M., Camanho, R.: Criteria in ahp: a systematic review of literature. Procedia Comput. Sci. **55**, 1123–1132 (2015). https://doi.org/10.1016/j.procs.2015.07.081
29. Saaty, R.W.: The analytic hierarchy process–what it is and how it is used. Math. Model. **9**(5), 161–176 (1987)
30. Saaty, T.L.: A scaling method for priorities in hierarchical structures. J. Math. Psychol. **15** (1977)

31. Saaty, T.L.: Rank from comparisons and from ratings in the analytic hierarchy/network processes. Eur. J. Oper. Res. **168**(2), 557–570 (2006). https://doi.org/10.1016/j.ejor.2004.04.032
32. Saeidnia, H.R., Hosseini, E., Abdoli, S., Ausloos, M.: Unleashing the power of ai: a systematic review of cutting-edge techniques in ai-enhanced scientometrics, webometrics and bibliometrics. Library Hi Tech (2024)
33. Samoili, S., Cobo, M.L., Gómez, E., De Prato, G., Martínez-Plumed, F., Delipetrev, B.: AI watch. defining artificial intelligence. Towards an operational definition and taxonomy of artificial intelligence (2020). https://doi.org/10.2760/382730
34. Scutella, M., Plewa, C., Reaiche, C.: Virtual agents in the public service: examining citizens' value-in-use. Public Manag. Rev. **26**(1), 73–88 (2024). https://doi.org/10.1080/14719037.2022.2044504
35. Straub, V.J., Morgan, D., Bright, J., Margetts, H.: Artificial intelligence in government: concepts, standards, and a unified framework. Gov. Inf. Q. **40**(4), 101881 (2023). https://doi.org/10.1016/j.giq.2023.101881
36. Vetan, J.: Design sprint 3.0 (2018). https://www.designsprint.academy/blog/design-sprint-3-0. Accessed 27 June 2024
37. Wang, C., Han, B., Patel, B., Rudin, C.: In pursuit of interpretable, fair and accurate machine learning for criminal recidivism prediction. J. Quant. Criminol. **39**(2), 519–581 (2023). https://doi.org/10.1007/s10940-022-09545-w
38. Xi, Z., et al.: The rise and potential of large language model based agents: a survey. arXiv preprint arXiv:2309.07864 (2023)
39. Yu, K.H., Beam, A.L., Kohane, I.S.: Artificial intelligence in healthcare. Nat. Biomed. Eng. **2**(10), 719–731 (2018). https://doi.org/10.1038/s41551-018-0305-z
40. Zhang, T., et al.: Raft: adapting language model to domain specific rag. arXiv preprint arXiv:2403.10131 (2024)

Low-Code Web Database Integration: Enhancing Workflow Efficiency and Collaboration with Web Components and Generic Web Services

Andreas Schmidt[1,2](✉) and Tobias Münch[3,4]

[1] Institute for Automation and Applied Informatics, Karlsruhe Institute of Technology, Karlsruhe, Germany
andreas.schmidt@kit.edu

[2] Department of Computer Science and Business Information Systems, Karlsruhe University of Applied Sciences, Karlsruhe, Germany
andreas.schmidt@h-ka.de

[3] Münch Ges. für IT Solutions mbH, Gewerbering 1, 49393 Lohne, Germany
to.muench@muench-its.de

[4] Chemnitz University of Technology, Chemnitz, Germany

Abstract. The demand for digital transformation in Germany and a persistent shortage of software engineers present significant challenges for businesses and public institutions. Traditional solutions for enterprises, such as ERP systems, require extensive customization, which is often time-consuming and costly. Low-code platforms offer an alternative by enabling a wider range of users to create and integrate software solutions with minimal coding effort. This paper presents BRIDGE (Business-Ready Integration and Development for Generic Environments), a low-code framework designed to simplify web-based database integration using web components and RESTful web services. Our approach leverages web standards to reduce complexity, making it accessible to users with basic HTML knowledge. We extend our previous work by introducing enhanced security mechanisms, a real-time configuration wizard, and new integration capabilities that improve usability and scalability in enterprise environments. To evaluate the effectiveness of BRIDGE, we explore its application in classical and agile project management scenarios, addressing key research questions related to system integration, project workflows, and technical constraints. Low-code web components can bridge the gap between non-technical users and software development, enabling faster prototyping and reducing engineering bottlenecks. Future research will focus on OpenAPI-based integrations, improved security policies, and a comprehensive evaluation in real-world enterprise settings.

Keywords: Web component · Relational database · Low-code · Prototyping

1 Introduction

Across Europe, particularly in Germany, private companies and public institutions are confronted with challenges of the so called VUCA (Volatility, Uncertainty, Complexity and Ambiugity) world and their digital transformation [14,65,66]. These challenges

M. Marchiori et al. (Eds.): WEBIST 2024, LNBIP 583, pp. 18–48, 2026.
https://doi.org/10.1007/978-3-032-25534-1_2

arise from limited financial resources for information technology (IT), and a shortage of IT personnel [2,58]. As a result, adopting complex enterprise software—such as Enterprise Resource Planning (ERP) or Customer Relationship Management (CRM) systems—can be both time-consuming and costly [32]. These systems often involve various distributed data sources that must be integrated by software engineers through Electronic Data Interchange (EDI), a shared database or Enterprise Service Bus (ESB) [43].

The current shortage of software engineers presents a significant challenge [58]. They are necessary for creating and maintaining huge, complex software solutions. Companies must respond quickly to emerging business opportunities and optimise internal processes to remain competitive [55]. However, the limited availability of qualified personnel within companies and in the broader job market can hinder these efforts. This situation raises an important question: How can organisations address the growing demand for software engineers, and how can we empower a wider group of individuals to tackle software-related challenges?

One way to reduce the workload of current software engineers is by utilising artificial intelligence (AI) [4]. For example, large technology companies like Facebook increasingly use AI-driven tools to automate certain aspects of software development [4]. This approach allows skilled engineers to concentrate on more complex tasks. Another approach is encouraging a wider range of users—beyond traditional software engineers—to solve software-related problems. For instance, Alan Blackwell has introduced the Moral codes, which stand for More Open Representations, Access to Learning, and Control Over Digital Expression [11]. He emphasises the importance of data sovereignty, human-centred interfaces, and accessible education [11]. Blackwell argues that developing more intuitive programming languages could enable diverse user groups to tackle software engineering challenges more effectively [11]. At least, low-code and no-code solutions offer programming for a wider range of humans, but are often hard to maintain in a broader setup [50].

Building on the idea of Blackwell and low-code approaches, we previously presented a low-code approach based on the composite standard of web components [55]. We call our approach **BRIDGE** – **B**usiness-**R**eady **I**ntegration and **D**evelopment for **G**eneric **E**nvironments. Our approach takes advantage of the fact that many potential users already have a basic understanding of HTML, and the declarative programming style makes it easier to apply this technology to solve business challenges [15,55]. It differs from existing approaches because it sets on 1) web standards, 2) reduced complexity for users, 3) focused on a specific scenario, and 4) uses generic RESTful web services to be suited for a wide range of usage. Our main research questions are:

- **RQ1:** How can another system be integrated into a web-based application over loosely coupled web components?
- **RQ2:** How does this approach fit into processes of traditional and agile project management with its stakeholders?
- **RQ3:** How is a solution of a declarative database integration approach with generic Webservices designed?

This paper introduces an extension of our previous work [55], that enhances security features for enterprise environments. We provide extensions like foreign key resolution, renaming of columns, support for parameterizable SQL statements, custom styles, and multi-selection of data with dependencies. In addition, we propose a configuration wizard with a real-time preview function to simplify the development process and encourage broader software creation participation and integrated a mechanism to link our components and/or HTML elements without additional Javascript code. Our research aims to outline a path toward more inclusive, secure, and efficient software engineering practices.

We have reached an early alpha version of BRIDGE, and our next steps are a quantitative and qualitative evaluation. In the quantitative analysis, we want to evaluate performance, maintainability, and traffic. In the qualitative evaluation, we want to evaluate how our stakeholders are able to use BRIDGE for their own purposes and what gaps in usage occur.

This paper is structured as follows. Section 2 explores real-world business scenarios where low-code solutions help address software development bottlenecks, particularly in classical and agile project management (RQ1, RQ2). Section 3 reviews related work on web database integration, low-code development, and web components, highlighting the gaps our approach fills. We describe the architecture and security aspects of BRIDGE in Sect. 4 (RQ3). Then, Sect. 5 details its core components (RQ3). Afterwards, in Sect. 6, we present two example application demonstrating its practical use (RQ1). Section 7 discusses limitations and possible improvements, and Sect. 8 concludes with conclusions and future research directions.

2 Business Scenarios

Because of a significant shortage of skilled software engineers in many industrialised countries, organisations face mounting pressure to digitise core operations and develop new digital services or support real-world services by digitalisation [13,33]. Low-code solutions have emerged as a promising strategy for addressing these challenges by enabling a broader array of stakeholders to participate in software-related tasks [21]. This chapter examines how our low-code framework, capable of integrating diverse data sources into existing enterprise systems, can help resource bottlenecks in two familiar project management contexts: classical and agile (RQ2).

In Germany, for instance, companies are categorised into micro, small, medium-sized, and large enterprises [60]. Micro and small firms often operate under tight financial constraints and rely extensively on multiple Software as a Service (SaaS) applications [2,5]. By contrast, medium-sized and larger organisations tend to maintain internal IT teams frequently overwhelmed with day-to-day administrative tasks, limiting their availability for new software development [25]. In both scenarios, non-technical users with a foundational understanding of HTML, commonly taught in secondary schools according to the Committee on European Computing Education (CECE) [15], could potentially address minor software needs if provided with the right tools.

2.1 Management Methods and Processes

Organisations typically adopt one of two high-level approaches to project governance: classical project management [28,56] or agile project management [6,52]. Sometimes there are hybrid approaches [59]. Each approach influences planning, execution, collaboration, and the degree to which a low-code framework can help engineering bottlenecks. While these approaches differ conceptually—particularly regarding flexibility and feedback loops [52]— the proposed low-code solution can be integrated into both models.

Once installed and configured by system administrators, BRIDGE empowers business developers and even end-users, operating within predefined security policies, to combine disparate data sources into a central Software as a Service (SaaS) application, such as an ERP or CRM system. This configuration establishes a secure, RESTful interface to existing databases (e.g., PostgreSQL, MySQL) and cloud-based services, thereby unifying otherwise isolated data streams. BRIDGE uses an easy-to-follow wizard for building applications, web components and straightforward programming. This wizard lets non-technical users quickly create forms and CRUD (Create-Read-Update-Delete) applications.

From a **classical project management** perspective, this low-code paradigm is woven into the established planning, implementation, and maintenance sequence. After defining the high-level scope and allocating resources, the system administrator sets up the low-code platform and configures data connections. Business developers or end-users then leverage these web components to build or modify front-end functionalities, such as reporting interfaces or process automation modules. Although the classic approach follows a more rigid, phase-based model, the availability of low-code tooling shortens development cycles. It reduces backlogs by distributing more straightforward tasks across a broader group of contributors.

Under **agile project management** (e.g., Scrum or Kanban), low-code solutions fit naturally into iterative sprints [52]. The approach's ability to rapidly prototype features with feedback loops [6]: new functionalities, like a quick data-integration module, can be implemented by business developers with HTML and a wizard in a few hours. As the sprint progresses, end-users provide feedback on these prototypes, prompting further refinements in subsequent iterations. By dispersing development responsibilities, agile teams can respond quickly to shifting requirements and emerging market opportunities, even when software engineering capacity is limited.

In both project management models, developing new software solutions starts with defining how existing and external data sources should interact. Once the core web service is configured, teams can incorporate new databases, SaaS platforms, or API endpoints by updating a central configuration file. The low-code library handles much of the underlying logic—querying databases, enforcing security rules, and rendering user-friendly interfaces—thus freeing software engineers to focus on complex or high-risk tasks beyond the scope of low-code components. BRIDGE streamlines integration with legacy databases and enables incremental rollout of new features, sustaining organisational agility regardless of the preferred project management methodology.

2.2 Stakeholders

Adopting BRIDGE hinges on effective collaboration among diverse stakeholders, each bringing specialised competencies and perspectives to the project.

The **Chief Financial Officer** oversees funding for software initiatives and evaluates return on investment to ensure that budget allocations reflect organisational priorities and outcomes [9]. He tracks performance metrics and potential cost savings [9]. Therefore, he has become a key supporter of low-code solutions, recognising that reduced development expenses and streamlined data integration can lower overall IT costs [35]. When two or more departments can more easily share or merge data through a centralised low-code platform, their collaboration grows more efficient, potentially leading to further cost reductions and operational improvements.

The **Business Developer** connects organisational strategy with practical workflows, continually seeking ways to optimise or innovate [7]. This role entails identifying specific processes or new market offerings that might be enhanced through low-code components, particularly when departmental silos impede information-sharing [7]. Business Developers promote solutions that integrate data sources from finance, marketing, logistics, and other departments to enhance team collaboration and ensure alignment with broader corporate objectives [7].

System Administrators maintain the organisation's technological backbone, focusing on secure deployment and ongoing reliability [39]. Their responsibilities include installing and monitoring software systems, role-based access control, and integrating data repositories [39]. These tasks ensure compliance with internal and external regulations and promote smoother information exchanges across departments [39].

Software Engineers handle advanced tasks—such as performance-critical integrations, complex analytics, and custom feature development—beyond the scope of low-code solutions. By managing quality assurance and architectural consistency, they preserve system integrity and support the continued scalability of organisational technologies. The availability of low-code components allows them to devote more time to these specialised areas, resulting in more sustainable, cost-effective, and robust solutions.

End-users interact with low-code applications in daily activities, such as data entry and process automation. Their engagement and feedback offer valuable insight. By optimising the data flow between various departments and minimising their reliance on software engineering resources, BRIDGE enhances user satisfaction, contributes to cost efficiencies, and improves collaboration.

2.3 Business Examples

To demonstrate the potential of BRIDGE, we present three scenarios from small and medium-sized enterprises in Lower Saxony and Baden-Wuerttemberg, Germany. While the use cases are grounded in real-world practices, the companies were guaranteed anonymity. In each case, our generic web service can be installed on-premises, or into a Software-as-a-Service (SaaS) environment and all scenarios allow for seamless API-based integration if needed. Moreover, BRIDGE can directly connect to existing infrastructures, offering flexibility in deployment and operation.

Scenario 1 Integration of Order Proposals Into CRM: In this scenario, we look at a distributor of food and beverages for the gastronomy sector that operates a web-based

Enterprise Resource Planning (ERP) system with a Customer Relationship Management (CRM) module, which is a common use case [16, 31]. Within the same organization, the purchasing department relies on a separate application that lacks API connectivity to the CRM. Therefore, employees must email requested items to the purchasing department. This approach can lead to inefficient and incorrect communication because of human errors.

Using BRIDGE, the company can integrate order proposals into the CRM without extensive custom coding or duplicating data. This integration makes the business process more efficient and reduces communication insufficiencies between the departments.

Scenario 2 Logistics Track-and-Trace for Shipments: Logistics providers commonly rely on a Transport Management System (TMS) connected to a Track-and-Trace (T&T) solution [18, 29]. Standard approaches to integrating these two systems involve duplicating data or manual synchronization, which can lead to inconsistencies [53]. Additionally, if a driver encounters technical issues (e.g., an offline mobile app), the dispatcher may need to override the shipment status manually.

BRIDGE enable seamless integration with existing T&T systems installed on-premise. This functionality lets users view delivery statuses directly within a TMS and update them without replicating data across multiple platforms.

Scenario 3 Veterinary Application and Laboratory Information System: In veterinary practices for poultry, samples are collected inside the barns and categorized with a label and a barcode. Additionally, a recipe is recorded in an ERP system alongside the relevant invoice or receipt. These samples must then be tracked through an internal Laboratory Information Management System (LIMS) to process diagnostic tests or other chemical or biological analyses [17]. Once results are available, the veterinarian requires immediate access to the results over the ERP environment. BRIDGE can facilitate direct communication between the ERP and LIMS, ensuring that veterinary professionals have up-to-date information on sample statuses and test outcomes.

3 Related Work

According to the scenarios described in the previous section, our focus lies on the related works of database access through the web, web components, and low-code development because each approach integrates different aspects of our work.

3.1 Database Access Through the Web

Several architectures have been proposed for publishing database content on the web, each differing in how data is retrieved, processed, and presented to end users. The following sections provide a concise overview of common approaches, ending with a discussion of BRIDGE.

Server-Side Web Applications. A foundational method is the server-side web application, in which a central server handles client requests, queries the database, and generates responses [23]. Frameworks such as Django (Python), Symfony (PHP), and Express (JavaScript) typically follow a Model-View-Controller (MVC) paradigm and often employ object-relational mapping (ORM) libraries [36]. This pattern simplifies development by separating business logic from presentation, but client-side interactivity is limited because each request requires a new HTTP communication with the server [34]. But it is very effective for Search Engine Optimization(SEO) [34].

Rich Internet Applications (RIAs). Rich Internet Applications (RIAs) are designed to create desktop-like experiences—rich means that the application has more interactive operation controls than previous web generations [24]. RIAs offload much of the processing to the client using JavaScript and AJAX to fetch and process data asynchronously [24]. Therefore, users benefit from faster updates and more interactive interfaces [22]. RIAs relied on browser plugins like Flash [45] or Silverlight [57].

RESTful Web Services and Progressive Web Apps (PWAs). Nowadays, web development shifted to Progressive Web Apps using modern implementations like HTML5, CSS3, and JavaScript frameworks (e.g., Angular, React, Vue.js) [20,26,49]. These frameworks improve responsiveness but introduce additional complexity in managing client-server communication. To create a shared state, REST-based architectures are used. Client applications—often single-page applications or PWAs—consume these endpoints through JSON or XML. PWAs enhance functionality with offline support and push notifications while maintaining the portability of web technologies. This approach decouples front-end and back-end development, enabling independent scaling of each layer.

Next.js and Content Delivery Networks (CDNs). Next.js is a React framework that supports both server-side rendering and static site generation [38,48]. Coupling Next.js with a CDN can reduce latency, since static assets are served from geographically distributed nodes [48]. Although database queries still occur on the main server, the combination of server rendering and CDN caching can speed up content delivery, especially for content-heavy sites.

Positioning BRIDGE. Our methodology aligns most closely with the RESTful Web Services plus PWA-model, but it differs by emphasizing a low-code strategy that reduces manual coding. By providing generic web services and customizable *web components* [64], our approach streamlines data-centric application development and fosters collaboration among domain experts and developers. Table 1 summarizes the key features of each approach. BRIDGE seeks to lower development barriers, use open technology, and facilitate iterative prototyping, distinguishing it from existing approaches that often require extensive hand coding.

Table 1. Comparision of BRIDGE approach with server-side Apps, RIAs, PWAs with REST and Next.js.

Approach	Tech Stack	Characteristics	Typical Use Cases
Server-side Apps	Django, Symfony, Express	Central server handles requests, MVC, ORM	Traditional sites with strong security needs
RIAs	AJAX, JavaScript frameworks	Enhanced interactivity, client-side updates	Apps needing frequent UI updates
REST + PWAs	REST APIs, JavaScript frameworks	Decoupled front/back ends, offline support	Scalable, cross-platform applications
Next.js + CDN	React, server-side rendering, CDNs	Faster load times, SEO benefits	Content-rich sites, global user bases
BRIDGE	Generic REST endpoints, web components	Reduced manual coding, easy customization	Data-centric apps, rapid prototyping

3.2 Web Components

Web components are a W3C standard that allows developers to define custom HTML elements with encapsulated functionality and reusable logic across web applications [64]. Modern web browsers fully support these components and enable modular development without requiring external dependencies or a dedicated server-side environment. A custom web component is implemented as a JavaScript class that extends the built-in `HTMLElement` class [64]. This class defines both the behavior and visual representation of the element, making it self-contained and independent. Once registered with the browser using the `customElements.define()` method, the component can be used like any standard HTML tag. For instance, a developer can create a `<db-table>` element that automatically renders database content in a structured format. Web components rely on several key technologies:

- Custom Elements: Allow developers to define new HTML tags with unique behaviour.
- Shadow DOM: Provides encapsulation, preventing styles and scripts from affecting or being affected by other parts of the entire application.
- HTML Templates & Slots: Enable reusable layouts while allowing dynamic content injection.

Web components support HTML attributes as configuration parameters [64]. These attributes act as input properties, enabling dynamic behaviour changes [64]. Furthermore, web components observe attribute changes and can re-render when necessary. This makes them interactive and responsive [64].

A naming convention ensures uniqueness and clarity: custom elements must contain a hyphen in their tag name (e.g., `<db-table>`). They also require both an opening and closing tag (`<db-table name="city" ...></db-table>`) unless they are self-closing elements.

By leveraging web components, BRIDGE ensures that database integration remains lightweight, modular, and maintainable. Unlike traditional low-code platforms that use specific components tied to certain frameworks, BRIDGE allows developers to add database-driven features to any web-based application without needing extra dependencies.

3.3 Low-Code Development

The rise of low-code development platforms (LCDPs) is reshaping software engineering by reducing the dependencies on coding [47]. Low-code platforms use visual programming, declarative logic, and pre-built components to enable faster application development, often allowing business users to participate [21,47]. Some LCDPs provide provide web applications as an output, such as the low-code platform Xelence by Sagitec Software [3].

Several low-code platforms dominate the market, each catering to different needs. For instance, Mendix [42] and OutSystems [40] are solutions with built-in integrations, workflow automation, and cloud-native deployments [51]. They provide drag-and-drop components and extensive connectors for third-party systems. These platforms require subscription-based licensing [40,42] and lead to vendor lock-in [12].

In contrast, BRIDGE is a lightweight, web component-based, low-code framework explicitly designed for database-driven applications. Instead of using a visual builder, it leverages standard web technologies (HTML + REST) to maintain low complexity and high flexibility. Unlike Mendix and OutSystems, BRIDGE avoids proprietary runtimes and lock-in, making integrating with existing enterprise environments easier.

A key differentiator is customization: BRIDGE provides direct access to underlying data structures through declarative web components, while traditional LCDPs abstract database interactions, sometimes limiting direct SQL-level manipulation. Additionally, BRIDGE is designed to be free and can be deployed anywhere on a web server. The client must have access to the generic web services and not the web server.

BRIDGE introduces a wizard-based configuration tool that allows users to generate a scenario for database connections and UI components. This feature simplifies onboarding, enabling non-technical users to quickly integrate relational databases without writing extensive code. While Mendix and OutSystems offer entirely visual programming environments [40,42], BRIDGE balances automation (via the wizard) with flexibility (through direct HTML and REST API control).

In summary, while Mendix and OutSystems are general-purpose low-code platforms optimized for enterprise workflows, BRIDGE is a specialized, minimalistic framework tailored for rapid database integration with maximum flexibility, control, and guided automation through its wizard (see Table 2).

3.4 Identity Management and Authorization

Identity management is crucial for securing systems at the enterprise scale by enforcing controlled resource access. The BRIDGE framework integrates authentication mechanisms through Keycloak [62], supporting various identity federation models, including LDAP [63], Kerberos [44], OAuth2 [27], and Active Directory (AD) [19]. These mechanisms ensure authentication across services while maintaining compliance inside an organization.

Table 2. Comparison of low-code approaches: BRIDGE, Mendix, and OutSystems.

Feature	BRIDGE	Mendix	OutSystems
Primary Focus	simple and small database web integration	Full-stack low-code development	Enterprise platform
Approach	Web components with REST API	Visual modeling	Visual development with workflows
Target Users	Business developers	Business & IT teams	Large enterprises, IT-heavy teams
Deployment Options	On-premises and cloud	Cloud, on-premises, or hybrid	Cloud, on-premises, hybrid, multi-cloud
Licensing & Costs	Open-source	Subscription-based	High-cost usage-based pricing
Vendor Lock-in	Minimal - web standards	Moderate (Mendix tools & runtime)	High – proprietary IDE and runtime dependency
Use Cases	Rapid database integration for web apps	General-purpose low-code applications	Enterprise-level apps

Federated identity management allows users to authenticate across systems using a single identity provider (IdP), reducing credential redundancy [10]. Keycloak enables federation by integrating with LDAP, Kerberos, and OAuth-based providersk [62]. Enterprises using Active Directory rely on LDAP for hierarchical credential management, while Kerberos SSO facilitates passwordless authentication via time-sensitive tickets [19,44,63]. OAuth2 is a de-facto standard for securing API access, particularly RESTful web services [27]. Many ERP systems support OAuth2 or backchannel authentication, enhancing security by separating authentication from front-end applications [8].

BRIDGE integrates authentication using Keycloak, focusing on four authentication strategies with different security levels and ease of integration (see Table 3):

- JWT Token Forwarding: The parent SaaS application authenticates users via Keycloak, and the JWT token is forwarded to BRIDGE's web services [62].
- Cookie-Based Authentication: Session-based authentication using secure HTTP cookies for persistent logins in web applications [61].
- Keycloak Token Exchange: A custom identity provider validates JWT tokens from external IdPs, facilitating federated authentication (Lodderstedt et al., 2021).
- Kerberos/LDAP SSO: Keycloak supports Active Directory integration, allowing seamless authentication within enterprise environments.

Currently, BRIDGE implements JWT token forwarding, while Keycloak token exchange and Kerberos integration are planned for future enhancements. Future work will focus on RBAC, multi-factor authentication (MFA), and OpenID Connect (OIDC) integration to enhance security and interoperability.

Table 3. Comparison of Authentication Methods in BRIDGE.

Authentication Method	Security Level	Ease of Integration	Use Case
JWT Token Forwarding	High	Easy	SaaS-based authentication
Keycloak Token Exchange	High	Moderate	Federated authentication
Kerberos/LDAP SSO	High	Complex	Enterprise Active Directory
Cookie Authentication	Medium	Easy	Web applications with session persistence

4 Overall Architecture

In this section we describe the architecture of BRIDGE and its components to answer RQ3. The overall architecture of the application can be seen in Fig. 1. The developed web components (left side, prefix `db-`) are executed in the browser and communicate with each other via method calls or a public-subscribe mechanism. Communication between the components and the databases does not take place directly, but via the component `db-connection` and a RESTful web service (`rdbms.php`, middle of the figure), which serves as an interface to the connected relational databases (right side).

We used Maurits van der Schee's `php-crud-api` module [54] as the basis for our RESTful backend service. The software is very easy to install and can be extended by the integration of so-called *customControllers*. In order to be able to work flexibly with multiple databases, we developed a new endpoint (`rdbms.php`) on the top of `php-crud-api` and also implemented two extensions in the form of custom controllers. The service provides the following functionality:

Database Selection: The new entry point (`rdbms.php`) has been implemented for the RESTful service to support multiple databases. All databases accessible from the RESTful service must be specified in a configuration file. Each database is specified by a logical name, under which it can then be accessed from the web components. Figure 2 (center) shows the structure of the entries in the configuration file. In addition, for each database connection, it is possible to specify which tables of the database can be accessed (default: all).

Access Control: The `php-crud-api`-server already offers an interface to use different authentication mechanisms like authentication via API key, username/password combination and JWT token [46]. The JWT token gets validated against an active Keycloak instance [62]. All these mechanisms are based on transporting authentication information in the HTTP header. To also support local HTML files accessed via the file URI schema [37], we have integrated an additional mechanism that sends an API key as an HTTP parameter. The reason for this are CORS [30] restrictions that would otherwise not allow access from the web components to the web service when accessing the HTML document via a file URI (like `file:///tmp/dbwc-demo.html`). This type of access places the least demands on a business developer, as only an editor to create the HTML documents and a browser with an internet connection are required to access and visualize the database content.

CRUD Functionality: To retrieve the data from a single table and to read and modify individual records, we use the functionality of the RESTful service `php-crud-api`.

Metadata Module: The metadata module was developed as a *customController* of the `php-crud-api` module. The module provides the following meta information: 1) available databases, 2) available tables per database, 3) columns, data types and constraints of each table. The constraints include primary keys, foreign key relationships, not null, and unique constraints. This information is consumed by the various components and the wizard we have created for the interactive generation of the markup code.

SQL Module: The SQL module was also realized as a *customController* extension of the `php-crud-api` service. It allows the direct execution of parameterized SQL statements in the specified database. The statements originate, for example, from the web component `db-query` (see Sect. 5.3), where they are passed to the web-component as an attribute value. In this case, `db-query` is also responsible for displaying the result records.

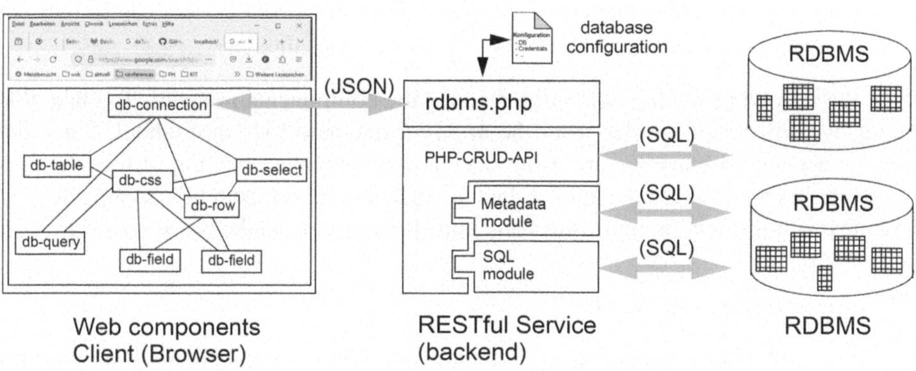

Fig. 1. Architecture of BRIDGE. The module *rdbms.php* receives the requests from the `db-connection` web-component and forwards them to the database specified in the request. The access information for the database is stored in the database configuration (see Fig. 2, middle) of the RESTful Webservice. The results are then returned to the web components via the *rdbms* module.

5 Components

In this section, the components we have realized are presented in detail. The individual components are as follows:

db-connection: This component must appear on every HTML page that uses our components. It acts as a link between the other components and the RESTful backend service. It has no visual representation except for authentication purposes. This component also obtains the JWT token for token-forwarding from the parent web application to hand it over to the generic web services.

db-table: This component is responsible for displaying table content. It can be adapted in a variety of ways to meet the requirements in terms of representation and interaction.

db-query: This component is responsible for displaying the results of an SQL select query.

db-row: This component represents a single record within a table. It can be used to create, modify, or display records.

db-field: This component represents a single attribute of a `db-row` component. It can used to display a data set when the internal representation options of the `db-row` component are insufficient.

db-select: The functionality of the component corresponds to that of the HTML select element, in which one or more entries can be selected from a series of predefined values. In the case of `db-select` components, the values come from the corresponding database. The values can be read in different ways. In the context of relational databases, the component plays a central role in the resolving of foreign key values.

db-css: This component can be used, if the overall *look & feel* should be changed dynamically. The component manages multiple sets of CSS files that can be dynamically swapped by changing an attribute for the path of the files.

In the following section, we will introduce the components in detail. To make this clearer, we will use examples from the *Mondial* database [41] throughout. Since the `php-crud-api` library we are using does not support the updating of records with composite keys, we have adapted the database schema by replacing the composite key attributes with artificial numeric keys and adjusting the foreign keys accordingly.

5.1 Connection-Component

First, the component responsible for communication between the other BRIDGE components and the RESTful service will be presented. This component must be present in every website that wants to use the BRIDGE components. If several databases are to be accessed within a page, it is possible to have multiple instances of the component. In this case, the id attribute must be set so that the other components can refer to the respective connection component.

In Fig. 2, the mapping process between the component `db-connection` and a specific database is shown. The component `db-connection` specifies the endpoint of the RESTful service with the attribute `url` and the logical database name with the attribute `database` (left side of the figure). The RESTful service (middle) running at the specified endpoint has a configuration file that maps the logical database name to a specific database (right side of the figure). Note that the databases can run on any computer and not necessarily on the computer with the REST-API endpoint.

For security considerations, we have to obtain the JWT token from the parent applications. The token can be shared over CustomEvents and a shared storage such as SessionStorage or LocalStorage. We prefer CustomEvents because of security best practices to expose the JWT token as little as possible. Therefore, our component sends the CustomEvent `requestToken` and listens to `receiveToken`. The parent application, which accesses the Keycloak instance (KeycloakJS), listens to the `requestToken` event and then sends back the JWT token over the event `receiveToken`. The `db-connection` component sends the JWT token with the requests to the generic web service.

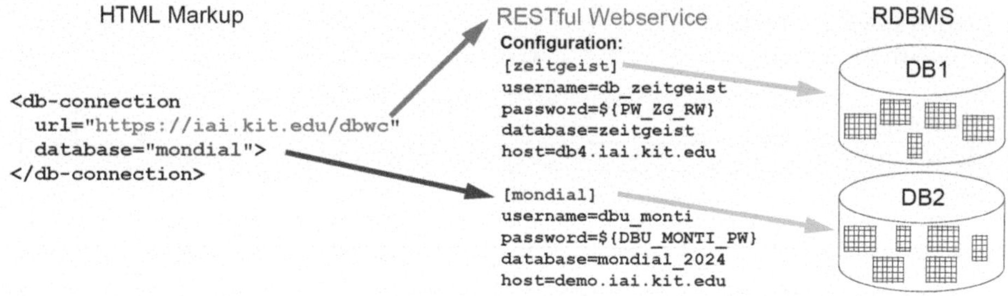

Fig. 2. Database mapping - the RESTful service maps the logical database name (*mondial*) specified in the web component (left-side) to the access information stored in the database configuration file (middle) and uses this to access the specified database (right side) (from [55]).

5.2 Table-Component

In the simplest case, the `db-table` web-component requires only one parameter that defines the table to be displayed. In this case, all data records with all columns are displayed by the component. If you are not interested in all columns and all data records, this can be restricted using the attributes `attribute-list` and `filter`. In addition, a sort order (attributes `sort`, `direction`) can be specified.

The component also provides a range of interactive elements that can be activated. This is shown using the table `country` in Fig. 3 as an example. The upper part of the figure shows the visual representation of the component, while the lower part shows the associated markup code. In this first example, the `db-connection` component from the previous section is also displayed in addition to the actual `db-table` component. For all further examples, only the markup code for the component currently being discussed is shown.

If the attribute `pagesize` is specified, a maximum of n data records per page are displayed and you can scroll through the data records page by page (1). Furthermore, it is possible to sort the data records by column values (2) or to formulate additional conditions on one or more columns (3).

The `db-table`-component also provides options for modifying records. On the one hand, direct inline edit (4) is possible and, furthermore, there is the option of deleting records from the table view or calling up an external edit view (5). These interaction elements are activated using the `actions` attribute.

Relational databases represent relationships between data sets using *foreign keys*. In the specific example, the name of the capital of a country is not stored in the `country` table, but rather a foreign key (column `Capital_fk`) exists in which the primary key value of the associated city is stored. This foreign key value is usually not helpful when visually inspecting the data records. For this reason, the `db-table` component allows

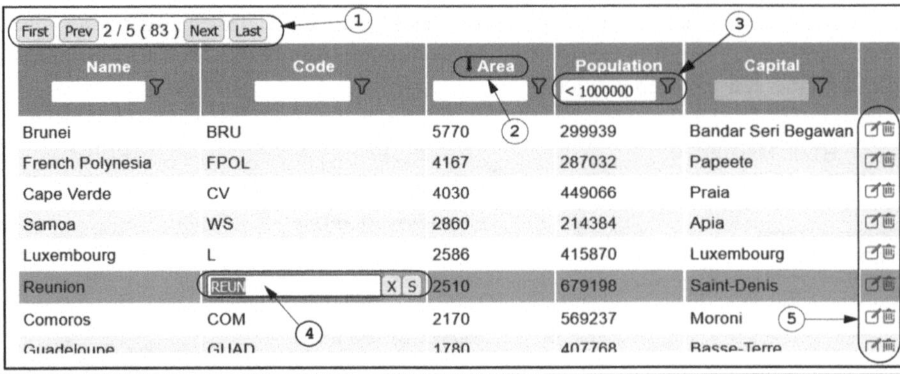


```
<db-connection
  url="https://it4edm.iai.kit.edu/dbwc"
  database="mondial-key">
</db-connection>

<db-table table="country"
  actions="filter,edit,delete,sort,inline-edit,paging"
  attribute-list="Name, Code, Area, Population, Capital_fk:city(Name) as Capital"
  pagesize="20">
</db-table>
```

Fig. 3. Visual appearance of the web component *db-table* (top) and the corresponding HTML code (bottom).

you to resolve this foreign key value and display the value of any column of the associated data record instead. This is done by tagging the entry for the foreign-key column in the attribute `attribute-list`. If a foreign key value is to be resolved, the name of the attribute is followed, separated by a double quotation mark, by the specification of the target table and the column to be displayed. In the specific example in Fig. 3, this has been done in the gray-shaded area of the markup code for the `Capital_fk` column. In addition, an alternative column name ("Capital") is specified using the `as` directive.

The visual appearance of the table can be defined by your own stylesheets. This can be done either directly by specifying a stylesheet URL (attribute `css`), or it can be defined centrally by the component `db-css` discussed later in Sect. 5.7. An overview of all possible attributes for the `db-table` component is given in Table 4.

5.3 Query-Component

The `db-query` component visualizes the result of an SQL select statement. The SQL statement can contain placeholders (parameters) whose values are read from other elements of the page. The component monitors the values of the placeholder elements and, if these change, the component executes the query again. The result is displayed in tabular form, analogous to the `db-table` component.

Figure 4 shows the functionality using a parameterized SQL statement that is supposed to display all cities between two specific latitudes. The values of the two latitudes

Table 4. Attributes of *db-table*.

Attribute	Description	Mandatory
table	Name of the table	yes
filter	Mandatory filter condition, every dataset must fulfill	no
pagesize	Maximum number of rows on a page	no
order	Sort order (column name)	no
direction	Sort direction (`asc`, `desc`)	no
page	Page to display	no
connection	Id of a *db-connection* web component. If the attribute is not set, the default connection component is chosen	no
attribute-list	Comma separated list of attributes to display (default: all)	no
actions	Allows the activation of "inline-edit", "delete", "edit", "filter", and "paging" functionality	no
refresh-rate	Time in seconds after which the table data is reloaded from the database	no
css	URL for a css file	no

are to be read from the HTML input fields at the beginning of the code fragment on the right side of the figure. Instead of specific values, the SQL statement contains question marks (?) as placeholders, which then have to be filled with values. The `params` attribute then references the source for the specific values (here: the elements with the id `min` and `max`, property `value`) and every time one of the two values is changed, the query is executed again. The left side of Fig. 4 shows the representation of the markup code (including input fields) in the browser.

Just as with the `db-table` component, additional optional parameters such as `refresh-rate`, `pagesize`, etc. can be specified. An overview of all supported attributes can be found in Table 5.

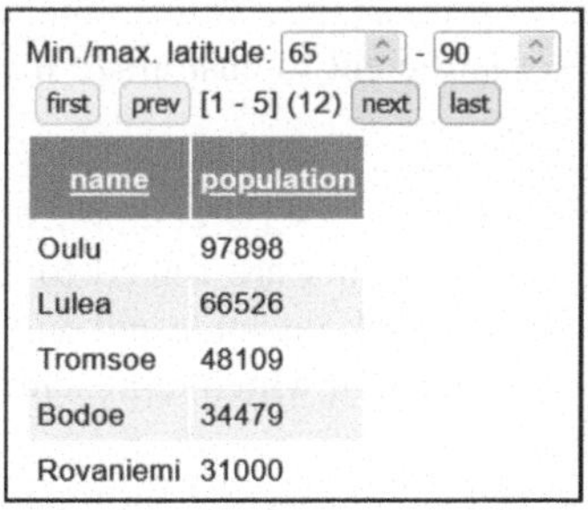


```
Min./max. latitude:
<input type="number" id="min" size="4"> -
<input type="number" id="max" size="4">
<db-query
    sql="select Name, Population
           from city
          where latitude >= ?
            and latitude <= ?
          order by Population desc"
    params="min.value max.value"
    pagesize="5">
</db-query>
```

Fig. 4. Visual appearance of the web component *db-query* (left) and the corresponding HTML code (right).

Table 5. db-query Attributes.

Attribute	Description	Mandatory
sql	SQL Statement to be executed	yes
connection	Id of a *db-connection* web component. If the attribute is not set, the default connection component is chosen	no
pagesize	Maximum number of datasets on a page	no
page	Page to display	no
refresh-rate	Duration (in seconds) until the query is resubmitted	no
css	URL for a css file	no

5.4 Row-Component

The component `db-row` represents a single data set of a table. It can be used to create a new data set, modify an existing data set or view (read only) an existing data set. The component provides an internal form for creating and modifying records. This form is constructed using the information from the metadata module (Sect. 4), such as primary and foreign keys, name and type of a column, and `not null` constraints. The form uses the information about the foreign key relationships to ensure that the value of the foreign key is not displayed, but that it is resolved and the value of the first textual column or a column to be specified of the target table is displayed. The `db-select` component described in Sect. 5.6 is used to display and select the related data record. The layout of the form or the read-only representation can be customized using CSS.

In Fig. 5 the data set of Andorra is presented using the `db-row` component. The left side shows the visual representation with the foreign key for the capital of the country resolved by the `db-select` component. Clicking on the arrow behind the name of the capital "Andorra la Vella" expands the `db-select` component and displays the list of cities from which the user can then select an entry. The associated markup code is shown on the right-hand side of the figure. The `table` attribute specifies the specific table of the data set and the `key` attribute specifies the data set within the table. The optional `display-key` attribute determines whether the primary key value should also be displayed or not. If the possibilities of CSS are not sufficient to customize the appearance to your own needs, there are two further options:

- For read-only views, any layout can be created using the `db-field` component presented next. To do this, one or more `db-field` components are linked to a `db-row` component. In this case, the `db-row` component is itself invisible and only functions as a data source for the `db-field` components, each of which represents a column of the data set.
- When creating or modifying data sets, it is possible to define an external form and link it to the component. In this case, this form is used instead of the component's internal form.

The `db-row` component can also be used in `controller-mode` as part of a Model View Controller (MVC) scenario. In this case, it has no visual representation and is only responsible for saving the data set. Depending on the parameterization, it expects the data from the URL (GET mode) or a JSON object. The component then executes an SQL insert or update statement depending on the transferred parameters. After the database operation, either the calling page is reloaded or a specified page (a view) is loaded. Table 6 gives an overview of the possible attributes of the component.

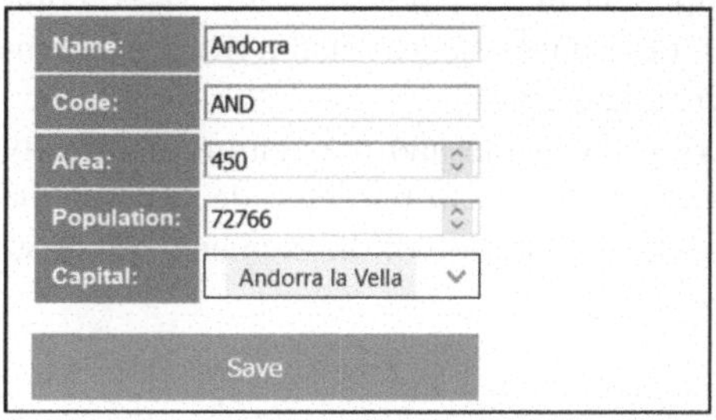


```
<db-row
    table="country"
    display-key="off"
    key="5">
</db-row>
```

Fig. 5. Web component *db-row*: Visual presentation (left) and markup code inside the HTML page (right). The record with the primary key value 5 (attribute key) of table country (attribute table) is displayed. The foreign key column Capital is resolved and displayed as a db-select component in which the possible values can be selected.

Table 6. db-row Attributes.

Attribute	Description	Mandatory
table	Name of the table	yes
connection	Id of a *db-connection* web component. If the attribute is not set, the default connection component is chosen	no
is-editable	Specifies if the dataset should be editable. Possible values: yes/no(default: yes)	no
display-key	Flag, if the database key should be displayed or not	no
attribute-list	Comma separated list of attributes to be shown (default: all attributes). For a foreign-key-column, the format can be extended to include the column of the target table, which should be displayed instead	no
key	The value of the primary key of a dataset in this table.	no
visible	Indicates if the dataset should be displayed or not	no
form	the id of a form-element, the *db-row* component should work with. Additionally a mapping between the formular fields and the table columns can be specified using the *mapping* attribute (see below)	no
mapping	Mapping between form field name and table column name	no
controller	Enable "controller-mode". If the parameter is set to "true", the parameter action must also be set (store-from-get-request, store-from-data)	no
action	See description above (controller-mode).	no
target-url, error-url	Page to load after dataset is written (controller-mode)	no
refresh-rate	Duration (in seconds) until the dataset is read again	no
css	A URL specifying a CSS-file	no

In Sect. 6 an application in the context of the MVC paradigm is shown, in which a page containing a form acts as a view and the HTML page with the db-row component takes over the controller part.

5.5 Field-Component

As mentioned in the previous section, the `db-field` component is used to implement an arbitrary read-only layout of the `db-row` component. Each `db-field` component is responsible for displaying one column of the data set (attribute `attribute`). In this scenario, the display of the component `db-row` is switched off using the attribute `visible`. If there is only one `db-row` component in the page, the `db-field` components automatically link to this component; otherwise, the associated `db-row` component must be specified using the attribute `datasource`.

Figure 6 gives a simple example, displaying the name and population of the city with the primary key value of 107 ("Andorra la Vella"). On the left side you see the result in the browser, on the right side you see the declaration of the elements `db-row` and `db-field` (2 x) in the HTML page.

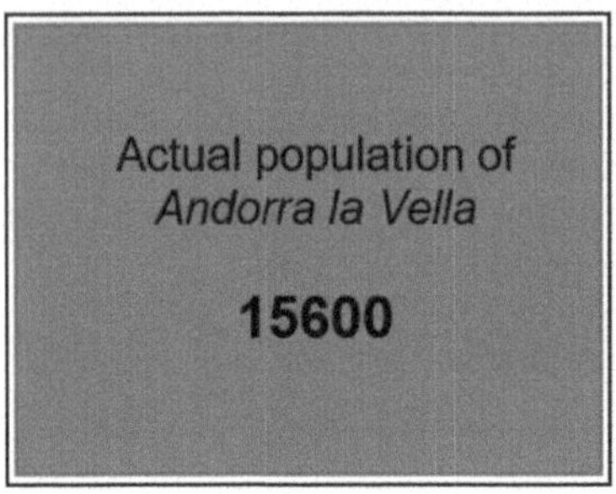


```
<db-row table="city" visible="off"
        key="107"
        refresh-rate="10">
</db-row>
<div class="large-box">
    Actual population of
    <db-field attribute="Name"
              class="cn">
    </db-field>
    <p/>
    <db-field attribute="Population"
              class="hb">
    </db-field>
</div>
```

Fig. 6. Two *db-field* components with an invisible `db-row` component.

An overview of the possible attributes of the `db-field` component is shown in Table 7.

Table 7. db-field Attributes.

Attribute	Description	Mandatory
attribute	name of the attribute to access	yes
datasource	id of the dataset component	no
css	URL for a css file	no

5.6 Selection-Component

The `db-select` component allows the selection of one (single-select) or more values (multi-select) from a list and was implemented on the basis of an extended version of the HTML select element from David Adams [1]. The values come from the database and can be formulated either by specifying a SQL select statement with one or two columns, or by specifying one or two columns, a table and an optional filter condition. If two columns are specified, the first column is used as the value and the second column as the text to be displayed for each option field. If only one column is specified, the displayed text and the value are the same. The component implements an infix and a prefix search. Figure 7 shows an example of the component. The prefix search (1) restricts the selection of displayed entries accordingly, so that you don't have to scroll through all the entries. If there is only one possible selection (attribute max=1 on the right-hand side), clicking on the desired entry closes the selection box and the entry is accepted. In multi-select mode, the menu remains open and you have the option of selecting further entries (see left side of Fig. 8 for an example). On the right side of Fig. 7 (markup) you can see the underlying SQL statement for the data, which reads the column Id of the country table as the value and the Name column as the text to be displayed. The parameter name specifies the name of the select box. The selected value is passed to the form under this name. By giving the element a unique id, it is possible to read the selected value(s) from another components as input. An example of this is given in Fig. 8, where the selected value of this component is read and used in a parameterized SQL statement.

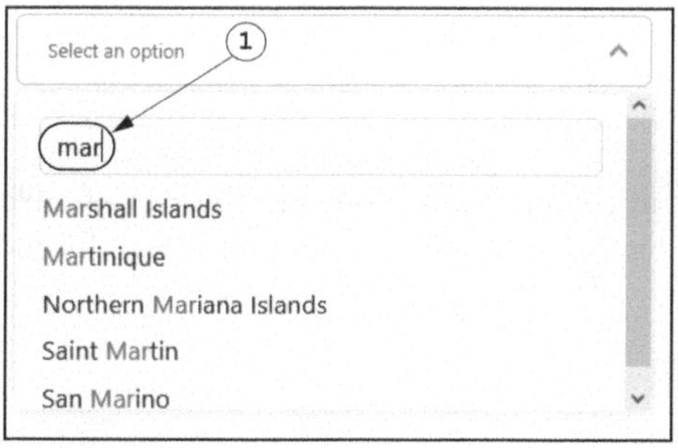


```
<db-select
   id="country-sel"
   name="country-sel"
   max="1"
   sql="select Id, Name from country">
</db-select>
```

Fig. 7. Web component *db-select* in single-selection mode (max="1"). Prefix search in column Name (attribute text) of table country (attribute table).

An central point is the display of the currently selected value(s). In the case of a one-to-many relationship (single-select mode), the current value can simply be passed to the default attribute of the component. In the case of an many-to-many relationship, which is realized in relational databases using relationship tables, it is more complicated. For this purpose, the component offers the option of specifying three columns when formulating the SQL statement. The third column then indicates whether the current option should be displayed as selected or not. If the value of the third column is NULL, the entry is not selected; otherwise it is. Displaying all potentially selectable values, in addition to the currently selected ones, can than easily be achieved by formulating an outer join. In Fig. 8, this is realized on the right-hand side by the outer join between the organization table and the ismember relationship table. Due to the outer join semantics, all entries from the organization table are displayed, but a value for the third column (the country ID) is only displayed for the organizations in which the specific country is a member. For all other organizations, the column value is NULL. This then leads to the display on the left, where all organizations are listed, but only the organizations for which the country has an entry in the `ismember` table are selected. As already explained in the introduction to the `db-query` component in Sect. 5.3, our components support parameterizable SQL statements, i.e., the statements can contain parameters (red question mark in the SQL statement), which are then replaced by the actual value. The value for a parameter comes from another element in the HTML page and is specified by the "`params`" attribute of the component. In this case, `params` has the value `country-sel.values` and references the property `values` from the `db-select` element in Fig. 7. Using this technology it is easy to build cascading components without any Javascript glue code.

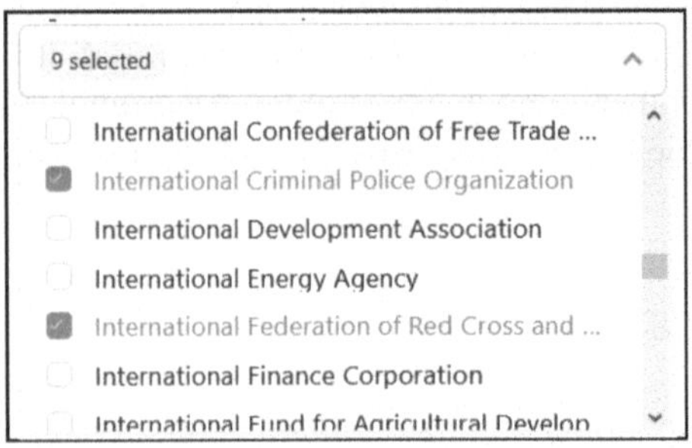


```
<db-select
  name="org-sel"
  sql="SELECT o.Id, o.Name, m.Country_fk
         FROM organization o
         LEFT JOIN ismember m
           ON o.Id= m.Organization_fk
          AND m.Country_fk = ?
        ORDER BY 2"
  params="country-sel.values" >
</db-select>
```

Fig. 8. Web component *db-select*. Prefix search in column `name` (attribute `label`) of table `country` (attribute `table`). The parameter in the SQL statement (?) and the source for the parameter value are indicated in red.

Table 8. db-select Attributes.

Attribute	Description	Mandatory
prefix-search	The term entered in the search field is considered as a prefix (Default: true)	No
default	Value(s) to be shown as selected	no
params	location (<elment-id>.<property>) of the values for the parameters ("?"-sign) in the SQL-Statement or `filter` attribute	
connection	Id of a *db-connection* web component. If the attribute is not set, the default connection component is chosen	no
css	URL for a css file	no
Variant I		
table-name	Name of the table	yes
key	Name of the attribute used for the value-attribute of the option element (returned by the form).	yes
text	Name of the attribute used for the text-node of the option element (value used for search).	yes
filter	Parameterizable condition the datasets must fulfill	no
Variant II		
sql	Parameterizable SQL-Statement with up to three columns	yes

5.7 Cascading Style Sheet Component

Each of our components can be adapted to your design requirements using the `css` attribute. If you want a different layout, you just need to change the URLs to the css-files. This can be done centrally in one place using the `db-css` component. The component expects the parameter `url`, which defines the path to a directory containing the css-files for the individual components. The name of the css-file corresponds to the name of the component with the extension `css`. For example, if the attribute `url` has the value https://www.smiffy.de/dbwc/LNBIP, the css-file for the component `db-table` is expected under the url https://www.smiffy.de/dbwc/LNBIP/db-table.css. The attribute `css` of the components and the component `db-css` are to be used either or. If both are specified, the attribute `css` has priority.

5.8 Parameter Binding

As described in the introduction to the individual components, these are configured by the attributes (Tables 4 to 8), such as the `table` attribute for the name of the underlying table of the components `db-table` and `db-row`. If the value of an attribute changes, the component is notified and can optionally re-render the component. Changing an attribute value is typically done using Javascript code that needs to be created. In order to further simplify the use of our components, we have implemented a mechanism that makes the creation of JavaScript code obsolete in many cases and enables the direct coupling of components. Analogous to the mechanism of parameterized SQL statements, in which the parameter values are read from the properties of other elements and monitored for changes, there is a mechanism for binding the attributes of our components to the values of other elements of the HTML page and monitoring them for changes.

The components support a special syntax that can be used to read attribute values from other HTML elements on the page. If the `id` of an HTML element is written in double curly brackets, the component interprets this in such a way that, on the one hand, it should read the value from there and, on the other hand, that it should be notified of any changes to the element's value so that it can react accordingly. Figure 9 shows this using the `pagesize` attribute of the `db-table` component, which gets its value from the HTML-select element with id `num-datasets`. By default, the property `value` of the element is used. If another property is to be used, it must be specified using the dot-notation.

```
<db-table table="country"
   actions="filter,edit,delete,sort,inline-edit,paging"
   attribute-list="Name, Code, Area, Population, Capital_fk:city(Name) as Capital"
   pagesize="{{num-datasets}}">
</db-table>

<select id="num-datasets">
   <option>10</option><option>20</option><option>50</option>
</select>
```

Fig. 9. Binding of an attribute value `pagesize` to an `select` element.

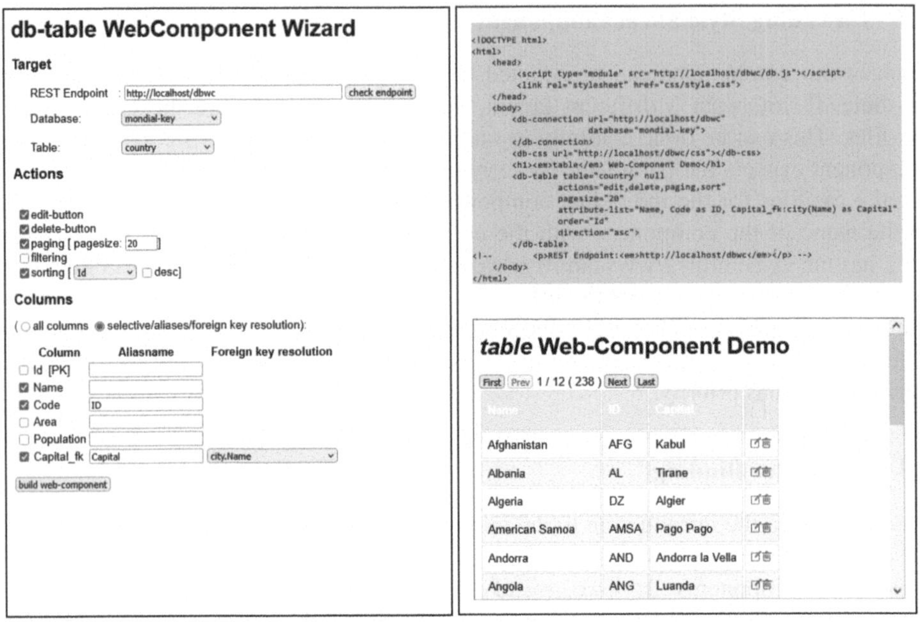

Fig. 10. Wizard for the creation of a `db-table` web-component.

5.9 Wizard

With the help of the schema information from the metadata module (Sect. 4), it is also possible to further simplify the realization of the HTML using our components by providing the developer with a wizard that enables the interactive creation of the markup code for a component. Figure 10 shows the `db-table` wizard in use. On the left side, you can see the configurator, which, after specifying the target (*REST endpoint*, *Database* and *Table*), presents the possible actions and columns to be displayed. On the right side, you can see the HTML code generated according to the settings in the configurator with our components and in the lower half the corresponding appearance, which is displayed in parallel.

6 Example Application

In this chapter we illustrate two different examples to highlight our achievements with BRDIGE to answer RQ2.

6.1 Example 1: Integration of Order Proposals

To illustrate the practical implementation of BRIDGE, we revisit Business Scenario I: Integration of Order Proposals into CRM. In this scenario, a food and beverage distributor operates a web-based ERP system with an integrated CRM module. However, the

View `webist-demo.html` (Screenshot)

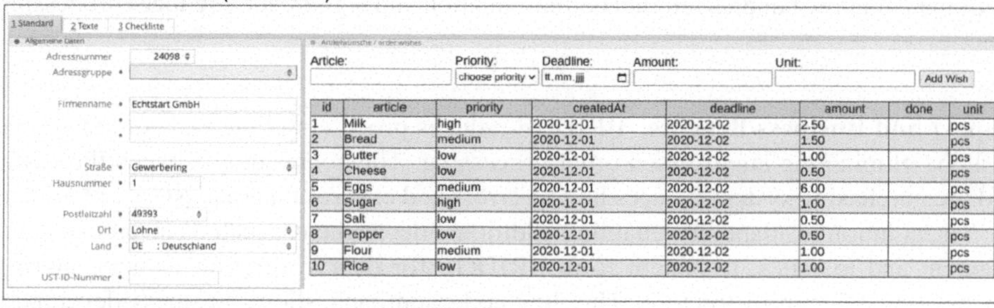

Controller `webist-demo-controller.html` (HTML Markup)

```
<script type="module" src="http://www.smiffy.de/dbwc/db.js"></script>
<db-connection database="webist-demo">
</db-connection>
<db-row controller="true"
        table="wishlist"
        action="store-from-get-request" >
</db-row>
```

Fig. 11. Example Application: Embedded web components in customer view of the SoftEngine ERP-Suite (View with HTML form and `db-table` component (top, right), controller markup (bottom) (from [55]).

purchasing department relies on a separate application that lacks direct API connectivity to the CRM. Therefore, an employee must transfer order requests via email, leading to inefficiencies and potential miscommunication.

Implementation with BRIDGE Components. The system administrator configures BRIDGE's RESTful service to connect the CRM with the purchasing system's database. To ensure data exchange, a new database user is created with appropriate read and write permissions. Authentication is managed through Keycloak, which enforces access control and ensures only authorized CRM users can submit and view order proposals. Once the database connection is established, the business developer integrates BRIDGE components into the CRM's web interface. A db-connection component establishes a link between the CRM and the purchasing system, allowing seamless data retrieval and submission. A db-row component is used to create a form where service agents can submit new order proposals, specifying article, priority, amount and unit. The customer is set implicitly. A db-table component displays a list of previously submitted requests.

User Workflow. When a service agent interacts with a customer, they can enter an order proposal into the CRM using the embedded BRIDGE form (see Fig. 11). The submitted request is stored in the purchasing system's database via the BRIDGE web service, eliminating the need for manual communication via email. The purchasing department can access the list of submitted order proposals in real time through the db-table component. Once an order is processed, the status is updated automatically, ensuring that service agents always have an up-to-date view of their customers' requests. This bidirectional data flow handles internal communication and significantly reduces processing time.

Impact and Business Benefits. BRIDGE reduces processing time and administrative costs by eliminating email-based order processing. The connection between the CRM and the purchasing system reduces human errors and ensures that requests are recorded.

The solution is adaptable, enabling additional departments, such as inventory management and logistics, to benefit from BRIDGE for data integration without altering the existing ERP infrastructure. This low-code approach allows business developers to quickly implement new workflows, reducing reliance on software engineers and enabling organizations to respond more swiftly to operational needs.

Integrating BRIDGE into the CRM facilitates order tracking, alleviates engineering bottlenecks, and streamlines the procurement process without requiring extensive backend development.

6.2 Example 2: Interactive Forms

A second example application in Fig. 12 demonstrates a simple, but functional query interface on top of a database. In this example, after selecting a country and subsequently selecting a province of that country, all cities in this province should be listed. This is shown in the figure on the left (after selecting the province of "Baden Württemberg" inside the country of "Germany").

The markup code of this application is shown on the right. The ability to formulate parameterized SQL statements (Sect. 5.3) and to access and monitor the properties of other elements on the page makes it easy to connect the developed components without having to write additional Javascript code.

In the example, two `db-select` and one `db-query` components are connected in a cascade (dashed arrows). The link is established by referencing the property of an element (`<element-id>.<property-name>`) in the `params` attribute of the component interested in the value.

The SQL statement of the first `db-select` component lists all countries in alphabetical order and displays them in the selection box. When a country is selected, the second `db-select` component is informed (solid red arrow in the figure) and executes an SQL statement that displays all the provinces of that country in the second selection box. Similarly, when a province is selected, the subsequently connected `db-query` component is informed of the change to the `values` property of the element with the id `province-sel` and then lists all the cities in that province.

7 Limitations and Improvements

While BRIDGE provides a low-code approach to database integration, several limitations must be addressed to improve its security, configurability, and extensibility. The main areas for improvement include authentication and security and integration with external business logic.

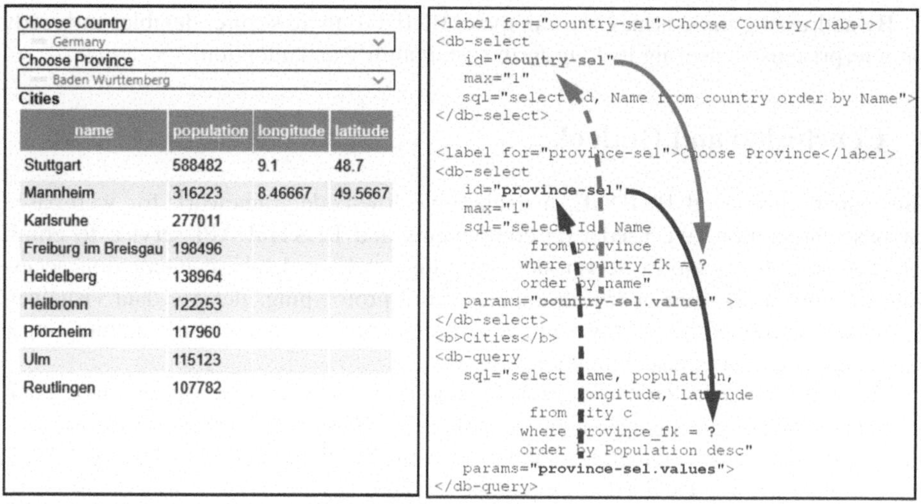

Fig. 12. Example Application 2: Cascading BRIDGE components, building a tiny interface on top of a relational database.

At the current stage of development, BRIDGE does not fully support OAuth2 or OpenID Connect, limiting its compatibility with modern federated authentication systems. In enterprise environments, AD integration would be an improvement, enabling user authentication across systems. RBAC (Role-Based Access Control) has not been fully implemented yet. Currently, the system does not support column-level access control, meaning users either have complete access to a dataset or none at all. By implementing fine-grained access policies, we can ensure that users only see or modify the data they are authorized to handle. At present, it is only possible to restrict a database connection to certain tables.

BRIDGE has some limitations: First, it does not allow file attachments, which makes it less useful for document storage. Second, it does not consider third-party business logic, making it tricky to integrate with external automation tools that have their own custom setups. To address these issues, we can use OpenAPI for integration. This would enable BRIDGE to connect with other business applications, allowing organizations to build custom workflows over several web services. In short, this would enhance BRIDGE's functionality beyond basic data operations.

To enhance the adoption of BRIDGE, we present a roadmap for further steps in the development. The following steps should be taken:

1. Conduct qualitative and quantitative evaluations to assess the developer experience, system performance, and overall business impact.
2. Refactor the code and expand the documentation to simplify maintenance and deployment processes.
3. Engage with the open-source community and onboard development partners to collaboratively improve BRIDGE.

By addressing these issues, we can make BRIDGE more secure, flexible, and ready for enterprise use, ensuring its long-term sustainability and adoption.

8 Conclusion and Outlook

This paper introduced BRIDGE, a declarative low-code framework for web-based database integration. We used web components and RESTful API service to eliminate the need for complex server-side scripting, making database interaction accessible to more users. Our approach enables rapid prototyping, flexible data visualization, and streamlined integration with existing enterprise systems while maintaining a lightweight, standards-based implementation.

The versatility of BRIDGE extends beyond traditional software development environments. For content management systems (e.g., WordPress) or enterprise applications, users can easily integrate database-driven functionalities by adapting HTML pages. Furthermore, BRIDGE components function within the browser's file URI schema, so they do not require a dedicated web server, reducing infrastructure dependencies.

While BRIDGE offers a solid foundation for low-code database integration, several areas require further development:

- **Security Enhancements:** Implementing RBAC and fine-grained access policies to improve data security.
- **Usability & Configurability:** Refining the developer experience, mainly through a guided wizard for OpenAPI-based integrations and configurable security policies.
- **Interoperability:** Expanding support for OData, OpenAPI-based data sources, and SOLID principles to enhance data portability and compliance.

The next step is to assess BRIDGE's real-world applicability through a structured evaluation. The evaluation includes quantitative benchmarks and qualitative feedback. We aim to optimize BRIDGE further, ensuring it becomes a practical solution for modern database-driven applications.

Acknowledgments. This publication was partly supported within the Hub Energy of the Helmholtz Metadata Collaboration (HMC), an incubator platform of the Helmholtz Association within the framework of the Information and Data Science strategic initiative.

Disclosure of Interests. The authors have no competing interests to declare that are relevant to the content of this article.

References

1. Adams, D.: Multi Select Dropdown with HTML and JavaScript. https://codeshack.io/multi-select-dropdown-html-javascript/. Accessed 19 Feb 2025
2. Almaree, K., et al.: The usefulness of cash budgets in micro, very small and small retail enterprises operating in the cape metropolis. Expert J. Bus. Manag. **3**(1) (2015)

3. Arora, R., Ghosh, N., Mondal, T.: Sagitec software studio (s3)-a low code application development platform. In: 2020 International Conference on Industry 4.0 Technology (I4Tech), pp. 13–17. IEEE (2020)
4. Bader, J., Seohyun Kim, S., Sifei Luan, F., Chandra, S., Meijer, E.: Ai in software engineering at facebook. IEEE Softw. **38**(4), 52–61 (2021). https://doi.org/10.1109/MS.2021.3061664
5. Bajenaru, A.: Software-as-a-service and cloud computing, a solution for small and medium-sized companies. Bulletin Of The Transilvania University Of Brasov. Series V: Economic Sciences, pp. 173–184 (2010)
6. Beck, K., et al.: Manifesto for agile software development (2001). http://www.agilemanifesto.org/
7. Berman, S.J.: Digital transformation: opportunities to create new business models. Strategy Leadership **40**(2), 16–24 (2012)
8. Bertocci, V.: Modern Authentication with Azure Active Directory for Web Applications. Microsoft Press, Hoboken (2015)
9. Bharadwaj, A., El Sawy, O.A., Pavlou, P.A., Venkatraman, N.V.: Digital business strategy: toward a next generation of insights. MIS Q. 471–482 (2013)
10. Bhargav-Spantzel, A., Squicciarini, A., Bertino, E.: Privacy preserving multi-factor authentication with biometrics. In: Proceedings of the Second ACM Workshop on Digital Identity Management, pp. 63–72 (2006)
11. Blackwell, A.F.: Moral Codes: Designing Alternatives to AI. MIT Press, Cambridge (2024)
12. Bock, A.C., Frank, U.: Low-code platform. Bus. Inf. Syst. Eng. **63**, 733–740 (2021)
13. Breaux, T., Moritz, J.: The 2021 software developer shortage is coming. Commun. ACM **64**(7), 39–41 (2021)
14. Cecchini, G., et al.: Digital transformation in Europe. In: Capogna, S., Greco, F. (eds.) The Digital Transformation of European Higher Education. Innovation, Technology, and Knowledge Management, LNCS, pp. 51–84. Springer, Cham (2024). https://doi.org/10.1007/978-3-031-70763-6_3
15. CECE: Informatics Education in Europe: Are We All In The Same Boat? Tech. rep., Association for Computing Machinery, New York, NY, USA (2017)
16. Chorafas, D.N.: Integrating ERP, CRM, Supply Chain Management, and Smart Materials. Auerbach Publications, Boca Raton (2001)
17. Croft, M., Fraser, G., Gaul, W.: Role of the new south wales department of primary industries' laboratory information management system (lims) in the 2007 equine influenza emergency animal disease response. Aust. Vet. J. **89**, 47–49 (2011)
18. Daithankar, J., Pandit, T., Daithankar, J., Pandit, T.: The need for tms: challenges, it landscape. Transportation Management with SAP TM 9.0: A Hands-On Guide to Configuring, Implementing, and Optimizing SAP TM, pp. 7–12 (2014)
19. Desmond, B., Richards, J., Allen, R., Lowe-Norris, A.G.: Active Directory: Designing, Deploying, and Running Active Directory. O'Reilly Media, Inc., Sebastopol (2008)
20. Domes, S.: Progressive Web Apps with React: Create Lightning Fast Web Apps with Native Power Using React and Firebase. Packt Publishing Ltd., Birmingham (2017)
21. Elshan, E., Dickhaut, E., Ebel, P.: An investigation of why low code platforms provide answers and new challenges. In: Hawaii International Conference on System Sciences (HICSS). Maui, Hawaii (2023). https://pubs.wi-kassel.de/wp-content/uploads/2023/01/JML_916.pdf
22. Farrell, J., Nezlek, G.S.: Rich internet applications the next stage of application development. In: 2007 29th International Conference on Information Technology Interfaces, pp. 413–418. IEEE (2007)
23. Florescu, D., Levy, A., Mendelzon, A.: Database techniques for the world-wide web: a survey. ACM SIGMOD Rec. **27**(3), 59–74 (1998)

24. Fraternali, P., Rossi, G., Sánchez-Figueroa, F.: Rich internet applications. IEEE Internet Comput. **14**(3), 9–12 (2010)
25. Grooss, O.F.: Digitalization of maintenance activities in small and medium-sized enterprises: a conceptual framework. Comput. Ind. **154**, 104039 (2024)
26. Hajian, M.: Progressive Web Apps with Angular: Create Responsive, Fast and Reliable PWAs Using Angular. Apress, New York (2019)
27. Hardt, D.: RFC 6749: the oauth 2.0 authorization framework. Tech. rep., RFC Editor, USA (2012)
28. Heagney, J.: Fundamentals of project management. Amacom (2016)
29. Helo, P., Thai, V.V.: Logistics 4.0–digital transformation with smart connected tracking and tracing devices. Int. J. Prod. Econ. **275**, 109336 (2024)
30. Hossain, M.: CORS in action: creating and consuming cross-origin APIs. Manning (2014). https://books.google.de/books?id=iFV8ngEACAAJ
31. Huiping, C.: An integration framework of erm, scm, crm. In: 2009 International Conference on Management and Service Science, pp. 1–4. IEEE (2009)
32. Hustad, E., Stensholt, J.: Customizing erp-systems: a framework to support the decision-making process. Procedia Comput. Sci. **219**, 789–796 (2023)
33. Hyrynsalmi, S.M., Rantanen, M.M., Hyrynsalmi, S.: The war for talent in software business-how are finnish software companies perceiving and coping with the labor shortage? In: 2021 IEEE International Conference on Engineering, Technology and Innovation (ICE/ITMC), pp. 1–10. IEEE (2021)
34. Iskandar, T.F., Lubis, M., Kusumasari, T.F., Lubis, A.R.: Comparison between client-side and server-side rendering in the web development. In: IOP Conference Series: Materials Science and Engineering, vol. 801, p. 012136. IOP Publishing (2020)
35. Jesse, N.: Agility eats legacy - the long good-bye. IFAC-PapersOnLine **52**(25), 154–158 (2019). https://doi.org/10.1016/j.ifacol.2019.12.464, https://www.sciencedirect.com/science/article/pii/S2405896319323730, 19th IFAC Conference on Technology, Culture and International Stability TECIS 2019
36. Kaluža, M., Kalanj, M., Vukelić, B.: A comparison of back-end frameworks for web ąpplication development. Zbornik veleučilišta u rijeci **7**(1), 317–332 (2019)
37. Kerwin, M.: The file URI Scheme. RFC 8089 (2017). https://doi.org/10.17487/RFC8089, https://www.rfc-editor.org/info/rfc8089
38. Lazuardy, M.F.S., Anggraini, D.: Modern front end web architectures with react. js and next. js. Res. J. Adv. Eng. Sci. **7**(1), 132–141 (2022)
39. Markus, M.L., Keil, M.: If we build it, they will come: designing information systems that people want to use. MIT Sloan Manag. Rev. **35**(4), 11 (1994)
40. Martins, R., Caldeira, F., Sa, F., Abbasi, M., Martins, P.: An overview on how to develop a low-code application using outsystems. In: 2020 International Conference on Smart Technologies in Computing, Electrical and Electronics (ICSTCEE), pp. 395–401. IEEE (2020)
41. May, W.: Information extraction and integration with florid: the mondial case study. Tech. rep, Citeseer (1999)
42. Mew, L., Field, D.: A case study on using the mendix low code platform to support a project management course. In: Proceedings of the EDSIG Conference ISSN, vol. 2473, p. 3857 (2018)
43. Mfanga, A., Sam, A., Kalegele, K.: An overview of existing frameworks for integrating fragmented information systems. Int. J. Inf. Sci. Tech. **6**, 13–23 (2016). https://doi.org/10.5121/ijist.2016.6602
44. Neuman, B.C., Ts'o, T.: Kerberos: an authentication service for computer networks. IEEE Commun. Mag. **32**(9), 33–38 (1994)

45. Noda, T., Helwig, S.: Rich internet applications. Technical Comparison and Case Studies of AJAX, Flash, and Java based RIA UW E-Business-Consortium Opinion Papers (2005) AJAX, Flash, and Java based RIA UW E-Business-Consortium Opinion Papers (2005)
46. Peyrott, S.: JWT Handbook (2024). https://auth0.com/resources/ebooks/jwt-handbook. Accessed 16 Sep 2024
47. Prinz, N., Rentrop, C., Huber, M.: Low-code development platforms-a literature review. In: AMCIS (2021)
48. Riva, M.: Real-World Next. js: Build Scalable, High-Performance, and Modern Web Applications Using Next. js, The React Framework for Production. Packt Publishing Ltd., Birmingham (2022)
49. Rojas, C.: Building Progressive Web Applications with Vue. js: Reliable, Fast, and Engaging Apps with Vue. js. Apress, New York (2019)
50. Rokis, K., Kirikova, M.: Challenges of low-code/no-code software development: a literature review. In: Nazaruka, ÄŠ., Sandkuhl, K., Seigerroth, U. (eds.) Perspectives in Business Informatics Research. BIR 2022. LNBIP, vol. 462, pp. 3–17. Springer, Cham (2022). https://doi.org/10.1007/978-3-031-16947-2_1
51. Sahay, A., Di Ruscio, D., Iovino, L., Pierantonio, A.: Analyzing business process management capabilities of low-code development platforms. Softw.: Pract. Exp. **53**(4), 1036–1060 (2023)
52. Salameh, H.: What, when, why, and how? A comparison between agile project management and traditional project management methods. Int. J. Bus. Manag. Rev. **2**(5), 52–74 (2014)
53. Schaupp, E., Abele, E., Metternich, J.: Potentials of digitalization in tool management. Procedia CiRp **63**, 144–149 (2017)
54. van der Schee, M.: PHP-CRUD-API (2024). https://github.com/mevdschee/php-crud-api. Accessed 16 Sep 2024
55. Schmidt, A., Münch, T.: Enable business users to embed dynamic database content in existing web-based systems using web components and generic web services. In: Proceedings of the 20th International Conference on Web Information Systems and Technologies - WEBIST, pp. 296–306. INSTICC, SciTePress (2024). https://doi.org/10.5220/0013000000003825
56. Schwalbe, K.: Introduction to Project Management. Course Technology Cengage Learning, Boston (2009)
57. Shi, Q., Wang, H., Wang, H., Chen, J.: Design of webgis rendering engine based on silverlight-based ria. In: 2011 Fourth International Conference on Intelligent Computation Technology and Automation, vol. 1, pp. 1050–1053. IEEE (2011)
58. Skare, M., de Obesso, M.D.L.M., Ribeiro-Navarrete, S.: Digital transformation and European small and medium enterprises (smes): a comparative study using digital economy and society index data. Int. J. Inf. Manag. **68**, 102594 (2023)
59. Špundak, M.: Mixed agile/traditional project management methodology-reality or illusion? Procedia Soc. Behav. Sci. **119**, 939–948 (2014)
60. Small and medium-sized enterprises (SME) - German Federal Statistical Office (2024). https://www.destatis.de/EN/Themes/Economic-Sectors-Enterprises/Enterprises/Small-Sized-Enterprises-Medium-Sized-Enterprises/ExplanatorySME.html. Accessed 07 Nov 2024
61. Stuttard, D., Pinto, M.: The Web Application Hacker's Handbook: Finding and Exploiting Security Flaws. John Wiley & Sons, Hoboken (2011)
62. Thorgersen, S., Silva, P.I.: Keycloak-Identity and Access Management for Modern Applications: Harness the Power of Keycloak, OpenID Connect, and OAuth 2.0 Protocols to Secure Applications. Packt Publishing Ltd., Birmingham (2021)
63. Wahl, M., Kille, S., Howes, T.: Lightweight Directory Access Protocol (v3). RFC 2251 (1997). https://doi.org/10.17487/RFC2251, https://www.rfc-editor.org/info/rfc2251

64. HTML Living Standard (2024). https://html.spec.whatwg.org/dev/. Accessed 16 Sep 2024
65. Wiechmann, D.M., Reichstein, C., Haerting, R.C., Bueechl, J., Pressl, M.: Agile management to secure competitiveness in times of digital transformation in medium-sized businesses. Procedia Comput. Sci. **207**, 2353–2363 (2022)
66. Wysokińska, Z.: A review of the impact of the digital transformation on the global and European economy. Comp. Econ. Res. Cent. Eastern Eur. **24**(3), 75–92 (2021)

Co-creative Robotics: Foundations, Challenges, and Collaborative Networks as a Mitigation Approach

Sanaz Nikghadam-Hojjati[1](✉), Eda Marchetti[2](✉), Jose Barata[3](✉), and Antonello Calabrò[2](✉)

[1] CTS- UNINOVA LASI, Nova University Lisbon, CNR-ISTI, 2829-516 Caparica, Portugal
sanaznik@uninova.pt

[2] Istituto di Scienza E Tecnologie dell'Informazione "A. Faedo", CNR, Pisa, Italy
{eda.marchetti,antonello.calabro}@isti.cnr.it

[3] CTS- UNINOVA, and LASI, Nova University Lisbon, 2829-516 Caparica, Portugal
jab@uninova.pt

Abstract. In the current polycrisis, volatile, uncertain, complex, and ambiguous world, traditional tools that once addressed isolated needs are no longer sufficient. There is a growing demand for solutions that provide diverse value and address multiple evolving challenges simultaneously. Robots also need to navigate an unpredictable world where adaptability, creativity, and collaboration are just as important as precision and speed. In response, Co-Creative Robotics (CCRs) has emerged as one of the transformative robotics subfields that integrates computational creativity and robotics to overcome these limitations. While research in this field has grown over the past two decades, gaps remain in understanding its foundations, key challenges, and strategies for advancement.

This conceptual expansion study investigates these gaps and explores the Collaborative Networks (CNs) as a possible strategic mitigation approach. To achieve the goals of this study, a mixed-method approach combining a narrative literature review and expert-focused group brainstorming was applied. The findings demonstrate CCRs considerably differ from traditional robotics and computational creativity across multiple dimensions. Additionally, 16 key challenges were identified. To address these challenges, seven categories of CNs were explored. Findings revealed CNs enhance human creativity, algorithmic efficiency, scalability, and resource management by integrating human insights, machine intelligence, and nature-inspired principles. They also improve human robot collaboration by strengthening communication, trust, interpretability, and ethical considerations. Furthermore, by embedding sustainability, regulatory compliance, and public acceptance, CNs support the development of robust, ethical, and culturally sensitive co-creative robotic systems.

Keywords: Co-creative robotics · Collaborative networks · Challenges

M. Marchiori et al. (Eds.): WEBIST 2024, LNBIP 583, pp. 49–89, 2026.
https://doi.org/10.1007/978-3-032-25534-1_3

1 Introduction

Over the past decade, robots have increasingly demonstrated their importance in our rapidly evolving world by contributing to various aspects of our daily lives. They profoundly transform our society, industries, and economies in ways that cannot be overlooked [1]. For instance, in industry, robots have revolutionized manufacturing processes, increasing efficiency, precision, and productivity while changing the skill and competence requirements for workers in these fields [2, 3]. They handle repetitive tasks quickly and accurately, freeing human workers to focus on more complex and creative endeavours, necessitating a shift in the skill sets and competencies needed for success [2–4]. In healthcare, robots assist surgeons in delicate procedures, provide support in rehabilitation therapies, and aid in tasks such as medication delivery and patient monitoring, altering the skill requirements for medical professionals [5–7]. In disaster management, they contribute to disaster response efforts, navigating hazardous environments to search for survivors and assessing damage, prompting a need for specialized training in robotic operation and coordination [8, 9]. In agriculture, they automate planting, harvesting, and crop monitoring, enhancing food production and sustainability and reshaping the skills of Agri-workers [10, 11]. Beyond these domains, robots play roles in entertainment [12], education [13], transportation [14], and even household chores [15], transforming the way humans live, work, and interact with technology, and requiring individuals to adapt to new skill demands in these evolving fields.

Robots designed for specific tasks across different fields provide a range of benefits, such as higher productivity and reliability [16], greater efficiency and quality [17], better consistency and accuracy [18], operators [19], human capabilities enhancement [20], reduced costs through automation [18], and the capacity for continuous operation [21]. These advantages are the results of the engineers tailored design to meet the requirements of specific applications in a particular field [22, 23]. Although specialized robots offer several benefits, they face several limitations, including inflexible operation, restricted autonomy [49], and inability to operate with creativity [24]. They can also challenge current human skills and job roles [25], and they often lack the versatility and adaptability needed in volatile, uncertain, complex, and ambiguous (VUCA) and polycrisis environments [26, 27]. Additionally, these robots may require specialized knowledge or struggle to address complex and poorly defined real-world problems [28]. To address these challenges, the emerging field of Co-Creative Robotics (CCRs) seeks to overcome these constraints by emphasizing adaptability, autonomy, and creativity in robotic systems [29, 30]. CCRs offers a transformative approach to robotics research, opening new possibilities for innovation, collaboration, and societal impact [31].

By focusing on adaptability, creativity, and inclusiveness, CCRs opens the path for a future where robots are central to solving complex challenges and enhancing the quality of life for humans [32]. However, CCRs advancement depends on mitigating its challenges and limitations, such as the complexity of human creativity [33], technological limitations [34], relevant skill constraints [33], adaptability and generalization [34], human-robot interaction (HRI) [35], ethical and social implications [34], interdisciplinary integration [33], resource constraints [35], and performance, effectiveness, and impact's validation and evaluation [36]. Collaborating with stakeholders is crucial to mitigate these challenges and limitations [37–39]. Collaboration fosters synergistic interactions, promotes knowledge sharing and exchange, and enables collective problem-solving, helping to overcome challenges and limitations [40, 41]. By working together, stakeholders can harness the collective expertise and resources needed to drive innovation, address societal challenges, and unlock the full potential of robotic systems to benefit humanity.

Thus, this Conceptual Expansion Research, aims to *explore the emerging field of CCRs by investigating its foundations, distinguishing it from Traditional Robotics and Computational Creativity, identifying its critical challenges, and examining how Collaborative Networks (CNs) can help mitigate these challenges.* To achieve its goals, by applying Mixed-Methods, it will answer the following Research Questions [RQs]:

[RQ1] What are the foundations of CCRs, and how do CCRs differentiate from Traditional Robotics and Computational Creativity?
[RQ2] What are the critical challenges of CCRs?
[RQ3] How can CNs serve as a mitigation approach to address the identified challenges in CCRs?

The current article will discuss and answer these RQs in Sects. 3, 4 and 5. Section 2 explains the research methodology, and Sect. 6 presents the conclusion, research contributions, and potential future work.

2 Methodology

This Conceptual Expansion Research to achieve its goals and answer the RQs applied Mixed-Methods approach include: i) **Narrative Literature Reviews**: this method has been used due to the trans-disciplinary nature of the current research. The Narrative Literature Review is used in the process of reviewing foundations of CCRs and its differences from traditional robotics [RQ1], the preliminary study of the challenges and limitations of advancement of CCRs [RQ2], and the initial research on the role of collaboration and CNs as a strategic mitigation approach for facing challenges of CCRs advancement [QR3]. ii) **Focused Group Brainstorming**: a structured approach for generating ideas, solutions, or creative insights within a group setting, combining the benefits of both brainstorming and focused discussions to identify the critical challenges and limitations of advancement of CCRs and the role of collaboration and CNs as a strategic mitigation approach for facing challenges of CCRs advancement [RQs 2 and 3]. It involves stating research questions, selecting participants, and setting ground rules. Participants engage in 5 in-person and five online brainstorming meetings, generating and discussing ideas. Results are anonymously presented to a validating group, and the best ideas are selected in individual meetings with each participant during the validating phase. The focused and validating groups were selected based on the current research and innovation activities oriented toward community and business environment needs. In particular, the focus group includes **10** experts from robotics, computational creativity, CNs, electronics and computing engineering, software and hardware engineering, informatics and computer science, and information and communication technologies. The brainstorming sessions results were validated anonymously by **8** experts from robotics, computational creativity, CNs, and computer science disciplines.

3 Foundations of CCRs

The growth of robotics has been driven by human creativity and continuous efforts to enhance efficiency and automate different tasks. Starting with the early mechanical birds of ancient civilizations, like Archytas's steam-powered invention from 350 B.C. [40], and evolving into today's advanced machines that aim to outperform human capabilities, robotics has progressed through several key milestones [42] The history of modern robotics can be traced back to the origins of the field's name.

The term "robot" was introduced by Karel Čapek in the 1920s, which comes from the Czech word "robota," meaning "forced labour." Karel Čapek described robots as mechanical beings capable of performing human tasks [43]. The Čapek vision took a concrete shape with the advent of the first industrial robot, UNIMATE, in the 1960s. Since then, UNIMATE and its descendants revolutionized manufacturing processes by undertaking repetitive and hazardous tasks [44].

In the last two decades of 20th century, as technology and interdisciplinary collaborations advanced, the capabilities of robots also improved. During the 1970s to 1990s, remarkable advancements in control systems and programming languages enabled robots to execute complex sequences of operations with greater precision and flexibility [45, 46]. In the 80s, the emergence of mobile and service robots expanded the realm of possibilities, allowing robots to navigate autonomously and perform various tasks in unstructured environments [45, 47].

Integrating artificial intelligence (AI) with robots started in the new 21st century and caused a paradigm shift. AI empowered robots to learn from their environment, make decisions, and interact more complexly [43]. The most recent developments in robotics (Since the 2010s) have been characterized by the rise of collaborative robots, or Cobots, which work alongside humans to enhance productivity and innovation [48].

In the meantime, the field of soft robotics has emerged. Soft robotics got inspiration from the natural world to create robots with unprecedented flexibility and adaptability [48]. These milestones, which are summarized in Fig. 1, not only highlight the technological progress in robotics but also underscore the potential of robots to transform industries and improve the quality of human life.

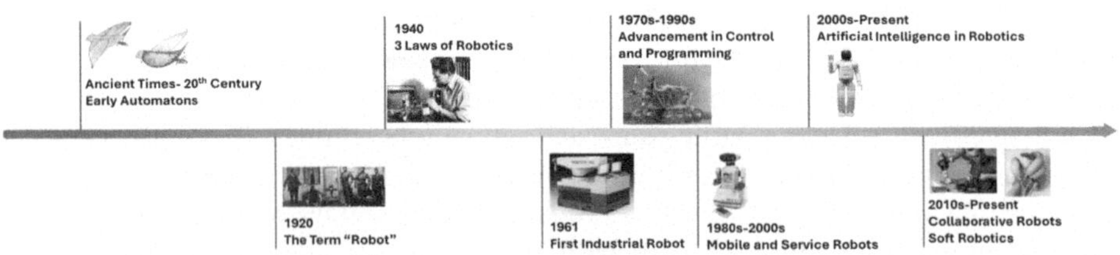

Fig. 1. Brief History of Robotics [30].

However, alongside technological evolvement, the real world's challenges and opportunities are becoming more VUCA [49]. This makes the current robotics ill-suited to address the real world's challenges and opportunities [50].

The traditional robots that are typically programmed to perform specific tasks in controlled environments struggle to adapt to dynamic and uncertain environments [51].

Most of them are designed for [30]repetitive and isolated tasks, which cause limitations in the social and emotional intelligence necessary to engage with humans and help them in their tasks [52]. Traditional robots are mainly programmed to follow pre-defined instructions and have difficulty adapting to new situations and problems [53].

Most industrial robots are optimized for efficiency and productivity [85], but they have severe limitations in the creativity and imagination required for creative endeavours [54]. Traditional robots follow predetermined rules and algorithms, with limitations in considering ethical dilemmas and making value-based judgments [55].

To overcome these limitations, it is essential to develop not only technically advanced but also socially adaptable, autonomous, creative, collaborative, and ethical robots. This enables them to navigate and contribute positively to diverse societal, economic, and environmental contexts and interact with human in their performance.

These robots should be able to learn and adapt to dynamic and uncertain environments rather than being confined to pre-programmed tasks in controlled settings [56]. They must be socially, physically, emotionally intelligent, adaptive, and safe to effectively engage and collaborate with humans in various contexts [57]. Also, these robots should prioritize creativity, innovation, and problem-solving capabilities to tackle new challenges and tasks with flexibility and ingenuity [54]. They must make human value-based judgments and consider ethical dilemmas to provide a higher level of autonomy and responsibility in decision-making processes [55, 58]. To develop robots with mentioned capabilities, one of the promising approaches is integrating two emerging fields of computational creativity and robotics through an interdisciplinary perspective.

Computational creativity uses computational methods and techniques to model, simulate, or enhance human creativity [59, 60]. It uses AI, cognitive psychology, philosophy, and the art fields to study, emulate, motivate, and enhance human creativity to reach one of the various ends [61]:

- Developing models, methods, and computer-based programs that can stimulate and enhance human creativity without necessarily being creative themselves.
- Developing models, methods, and computer-based programs that can generate human-level creative ideas.
- Better studying and understanding the nature and processes of human creativity and applying a computer perspective on human creative behaviour.

By getting an advantage from the power of computational creativity, researchers are exploring new ways to empower robots with creative abilities, enabling them to generate novel ideas, solutions, and expressions [62]. CCRs emerge as a natural extension of this concept, where the principles of computational creativity are applied to robotics to create not only technically proficient but also creatively capable robots.

In this regard, and in replying to the RQ1: "What are the foundations of CCRs, and how do CCRs differentiate from Traditional Robotics and Computational Creativity?" authors adopt the following definition for CCRs [30] as *"an interdisciplinary field that integrates computational creativity and robotics principles to develop machines capable of demonstrating or supporting creative behaviour by generating human-like novel ideas, solutions, and artistic expressions, or collaborating in the creative tasks."*

CCRs, in a broader context, encompasses the following aspects [30]:

- Developing computational creativity-based robots that support humans in their creative tasks and stimulate and enhance their creative behaviour without necessarily being creative themselves.
- Developing computational creativity-based robots that can generate human-level creative ideas and learn and demonstrate creative behaviour.
- Better studying and understanding the nature and processes of human creativity, from different perspectives such as philosophy, neuroscience, psychology, anatomy and biology, cognitive science, and art.

Table 1 presents an overview of the different characteristics of CCRs compared to computational creativity and traditional robotics regarding various criteria such as creativity, autonomy, physical capabilities, human interaction, adaptability, ethical considerations, and learning.

As evidenced by Table 1, the main limitations of traditional robotics and computational creativity are the lack of dynamic included tasks and environments, with the concrete risk of struggling with adaptability or understanding in dynamic or uncertain situations, and the difficulty in simulating human creativity because seriously bounded by the intuition and insight of human creators. CCRs overcome the above-mentioned limitations even if they could have restrictions in their human-behaviour representation due to physical capabilities, complexity of tasks, and interaction with unpredictable environments. As schematized in Fig. 2, from a technological perspective, CCRs encompasses components and principles that enable robots to engage in creative tasks and behaviours as the main actors. Key technological aspects of CCRs are computational creativity, affective computing, sensory perception, HRI, autonomous decision-making, physical embodiment, feedback mechanism, ethics, and cybersecurity.

Computational Creativity, which incorporates AI, focuses on developing algorithms, methods, models, and computer programs that simulate or enhance human creativity, allowing robots to produce innovative ideas, solutions, and artistic expressions [63]. It will use AI techniques such as Machine Learning (ML), deep learning, and Natural Language Processing (NLP) to enable robots to autonomously learn, reason, and generate novel and appropriate ideas and solutions [64].

Affective Computing involves the development of algorithms and systems that enable robots to understand, interpret, and respond to human emotions, which is fundamental in HRI [65]. HRI technologies facilitate seamless collaboration between humans and robots in creative endeavours, providing interfaces for NLP, Gesture Recognition, and emotional understanding. Advanced sensory systems, including cameras, microphones, and tactile sensors, enable robots to perceive and understand their environment and interact with objects, people, and surroundings [66]. Additionally, robots require algorithms for planning, reasoning, and adapting creatively to dynamic conditions, enabling them to make independent decisions based on task comprehension, environmental factors, and objectives [67, 68].

The physical manifestation of robots, such as robotic arms, hands, or humanoid bodies, plays a pivotal role in CCRs by serving as the medium through which creative outputs are expressed [69, 70]. Furthermore, co-creative robots integrate feedback mechanisms that enable them to assess and learn from their actions, refining their creative abilities over time through iterative processes [71].

Table 1. CCRs, Computational Creativity, Traditional Robotics Differences (adopted from [30]).

Criteria	Traditional Robotics	Computational Creativity	CCRs
Creativity	They are not intended for creative tasks and are restricted to predefined tasks and environments	May(not) involve the creative generation of ideas, solutions, and expressions	Able to produce original solutions, concepts, and artistic works alone or through collaboration
Autonomy	They typically need human oversight or intervention and are limited in their ability to adapt beyond their specified functions	May(not) operate autonomously often requires human input or supervision	Able to function independently in different settings and adjust to evolving circumstances resourcefully and creatively
Physical Capabilities	May have enhanced physical abilities for manipulation, navigation, or assembly tasks	May(not) involve physical capabilities, depending on the specific application	Able to physically handle objects, engage with the surroundings, and demonstrate creative behaviour
Human-Interaction	Restricted capacity for spontaneous interactions or understanding human emotions; Frequently exhibits a deficiency in social and emotional intelligence	May involve human collaboration or feedback in the creative process but does not necessarily engage in direct HRI	They can participate in meaningful exchanges with people, work together on creative projects, and respond to emotional signals
Adaptability	Limited flexibility in adjusting to new circumstances beyond established tasks and environments	Can adapt to new situations and problems but may not be as flexible or versatile as robots	Able to creatively adjust to changing and unpredictable environments and tasks
Ethical Considerations	They adhere to established rules and algorithms without considering broader ethical considerations	May or may not involve ethical decision-making, depending on the specific application	They can examine ethical and cultural dilemmas and make judgments based on our values
Learning	Restricted ability to learn beyond specified tasks and settings	May incorporate learning mechanisms to improve creative output	Able to improve creativity over time by learning from past experiences

Moreover, ethical considerations gain significance as robots engage in creative tasks and interact with humans. It is imperative to uphold fairness, transparency, and accountability throughout the creative process while addressing privacy, safety, and societal impact concerns [72, 73].

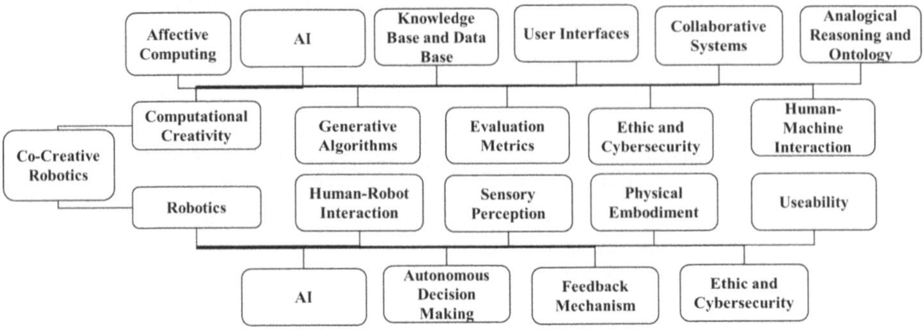

Fig. 2. Primary CCRs Technological Dimensions [30].

Given the complexity of designing, developing, and implementing CCRs, adopting a collaborative and interdisciplinary approach for advancements in this field is essential. By uniting experts from various disciplines, they can effectively address the multifaceted challenges of CCRs. This collaboration fosters the development of innovative solutions that expand the possibilities of what CCRs can achieve.

4 CCRs Challenges

As previously mentioned, CCRs is one of the emerging approaches that have the potential to impact VUCA environments, societies, tasks, and problems by providing, executing, or collaborating on adaptive, creative, and inclusive solutions. Benefiting from creative robots, deepening our understanding of them and identifying their challenges for advancement, is fundamental. As schematized in Fig. 3, and to answer the second research question **[RQ2]:** "*What are the critical challenges of CCRs?*", the most significant challenges of advancing co-creative robots are as follows:

Lack of Knowledge and Deep Understanding of the Nature of Human Creativity: Considering the limited knowledge and understanding of the nature of human creativity, it isn't easy to replicate it in robotic systems. Human creativity is a multifaceted phenomenon shaped by various factors such as cognitive, emotional, sociocultural, and personal factors [74]. Human cognitive processes (which are studied in cognitive science), such as divergent thinking, associative thinking, and insight, are not fully understood. These processes interact with memory, attention, and problem-solving abilities in complex ways, creating novel human ideas and solutions [75]. In addition, fields such as emotional creativity, affective computing, and the science of emotion still study the mystery of human emotions, motivations, and affective states [76]. Various

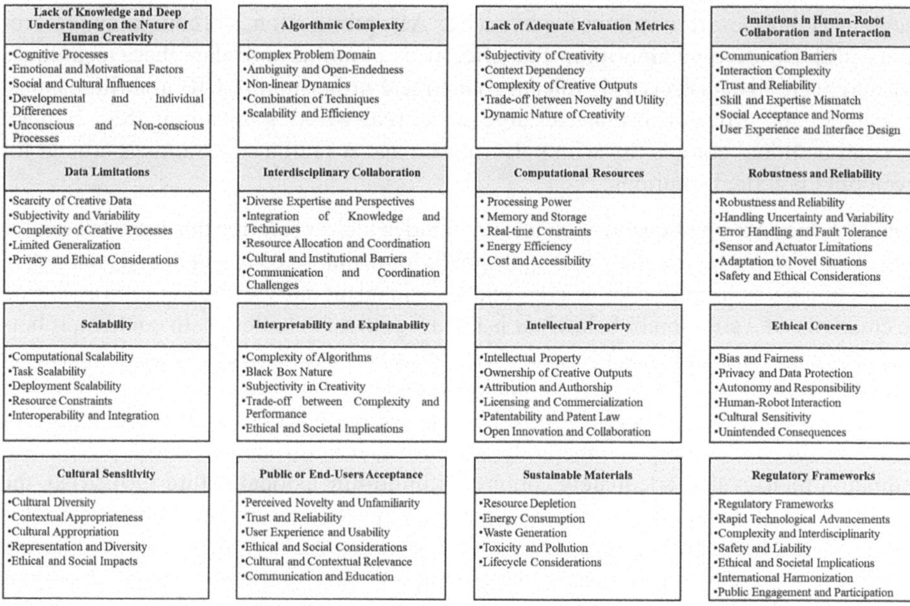

Fig. 3. Most Important Challenges of Advancing Creative Robots.

evidence demonstrates that human emotions play crucial roles in creativity, influencing the generation, evaluation, and selection of creative ideas and solutions (e.g., [77]). Furthermore, social interactions, collaboration, and cultural knowledge shape creative expression and innovation [78], posing challenges for robots operating in diverse cultural settings. Creativity varies across individuals, and developmental stages are influenced by factors such as personality traits [79], domain expertise [80], and life experiences [81]. Understanding the individual differences in creativity is essential for designing personalized and adaptive CCRs systems. Much human creativity occurs unconsciously, involving intuitive insights, analogical reasoning, and implicit knowledge [82, 83]. These processes are challenging to be replicated in computational models, limiting our ability to capture the full richness of human creativity in robots.

Algorithmic Complexity: In CCRs, algorithmic complexity refers to the difficulty of creating algorithms that can generate or contribute to creative outputs [84]. Creative tasks typically deal with complex problem spaces, which include multiple interacting factors and uncertainties [85]. Developing algorithms that can effectively navigate and explore these complex problem spaces is challenging. The complex problem spaces of creative tasks also cause uncertainty in the possible solutions [86]. Thus, developed algorithms must be able to tolerate VUCA and explore diverse possibilities to produce innovative outputs. In addition to these challenges, creative processes tend to have non-linear dynamics, where slight changes can lead to abnormally large effects [87]. That is why CCRs-developed algorithms should capture these non-linear dynamics and leverage them to generate creative solutions dynamically and adaptively. Also, they should integrate techniques from various fields, such as AI, optimization, and computational creativity [88]. Developing algorithms that effectively combine and adapt these techniques to different creative tasks is a significant challenge. Furthermore, CCRs algorithms must be scalable and efficient to manage large-scale, real-world applications [89]. Balancing computational complexity with performance and resource constraints is crucial for developing practical solutions.

Lack of Adequate Evaluation Metrics: A creative idea or solution that leads to creative behaviour needs to be adequate and appropriate for the targeted problem and its novelty. Due to human's rich cultural knowledge and associated memory, evaluating and assessing the creativity of a solution or behaviour is not a significant challenge. In contrast, robots have serious issues in this respect. This challenge arises due to several reasons, including (i) the subjectivity of creativity, (ii) context dependence, (iii) the complexity of creative output, (iv) the trade-off between novelty and utility, and (v) the dynamic nature of creativity. Since creativity is inherently subjective, it is difficult to develop objective evaluation metrics that adequately capture its multidimensional nature [90]. Also, the context in which creativity occurs significantly impacts how it is evaluated [91]. This makes developing universal evaluation metrics for co-creative robots more difficult. In addition, co-creative robots have the potential to produce a wide range of outputs [54, 92]. Developing evaluation metrics that can measure these outputs requires careful consideration of multiple dimensions and criteria and interdisciplinary collaborations. Co-creative robots should be able to balance the trade-off between their outputs' novelty and utility [93]. Another challenge that needs to be considered is developing metrics that can provide this balance. Lastly, since creativity is a dynamic and iterative process that evolves, traditional evaluation metrics may have difficulties capturing this dynamic nature [94].

Limitations in Human-Robot Collaboration (HRC) and Interaction: One of the most fundamental aspects of CCRs is HRC and interaction. These collaboration and interaction are essential for human and robot skills complementarity, creativity enhancement, improved adaptability and flexibility in developing creative tasks, enhanced learning process, ethical inclusion, improved user experience, increased outputs, cultural and social relevance, and inclusivity. Limitations in HRC reduce effective collaboration between humans and robots in creative endeavours. These challenges include (i) communication barriers which rising from differences in language and sensory perception and hindering seamless interaction and understanding [95]; (ii) interaction complexity between human and robots which demands multifaceted coordination and mutual comprehension between human and robot through adaptability and interpretive skills from robots [96]; (iii) trust and reliability issues also increase the difficulty of collaboration, as humans may hesitate to entrust critical or creative responsibilities to robots without assurance of safety and predictability [97]; moreover (iv) disparities in skill sets and expertise levels between humans and robots lead to challenges in task allocation and coordination [37, 38]; (v) cultural norms and social acceptance influence interaction dynamics which emphasizing the importance of designing robots to respect social conventions and preferences [98]; lastly (vi) the use interface design plays a crucial role in shaping the user experience. Intuitive and responsive user interface design is a fundamental challenge to facilitate effective HRC [99].

Data Limitations: Data is a critical component in CCRs advancement. Any limitation on data availability, quality, and diversity will reduce the creative robots' capability in learning, adaptation, and personalization. Several factors contribute to these limitations: (i) generating labelled data for training CCRs algorithms can be time-consuming, resource-intensive, and subjective, limiting the availability of training data [100]; (ii) creative outputs may vary widely across individuals, domains, and cultural contexts, leading to variability and uncertainty in the training data [100]; (iii) capturing the richness and complexity of ideation, experimentation, and iteration processes of creative tasks, in data is challenging, as they may unfold over time and involve non-linear dynamics [54]; (iv) training on diverse and representative datasets is a significant challenge for developing robust and generalizable CCRs systems [101]; and (v) collecting and sharing creative data may raise privacy concerns and ethical considerations, mainly when dealing with sensitive or proprietary information [102].

Interdisciplinary Collaboration: Interdisciplinary collaboration is essential for advancing CCRs as it brings together diverse expertise, enhances innovation, solves complex problems, centres on human needs, addresses ethical concerns, fosters educational synergies, and ensures practical, real-world applications. However, this collaboration is not without challenges and barriers. Some of the main barriers to interdisciplinary collaboration in CCRs fields include: (i) bringing together experts from different domains and facilitating effective communication and collaboration between them is challenging due to differences in terminology, methodologies, and priorities [92]; (ii) integrating knowledge across disciplines is difficult, as it requires bridging conceptual and methodological gaps and fostering mutual understanding and appreciation of diverse perspectives [103]; (iii) interdisciplinary collaboration requires allocating resources and coordinating and managing these resources effectively to support collaborative research agendas and achieve shared goals is complex and time-consuming [104]; (iv) cultural and institutional factors, such as academic silos, disciplinary boundaries, and incentive structures, challenging interdisciplinary collaboration [105]. To overcome these barriers, cultural shifts, policy changes, and institutional support are significant to foster a collaborative and inclusive research environment; (v) communication challenges, such as language barriers, differing communication styles, and conflicting priorities, can reduce collaboration and slow down progress [106].

Computational Resources: These resources are fundamental because they provide the necessary processing power, support machine learning, and AI, manage large datasets, enable extensive simulation and testing, facilitate real-time interaction, execute complex algorithms, and ensure scalability and flexibility. These capabilities are crucial for developing and deploying innovative and effective creative robotic systems. However, having adequate computational resources facing several challenges include: (i) CCRs tasks such as generating and analysing large datasets, running advanced algorithms for creativity, and simulating complex environments require significant processing power that goes beyond the existing hardware [54]; (ii) CCRs systems may not be able to handle the large volume of data generated during training, testing, and deployment, leading to performance bottlenecks and scalability issues [33]; (iii) many CCRs applications, such as interactive art installations, live performances, and real-time design tools, require real-time processing and responsiveness, which posing additional challenges in meeting real-time constraints while maintaining high computational performance [107]; (iv) energy consumption is a critical consideration for mobile and autonomous robots, making it essential to balance computational performance with energy efficiency to extend battery life, reduce operating costs, and minimize environmental impact [108]; (v) finding and maintaining computational resources, such as high-performance computing clusters, cloud infrastructure, and specialized hardware, can be costly and difficult for small research groups, startups, or individuals [109].

Robustness and Reliability: Robustness and reliability ensure consistent performance, adaptability, minimal downtime, user trust, safety, long-term viability, adherence to ethical and quality standards, and overall technical and economic feasibility. These factors are essential for the successful integration and sustained use of creative robotic systems. Due to the complexity and unpredictability of creative tasks and real-world environments, robustness and reliability pose significant challenges in advancing CCRs. Some of these challenges include: (i) CCRs systems must operate effectively in dynamic and unpredictable environments, which require algorithms and control systems that ensure robustness and reliability by adapting and responding to uncertainty and variability [110]; (ii) CCRs systems are highly vulnerable to errors, failures, and malfunctions, which can arise from hardware failures, software bugs, or unexpected interactions with the environment [111]; (iii) co-creative robots rely on sensors and actuators which can be vulnerable to noise, drift, or wear and tear, leading to inaccuracies and performance degradation over time [112]; (iv) Creative tasks involve encountering novel situations or scenarios that depend on algorithms and learning mechanisms that can generalize from experiences and adapt to new challenges [113]; (v) ensuring the safety, ethical behaviour, and responsible deployment of CCRs systems is essential, particularly when interacting with humans or operating in shared spaces [114].

Scalability: "Scalability" enables systems to expand capabilities, adapt to diverse applications, future-proof against technological advancements, ensure economic efficiency, meet fluctuating demands, optimize resources, enhance collaboration and integration, and allow customization and personalization. Scalability imposes challenges in advancing CCRs due to their need for effective performance across various scales, which include: (i) scaling algorithms and architectures to accommodate larger datasets, more powerful hardware, and more sophisticated tasks without sacrificing performance or efficiency is a significant challenge [54]; (ii) designing algorithms and architectures that are flexible and adaptable enough to scale to different task requirements, contexts, and user needs is essential and challenging for advancing CCRs [115]; (iii) deploying co-creative robots in real-world or VUCA environments requires scalability in terms of robustness, reliability, and usability, as well as, safety, regulatory, and ethical requirements [116]; (iv) ensuring interoperability and integration across multiple systems and environments is essential for scalability and collaboration in CCRs applications [117].

Interpretability and Explainability: Interpretability and explainability build user trust, enhance collaboration, facilitate debugging and improvement, ensure ethical practices, support compliance and accountability, enable personalization, and improve creativity. These factors that are essential for the effective and responsible integration of co-creative robots into various fields pose a significant challenge in advancing CCRs including: (i) complex and opaque models that are used in CCRs may produce highly intricate and non-linear decision boundaries, which interpreting their inner workings process to reach the creative outputs is challenging [118]; (ii) many state-of-the-art machine learning and AI approaches are "black box" models with underlying mechanisms that are difficult to comprehend, making it challenging to grasp their specific decisions or results [119]; (iii) interpreting and explaining the creative process requires accounting for subjective preferences, cultural influences, and personal biases, which can be challenging to formalize and articulate [54]; (iv) simplifying CCRs' complex models for interpretability can reduce its creative capabilities, while increasing complexity of models can reduce transparency for improved performance [120]; (v) lack of interpretability and explainability may raise concerns about bias, fairness, accountability, and safety in autonomous co-creative robots [121].

Ethical Concerns: CCRs must address ethical concerns to ensure bias-free outputs, respect intellectual property, maintain transparency and accountability, respect cultural differences, protect employment, safeguard privacy, uphold moral and aesthetic values, and consider long-term societal impacts. However, to develop ethical CCRs scientist and practitioners need to address challenges such as: (i) ensuring fairness, transparency, and accountability in the design and implementation of CCRs algorithms to mitigate bias and promoting equitable outcomes [122]; (ii) protecting privacy, confidentiality, and data security to respect individual rights and ensuring trust and confidence in autonomous creative systems [101]; (iii) clarifying the legal, ethical, and moral implications of autonomous creative robots, including issues of liability, culpability, and agency, to foster trust and ethical governance [123]; (iv) designing HRI interfaces that respect human values, preferences, and rights to promote ethical behaviour and foster positive interactions [124]; (v) ensuring cultural sensitivity and inclusivity in the design, development, and deployment of co-creative robots to respect cultural diversity and avoid unintended harm or offense [125]; (vi) mitigating potential risks associated with CCRs deployment for responsible innovation and ethical governance [126].

Cultural Sensitivity: Cultural sensitivity in developing the CCRs field ensures respect for diversity, prevents misrepresentation, enhances user experience, builds trust and acceptance, fulfils ethical responsibilities, increases global market relevance, fosters creativity and innovation, and prevents harm. To implement cultural sensitivity, it is essential to address several challenges, including (i) sensitivity to this diversity and avoid imposing culturally specific assumptions or biases that may not be universally applicable or acceptable [125]; (ii) recognizing and respecting cultural difference, adapting creative robots' behaviour and outputs with the cultural characteristics and preferences of diverse audiences [127]; (iii) ensuring that co-creative robots engage with cultural materials and references respectfully and responsibly to avoid cultural appropriation and foster cultural appreciation and understanding [125]; (iv) incorporating diverse cultural inputs, narratives, and aesthetics into the design and content of co-creative robots to promote inclusivity and cultural diversity [128]; (v) ensuring cultural sensitivity in the design and deployment of co-creative robots to promote ethical behaviour, social cohesion, and mutual respect in diverse cultural contexts [121].

Public or End-Users Acceptance: Public acceptance of CCRs drives widespread adoption, builds trust and confidence, enhances user engagement and satisfaction, ensures market success, facilitates feedback and improvement, addresses ethical and social considerations, promotes collaboration and integration, and influences educational and cultural impact. To increase CCRs public and end-user acceptance, it is necessary to address the several challenges include: (i) fear or resistance towards adapting CCRs systems which raised from perceptions of novelty and unfamiliarity within end-users or public [129]; (ii) lack of trust and adoption, particularly in critical or high-stakes applications which raised from concerns about reliability, errors, or malfunctions [130]; (iii) complex interfaces, unintuitive controls, or time-consuming interactions affects adoption and satisfaction among end-users [131]; (iv) end-users' ethical or social concerns about the impact of CCRs on society, such as job displacement, privacy invasion, or cultural implications can reduce their trust and acceptance [132]; (v) lack of attention to cultural and contextual factors lead to misalignment with user needs and preferences [133]; (vi) lack of clear and accessible information about the benefits, risks, and capabilities of CCRs systems [92].

Sustainable Materials: Utilizing sustainable materials in CCRs reduces environmental impact, ensures long-term viability, supports regulatory compliance, enhances public perception and acceptance, drives innovation, offers cost efficiency, improves health and safety, and upholds corporate responsibility. However, to use sustainable materials in creative robots, scientist and practitioners need to address challenges such as: (i) finding sustainable alternatives to fossil fuels, metals, and plastics materials to reduce environmental impact and conserving finite resources [134]; (ii) developing energy-efficient robotics technologies and utilizing renewable energy sources to reduce the carbon footprint of co-creative robots and promote environmental sustainability [135]; (iii) implementing waste reduction strategies, such as recycling, reusing, and refurbishing robotic components, to minimize waste generation and promote circular economy principles [136]; (iv) choosing environmentally friendly materials and manufacturing methods that minimize toxic emissions and pollution to protect human health and ecosystems [137]; (v) implementing life cycle assessment (LCA) methodologies and eco-design principles to identify opportunities for reducing environmental impact at each stage of the product lifecycle [92].

Regulatory Frameworks: Regulatory frameworks are essential in advancing CCRs to ensure safety and reliability, enforce ethical compliance, protect consumers, foster market stability and trust, drive innovation and standardization, promote environmental protection, address social impacts, enhance global competitiveness, and provide legal clarity and compliance. Several factors challenges developing regulatory frameworks for CCRs, which include: (i) the rapid pace of technological innovation cause legal and regulatory gaps and limits the responsible deployment and governance of autonomous creative systems [138]; (ii) the convergence of diverse technologies limits development of comprehensive regulatory frameworks that address the multifaceted nature of autonomous co-creative robots [127]; (iii) clarifying legal frameworks and liability standards to mitigate risks and ensuring accountability, responsibility, and liability of co-creative robots in the event of accidents, errors, or harm caused by them [139]; (iv) developing regulatory frameworks that address ethical and societal challenges, such as privacy infringement, algorithmic bias, cultural appropriation, and job displacement, to promote responsible innovation and safeguarding societal values and interests [140]; (v) harmonizing regulatory standards at the international level to facilitate cross-border collaboration, trade, and innovation while ensuring consistent protection of human rights and ethical principles [100]; (vi) establishing mechanisms for public consultation, stakeholder engagement, and democratic decision-making to promote transparency, accountability, and legitimacy in the regulation of autonomous CCRs [141].

Intellectual Property (IP): IP protection in advancing CCRs encourages innovation, protects investments, facilitates collaboration, ensures ethical use, provides legal clarity, supports economic growth, promotes global competitiveness, and encourages ethical and responsible innovation. However, to protect IP in CCRs it is necessary to face several challenges include: (i) determining the rightful ownership of creative outputs generated by robotic systems, particularly in collaborative or co-creative contexts [100]; (ii) establishing clear guidelines and protocols for attributing authorship and acknowledging contributions to promote fairness, transparency, and ethical conduct in CCRs research and practice [100]; (iii) negotiating licensing agreements, determining royalty rates, and protecting intellectual property rights to ensure fair compensation and incentivizing innovation in CCRs [53]; (iv) possibility of potentiating the co-co-creative robots inventions raises novel legal and technical challenges that require careful consideration and interpretation of patent law [142]; (v) balancing the principles of open innovation with the protection of IP rights to foster collaboration, innovation, and knowledge exchange in the CCRs community [38].

A collaborative, multidisciplinary and multidimensional approach is essential to mitigate the challenges of advancing CCRs. Depending on the nature and constraints of each challenge, diverse types of collaboration in other networks can be employed.

5 Collaborative Networks to Mitigate CCRs Challenges

Carlo Bellieni and the Mexican philosopher Lourdes Velazquez proposed a new understanding of evolution in the recently published book "The True Secret of Evolution: From Conflict to Collaboration" (2023). They suggested that although evolution in life is based on random mutations, it is also based on collaboration between species and the environment [143]. The human species has also developed a fundamental need for social connection, interaction, and cooperation, essential for survival and evolution. We have even evolved an evolutionary warning signal that alerts us when the need for connection, interaction, and collaboration is not fulfilled [144]. This connection, interaction, and cooperation is not limited to human-human; it also extends to relationships with other species in nature and even with artificial entities and intelligent machines [145]. Nikghadam-Hojjati, Marchetti, Barata, and Calabro (2024), based on the entities involved, classified CNs into seven main categories of Human-Haman Collaborative Networks (HHCNs), Human-Machine Collaborative Networks (HMCNs), Human-Nature Collaborative Networks (HNCNs), Machine-Machine Collaborative Networks (MMCNs), Machine-Nature Collaborative Networks (MNCNs), Nature-Nature Collaborative Networks (NNCNs), and Human-Machine-Nature Collaborative Networks

(HMNCNs) [30], which illustrated in Fig. 4 The authors proposed this classification, inspired by hybridization as one of the main characteristics of the fourth [146] and fifth [147] generations of CNs, which represent a collaboration between diverse entities, especially between human and intelligent autonomous systems.

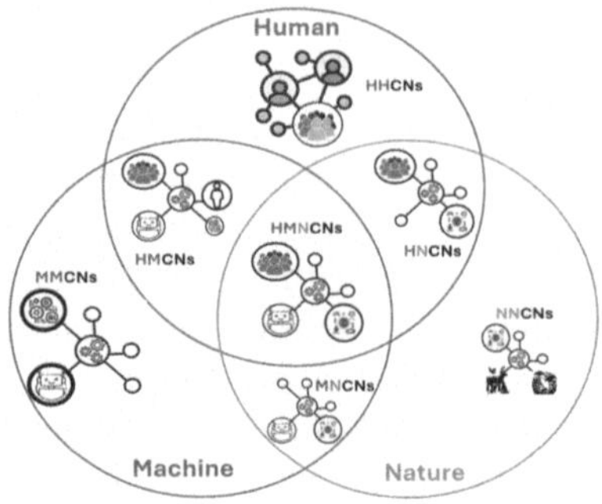

Fig. 4. Classification of CNs based on the involved entities [30].

Within the evolving field of CCRs, collaboration across distinct types of CNs acts as a significant accelerator, driving progress more rapidly. Interdisciplinary, multidimensional, multifaceted, and hybrid (cross-entity) CNs empower stakeholders to address challenges in CCRs effectively. CNs facilitate the integration of diverse expertise [39], accelerating knowledge sharing [148], pooling resources [148], enhancing problem-solving capabilities [150], addressing ethical concerns [151], fostering cross-disciplinary innovation [152], and promoting global standards [153]. To answer this research's third question **[RQ3]: "***How can CNs serve as a mitigation approach to address the identified challenges in CCRs?***"**, Table 2 presents the result of focused group brainstorming sessions, which explain how the seven categories of CNs contribute to mitigating and addressing CCRs challenges.

Based on the collective information provided in Table 2, we can respond to the **RQ3** as follows:

- CNs mitigate the *"Lack of Knowledge and Deep Understanding of the Nature of Human Creativity"* challenge by fostering interdisciplinary collaboration, integrating human, machine, and nature-inspired insights, and leveraging AI for pattern recognition. They enhance creativity models by studying cognitive, emotional, and biological processes, drawing from natural adaptation and emergent behaviours. CNs identify creativity patterns through data analysis and distributed computing, leading to more comprehensive and adaptive CCRs solutions.
- CNs mitigate *"Algorithmic Complexity"* by integrating human insights, machine intelligence, and nature-inspired principles to develop innovative and efficient algorithms. They enhance computational models by leveraging human intuition, AI-driven optimization, and biological problem-solving techniques such as biomimicry and collective intelligence. Through high-performance computing and interdisciplinary collaboration, CNs refine algorithmic structures, ensuring adaptability, scalability, and a balance between novelty and utility in CCRs.

Table 2. Contribution of CNs to Mitigate and Address CCRs Challenges (Ch.).

Ch.	CNs	Contribution of CNs to Mitigate CCRs Challenges
Lack of Knowledge of human Creativity	HH	Enable interdisciplinary peer-to-peer knowledge exchange and collaboration among stakeholders through workshops, shared research initiatives, and collaborative platforms
	HM	Integrate diverse cognitive, emotional, and socio-cultural perspectives to enhance human creativity models by enabling continuous human and AI interaction, allowing systems to learn from human behaviour
	HN	Integrate diverse human perspectives with natural models of creativity observed in biological systems by studying biological creativity (e.g., swarm intelligence) to develop new insights into creative processes
	MM	Aggregating and analysing enormous amounts of data from various sources by leveraging distributed computing for patterns detection and correlations
	MN	Providing novel solutions to complex problems by integrating machine intelligence with natural world insights by studying emergent behaviours in nature, such as evolution, to inspire robotic creativity models
	NN	Provide insights from biological systems to inform the design of adaptive and resilient robotic algorithms by studying how organisms respond to environmental changes and applying these principles to CCRs
	HMN	Enhance understanding of human creativity by integrating human expertise, machine learning algorithms, and insights from natural systems by combining cognitive science, AI analysis, and nature-inspired creativity models to develop more comprehensive theories of creativity

(*continued*)

Table 2. (*continued*)

Ch.	CNs	Contribution of CNs to Mitigate CCRs Challenges
Algorithmic Complexity	HH	Integerating human insights into developing algorithms, optimizing computational resources, and promoting model transparency by allowing AI and ML experts to collaborate and incorporate socio-cultural creativity patterns into algorithm design while ensuring computational efficiency
	HM	Combine human creativity with machine efficiency to develop innovative algorithms for solving complex problems by leveraging human intuition in problem formulation while using machine computational power for optimization and execution
	HN	Inform the development of sophisticated algorithms by leveraging natural inspiration by analysing biological problem-solving techniques (e.g., evolutionary computing) to enhance robotic and AI-based creativity
	MM	Enable the development of complex algorithms that navigate uncertain and dynamic problem spaces while balancing novelty and utility by using high-performance computing and autonomous machine-learning models to refine algorithmic structures
	MN	leveraging biomimicry to simulate creative processes observed in nature by replicating patterns from social insect colonies, neural networks, and adaptive animal behaviours to refine robotic algorithms
	NN	Inspire the development of more adaptive and dynamic robotic algorithms by analysing natural self-regulation, collective intelligence, and feedback-driven adaptation in ecosystems
	HMN	Leveraging interdisciplinary collaboration to develop innovative solutions by using AI to model human creativity while incorporating adaptive natural processes for more flexible and scalable algorithms

(*continued*)

Table 2. (*continued*)

Ch.	CNs	Contribution of CNs to Mitigate CCRs Challenges
Lack of Adequate Evaluation Metrics	HH	Help design creativity evaluation metrics that balance computational analysis with human subjectivity and socio-cultural context by involving psychologists and human factors experts to develop more meaningful and context-aware assessment frameworks
	HM	Create evaluation metrics that balance subjective human insights with objective machine analysis by incorporating human feedback into AI-driven assessment frameworks, ensuring a nuanced evaluation of creative ideas
	HN	Using nature-inspired benchmarks (e.g., efficiency, adaptability, and emergent creativity) to assess CCRs performance
	MM	Analysing large datasets and computational models to establish objective benchmarks for assessing creative outputs
	MN	Help design nature-inspired evaluation metrics for creativity by applying ecological and biological assessment principles, such as efficiency, resilience, and adaptability, to robotics
	NN	Applying ecological assessment principles to CCRs using resilience, adaptability, and efficiency as measurable indicators
	HMN	Balancing human subjectivity, machine analysis, and natural efficiency principles by integrating human perception-based scoring with AI-driven assessments and nature-based efficiency mode
Limitations in HRC and Interaction	HH	Incorporating psychological, Neurological, and design expertise by engaging psychologists, neurologists, and interaction designers to refine communication protocols, interfaces, and trust-building mechanisms

(*continued*)

Table 2. (*continued*)

Ch.	CNs	Contribution of CNs to Mitigate CCRs Challenges
	HM	Improve communication and understanding to enhance trust and reliability in HRC by refining human-robot interfaces, improving natural language processing, and implementing adaptive response mechanisms
	HN	Applying biomimetic principles to robotic behaviour, making interactions more intuitive and adaptive to human responses
	MM	Improving communication, adaptability, and trust through interaction and intuitive machine interfaces that adjust dynamically to human feedback
	MN	Incorporating nature-inspired adaptability by designing robotic interactions based on biological communication models, improving intuitiveness and efficiency in human-robot cooperation
	NN	Mimicking biological communication and cooperation strategies by studying how organisms collaborate to optimize coordination in HRI
	HMN	Facilitating robust HRC by integrating machine intelligence with human intuition and natural adaptability by designing robots that adjust dynamically based on human feedback and biomimetic interaction strategies
Data Limitation	HH	Support trustworthy sharing of high-quality data among stakeholders by creating shared repositories, open platforms, and interdisciplinary communication channels that ensure broad access and practical use
	HM	Streamline the collection and sharing of data, improving dataset quality by facilitating collaborative data-gathering processes, using AI to analyse and preprocess data, and maintaining diverse and high-quality datasets

(*continued*)

Table 2. (*continued*)

Ch.	CNs	Contribution of CNs to Mitigate CCRs Challenges
	HN	Optimize data collection by leveraging biological patterns for data organization and learning by implementing bio-inspired data filtering, pattern recognition, and self-organizing information structures
	MM	Pooling resources and automating data processing to ensure high-quality, diverse, and representative dataset collection
	MN	Employing bio-inspired data collection and processing techniques using distributed, self-organizing systems modelled after nature to improve data acquisition and management
	NN	Enhancing data processing and organization by leveraging naturally occurring information-sharing mechanisms by modelling robotic data collection on ecological systems that optimize resource distribution
	HMN	Improving data collection and sharing through machine-driven automation and human oversight by using AI to aggregate data efficiently while ensuring human validation for accuracy and ethical considerations
Interdisciplinary Collaboration	HH	Facilitate breaking down disciplinary barriers and solving complex problems by establishing collaborative platforms and workshops to exchange ideas, coordinate efforts, and leverage collective expertise across multiple, traditionally isolated disciplines
	HM	Promote knowledge exchange and resource management by facilitating interdisciplinary collaboration within HMCNs by connecting experts from various domains to develop well-rounded robotic systems

(*continued*)

Table 2. (*continued*)

Ch.	CNs	Contribution of CNs to Mitigate CCRs Challenges
	HN	Bringing together experts in biology, engineering, AI, psychology, and environmental sciences to develop nature-inspired solutions
	MM	Integrating multi-domain knowledge and bridging conceptual gaps by enabling cross-domain AI and ML applications that enhance CCRs innovation
	MN	Serve as platforms for integrating expertise from diverse fields, mirroring the interconnectedness of ecosystems by combining insights from biology, ecology, robotics, and AI to develop CCRs solutions
	NN	Connecting biology, engineering, and computer science experts by fostering cross-domain knowledge exchange to create biomimetic robotic systems
	HMN	Bringing together robotics, AI, cognitive sciences, and environmental experts by establishing shared research initiatives that combine human creativity, machine intelligence, and natural insights
Computational Resources	HH	Effectively distributing workloads among interdisciplinary teams, ensuring efficient use of shared resources (e.g., cloud-based collaboration), and distributing workloads effectively
	HM	Assigning tasks based on the strengths of both humans and machines by dynamically distributing workload, ensuring that humans handle abstract and creative tasks while machines handle high-speed computations
	HN	Using bio-inspired algorithms (e.g., swarm intelligence, genetic algorithms) enhances robotic processing and problem-solving efficiency
	MM	Distributing tasks across multiple autonomous systems, ensuring efficient processing and energy use

(*continued*)

Table 2. (*continued*)

Ch.	CNs	Contribution of CNs to Mitigate CCRs Challenges
	MN	Optimize computational efficiency using self-organizing and decentralized models inspired by nature by implementing swarm intelligence and decentralized processing methods found in biological networks
	NN	Applying natural distributed problem-solving models by replicating decentralized processing and emergent behaviours observed in natural networks
	HMN	Distributing tasks between humans, machines, and nature-inspired models by assigning abstract creative tasks to humans, high-speed processing to AI, and adaptive system modelling to nature-inspired algorithms
Robustness and Reliability	HH	Promoting interdisciplinary collaboration that validates robotic models and ensures real-world applicability
	HM	Combining human oversight with machine precision through human validation of AI-generated outputs, reduces errors and improves adaptability
	HN	Incorporating biological resilience principles, e.g., self-repair, redundancy, and adaptability
	MM	Leveraging machine-to-machine (M2M) communication to enhance system resilience, fault tolerance, and adaptability
	MN	Applying natural resilience mechanisms by mimicking fault-tolerant and self-repairing behaviours found in biological organisms
	NN	Mirroring the resilience of natural ecosystems by implementing redundancy, self-repair, and adaptive response mechanisms
	HMN	Incorporating self-adaptive mechanisms inspired by nature, machine-learning-based error correction, and human oversight for validation

(*continued*)

Table 2. (*continued*)

Ch.	CNs	Contribution of CNs to Mitigate CCRs Challenges
Scalability	HH	Leveraging multi-disciplinary approaches that enable seamless human knowledge and integration of computational resources
	HM	Managing larger datasets and complex tasks by automating data processing allowing robots to adapt and expand as data and problem complexity grow
	HN	Using natural models of evolution by applying principles from ecosystems and biological adaptation to enable robotics systems to scale efficiently
	MM	Utilizing distributed networks that allow seamless expansion and adaptation to larger datasets and more complex robotic systems
	MN	Leveraging self-organization and natural growth principles by designing robotic networks that can dynamically expand and adjust based on environmental inputs
	NN	Support scalability in robotics by using natural growth and self-regulation principles by structuring robotic networks to expand and function autonomously, like ecological development
	HMN	Improving scalability by combining self-organizing biological systems with machine intelligence by designing robotic networks that can expand and function autonomously, adapting to changing environments
Interpretability and Explainability	HH	Promote models' transparency, interpretability, and comprehensibility by incorporating diverse human expertise, ensuring robotic models are understandable to a broader audience

(*continued*)

Table 2. (*continued*)

Ch.	CNs	Contribution of CNs to Mitigate CCRs Challenges
	HM	Improve model transparency through transparent and interpretable machine outputs, making them understandable and culturally relevant by refining AI-generated explanations using human-driven interpretability frameworks
	HN	Natural analogies (e.g., neural networks modelled after brain function) can be used to make AI and robotic decisions more comprehensible to humans
	MM	Structuring machine-generated insights into understandable formats, ensuring transparency in decision-making
	MN	Using nature-based analogies in AI and robotics by structuring machine-learning models after recognizable natural processes makes output more intuitive and understandable
	NN	Improve interpretability by making AI and robotics more understandable through nature-inspired structures using analogy-based reasoning modelled after natural systems for more precise decision-making
	HMN	Enhancing interpretability using nature-based analogies and human-centred AI models ensures that machine-generated outputs are transparent, understandable, and aligned with human cognitive processes
Ethical Concerns	HH	Address ethical concerns by integrating diverse stakeholders and embedding ethical considerations into technological development. Also, it ensures fairness and responsibility in CCRs by considering socio-cultural implications and ethical frameworks
	HM	Incorporating human values into robot design and deployment by embedding ethical constraints into AI decision-making and ensuring bias mitigation strategies

(*continued*)

Table 2. (*continued*)

Ch.	CNs	Contribution of CNs to Mitigate CCRs Challenges
	HN	Incorporating human values and natural principles ensures that CCRs align sustainability, fairness, and ecological responsibility
	MM	Embedding transparency and accountability mechanisms in M2M interactions to ensure fairness and prevent biases in automated processes
	MN	Aligning robotic systems with natural balance and sustainability principles by integrating ecological values into AI and robotics decision-making
	NN	Aligning robotics with ethical considerations by embedding sustainability and ecological responsibility into design ensures that co-creative robotic innovations do not disrupt the natural balance
	HMN	Embedding human values, regulatory guidelines, and ecological principles into CCRs by integrating ethical AI frameworks, sustainability considerations, and human decision-making in robotic operations
Cultural Sensitivity	HH	Involving experts from diverse backgrounds, embedding inclusivity and representation in robotics development
	HM	Involving diverse human inputs in CCRs development by integrating multi-cultural datasets and human feedback loops to ensure inclusivity in robotic behaviour and decision-making
	HN	Integrating nature-inspired perspectives from various cultures that view nature and creativity differently, making robotic applications more inclusive
	MM	Adapting machine-generated outputs to diverse cultural contexts, ensuring inclusive CCRs applications

(*continued*)

Table 2. (*continued*)

Ch.	CNs	Contribution of CNs to Mitigate CCRs Challenges
	MN	Drawing from nature-based philosophies and Indigenous knowledge systems, respecting diverse environmental perspectives in robotics design
	NN	Incorporating ecological perspectives from diverse traditions and philosophies by respecting Indigenous and local knowledge about nature's role in human-technology interaction
	HMN	Engaging diverse stakeholders and aligning CCRs with societal values by incorporating multi-cultural perspectives and inclusive design approaches in robotic development
Public or End-Users Acceptance	HH	Enhancing stakeholder engagement by involving communities and policymakers early and addressing societal concerns proactively
	HM	Fostering user-friendly and culturally relevant robots by designing human-centred interfaces and personalizing interactions based on user feedback
	HN	Fostering user-friendly and culturally relevant robots by designing systems that reflect familiar natural behaviours and ethical considerations, making them more relatable
	MM	Ensuring reliability, safety, and adherence to ethical standards through autonomous quality control and compliance verification mechanisms
	MN	Designing robots that function harmoniously with natural ecosystems by ensuring robotic systems interact safely with their surroundings
	NN	Demonstrating the benefits of robotics inspired by natural ecosystems by ensuring that robotic systems align with ecological values and serve sustainability goals

(*continued*)

Table 2. (*continued*)

Ch.	CNs	Contribution of CNs to Mitigate CCRs Challenges
	HMN	Supporting the design of robotics solutions that align with ethical, social, and environmental priorities by engaging communities in decision-making, ensuring transparency, and demonstrating societal benefits
Sustainable Material	HH	Contribute to sustainable materials research by facilitating collaboration with environmental scientists and material experts
	HM	Combining human expertise in sustainability with machine capabilities by leveraging AI to optimize material selection and reduce environmental impact while allowing human experts to guide decisions
	HN	Encouraging biomaterial integration and eco-friendly design principles in robotics manufacturing
	MM	Optimizing robotic operations for energy efficiency and minimizing material waste through intelligent automation
	MN	Promoting sustainable materials and eco-friendly design principles by incorporating biodegradable, recyclable, and nature-inspired materials into robotic manufacturing
	NN	Promoting biomimicry and eco-friendly materials by designing robots with biodegradable components and renewable energy sources
	HMN	Integrating eco-friendly materials, energy-efficient designs, and bio-inspired processes by leveraging biomaterials, reducing energy consumption, and ensuring environmentally responsible robotic production

(*continued*)

Table 2. (*continued*)

Ch.	CNs	Contribution of CNs to Mitigate CCRs Challenges
Regulatory Frameworks	HH	Facilitate regulatory compliance by involving legal professionals who establish clear guidelines for robotics governance. They support aligning robotics innovations with international standards through policy engagement and legal expertise
	HM	Supporting interdisciplinary collaboration, ensuring alignment with technological advancements and ethical considerations by involving legal professionals and AI ethicists to shape policies and compliance mechanisms
	HN	Aligning CCRs with environmental regulations and sustainability policies
	MM	Facilitate regulatory compliance by ensuring M2M interactions align with legal and ethical standards via built-in regulatory monitoring mechanisms
	MN	Aligning robotic innovations with environmental policies and sustainability guidelines by ensuring CCRs follow ecological impact assessments and regulatory requirements
	NN	Aligning CCRs with conservation laws, environmental protection policies, and sustainability standards
	HMN	Aligning robotic innovation with environmental and societal policies by collaborating with policymakers, legal experts, and industry stakeholders to ensure ethical and legal adherence
IP	HH	Involving legal and business professionals who ensure alignment with regulatory frameworks and intellectual property standards
	HM	Guidelines for ownership and authorship by integrating AI-tracked contributions, ensuring proper credit attribution between humans and machines

(*continued*)

Table 2. (*continued*)

Ch.	CNs	Contribution of CNs to Mitigate CCRs Challenges
	HN	Guidelines for IP protection by ensuring that nature-inspired innovations are attributed and legally protected
	MM	Help manage IP concerns by automating authorship tracking, ensuring proper attribution and protection of AI-generated innovations
	MN	Help define IP protection for nature-inspired robotics by establishing legal frameworks that recognize contributions derived from biological and ecological research
	NN	Defining legal frameworks for nature-inspired innovation by ensuring fair and ethical recognition of biological principles used in robotic designs
	HMN	Developing clear guidelines for ownership in human-machine collaborations by establishing AI-generated content attribution models and ethical frameworks for nature-inspired innovations

- CNs address "*Lack of Adequate Evaluation Metrics*" by balancing human subjectivity, machine analysis, and nature-inspired benchmarks. They integrate socio-cultural insights, psychological factors, and large-scale data analysis to refine creativity assessment. By leveraging computational models and ecological principles, CNs establish adaptable and reliable evaluation frameworks for CCRs.
- CNs mitigate "*Limitations in HRC and Interaction*" by enhancing communication, trust, and adaptability through interdisciplinary expertise, AI-driven refinements, and nature-inspired strategies. They improve interfaces, natural language processing, and adaptive response mechanisms to make interactions more intuitive. By mimicking biological communication models, CNs design robotic behaviours that dynamically adjust to human feedback, fostering efficient collaboration.
- CNs mitigate "*Data Limitations*" by facilitating the collection, sharing, and processing of high-quality datasets through collaborative platforms, AI-driven automation, and bio-inspired techniques. They enhance data diversity and reliability by leveraging machine intelligence for preprocessing, biological models for self-organizing data structures, and ecological systems for optimized resource distribution. By integrating human oversight with automated data acquisition, CNs ensure accuracy, accessibility, and ethical use in CCRs.
- CNs mitigate "*Interdisciplinary Collaboration*" challenges by breaking down disciplinary barriers and fostering knowledge exchange across traditionally isolated fields.

They establish collaborative platforms that connect experts from robotics, AI, cognitive sciences, biology, and environmental sciences to develop holistic solutions. By integrating diverse perspectives and bridging conceptual gaps, CNs enhance CCRs innovation, ensuring a balanced fusion of human creativity, machine intelligence, and nature-inspired principles.

- CNs mitigate "*Computational Resource*" challenges by optimizing workload distribution across humans, machines, and nature-inspired systems. They enhance efficiency by assigning creative tasks to humans, high-speed processing to AI, and adaptive problem-solving to bio-inspired models. By leveraging decentralized and self-organizing computing approaches, CNs improve processing speed, energy use, and scalability, ensuring CCRs operate efficiently in complex environments.
- CNs enhance "*Robustness and Reliability*" in CCRs by integrating interdisciplinary validation, human oversight, and nature-inspired resilience mechanisms. They improve fault tolerance and adaptability by combining human verification with machine precision, leveraging biological principles such as self-repair, and utilizing M2M communication for system resilience. By mirroring the stability of natural ecosystems and applying AI-driven error correction, CNs ensure robotic systems remain reliable, adaptive, and effective in real-world applications.
- CNs enhance "*Scalability*" in CCRs by integrating human expertise, machine intelligence, and nature-inspired self-organizing principles. They automate data processing and utilize distributed networks to manage larger datasets and more complex tasks. By applying biological adaptation and ecosystem-based growth models, CNs enable robots to expand dynamically and function autonomously, ensuring seamless adaptation to increasing computational demands and evolving environments.
- CNs improve "*Interpretability and Explainability*" in CCRs by integrating human expertise, AI-driven transparency, and nature-inspired analogies. They refine AI-generated explanations to ensure clarity and cultural relevance while structuring machine-learning models after recognizable natural processes. Using analogy-based reasoning and human-centred frameworks, CNs make robotic decisions more intuitive, transparent, and aligned with human cognitive understanding, enhancing trust and usability.
- CNs address "*Ethical Concerns*" in CCRs by embedding human values, transparency, and sustainability into design and decision-making. They ensure fairness and bias mitigation in AI, integrate socio-cultural and ecological principles and promote accountability in machine interactions. By aligning robotics with ethical frameworks, sustainability goals, and regulatory guidelines, CNs foster responsible innovation that respects both human and environmental well-being.
- CNs enhance "*Cultural Sensitivity*" in CCRs by integrating diverse human perspectives, multi-cultural datasets, and nature-based philosophies. They ensure inclusivity in robotic behaviour, decision-making, and machine-generated outputs by incorporating Indigenous knowledge, ecological traditions, and societal values. By embedding representation and inclusivity into design, CNs create globally adaptable and culturally aware robotic systems.
- CNs enhance "*Public and End-user Acceptance*" by engaging stakeholders early, ensuring cultural relevance, and aligning robotics with societal and environmental priorities. They create user-friendly systems with personalized interactions, foster trust

through ethical standards, and design robots that integrate harmoniously with natural ecosystems. By promoting transparency, sustainability, and real-world benefits, CNs ensure robotics are widely accepted and valued by communities.

- CNs promote "*Sustainability*" in robotics by integrating eco-friendly materials, optimizing energy efficiency, and leveraging biomimicry in design. They facilitate collaboration with environmental experts, use AI to enhance material selection and incorporate biodegradable and recyclable components. By minimizing waste and ensuring responsible production, CNs support the development of sustainable, energy-efficient, and environmentally conscious robotic systems.
- CNs support "*Regulatory*" compliance by aligning robotics innovation with legal, ethical, and environmental policies. They facilitate collaboration with legal professionals, AI ethicists, and policymakers to establish clear governance frameworks and ensure adherence to international standards. By integrating sustainability guidelines, ecological impact assessments, and automated regulatory monitoring, CNs help robotics operate responsibly within legal and societal expectations.
- CNs facilitate "*IP*" protection by establishing clear legal frameworks for ownership, authorship, and attribution in CCRs. They ensure AI-generated and nature-inspired innovations are properly credited, integrating automated authorship tracking and ethical guidelines. By involving legal and business professionals, CNs align robotics development with regulatory standards, ensuring fair and transparent IP protection across human, machine, and nature-driven contributions.

6 Conclusion

The growing integration of robotic systems in various sectors has significantly transformed various aspects of our personal and professional lives. In the last decades, robotic systems, through enhancing efficiency, precision, and productivity, have been able to improve quality-of-service delivery in diverse fields like medicine, manufacturing, agriculture, and even disaster management. However, traditional robotics face limitations such as inflexibility, restricted autonomy, and limited creative and collaborative capacities. These shortcomings highlight the necessity of developing a new generation of robotic systems that can be involved in creative and collaborative tasks and foster adaptability, autonomy, and ethical decision-making capabilities. CCRs is an interdisciplinary field that integrates computational creativity and robotics principles to develop robots with such abilities and characteristics.

This study aimed to address three central research questions including i) the foundations of it and how it could distinguish it from traditional robotics and computational creativity, ii) critical challenges hindering its advancement, and iii) exploring how CNs could be considered as a mitigation approach to address these challenges.

This conceptual expansion research utilized a mixed method to respond to these research questions. To address RQ1, the study presents a brief review of CCRs, the conceptual foundation, and the technological dimensions of it as well as a comparison of between CCRs, computational creativity, and traditional robotics based on seven criteria (creativity, autonomy, physical capabilities, human-interaction, adaptability, ethical considerations, and learning).

The study, in response to RQ2, identified 16 critical challenges, including Lack of Knowledge and Deep Understanding of Human Creativity; Algorithmic Complexity; Lack of Adequate Evaluation Metrics; Limitations in HRC and Interaction; Data Limitations; Interdisciplinary Collaboration; Computational Resources; Robustness and Reliability; Scalability; Interpretability and Explainability; Ethical Concerns; Cultural Sensitivity; Public or End-User Acceptance; Sustainable Materials; Regulatory Frameworks; Intellectual Property.

To mitigate these challenges, in response to RQ3, seven categories of CNs, developed through hybridization of different entities, were explored. The findings demonstrated that CNs effectively enhance the understanding of human creativity, algorithmic efficiency, scalability, and computational resource management by integrating human insights, machine intelligence, and nature-inspired adaptation principles. Also, they improve HRC by refining communication, trust, interpretability, ethical considerations, and cultural sensitivity. CNs by embedding sustainability practices, regulatory compliance, and promoting public acceptance, CNs facilitate robust, ethical, and culturally sensitive co-creative robotic systems.

The primary innovation of this research lies in defining the conceptual and technological foundations of CCRs and differentiating them from traditional robotics and computational creativity. Additionally, after identifying CCRs' advancement 'challenges, it introduces distinct types of CNs as a strategic solution to overcome, filling the gap in systematic mitigation approaches.

The results of this research contribute to both theory and practice by defining CCRs, identifying key challenges, and introducing CNs as a mitigation approach. By establishing a clear conceptual foundation and distinguishing CCRs from traditional robotics and computational creativity, this study contributes to developing a framework that researchers, engineers, and policymakers can use to develop and evaluate CCRs systems. The identification of critical challenges offers a structured approach for future research and development. In real-world applications, CNs enhance CCRs across different sectors. For instance, it helps optimize automation in manufacturing, patient-robot interactions in healthcare, and fostering AI-driven innovation in creative industries.

Considering the conceptual nature of this study, future research is suggested to focus on deepening the empirical understanding of CCRs by conducting case studies, prototype development, and experimental validation of CN-based mitigation strategies. Further exploration of CCRs' real-world applications, industry-specific constraints, and long-term impacts also can provide practical insights.

7 Disclosure of Interests.

The authors have no competing interests to declare that are relevant to the content of this article.

Acknowledgments. This research was partly supported by the Portuguese FCT program, Centre of Technology and Systems (CTS) CTS/00066, the project SER-ICS (PE00000014) under the NRRP MUR program funded by the EU – NGEU, and Nova University Lisbon.

References

1. Cai, X., et al.: Robot and its living space: a roadmap for robot development based on the view of living space. Digit. Commun. Netw. **7** (2021). https://doi.org/10.1016/j.dcan.2020.12.001
2. Leigh, N.G., Kraft, B., Lee, H.: Robots, skill demand and manufacturing in US regional labour markets. Camb. J. Regions Econ. Soc. **13** (2020). https://doi.org/10.1093/cjres/rsz019
3. Fragapane, G., Ivanov, D., Peron, M., Sgarbossa, F., Strandhagen, J.O.: Increasing flexibility and productivity in Industry 4.0 production networks with autonomous mobile robots and smart intralogistics. Ann. Oper. Res. **308** (2022). https://doi.org/10.1007/s10479-020-03526-7
4. Dauth, W., Findeisen, S., Suedekum, J., Woessner, N.: German robots - the impact of industrial robots on workers. Centre for Economic Policy Research (2017)
5. Cresswell, K., Cunningham-Burley, S., Sheikh, A.: Health care robotics: qualitative exploration of key challenges and future directions. J. Med. Internet Res. **20** (2018). https://doi.org/10.2196/10410
6. Bathirappan, K., Pandurengan, D.B., Nawaz, J.Y.A., Arulrajan, J.R.: Patient monitoring and medicine dispenser robot. In: AIP Conference Proceedings (2022). https://doi.org/10.1063/5.0106604
7. Bogue, R.: Rehabilitation robots. Industr. Robot. **45** (2018). https://doi.org/10.1108/IR-03-2018-0046
8. Habib, M.K., Baudoin, Y.: Robot-assisted risky intervention, search, rescue and environmental surveillance. Int. J. Adv. Robot. Syst. **7** (2010). https://doi.org/10.5772/7249
9. Narayan, S., Aquif, M., Kalim, A.R., Chagarlamudi, D., Harshith Vignesh, M.: Search and reconnaissance robot for disaster management. In: Lecture Notes in Mechanical Engineering (2022). https://doi.org/10.1007/978-981-16-0550-5_17
10. Sparrow, R., Howard, M.: Robots in agriculture: prospects, impacts, ethics, and policy. Precis Agric. **22** (2021). https://doi.org/10.1007/s11119-020-09757-9
11. Mor, R.S., Kumar, D., Singh, A., Neethu, K.: Robotics and automation for agri-food 4.0: innovation and challenges. In: Advanced Series in Management (2022). https://doi.org/10.1108/S1877-636120220000027013
12. Bogue, R.: The role of robots in entertainment. Industr. Robot. **49** (2022). https://doi.org/10.1108/IR-02-2022-0054
13. Belpaeme, T., Kennedy, J., Ramachandran, A., Scassellati, B., Tanaka, F.: Social robots for education: a review (2018). https://doi.org/10.1126/scirobotics.aat5954
14. Dang, Q.V., Nguyen, C.T., Rudová, H.: Scheduling of mobile robots for transportation and manufacturing tasks. J. Heurist. **25** (2019). https://doi.org/10.1007/s10732-018-9391-z
15. Pantofaru, C., Takayama, L., Foote, T., Soto, B.: Exploring the role of robots in home organization. In: HRI 2012 - Proceedings of the 7th Annual ACM/IEEE International Conference on Human-Robot Interaction (2012). https://doi.org/10.1145/2157689.2157805
16. Hoeckelmann, M., Rudas, I.J., Fiorini, P., Kirchner, F., Haidegger, T.: Current capabilities and development potential in surgical robotics. Int. J. Adv. Robot. Syst. **12** (2015). https://doi.org/10.5772/60133
17. Javaid, M., Haleem, A.: Impact of industry 4.0 to create advancements in orthopaedics. J. Clin. Orthop. Trauma. **11** (2020). https://doi.org/10.1016/j.jcot.2020.03.006
18. Javaid, M., Haleem, A., Singh, R.P., Suman, R.: Substantial capabilities of robotics in enhancing industry 4.0 implementation (2021). https://doi.org/10.1016/j.cogr.2021.06.001
19. Lindner, T., Wyrwał, D., Milecki, A.: An autonomous humanoid robot designed to assist a human with a gesture recognition system. Electron. (Switz.) **12** (2023). https://doi.org/10.3390/electronics12122652

20. Ferris, D.P., Schlink, B.R.: Robotic devices to enhance human movement performance. Kinesiol. Rev. **6** (2017). https://doi.org/10.1123/kr.2016-0040
21. Tao, F., Cheng, Y., Zhang, L., Nee, A.Y.C.: Advanced manufacturing systems: socialization characteristics and trends. J. Intell. Manuf. **28** (2017). https://doi.org/10.1007/s10845-015-1042-8
22. Liu, J., Wang, Z., Qian, L., Luo, R., Luo, X.: Task-oriented systematic design of a heavy-duty electrically actuated quadruped robot with high performance. Sensors. **23** (2023). https://doi.org/10.3390/s23156696
23. Schweighofer, N., Choi, Y., Winstein, C., Gordon, J.: Task-oriented rehabilitation robotics (2012). https://doi.org/10.1097/PHM.0b013e31826bcd42
24. Li, J., Storie, J., Clune, J.: Encouraging creative thinking in robots improves their ability to solve challenging problems. In: GECCO 2014 - Proceedings of the 2014 Genetic and Evolutionary Computation Conference (2014). https://doi.org/10.1145/2576768.2598222
25. Chuang, S.: An empirical study of displaceable job skills in the age of robots. Eur. J. Train. Dev. **45** (2020). https://doi.org/10.1108/EJTD-10-2019-0183
26. Yao, Y., Marchal, K., Van De Peer, Y.: Improving the adaptability of simulated evolutionary swarm robots in dynamically changing environments. PLoS One **9** (2014). https://doi.org/10.1371/journal.pone.0090695
27. Booth, J.W., et al.: OmniSkins: robotic skins that turn inanimate objects into multifunctional robots. Sci. Robot. **3** (2018). https://doi.org/10.1126/scirobotics.aat1853
28. Wong, C., Yang, E., Yan, X.-T., Gu, D.: Autonomous robots for harsh environments: a holistic overview of current solutions and ongoing challenges. Syst. Sci. Control Eng. **6** (2018). https://doi.org/10.1080/21642583.2018.1477634
29. Gizzi, E., Nair, L., Chernova, S., Sinapov, J.: Creative problem solving in artificially intelligent agents: a survey and framework. J. Artif. Intell. Res. **75** (2022). https://doi.org/10.1613/jair.1.13864
30. Nikghadam-Hojjati, S., Marchetti, E., Barata, J., Calabrò, A.: Moving into co-creative robotics. In: Proceedings of the 20th International Conference on Web Information Systems and Technologies, pp. 307–314. SCITEPRESS - Science and Technology Publications (2024). https://doi.org/10.5220/0013000400003825
31. Andrey, A., Todor, P.: The principles of creative robotics. Technologos (2020). https://doi.org/10.15593/perm.kipf/2020.4.01
32. Samani, H.: Creative robotics (2023)
33. Sullivan, F.R.: The creative nature of robotics activity: design and problem solving. In: Robotics in STEM Education, pp. 213–230. Springer International Publishing, Cham (2017). https://doi.org/10.1007/978-3-319-57786-9_9
34. Kennerley, B.: 10 challenges for the future of robotics. https://www.imperial.ac.uk/news/185792/10-challenges-future-robotics/. Accessed 29 Apr 2024
35. Freekly: Challenges in AI Driven Robotics. https://aitrot.com/challenges-in-ai-driven-robotics/robots/. Accessed 29 Apr 2024
36. Fuge, L.: The 10 "great challenges" for robots. https://cosmosmagazine.com/technology/robotics/the-10-great-challenges-for-robots/. Accessed 29 Apr 2024
37. Natarajan, M., et al.: Human-robot teaming: grand challenges. Curr. Robot. Rep. **4** (2023). https://doi.org/10.1007/s43154-023-00103-1
38. Patil, S., Vasu, V., Srinadh, K.V.S.: Advances and perspectives in collaborative robotics: a review of key technologies and emerging trends. Discov. Mech. Eng. **2** (2023). https://doi.org/10.1007/s44245-023-00021-8
39. Zeller, F., Dwyer, L.: Systems of collaboration: challenges and solutions for interdisciplinary research in AI and social robotics. Discov. Artif. Intell. **2** (2022). https://doi.org/10.1007/s44163-022-00027-3

40. Yao, B.: International research collaboration: challenges and opportunities (2021). https://doi.org/10.1177/8756479320976130
41. Crippen, K.J., Antonenko, P.D.: Designing for collaborative problem solving in STEM cyberlearning. Presented at the (2018). https://doi.org/10.1007/978-3-319-66659-4_5
42. Horáková, J., Kelemen, J.: The robot story: why robots were born and how they grew up. In: The Mechanical Mind in History (2023). https://doi.org/10.7551/mitpress/7626.003.0013
43. Dzedzickis, A., Subačiūtė-žemaitienė, J., Šutinys, E., Samukaitė-Bubnienė, U., Bučinskas, V.: Advanced applications of industrial robotics: new trends and possibilities, (2022). https://doi.org/10.3390/app12010135
44. Wallén, J.: The history of the industrial robot (2008)
45. Fukuda, T., Dario, P., Yang, G.Z.: Humanoid robotics—history, current state of the art, and challenges (2017). https://doi.org/10.1126/scirobotics.aar4043
46. Bilancia, P., Schmidt, J., Raffaeli, R., Peruzzini, M., Pellicciari, M.: An overview of industrial robots control and programming approaches (2023). https://doi.org/10.3390/app13042582
47. Sharma, N., Pandey, J.K., Mondal, S.: A review of mobile robots: applications and future prospect (2023). https://doi.org/10.1007/s12541-023-00876-7
48. Hazarika, S.M., Dixit, U.S.: Robotics: history, trends, and future directions. Presented at the (2018). https://doi.org/10.1007/978-3-319-78488-5_7
49. Roser, M.: This timeline charts the fast pace of tech transformation across centuries. https://www.weforum.org/agenda/2023/02/this-timeline-charts-the-fast-pace-of-tech-transformation-across-centuries/. Accessed 06 May 2024
50. Kennerley, B.: 10 challenges for the future of robotics. https://www.imperial.ac.uk/news/185792/10-challenges-future-robotics/. Accessed 06 May 2024
51. Wijayathunga, L., Rassau, A., Chai, D.: Challenges and solutions for autonomous ground robot scene understanding and navigation in unstructured outdoor environments: a review (2023). https://doi.org/10.3390/app13179877
52. Marcos-Pablos, S., García-Peñalvo, F.J.: Emotional intelligence in robotics: a scoping review. Presented at the (2022). https://doi.org/10.1007/978-3-030-87687-6_7
53. Tong, Y., Liu, H., Zhang, Z.: Advancements in humanoid robots: a comprehensive review and future prospects. IEEE/CAA J. Autom. Sinica. **11** (2024). https://doi.org/10.1109/JAS.2023.124140
54. Gomez Cubero, C., Pekarik, M., Rizzo, V., Jochum, E.: The robot is present: creative approaches for artistic expression with robots. Front. Robot. AI. **8** (2021). https://doi.org/10.3389/frobt.2021.662249
55. Robotics and Automation News: Ethical Considerations in Robotics: Balancing Innovation with Responsibility. https://roboticsandautomationnews.com/2024/01/25/ethical-considerations-in-robotics-balancing-innovation-with-responsibility/79099/. Accessed 06 May 2024
56. Shahid, A.A., Piga, D., Braghin, F., Roveda, L.: Continuous control actions learning and adaptation for robotic manipulation through reinforcement learning. Auton. Robots. **46** (2022). https://doi.org/10.1007/s10514-022-10034-z
57. Devillers, L.: Social and emotional robots: useful artificial intelligence in the absence of consciousness. In: Healthcare and Artificial Intelligence (2020). https://doi.org/10.1007/978-3-030-32161-1_32
58. Sheir, S., Manzini, A., Smith, H., Ives, J.: Adaptable robots, ethics, and trust: a qualitative and philosophical exploration of the individual experience of trustworthy AI. AI Soc. (2024). https://doi.org/10.1007/s00146-024-01938-8
59. Duch, W.: Computational creativity. In: The 2006 IEEE International Joint Conference on Neural Network Proceedings, pp. 435–442. IEEE (2006). https://doi.org/10.1109/IJCNN.2006.246714

60. Nikghadam-Hojjati, S., Barata, J.: Computational creativity to design cyber-physical systems in industry 4.0. In: IFIP Advances in Information and Communication Technology (2019). https://doi.org/10.1007/978-3-030-28464-0_4
61. Colton, S., de Mántaras, R.L., Stock, O.: Computational creativity: coming of age. AI Mag. **30**, 11–14 (2009). https://doi.org/10.1609/aimag.v30i3.2257
62. Gemeinboeck, P., Saunders, R.: Creative machine performance: computational creativity and robotic art. In: Proceedings of the 4th International Conference on Computational Creativity, ICCC 2013 (2013)
63. Ventura, D.: Autonomous intentionality in computationally creative systems. Presented at the (2019). https://doi.org/10.1007/978-3-319-43610-4_3
64. Alves-Oliveira, P., LaViers, A., Kahn, P.H., Gordon, G., Cakmak, M., Sarathy, V. (eds.): Creativity and robotics. Frontiers Media SA (2022). https://doi.org/10.3389/978-2-83250-384-3
65. Kappas, A., Gratch, J.: These aren't the droids you are looking for: promises and challenges for the intersection of affective science and robotics/AI (2023). https://doi.org/10.1007/s42761-023-00211-3
66. Thuruthel, T.G., Shih, B., Laschi, C., Tolley, M.T.: Soft robot perception using embedded soft sensors and recurrent neural networks. Sci. Robot. **4** (2019). https://doi.org/10.1126/SCIROBOTICS.AAV1488
67. Maroto-Gómez, M., Castro-González, Á., Malfaz, M., Salichs, M.Á.: A biologically inspired decision-making system for the autonomous adaptive behavior of social robots. Complex Intell. Syst. **9** (2023). https://doi.org/10.1007/s40747-023-01077-5
68. Maroto-Gómez, M., Alonso-Martín, F., Malfaz, M., Castro-González, Á., Castillo, J.C., Salichs, M.Á.: A systematic literature review of decision-making and control systems for autonomous and social robots (2023). https://doi.org/10.1007/s12369-023-00977-3
69. Deng, E., Mutlu, B., Mataric, M.J.: Embodiment in socially interactive robots. Found. Trends® Robot. **7** (2019). https://doi.org/10.1561/2300000056
70. Moruzzi, C.: The (artificial) physicality of creativity: how embodiment influences perceptions of creativity. In: Proceedings of the 13th International Conference on Computational Creativity, ICCC 2022 (2022)
71. Vollmer, A.L., et al.: Robots show us how to teach them: Feedback from robots shapes tutoring behavior during action learning. PLoS One **9** (2014). https://doi.org/10.1371/journal.pone.0091349
72. Bossema, M., Allouch, S. Ben, Plaat, A., Saunders, R.: Human-robot co-creativity: a scoping review : informing a research agenda for human-robot co-creativity with older adults. In: IEEE International Workshop on Robot and Human Communication, RO-MAN (2023). https://doi.org/10.1109/RO-MAN57019.2023.10309458
73. Mayoral-Vilches, V.: Robot cybersecurity, a review. Int. J. Cyber Forensics .... x (2022)
74. Shevlin, H.: Rethinking creative intelligence: comparative psychology and the concept of creativity. Eur. J. Philos. Sci. **11** (2021). https://doi.org/10.1007/s13194-020-00323-8
75. Schmid, U., Ragni, M., Gonzalez, C., Funke, J.: The challenge of complexity for cognitive systems (2011). https://doi.org/10.1016/j.cogsys.2010.12.007
76. Fellous, J.M.: From human emotions to robot emotions. In: AAAI Spring Symposium - Technical Report (2004)
77. Alex, C., Gillier, T., Haon, C.: How do emotions impact creativity ? A meta-analysis of dual pathway creativity model. Acad. Manage. Proc. **2023** (2023). https://doi.org/10.5465/amproc.2023.18558abstract
78. Barrett, M.S., Creech, A., Zhukov, K.: Creative collaboration and collaborative creativity: a systematic literature review (2021). https://doi.org/10.3389/fpsyg.2021.713445
79. Jirásek, M., Sudzina, F.: Big five personality traits and creativity. Qual. Innov. Prosperity **24** (2020). https://doi.org/10.12776/QIP.V24I3.1509

80. Baer, J.: The importance of domain-specific expertise in creativity. Roeper Rev. **37** (2015). https://doi.org/10.1080/02783193.2015.1047480
81. Pluut, H., Curşeu, P.L.: The role of diversity of life experiences in fostering collaborative creativity in demographically diverse student groups. Think. Skills Creat. **9** (2013). https://doi.org/10.1016/j.tsc.2013.01.002
82. Schwartz, S.A.: Consciousness, creativity, innovation, and survival. Explore **18** (2022). https://doi.org/10.1016/j.explore.2021.12.011
83. Andreasen, N.C.: A journey into chaos: creativity and the unconscious (2011). https://doi.org/10.4103/0973-1229.77424
84. Roitblat, H.L.: Algorithms are not enough: creating general artificial intelligence (2020)
85. Badke-Schaub, P., Buerschaper, C.: Creativity and complex problem solving in the social context. In: Decision Making: Social and Creative Dimensions (2001). https://doi.org/10.1007/978-94-015-9827-9_9
86. Wang, R., et al.: Enhanced poet: open-ended reinforcement learning through unbounded invention of learning challenges and their solutions. In: 37th International Conference on Machine Learning, ICML 2020 (2020)
87. Livingston, I.: Nonlinearity, writing, and creative process. In: The Palgrave Handbook of Literature and Mathematics (2020). https://doi.org/10.1007/978-3-030-55478-1_15
88. Anantrasirichai, N., Bull, D.: Artificial intelligence in the creative industries: a review. Artif Intell Rev. **55** (2022). https://doi.org/10.1007/s10462-021-10039-7
89. Nagarajan, T., Thondiyath, A.: An algorithm for cooperative task allocation in scalable, constrained multiple robot systems. Intell. Serv. Robot. **7** (2014). https://doi.org/10.1007/s11370-014-0154-x
90. Long, H., Wang, J.: Dissecting reliability and validity evidence of subjective creativity assessment: a literature review (2022). https://doi.org/10.1007/s10648-022-09679-0
91. Lloyd-Cox, J., Pickering, A., Bhattacharya, J.: Evaluating Creativity: How Idea Context and Rater Personality Affect Considerations of Novelty and Usefulness. Creat Res J. 34, (2022). https://doi.org/10.1080/10400419.2022.2125721
92. Gubenko, A., Kirsch, C., Smilek, J.N., Lubart, T., Houssemand, C.: Educational robotics and robot creativity: an interdisciplinary dialogue. Front. Robot AI **8** (2021). https://doi.org/10.3389/frobt.2021.662030
93. Mukherjee, A., Chang, H.H., Kong Chian, L.: The creative frontier of generative AI: managing the novelty-usefulness trade-off (2023)
94. Corazza, G.E., Lubart, T.: The big bang of originality and effectiveness: a dynamic creativity framework and its application to scientific missions. Front Psychol. **11** (2020). https://doi.org/10.3389/fpsyg.2020.575067
95. Bonarini, A.: Communication in human-robot interaction. Curr. Robot. Rep. **1** (2020). https://doi.org/10.1007/s43154-020-00026-1
96. Robinson, N., Tidd, B., Campbell, D., Kulić, D., Corke, P.: Robotic vision for human-robot interaction and collaboration: a survey and systematic review. ACM Trans. Hum. Robot. Interact. **12** (2023). https://doi.org/10.1145/3570731
97. Loizaga, E., Bastida, L., Sillaurren, S., Moya, A., Toledo, N.: Modelling and measuring trust in human–robot collaboration. Appl. Sci. **14** (2024). https://doi.org/10.3390/app14051919
98. Rossi, A., Holthaus, P., Perugia, G., Moros, S., Scheunemann, M.: Trust, acceptance and social cues in human–robot interaction (SCRITA) (2021). https://doi.org/10.1007/s12369-021-00844-z
99. Apraiz, A., Lasa, G., Mazmela, M.: Evaluation of user experience in human–robot interaction: a systematic literature review (2023). https://doi.org/10.1007/s12369-022-00957-z

100. Sandoval, E.B., Sosa, R., Cappuccio, M., Bednarz, T.: Human–robot creative interactions: exploring creativity in artificial agents using a storytelling game. Front. Robot. AI. **9** (2022). https://doi.org/10.3389/frobt.2022.695162
101. Agarwal, A., Veer, S., Ren, A.Z., Majumdar, A.: Stronger generalization guarantees for robot learning by combining generative models and real-world data. In: Proceedings - IEEE International Conference on Robotics and Automation (2022). https://doi.org/10.1109/ICRA46639.2022.9811565
102. Chatzimichali, A., Harrison, R., Chrysostomou, D.: Toward privacy-sensitive human-robot interaction: privacy terms and human-data interaction in the personal robot era. Paladyn. **12** (2021). https://doi.org/10.1515/pjbr-2021-0013
103. Hautala, J., Jauhiainen, J.S.: Co-creating knowledge with robots: system, synthesis, and symbiosis. J. Knowl. Econ. **14** (2023). https://doi.org/10.1007/s13132-022-00968-1
104. Lanier, A.L., et al.: Facilitating integration in interdisciplinary research: lessons from a south florida water, sustainability, and climate project. Environ. Manage. **62** (2018). https://doi.org/10.1007/s00267-018-1099-1
105. Reich, S.M., Reich, J.A.: Cultural competence in interdisciplinary collaborations: a method for respecting diversity in research partnerships. Am. J. Commun. Psychol. **38** (2006). https://doi.org/10.1007/s10464-006-9064-1
106. Liu, P., Lyndon, A., Holl, J.L., Johnson, J., Bilimoria, K.Y., Stey, A.M.: Barriers and facilitators to interdisciplinary communication during consultations: a qualitative study. BMJ Open. **11** (2021). https://doi.org/10.1136/bmjopen-2020-046111
107. The Robotics Back-End: What are Real-Time Constraints in Robotics?. https://roboticsbackend.com/what-are-real-time-constraints-in-robotics/. Accessed 20 May 2024
108. Kashiri, N., et al.: An overview on principles for energy efficient robot locomotion (2018). https://doi.org/10.3389/frobt.2018.00129
109. Dromnelle, R., et al.: Reducing computational cost during robot navigation and human–robot interaction with a human-inspired reinforcement learning architecture. Int. J. Soc. Robot. **15** (2023). https://doi.org/10.1007/s12369-022-00942-6
110. Wang, H.: Adaptive control of robot manipulators with uncertain kinematics and dynamics. IEEE Trans. Automat Contr. **62** (2017). https://doi.org/10.1109/TAC.2016.2575827
111. Muzakkir Quamar, M., Ali Nasir, A.: Review on fault diagnosis and fault-tolerant control scheme for robotic manipulators: recent advances in AI, machine learning, and digital twin. arXiv preprint arXiv:2402.02980 (2024)
112. Zaidi, S., Maselli, M., Laschi, C., Cianchetti, M.: Actuation technologies for soft robot grippers and manipulators: a review. Curr. Robot. Rep. **2** (2021). https://doi.org/10.1007/s43154-021-00054-5
113. Donald, R., Hertel, B., Misenti, S., Gu, Y., Azadeh, R.: An adaptive framework for manipulator skill reproduction in dynamic environments (2024)
114. Różańska-Walczuk, M.: Collaborative robotics. Safety and ethical considerations. In: Lecture Notes in Networks and Systems (2023). https://doi.org/10.1007/978-3-031-37649-8_26
115. Chen, Y., Arkin, J., Zhang, Y., Roy, N., Fan, C.: Scalable multi-robot collaboration with large language models: centralized or decentralized systems? In: The 2024 International Conference on Robotics and Automation (2024)
116. Soma, K., Vardharajan, V.S., Hamann, H., Beltrame, G.: Congestion and scalability in robot swarms: a study on collective decision making. In: 2023 International Symposium on Multi-Robot and Multi-Agent Systems, MRS 2023 (2023). https://doi.org/10.1109/MRS60187.2023.10416793
117. Pilkington, B.: Interoperability, and Why Robot-Robot Partnerships Matter. https://www.azorobotics.com/Article.aspx?ArticleID=536. Accessed 22May 2024

118. Zhou, C., Huang, B., Fränti, P.: A review of motion planning algorithms for intelligent robots (2022). https://doi.org/10.1007/s10845-021-01867-z
119. Hassija, V., et al.: Interpreting black-box models: a review on explainable. Artif. Intell. (2024). https://doi.org/10.1007/s12559-023-10179-8
120. Saberifar, F.Z., Shell, D.A., O'Kane, J.M.: Charting the trade-off between design complexity and plan execution under probabilistic actions. In: Proceedings - IEEE International Conference on Robotics and Automation (2022). https://doi.org/10.1109/ICRA46639.2022.9811751
121. Veruggio, G., Operto, F.: Roboethics: social and ethical implications of robotics. In: Springer Handbook of Robotics (2008). https://doi.org/10.1007/978-3-540-30301-5_65
122. Londoño, L., Hurtado, J.V., Hertz, N., Kellmeyer, P., Voeneky, S., Valada, A.: Fairness and bias in robot learning (2022)
123. Alaieri, F., Vellino, A.: Ethical decision making in robots: autonomy, trust and responsibility autonomy trust and responsibility. In: Lecture Notes in Computer Science (including subseries Lecture Notes in Artificial Intelligence and Lecture Notes in Bioinformatics) (2016). https://doi.org/10.1007/978-3-319-47437-3_16
124. Sequeira, J.S.: Ethics in human-robot interaction. Presented at the (2019). https://doi.org/10.1007/978-3-319-96722-6_7
125. Ornelas, M.L., Smith, G.B., Mansouri, M.: Redefining culture in cultural robotics. AI Soc. **38** (2023). https://doi.org/10.1007/s00146-022-01476-1
126. Colton, S., Pease, A., Saunders, R.: Issues of authenticity in autonomously creative systems. In: Proceedings of the 9th International Conference on Computational Creativity, ICCC 2018 (2018)
127. Obaid, M., Muller, C., Cerna, K.: Creative Approaches to Appropriation and Design: Novel Robotic Systems for Heterogeneous Contexts. https://www.frontiersin.org/research-topics/48274/creative-approaches-to-appropriation-and-design-novel-robotic-systems-for-heterogeneous-contexts. Accessed 27 Apr 2024
128. Pereida, K., Greef, M.: Diversity in Robotics: From Diverse Teams to Diverse Impact (2020). https://www.dynsyslab.org/wp-content/papercite-data/pdf/pereida-icra19b.pdf
129. Smedegaard, C.V.: Novelty knows no boundaries: why a proper investigation of novelty effects within SHRI should begin by addressing the scientific plurality of the field. Front. Robot. AI **9** (2022). https://doi.org/10.3389/frobt.2022.741478
130. Kok, B.C., Soh, H.: Trust in robots: challenges and opportunities. Curr. Robot. Rep. **1** (2020). https://doi.org/10.1007/s43154-020-00029-y
131. Shamonsky, D.: User experience best practices for human-robot interaction. In: Lecture Notes in Computer Science (Including Subseries Lecture Notes in Artificial Intelligence and Lecture Notes in Bioinformatics) (2021). https://doi.org/10.1007/978-3-030-78465-2_24
132. Boada, J.P., Maestre, B.R., Torras, C.: Ethics for social robotics: a critical analysis (2022)
133. Dunstan, B.J., Silvera-Tawil, D., Koh, J.T.K.V., Velonaki, M.: Cultural robotics: robots as participants and creators of culture. In: Lecture Notes in Computer Science (Including Subseries Lecture Notes in Artificial Intelligence and Lecture Notes in Bioinformatics) (2016). https://doi.org/10.1007/978-3-319-42945-8_1
134. Keating, S.J., Leland, J.C., Cai, L., Oxman, N.: Toward site-specific and self-sufficient robotic fabrication on architectural scales. Sci Robot. **2** (2017). https://doi.org/10.1126/scirobotics.aam8986
135. Sękala, A., Blaszczyk, T., Foit, K., Kost, G.: Selected issues, methods, and trends in the energy consumption of industrial robots (2024). https://doi.org/10.3390/en17030641
136. Satav, A.G., Kubade, S., Amrutkar, C., Arya, G., Pawar, A.: A state-of-the-art review on robotics in waste sorting: scope and challenges (2023). https://doi.org/10.1007/s12008-023-01320-w

137. Han, D., Wu, H., Zhu, Y., Diao, Y.: The road to carbon win, the wise first: evidence of robot impact enabling the synergistic effects of pollution reduction and carbon emissions. Air Qual. Atmos. Health (2024). https://doi.org/10.1007/s11869-024-01542-1
138. Song, Q., Zhao, Q.: Recent advances in robotics and intelligent robots applications. Appl. Sci. **14**, 4279 (2024). https://doi.org/10.3390/app14104279
139. Vecellio Segate, R., Daly, A.: Encoding the enforcement of safety standards into smart robots to harness their computing sophistication and collaborative potential: a legal risk assessment for european union policymakers. Eur. J. Risk Regul. 1–40 (2023). https://doi.org/10.1017/err.2023.72
140. Funk, M., Lin, P., Abney, K., Bekey, G.A. (eds.): Robot Ethics: The Ethical and Social Implications of Robotics. Ethical Theory and Moral Practice, vol. 19, (2016). https://doi.org/10.1007/s10677-015-9638-9
141. Robb, D.A., et al.: Robots in the danger zone: exploring public perception through engagement. In: ACM/IEEE International Conference on Human-Robot Interaction (2020). https://doi.org/10.1145/3319502.3374789
142. Abbott, R.: I think, therefore i invent: creative computers and the future of patent law. SSRN Electron. J. (2016). https://doi.org/10.2139/ssrn.2727884
143. Bellieni, C., Velazquez, L.: The True Secret of Evolution: From Conflict to Collaboration (Spanish Edition). (2023)
144. Braren, S.: The evolution of social connection as a basic human need. https://www.thesocialcreatures.org/thecreaturetimes/evolution-of-social-connection. Accessed 25 May 2024
145. Mattioli, F., Coghlan, S., Tomko, M., Tolmeijer, S., Kneer, M.: Beyond anthropomorphism? The AI - machine - human - animal continuum. https://www.unimelb.edu.au/caide/research-archive/beyond-anthropomorphism-the-ai-machine-human-animal-continuum. Accessed 24 May 2024
146. Camarinha-Matos, L.M., Afsarmanesh, H.: The evolution path to collaborative networks 4.0. In: IFIP Advances in Information and Communication Technology (2021). https://doi.org/10.1007/978-3-030-81701-5_7
147. Marchetti, E., Nikghadam-Hojjati, S., Barata, J.: Collaborative network 5.0: by design human values and human-centred based extended collaborative networks. In: IFIP Advances in Information and Communication Technology (2023). https://doi.org/10.1007/978-3-031-42622-3_29
148. Cormican, K., Dooley, L.: Knowledge sharing in a collaborative networked environment. J. Inf. Knowl. Manage. **6** (2007). https://doi.org/10.1142/S0219649207001706
149. Camarinha-Matos, L.M., Abreu, A.: Performance indicators for collaborative networks based on collaboration benefits. Prod. Plann. Control **18** (2007). https://doi.org/10.1080/09537280701546880
150. Sridharan, S., Gillespie, D.: Sustaining problem-solving capacity in collaborative networks. Criminol. Public Policy. **3** (2004). https://doi.org/10.1111/j.1745-9133.2004.tb00038.x
151. Patel, M., et al.: Harnessing interdisciplinarity to promote the ethical design of AI systems. In: Proceedings of the European Conference on the Impact of Artificial Intelligence and Robotics (Eciair 2019) (2019)
152. Igbinenikaro, O.P., Adekoya, O.O., Etukudoh, E.A.: Fostering cross-disciplinary collaboration in offshore projects: strategies and best practices. Int. J. Manage. Entrep. Res. **6**, 1176–1189 (2024). https://doi.org/10.51594/ijmer.v6i4.1006
153. Feng, K., Karreman, B., Zeng, D., Pennings, E.: R&D collaboration, social coordination, and standardization: evidence from the Chinese automotive industry. J. Technol. Transf. **49** (2024). https://doi.org/10.1007/s10961-022-09972-8

Impact of the Number of Items on the Response Rate of User Experience Surveys

Marco Schaa[1], Jessica Kollmorgen[2], Martin Schrepp[3], and Jög Thomaschewski[2(✉)]

[1] Allpax GmbH & Co. KG, Papenburg, Germany
marco.schaa@ux-researchgroup.com

[2] University of Applied Sciences Emden/Leer, Emden, Germany
jessica.kollmorgen@ux-researchgroup.com,
joerg.thomaschewski@hs-emden-leer.de

[3] SAP SE, Hasso-Plattner-Ring 7, 69190 Walldorf, Germany
martin.schrepp@sap.com

Abstract. Standardized questionnaires are a popular method to evaluate the user experience of a product. A common problem of this approach are low response rates. Many products request user feedback and therefore the willingness to fill out a UX survey is often quite low. This makes it difficult to collect enough data to derive meaningful conclusions. Of course, it is natural to assume that the length of a survey impacts the response rate. We describe in this paper two mechanisms to implement short surveys in a web shop. In the first study customers are either asked on the order confirmation page of a web shop to answer all 8 items of the UEQ-S questionnaire or to answer just one randomly selected item. The presentation of single items increased the response rate. The increase was statistically significant, but from a practical point of view not really relevant. In addition, there were some context effects that caused a statistically significant difference of some item scores between the full UEQ-S and the single item display. In a second study we compared the full UEQ-S with the Net Promoter Score (NPS), a classical single item questionnaire. Again, there was no practically relevant increase of the response rate. Using this example, we discuss also the trade-off between very condensed single item scales and detailed UX questionnaires like the UEQ-S.

Keywords: Response rates · User experience · UX measurement · UX questionnaire · UEQ-S · Single item version · Net promoter score

1 Introduction

A good user experience (UX) of products is important to stay competitive in the market. UX is a holistic concept that goes beyond pure usability. Depending on the product category [10] UX aspects like, for example, aesthetics, fun of use or trust must be taken into account in addition to pure usability aspects, like for example, efficiency or learnability. Since products evolve over time, it is important to constantly measure the UX quality to react on changes. For example, to check if a redesign of a web shop has a positive or negative impact on its perceived UX.

M. Marchiori et al. (Eds.): WEBIST 2024, LNBIP 583, pp. 90–108, 2026.
https://doi.org/10.1007/978-3-032-25534-1_4

A popular method to collect user feedback and to measure UX quality is surveys. They can easily be distributed over different channels (for example, email campaigns, feedback buttons inside a product, or links in posts on social media) and allow to collect feedback from larger user groups with low effort. If a standardized UX questionnaire, for example the UEQ [11], the SUS [1], or the UMUX [5] is incorporated in a survey, then quantitative measurements are possible that allow to compare products or product versions concerning their UX quality.

These advantages made especially online surveys quite popular. But this success created also some problems for the method. People are constantly asked to provide feedback over surveys for different products. This naturally creates survey fatigue and response rates for surveys are often quite low [21].

Therefore, it is practically highly relevant to present a survey in a way that attracts as many users as possible. Some incentives to give feedback can increase the response rate, but may also decrease the quality of the responses, since many participants just take part in the survey to get the incentive and minimize the time they spend to think about their answers.

Another way to achieve a high response rate is the usage of very short surveys. However, such short surveys create less detailed insights compared with a longer standardized UX questionnaire. Of course, the more items are used, the more detailed is the information that can be collected. One idea to overcome this problem is to split the items of a longer survey into smaller groups and to show each user only one randomly selected group. Thus, per user the number of items is small, but since each user responds to different items we still collect data for all items. The most extreme version of this strategy is to show each user only one randomly selected item of the questionnaire. In many situations, especially in e-commerce, there is a high number of potential respondents. Thus, this strategy will still generate enough responses for each item. This leads to our first research question.

RQ1: Do The Item and Scale Scores Collected Over Single Item Presentation Differ from the Corresponding Scores Collected with the Full Version?
We use the UEQ-S questionnaire [16] in our study. We investigate if it is possible to estimate the results of the full UEQ-S from the responses to single items. Items are always interpreted in a context. This context is mainly defined by the evaluated product, but neighboring items can also influence the interpretation. Therefore, it is important to investigate if the isolated presentation of single items has an effect on the results.

The goal of the split of a questionnaire into single items is to increase the willingness of users to respond. This directly leads to our second research question.

RQ2: How Does a Split into Single Items Impact the Response Rate?
Of course, we assume that the response rate increases for the single item version - but how big is the increase and is it big enough to be of practical relevance?

The items of a longer UX questionnaire are of course designed to be used within the context of the complete set of items. Thus, a possible effect that may in fact negatively influence the response rate of single item presentations is that the isolated items may look a bit unnatural. To control this effect we replicate the study used to answer the first two research questions with a different setting. We compare the response rate of the

UEQ-S to the response rate of the NPS [14], which is a single item questionnaire, i.e. the item is designed and optimized to be displayed in isolation.

RQ3: How Does the Response Rate of a Multi-item Questionnaire Differ from the Response Rate of a Single Item Questionnaire?

Classical single item questionnaires, for example the NPS [14] or the Product Satisfaction Question (PSAT), just measure a high level UX impression. Customer loyalty in the case of the NPS and overall user satisfaction in the case of the PSAT. We investigate in the second study also the benefits of a more detailed measurement approach that takes distinct UX qualities into account compared to an approach that concentrates of a single high-level UX concept.

First insights concerning our first two research questions were already described in [15]. This paper extends these results by presenting a second study that replicates the basic settings of the study described in this paper and enhances the insights by adding a third research question.

The article structures as follows: Sect. 2 presents related work. Section 3 then describes a study that tries to answer the first two research questions. Section 4 presents a second study targeted to the third research question. Section 5 summarizes the results and limitations of both studies.

2 Related Work

We present in this section several results related to our three research questions and some background information about the questionnaires used in our studies.

2.1 Survey Length and Response Rate

It is a natural assumption that the length of a survey will have an impact on the willingness of people to fill it out. The more questions a survey contains, the higher is the probability that participants do not even start. In addition, participants can easily get bored if a survey contains too many questions and then quit without submitting their responses. It is thus wise to include only questions that are crucial for the research question in a survey.

Research shows that not the actual number of questions but the perceived length of a survey is the real problem [19]. Perceived length can be influenced by several factors of survey design. It is, for example, a common practice to mention the time required to complete the survey in the instruction. The longer the announced time is, the lower is the rate of participants that enter the survey [3].

Another element that impacts perceived length are progress indicators that show how many of the questions are already answered. If the displayed progress is behind the expectation of participants, then the drop-out rates will increase [2]. In a meta-analysis of studies that compared different progress indicators [20] it was found that indicators that show a fast progress in the beginning and a slower progress closer to the end reduced drop-off rates. Contrary progress indicators that show a slow progress in the beginning and a fast progress close to the end increased drop-out rates.

Of course, the most direct and efficient way to reduce perceived length of a survey is to reduce the number of questions and the most radical way is to use only a single question. We investigate in this paper two methods to reduce survey length. First, the split of a longer survey into single questions. Each respondent is shown randomly one of the items in the questionnaire, but by this mechanism still answers to all items are collected. A second method is the use of dedicated single item questionnaires.

2.2 Single Item Questionnaires

Single item scales or questionnaires are a simple and direct approach to measure impressions of users. This make them quite popular in practice and research. However, they are often seen as dubious because of a low reliability and an inadequate coverage of complex constructs [18].

The possibility of using single items to measure a construct and still collecting valuable and reliable information depends on the construct itself. Fuchs et al. [6] found that the use of single item measurement can be appropriate under certain conditions. The authors created guidelines for relevant criteria to evaluate single item measurements for use in business administration.

Cuvillier et al. [4] came to a similar conclusion using the example of financial institution websites. They investigated functional and non-functional user requirements using the Net Promoter Score (NPS) and the Product Satisfaction Score (PSAT). They investigated the influence of the context on the hedonic and pragmatic experiences of the users, whereby it was shown that hedonic features correlated slightly better with the single-item scales.

There are also systematic studies on this topic for other fields, such as Organizational Psychology. Matthews et al. [12] developed corresponding single item alternatives for 91 questionnaires that have proven effective in this area. The authors analyzed them for criteria and content validity, reliability and usability and also investigated if there is a negative relation between the construct breadth (near vs. broad) and the validity and reliability. Their approach was to develop new, more comprehensive items instead of just splitting the existing surveys into their single item pieces. As a result, they showed that the use of single item measurements does not automatically mean the sacrifice of validity and reliability but has to be considered due to the advantages of short surveys.

Single item measuring in the field of user experience was already investigated for the System Usability Scale (SUS) [1] in relation to automated driving. Himmels et al. [7] developed a single item version of the SUS (called SIUX scale) and compared it to the multi-item measures SUS and UMUX in terms of stability, reliability and validity. Their results supports the hypotheses that the SIUX is even more sensitive to differences in event related user experience than the UMUX and more sensitive to cumulative user experience than the SUS.

The related work shows that single item surveys are not in general a bad research approach, but have to be individually examined for each construct.

2.3 UX Questionnaires in Our Studies

We introduce in the following two established UX questionnaires that we use in our studies.

The User Experience Questionnaire (UEQ) [11] is a standardized questionnaire that allows to measure several task-related (pragmatic) and non-task-related (hedonic) UX aspects by 26 items. The item format is a semantic differential with a 7-point answer scale (scored from −3 to +3). An example of an item is:

inefficient o o o o o o o efficient

Filling out a complete UEQ can be done in approximately 3 to 5 min. Nevertheless, this is still too much effort for several typical application scenarios. For example, if the questionnaire should be filled after completing an order in a web shop.

For scenarios that require a low completion time a short version, called UEQ-S, with just 8 items was developed [16]. The items of the English version (translation can be found on www.ueq-online.org) are shown in Table 1.

Table 1. UEQ-S items (English version).

UEQ1	obstructive	supportive
UEQ2	complicated	easy
UEQ3	inefficient	efficient
UEQ4	confusing	Row clear
UEQ5	boring	exciting
UEQ6	not interesting	interesting
UEQ7	conventional	inventive
UEQ8	usual	leading edge

The first four items form the scale *Pragmatic Quality*, the last four items the scale *Hedonic Quality*. The labels in parentheses are used in Sect. 3.3 to refer to the items. A benchmark for the UEQ-S is described in [8].

A quite popular single item scale is the Net Promotor Score (NPS) [14]. It consists of a single question:

How likely is it that you would recommend < product > to a friend or colleague?
Not at all likely o o o o o o o o o o o *Extremely likely*

Answers are scored from left to right from 0 to 10 and classified into three categories as seen in Table 2.

The NPS score is calculated as *Percentage of Promoters – Percentage of Detractors*, thus it ranges from -100 (worst) to 100 (best).

The idea behind this scoring scheme is that promoters are extremely impressed by the product and suggest it to other people, thus influencing their buying decisions

Table 2. NPS Answer Scoring Classification.

Answer score from..to	Classification
0..6	Detractors
7..8	Passives
9..10	Promoter

positively. A high NPS should thus indicate a growing customer base. Reichheld [13, 14]) suggests a positive influence of the measured NPS score on the further growth of a company relative to its competitors in the market. However, other studies [9] failed to reproduce these results.

3 First Study: Split a Longer Questionnaire into Single Items

The following section outlines the study design, detailing the web shop utilized, the implementation of both the full UEQ-S and its single-item variant, as well as the data collection process and the evaluation methodology employed to address the research questions RQ1 and RQ2.

3.1 Investigated Web Shop

Data for this study were obtained from a German online store specializing in a diverse range of product categories, including vacuum technology, cleaning technology, infrared heaters, gastronomy supplies, and laboratory equipment. The company primarily serves commercial customers (90%) but also sells to private customers (10%). Private customers predominantly purchase gastronomy-related products, like household vacuum sealers, low-temperature cooking devices or other articles like infrared heaters. At the time of the study, the online store listed approximately 13,000 products.

Given the relatively high visitor traffic, with an average of 117 daily purchases, a sufficiently representative dataset could be collected. Furthermore, the webshop follows strict data protection regulations, ensuring the anonymity of all participants.

3.2 Implementation of the Feedback Mechanism and Data Collection

The UX assessment using the UEQ-S was integrated into the online shop's checkout process, appearing on the checkout success page immediately after a completed purchase and payment. This placement was chosen to minimize any disruption to the purchasing experience and to mitigate the risk of cart abandonment.

During the data collection period from February 2, 2024, to June 2, 2024 (four months), the questionnaire was presented to a total of 14,469 customers, averaging 119 participants per day.

As the shop system in use is proprietary and closed-source—developed in ASP.NET by 4Sellers, Rain am Lech—a direct integration of a survey module was not pursued due to cost considerations. Instead, a PHP script was implemented on a separate Apache server and incorporated into the shop template through an iFrame.

This PHP script assigned a random number between 1 and 12 to each request, determining whether the participant would receive (a) a single UEQ-S item or (b) the complete UEQ-S questionnaire. To ensure a sufficient dataset of complete UEQ-S responses for comparative analysis, the full questionnaire was displayed four times more often than each individual item (i.e., four of the 12 random numbers corresponded to the full UEQ-S, while each of the remaining numbers triggered a single item). Upon submission, the collected responses, along with timestamps for both display and submission, were stored in a CSV file on the server.

In addition, every survey display was recorded in a separate CSV file, which captured the randomly assigned identifier, the timestamp of the display, and the customer GUID. This enabled an analysis of response rates and an investigation if some UEQ-S items were answered more or less frequently.

The frequency with which individual UEQ-S items were answered varied between the full and single-item versions. Some participants did not complete the full questionnaire before leaving the online shop, leading to differences in response counts. The number of responses per item for both versions is presented in Table 3. In total, 1,387 responses were collected, consisting of 413 from the full UEQ-S and 964 from the single-item version.

Table 3. Number of answers per item in the full and single item UEQ-S version.

Item	N (full)	N (single)
obstructive/supportive	373	114
complicated/easy	407	165
inefficient/efficient	377	149
confusing/clear	402	141
boring/exciting	338	102
not interesting/interesting	344	110
conventional/inventive	343	102
usual/leading edge	342	90

3.3 Results

We present in this section some analyses required to answer our first two research questions.

Our first research question RQ1 asked if the item and scale scores collected using the single item version differs from the corresponding scores collected by using the full UEQ-S? Thus, this research question focus on potential context effects that cause different responses if an item is presented within the context of other items.

As a first analysis we present results concerning the observed means and confidence intervals of the items in both conditions. Figure 1 shows the scale scores and confidence intervals for the 8 UEQ-S items in both versions.

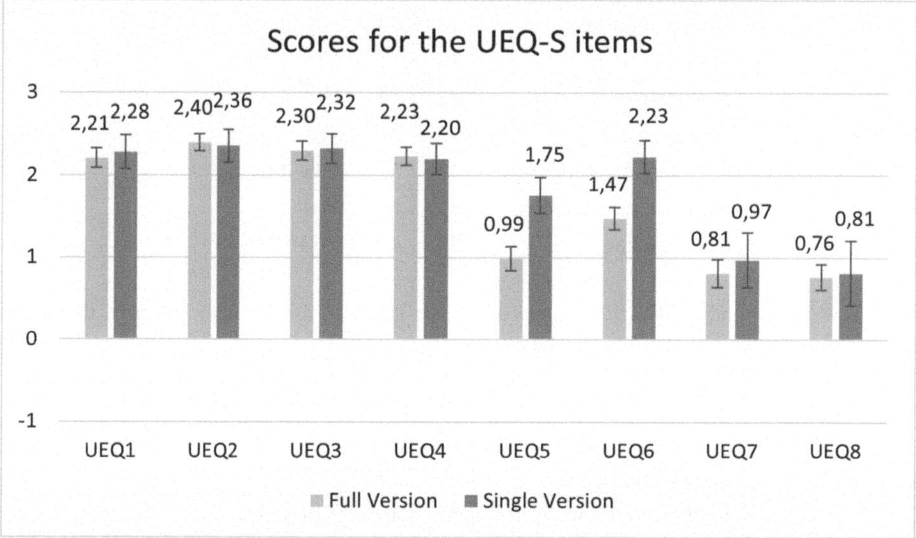

Fig. 1. Mean item scores and the corresponding confidence intervals for the investigated web shop measured with the full and single item UEQ-S version (number of answers per item is shown in Table 3). The scale ranges from −3 to +3 but is reduced in the figure to the range of −1 to +3 to enhance readability as already described in [15].

The detailed scores, standard deviations and confidence intervals are shown in Table 4 for the full version and in Table 5 for the single item version.

To decide if the differences between the mean scores are statistically significant two-sample t-tests assuming equal variances ($p<0.05$) were performed for all 8 items.

For the items UEQ5 ($t = 5.29$, $df = 421$, $p <0.0000002$) and UEQ6 ($t = 5.96$, $df = 429$, $p<0.000000005$), the mean score resulting from the single item display is significantly higher than the corresponding score resulting from the full UEQ-S display. In addition, the strength of the significant influence was checked using the effect size (Cohen's d). The result was an effect size of $d = 0.59$ for UEQ5 and $d = 0.61$ for UEQ6, so that a medium effect (>0.5, <0.8) was determined for both items.

For all other items, the differences between the item scores resulting from the two display variants are not statistically significant.

The mean scale scores for the *Pragmatic Quality* (PQ, items UEQ1-UEQ4), *Hedonic Quality* (HQ, items UEQ5-UEQ8) and the overall score (all items) are displayed in Fig. 2. The exact scores are shown in Table 6. Statistically significant differences with a strong effect were found for both the HQ dimension ($t = 5.54$, $df = 1769$, $p = 0.000000034$; Cohen's $d = 1.80$) and the overall value ($t = 4.89$, $df = 3888$, $p = 0.000001$; Cohen's $d = 3.17$).

Table 4. Means, standard deviations and confidence intervals for the item scores of the **full version** (number of answers per item is shown in Table 3).

Item	Mean	St.Dev.	Confidence Int.
obstructive/supportive	2.21	1.18	2.09–2.33
complicated/easy	2.40	1.09	2.29–2.50
inefficient/efficient	2.30	1.15	2.18–2.42
confusing/clear	2.23	1.14	2.12–2.34
boring/exciting	0.99	1.36	0.84–1.13
not interesting/interesting	1.47	1.28	1.33–1.61
conventional/inventive	0.81	1.59	0.64–0.98
usual/leading edge	0.76	1.49	0.60–0.92

Table 5. Means, standard deviations and confidence intervals for the item scores of the **single item version** (number of answers per item is shown in Table 3).

Item	Mean	St.Dev.	Confidence Int.
obstructive/supportive	2.28	1.17	2.08–2.49
complicated/easy	2.36	1.31	2.16–2.56
inefficient/efficient	2.32	1.10	2.14–2.50
confusing/clear	2.12	1.15	2.01–2.39
boring/exciting	1.76	1.14	1.53–1.98
not interesting/interesting	2.23	1.06	2.03–2.43
conventional/inventive	0.97	1.70	0.64–1.30
usual/leading edge	0.81	1.90	0.42–1.20

Now we move our attention to our second research question RQ2 and investigate if a split into single items impacts the response rate. The response rate is the number of participants who submitted an answer divided by the number of participants who see the corresponding version on the checkout page. Thus, for the full UEQ-S version it is the number of submitted UEQ-S responses divided by the number of all customers who see the full UEQ-S on their checkout page. Similar for the single item version.

Overall, 14,469 participants reached the checkout page during the period of the study. For 4,809 participants, the full UEQ-S was presented and for 9,660 only a single item was shown.

The Overall Response Rate for the full UEQ-S Version was 8% and the Response Rate for the Single Item Version was 10%.

There is a statistically significant dependency (Chi-Square = 7.21, df = 1, $p<0.0072$) between the display condition (single item versus full UEQ-S) and the willingness to respond. The single item version increased the response rate (two-sample T-test assuming unequal variances, $t = 2.75$, $df = 10198$, $p = 0.006$). Furthermore, the strength of the significant influence was checked using the effect size (Cohen's d). The result was

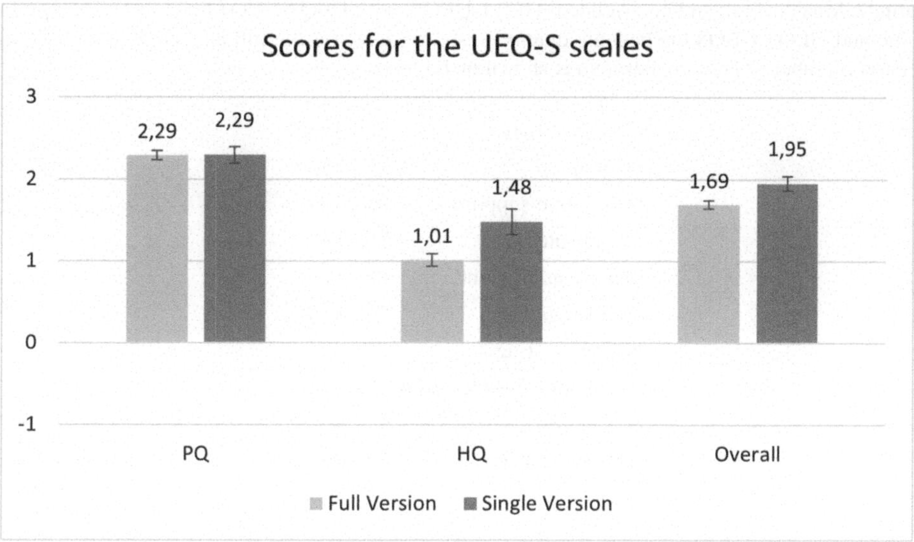

Fig. 2. Mean scale scores for the investigated web shop measured with the full and single item UEQ-S version (number of answers per item is shown in Table 3). The scale ranges from −3 to +3 but is reduced to −1 to +3 to enhance readability as already described in [15].

Table 6. Means, standard deviations and confidence intervals for the scale scores (PQ, HQ and overall) of both versions (number of answers per item is shown in Table 3).

Scale	Full UEQ-S			Single item version		
	Mean	St.dev.	Conf.Interval	Mean	St.dev.	Conf.Interval
PQ	2.31	1.04	2.21–2.41	2.29	1.18	2.11–2.47
HQ	1.05	1.33	1.92–1.18	1.48	1.58	1.23–1.72
Overall	1.80	1.07	1.70–1.91	1.95	1.42	1.73–2.17

an effect size of d = 1.98, so that a strong effect (>0.8) exists. The response rate in the single item version differs between the 8 items (see Table 7).

The pragmatic items (items UEQ1-UEQ4) showed higher response rates than the hedonic items (UEQ5-UEQ8). The mean response rate in the single item version for pragmatic items was 12% and for hedonic items 8%. There is a statistically significant dependency between the UEQ-S subscale (PQ or HQ) and the willingness to answer the item (Chi-Square 29.06, df = 1, p<0,00000007). Pragmatic items have a statistical significantly higher response rate than hedonic items (two-sample T-test assuming unequal variances, t = −55.24, df = 550, p<1.3e-226). A strong effect (d = 1.99) was also detected in this case.

Concerning the time required to create an answer (time between showing the order confirmation screen and clicking the submit button), there is also a difference between

Table 7. Mean overall and item-related (UEQ1-UEQ8, with UEQ1-UEQ4 for assessing the pragmatic and UEQ5-UEQ8 the hedonic quality) response rates for the full and single item UEQ-S version (number of answers per item is shown in Table 3).

Response Rate	Full	Single
Overall	8%	10%
obstructive/supportive	8%	9%
complicated/easy	8%	14%
inefficient/efficient	8%	11%
confusing/clear	8%	12%
boring/exciting	7%	9%
not interesting/interesting	7%	9%
conventional/inventive	7%	8%
usual/leading edge	7%	7%

the two versions. The median time required to answer was 21 s for the single item version and 43 s for the full UEQ-S version.

3.4 Discussion of the Results for the First Study

We start with a discussion of our first research question **RQ1: Do the item and scale scores collected over single item version differ from the corresponding scores collected with the full UEQ-S version?** A negative answer, i.e. no differences between both versions, would allow to estimate the result of a full UEQ-S questionnaire based on the results of the single items. Thus, such a negative answer is required to justify the approach to split a longer questionnaire into single items to increase the response rate.

Our results show that the mean values of the full and single item version do not differ with regard to the four items UEQ1-UEQ4 belonging to the *Pragmatic Quality* scale (see Sect. 2.3). Thus, for this scale the results of the single items can be used to estimate the scale score of the full version.

The situation is different for the items UEQ5-UEQ8 of the scale *Hedonic Quality*. Significant differences with a strong effect were found for UEQ5 (boring/exciting) and UEQ6 (not interesting/interesting). In both cases the mean score for the single item version was higher than for the full version. As a result of the significant differences for these two items, the mean rating of the dimension *Hedonic Quality* and the overall rating of the full and single item version also differed significantly from each other.

How can these differences be explained? One potential explanation is a context effect. Thus, if an item is shown in context with other items it may be interpreted differently compared to a situation where it is shown in isolation. The investigated web shop is used in a more pragmatic intention by customers. Given the available products in the shop, customers place orders to fulfill concrete demands. Thus, fun or pleasure do not play a big role for the shopping experience. Therefore, the pragmatic items will look more natural and are more aligned with the expectations of customers than the hedonic items. This will most likely cause a more direct and stable interpretation that is less influenced by a context effect. This interpretation is also supported by the fact that the hedonic items are less frequently answered than the pragmatic items (See Table 7) in both conditions. This may result from a higher difficulty to interpret the hedonic items.

Another explanation could be a different importance of pragmatic and hedonic items for the overall impression of customers [17]. The more important a UX aspect is the higher is the willingness to answer the corresponding items and the more carefully will a participant of a study answer. As we already explained above the pragmatic quality is much more important than the hedonic quality for the investigated web-shop. And in addition, the pragmatic items were rated very positively. Thus, customers seems to be quite satisfied with the pragmatic quality. If less effort is spend to decide on the rating of the hedonic items this will naturally cause a lower rating, since the rating may reflect the lower importance.

Thus, to summarize these findings we can conclude that the answer to the first research question depends on the scales and items. It can not be generally answered. If the items are fitting quite well to the expectations of the participants in an evaluation and if there are no strong context effects that influence their interpretation of the items it is possible to estimate the scale scores from single items. But this must be investigated and confirmed for each combination of product and questionnaire. If these conditions are not met, then the use of single item scores to estimate a full scale can lead to severe errors.

Now we move our attention to our second research question **RQ2: How does a split into single items impact the response rate?**

As expected the response rate for the single item version was higher. There was a small but significant increase of 2% overall.

From a practical point of view the increase is not relevant and for sure not big enough to justify a switch to a single item display. It seems that the willingness to respond is not much influences by the pure length of a questionnaire. However, we must note here that the UEQ-S is with 8 items already a relatively short questionnaire. The time required to answer the full UEQ-S was with 43 s nearly twice as long as the time required to answer the single item (21 s), but still relatively short. Thus, if the study would, for example, be repeated with a full 26 item UEQ instead of the UEQ-S, then results will look of course quite different. In such cases a split into smaller sets of items will for sure create higher effects.

We also observed differences in the increase in response rates for the two dimensions PQ and HQ. The response rates for the pragmatic items rose from an average of 8% to 12%, while the increase in the response rate is much lower for the hedonic items. This effect can again be explained by the type of the investigated web shop, which supplies goods that customers need for their work and is mainly used by commercial customers (90%). In this case, shopping is not a fun task, but above all a pragmatic need. Therefore, the hedonic items do not match the customers' expectations as well as the pragmatic ones.

4 Second Study: Using Single Item Questionnaires

The following section outlines the design of our second study. This study compares a usage of the UEQ-S and the single item NPS questionnaire and is targeted towards research question RQ3.

4.1 Investigated Web Shop and Feedback Mechanism

The same web shop as in the first study was used. In addition, the mechanism to collect feedback is nearly identical. The only difference was that in the second study the NPS was displayed instead of a single UEQ-S item.

During the data collection period from January 23, 2025 to February 25, 2025 (34 days), the questionnaires were presented to a total of 4757 customers, averaging 140 participants per day. It was randomly decided (with equal probabilities) if the UEQ-S or NPS was displayed on the checkout page.

4.2 Results

As a first analysis for the second study, we present the results regarding the observed mean scores and confidence intervals of the items for the full UEQ-S. Figure 3 shows the scale scores and confidence intervals for the 8 UEQ-S items. Overall 176 customers answered the UEQ-S, but not all participants answered all items. This corresponds to an answer rate of 7%. If we compare the scores for the items we see that they are quite similar to the scores measured in the first study (see Table 4).

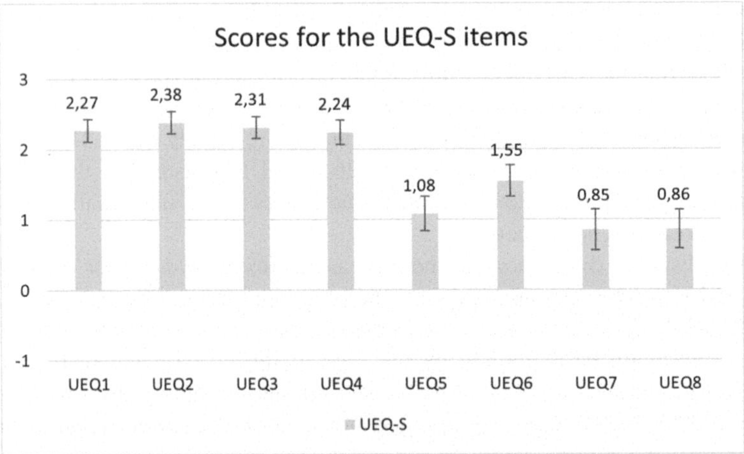

Fig. 3. Mean item scores and the corresponding confidence intervals for the investigated web shop measured with the full UEQ-S version in the second study in 2025 (number of answers per item is shown in Table 8). The scale ranges from −3 to +3 but is reduced in the figure to the range of −1 to +3 to enhance clarity.

Table 8. Means, standard deviations and confidence intervals for the item scores of the **full version** in the second study.

Item	N	Mean	St.Dev.	Confidence Int.
obstructive/supportive	141	2.27	0.97	2.11–2.43
complicated/easy	161	2.38	1.03	2.22–2.54
inefficient/efficient	140	2.31	0.93	2.16–2.47
confusing/clear	155	2.24	1.12	2.06–2.42
boring/exciting	128	1.08	1.40	0.84–1.32
not interesting/interesting	134	1.55	1.34	1.33–1.78
conventional/inventive	127	0.85	1.68	0.56–1.14
usual/leading edge	129	0.86	1.59	0.69–1.14

Detailed scores, standard deviations, and confidence intervals are shown in Table 8.

Compared to the first study, the questionnaire was therefore answered by fewer participants due to the time frame, so discrepancies could be expected. However, the ratings measured with the UEQ-S are similar compared to the first study (see Table 4, largest difference of 0.1 for UEQ8). The measured data from the second study therefore provide a good supplement. Similar findings can also be seen in the scale-related mean values for PQ, HQ and Overall (see Fig. 4). There, the largest difference to the first study is 0.16 for the overall value (see Table 6).

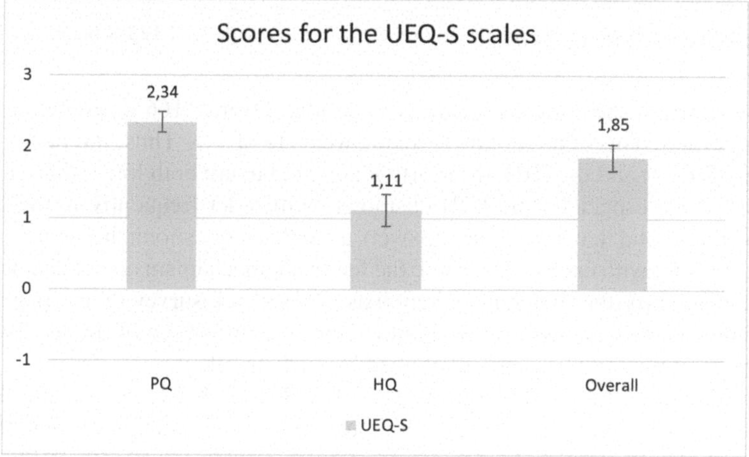

Fig. 4. Mean scale scores for the investigated web shop measured with the full UEQ-S version in the second study in 2025 (number of answers per item is shown in Table 9).

The following Fig. 5 shows a comparison of the PQ, HQ and Overall result to the UEQ-S benchmark [8]. The results implies an *Excellent* pragmatic quality and overall

Table 9. Means, standard deviations and confidence intervals for the scale scores (PQ, HQ and overall) of the full UEQ-S version.

Scale	Full UEQ-S		
	Mean	St.dev.	Conf.Interval
PQ	2.34	0.94	2.20–2.49
HQ	1.11	1.44	0.89–1.36
Overall	1.85	1.19	1.67–2.03

impression (this means that the results are in the range of the best 10% of results in the underlying benchmark data set that contains the results of 468 studies). The result for the hedonic quality is *Above average* (within the best 50% of results).

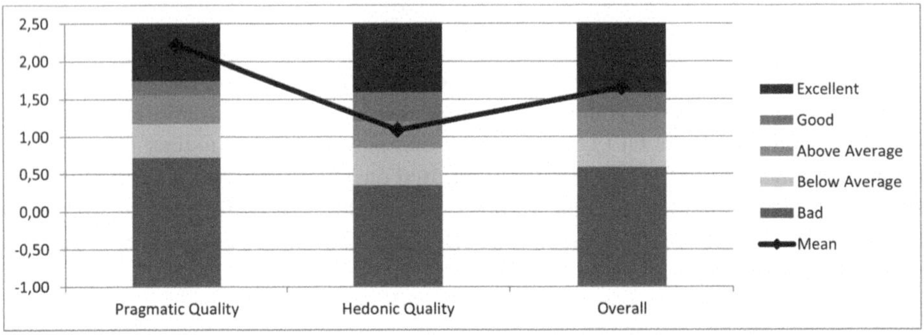

Fig. 5. Comparison of the results in our second study with the UEQ-S benchmark.

Now we turn to the analysis of the NPS results. Overall 166 customers answered the NPS question. This corresponds to an answer rate of 7%. Thus, the response rates of the UEQ-S (7%) and the NPS are nearly identical, but are both lower than in the first study. Customers, especially the B2B customers will order frequently in the shop. Of course, the likelihood that a customer answers a feedback questionnaire on the checkout page is decreasing with each order. Since the feedback mechanism on the checkout page was implemented for the first study (there was no feedback survey on the page before) this mechanism runs now for several month. Thus, the difference of the feedback rates between both studies can be easily explained by such an effect.

The median time required to fill out the UEQ-S (time between showing the order confirmation screen and pressing the submit button) was 46 s and thus close to the result (43 s) measured in the first study. The median time required to answer the NPS question was 19 s and thus similar to the time required to respond in a single item display in the first study (21 s).

We count 127 Promoters, 28 Passives and 11 Detractors, which already points to a very high customer loyalty and satisfaction.

The resulting NPS score is 70 (standard deviation 5.87 and confidence interval [61,79]). Figure 6 shows the distribution of single scores.

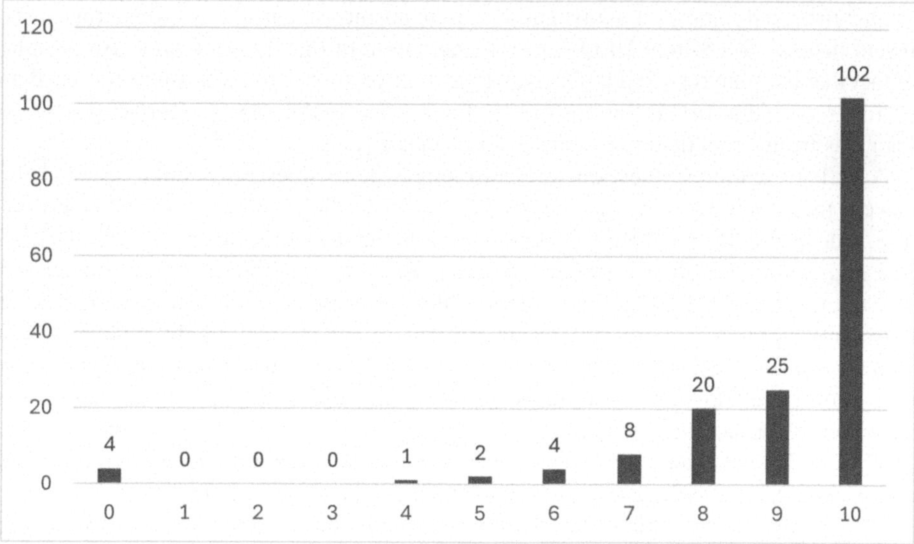

Fig. 6. Distribution of the single ratings for the NPS question.

Therefore, we have not only an impressively high NPS score, but a look at the distribution of the single scores shows that nearly all customers gave very high ratings.

4.3 Discussion of the Results for the Second Study

The results of our second study confirm the main result of the first study concerning our second research question RQ2. The reduction of the item number from 8 to a single item did not increase the response rate in a range that is practically relevant (both response rates are 7%). The time needed to fill out the complete UEQ-S was again nearly twice the time required to fill the NPS, but seems to be still in a range that does not impact the willingness to provide feedback.

We measured for both questionnaires quite positive results. The NPS is impressively high. A comparison of the PQ and HQ scales with the benchmark indicate also a high UX quality. However, we can see directly that the UEQ-S provides much more insights into the UX than the single question of the NPS. We can conclude from both results that the satisfaction with the current implementation is high. But from the UEQ-S we see in addition that there is some potential to improve the shop concerning hedonic quality.

The natural assumption that the usage of shorter questionnaires will always lead to an increased response rate is at least for the comparison of an 8-item UEQ-S to a single item NPS not true. Of course, if we compare a much longer questionnaire, for example a 26-item full UEQ, to a single item questionnaire such an effect may be bigger, thus the result can not be generalized to all situations.

5 Conclusion and Limitations

We examined in a live web shop whether an increase in the response rate can be achieved by splitting a UX questionnaire (UEQ-S) into individual items or by using dedicated single item measures, like the NPS.

Our first study shows a statistically significant increase in the response rate if we present instead of a 8-item UEQ-S just a single item of this questionnaire. But despite the fact that the time required to fill the single item version (21 s) was much shorter than the time required to fill all 8-items (43 s), the increase in the response rate (from 9% to 10%) was from a practical perspective not of much value.

A split of a longer questionnaire into single items does only make sense if the answers to the single items can be used to estimate the results of the full questionnaire. Our results showed that this depends on the nature of the scales. For the UEQ-S scale *Pragmatic Quality* it is possible to infer the score resulting from the full version from the results of the single item version. For the scale *Hedonic Quality* there were statistically significant differences. This differences can be most likely explained by a different relevance of both scales for the user experience in the investigated web shop and by context effects, i.e. some items are interpreted differently if they are not shown in the context of the other items.

Thus, it depends on the investigated product and the scale if the result of a full scale can be estimated from the answers to items that are shown in isolation.

At least for our example of the Allpax web show and the UEQ-S a split to a single item version can not be recommended. There is no practically relevant increase in the response rate and showing the full UEQ-S creates more reliable results.

Our second study replicated the design of the first study comparing the UEQ-S [16] with the Net Promoter Score [14] that contains just a single item. The items of the UEQ-S were initially selected for a display in context of the other UEQ-S items. Thus, there is the danger that the low increase of the response rate in the single item condition results to some extent from the fact that they look a bit unnatural in isolation and are thus answered less frequently. To rule this effect out, we used in our second study a single item that was explicitly designed to be displayed standalone.

However, we found no difference in the response rates of UEQ-S and NPS. Again using a single item instead of the 8 items of the UEQ-S did not create a higher response rate.

Overall both the UEQ-S and the NPS result indicate a high level of satisfaction with the web shop. But the UEQ-S creates some additional insights, since the results show clear differences between the pragmatic and hedonic aspects of the interaction. Thus, switching to the NPS would not create any benefits concerning the response rate and delivers less insights, i.e. is not a good idea for the Allpax web shop.

However, it is important to notice that depending on the product, the used questionnaire and the way it is presented to participants different results may be observed. In our case the questionnaire was presented on the checkout page of the shop. Thus, customers have just finished their shopping task successfully and are now asked to provide feedback. Such a scenario is not disruptive. The time spent on giving feedback may thus be not so important from the users perspective than in a scenario where the questionnaire pops-up automatically in the middle of a task. Thus, it is important to conduct similar studies for different display modes (middle of a task, end of a task, survey sent by email, survey available as a link on a web page, etc.) and different combinations of product and UX questionnaire (Fig. 7).

Appendix

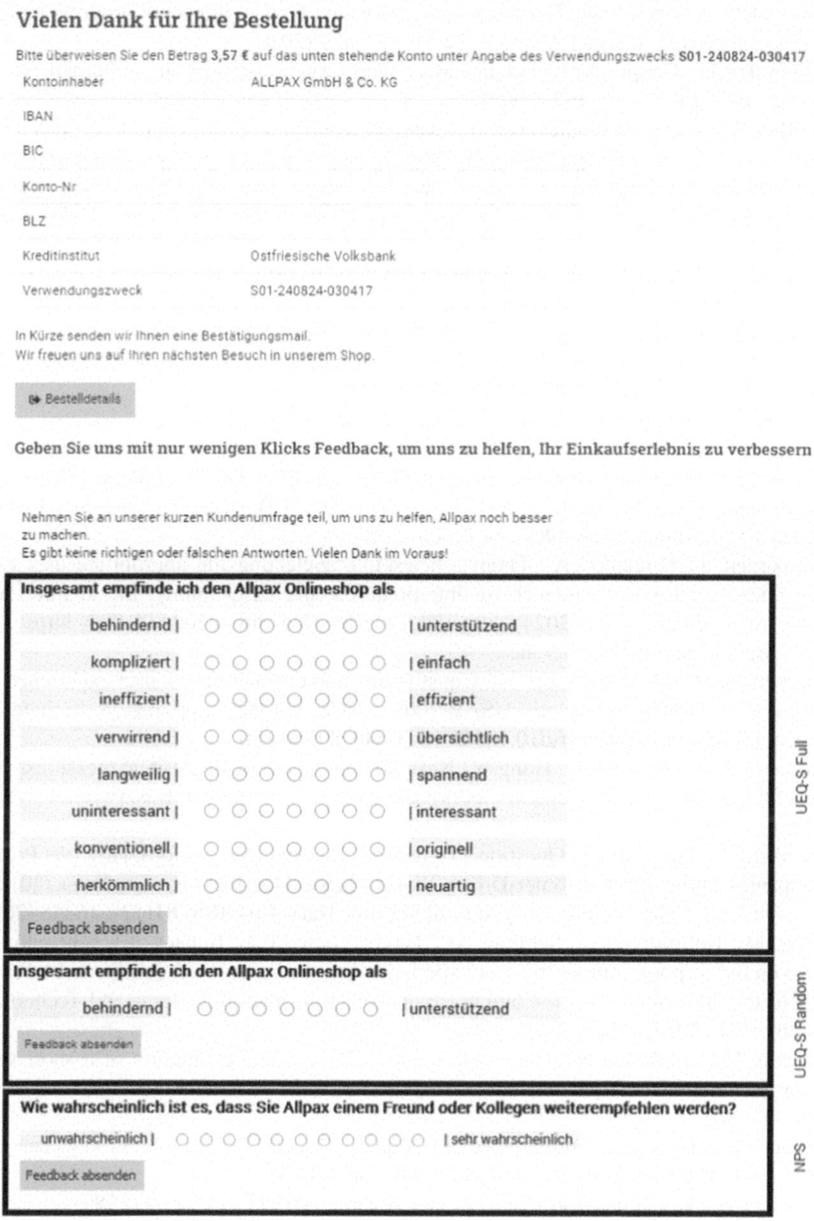

Fig. 7. Below the order confirmation each customer sees one questionnaire. It was per participant randomly decided, which one was displayed. In study 1 UEQ-S and a single item were used. In study 2 UEQ-S and NPS.

References

1. Brooke, J.: SUS: a "quick and dirty" usability scale. Usability Eval. Ind. **189**, 189–194 (1996)
2. Conrad, F.G., Couper, M.P., Tourangeau, R., Peytchev, A.: The impact of progress indicators on task completion. Interact. Comput. **22**(5), 417–427 (2010)
3. Crawford, S.D., Couper, M.P., Lamias, M.J.: Web surveys: perceptions of burden. Soc. Sci. Comput. Rev. **19**(2), 146–162 (2001)
4. Cuvillier, M., Léger, P.M., Sénécal, S.: Quantity over quality: do single-item scales reflect what users truly experienced? Comput. Hum. Behav. Rep. (2021). https://doi.org/10.1016/j.chbr.2021.100097, https://www.sciencedirect.com/science/article/pii/S2451958821000452
5. Finstad, K.: The usability metric for user experience. Interact. Comput. **22**(5), 323–327 (2010)
6. Fuchs, C., Diamantopoulos, A.: Using single-item measures for construct measurement, 195–210 (2009)
7. Himmels, C., Jarosch, O., Omozik, K., Buchner, A.: Measuring user experience in automated driving. In: AutomotiveUI '21, pp. 09–14. Association for Computing Machinery, Leeds (2021). https://doi.org/10.1145/3409118.3475135
8. Hinderks, A., Schrepp, M., Thomaschewski, J.: A benchmark for the short version of the user experience questionnaire. In: Proceedings of the 14th International Conference on Web Information Systems and Technologies-APMDWE, pp. 373–377. SciTePress (2018)
9. Keiningham, T.L., Aksoy, L., Cooil, B., Andreassen, T.W.: Linking customer loyalty to growth. Sloan Manag. Rev. **49**(4), 51 (2008)
10. Kollmorgen, J., Hinderks, A., Thomaschewski, J.: Selecting the appropriate user experience questionnaire and guidance for interpretation: the UEQ family. Int. J. Inter. Multimedia Artif. Intell., 1–14 (2024). https://doi.org/10.9781/ijimai.2024.08.005, https://www.ijimai.org/journal/bibcite/reference/3481
11. Laugwitz, B., Held, T., Schrepp, M.: Construction and evaluation of a user experience questionnaire. In: Holzinger, A. (ed.) USAB 2008. LNCS, vol. 5298, pp. 63–76. Springer, Heidelberg (2008). https://doi.org/10.1007/978-3-540-89350-9_6
12. Matthews, R.A., Pineault, L., Hong, Y.: Normalizing the use of single-item measures: validation of the single-item compendium for organizational psychology. J. Bus. Psychol., 639–673 (2022)
13. Reichheld, F.: The Ultimate Question 2.0 (revised and expanded edition): How Net Promoter Companies Thrive in a Customer-Driven World. Harvard Business Review Press (2011)
14. Reichheld, F.F.: The one number you need to grow. Harv. Bus. Rev. **81**(12), 46–55 (2003)
15. Schaa, M., Kollmorgen, J., Schrepp, M., Thomaschewski, J.: Impact of a split into single items on the response rate of the user experience questionnaire Short (UEQ-S). In: Proceedings of the 20th International Conference on Web Information Systems and Technologies, pp. 363–371 (2024)
16. Schrepp, M., Hinderks, A., Thomaschewski, J.: Design and evaluation of a short version of the user experience questionnaire (UEQ-S). Int. J. Inter. Multimedia Artif. Intell. **4**(6), 103–108 (2017)
17. Schrepp, M., et al.: On the importance of UX quality aspects for different product categories. Int. J. Inter. Multimedia Artif. Intell. **8**(2), 232–246 (2023)
18. Straub, D.W.: Validating instruments in mis research. MIS Q., 147–169 (1989)
19. Vicente, P., Reis, E.: Using questionnaire design to fight nonresponse bias in web surveys. Soc. Sci. Comput. Rev. **28**(2), 251–267 (2010)
20. Villar, A., Callegaro, M., Yang, Y.: Where am I? A meta-analysis of experiments on the effects of progress indicators for web surveys. Soc. Sci. Comput. Rev. **31**(6), 744–762 (2013)
21. Whelan, T.J.: Antecedents of anonymity perceptions in web-based surveys (2008)

Leveraging IoT Cybersecurity Through RED-Based Testing

Tauheed Waheed(✉), Eda Marchetti, and Antonello Calabrò

CNR Istituto di Scienza e Tecnologie dell'Informazione "A. Faedo", Via Giuseppe Moruzzi, 1, 56124 Pisa, Italy
{tauheed.waheed,eda.marchetti,antonello.calabro}@isti.cnr.it

Abstract. The rapid growth of smart home systems has changed how we engage with technology, offering significant convenience and efficiency. This ubiquitous connectivity also introduces serious cybersecurity risks. As smart devices become more integral to our everyday routines, it is essential to implement robust cybersecurity measures. The SECURER-RED framework provides a user-centered, flexible, and all-encompassing strategy for cybersecurity testing. Its goal is to enhance the security of smart home systems by focusing on user behavior, adapting to changing cyber threats, leveraging existing testing suites, and ensuring compliance with RED directives. We aim to demonstrate the capabilities and usefulness of our user-centric cybersecurity testing framework (SECURER-RED) by presenting a practical testing methodology to address cyber threats at the keyless entry systems within smart home environments.

Keywords: Smart home systems · RED · Cybersecurity testing · User-centric

1 Introduction

Every month, thousands of smart devices connect to the internet, making them vulnerable to various privacy and security concerns that malicious actors and cyber-attackers can exploit. There are about 8 billion devices online, which is estimated to reach between 25 and 35 billion IoT devices worldwide by early 2025.

In recent years, cybersecurity has exhibited paramount and complex challenges for disruptive technologies such as the Internet of Things (IoT); there should be a strategic approach to protect business infrastructure and user trustworthiness. Moreover, these disruptive technologies can substitute existing services, systems, and products, leading to new industry leaders' rise and putting various reputed organizations at risk if they do not evolve their security.

Cybersecurity is vital for developing secure IoT systems that protect users' sensitive information, which is significantly related to current challenges in IoT security. Moreover, there is a critical need for appropriate privacy standards and testing strategies. Therefore, the prioritization of robust cybersecurity measures becomes essential for maintaining trust.

It's paramount to understand that smart home systems comprise sensors, intelligent thermostats, and security cameras that enable users to automate tasks, control systems

M. Marchiori et al. (Eds.): WEBIST 2024, LNBIP 583, pp. 109–137, 2026.
https://doi.org/10.1007/978-3-032-25534-1_5

remotely, and optimize energy consumption, enhancing the overall quality of life. However, this technological advancement comes with numerous risks, mainly due to the lack of comprehensive cybersecurity testing for these smart home devices. It has been evident that many smart home systems are inadequately protected, exposing them to malicious actors and cyber threats.

The vulnerabilities in IoT devices and insufficient encryption strategies can open networks to unauthorized access and exploitation [12]. However, the rapid development of these IoT devices often leads to quickened deployments without comprehensive security testing [8] and assessment, leaving gaps that intruders and cyber-attackers can exploit.

The recent cyber-attacks targeting smart home devices have increased, resulting in breaches of personal privacy, data theft, and even physical damages [16]. Users remain vulnerable to threats compromising their devices and personal safety and data integrity. Therefore, it emphasizes the need to establish standardized testing and regulatory frameworks that prioritize security and ensure manufacturers comply with best cybersecurity practices.

The implementation of smart home systems extensively relies on wireless communication, which, while promoting convenience and scalability, also increases the risk of various cyber threats. The research indicates that [9, 18] wireless channels are generally more exposed to security breaches than their wired counterparts, leading to vulnerabilities such as eavesdropping and man-in-the-middle attacks.

The most adequate approach to leverage the cybersecurity of smart home systems is through rigorous and comprehensive testing. Moreover, it identifies potential vulnerabilities that malicious actors could exploit and ensures that the systems comply with industry standards and regulations. Furthermore, this chapter aims to provide a testing platform for users/prosumers to test their IoT devices themselves; homeowners protect the integrity of their devices and the sensitive data they handle simultaneously, ultimately creating a safer and more reliable smart home environment.

It has been evident [22] that IoT devices are more vulnerable to cyberattacks when they cannot receive updates. Moreover, recently, when the Mirai Botnet has been widely used, it is one of the situations in which we may have heard about firmware security. User access is granted to the equipment using the default credentials, and the Mirai Botnet infects devices. Therefore, analyzing the firmware's contents for alteration during runtime is also critical for smart home systems.

In response to these cybersecurity challenges for smart home systems, we are leveraging and implementing a comprehensive framework known as SECURER [39] (User-Centric Cybersecurity Testing Framework). As better detailed in the next sections, SECURER has been developed considering the following principal critical needs: ensuring robust security measures, enhancing user involvement, providing adaptable testing strategies, and cybersecurity awareness [32]. Additionally, SECURER has been conceived to be flexible and robust enough to be utilized for various application domains, recognizing the diverse nature of IoT infrastructure.

In this study, we introduce an innovative characterization known as SECURER_RED, designed to tailor the SECURER testing environment for smart home devices. This framework ensures these devices adhere to the rigorous standards outlined in a RED security directive, enhancing their protection and compliance in an increasingly connected world, Indeed the RED Directive can refer to various contexts, but it generally implies a set of strict guidelines or instructions that must be adhered to, often in high-stakes or emergency situations. In many organizations, it signifies protocols initiated when specific criteria are met, such as security threats or critical operational decisions.

In this book chapter, Sect. 2 presents the motivations and overview of cybersecurity testing and the importance of RED directives for adequate user specifications and cybersecurity testing. Section 3 discusses current state-of-the-art cybersecurity strategies and solutions, and Sect. 4 presents the cybersecurity challenges in smart home systems and our solution in shape for SECURER-RED workflow.

Sections 5 and 6, respectively, present its in-depth detail and preliminary implementation. Furthermore, Sect. 7 comprises showcase examples to conduct user-centric cybersecurity testing through SECURER-RED, and Sect. 8 discusses the book chapter conclusion.

2 Background

Several basic concepts must be introduced to clarify the proposed SECURER_RED instantiation for smart home devices, such as the role of Smart home vulnerabilities, user satisfaction, the RED directive, a way to manage user requirements, and an overview of Cybersecurity testing.

In the following, a short introduction is provided for each of them.

2.1 Vulnerabilities

Cybersecurity vulnerabilities within smart home systems are growing as these environments are increasingly interconnected. The reliance on cloud-based architectures for managing smart home devices limits long-term effectiveness and raises significant security issues. While edge computing solutions like Databox [27] present enhanced security, privacy, and compliance benefits, massive vulnerabilities remain largely unaddressed. Researchers in [28] have identified 17 unique vulnerabilities across 22 smart home devices, among which many have been classified as critical by the National Vulnerability Database (NVD). Alarmingly, these insecure devices are still commercially available and actively utilized in households worldwide. This highlights a major oversight in cybersecurity standards, which often overlook internal human threats such as social surveillance and domestic abuse that can also compromise the safety of smart home systems [28].

The implications of these vulnerabilities are severe. Cyber attackers could exploit these weaknesses to gain unauthorized access, jeopardizing property security and the well-being of residents. The potential for an attacker to infiltrate a home underscores the urgent need for comprehensive cybersecurity testing and enhancements. With a substantial number of smart home IoT devices exhibiting serious security threats, prioritizing robust security measures is essential for the safety and privacy of users in an increasingly digitized living environment.

2.2 User Satisfaction

User satisfaction in smart home systems is significantly influenced by integrating security features, ease to use, and overall functionality [15]. As these systems become pervasive, users expect not only convenience and automation but also robust cybersecurity protections that safeguard their privacy and personal data. Several aspects can be considered in user satisfaction. Cultural differences play a significant role in understanding smart-home users' satisfaction and their preferences for non-financial rewards related to cybersecurity behaviors [15]. For example, British users often prefer discount offers associated with cyber insurance, whereas Japanese users favor virtual point rewards.

When users invest in smart home technology, they seek peace of mind knowing that their devices are secure against potential cyber threats. A lack of confidence in the security of these systems can lead to dissatisfaction, as users may feel vulnerable to breaches that could compromise their home and personal safety.

Moreover, the user experience plays a crucial role in satisfaction. If devices are difficult to set up or manage due to complex security protocols, users may become frustrated. Conversely, those systems that offer seamless integration of security measures, such as automatic updates and user-friendly privacy settings, tend to enhance user satisfaction.

Furthermore, the scope and standards of cybersecurity training programs should be tailored to align with the user's socioeconomic status and security culture. Keeping users informed about potential vulnerabilities and providing clear guidance on protecting their devices can significantly boost their confidence in the system's security. When users feel well-informed and equipped to handle security, their overall satisfaction with the smart home experience will likely improve. As a brief overview in the remainder of this section, or increasing user satisfaction, several initiatives can be considered.

The researchers [3] developed an innovative 3-phase strategy that improves the security of sensor identities in smart home systems. The approach safeguards privacy by protecting sensor data against external threats. Moreover, the critical factor influencing the effectiveness of this approach is the threshold value, which establishes the specific time interval each sensor operates. Furthermore, the researchers optimized the system's performance, reliability, and security, minimizing the risk of unauthorized access while maintaining efficient sensor functionality.

The researchers [1] developed a network intrusion detection system (IDS) specifically for smart home systems. Moreover, the system comprises an effective deployment strategy to address various network security challenges, such as unauthorized access and data breaches, using machine learning (ML) algorithms and real-time monitoring to enhance overall security for IoT devices.

The researchers [36] conducted hands-on lab exercises and effectively accomplished their academic goals, as evidenced by students' positive feedback and confident self-assessments of the skills they acquired throughout the experience. However, students expressed various concerns that the knowledge they acquired was insufficient when evaluating the vulnerabilities of IoT devices from a broader perspective.

Moreover, this drawback emerges because the activities are primarily focused on a few IoT devices, leaving individuals expecting a more robust learning experience. Furthermore, the lab activities lacked coverage of a diverse range of IoT devices and various cyber-attack techniques, indicating a significant gap in the curriculum that could be the point of concern and focus on providing a more comprehensive education in the critical field of IoT security. The scope of the exercises should ensure that students are better prepared to face real-world challenges related to IoT vulnerabilities and security threats.

The researchers [13] have developed a home monitoring system that integrates beacon technology to systematically track the location and movement of elderly residents within their homes. The system automatically identifies potential safety hazards, such as prolonged periods in risky areas, including kitchens or staircases, where possible accidents may occur. The methodology employs federated learning to enhance operational performance while protecting user privacy.

This strategy significantly improves the object recognition capabilities of the faster R-CNN model, allowing for the accurate identification of various objects and situations. Moreover, it protects sensitive information by securely storing data on a local server, preventing unauthorized access. In addition to tracking mobility, the system offers continuous monitoring of household appliances that may pose safety risks. It assesses their operational status and promptly alerts caretakers if any issues are detected. This functionality facilitates immediate intervention, ultimately promoting a safer living environment for elderly residents. Furthermore, this home monitoring system represents a fusion of advanced technology and essential safety measures, enhancing the quality of life for residents and their guardians.

2.3 RED Directives

The rapid growth of smart home systems has changed how we use technology, offering great convenience and efficiency. However, this connectivity also introduces significant cybersecurity risks. As smart devices become more integral to our lives, robust cybersecurity measures are essential. The recent introduction of the EU Cybersecurity Directive 2014/53/EU [14], commonly called the RED (Radio Equipment Directive), underscores the urgent need for standardized security protocols in smart home systems. This directive aims to enhance the security of networked devices by mandating comprehensive risk assessments, vulnerability disclosures, and incident response strategies.

About existing security standards, the RED emphasizes a holistic approach to cybersecurity, aligning itself with frameworks such as GDPR [26] and the NIS Directive [24]. By fostering a unified standard that prioritizes user privacy and data protection, the RED aims to create a safer digital environment for consumers. As we continue to embrace the potential of interconnected smart home devices, it is essential that we prioritize the development of user-centered security features, ultimately fostering trust and empowering users to engage confidently with their smart environments.

In detail, the directive establishes a comprehensive legal framework governing the operation and compliance of radio equipment within the European Union. It outlines critical requirements to ensure electromagnetic compatibility, safety, health standards, and the efficient utilization of the radio infrastructure. However, Article 3(3) points d, e, and f of the Directive are further explained through the Delegated Regulation (EU) 2022/30. Moreover, this regulation specifies the cybersecurity mandates essential for improving network performance and integrity.

It emphasizes the importance of protecting sensitive personal data and maintaining user privacy, addressing potential vulnerabilities that could lead to fraud or unauthorized access. By setting these rigorous standards, the regulation ensures that radio equipment meets operational efficiency and strengthens users' trust and safety in an increasingly connected environment.

The RED Delegated Act (2022/30), the legislation to enhance the regulatory framework for IoT devices and services, was officially published on February 1, 2022. The act was initially planned to take effect on August 1, 2024; however, in response to industry feedback and the need for adequate preparation, the European Commission has officially extended this deadline, now mandating that electronic and IoT devices should be compliant with the act starting August 1, 2025.

It's essential to understand that extension time provides manufacturers and stakeholders within the electronics sector additional time to ensure that their products meet the comprehensive requirements established by the act, including safety standards, electromagnetic compatibility, and efficient utilization of IoT services. However, any devices that fall within the scope of the RED Delegated Act, as schematized in Fig. 1, must be fully compliant before their introduction into the European market after this new deadline. Furthermore, this regulatory transition aims to safeguard consumer interests and promote innovation while ensuring that all electronic devices operate within an environmentally secure and reliable framework.

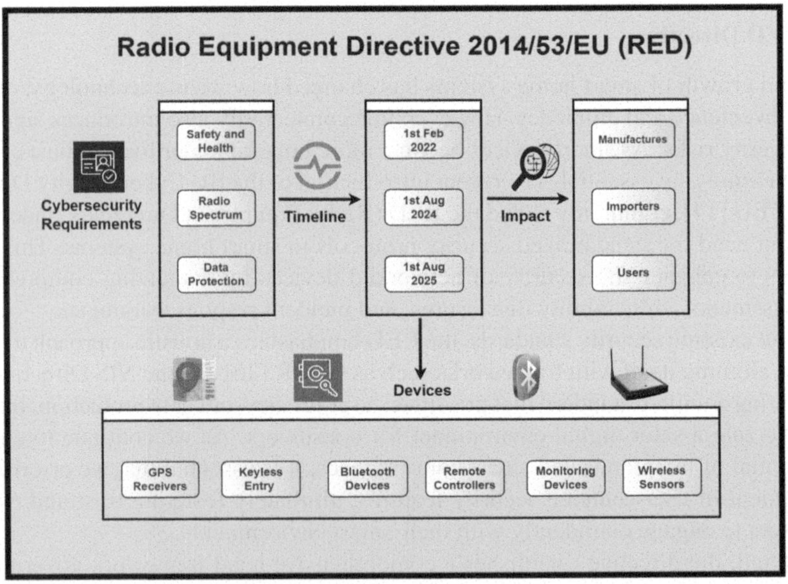

Fig. 1. RED Directives. (Color figure online)

Figure 1 demonstrates that various Internet of Things (IoT) devices and different forms of integrated equipment may fall under the regulatory framework established by the Radio Equipment Directive (RED). However, stakeholders must adhere to appropriate cybersecurity standards and best practices, as compliance is critical for safeguarding the integrity and security of these devices. Moreover, by diligently following these established standards, manufacturers can significantly enhance security protocols, protect user privacy, and improve the overall reliability of both radio equipment and consumer IoT devices. Furthermore, this proactive approach not only meets compliance requirements but also aligns with the fundamental objectives of the RED, which ensures the growth of a safe and trustworthy technological environment for consumers while promoting innovation and development in the industry.

2.4 Managing User Requirements

Questionnaires are valuable in eliciting cybersecurity requirements and offering a structured approach to gathering stakeholder information. They are often used alongside other techniques, such as interviews, observations, and document analysis, to ensure a comprehensive understanding of security needs [17]. In the context of Cyber-Informed Engineering (CIE) [42], the requirements elicitation phase is critical for identifying all necessary engineering-based protections and layered defenses. The process involves multiple techniques, including interviews, surveys/questionnaires, observations, and document analysis, each providing unique insights that contribute to a comprehensive understanding of cybersecurity requirements.

Various methodologies have been proposed in the literature to identify and address security needs systematically [4,33]. This methodology prioritizes the early identification of security threats within the software development process and proposes systematic approaches to gathering the necessary security requirements to elicit threats and define security objectives [43]. These literature proposals aid in developing structured methods for identifying and addressing security requirements, thus improving the security posture of software systems.

In addition, several tools and frameworks that are currently available to facilitate the elicitation of cybersecurity requirements. Among threat modeling Tools (such as (Microsoft Threat Modeling Tool[1] and IriusRisk[2]) use questionnaires and risk model libraries to create and maintain threat models throughout the Software Development Life Cycle (SDLC) and be used to assist in identifying potential threats and vulnerabilities within a system, enabling the development of appropriate security requirements.

2.5 Cybersecurity Testing

Regulatory frameworks and international standards are crucial in shaping security assurance and testing methodologies in the evolving cybersecurity landscape. Ensuring compliance with regulations such as the EU Artificial Intelligence Act[3] (AI Act), the Radio

[1] https://learn.microsoft.com/en-us/azure/security/develop/threat-modeling-tool.
[2] https://www.iriusrisk.com/threat-modeling-platform.
[3] https://artificialintelligenceact.eu/.

Equipment Directive[4] (RED Directive), and the General Data Protection Regulation[5] (GDPR), alongside globally recognized cybersecurity standards like ISO/IEC 27001[6], enhances security, privacy, and resilience in industry [23] and digital systems.

Cybersecurity testing [25] must align with key legislative and industry standards to mitigate risks effectively. A structured approach to testing involves risk-based cybersecurity assessments, rigorous development methodologies, attack resistance validation [41], and continuous monitoring. ISO/IEC 27001 emphasizes the importance of risk-based cybersecurity assessments, ensuring that potential threats and vulnerabilities are systematically identified and mitigated. In the context of AI systems, the EU AI Act introduces a risk-based categorization that mandates heightened levels of testing and validation for high-risk AI applications, such as biometric identification and AI-driven critical infrastructure. Similarly, ISO-based security assessments help ensure that vulnerabilities in AI and other digital systems are addressed in line with international best practices.

Development rigor and security validation play a crucial role in cybersecurity testing. The RED Directive (2014/53/EU) mandates that wireless and IoT devices comply with cybersecurity and privacy requirements, ensuring that security testing aligns with industry standards. Secure software development practices, as outlined in ISO/IEC 62443 (Industrial Cybersecurity) and ISO 27034[7] (Application Security), establish the necessary level of development rigor needed to build resilient systems. Security-by-design and privacy-by-design principles guide selecting secure coding practices, penetration testing, and vulnerability assessments to prevent exploitation.

Defining necessary attack resistance involves implementing security measures such as encryption, access controls, and intrusion detection systems, which align with ISO 27001 requirements [21]. Article 32 of GDPR mandates strong data protection mechanisms, requiring cybersecurity testing to assess resilience against data breaches and unauthorized access. Testing methodologies such as red teaming, ethical hacking, and penetration testing ensure that systems can withstand cyberattacks while adhering to compliance requirements.

Vulnerabilities in cybersecurity can arise from multiple sources. One common origin is specification flaws, such as selecting a cryptographic protocol with known security weaknesses. Another source is design flaws, where an otherwise robust algorithm is misapplied in an inappropriate context or configured with ineffective parameters. Additionally, implementation defects can introduce security risks, such as buffer overflows resulting from coding errors during software development.

Cybersecurity testing aims to detect and analyze these vulnerabilities [40], tracing them back to their root causes. However, a fundamental challenge in this process is that testing can confirm the existence of vulnerabilities but cannot definitively prove their absence. This limitation underscores the need for continuous security assessments and proactive threat mitigation strategies.

---

[4] https://single-market-economy.ec.europa.eu/sectors/electrical-and-electronic-engineering-industries-eei/radio-equipment-directive-red_en.

[5] https://eur-lex.europa.eu/eli/reg/2016/679/.

[6] https://www.iso.org/standard/27001.

[7] https://www.iso.org/standard/44378.html.

Security testing must also define the scope and depth of cybersecurity validation, ensuring continuous monitoring and auditing to detect emerging threats. ISO/IEC 27001 mandates ongoing security assessments, aligning with the AI Act's lifecycle security requirements for AI models and the RED Directive's wireless security compliance. GDPR enforcement requires impact assessments and security validation to ensure that organizations proactively safeguard personal data and system integrity.

Integrating cybersecurity testing with regulatory frameworks ensures traceability and accountability across the entire development and deployment lifecycle, aligning with GDPR's accountability principle and the AI Act's transparency requirements. By enforcing security compliance, organizations can establish resilience and interoperability, ensuring that AI, IoT, and digital infrastructure adhere to standards such as ISO 27001, ISO 62443, and the RED Directive. Furthermore, adaptability to evolving threats is critical, necessitating the continuous evaluation of cybersecurity assurance levels through risk management and compliance-driven audits. Embedding cybersecurity testing [37] within internationally recognized standards and legal frameworks is fundamental to building secure, compliant, and resilient systems while fostering trust in digital and AI-driven technologies.

3 State-of-the-Art

This section, while not comprehensive, contextualizes the SECURER_RED proposal within the existing landscape and offers an overview of the available testing frameworks and current cybersecurity strategies.

In particular, similarities can be experienced in the Multi-Access Edge Computing (MEC) [29]. This computing framework aims to bring computation and data storage nearer to the user, ensuring quick access to applications while optimizing network resource utilization. MEC promotes the smooth integration of new Internet of Things (IoT) applications, improving scalability, reliability, and real-time responsiveness. This is particularly beneficial in tackling cybersecurity issues and strengthening the resilience of IoT applications against cyber threats. Compared with SECURER_RED, both proposals focus on users and devices to reduce latency, improve performance, and optimize resource utilization. By offloading tasks from centralized data centers, both can reduce network congestion and optimize data efficiency and security. However, SECURER_RED is targeted primarily at data protection and access control, while it is more about optimizing network resources and enabling real-time, data-intensive applications near the end user.

Another proposal is the multifunctional testbed proposed by [12]. This framework involves the Mirai botnet [2] proposal and additional red-teaming tools. It focuses on the identification of botnets and performing denial-of-service (DoS) attacks, scanning activities, and targeting of Internet of Things (IoT) protocols. The multifunctional testbed serves as a cyber range for simulating cyber attacks, testing and validating security solutions, and gathering network and application data to generate comprehensive datasets for analysis and research purposes. Compared with SECURER_RED, both are designed to address security challenges in networked environments, especially IoT computing, and focus on the detection, analysis, and mitigation of cybersecurity threats. Additionally, both provide testing and validation features. However, SECURER_RED is a testbed for analyzing and validating defenses against cyber threats specifically focused on RED directives for data privacy, protection, and access control. The multifunctional testbed is designed to understand cyber threats through simulated attacks, focusing on botnets, DoS, and IoT vulnerabilities. It serves as a cyber range for training, testing, and research.

Recent research [19] highlights the importance of comprehensive vulnerability assessments in penetration testing. The study involved extensive cybersecurity evaluations of 22 devices from five categories related to connected homes: smart door locks, security cameras, smart car adapters/garages, smart appliances, and various other smart home gadgets. Compared with SECURER_RED, this uses penetration testing to strengthen cybersecurity by identifying vulnerabilities and implementing protective measures for IoT devices, which are increasingly integrated into smart homes and edge environments. It also adopts the proposed rigorous testing methods to validate security solutions and identify and address weaknesses in connected devices to prevent unauthorized access.

Traditional security protocols frequently permit communication before proper authentication, creating opportunities for exploitation by malicious actors. The approach outlined in [31] seeks to ensure user and device authentication before any communication occurs, thereby establishing a secure channel. This improves security and network performance within IoT systems and distributed Edge data center environments. Compared with SECURER_RED, both use authentication techniques to ensure only authorized devices and users can access network resources and to minimize the risk of data breaches. However, SECURER_RED is a comprehensive, multi-layered security solution targeting the RED directives. It goes beyond authentication to secure edge environments with a strong emphasis on compliance with data protection, privacy, and secure access regulations. The solution outlined in [31] s is more focused on securing communication channels by strictly verifying user and device identities.

Researchers have developed an innovative security strategy known as DecisionTSec [30], which uses decision trees to bolster communication security in IoT networks. This approach leverages edge data centers situated at the network's edge to strengthen security protocols. Tests conducted on a real-time testbed have demonstrated its effectiveness and theoretical soundness in assessing both system performance and the integrity of security measures. Compared with SECURER_RED, similar considerations of the previous proposal can be outlined. However, DecisionTSec is a data-driven, dynamic security approach for real-time detection and classification in IoT networks focused on communication security and adaptive threat assessment.

The researchers [5] conduct a case study to investigate the requirements that future data collection frameworks need to meet in order to provide strong privacy protection for users, focusing on user-centric privacy engineering strategies. Similarly, [34] examines user-centric privacy preservation models in the context of the Internet of Things (IoT), identifying unresolved challenges and potential avenues for research. Additionally, creating frameworks that prioritize the user in data management ensures individuals have full control and decision-making power over how their data is utilized, while also emphasizing the importance of protecting their privacy. Compared with SECURER_RED, both prioritize privacy protection and secure data management, provide alignment with data protection regulations, and highlight the importance of user control over data, However, SECURER_RED provides a multilayer solution with a strong focus on preventing unauthorized access and data breaches while the user-centric privacy preservation models prioritize user control, consent management, and transparency in data handling.

As a conclusion, current strategies for addressing cybersecurity and privacy in the Internet of Things (IoT) often lack a focus on user-centric solutions and typically do not include simultaneous testing. It is crucial to create a comprehensive framework that improves cybersecurity through user-centered testing to ensure the responsible and effective deployment of IoT technologies. The SECURER_RED testing process aims to safeguard against potential breaches, making sure that technologies are secure, reliable, and compliant with regulatory standards, which is essential for maintaining user trust. Moreover, SECURER_RED targets cybersecurity from the user's perspective, in line with current RED directives. It focuses on identifying vulnerabilities in IoT systems, protecting against evolving cyber threats, and providing accessible and understandable solutions for non-expert users. This approach seeks to enhance the adoption of security standards and promote proper usage of IoT technologies.

4 Challenges and Solution

Leveraging smart home systems to address critical cybersecurity aspects presents several challenges that adopting a suitable cybersecurity testing process can mitigate. The next sections discuss the most important challenges and the proposed solution.

4.1 Cybersecurity Challenges

Protection Against Vulnerabilities. Cybersecurity testing is important in safeguarding Internet of Things (IoT) systems and devices. By meticulously identifying and addressing potential vulnerabilities, testing helps prevent threats and malicious attacks and ensure cybersecurity quality level, avoiding misuse of sensitive data and the execution of critical functions. By prioritizing cybersecurity testing, organizations can effectively strengthen their defenses, enhance the reliability of their IoT devices, and ultimately protect both user data and system integrity. Implementing regular security assessments not only mitigates risks but also fosters trust among users and stakeholders.

Maintaining User Trust. Any security breach or lapse in the Internet of Things (IoT) ecosystem has the potential to undermine public confidence in these technological innovations severely [20]. Implementing stringent cybersecurity protocols is an effective means for ensuring the safety and reliability of such technologies, safeguarding user data, protecting the integrity of the systems involved, and assuring continued growth and acceptance of IoT solutions. As trust erodes, the willingness of users to adopt new technologies diminishes, making it imperative that organizations prioritize robust security measures to foster a safe and dependable environment for all. Building a culture of transparency and proactive communication regarding security practices can further enhance user confidence and engagement in the IoT space.

Regulatory Compliance. Regulation compliance is an important objective for businesses because it can avoid severe legal repercussions, including fines and sanctions. In this context, cybersecurity testing can be an effective means for assessing and assuring compliance with cybersecurity regulations, adhering to legal standards, and demonstrating a commitment to safeguarding sensitive information. Furthermore, in the event of failures, cybersecurity testing encourages the adoption of measures that establish a necessary foundation of trust with customers and stakeholders. This approach helps mitigate risks, enhance operational resilience, and foster a culture of security awareness that supports long-term success.

Enabling Innovation. Implementing strong cybersecurity measures at both the business and individual levels can accelerate the innovation process. It helps alleviate concerns about intellectual property theft and cyber threats that often hinder the open exchange of ideas and slow technological advancements. When organizations feel confident that their proprietary information is secure, they are more inclined to collaborate, share insights, and take risks that can lead to groundbreaking developments. Investing in cybersecurity protects assets and fosters an environment where creativity can flourish, resulting in a more dynamic and forward-thinking technological landscape.

Business Continuity. The repercussions of a cyberattack can be extensive, affecting service delivery, resulting in significant financial losses, and damaging the organization's reputation. Cybersecurity testing can be an effective solution to create and validate defense mechanisms and enables organizations to maintain continuity in the face of cyber threats. As the digital landscape evolves, it is imperative for companies to regularly evaluate and improve their security protocols, investing in advanced technologies and strategies that will empower them to respond swiftly and effectively to any potential cyber incidents, ultimately ensuring long-term resilience and trust with their clients and stakeholders.

Protecting User Data. Due to the extensive data managed by these devices, it is crucial to conduct cybersecurity testing to identify and address potential vulnerabilities. Testing can help identify and address potential vulnerabilities leading to unauthorized access or data breaches. Cybersecurity measures protect user information and ensure its integrity, privacy, and security. Indeed, adopting regular and comprehensive cybersecurity assessments can safeguard sensitive data and reinforce user trust in the interconnected ecosystem of IOT devices. It also creates more secure architectures for managing and protecting user data, fostering a safer environment for all participants in the IoT landscape. This allows for the secure and efficient connection and integration of various devices without compromising user privacy.

Leveraging Human-Centric Testing. Incorporating user behavior into cybersecurity strategies significantly improves the effectiveness of testing and strengths defenses against cyber attacks. By emphasizing the human element in cybersecurity, organizations can cultivate a robust security culture that raises awareness and vigilance among users, equipping them to recognize and respond to potential threats more effectively. This user-focused strategy not only enhances security measures but also engages individuals as active participants in safeguarding their digital environments. Overall, fostering a deeper understanding of user interactions with technology can lead to more resilient and proactive cybersecurity initiatives.

4.2 SECURE_RED Solution

Considering the above-mentioned challenges and the preliminary SECURER proposal presented in [39], in this paper, we target a specific SECURER customization (called SECURE_RED) to be applied in the smart home environment. In particular, SECURE_RED customizes the SECURER testing environment to target and assure Smart home device compliance to a RED [14] security directive. Therefore the main SECURE_RED objectives can be summarized below:

- **Target User-Centric Testing.** Smart home systems are inherently diverse, incorporating various devices with different capabilities, communication protocols, and security challenges. In alignment with the RED Directive, SECURE_RED addresses this complexity by offering a comprehensive and adaptable security testing environment. In its assessments, it considers the heterogeneous nature of IoT ecosystems and user behaviors, preferences, and usability requirements. This approach wants to ensure regulatory compliance while maintaining robust security. Aligned with the Rapid Evolution of Cyber Threats
- **Address Cyber Threats.** Cyber threats are evolving at an unprecedented pace, requiring proactive and adaptive security measures. SECURE_RED, in compliance with the RED Directive, provides a cybersecurity testing framework designed to anticipate, detect, and mitigate potential vulnerabilities before exploitation occurs. This strengthens the security posture of Smart home systems while ensuring alignment with regulatory requirements.
- **Increase Test Suites Effectiveness.** Rather than building security testing from scratch, SECURE_RED maximizes efficiency by integrating, customizing, and enhancing RED existing conformance test suites. This allows for a more targeted and resource-efficient evaluation of system security, ensuring compliance with RED Directive guidelines on security assessments while reducing testing costs and implementation time.
- **Improve Compliance.** A structured approach to security validation is essential for meeting security requirements. SECURE_RED provides organizations with customized security testing frameworks that facilitate RED directive regulatory compliance, enhance security assurance, and build trust among users and stakeholders.
- **Increase Cybersecurity Awareness.** SECURE_RED adopts a holistic approach to cybersecurity risk assessment, ensuring compliance with RED Directive principles. It integrates technical safeguards, user awareness, and ethical data-handling frameworks to enhance security knowledge and best practices. This comprehensive strategy reinforces compliance and improves overall system resilience.

To ensure compliance with the RED Directive, SECURE_RED establishes a testing and validation process focusing on the following objectives: i) Ensuring that smart home systems comply with RED requirements. ii) Facilitating early detection and mitigation of vulnerabilities, which aligns with the directive's goals of enhancing cybersecurity resilience. iii) Customizing existing RED test suites to meet specific user needs, promoting efficiency and resource optimization and reducing the compliance burden. iv) Integrating security best practices, technical safeguards, and user awareness to strengthen overall cybersecurity in smart homes. v) Providing a dynamic approach to cybersecurity that ensures systems remain resilient against emerging threats.

5 Leveraging SECURER Architecture for RED Directive

The section describes the SECURER proposal used for implementing the SECURER_RED characterization to tailor the application of the RED directive to smart home devices. In particular, the SECURER_RED customized of the different components has been performed. For completeness, in the next sections, the SECURER's original architecture and its behavioral model are reported [39]. In Sect. 5.2, a detailed description of some of the SECURER_RED components in line with the RED directive is provided.

5.1 SECURER Architecture

The SECURER framework is a user-centric approach focusing on users' cybersecurity needs and testing experiences. Moreover, this framework aims to improve users' confidence in their systems and data security and foster a proactive cybersecurity awareness and shared responsibility culture For this, two crucial activities have received specific attention: the requirements collections and the test strategy application. As detailed in Sect. 2.4, using a questionnaire to gather user specifications and cybersecurity experiences is an important contribution. This way, providing facilities for realizing effective requirements through questionnaire collection is a core part of the proposed framework's core. Additionally, user-centric testing strategies for improving cybersecurity measures and promoting a proactive and reliable IoT environment is also a fundamental part.

As schematized in Fig. 2, for realizing the required features, the improved SECURE_RED architecture has been realized starting from the initial proposal presented in [39]. For completeness, we briefly describe the SECURER reference architecture, its components, and the interconnected elements in the following. Customization of SECURER architecture for the RED directive is described in the rest of this section.

User-Centric Test Manager (UCTM). A user-centric test manager is dedicated to comprehensively understanding users' needs, with the primary goal of identifying specific and detailed testing objectives. This component uses crafted questionnaires designed considering the RED principles to illuminate and close the gap between user expectations and their actual testing requirements. Additionally, the test manager oversees the collection and analysis of feedback during the testing activities and the various decisions made throughout the testing execution process. All user interactions occur through a graphical user interface (GUI), ensuring a seamless and engaging experience for all participants involved in the testing process.

Test Generator: Is the component that selects a set of suitable test cases from those available from the RED conformance test suite or generates test cases tailored to meet specific user requirements and needs. Depending on various conditions, it can propose testing strategies and assist users in choosing the most suitable option. Among the available test cases, a selection will focus on those most effective at identifying and mitigating potential security risks. By executing these test cases, users can ensure the continuous availability, confidentiality, and overall cybersecurity of vital information within an IoT system.

Test Executor. Based on the available testing libraries, this component finalizes test cases tailored for the application's unique execution environment, whether provided by users or sourced from open-source initiatives.

Test Controller. It offers a comprehensive collection of test strategies and, where applicable, pre-defined test cases. It assists in crafting questionnaires specifically designed for user-centric test managers, ensuring test cases align with the established requirements. Furthermore, it leverages Generative AI to develop test case instances and broaden test suites, thereby upholding quality standards in light of the continually evolving cybersecurity threats.

Analysis and Results. This component aids in understanding vulnerabilities and identifying unnecessary paths in the source code of applications, IoT devices, and third-party libraries or APIs (Application Programming Interface). The analysis is conducted by utilizing coverage testing and inspecting all possible execution paths for a thorough assessment. Moreover, this component reviews the test results generated by SECURER and creates detailed test reports for our users, accessible through our user-centered test manager's user interface (UI). Furthermore, it enables users to interpret results.

Test DB. The component collects knowledge and results from testing activities, providing resources to other components like GitHub. It facilitates the creation of questionnaires and datasets for predefined test cases and maintains user feedback and test reports. This process enhances the design of future questionnaires and improves overall testing efficiency.

The architecture of SECURER is developed to adapt and collaborate with various advanced technologies, including collaborative robots (cobots), drones, the Internet of Vehicles (IoV), and the Internet of Things (IoT). This user-centered approach to cybersecurity enables the formulation of tailored testing scenarios that meet specific user requirements. SECURER encourages users to recognize and mitigate risks by simulating malicious behaviors and identifying system vulnerabilities. This process ultimately enhances their understanding of the testing process and cybersecurity measures.

The SECURER framework significantly advances cybersecurity testing to address the complex risks of interconnected Internet of Things (IoT) systems. This initiative aims to create a collaborative security ecosystem where the responsibility for mitigating cyber threats is shared among all stakeholders, strongly emphasizing resilience and recovery strategies. The user involvement in the testing process enhances understanding of security behaviors and expectations, promoting greater awareness and ownership of security practices. This collaboration is essential for developing secure systems that meet user needs.

The customized version SECURER_RED shifts from traditional reactive quality governance to a powerful, all-encompassing framework. Not only does it boost operational efficiency, but it also tackles cybersecurity challenges head-on. With this resilient

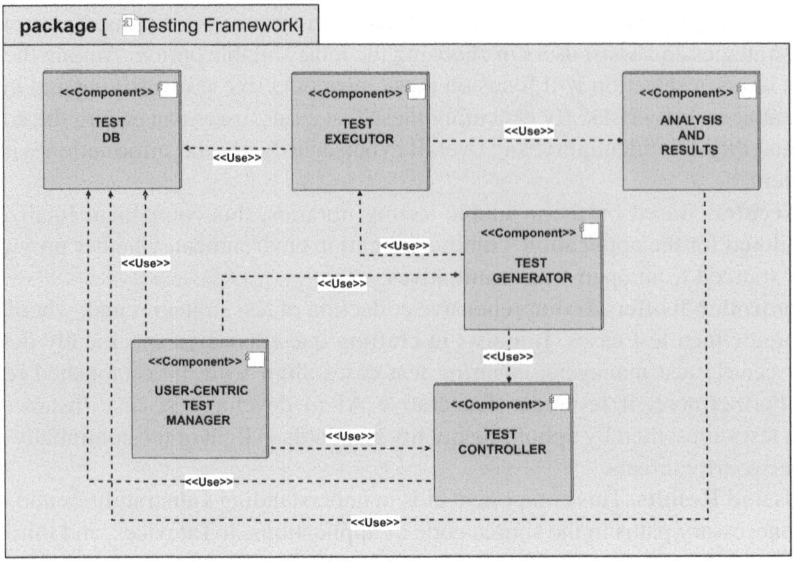

Fig. 2. SECURER [39] Architecture.

architecture, organizations can protect their reputations and foster deeper trust among users in smart home systems, paving the way for a brighter, more secure future.

It also contributes to compliance with standards and increases cybersecurity awareness by guiding users in requirements collection and testing execution. The improved SECURER-RED framework allows organizations to identify vulnerabilities, establish defenses, and secure data throughout its life cycle, even without requiring a deep knowledge of the directive provisions. Additionally, integrating user-centric cybersecurity testing with RED directives enables organizations to address emerging challenges while resolving current issues proactively. This approach helps anticipate and prevent future threats, creating a more secure environment for users and stakeholders.

In the next section, we provide a detailed description of the specific component customization for targeting the RED directive. In particular, we specify User-Centric Test Manager (UCTM) because it is one of the most important components for the RED directive analysis and application.

5.2 User-Centric Test Manager Details

The proposed SECURER-RED framework has been instantiated to address the complex risks that may arise in smart home systems, developing a collaborative strategy with the involved stakeholders to safeguard the overall system against cyber-attacks. The proposed recovery strategies are designed to improve response time in recovery and the system's resilience.

The innovative aspect of the User-Centric Test Manager (UCTM) lies in its approach to actively engage users in the testing process. It empowers users to enhance their understanding of their behaviors and expectations concerning secure technological architectures. This involvement is essential, fostering a sense of ownership and awareness about security practices. Ultimately, this leads to developing secure and well-aligned systems with RED cybersecurity requirements and user needs. The architecture of the UCTM is illustrated in Fig. 3, and further details of its components are outlined as follows:

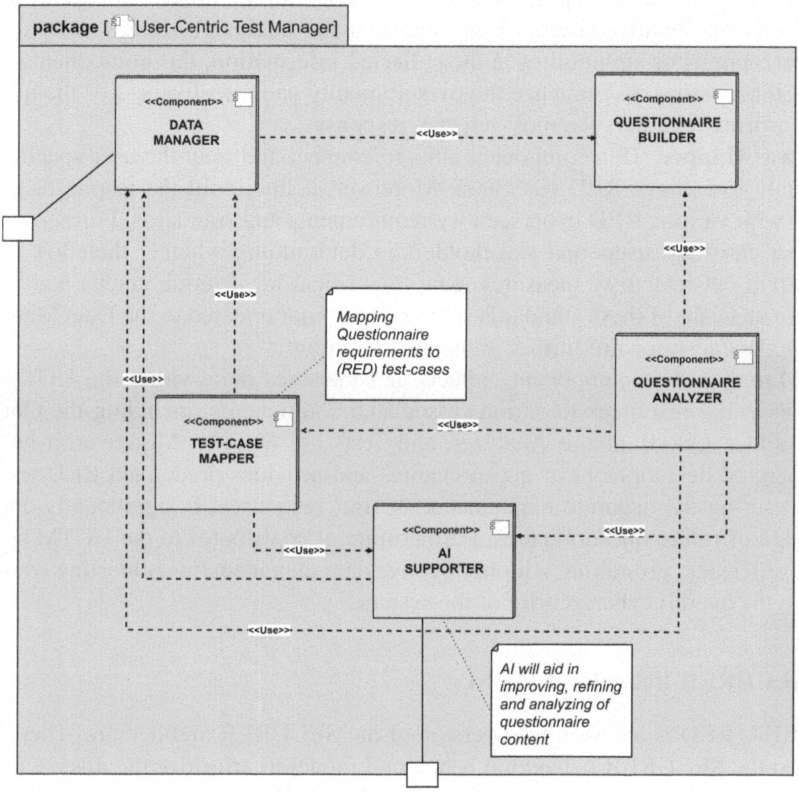

Fig. 3. UCTM components.

Questionnaire Builder. The primary purpose of a questionnaire builder is to create a comprehensive questionnaire for users. This tool helps formulate effective and structured questions to assess the security awareness of users involved with IoT devices. By focusing on critical security practices, such as password management, software updates, and default settings, the questionnaire proposes questions on areas where users may be more vulnerable to cyber-attacks. Additionally, this process enhances the overall cybersecurity of IoT infrastructure through user-based interactive testing.

Questionnaire Analyzer. The questionnaire analyzer is vital to the comprehensive assessment and systematic organization of user responses. Moreover, this component effectively evaluates data from a well-structured questionnaire; it facilitates the identification of crucial user opinions, complex behaviors, and emerging trends related to cybersecurity testing and user interaction patterns. Such insightful information deepens our understanding of user experiences. Furthermore, it provides a robust foundation for making proactive, evidence-based decisions that leverage our cybersecurity testing strategy and the effectiveness of our UCTM.

AI Supporter. This component aims to refine and improve the questionnaire's content through AI when the user specifications lack clarity and completeness, and it tends to fail to meet the quality criteria of the questionnaire analyzer. Moreover, by identifying shortcomings or ambiguities in the collected information, this component seeks to address those issues and enhance the overall quality and effectiveness of the questionnaire, ensuring it gathers the most relevant responses.

Test-Case Mapper. This component aims to connect and map the user specifications adequately to achieve RED test cases. Moreover, it filters out the responses to compliance with various RED cybersecurity requirements and standards. Furthermore, the RED test cases aid users and stakeholders in determining whether their IoT systems and current cybersecurity measures meet the critical legal requirements and whether users are unaware of these standards so it can be communicated to the Data Manager to improve the questionnaire further in the next iteration.

Data Manager. The component collects and manages data within the UCTM, providing essential resources to various associated components, including the Questionnaire Builder, Questionnaire Analyzer, and Test-case Mapper. Moreover, it leverages the structured development of questionnaires and provides predefined RED test cases while ensuring the accurate maintenance of user responses. It significantly enhances the design of future questionnaires. Furthermore, it contributes to the UCTM system's overall efficiency, promoting a more effective data management and testing strategy to improve the overall cybersecurity of the system.

5.3 SECURER Behavioral Model

SECURER_RED is a customized version of the SECURER architecture. Therefore, it inherited the SECURER behavioral behavioral model to prioritize the diverse needs of users. For completeness, we report the main SECURER's comprehensive behavioral model, describing the specific customization inside the activities description.

As schematized in Fig. 4 the model showcases the various phases of interaction that users can have with the SECURER platform and emphasizes the systematic approach required to carry out comprehensive cybersecurity testing as follows:

UTM GUI. To utilize the graphical user interface (GUI) of the User-Centric Testing Manager (UCTM), it is imperative that users complete the registration process and successfully log in to the User Testing Manager (UTM). This procedure is essential for conducting robust cybersecurity testing, as it enables users to specify their requirements and testing environments and select the relevant application domain. Furthermore, UCTM can utilize the collected information to develop an ad-hoc questionnaire tailored to the user's needs, enhancing the overall testing experience.

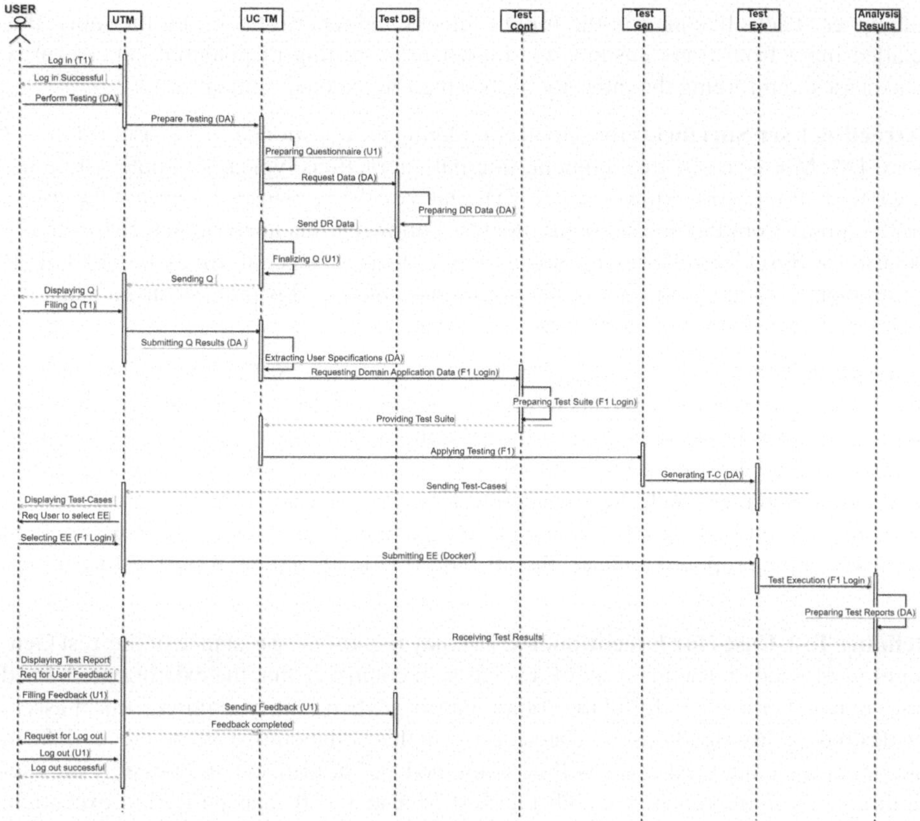

Fig. 4. SECURER [39] Sequence Diagram Note: **DA**: Domain Application; **U1**: User-1;**Q**: Questionnaire; **DR**: Domain Requirements; **T1**: Testing-1/Tester-1; **F1**: Feature 1 (Feature to be tested against cyber-attacks and vulnerabilities);**T-C**: Test-cases (Generating test-cases for the feature to be tested by the user as per their domain requirements).

Preparing Questionnaire. The UCTM actively seeks collaboration with Test DB to construct the questionnaire. This collaboration is vital, as Test DB is not just a repository; it is a detailed repository of predefined test cases and domain-specific information that can be instrumental in shaping the questionnaire. Moreover, by utilizing data from Test DB, the UCTM aims to design the questionnaire with depth and relevancy, ensuring that it effectively addresses user specifications and gathers appropriate feedback. Furthermore, this collaborative effort will ultimately enhance the quality and applicability of the questionnaire.

Finalizing Questionnaire. UCTM offers an interactive questionnaire for users to complete, enabling them to input detailed and precise information essential for defining test cases during the generation phase. For instance, users can identify specific components within smart home systems such as smart locks (keyless entry), security cameras, and home automation hubs that require rigorous testing for vulnerabilities associated with cyber-attacks like man-in-the-middle attacks and replay attacks. Furthermore, this detailed input from users ensures a comprehensive testing of potential cybersecurity weaknesses, reinforcing the integrity of the smart home environment.

Extracting User Specifications. Upon completing the questionnaire, the user submits it to UCTM. Moreover, by this moment, internal interactions typically initiate within the SECURER framework. However, UCTM analyzes the responses to extract the user's specifications from the questionnaire results. Following this analysis, UCTM formally requests the Test Controller to develop a set of test cases that conform to the SECURER requirements stated by the user in the preliminary phase. This process ensures that the testing procedures meet the user's specific needs.

Generating Test-Cases. Following the request made by UCTM, the Test Controller initiates a comprehensive analysis to identify an appropriate test suite and testing strategy that effectively satisfies the outlined requirements. However, when a predefined test suite is available, the Test Controller will offer functionalities to refine and update the suite in alignment with the specified testing criteria. Furthermore, the adoption of generative AI support may be employed in this context to enhance the precision and efficiency of the proposed updates, thereby contributing to a more robust testing framework.

Refining Test-Cases for Execution. UCTM may request the assistance of the Test Generator to provide an adequate set of test cases, recognizing that the existing predefined cases may not effectively fulfill the comprehensive cybersecurity requirements or assess the desired quality standards in cybersecurity. In this collaborative effort, the predefined and newly generated test cases will be combined and prioritized, and possibly an integration of these approaches, which the Test Manager will manage during execution, ensuring a robust and thorough evaluation process.

Generating Test Report. The Analysis and Results component is a crucial part of the testing framework, responsible for collecting and analyzing test results. It offers users detailed statistical evaluations and provides specific recommendations to address vulnerabilities identified during cybersecurity testing. These findings are demonstrated via a user-centric UTM GUI or UI (User Interface), which enhances user experience and encourages feedback. This approach promotes ongoing improvement and optimization of the SECURER-RED testing process, ensuring a more effective security assessment.

In the next section, a realization of the SECURER-RED implementation is provided.

6 Implementation

The architecture and behavioral model discussed in the previous section have been implemented in a prototype solution. The main goal of this implementation is to showcase the feasibility of the SECURER_RED proposal, albeit with some compromises on its effectiveness and overall performance. Moreover, all components of SECURER_RED, illustrated in Fig. 4 [39], were developed using open-source solutions and tools, involving minimal integration and some manual interactions.

The *Test Generator, Test Executor, Test Controller*, and *Test DB* have been developed employing available (open-source) tools such as IDE's (Integrated Development Environment) and XAMPP[8] for testing.

However, frameworks such as the OWASP Top Ten[9], CVE (Common Vulnerabilities and Exposures)[10] databases and MITRE ATT&CK[11] have been given due importance for adequate functionality of UCTM.

The generation of a questionnaire to gather needs and requirements for cybersecurity testing has been done using the JOTFORM tool, the Questionnaire for SECURER-RED Cybersecurity Requirements[12], while Mongo DB[13], has been used for *Test DB* realization.

A preliminary version of the User Interface (UI) and Graphical User Interface (GUI) for the UCTM component has been developed using React[14].

The Test Generator engine is a key component of this implementation. Various open-source test generation tools and resources from GitHub were explored in developing it. These have been incorporated into the proposed first implementation of our UCTM [39]. We also considered the integration of language learning models (LLMs) using OPEN API[15].

For executing test cases, we evaluated several testing libraries, extensions, and frameworks, including Pytest[16], JUnit[17], and NUnit[18]. Additionally, a *Test DB* has been instantiated to record details about executed test cases, including identified vulnerabilities classified by severity and mitigation recommendations to be included in the final report.

In the following, we provide technical details regarding the tools used to implement the SECURER-RED proposal components and discuss their compliance and optimization. Specific components like UI of UCTM was implemented using stubs or required manual interaction.

The current SECURER-RED prototype implementation is focused on various IoT domains: smart home systems, drone systems, and collaborative robots (cobots). Specifically, we used the following tools for robust cybersecurity testing and reducing the attack surface in the different phases of the process:

Metasploit[19]. A robust platform that simplifies the process of penetration testing. It allows users to select exploits, pick payloads, configure options, and execute attacks

[8] https://www.apachefriends.org/.
[9] https://owasp.org/www-project-top-ten/.
[10] https://cve.mitre.org/.
[11] https://attack.mitre.org/.
[12] https://form.jotform.com/250737176517361/.
[13] https://www.mongodb.com/.
[14] https://react.dev/learn/describing-the-ui.
[15] https://openapi.it/.
[16] https://docs.pytest.org/en/8.2.x/.
[17] https://junit.org/junit5/.
[18] https://nunit.org/.
[19] https://www.metasploit.org/.

on target systems. Metasploit has been employed in our Test Executor as illustrated in Fig. 4.

Aircrack-ng[20]**.** A suite of tools used for evaluating the security of WiFi networks, employed to assess the wireless communication security of IoT devices. Aircrack-ng has also been used in our Test Executor, as shown in Fig. 4.

OWASP ZAP (Zed Attack Proxy)[21]**.** An open-source web application security scanner that can be used to test web interfaces present in cobot systems. OWASP ZAP features in our Test Executor as depicted in Fig. 4.

Wireshark[22]**:** A network protocol analyzer that captures real-time network data, utilized for gathering information for our Test Controller, which supports the Test Generator as shown in Fig. 4.

CONCERN[23]**.** An open-source, customizable Complex Event Processing Monitor Infrastructure [11] that facilitates monitoring of test case executions and vulnerability detection. It has been tested in various contexts and application areas [6,7,10]. This component has been integrated into our Test Executor, illustrated in Fig. 4.

The SECURER-RED prototype is designed with a strong commitment to adhere to international security standards and regulations. Its primary objective is to significantly enhance the security landscape of the IoT while also developing reliable and robust components. These advancements are intended to maintain safety measures and promote more efficient and streamlined operations within industrial settings. Integrating these high-security protocols and dependable components, the SECURER-RED prototype aims to create a more secure and efficient industrial environment, ultimately contributing to increased operational resilience and safeguarding against potential cybersecurity threats.

7 Example Smart Home

The proposed implementation has been focused on cyber-attacks directed at smart home systems. This would showcase the SECURER-RED prototype practically. We examined the devices encompassed by RED, as outlined in the accompanying Fig. 1, which includes keyless entry systems. These systems enable authorized individuals to access secured areas without needing a physical key. We aim to assess these systems for vulnerabilities and potential cyber threats, including the common replay attacks and Man-in-the-middle attacks. Unauthorized access to keyless entry systems can disrupt the entire smart home installation.

In addition, like many other fields, the Internet of Things (IoT) and the broader industry must focus on developing strong cybersecurity testing practices. These practices are essential for identifying and addressing vulnerabilities in the firmware of smart home systems. The nature of attacks can vary greatly depending on the attackers' skills and the specific targets they choose to pursue [38].

[20] https://www.aircrack-ng.org/.

[21] https://www.zaproxy.org/.

[22] https://www.wireshark.org/.

[23] https://github.com/ISTI-LABSEDC/Concern.

7.1 Instantiating the UCTM

For our experiment, we filled the *Data Manager* component of UCTM, as illustrated in Fig. 3, with essential information regarding the most common threats and attacks targeting keyless entry systems in smart homes. Test cases that specifically address RED cybersecurity requirements have been chosen to cover a range of roles and scenarios, allowing for the development of appropriate test cases. The data has been organized into distinct categories, each presenting its own unique set of threats and challenges.

Cyber-attacks on smart home systems are prioritized by *Data Manager* of UCTM into distinct categories to enhance the effectiveness of our *Questionnaire Builder* and *Test-case Mapper*.

7.2 Questionnaire Process

The questionnaire process generation relies on a massive interaction among two components: the *Questionnaire Builder* and the *Questionnaire Analyzer*. These interconnected tools work collaboratively to construct a thorough and well-structured questionnaire. Furthermore, to improve questionnaire quality, the *AI Supporter* component plays a crucial role in this process by providing insightful guidance to clarify and refine user specifications.

Going into detail, the *Questionnaire Analyzer* evaluates the user response to replicate effective and targeted questions that assess users' security awareness concerning their interactions with IoT devices such as keyless entry system devices. Moreover, it places a strong emphasis on vital security practices, including robust password management, timely software updates, and prudent handling of default settings. The generated questionnaire seeks to uncover potential vulnerabilities in user behavior that could heighten the risk of cyber-attacks as illustrated in detail through Figs. 5, 6 and 7, which enhance overall cybersecurity awareness among users.

7.3 Mapping RED Test-Cases

The effective mapping of RED test cases is crucial for creating a strong framework that aligns user specifications with the relevant RED test cases. Additionally, as illustrated in Fig. 6, we have designed a detailed and focused questionnaire to gather specific user input regarding their cybersecurity needs and practices. This precise filtering of responses helps us evaluate the level of compliance with the various mandates set forth by RED.

Identifying potential vulnerabilities or deficiencies in current IoT systems and their cybersecurity measures is crucial. The *Test-case Mapper* has facilitated a systematic mapping process that correlates user responses with the applicable RED test cases [35] inspired by RED cybersecurity requirements and standards as follows:

TSO 5.1: No universal default passwords
TSO 5.11: Make it easy for users to delete user data
TSO 5.12: Make installation and maintenance of devices easy

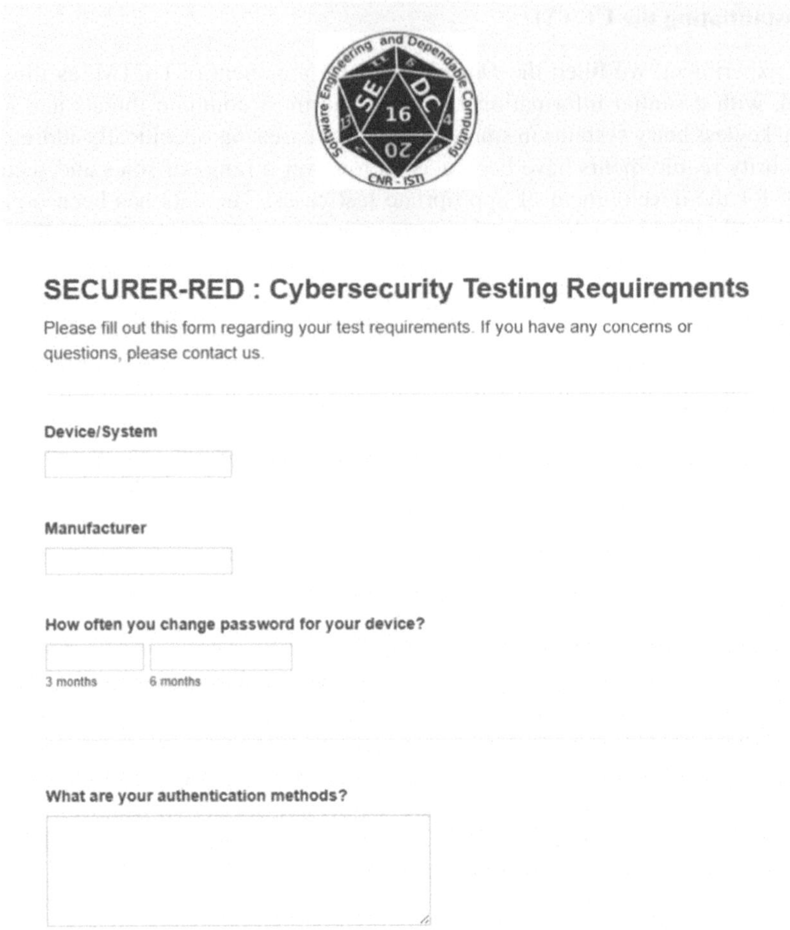

Fig. 5. SECURER-RED Questionnaire. (Color figure online)

TSO 5.13: Validate input data

The RED test cases have provided valuable insights for users and stakeholders, helping them determine whether their existing systems meet essential legal requirements. A critical part of this process is identifying areas where users may be unaware of specific cybersecurity standards. Gathering this information enables us to communicate effectively with the Data Manager, ensuring that insights from user experiences can guide iterative improvements in the questionnaire. This ongoing refinement of our testing process aims to better address user needs and enhance the overall accuracy and effectiveness of compliance assessments in future iterations.

Do you have two-factor authentication?

How your system behave in case of wrong password?

How does the system ensure the complete removal of personal data?

Do you receive any confirmation Email/message to verify that data has been successfully removed?

Is user authentication required before allowing access to personal data removal functionalities?

Fig. 6. Q 2.

The findings reveal a significant vulnerability in keyless entry systems employed in smart home systems. These systems fail to automatically realign their rolling codes when consecutive lock or unlock commands are received from various sources. Moreover, in connection with the adequate mapping of RED test cases and the analysis of real-time replay attacks, the identified vulnerability is expected to enhance our cybersecurity strategy substantially, emphasizing ensuring user safety and maintaining trust. We have developed the SECURER-RED architecture and operational model, underscoring the importance of ongoing user feedback and continuous optimization.

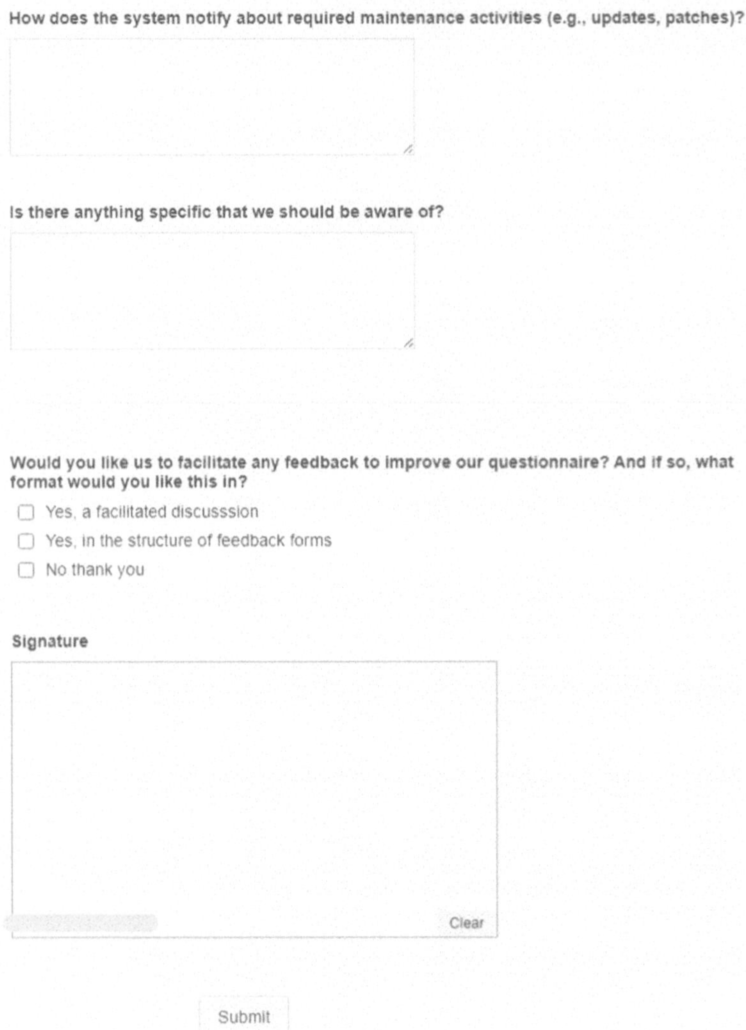
How does the system notify about required maintenance activities (e.g., updates, patches)?

Is there anything specific that we should be aware of?

Would you like us to facilitate any feedback to improve our questionnaire? And if so, what format would you like this in?

- [ ] Yes, a facilitated discusssion
- [ ] Yes, in the structure of feedback forms
- [ ] No thank you

Signature

Clear

Submit

Fig. 7. Q 3.

This framework aims to encourage a more resilient and responsive cybersecurity culture through user-centric testing depicted through our comprehensive questionnaire. However, ensuring the robust integration of the UCTM components within the SECURER-RED is critical for our cybersecurity testing framework to achieve its intended effectiveness. Such integration is essential for delivering a comprehensive security solution that effectively mitigates emerging threats.

8 Conclusion and Future Work

The SECURER-RED framework provides a comprehensive user-centric strategy for testing cybersecurity measures aimed at defending against replay attacks on smart home systems. This approach is vital for safeguarding both users and the broader Internet of Things (IoT) infrastructure. The book chapter outlines the design and key features of the framework and presents a preliminary prototype to demonstrate its significant potential and feasibility. Future work will focus on improving the framework by incorporating updated cybersecurity tools to cater to a wider audience and various application fields. Additionally, efforts will be made to refine the process of gathering user testing requirements and to explore the integration of DevSecOps (Development Security Operations) and GitHub Labs. This integration aims to effectively align RED test cases with user specifications, thereby enhancing the cybersecurity of IoT devices and smart home systems.

Acknowledgements. This work was partially supported by the project RESTART (PE00000001) and the project SERICS (PE00000014) under the NRRP MUR program funded by the EU - NextGenerationEU.

References

1. Abdusalomov, A.B., Kilichev, D., Nasimov, R., Rakhmatullayev, I., Cho, Y.I.: Optimizing smart home intrusion detection with harmony-enhanced extra trees. IEEE Access **12**, 117761–117786 (2024). https://api.semanticscholar.org/CorpusID:271005710
2. Ali, M., Shahroz, M., Mushtaq, M.F., Alfarhood, S., Safran, M.S., Ashraf, I.: Hybrid machine learning model for efficient botnet attack detection in IoT environment. IEEE Access **12**, 40682–40699 (2024). https://doi.org/10.1109/ACCESS.2024.3376400
3. Alshboul, Y., Bsoul, A.A.R., Al Zamil, M., Samarah, S.: Cybersecurity of smart home systems: sensor identity protection. J. Netw. Syst. Manag. **29**(3), 22 (2021)
4. Ansari, M.T.J., Pandey, D., Alenezi, M.: STORE: security threat oriented requirements engineering methodology. J. King Saud Univ.-Comput. Inf. Sci. **34**(2), 191–203 (2022)
5. Barhamgi, M., Perera, C., Ghedira, C., Benslimane, D.: User-centric privacy engineering for the internet of things. IEEE Cloud Comput. **5**(5), 47–57 (2018)
6. Barsocchi, P., et al.: COVID-19 & privacy: enhancing of indoor localization architectures towards effective social distancing. Array **9**, 100051 (2021). https://doi.org/10.1016/j.array.2020.100051
7. Barsocchi, P., Calabrò, A., Ferro, E., Gennaro, C., Marchetti, E., Vairo, C.: Boosting a low-cost smart home environment with usage and access control rules. Sensors **18**(6), 1886 (2018). https://doi.org/10.3390/s18061886
8. Bella, G., Biondi, P., Bognanni, S., Esposito, S.: PETIoT: penetration testing the internet of things. Internet Things **22**, 100707 (2023)
9. Borgosz, L., Dikicioglu, D.: Industrial internet of things: what does it mean for the bioprocess industries? Biochem. Eng. J. **201**, 109122 (2024)
10. Calabrò, A., Cioroaica, E., Daoudagh, S., Marchetti, E.: BIECO runtime auditing framework. In: 14th (CISIS and ICEUTE) 2021. Advances in Intel. Systems and Computing, vol. 1400, pp. 181–191. Springer (2021)

11. Calabrò, A., Marchetti, E., Skrzypek, P., Marchel, J.: Concern: a model-based monitoring infrastructure. Internet Things **31**, 101557 (2025). https://doi.org/10.1016/j.iot.2025.101557, https://www.sciencedirect.com/science/article/pii/S2542660525000708
12. Sáez-de Cámara, X., Flores, J.L., Arellano, C., Urbieta, A., Zurutuza, U.: Gotham testbed: a reproducible IoT testbed for security experiments and dataset generation. IEEE Trans. Dependable Secure Comput. (2023)
13. Chen, M.Y.: Establishing a cybersecurity home monitoring system for the elderly. IEEE Trans. Industr. Inf. **18**(7), 4838–4845 (2021)
14. Chiara, P.G.: The EU legal frameworks regulating IoT cybersecurity. In: The Internet of Things and EU Law: Cybersecurity, Privacy and Data Protection Challenges, pp. 65–148. Springer (2024)
15. Douha, N.Y.R., Renaud, K., Taenaka, Y., Kadobayashi, Y.: Smart home cybersecurity awareness and behavioral incentives. Inf. Comput. Secur. **31**(5), 545–575 (2023)
16. Dritsas, E., Trigka, M.: A survey on cybersecurity in IoT. Future Internet **17**(1) (2025)
17. Etigowni, S., Macwan, R., Welsh, J.: Requirements framework for cyber-informed engineering: cyber-informed engineering (2025). https://doi.org/10.2172/2497726
18. Gulati, K., Boddu, R.S.K., Kapila, D., Bangare, S.L., Chandnani, N., Saravanan, G.: A review paper on wireless sensor network techniques in internet of things (IoT). Mater. Today: Proc. **51**, 161–165 (2022)
19. Heiding, F., Süren, E., Olegård, J., Lagerström, R.: Penetration testing of connected households. Comput. Secur. **126**, 103067 (2023)
20. Huang, H.C., Liu, I.H., Lee, M.H., Li, J.S.: Anomaly detection on network traffic for the healthcare IoT. Eng. Proc. **55**(1) (2023). https://doi.org/10.3390/engproc2023055003
21. Kaksonen, R., Halunen, K., Röning, J.: Common cybersecurity requirements in IoT standards, best practices, and guidelines. In: Proceedings of the 7th International Conference on Internet of Things, Big Data and Security-IoTBDS. SciTePress (2022)
22. Kaushik, K., Bhardwaj, A., Dahiya, S.: Framework to analyze and exploit the smart home IoT firmware. Meas.: Sens. **37**, 101406 (2025)
23. Kayan, H., Nunes, M., Rana, O., Burnap, P., Perera, C.: Cybersecurity of industrial cyber-physical systems: a review. ACM Comput. Surv. (CSUR) **54**(11s), 1–35 (2022)
24. Kun, E.: Searching for the appropriate legal basis for personal data processing for cybersecurity purposes under the NIS 2 directive: legal obligation and/or legitimate interest? Comput. Law Secur. Rev. **56**, 106098 (2025)
25. Marchetti, E., Waheed, T., Calabrò, A.: Cybersecurity testing in drones domain: a systematic literature review. IEEE Access (2024)
26. Negri-Ribalta, C., Lombard-Platet, M., Salinesi, C.: Understanding the GDPR from a requirements engineering perspective–a systematic mapping study on regulatory data protection requirements. Requirements Eng. **29**(4), 523–549 (2024)
27. Orlowski, A., Loh, W.: Data autonomy and privacy in the smart home: the case for a privacy smart home meta-assistant. AI & SOCIETY, 1–14 (2025)
28. Piasecki, S., Urquhart, L., McAuley, D.: Defence against the dark artefacts: smart home cybercrimes and cybersecurity standards. Comput. Law Secur. Rev. **42**, 105542 (2021)
29. Pietrantuono, R., Ficco, M., Palmieri, F.: Testing the resilience of MEC-Based IoT applications against resource exhaustion attacks. IEEE Trans. Dependable Secure Comput. (2023)
30. Puthal, D., Wilson, S., Nanda, A., Liu, M., Swain, S., Sahoo, B.P., Yelamarthi, K., Pillai, P., El-Sayed, H., Prasad, M.: Decision tree based user-centric security solution for critical IoT infrastructure. Comput. Electr. Eng. **99**, 107754 (2022)
31. Puthal, D., et al.: A user-centric security solution for internet of things and edge convergence. ACM Trans. Cyber-Phys. Syst. **4**(3), 1–19 (2020)
32. Quayyum, F., Jaccheri, L.: CyberFamily: a collaborative family game to increase children's cybersecurity awareness. Entertainment Comput. **52**, 100826 (2025)

33. Ramzan, F., et al.: New requirement elicitation techniques, processes, and frameworks: innovation to requirement engineering. J. Softw. Eng. Pract. **5**(2), 1–12 (2024)
34. Rivadeneira, J.E., Silva, J.S., Colomo-Palacios, R., Rodrigues, A., Boavida, F.: User-centric privacy preserving models for a new era of the internet of things. J. Netw. Comput. Appl., 103695 (2023)
35. Siavvas, M., Xanthopoulou, G., Kalouptsoglou, I., Kehagias, D., Tzovaras, D.: Digital transformation of security standards: requirements extraction using large language models. In: 2024 11th International Conference on Dependable Systems and Their Applications (DSA), pp. 430–431. IEEE (2024)
36. Trabelsi, Z.: IoT based smart home security education using a hands-on approach. In: 2021 IEEE Global Engineering Education Conference (EDUCON), pp. 294–301. IEEE (2021)
37. Waheed, T., Marchetti, E.: The impact of IoT cybersecurity testing in the perspective of industry 5.0. In: WEBIST, pp. 480–487 (2023)
38. Waheed, T., Marchetti, E., Calabrò, A.: Cybersecurity testing for cobots. In: García-Peñalvo, F.J., Aberer, K., Marchiori, M. (eds.) Proceedings of the 20th International Conference on Web Information Systems and Technologies, WEBIST 2024, Porto, Portugal, 17–19 November 2024, pp. 449–456. SCITEPRESS (2024). https://doi.org/10.5220/0013071000003825
39. Waheed, T., Marchetti, E., Calabrò, A.: SECURER: user-centric cybersecurity testing framework for IoT system. In: García-Peñalvo, F.J., Aberer, K., Marchiori, M. (eds.) Proceedings of the 20th International Conference on Web Information Systems and Technologies, WEBIST 2024, Porto, Portugal, 17–19 November 2024, pp. 393–400. SCITEPRESS (2024). https://doi.org/10.5220/0013062900003825
40. Waheed, T., Marchetti, E., Calabro, A.: Vulnerability mapping and mitigation through AI code analysis and testing. In: Proceedings of the 13th International Conference on Model-Based Software and Systems Engineering (MODELSWARD 2025), pp. 363–370 (2025)
41. Wooderson, P., Ward, D.: Cybersecurity testing and validation. Tech. rep., SAE Technical Paper (2017)
42. Wright, V.L., et al.: Cyber-informed engineering implementation guide. Tech. rep., Idaho National Laboratory (INL), Idaho Falls, ID (United States) (2023)
43. Yigit Ozkan, B., Spruit, M.: A questionnaire model for cybersecurity maturity assessment of critical infrastructures. In: International Workshop on Information and Operational Technology Security Systems, pp. 49–60. Springer (2018)

Malicious Web Links Detection with Large Language Models

Claudia-Ioana Coste(✉) and Thomas Kaisser

Faculty of Mathematics and Computer Science, Babeș-Bolyai University, Cluj-Napoca, Romania
claudia.coste@ubbcluj.ro, thomas.kaisser@stud.ubbcluj.ro
https://www.cs.ubbcluj.ro/

Abstract. The Internet and the World Wide Web have now become the medium for information, socializing, entertainment, learning, shopping and so on. Because the online environment is used on such a large scale, many inexperienced users can be vulnerable and may fall victim to very sophisticated attacks through clicking a malicious web link, the main propagating vector for web malware. The present approach proposes to advance the research in this domain by classifying websites and making use of the functionalities of Large Language Models, especially Chat GPT. First, a three-step modelling process is described using hand-crafted features. Additional experiments with OpenAI's models are delivered, and then a GPT-2 model is fine-tuned for detecting malicious web links. The last model managed to reach an accuracy of 97.67%, outperforming other relevant solutions from the State-of-the-Art. In addition, a new feature was developed that included the GPT-2's annotation. To be able to analyze whether this feature was relevant, a diverse group of intelligent methods was used to test if any improvements were made by adding it. Overall, a small improvement was noticeable.

Keywords: Malicious web links detection · Large language models · Ensembles · OpenAI API · Chat GPT · Machine learning

1 Introduction

Surfing the Internet comes with a lot of challenges, considering user privacy and cybersecurity. Most online users do not possess the required digital skills and abilities to properly identify attacks. According to [11] there are approximately 5.56 billion people using the Internet, which accounts for almost 68% of the world's population. The most common type of attack is phishing, spread mostly through email. It was estimated that 3.4 billion spam emails are sent every day [6]. Most emails include malicious URLs in their text or malware attachments, trying to deceive users into accessing the link or the bad-intended attached file. Most links will imitate legitimate links, for example, being under ".com", ".net" top-level domains and use other common domain names, such as: "Adobe", "Google", "Myportofolio", etc. [6]. Moreover, from the malicious emails reported, 38% of them had a URL inserted [6].

M. Marchiori et al. (Eds.): WEBIST 2024, LNBIP 583, pp. 138–158, 2026.
https://doi.org/10.1007/978-3-032-25534-1_6

With the launch of Chat GPT 3 in 2022, Large Language Models (LLMs) received major attention from the public and the scientific community. The GPT-3 model was working very well, it provided human-like responses, proved a deep understanding of human language, and was able to respond empathetically and appropriately to the context. LLMs were constructed based on the Transformer architecture, an encoder-decoder model, with multiple attention heads that selected relevant information for the context [39]. The attention mechanism was initially proposed for the translation problem. Chat GPT and other models launched later (e.g., Llama, Gemini, GPT-4o) demonstrated good accuracy when dealing with human-like monotone tasks. AI was quickly adopted and employed for a large variety of tasks. However, LLMs present some disadvantages, such as hallucinations, biased information, false explanations, etc. The systematic literature review from [44] uncovers many aspects: positive and negative regarding LLMs and cybersecurity. There are papers which proven that LLMs, and mostly Chat GPT, are used for generating malware software by "hacking" the prompt. Moreover, it was observed that LLMs are very efficient for phishing attacks, generating personalized emails to achieve higher click rates from users. Additionally, these language models can be used to drive user-oriented attacks by generating misinformation, establishing a connection between topics that are not accurately related. LLMs can contribute to social engineering attacks, which will aggregate a large amount of data gathered from data breaches targeting each user in particular. Other mischievous methods employed by LLMs are scientific misconduct and fraud generation. There is FrandGPT available on the Dark Web, which enables attackers to use the chatbot, bypassing its protection mechanisms against biases, malicious intents, etc. Nevertheless, LLMs as AI models can present several vulnerabilities and threats, such as prompt injection, data poisoning, exploiting biases, backdoor attacks, and many others. Considering specifically malicious web links, Roy et al. [34] investigate the utilization of chatbots for crafting phishing websites. It was observed that, without any computer science knowledge, just by crafting prompts, malicious users are able to clone well-known websites and generate phishing content. Roy et al. [34] propose a BERT detection solution that can be used by LLMs to block them from generating deceiving content.

The present paper is an extension of the paper [10] and proposes to continue investigating the usage of Chat GPT models in detecting malicious tasks. Present contributions can be summarised as follows:

- A three-step routine for feature extraction;
- Experiment with OpenAI's two mini models (GPT-4o-mini and o1-mini);
- Fine-tune a GPT-2 model for classification;
- Test multiple machine learning models with hand-crafted features and by adding a GPT-2's prediction as a new feature;
- Run algorithms for two dataset configurations: one with 4,000 randomly picked samples and the other with 40,000 samples.

This research paper is split into five chapters. First, the Introduction 1 is discussed, then the paper follows with a Sect. 2 reviewing the previous works proposed in the domain of malicious web links detection. The next Sect. 3 describes the present approach and the idea of research using Large Language Models for the detection of malicious websites. Next, Sect. 4 tackles the experiments, computations, and the final results obtained. The proposed approach is thoroughly compared with other literature ideas. Lastly, the main contributions are reiterated, and the future areas of research are discussed.

2 State-of-the-Art

With the rise of many AI-based systems, web attacks have become more and more sophisticated and easy to develop. Thus, new methods need to leverage the capabilities of the most complex AI systems: LLMs. So far, not many solutions have focused on detecting malicious web links by employing LLMs. Most detection systems revolve around classic machine learning (ML) methods, blacklists, ant-viruses and sometimes complex networks. Considering the information given as input, approaches could be split into content-dependent and content-independent solutions. The first category will take as input data retrieved from the content of the web page, extracting features from the HyperText Markup Language (HTML), Cascading Style Sheets (CSS), JavaScript (JS), and visual cues. The second group of features consists of gathering data from the URL, third parties (e.g., Google Safe Browning, Google index, DNS, WHOIS services, blacklists etc.) or other networking information (e.g., HTTP headers, IP of the server, port and others).

2.1 Content-Dependent Solutions

Many papers extract content-dependent features manually, which are considered relevant by computer scientists. However, there are ideas automatically extracting attributes using deep learning techniques, as is the example from [35]. Rozi et al. [35] are parsing the JS code, resulting in the Abstract Syntactic Tree (AST). The AST is then encoded with graph2vec in a format suitable for the input of the classification models. There is delivered a comparative analysis with a large range of ML techniques, from which one could recall: a Simple Neural Network (NN), a Multi-layer Perceptron, Logistic Regression (LR), tree models (e.g., Decision Tree, Extreme Gradient Boosting), statistical methods (e.g., Naive Bayes) and Support Vector Machine (SVM) using the Radial Basis Function (RBF).

Articles considering mostly hand-crafted characteristics will apply different feature selection methods to select the most suitable and important attributes. For example, Wejinya et al. [43] are depicting 15 features out of 30 content-based, lexical, and network-related attributes. The model used in classification is Naive Bayes (NB). Kumi et al. [16] in a comparable approach using data retrieved from the web content, mostly from HTML or JS code, will conclude that after classification, the most promising attributes are: the entropy of the domain, script tags, functions which manipulate the DOM, etc. The classification is done through an association classifier (95.8% accuracy), compared with other ML algorithms such as LR, SVM, and NB. Similarly, Nagy et al. [28] will sort out the most relevant features using the chi-square test. Just 15 characteristics picked from the HTML or JS contained by the web link are used in the final model, NB. Other AI methods were used in detection (e.g., Random Forest (RF), Convolutional Neural Network (CNN), and Long-Short Term Memory (LSTM)), however, none of them outperformed NB, which reached 96.01 % accuracy.

2.2 Content-Independent Solutions

Content-independent detection systems have the advantage that they do not require to access the web page and downloading its content which could be perfoming malicious routines. Collected content-independent information is relatively safe.

The first idea is to filter URLs based on blacklists, which are public domain lists containing untrustworthy domains, that have been previously reported as performing malicious actions. Maintaining these lists is a community effort, and they are not protecting users against 0-day attacks, malicious activities that have not been reported yet. An example of a blacklist-based solution is detailed in [23].

Another type of solution selecting characteristics from the URL is [31], which chooses multiple textual features (i.e., N-grams, word2vec, and others). For experiments, multiple datasets are merged, and ten models (e.g., LR, Linear SVM, DT, RF, K-Nearest Neighbor (KNN), NN, NB, K-Means, Gaussian Mixture Model, and Categorical Boosting) are compared, the best performing one being K-Nearest Neighbor (KNN). Similarly, but collecting a more diversified range of attributes from the URL, Mahdavifar et al. [24] deliver a KNN-detection system with a 98.9% detection rate. The features extracted are lexical, and many are retrieved from the DNS and other external services. For feature selection, the information gain formula is applied, leading to 13 final attributes. Experiments include a comparative analysis with other models, such as SVM, MLP, an NB variant, and LR. Tests were run on a dataset collected in [24] with 400,000 benign URLs and a disproportionate number of 13,011 suspicious links. The study concluded that information gathered from external services was more pertinent to the classification.

The present approach uses a dataset [37] frequently employed in literature. For example, Alsaedi et al. [3] sample just 20,000 URLs for each class to train and test their solution. The detection system includes an RF model for each category of attributes, and then these models are merged into an ensemble with the assistance of an MLP classifier. The developed algorithm reaches 96.8% accuracy. Moreover, besides the RF, other intelligent methods are used for comparisons. Still, RF surpasses the other in terms of accuracy rate. The feature categories are lexical, computer network related (WHOIS), and information retrieved from a third party (Google Cyber Threat Intelligence). Similarly, proposing an ensemble model and using the same dataset, Coste [5] tackles the problem of malicious web links detection by testing a Particle Swarm Optimization (PSO) ensemble with a large variety of ML models.

From the multi-label viewpoint, Shetty et al. [36] provide a solution with an RF model achieving almost 97% accuracy. Likewise, Zhang et al. [45] propose a Multi-filter CNN with word-level embeddings, and it was tested in both multi-class and binary-class environments. The system proved outstanding in comparison with other literature proposed ideas. Another interesting approach considering binary classification for malicious links can be found in [4], where URLs are mapped to images and then deep learning methods are applied to classify. Tested on [37] dataset, this method reached 94% accuracy for 40K of the samples and 96% for all data.

2.3 LLM-Based Solutions

Approaches making use of LLMs are not many but they seem to be the next topical field of research because of their extraordinary capabilities. LLMs have many applications in education, translation, summarizing, rephasing, cybersecurity and many others.

A newly developed solution is proposed by Koide et al. [12] entitled ChatPhishDetector, where multiple LLMs are used for phishing detection. The system build is complex, has multiple types of inputs, such as the URL, the HTML, and the screenshot of the website. Prompt engineering is thoroughly analyzed to retrieve additional explanatory information besides the class (phishing or not) and identify the impersonated brand. Multiple LLMs are tried (e.g., Chat GPT 4, 4 Vision, 3.5 Turbo, Gemini Pro, Pro Vision, and Llama 2), yet the best performance was reached with Chat GPT 4 Vision. The dataset consisted of 1,000 private URLs for each class and achieved an outstanding accuracy of 99.2%.

Similarly, Lee et al. [19] are building a Multimodal LLM to detect phishing web links. They focus their research on identifying the brand impersonated in the phishing webpage, creating two phases for the detection strategy. The first phase takes as input the HTML content and the screenshot of the URL to pick out the brand. Then the output for the first phase is concatenated with the URL information, such that the system will cross-check if the previously identified brand matches the domain of the URL. After phase two, the detection result is determined. Lee et al. [19] are comparing multiple LLMs for the experiments, such as Anthropic Claude 3, Gemini ProVision 1.0, and GPT-4-turbo, from which GPT-4 and Claude are the best performing ones. The dataset is collected by the authors during the October-December months. The legitimate URLs were extracted from the Tranco list [17], and the phishing samples were scraped from OpenPhish [30]. The experiments conducted are investigating whether there is a need to provide both the screenshot of the website and its HTML, or just one of the elements. The best performance is reached when both datasets are given as input. Moreover, there is an analysis to observe if both stages of the detection strategy are required. Additionally, adversarial attacks are generated in two ways: by adding modifications to the HTML content and by adding noise to the logo images. The last type of adversarial attack was most effective, however, LLMs demonstrate resilience with a few URLs mistakenly classified. The usage of LLMs for this problem type included additional details for the LLM to respond, such as: confidence score, explanation, genuine URL, etc.

A series of simple experiments provided as a tutorial article, which can be found at [38] presented how to use OpenAI's chatbot to annotate phishing web pages. Two rounds of tests were done, and the overall performance was around 87% detection rate, however, with numerous false positives.

From another cybersecurity perspective, VirusTotal implemented a tool, Code Insight, whose purpose was to signal any logical problems from the code. Developers used Sec-PaLM, a LLM certified by Google and the system will translate code into natural language to mitigate the difficulties with code understanding.

On the same note, Kulkarni et al. [15] propose to generate adversarial phishing attacks through the PhishOracle system to test several solutions for phishing web links detection. The proposed system should retrieve from the Internet legitimate web pages and randomly insert phishing features from a curated selection of visual and /or content-based attacks. Some examples of phishing characteristics inserted could be: disabling anchor tags, login buttons, right click, CTRL and Fn keys, logo transformations, etc. For the experiments, Kulkarni et al. [15] depicted a Stack model provided by [20], two deep learning solutions: VisualPhishNet [1] and Phishpedia [22]. Additionally, there were added experiments with a Multimodal LLM developed in [19]. The Stack model is constructed from a Gradient Boosted Decision Tree, an Extreme Gradient Boosting, and a Light Gradient Boosting Machine. Kulkarni et al. [15] retrained all algorithms on a newly collected dataset and generated EvasionSets for each of them. According to their study, all solutions suffered a decrease in detection rate; the most severe was from Phishpedia, which dropped by at most 40%. The LLM model proved to be the more robust one, with only 10% descrese at most. The security vendor from Virus Total [41], did not do a very good job in identifying these adversarial-generated attacks. Moreover, the same experiment was conducted on human subjects as well, they were asked to label webpages as phishing or legitimate. It was computed that 48% of phishing web pages were annotated as safe links.

In other connected fields, LLMs are employed for phishing email detection, such as in [13] and in [7]. The solution provided by Koide et al. [13] used four models to compare their performance (i.e., GPT-3.5-turbo, GPT-4, Llama2-70B, GeminiPro) and the best one proved to be GPT-4 achieving 99.7% accuracy. Heiding et al. [7] used for experiments GPT, Claude, PaLM and Llama2. The most stable model was Claude, however, their testing environment is not very diverse, giving just 20 emails as input.

Therefore, not many ideas were previously provided in the literature regarding the usage of LLMs in malicious web links detection, but they constitute a field of interest for many researchers. The present paper proposes to further develop experiments with LLMs, continuing the work by [10] and advancing research in web links classification by leveraging LLMs.

3 Proposed Approach

The present approach is based on the work developed by Kaisser et Coste in [10]. The experiments are continued and elaborated. The current research approach could be reduced to the following phases:

1. Dataset;
2. Preprocessing;
3. Feature selection and extraction;
4. ML models and ensembles;
5. OpenAI's models.

3.1 Dataset

The chosen dataset is, to our knowledge, one of the most comprehensive, and it can be accessed for free on the Kaggle website at [37]. It includes 651,191 URLs, both benign and malicious in total. The malicious samples are further split into three other categories: malware, defacement, and phishing. There are 428,103 legitimate samples,

96,457 defacements, 94,111 phishing URLs, and 32,520 malware ones. This dataset was created by aggregating information from multiple resources. One source is the ISCX-URL-2016 dataset from [26], another one is Faizan's repository on GitHub [9]. Other websites that provide malicious URLs are PhishTank [33], PhishStorm [27], and the webpage entitled "malwaredomainlist.com" [25].

3.2 Preprocessing

Our first experiments started considering multi-classification, but because we wanted to make comparisons easier with other detection approaches, we propose to see the malicious web links detection problem as a binary one. The initial malicious labels found in the dataset (i.e., malware, phishing, and defacement) were mapped to "unsafe". The benign ones were mapped to "safe". Finally, the binary dataset would contain 428,103 "safe" URLs and 223,008 "unsafe" ones. As an observation, the database is not balanced. In some experiments, we considered a balanced data split; however, in other cases, we considered that it is relevant to get results similar to a real-case scenario, where legitimate URLs outnumber the malicious ones.

3.3 Feature Selection and Extraction

The proposed features for this approach are detailed in Table 1, where all features are named, described, and their datatype is also included. These features were extracted because of previous literature results, where these types of attributes proved to be relevant in the classification of malicious web links. These hand-crafted features are both host-based and lexical. From the host-based category, we can exemplify Google Index, port indicator, etc., and from the second category, one could include here: the total length of the URL, number of special characters, or other specific signs, and others. The elected attributes can be taken from the URL alone.

For feature extraction, there were elaborated three methods applied successively to depict the most important characteristics for our case.

1. Adding/ Dropping features according to how the accuracy score evolved;
2. Eliminating attributes in the model based on their obtained relevance score;
3. Deleting the highly coupled characteristics based on the covariance matrix.

In the first stage, experiments started with an initial set of features, which were depicted from the literature. To this initial set, other features were added. If the accuracy of the RF model improved, then the feature was kept. A figure representing this heuristic is presented in Fig. 1. The primary set of characteristics is displayed in Table 1 with the green color. The rest of the features are either added or dropped after the feature selection process.

The second phase of feature selection is considering the relevance score obtained by each attribute. If the significance score was one of the lowest, we chose to eliminate those features. The importance score was computed in the RF model implemented in the scikit-learn Python library [32], version 1.6.1. The relevance score is the average reduction in impurity for all estimator trees forming the RF model.

Table 1. The features selected and their descriptions [10].

Feature name	Feature type	Description
IP address	Boolean	checks whether the web link contains an IP address
no. "." sign	Number	number of the "." sign
no. "@" sign	Number	number of the "@" sign
Google Index	Boolean	using Google service [40] checks whether the URL was indexed
no. embedded domains	Number	the number of domains found within the weblink (domains are separated by "//")
no. directories	Number	the number of directories found in the path of the URL (directories are separated by "/")
URL length	Number	total length of the weblink
no. digits	Number	the number of digits contained by the URL
no. special chars.	Number	number of all special characters ("/", "%", "#", "&", "=", "?") found in the web link
Shannon entropy	Float number	calculate based on the formula from [21] considering the domain, port or subdomains if there are any
longest FQDN token	Number	the length of the longest token found in the Fully Qualified Domain Name (FQDN) considering the hostname (domain, port, and subdomains)
no. vowels	Number	the number of vowels ("a", "e", "i", "o", "u") found in the path of the URL
query length	Number	number of characters representing the query string (i.e, the characters between the "?" and the fragment sign "#")
is HTTPS	Boolean	checks the presence of the HTTPS certificate
no. phishing words	Number	based on the phishing words identified by [2] (e.g., "webscr", "secure", "banking", "ebayisapi", "account", "confirm", "login', "signing") count if any of these words appear in the URL
port indicator	Boolean	set to True if the port was included in the URL; set to False otherwise

On the third step, the covariance matrix is computed, and features found to be highly dependent on each other are discarded. The covariance matrix is calculated on pairs of columns from the dataset to analyze their correlation. If the value from the matrix is high, then the features from the corresponding column and row are highly correlated, and if the value is negative, then the features have a low correlation.

3.4 OpenAI's Models

The empirical studies concerning OpenAI's model could be split into multiple categories:

1. Prompt engineering;
2. OpenAI's classification (simple models and mini models);
3. Train an LLM for the web link classification tasks.

Prompt engineering was the first stage for experimenting with OpenAI's models. The prompts designed in the present approach are presented in Table 2. The first prompt

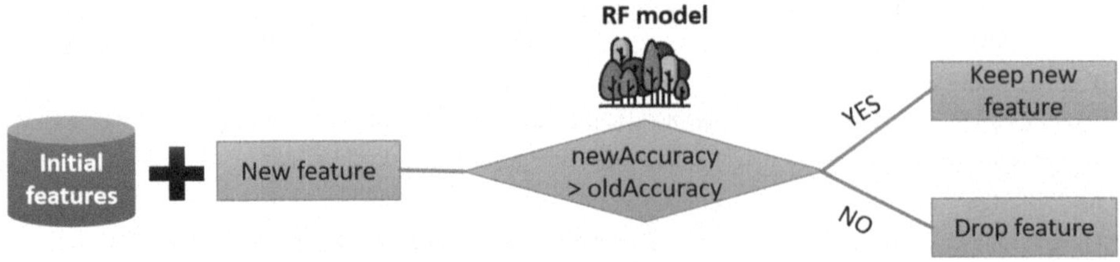

Fig. 1. Heuristic for the first stage of feature selection.

is the simplest one, stating just the task for the GPT model. The next two prompts add more details, making use of the Zero-Shot technique [14]. The third prompt includes examples, while the second one does not. Those examples should help the chatbot in classification. The last prompt is employing strategies from the Chain-of-Thought technique [42], where examples are given and explained based on a list of features extracted. The attributes of a web page listed in the prompt are selected based on our considerations to be relevant for the maliciousness detection process.

The round of experiments started with using just OpenAI's models for classification. Firstly, two GPT models were used: GPT-3.5 Turbo and GPT-4 with all four prompts, leading to eight configurations. Due to limited financial resources, we decided to experiment with just 1,000 randomly sampled web links from the dataset. The cost associated with GPT-3.5 Turbo at the time of developing this study was between an interval of 0.12 and 0.27$ per testing round. By contrast, GPT-3.5 Turbo is significantly cheaper than GPT-4. For GPT-4 which at the time was the latest model, we paid between 1.72$ and 9.06$ per set.

In the code development, the OpenAI Python library was used as exemplified in OpenAI's documentation [29].

The following experiments considered the most performing prompt according to the previous iteration. The next study involved two mini models proposed by OpenAI [29], such as GPT-4o-mini (i.e., gpt-4o-mini-2024-07-18) and o1-mini (i.e., o1-mini-2024-09-12). To minimize the cost of requests, the development included using the Batch API. GPT-4o-mini model has a system/developer option with which users can explain the task once and then give successively just the URLs to be classified. Thus, this convenient option enabled programmers to minimize the costs associated. However, this option was not yet available for o1-mini at the time of running the experiments. For GPT-4o-mini, the prompt was slightly modified to express how the URLs are going to be passed and that the model should output a JSON. The financial costs associated with these experiments enabled us to use 4,000 web links for testing. All URLs were randomly sampled, and the classes are balanced. For GPT-4o-mini we paid 0.5$ per round of testing, and for o1-mini the costs ranged from 20–25$. O1-mini was more expensive because their Batch API did not have implemented the option for the system or developer through which we would have been able to state the task once.

The last part of the experiments proposes to train a GPT-2 model, available for free on Hugging Face [8] for the specific classification task of malicious web links detection. For implementation, additional libraries (e.g., huggingface-hub version 0.29.3, trans-

Table 2. The prompts engineered for the GPT models (GPT-4 and GPT-3.5 Turbo) [10].

No.	Prompt
1	Check if the url is safe or not, respond with SAFE for safe url and UNSAFE for unsafe url
2	Check if the url is safe or not, respond with SAFE for safe url and UNSAFE for unsafe url. Try to look at the entropy of the domain, the length of the domain, the number of the special characters, the longest token in the url
3	Check if the url is safe or not, respond with SAFE for safe url and UNSAFE for unsafe url. Try to look at the entropy of the domain, the length of the domain, the number of the special characters, the longest token in the url Examples: 1. http://www.ikenmijnkunst.nl/index.php/exposities/exposities-2006,unsafe 2. http://peluqueriadeautor.com/index.php?option=com_virtuemart&page=shop.browse &category_id=31&Itemid=70,unsafe 3. movies.yahoo.com/shop?d=hv&cf=info&id=1800340831,safe 4. duckduckgo.com/1/c/Roman_Catholic_cathedrals_in_Canada,safe 5. alexpay2.beget.tech,unsafe 6. http://worldoftanks.ru/ru/content/guide/payments_instruction/mobile-payments-rostelekom-ural-utel/,safe 7. http://www.artedesignsas.it/catalogo.html?page=shop.browse&category_id=14,unsafe
4	Check if the url is safe or not, respond with SAFE for safe url and UNSAFE for unsafe url. Look at these features: - Number of directory levels - Length of the URL: 38 characters - Number of special characters (from "/%#&=?") - Shannon entropy of the domain - Length of the longest token in the FQDN - Number of dots in the URL - Number of vowels in the path Examples: friars.com/sports/m-baskbl/archive/prov-m-baskbl-2003.html is Safe because the values of the extracted features are: [4, 58, 4, 0.0, 0, 2, 10] http://www.martin-busker.de/administrator/help/en-GB/css/Facture/c4d12146ebce8e1684d3542308399779/8fa39dab95edb1b676b638a672278eae/particuliers-45636.php is Unsafe because the values of the extracted features are: [8, 153, 10, 3.78, 13, 3, 25]

formers 4.50.1, torch 2.6.0, etc.) are added, and the configuration is inspired by web articles on the topic, such as [18].

Finally, by comparing all LLMs used, we propose to build a feature that will include the GPT's prediction on a malicious website.

3.5 ML Models and Ensembles

The baseline model is represented by the RF model imported from the scikit-learn library [32], which was trained both for multi-classification and for binary detection to provide a full understanding of the problem of malicious web links. All experiments regarding ML models could be categorized into the following steps:

1. Multi-label and binary classification for the baseline model;
2. Comparisons with other ML models;
3. Ensemble models;
4. Adding a GPT-prediction feature.

Firstly, the base model was trained in a multi-class environment and then in a binary one. For the next empirical studies, we choose to continue with binary classification because of the ease of comparisons with other literature results, where mostly binary classification is done.

Besides using the RF model, other ML algorithms were chosen to build a hierarchy of models and analyze their performance. The models depicted are all implemented with the Scikit-learn library [32] and their parameters are set to the default ones. The algorithms are: Gradient Boosted Tree (XGB), Adaptive Boosting (ADA), Logistic Regression (LR), Decision Tree (DT), Gaussian Naive Bayes (GNB), Multinomial Naive Bayes (MNB), Complement Naive Bayes (CNB), Quadratic Discriminant Analysis (QDA), Linear Discriminant Analysis (LDA), Passive Aggressive Classifier (PAC), Support Vector Machine (SVM), and K-Nearest Neighbor (KNN). One could observe that we tried to cover a wide range of classifiers: based on trees, ensembles, statistics, and so on.

The following step will try to aggregate the best performing algorithms into an ensemble to benefit from their internal detection mechanisms and improve the robustness of the overall classification. The ensemble model is a weighted-voting ensemble type and it will use weights generated from the accuracy rates obtained. Ensembles are fine-tuned considering the voting mechanisms (i.e., "hard" or "soft").

Lastly, all ML models developed will test a novel proposed feature represented by the GPT's prediction on a web link. We propose to observe if any improvements can be made by adding such a feature.

All experiments used 80% of the data for training and 20% of the data for testing.

4 Evaluation and Results

In the current section, there are presented all the computations and results obtained for all experiments: feature selection, performance metrics for OpenAI's models and the achievements obtained by the ML models. Lastly, comparisons are done and observations are discussed.

4.1 Feature Selection

Considering the feature selection process, this was done in three steps as described in the Subsect. 3.3 from Methodology 3. During the first stage, we will start with a primary set of attributes displayed in Table 1 with green color. Then, one new feature was added, and if the accuracy of the baseline RF model increased, then the feature is kept; otherwise, it is not. The characteristics shown in Table 1 with blue color improved the performance, and the remaining ones in white did not lead to a growth in accuracy.

During the second phase of feature selection, over five steps of experiments, features achieving a low relevance score were dropped. All steps are detailed in Table 3, where the green colored features represent the initial set and the blue ones were added earlier during the first stage of feature selection. The Table 3 provided importance scores and a view on how the accuracy of the RF model evolved. One could observe that during the first four steps, the accuracy is not significantly modified. However, by eliminating the count of digits, the performance drops by approximately 0.4% which, to our considerations, was important, and we decided to keep the attribute for the number of digits. The final feature set is represented by: count of dots, number of directories, total length of the URL, the number of digits, or special characters, or vowels, the Shannon entropy, and the size of the longest FQDN token.

Table 3. The feature importance scores according to the RF model and across all five steps.

Feature names	1	2	3	4	5
IP address	0	-	-	-	-
number of "." sign	0.1075	0.1022	0.1017	0.1035	0.1132
number of "@" sign	0.0014	0.0012	0.0012	-	-
Google Index	0	-	-	-	-
number of embedded domains	0.0007	0.0007	-	-	-
number of directories	0.1022	0.0974	0.0975	0.1035	0.106
URL length	0.1193	0.1176	0.1173	0.1151	0.1301
number of digits	0.0857	0.0835	0.0835	0.0848	-
number of special characters	0.0997	0.1079	0.1102	0.106	0.1095
Shannon entropy	0.1808	0.2014	0.2041	0.1908	0.2554
longest FQDN token	0.1991	0.1612	0.173	0.1745	0.1589
number of vowels	0.1032	0.1264	0.111	0.1213	0.1266
ACCURACY	93.7706	93.7898	93.7574	93.7898	93.3161

The last study for choosing the most relevant features was done by calculating the Covariance Matrix, as it can be seen in Table 4. The correlation between any two attributes is computed in the matrix. It can be observed that the total length of the web link is highly correlated with the number of special characters and the count of digits. Therefore, a decision to eliminate the one (i.e., number of digits) having the lowest relevance score according to Table 3 was made. It is expected to have such a dependency between these features because the number of digits and the number of special characters are included in the length of the URL.

4.2 OpenAI's Models Results

In [10], the GPT's experiments were done with two models: GPT-3.5-turbo and GPT-4 [29]. The results for all configurations between OpenAI's models and the prompts are presented in Table 5. One could observe that the best obtained accuracy is for Prompt 3 and GPT-4. However, the achieved performance is not comparable with other literature

Table 4. The covariance matrix computed on the third experiment.

Feature	no. directories	len. URL	no. special chars.	no. digits	Shannon entropy	longest FQDN	no. dots	no. vowels
no. directories	2.45	21.26	1.9	3.76	0.05	−0.02	0.07	6.34
len. URL	21.26	2002.91	168.4	359.64	25.57	87.48	25.53	137.88
no. special chars.	1.9	168.4	35.22	35.16	3.97	11.71	1.29	−0.45
no. digits	3.76	359.64	35.16	136.9	2.81	6.55	5.16	16.18
Shannon entropy	0.05	25.57	3.97	2.81	2.27	7.54	0.5	−2.53
longest FQDN	−0.02	87.48	11.71	6.55	7.54	31.14	1.637	−9.41
no. dots	0.07	25.53	1.29	5.16	0.5	1.637	2.22	0.58
no. vowels	6.34	137.88	−0.45	16.18	−2.53	−9.41	0.58	61.4

Table 5. The performance of the chat GPT models (3.5-turbo, 4) resulted from [10] and GPT mini models (4o-mini, o1-mini) for link classification (testing set).

Prompt	Acc.(%)	Precision	Recall	F1	Cost
GPT-3.5-turbo					
1	48.5	65	54	40	0.12 $
2	63	66	65	62	0.15 $
3	54.5	65	58	51	0.24 $
4	44.5	64	51	34	0.23 $
GPT-4					
1	60	64	60	60	1.72 $
2	61	67	64	60	3.15 $
3	65	65	65	65	7.35 $
4	64	66	65	64	9.06 $
GPT-4o-mini					
3	63.98	59.78	85.41	70.34	0.43 $
o1-mini					
3	59.7	58.98	65.36	62.01	22.7 $
GPT-2 fine-tuned					
no prompt	97.67	98.19	98.18	98.18	0 $

solutions, being considerably lower. By deciding to elaborate on the previous experiments, we proposed to experiment with mini models from OpenAI, such as gpt-4o-mini and o1-mini. These models were configured with the third prompt and tested on 4,000 samples, 2,000 links per class. Unfortunately, as can be seen from Table 5, the accuracies did not manage to outperform GPT-4 model. GPT-4o-mini comes closest with almost 64% accuracy score and a higher recall (85.41%) and F1 score (70.34%). The dissimilarities obtained for recall and F1 score may be due to the fact that the testing set had a larger number of samples, and we explicitly selected the same quality from each class (i.e., malicious or legitimate).

Furthermore, the present approach proposes to experiment with a fine-tuned LLM. Therefore, GPT-2 model was taken from HuggingFace, configured according to online tutorials, trained on 40K samples (20K for each class), and tested. The accuracy obtained (i.e., 97.67%) manages to outperform the rest of OpenAI's models. The GPT-2 was specifically tuned for classification, no prompt engineering was made, and the batch size for both training and testing was 1, such that parameters would be updated very frequently. Besides, the parameter for *gradient_accumulation_steps* was set to 4.

As observations regarding working with LLMs, more ideas could be studied in depth, especially elaborating more on prompt engineering, which has the potential to improve the performance of the models. Additionally, more LLM models could be tested (e.g., Gemini, Llama etc.) and as well train and fine-tune a pre-trained LLM or elaborate more with a Small Language Model (SLM).

4.3 ML Models Results

The very first experiments proposed involve training the baseline model, RF, in a binary-label and multi-label environment. The results are presented in Table 6. The overall accuracy was 93.31%. Additionally, it can be observed that for the malware class, the model achieves the lowest metric score. This may be happening because the "malware" class is under-represented in the dataset compared to the other labels. All the following experimental studies are considering a binary classification because of the ease of comparison with other literature solutions.

Table 6. The classification report for the baseline model RF trained and tested for the whole dataset.

Class	Precision	Recall	F1-score	Support
Benign	0.95	0.97	0.96	85,778
Phishing	0.95	0.98	0.97	19,104
Defacement	0.98	0.93	0.95	6,521
Malware	0.81	0.72	0.76	18,836
Accuracy			0.93	130,239
Macro Avg.	0.92	0.90	0.91	130,239
Weighted Avg.	0.93	0.93	0.93	130,239

By continuing the work done in [10], we choose to experiment with the same algorithms but with more samples (4,000 and 40,000). The GPT feature comes from the

Table 7. The accuracy of all ML models (testing set). Results for 1K links are taken from [10].

Model	Acc. (1K) [10]	Acc. with GPT-4 (1K) [10]	Diff. (1K)	Acc. (4K)	Acc. with GPT-2 (4K)	Diff. (4K)	Acc. (40K)	Acc. with GPT-2 (40K)	Diff. (40K)	Acc. (all) [10]
RF	88.8	89	0.2	91.72	91.25	−0.47	93.22	92.7	−0.51	95
XGB	93.4	93.3	−0.1	92.12	91.85	−0.27	91.82	91.72	−0.1	92.86
ADA	92.6	93.3	0.7	88.55	88.95	0.4	88.42	88.47	0.045	91.08
DT	91	90.9	−0.1	89.02	87.57	−1.45	92.065	92	−0.06	94.35
LR	87.9	88.3	0.4	82.25	82.35	0.1	82.1	82.062	−0.04	85.43
GNB	85.1	86.2	1.1	79.02	79.95	0.92	80.42	80.51	0.092	84.56
MNB	86.9	87.8	0.9	79.92	80.7	0.77	80.12	79.81	−0.31	84.55
CNB	86.6	86.9	0.3	79.65	79.85	0.2	79.90	80.01	0.11	84.47
MLP	90.8	91.2	0.4	88.75	88.35	−0.4	91.34	91.81	0.47	93.3
KNN	87.8	88.5	0.7	87.2	86.42	−0.77	91.02	91.09	0.067	93.38
QDA	88.2	87.3	−0.9	80.87	79.97	−0.9	79.77	79.81	0.04	84.67
LDA	88.1	87.9	−0.2	78.42	79.75	1.32	80.37	79.86	−0.51	84.99
PAC	87.7	72.1	−15.6	79.15	78.1	−1.05	70.96	74.53	3.57	83.84
SVC	86.9	87.9	1	81.57	81.39	−0.17	82.67	82.17	−0.5	87.33
AVG.	88.7	87.9	−0.8	84.16	84.03	−0.12	84.58	84.75	0.168	88.55

prediction made by GPT-2 fine-tuned, whose performance was described in the previous Subsect. 4.2. The samples were randomly selected, and each set is balanced, having the same number of malicious and legitimate URLs. The results for single ML models are detailed in Table 7, where we included the results from [10] to be able to compare. The individual ML algorithms were first trained and tested without the GPT feature and then by including this feature. Since GPT-2, after its fine-tuning process, obtained a rather high accuracy, there was an expectation that it should improve the performance of individual models. However, none of the models managed to reach the LLM's accuracy rate. The last row from Table 7 computes the average for the column. Besides, there is a column that computes the difference in accuracy between the method including GPT's classification and the one not including it. The base model runs with eight host-based or lexical features selected after the selection process described in Subsect. 4.1. In Table 7, it can be observed that overall the accuracy decreased when training on more samples (4K), but there is a low increase from 4K to 40K and from 40K to all data. The differences in performance obtained on 1K and 4K may be due to the fact that 1,000 links is not relevant in training, and the input data may be too small for that case. Related to the difference in performance when adding the GPT's label, on more data, the increase is reduced; some of the best-performing algorithms (e.g., RF, XGB, DT, etc.) do not benefit from this characteristic. However, the annotation from GPT managed to improve the detection rate for almost half of the models tested in both cases, for 4,000 and 40,000 samples. The conclusion from [10] can be applied in this case as well, that adding this feature, there is a minor growth in reliability. By observing the overall variation in differences, with more data, the difference is compressed.

For each configuration of training and testing sets, we depicted the top three most performant intelligent methods to form ensembles. The ensemble is a Weighted Voting heterogeneous one implemented with the help of the Scikit-learn Python library [32]. The voting strategy was varied (i.e., hard or soft), and the weights were according to the accuracy performance. The parameters for the ensembles are displayed in Table 8. In most cases, the ensemble contained XGB or RF models, which are according to the individual performance from Table 7.

Table 8. The weights used for the ensemble according to each dataset configuration.

Ensemble	Models	Weights
1K [10]	DT, XGB, ADA	0.91; 0.934; 0.926
1K + GPT-4 [10]	DT, XGB, ADA	0.909; 0.933; 0.933
4K	XGB, RF, DT	0.92125; 0.91725; 0.89025
4K + GPT-2	XGB, RF, ADA	0.9185; 0.9125; 0.8895
40K	RF, DT, XGB	0.932225; 0.92065; 0.918275
40K + GPT-2	RF, DT, MLP	0.92705; 0.920025; 0.918175
all [10]	DT, XGB, ADA	0.9435; 0.9286; 0.9108

Table 9 contains all results for the hybrid models with different parameter variations or datasets. The last row includes a mean computation of the column, and after each dataset configuration, a calculation column is inserted computing the between the accuracy when adding the GPT feature and when not adding it. Results for 1000 samples and the complete dataset were computed in [10]. As can be seen from Table 9, for the added experiments, there is a light enhancement in accuracy when adding the GPT feature. Moreover, when training on more data, the detection rate was boosted. The classification correctness was rather close, with not a considerable difference when varying the parameters. The training on 4000 randomly sampled data did not lead to a rise in accuracy when grouping multiple classifiers in an ensemble. However, for more data (i.e., 40,000), the performance improved to some degree.

As observations, we should add that supplementary empirical work is much needed in this case to properly adjust the weights and deliver a more robust and reliable model. Moreover, multiple LLMs or SLMs could be grouped in a hybrid model to collaborate when detecting links.

Table 9. The testing accuracy on the formed ensembles.

Ensemble	Acc. (1K) [10]	Acc. with GPT-4 (1K) [10]	Diff. (1K)	Acc. (4K)	Acc. with GPT-2 (4K)	Diff. (4K)	Acc. (40K)	Acc. with GPT-2 (40K)	Diff. (40K)	Acc. (all) [10]
voting soft	90.7	90.8	0.1	90.9	91.97	1.075	93.042	93.047	0.005	94.29
voting hard	92.7	92	−0.7	90.45	90.8	0.35	93.022	92.86	−0.162	93.06
voting soft + weights	90.7	89.3	−1.4	90.425	91.4	0.975	92.89	93.102	0.212	94.29
voting hard + weights	92.8	92.6	−0.2	91.075	90.375	−0.7	93.007	93.215	0.207	93.19
AVG.	91.725	91.175	−0.55	90.712	91.137	0.425	92.99	93.056	0.065	93.707

4.4 Comparisons and Discussion

Taking into consideration all empirical studies delivered, we proposed to develop a deep understanding of how these solutions account for other literature work. Figure 2 produces a graph where all solutions are visually represented and can be comfortably compared. The blue lines are accuracy scores obtained on the whole dataset. The red ones depict the performance achieved on 40,000 samples of URLs, and lastly, the yellow ones represent the small dataset with 4,000 samples, except for Koide et al. [12], which tested on a 2,000-link private dataset.

By comparing results obtained on the whole dataset, the performance produced by [10] is over the one from [45]. However, solutions from [10] did not surpass much more performant ideas from [36] or [4].

Setting side by side results obtained for the 40,000 dataset selected from [37], one could observe that GPT-2 fine-tuned outperforms the rest of the literature solutions, such as [3] or [4], or [5]. Moreover, the GPT-2 model trained on malicious web links detection is more accurate than other algorithms, integrating a feature based on its prediction.

Considering the small dataset of 2,000 records per class (safe or unsafe), the state-of-the-art approach from [12] tested on half of our data (i.e., 2000 samples) is closely followed by our fine-tuned LLM. The mini models from OpenAI do not reach a desirable accuracy. We think that more research should be done in prompt engineering to properly calibrate the chatbots. Our other proposed models using hand-crafted features and the GPT's prediction are over 90%, but not not pass over 94% accuracy. They are not near enough to the state-of-the-art model to be comparable.

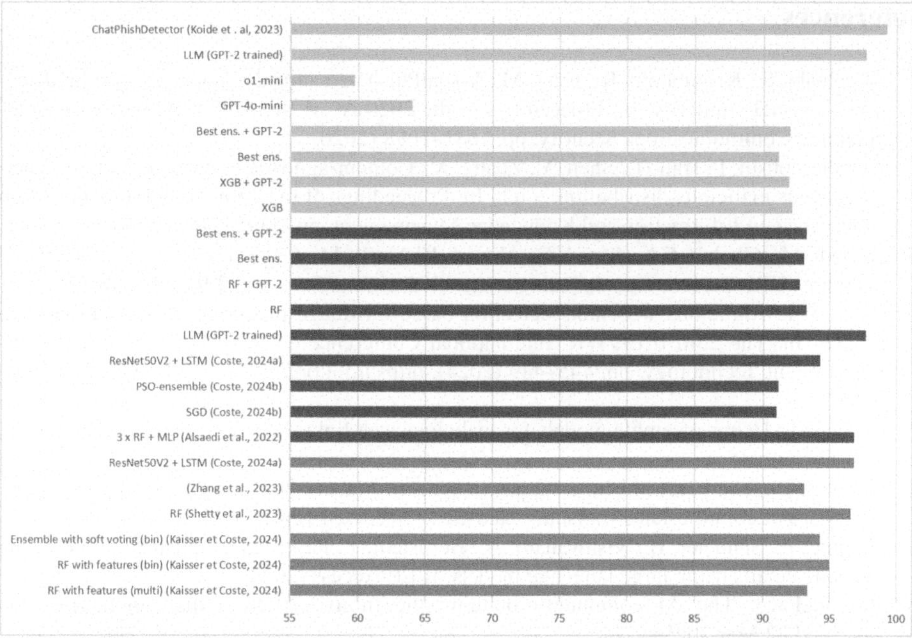

Fig. 2. Compilation of our proposed solutions and other state-of-the-art results.

5 Conclusions and Future Work

Malicious web links detection is a challenging field with many novel solutions emerging over the last years. Nonetheless, there are still things to research because of the dynamism of the domain and the sophistication of the web attacks. Leveraging Large Language Models for such complex fields can pave the way for accurate, performant, and robust solutions. The present paper proposed to train a Large Language Model (i.e., GPT-2) on detecting malicious websites. It proved a rather stable accuracy of 97%, which is surpassing other classical machine learning methods. Although adding the prediction as a feature in intelligent models, their detection rate can increase to a small degree. The tests were run under more dataset configurations and with various types of algorithms, for example, tree models, ensembles, statistical approaches, etc.

For the next ideas of research, multiple large or small language models could be tuned for the specific task of malicious web links detection. Moreover, these models could provide a factful and plausible explanation for the labeling of the URL which could help every day users to raise awareness over web threats. Additionally, a browser extension could assist consumers in protecting them from malicious attacks on the Internet and help them understand the online dangers.

Disclosure of Interests. The authors have no competing interests to declare that are relevant to the content of this article.

References

1. Abdelnabi, S., Krombholz, K., Fritz, M.: VisualPhishNet: zero-day phishing website detection by visual similarity. In: Proceedings of the 2020 ACM SIGSAC Conference on Computer and Communications Security, pp. 1681–1698 (2020)
2. Alabdulmohsin, I., Han, Y., Shen, Y., Zhang, X.: Content-agnostic malware detection in heterogeneous malicious distribution graph. In: Proceedings of the 25th ACM International on Conference on Information and Knowledge Management, pp. 2395–2400 (2016)
3. Alsaedi, M., Ghaleb, F.A., Saeed, F., Ahmad, J., Alasli, M.: Cyber threat intelligence-based malicious URL detection model using ensemble learning. Sensors **22**(9), 3373 (2022)
4. Coste, C.I.: Malicious web links detection based on image processing and deep learning models. In: The 23rd IEEE/WIC International Conference on Web Intelligence and Intelligent Agent Technology, pp. 445–449 (2024). https://doi.org/10.1109/WI-IAT62293.2024.00071
5. Coste, C.I.: Using ensemble models for malicious web links detection. In: ICAART (3), pp. 657–664 (2024)
6. Griffiths, C.: The latest phishing statistics (updated January 2025): AAG it support (2025). https://aag-it.com/the-latest-phishing-statistics/. Accessed 1 Mar 2025
7. Heiding, F., Schneier, B., Vishwanath, A., Bernstein, J., Park, P.S.: Devising and detecting phishing emails using large language models. IEEE Access (2024)
8. HuggingFace: The AI community building the future (2025). https://huggingface.co/. Accessed 22 Mar 2025
9. Joerg, S.: Using-machine-learning-to-detect-malicious-URLs (2017). https://github.com/faizann24/Using-machine-learning-to-detect-malicious-URLs/tree/master/data. Accessed 22 Mar 2025
10. Kaisser, T., Coste, C.I.: Using chat GPT for malicious web links detection. In: Proceedings of the 20th International Conference on Web Information Systems and Technologies, pp. 425–432 (2024)
11. Kepios: Digital around the world - datareportal – global digital insights. https://datareportal.com/global-digital-overview. Accessed 1 Mar 2025
12. Koide, T., Fukushi, N., Nakano, H., Chiba, D.: Detecting phishing sites using chatGPT. arXiv preprint arXiv:2306.05816 (2023)
13. Koide, T., Fukushi, N., Nakano, H., Chiba, D.: ChatSpamDetector: leveraging large language models for effective phishing email detection. In: 20th EAI International Conference on Security and Privacy in Communication Networks (SecureComm 2024) (2024)
14. Kojima, T., Gu, S.S., Reid, M., Matsuo, Y., Iwasawa, Y.: Large language models are zero-shot reasoners. Adv. Neural. Inf. Process. Syst. **35**, 22199–22213 (2022)
15. Kulkarni, A., Balachandran, V., Divakaran, D.M., Das, T.: From ML to LLM: evaluating the robustness of phishing webpage detection models against adversarial attacks. arXiv preprint arXiv:2407.20361 (2024)
16. Kumi, S., Lim, C., Lee, S.G.: Malicious URL detection based on associative classification. Entropy **23**(2), 182 (2021)
17. Le Pochat, V., Van Goethem, T., Tajalizadehkhoob, S., Korczyński, M., Joosen, W.: Tranco - a research-oriented top sites ranking hardened against manipulation. https://tranco-list.eu/. Accessed 1 Mar 2025
18. Lee, E.: Fine-tuning GPT-2 for sentiment analysis (2024). https://drlee.io/fine-tuning-gpt-2-for-sentiment-analysis-94ebdd7b5b24. Accessed 12 Mar 2025
19. Lee, J., Lim, P., Hooi, B., Divakaran, D.M.: Multimodal large language models for phishing webpage detection and identification. arXiv preprint arXiv:2408.05941 (2024)

20. Li, Y., Yang, Z., Chen, X., Yuan, H., Liu, W.: A stacking model using URL and html features for phishing webpage detection. Futur. Gener. Comput. Syst. **94**, 27–39 (2019)
21. Lin, J.: Divergence measures based on the Shannon entropy. IEEE Trans. Inf. Theory **37**(1), 145–151 (1991)
22. Lin, Y., et al.: Phishpedia: a hybrid deep learning based approach to visually identify phishing webpages. In: 30th USENIX Security Symposium (USENIX Security 21), pp. 3793–3810 (2021)
23. Ma, J., Saul, L.K., Savage, S., Voelker, G.M.: Beyond blacklists: learning to detect malicious web sites from suspicious URLs. In: Proceedings of the 15th ACM SIGKDD International Conference on Knowledge Discovery and Data Mining, pp. 1245–1254 (2009)
24. Mahdavifar, S., Maleki, N., Lashkari, A.H., Broda, M., Razavi, A.H.: Classifying malicious domains using DNS traffic analysis. In: 2021 IEEE International Conference on Dependable, Autonomic and Secure Computing, International Conference on Pervasive Intelligence and Computing, International Conference on Cloud and Big Data Computing, International Conference on Cyber Science and Technology Congress (DASC/PiCom/CBDCom/CyberSciTech), pp. 60–67. IEEE (2021)
25. malwaredomainlist: Malware domain list (2010). https://www.malwaredomainlist.com/mdl.php. Accessed 2 Apr 2025
26. Mamun, M.S.I., Rathore, M.A., Lashkari, A.H., Stakhanova, N., Ghorbani, A.A.: Detecting malicious URLs using lexical analysis. In: Chen, J., Piuri, V., Su, C., Yung, M. (eds.) NSS 2016. LNCS, vol. 9955, pp. 467–482. Springer, Cham (2016). https://doi.org/10.1007/978-3-319-46298-1_30
27. Marchal, S., François, J., State, R., Engel, T.: Phishstorm: detecting phishing with streaming analytics. IEEE Trans. Netw. Serv. Manage. **11**(4), 458–471 (2014)
28. Nagy, N., et al.: Phishing URLs detection using sequential and parallel ml techniques: comparative analysis. Sensors **23**(7), 3467 (2023)
29. OpenAI: OpenAI platform (2025). https://platform.openai.com/docs/overview. Accessed 22 Mar 2025
30. OpenPhish: Open phish - phishing intelligence (2018). https://openphish.com/. Accessed 1 Mar 2025
31. Oshingbesan, A., Okobi, C., Ekoh, C., Richard, K., Munezero, A.: Detection of malicious websites using machine learning techniques. Preprint 1–5 (2021). https://doi.org/10.13140/RG.2.2.30165.14565
32. Pedregosa, F., et al.: Scikit-learn: machine learning in Python. J. Mach. Learn. Res. **12**, 2825–2830 (2011)
33. PhishTank: PhishTank - Out of the Net, into the Tank - Developer Information (2023). https://www.phishtank.com/developer_info.php. Accessed 22 Mar 2025
34. Roy, S.S., Thota, P., Naragam, K.V., Nilizadeh, S.: From chatbots to phishbots?: phishing scam generation in commercial large language models. In: 2024 IEEE Symposium on Security and Privacy (SP), pp. 36–54. IEEE (2024)
35. Rozi, M., Ban, T., Kim, S., Ozawa, S., Takahashi, T., Inoue, D.: Detecting malicious websites based on JavaScript content analysis. In: Computer Security Symposium 2021. Computer Security Symposium 2021, Dubrovnik, Croatia (2021)
36. Shetty, U., Patil, A., Mohana, M.: Malicious URL detection and classification analysis using machine learning models. In: 2023 International Conference on Intelligent Data Communication Technologies and Internet of Things (IDCIoT), pp. 470–476. IEEE (2023)
37. Siddhartha, M.: Malicious URLs dataset (2021). https://www.kaggle.com/datasets/sid321axn/malicious-urls-dataset. Accessed 4 Apr 2025
38. Tushkanov, V.: Investigating chatGPT phishing detection capabilities (2023). https://securelist.com/chatgpt-anti-phishing/109590/. Accessed 22 Mar 2025

39. Vaswani, A., et al.: Attention is all you need. Adv. Neural Inf. Process. Syst. **30** (2017)
40. Vikramaditya, N.: Googlesearch-python (2025). https://pypi.org/project/googlesearch-python/. Accessed 22 Mar 2025
41. VirusTotal: Virustotal: Analyse suspicious files, domains, IPs and URLs. https://www.virustotal.com. Accessed 1 Mar 2025
42. Wei, J., et al.: Chain-of-thought prompting elicits reasoning in large language models. Adv. Neural. Inf. Process. Syst. **35**, 24824–24837 (2022)
43. Wejinya, G., Bhatia, S.: Machine learning for malicious URL detection. In: Tuba, M., Akashe, S., Joshi, A. (eds.) ICT Systems and Sustainability. AISC, vol. 1270, pp. 463–472. Springer, Singapore (2021). https://doi.org/10.1007/978-981-15-8289-9_45
44. Yao, Y., Duan, J., Xu, K., Cai, Y., Sun, Z., Zhang, Y.: A survey on large language model (LLM) security and privacy: the good, the bad, and the ugly. High-Confidence Comput. 100211 (2024)
45. Zhang, L., Yan, Q.: Detect malicious websites by building a neural network to capture global and local features of websites. Research Square (2023)

Web Intelligence and Semantic Web

Efficient Fine-Tuning for Domain-Specific Language Models: SLIM-RAFT

Vinícius Di Oliveira[1,2(✉)], Pedro Carvalho Brom[1,3], Yuri Façanha Bezerra[1], Li Weigang[1], and Victor Rafael R. Celestino[4]

[1] TransLab, University of Brasilia, Brasilia, Federal District, Brazil
vinidiol@gmail.com, weigang@unb.br
[2] Secretary of Economy, Brasilia, Federal District, Brazil
[3] Instituto Federal de Brasilia, Brasilia, Federal District, Brazil
[4] LAMFO, Department of Administration, University of Brasilia, Brasilia, Federal District, Brazil
https://www.translab.unb.br

Abstract. Natural Language Processing (NLP) has witnessed significant advancements with the emergence of Large Language Models (LLMs). However, considerable improvements remain necessary for languages other than English, particularly in specialised domains such as the application of the Mercosur Common Nomenclature (NCM)—an adaptation of the Harmonised System (HS) for the Mercosur countries—and the Brazilian ZIP Code system, known as CEP. The limited availability of high-performance LLMs tailored for these tasks presents a critical challenge for accurate and efficient classification and retrieval processes. This study employs TeenyTineLLaMA, a foundational Portuguese LLM, as the base model for two specialised applications to address this gap. A novel approach, Simplified Retrieval-Augmented Fine-Tuning (SLIM-RAFT), is introduced to facilitate LLMs' efficient, task-specific fine-tuning. This technique introduces the Sequence-of-Sets (SoS) prompting strategy—a refined chain-of-thought (CoT) methodology—by leveraging the transitivity property of sets to streamline prompt development concisely and in a structured manner. The proposed model is a cost-effective and computationally efficient alternative for fine-tuning smaller-scale LLMs, significantly surpassing the performance of both TeenyTineLLaMA and ChatGPT-4 in the designated classification tasks. Although this research primarily focuses on NCM and CEP applications, the methodology is readily adaptable to broader international contexts, including HS and ZIP Code applications worldwide, thereby demonstrating its broader applicability and scalability.

Keywords: Fine-tuning · HS · Large language model · NCM · Portuguese language · Retrieval augmented generation · Prompting engineering

1 Introduction

The widespread application of Generative Artificial Intelligence (GenAI) systems has significantly advanced the development of artificial intelligence [21,22]. On the one

M. Marchiori et al. (Eds.): WEBIST 2024, LNBIP 583, pp. 161–182, 2026.
https://doi.org/10.1007/978-3-032-25534-1_7

hand, more sophisticated large language models (LLMs), such as ChatGPT, possess multilingual capabilities to process multimodal information and have become key drivers for AI applications [33]. However, for most users, effective use of these models requires enhancing prompt engineering skills. On the other hand, open-source large language models, such as LLaMA 3, can locally fine-tune models, catering to specific security and flexibility needs. Nonetheless, non-English users may encounter limitations due to the composition of LLaMA's training corpus, predominantly English-based (90%), with only a tiny portion (10%) dedicated to other languages, including French, Spanish, and Portuguese.

While LLMs offer cross-language processing capabilities, enabling some understanding of related languages, particularly within the Latin language group, these capabilities are often insufficient for more nuanced language processing tasks [24]. This is especially true for tasks involving technical terminology and enterprise-specific privacy data requirements. The limited proportion of pre-trained Portuguese corpus in models like LLaMA highlights these constraints, revealing significant limitations in their language processing capabilities for non-English languages.

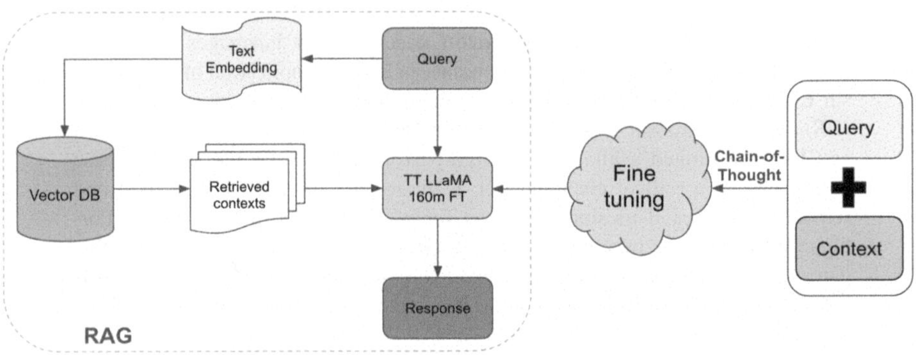

Fig. 1. The SLIM-RAFT diagram [1].

Another way to tackle these downstream tasks could be to use significantly smaller LLMs and perform fine-tuning by retraining the model parameters, as demonstrated in the TeenyTineLLaMA model [3], which is the approach addressed in this work. This approach considers that subsequent tasks have a well-defined and reduced scope but preserves the essence of using LLMs.

Retrieval-Augmented Generation (RAG) addresses several critical challenges inherent in LLMs [7,13]. These challenges encompass hallucinations, outdated knowledge, and nontransparent, untraceable reasoning processes. By incorporating information from external databases, RAG significantly improves the accuracy and credibility of generated content, particularly for knowledge-intensive tasks. This approach facilitates continuous updates of knowledge and the integration of domain-specific information, effectively merging the intrinsic capabilities of LLMs with the extensive and dynamic repositories of external databases. Consequently, RAG provides a robust solution for improving the performance and reliability of language models, making it an invaluable approach across diverse applications.

In pursuit of enhancing the performance of LLM in downstream applications, Retrieval-Augmented Fine-Tuning (RAFT) presents numerous significant benefits [30,35]. Although pretraining LLMs on extensive corpora of textual data is now standard practice, integrating new, time-sensitive, or domain-specific knowledge remains a complex challenge. Traditional methodologies such as RAG-based prompting or fine-tuning are frequently employed; however, RAFT offers a more optimal approach to embedding such knowledge. RAFT distinguishes itself by training the model to ignore distractor documents, those that do not contribute to answering the query. By concentrating on pertinent documents and accurately citing the sequences necessary for responding to questions, RAFT substantially enhances the model's reasoning abilities. This chain-of-thought response mechanism refines the model's overall performance. Despite the positive results of this technique, producing the training base according to the chain-of-thought model is difficult and expensive, as another powerful LLM is required.

This work focuses on the MERCOSUR Common Nomenclature (NCM) code system, which is used by all member countries of MERCOSUR. The NCM code system is derived from the Harmonized Commodity Description and Coding System, commonly known as the "Harmonized System" (HS), which is a multipurpose international product nomenclature developed by the World Customs Organization and used by more than 200 countries. The NCM code is widely used in Brazil and is mandatory for all domestic sales operations and international import and export transactions. Due to the complexity of the NCM system, which involves product classification, specifications, and tax ranges, advanced language processing capabilities are required. Ordinary English-Portuguese translation is inadequate for this process, as it requires a sophisticated understanding of Portuguese and precise handling of proper nouns. Preliminary experiments indicate that using only ChatGPT or TeenyTineLLaMA, a Portuguese LLM, is insufficient for effectively processing these tasks.

The simple task of classifying commodity descriptions can be handled with more straightforward techniques like neural networks by a hierarchical sequence learning [6]. This study aims not merely to classify product descriptions but to extract the inherent knowledge within the NCM code system. The model can be enriched with specialised knowledge by elucidating the semantic relationships between product descriptions and their respective classifications. Such enhancements hold considerable potential for commerce, compliance, and taxation applications.

This study extends the research introduced for the "Simplified Logical Intelligent Model Retrieval-Augmented Fine-Tuning" - SLIM-RAFT [1] model to effectively address the challenges associated with the NCM code. It considers the constraints of developing a comprehensive training base akin to the original RAFT model. The SLIM-RAFT model can be applied to any element description and multi-classification problems. To demonstrate this capability, we extend the experiment to tackle the classification challenge of the CEP code (the Brazilian ZIP code for addresses). Like the problem of interpreting product descriptions in the NCM code, interpreting addresses for the CEP code brings many abbreviated, truncated, and misspelled words. Therefore, this is a significant challenge for language models.

A distinguishing feature of the SLIM-RAFT model is its significantly smaller LLM source use than traditional models. Specifically, the TeenyTineLLaMA model, comprising only 160 million parameters, was utilised in constructing SLIM-RAFT as the fine-tuned LLM. The results achieved by our model substantially outperform those of ChatGPT 4 in the proposed challenge: ChatGPT 4 scored 4.5/10, whereas SLIM-RAFT achieved an impressive score of 8.67/10. The SLIM-RAFT scheme can be seen in Fig. 1.

This paper is organized as follows:

- Section 2 presents the works directly related to the ideas proposed in constructing SLIM-RAFT;
- Section 3 shows the structure of the HS and NCM codes and the Brazilian ZIP Code;
- Section 4 properly demonstrates the construction of the SLIM-RAFT model;
- Section 5 presents the results obtained in the comparative evaluations of the models and discusses what was found;
- Section 6 concludes the work and suggests future work related to the presented model.

2 Related Works

This section presents the related work in two areas: 1) research on the implementation of LLMs with Portuguese as the primary language and 2) studies on Retrieval-Augmented Generation (RAG) and Retrieval-Augmented Fine-Tuning (RAFT).

2.1 Portuguese LLM's

The introduction of LLaMA [25] as an open and efficient foundational language model marked a significant milestone in the evolution of language processing. With models spanning 7 billion to 65 billion parameters, LLaMA underscored the viability of training cutting-edge models exclusively on publicly available datasets. Notably, the LLaMA-13B model surpassed GPT-3 in various benchmarks, demonstrating its remarkable performance despite a comparatively smaller parameter count. This initial success paved the way for subsequent iterations, with LLaMA 2 and 3 [19,26] further refining the models. These later versions, particularly tailored for dialogue applications, introduced fine-tuned language models optimized for chat interfaces. Consequently, these early advancements laid a robust foundation for future progress in natural language processing.

Although ample data exists for training transformer-based language models in Portuguese, native speakers can readily discern limitations in the text generation and performance of pre-trained models primarily derived from English language data. In recent years, there has been a rising interest in the development and enhancement of large-scale language models tailored to the Portuguese language. This trend has been propelled by pioneering and innovative research efforts, as evidenced by numerous recent contributions to the field.

In European Portuguese (PT-PT), the initiative known as GlórIA [14] merits particular attention. This project involves a trained decoder language model meticulously constructed from a corpus comprising 35 billion tokens from various sources.

For Brazilian Portuguese (PT-BR), the first relevant LLM encountered was Sabiá [20]. This initiative underscores the development of robust and scalable language models for the Portuguese language. Leveraging advanced machine learning architectures, these models have been instrumental in advancing natural language processing applications in Brazilian Portuguese.

The Cabrita model [12] was launched as a low-cost alternative for training LLMs. The authors posited that their methodology could be extended to any transformer-like architecture. To substantiate their hypothesis, they undertook continuous pre-training exclusively on Portuguese text using a 3-billion-parameter model known as OpenLLaMA. This effort culminated in the creation of openCabrita 3B. Remarkably, openCabrita 3B incorporates a novel tokenizer, significantly reducing the number of tokens necessary to represent the text. Subsequently, in a comparable approach, a new study introduced a model predicated on LLaMA 2, designed specifically for handling prompts in Portuguese. This model, named Bode [8], is available in two versions: one with 7B and 13B parameters. Both models used the LoRa [10] fine-tuning method over an open-source LLM. This technique preserves the original parameters intact while introducing a new terminal layer atop the model, which is subsequently trained to achieve the desired fine-tuning outcome.

A noteworthy recent publication entitled "TeenyTinyLlama: Open Source Tiny Language Models Trained in Brazilian Portuguese" [3] offers a valuable perspective on developing compact, open source language models tailored to Brazilian Portuguese. Despite their reduced scale, these models hold significant potential for democratizing access to natural language processing technology, particularly within resource-limited communities.

Collectively, these works signify substantial advancements in implementing language models for the Portuguese language. They underscore the diversity of methodologies and the abundance of resources that bolster research and applications in natural language processing and related fields. These ongoing initiatives are poised to continue influencing the future of language technology for Portuguese speakers globally.

2.2 Retrieval-Augmented Approach

Retrieval Augmented Generation - RAG [13] represents a transformative approach to enriching the quality and pertinence of generated content by integrating external insights derived from extensive datasets or repositories of knowledge. By embedding pertinent external knowledge sources into the generation process, RAG is designed to elevate the coherence, factual precision, and overall utility of generated text. This methodology proves advantageous in domains necessitating precise and contextually nuanced content generation, such as question-answering, summarizing, and advanced dialogue systems. By controlling retrieval mechanisms, RAG ensures that the resultant outputs are provided with high accuracy and contextual relevance, thereby advancing the frontiers of natural language processing applications.

In pursuit of enhancing the precision of model responses and mitigating the phenomenon of LLM hallucinations, a novel approach has emerged: Retrieval Augmented Fine-Tuning (RAFT) [35]. This methodology integrates the RAG framework with fine-tuning techniques, empowering models not only to acquire domain-specific knowledge but also to adeptly retrieve and comprehend external contexts crucial for task execution. RAFT introduces the idea of chain-of-thought prompting for building the fine-tuning data set. This prompting technique enables the model's answers to show its reason line with a sequence of arguments, enhancing its explicability.

RAG and RAFT were designed to confront the complexity of tailoring LLMs to specialized domains. Within these realms, the emphasis pivots from general knowledge reasoning to optimizing accuracy *vis-à-vis* a meticulously defined array of domain-specific documents.

2.3 NCM Data Set

The ELEVEN data set, ELEctronic inVoicEs in the Portuguese language [5], was meticulously curated to furnish researchers and entrepreneurs with a repository of product descriptions categorized under the Mercosur Common Nomenclature (NCM). This extensive database comprises over a million meticulously labelled records, each scrutinized by taxation experts. These descriptions are short texts, limited to 120 characters, and extracted from authentic electronic invoices documenting purchase and sales transactions.

Labelled datasets are a rare commodity, yet they provide indispensable resources for applications reliant on supervised learning [28]. The ELEVEN dataset has served as a cornerstone for several noteworthy academic endeavours: 1) the development of a CNN-based system for classifying goods [11]; 2) the creation of data visualization tools aimed at identifying outliers and detecting fraud [16]; and 3) the establishment of a framework utilizing automatic encoders to cluster short-text data extracted from electronic invoices, thereby enhancing anomaly detection within numeric fields [23].

3 HS, NCM and CEP Codes

In the dynamic realm of international trade, customs brokers, exporters, and importers confront the critical task of accurately classifying goods under the Harmonized System (HS) Code, which underpins the Mercosur Common Nomenclature (NCM) code [27].

The Harmonized System (HS) is the foundation for customs tariffs and the compilation of international trade statistics in over 200 countries and economies. Beyond these primary functions, the HS is employed for various other purposes, including the monitoring of controlled goods, establishing rules of origin, and facilitating trade negotiations. It is also a crucial component of fundamental customs controls and procedures [32].

The MERCOSUR Common Nomenclature - NCM code system (*Nomenclatura Comun do Mercosul* in Portuguese) is utilized by all member countries of MERCOSUR: Argentina, Brazil, Paraguay, Uruguay, and Venezuela [18]. In Brazil, including the NCM code is a legal requirement on every electronic invoice issued. Consequently, all commercial transactions, whether domestic or international, must incorporate this code [2].

The Harmonized Commodity Description and Coding System, generally called the "Harmonized System" or simply "HS," is a multipurpose international product nomenclature developed by the World Customs Organization [31]. The HS structure is shown in Table 1. The NCM, structured hierarchically in the same way as HS, consists of numerical codes assigned to various products, thereby facilitating their identification and categorization in trade agreements and customs processes [17].

Table 1. Structure of the HS Codes [31].

2 digit (01–97)	Chapter
4 digit (01.01–97.06)	Heading
6 digit (0101.21–9706.00)	Subheading

Table 2 shows an HS list cutout, showing the distinction in classification codes for fresh and dried apples. While this differentiation may appear trivial, in an import operation where each type of apple is subject to different tax treatments, an error in code designation can result in significant repercussions. On one hand, the seller faces the risk of tax penalties, while on the other, customs authorities may encounter a loss of revenue.

Table 2. Headings 08.08 and 08.13 in the HS [31].

08.08	Apples, pears and quinces, fresh.
0808.10	- Apples
0808.30	- Pears
0808.40	- Quinces
...	...
08.13	- Fruit, dried, other than that of headings 08.01 to 08.06; mixtures of nuts or dried fruits of this Chapter.
0813.10	- Apricots
0813.20	- Prunes
0813.30	- Apples
0808.40	- Other Fruit
0808.50	- Mixtures of nuts or dried fruits of this Chapter

Accurate classification of goods is paramount, as it directly impacts taxation, compliance with specific regulations such as sanitary and phytosanitary standards, and eligibility for benefits under international trade agreements. Misclassification can lead to penalties, delays in customs clearance, and substantial financial losses [34].

The MERCOSUR Common Nomenclature code system adds two digits to the HS structure, making it possible to address new items and their respective subgroups, as seen in Table 3. This system allows for a more precise and specialized classification of products, enabling more items to be catalogued distinctly by accounting for their specific characteristics.

Table 3. Structure of the NCM Codes [17].

2 digit (01–97)	Chapter
4 digit (01.01–97.06)	Heading
6 digit (0101.21–9706.00)	Subheading
7 digit (0101.21.1–9706.00.9)	Item
8 digit (0101.21.10–9706.00.90)	Sub-item

The Brazilian Postal Code - CEP (*Código de Endereçamento Postal* in Portuguese) is made up of eight digits, five main digits and three additional digits. The standard format is "nnnnn-nnn". The first digit represents a large geographic region. In Brazil, each number from 0 to 9 is assigned to a specific region. The second two digits, together with the first digit, identify a sub-region or sector within the large region [4]. The last three digits, help identify specific neighborhoods, streets or businesses. The Table 4 shows the CEP Code components.

This coding can be illustrated with the example of the CEP code of the University of Brasilia Campus: 70.910-900. The first digit, "7", indicates the Central-West region of Brazil, and the second digit "0" indicates the city of Brasilia. The triplet formed by the third, fourth, and fifth digits "910" indicate the sector and subsector of the town where the university is located, while the suffix "900" at the end indicates a code for a large correspondence receiver.

Table 4. Components of the CEP Code [4].

X0000-000:	Region
0X000-000:	Sub-region
00X00-000:	Sector
000X0-000:	Subsector
0000X-000:	Subsector divisor
00000-XXX:	Distribution suffix

The task of classifying product descriptions within the HS or NCM system has been explored in academic literature [6, 11, 23]. Techniques such as neural networks with hierarchical learning and convolutional neural networks (CNNs) have been effectively employed to address this task. Nevertheless, certain challenges associated with this domain remain insufficiently addressed.

One notable challenge is the variability in product descriptions: the same product can be described in multiple ways, and context-dependent synonyms and abbreviations further complicate classification. This complexity makes using LLMs a compelling alternative for interpreting product descriptions. Beyond simple classification, LLMs offer the potential to extract deeper knowledge by identifying relationships between products. Table 5 shows some abbreviations that can be easily found.

Table 5. Abbreviation examples of some product descriptions [1].

English	
Coc. 2L	= Coca-Cola 2 Liters
P. W. Rice	= Parboiled White Rice
Portuguese	
Fr. Desc.	= Fralda descartável (*Disposable diaper*)
T. Pap. FDupla	= Toalha de Papel Folha Dupla (*Double Ply Paper Towel*)
French	
EDT	= Eau de Toilette
EDP	= Eau de Parfum

Context is crucial in language processing, as it can help resolve ambiguities that often arise when considering abbreviations in isolation. This is where TRANSFORMER-based algorithms shine, as their ability to understand context is key [29]. For example, the abbreviation "fr." in Portuguese could refer to "fralda" (diaper), as shown in Table 5, or it could mean "fruta" (fruit). However, when the term "desc" (meaning "descartável" or disposable) follows, the context effectively resolves the ambiguity between "fralda" and "fruit".

When we look at the problem of interpreting address descriptions for their CEP codes, we also face the same challenge of understanding the address without knowing the context. Let us examine the following variations of the descriptions for the same CEP code in Table 6.

This type of problem can be understood as a lexical normalization challenge, which is also observed in residential and commercial addresses. In the case of the classification of the CEP code for a given address, the context would disambiguate the terms, but unfortunately, as in the case of NCM codes, this does not always happen.

Therefore, developing LLMs capable of dealing with NCM, HS and CEP codes is useful in many fields, especially compliance and tax inspection for NCM and HS codes.

Import and export companies, as well as trading companies in general, are interested in issuing their invoices correctly under current regulations. Errors in product descriptions or their classification according to HS and NCM codes may result in financial penalties or even legal prohibitions of trading.

Customs authorities carefully observe the correct indication of HS and NCM codes, as the tax treatment of those products will be defined through this classification. Misguided indications in these codes can be interpreted as an intention to circumvent the

Table 6. Address descriptions for the CEP Code 70.854-050.

English	
1	Super Block North 209, Block E, Asa Norte Neighbor., City: Brasília
2	SBN 209, bl E, Asa N. Brasília
3	SBNorth 209, block E, A. Norte BSB
Portuguese	
1	Super Quadra Norte 209, Bloco E, Bairro Asa Norte, Cidade: Brasília
2	SQN 209, bl E, Asa N. Brasília
3	SQNorte 209, bloco E, A. Norte Brasília

rules to pay less taxes. Of course, fines or other sanctions may be applied to those responsible for the commercial transaction involved.

Therefore, using AI models can improve controlling and correcting the issuance of invoices and related documents [11, 16].

4 SLIM-RAFT Model

The SLIM-RAFT model simplifies RAFT logically and intelligently. Just as RAFT maintains the RAG in its designed form, SLIM-RAFT also maintains the RAG mechanism in its structure; see Fig. 1.

The preceding sections have elucidated that constructing the training base in the original RAFT model is an expensive endeavour, frequently necessitating the deployment of another powerful LLM. This substantial cost is predominantly attributable to two features of RAFT: the chain-of-thought reasoning and the inclusion of irrelevant documents. While the concept of learning to disregard irrelevant documents is both valid and logical within the context of RAFT's objectives, it is not a requisite for all applications. This insight prompted the exclusion of this feature in the development of SLIM-RAFT.

SLIM-RAFT retains the chain-of-thought concept in its fine-tuning process, albeit simplified. Instead of using lengthy texts or entire documents as input, the approach employs logical arguments derived from the knowledge base. For instance: 1) element "a" belongs to set A; 2) set A is contained within set B; 3) consequently, "a" belongs to set B. The next subsection will explain how it was done.

4.1 Fine-Tuning Database and Prompting

The simplified chain of thought prompting technique created for SLIM-RAFT was named "Sequence-of-Sets" (SoS). It is a reasoning based on the **property of transitivity** between sets, which is a property that is established when an element has a relationship with a second element, and this has a relationship with a third, then the first element has a relationship with the third.

- Doc. 1:

$$a \in A \tag{1}$$

- Doc. 2:

$$A \subseteq B \tag{2}$$

- Doc. 3: Consequently,

$$\therefore a \in B \tag{3}$$

This was an application of the training base built for fine-tuning within the idea of the simplified chain-of-thought named "Sequence-of-Sets" (SoS). See below for a generic example of a prompt:

```
[
  {
    "content":
   [context 1 ]....\n
   [context 2 ]...\n
   [context 3 ]...\n
   [...] ... \n
   [context n]... \n
   \n
   Answer the following question using information
   from the previous context: question", "role":
   "user"
  },
  {
  "content": "response + reasoning based on context",
  "role": "assistant"
 }
]
```

Even with the prompting strategy for fine-tuning defined, it is still necessary to build the training base with a few thousand samples. The process of building the base for fine-tuning will be described below.

An expert in the NCM code developed a series of question-and-answer sets, complete with their respective arguments. Utilising the open version of ChatGPT 3.5, numerous variations of these questions were generated. Subsequently, a Python script was employed to create thousands of pairs [question + argument, answer + argument], wherein information derived from the NCM database populated the generic questions.

An example of a generic question used in constructing the NCM base is as follows:

```
[
 {
  "content":
```

```
        [product {{product}} has NCM code {{NCM}}], \n
        [which refers to the category {{category}}] \n
        \n
        Answer the following question using information
        from the previous context: What is the 'category' of
        the 'product' {{product}}?", "role": "user"
      },
      {
        "content": "the product {{product}} has the NCM code
        {{NCM}}, which refers to the category {{category}},
        "role": "assistant"
      }
    ]
```

A sample record in Portuguese as it was recorded is provided in the Appendix of this work.

Then, for building a data training base in SLIM-RAFT mode, there are three steps:

1. A domain expert creates a small question-and-answer set, e.g. *"What is the category of the product ''product'?"*;
2. Construct question-and-answer set variations (an LLM could be used), e.g. *"Could you specify the category to which the product 'product' belongs?"*;
3. Populate de question-and-answer set mask. e.g. *"What is the category of the product 'fresh apple package'?", "Could you specify the category to which the product 'fresh apple package' belongs?"*

The total number of records in the data training base will be:

$$N = q \times v \times n \tag{4}$$

where q is the number of question-and-answer created by the domain expert, v is the number of variations from each question-and-answer unit, and n is the total number of samples from the NCM database.

As delineated earlier, a notable distinction between SLIM-RAFT and the original RAFT lies in the simplified approach to constructing the fine-tuning base while preserving the chain-of-thought methodology.

According to the procedure reported above, a database of 100k records was built and made available[1]. For comparison and evaluation purposes, a database with 240k queries (simple questions and answers) was also made available without the use of the Sequence-of-Sets (SoS) prompt technique[2].

The CEP code challenge was addressed in the same way as described above. For this purpose, a database of 48k samples was constructed and made available using the Sequence-of-Sets technique to fine-tune models[3].

[1] https://huggingface.co/datasets/yurifacanha/NCM-RAFT-samall.
[2] https://huggingface.co/datasets/yurifacanha/NCM-dataset.
[3] https://huggingface.co/datasets/vinidiol/FT_CEP.

4.2 Source LLM and Fine-Tuning

The LLM source chosen for this work was Teeny TinyLLaMA - TTL, available in two sizes: 460 million and 160 million parameters. Two primary characteristics of TTL guided this selection: its compact size and the training on a corpus in Brazilian Portuguese.

While other source models trained in Brazilian Portuguese exist, as discussed in Sect. 2, their substantial size can make fine-tuning costly, even when employing optimised techniques such as LoRa [10]. In contrast, the compact size of TTL made our fine-tuning process more cost-effective, demonstrating its practicality and potential for wider application.

The Fine-tuning process adjusts all model parameters. The reduced size of TTL facilitated this task. The codes employed were adapted from those provided by the authors of the original TTL paper (available on GitHub[4]) with minor modifications.

The total cost of building the fine-tuning database shown here, including the experimental tests, was less than 100 USD with the ChatGPT API. The fine-tuning processing was done using Google Colab, an A100 GPU was used for this task. The total training time was around two hours.

All codes developed for SLIM-RAFT are accessible on SLIM-RAFT's GitHub repository. Both TTL models, 160 million and 460 million parameters, were fine-tuned to create SLIM-RAFT. The 160 million parameter version was used in SLIM-RAFT, while the 460 million parameter version was used for comparative analysis during the final model evaluation.

The SLIM-RAFT GitHub repository[5] is a valuable resource that provides the codes used in this study. This open access not only allows the community to reproduce and assess this experiment but also encourages further collaboration and potential contributions to natural language processing.

5 Results and Discussion

The results were evaluated through a comparative analysis of the responses delivered by the tested models. Three other models were chosen for this comparison: TeenyTinyLLaMA 460 m, TeenyTinyLLaMA 460 m + NCM fine-tuning, and ChatGPT 4. In the end, four models were tested and evaluated by ChatGPT 4.0:

- Model 1: TeenyTinyLlama with tiny460M without fine-tuning on the dataset, defined as TTL.
- Model 2: ChatGPT 4.0, defined as GPT.
- Model 3: TeenyTinyLlama with fine-tuning on the NCM dataset, defined as NCM-TTL.
- Model 4: TinyLlama with fine-tuning on the NCM dataset and using SLIM RAFT, defined as SLIM-RAFT.

[4] https://github.com/Nkluge-correa/TeenyTinyLlama.
[5] https://github.com/yurifacanha/ncmrag.

The model responses were then submitted to ChatGPT-4, which compared the outputs produced with the desired outputs. To ensure impartiality in the evaluation, it is important to note that ChatGPT-4 was not informed of the model to which each response was referred.

The same experiment was replicated for the CEP code problem to demonstrate the flexibility of using SLIM-RAFT, as well as the efficiency of the Sequence-of-Sets (SoS) prompting technique. To evaluate the model built for the CEP code, SLIM-RAFT-CEP, the results were compared with the TeenyTinyLLaMA 460 m and ChatGPT 4.0 models.

5.1 Results Presentation

The evaluation used 100 questions and answers not included in the fine-tuning training base. These 100 questions were presented to various models and their responses were recorded and compared. ChatGPT-4 assessed the quality of each response, scoring it on a scale of 0 to 10. The final score for each model represents the average of the scores assigned to each response. Table 7 presents the results of this evaluation. It is clear that Model 4 of SLIM RAFT achieved the best score of 8.63 with a standard deviation of 2.30 across the 100 Q/As.

Table 7. NCM Score results between the four models. [1].

Model	Aver.	St. Dev.	Min.	Max.
TTL	0.2	0.98	0	5
NCM-TTL	4.71	3.53	0	10
GPT 4.0	4.5	1.39	0	5
SLIM-RAFT	8.63	2.30	0	10

Table 9 and Table 10 provides a clear comparison of the responses generated by all models, with the desired response serving as the benchmark for evaluation. This benchmark response sets a standard against which the models' performance can be measured.

Table 8. CEP Score results between the three models.

Model	Aver.	St. Dev.	Min.	Max.
TTL	0.39	0.063	0	2
GPT 4.o mini	1.90	0.067	0	3
SLIM-RAFT-CEP	1.92	0.039	0	2

The evaluation of the SLIM-RAFT for CEP code model was carried out in the same way as that presented for SLIM-RAFT previously. 100 new questions were asked of the model, and its results were compared with TTL and ChatGPT 4.o mini, as can be seen in Table 8. The score achieved by the SLIM-RAFT model was similar to that achieved by OpenAI's 4.o mini model. We highlight that our model uses an open-source LLM with 160M parameters, while the 4.o mini is a state-of-the-art LLM with billions of parameters. Therefore, the application of SLIM-RAFT was successful in both tested domains. All codes used for the CEP applications are available on GitHub[6].

5.2 LLM Justification

It is essential to underscore the potential utility of an LLM specialized in this type of task, as it extends beyond mere classification. Whereas a straightforward input-output classification system is confined to specific subjects and input formats, an LLM system can extract semantic knowledge from the training base and demonstrates flexibility in handling various input formats.

Answering a simple direct question like "What is the NCM code for the product *fresh apple package*" is not enough. The question can come in several forms or be embedded in a larger context, for example: "I don't know the NCM code for *fresh apple package*, can you help me?".

Another pertinent scenario involves cases of attempted tax evasion. For instance, if the product *fresh apple package* is exempt from taxation while *apple juice package* is subject to tax, it could be misleadingly described in a tax document as *apple j. pack.* but assigned the NCM code for *fresh apples package*, which is tax-exempt. If this discrepancy goes undetected by customs authorities, it could result in a loss of revenue due to the uncollected tax.

The SLIM-RAFT model can effectively help a system for controlling and inspect documents regarding the NCM Code misuse. But, because of its reduced size, the capability of extracting the right question embedded in a bigger context is limited. Let us consider the following example:

Portuguese - *Fui na padaria e comprei um suco de laranja, percebi que na nota fiscal aparecia um código chamado NCM, mas estava com a impressão borrada. Qual seria o código impresso?*

English - at the bakery and bought some orange juice, I noticed that a code called NCM appeared on the invoice, but the print was blurry. What would be the printed code?

When presented with this query, our model may not discern the central issue, namely, "What is the NCM category for orange juice?" Integrating an additional LLM into the system could mitigate this limitation.

The Few-shot prompting technique [9, 15] can enable other large language models (LLMs) to reformulate queries, thereby adapting the context to enhance comprehension by the smaller LLM integrated within the SLIM-RAFT model. This approach is shown above.

[6] https://github.com/pcbrom/webist_cep.

Table 9. Comparison of Q/A results of four models in Portuguese [1].

Q/A and Models	Sample question - Portuguese
Prompting	Qual a categoria NCM correta para o produto : LIMPADOR VEJA PERF.NAT PERF.SUAVE 1LT? Responda apenas a descrição da categoria . Caso não saiba responda a categoria que mais se aproxima. Não adicione qualquer qualquer outro comentário à sua resposta
Expected Answear	Outros agentes orgânicos de superfície (exceto sabões); preparações tensoativas, preparações para lavagem (incluídas as preparações auxiliares para lavagem) e preparações para limpeza (inclusive multiuso e limpadores), mesmo contendo sabão, exceto os produtos descritos nos CEST 11.001.00, 11.004.00, 11.005.00 e 11.006.00; em embalagem de conteúdo inferior ou igual a 50 litros ou 50 kg
TeenyTinyLLaMA	Não consigo responder com base nas informações fornecidas. No entanto, posso fornecer uma explicação geral de como categorizar produtos NCM, incluindo categorias específicas e suas respectivas categorias
ChatGPT 4.0	Preparações para limpeza
TeenyTinyLLaMAFT PT NCM	A categoria NCM correta é: Agentes orgânicos de superfície (exceto sabões); preparações tensoativas, preparações para lavagem (incluindo as preparações auxiliares para lavagem) e preparações para limpeza, mesmo que contenham sabão, exceto as da posição 34.01. - Preparações acondicionadas para venda a retalho
SLIM-RAFT	o produto LIMPADOR VEJA PERF.NAT PERF. SUAVE 1LT possui categoria: Sabões, agentes orgânicos de superfície, preparações para lavagem, preparações lubrificantes, ceras artificiais, ceras preparadas, produtos de conservação e limpeza, velas e artigos semelhantes, massas ou pastas para modelar, "ceras para odontologia" e composições para odontologia à base de gesso. - Agentes orgânicos de superfície (exceto sabões); preparações tensoativas, preparações para lavagem (incluindo as preparações auxiliares para lavagem) e preparações para limpeza, mesmo que contenham sabão, exceto as da posição 34.01. - - - Preparações acondicionadas para venda a retalho

Table 10. Comparison of Q/A results of four models in English [1].

Q/A and Models	Sample question - English
Prompting	What is the correct NCM category for the product: CLEANER VEJA PERF.NAT PERF. SOFT 1LT? Respond only to the category description. If you don't know, answer the category that comes closest. Do not add any other comments to your answer
Expected Answear	Other organic surface agents (except soaps); surfactant preparations, washing preparations (including auxiliary washing preparations) and cleaning preparations (including multipurpose preparations and cleaners), whether or not containing soap, except the products described in CEST 11.001.00, 11.004.00, 11.005.00 and 11.006.00; in packaging with a content of less than or equal to 50 liters or 50 kg
TeenyTinyLLaMA	I am unable to respond based on the information provided. However, I can provide a general explanation of how to categorize NCM products, including specific categories and their respective categories
ChatGPT 4.0	Cleaning preparations
TeenyTinyLLaMAFT PT NCM	The correct NCM category is: Organic surface agents (except soaps); surfactant preparations, washing preparations (including auxiliary washing preparations) and cleaning preparations, whether or not containing soap, other than those of heading 34.01. - Preparations packaged for retail sale
SLIM-RAFT	The CLEANER VEJA PERF.NAT PERF. SOFT 1LT product has a category: Soaps, organic surface agents, washing preparations, lubricating preparations, artificial waxes, prepared waxes, conservation and cleaning products, candles and similar articles, modeling masses or pastes, "dental waxes" and plaster-based dental compositions. - Organic surface agents (except soaps); surfactant preparations, washing preparations (including auxiliary washing preparations) and cleaning preparations, whether or not containing soap, other than those of heading 34.01. - - - Preparations put up for retail sale

Portuguese:

```
Possuo um modelo capaz de responder questões diretas, mas não
consegue responder quando ela não vem nos padrões em que foi
treinado. O padrão de pergunta correto é "Qual a categoria NCM
correta para o produto: A?",onde A é a descrição do produto.
Sua missão é reformular os prompts para que meu modelo entenda:
Exemplo 1:
Pergunta original na padaria e comprei um suco de laranja,
percebi que na nota fiscal aparecia um código chamado NCM, mas
estava com a impressão borrada. Qual seria o código impresso?
pergunta reforumulada: Qual a categoria NCM correta para o
produto:suco de laranja?
Exemplo 2:
Pergunta original: Sou um importador de produtos cosméticos e
vou preencher um documento fiscal para a importação do produto
"TINT MAXTON 10.0 UN". Perdi minha planilha de códigos NCM,
então pergunto qual NCM usar neste caso?
Pergunta reforumulada:
Qual a categoria NCM correta para o produto: TINT MAXTON 10.0
UN?

Agora é sua vez, faça o mesmo para as perguntas abaixo:

1) Eu sou um comerciante que acabou de iniciar as atividades.
Vou vender cerveja e não sei qual código NCM lançar na nota
fiscal. Pode me ajudar?
2) Meu filho foi no mercado e comprou uma bebida deixando a nota
fiscal em cima da mesa da sala, onde estava escrito "V. ITAL.
CORBELLI PRIMITIVO TTO 750 ML". Qual bebida meu filho comprou?
E qual o código NCM?
3) Sabendo que frutas frescas são isentas de impostos e que
sucos de frutas industrializado são tributados, pergunto se o
produto Dell Vale Laranja é isento ou tributado? E qual o seu
código NCM?
```

ChatGPT output:

```
Aqui estão as perguntas reformuladas para o formato adequado ao
seu modelo:
1. Pergunta reformulada: Qual a categoria NCM correta para o
produto: cerveja?
2. Pergunta reformulada: Qual a categoria NCM correta para o
produto: V. ITAL. CORBELLI PRIMITIVO TTO 750 ML?
3. Pergunta reformulada: Qual a categoria NCM correta para o
produto: Dell Vale Laranja?
```

English translation:

```
I possess a model capable of answering direct questions, but it
struggles to respond when they do not conform to the patterns in
```

```
which it was trained. The correct question format is "What is
the correct NCM category for the product: A?", where A is the
product description. Your task is to rephrase the prompts so
that my model can understand them:
Example 1:
Original question:
I was at the bakery and bought orange juice, but I noticed that
the invoice had a smudged code called NCM. What would be the
printed code?
Rephrased question: What is the correct NCM category for the
product: orange juice?
Example 2:
Original question:
I am a cosmetic product importer and need to fill out a tax
document for the import of the product "TINT MAXTON 10.0 UN." I
lost my NCM codes spreadsheet, so I'd like to know which NCM to
use in this case.
Rephrased question: What is the correct NCM category for the
product: TINT MAXTON 10.0 UN?

Now it's your turn; do the same for the questions below:

1) I am a merchant who has just started a business. I will sell
beer and do not know Which NCM code should be used on the
invoice? Can you help me?
2) My son went to the market and bought a drink, leaving the
invoice on the living room
table, which read "V. ITAL. CORBELLI PRIMITIVO TTO 750 ML". What
drink did my son buy? And what is the NCM code?
3) Knowing that fresh fruits are exempt from taxes and that
industrialised fruit juices are taxed, I ask if the product Dell
Vale Orange is exempt or taxed? And what is its NCM code?
```

ChatGPT output English translation:

```
Here are the questions rephrased to the the appropriate format
for your model:
1. Rephrased question: What is the correct NCM category for the
product: beer?
2. Rephrased question: What is the correct NCM category for the
product: V. ITAL. CORBELLI PRIMITIVO TTO 750 ML?
3. Rephrased question: What is the correct NCM category for the
product: Dell Vale Orange?
```

Nonetheless, it is important to acknowledge that our model, given its current limited size, may not fully comprehend all contexts. The objective, however, is to expand the model as more resources become available, thereby enhancing its capacity and performance; as the model becomes larger, the need for integration with another model will be suppressed.

5.3 Limitations

The SLIM-RAFT model is a prototype developed to illustrate the simplification of the original RAFT methodology and propose its application within the NCM domain. Consequently, it is a highly specialised tool tailored for its designated task.

It is not recommended for use in ChatBot applications, as TeenyTinyLLaMA (TTL) creators have advised against employing the TTL 160 m model for such purposes. The TTL 460 m model is recommended for chatbot functionalities.

A simplified chain-of-thought approach is employed when constructing the training base for fine-tuning. However, it's crucial to remember that the involvement of a domain expert is beneficial and necessary for developing the reference lines of reasoning, highlighting the irreplaceable role of human expertise in this process.

6 Conclusions

The SLIM-RAFT model has demonstrated markedly superior performance compared to ChatGPT-4 in interpreting and classifying product descriptions according to the NCM code and allocating descriptions based on the CEP code.

These findings suggest that when equipped with domain-specific knowledge and appropriately fine-tuned, a smaller-scale LLM can outperform a more powerful general-purpose LLM in specialized tasks while maintaining significantly lower computational and operational costs. This underscores the potential of targeted model adaptation to achieve high precision in niche applications without excessive resource expenditure.

The innovative approach employed in SLIM-RAFT, particularly the Sequence-of-Sets (SoS) method for simplifying chain-of-thought reasoning, not only reduces costs but also represents a viable and efficient strategy for developing specialized LLMs with enhanced accuracy. This method provides a structured yet computationally efficient means of reasoning, thereby improving interpretability and decision-making in complex classification tasks.

Given that NCM coding plays a crucial role not only in the administration, transportation, taxation, and pricing of goods in the import and export sector across MERCOSUR countries but also in the taxation of goods, commodities, and restaurant services within Brazil, the practical implications of this research are considerable. The findings offer tangible benefits to government agencies involved in customs operations, taxation, trade regulation, financial institutions, logistics providers, and manufacturers. Furthermore, since the HS system serves as the global standard for the classification of import and export in more than 200 countries, the proposed LLM-NCM solution can contribute significantly to the greater adoption and refinement of LLM-HS applications globally.

Future research will focus on extending the application of SLIM-RAFT to larger-scale LLMs, such as LLaMA 3, with a particular emphasis on multilingual processing capabilities. Furthermore, subsequent studies will explore comparative analyses with other fine-tuning methodologies, such as LoRa, to evaluate their relative effectiveness in improving model performance in various linguistic and classification tasks.

Acknowledgments. ChatGPT 4 was used in all sections of this work to standardize and improve the writing in British English. This research is partially funded by the Brazilian National Council for Scientific and Technological Development (CNPq).

References

1. Di Oliveira, V., Bezerra, Y.F., Brom, P.C., Weigang, L., Celestino, V.R.: SLIM-RAFT: a novel fine-tuning approach to improve cross-linguistic performance for mercosur common nomenclature. In: Proceedings of WEBIST 2024, pp. 234–241 (2024). ISBN 978-989-758-718-4
2. Brazil, C.: Ajuste sinief 17 (2016). https://www.confaz.fazenda.gov.br/legislacao/ajustes/2016/AJ_017_16. Accessed 6 June 2024
3. Corrêa, N.K., Falk, S., Fatimah, S., Sen, A., de Oliveira, N.: Teenytinyllama: open-source tiny language models trained in brazilian portuguese. arXiv preprint arXiv:2401.16640 (2024)
4. CORREIOS. Correios do Brasil - Tudo sobre CEP (2025). https://www.correios.com.br/enviar/precisa-de-ajuda/tudo-sobre-cep. Accessed 4 Mar 2025
5. Di Oliveira, V., Weigang, L., Rocha Filho, G.P.: Eleven data-set: a labeled set of descriptions of goods captured from Brazilian electronic invoices. In: Proceedings of WEBIST 2022, pp. 257–264 (2022). ISBN 978-989-758-613-2
6. Du, S., Wu, Z., Wan, H., Lin, Y.F.: HScodeNet: combining hierarchical sequential and global spatial information of text for commodity hs code classification. In: Karlapalem, K., Cheng, H., Ramakrishnan, N., Agrawal, R.K., Reddy, P.K., Srivastava, J., Chakraborty, T. (eds.) PAKDD 2021. LNCS (LNAI), vol. 12713, pp. 676–689. Springer, Cham (2021). https://doi.org/10.1007/978-3-030-75765-6_54
7. Gao, Y., et al.: Retrieval-augmented generation for large language models: a survey. arXiv preprint arXiv:2312.10997 (2023)
8. Garcia, G.L., et al.: Introducing bode: a fine-tuned large language model for Portuguese prompt-based task. arXiv preprint arXiv:2401.02909 (2024)
9. Gu, Y., Han, X., Liu, Z., Huang, M.: PPT: pre-trained prompt tuning for few-shot learning. arXiv preprint arXiv:2109.04332 (2021)
10. Hu, E.J., et al.: LoRA: low-rank adaptation of large language models. arXiv preprint arXiv:2106.09685 (2021)
11. Kieckbusch, D.S., Geraldo Filho, P., Di Oliveira, V., Weigang, L.: Scan-NF: a CNN-based system for the classification of electronic invoices through short-text product description. In: WEBIST, pp. 501–508 (2021)
12. Larcher, C., Piau, M., Finardi, P., Gengo, P., Esposito, P., Caridá, V.: Cabrita: closing the gap for foreign languages. arXiv preprint arXiv:2308.11878 (2023)
13. Lewis, P., Perez, E., Piktus, A., Petroni, F., Karpukhin, V., Goyal, N., Küttler, H., Lewis, M., Yih, W.-T., Rocktäschel, T., et al.: Retrieval-augmented generation for knowledge-intensive NLP tasks. Adv. Neural. Inf. Process. Syst. **33**, 9459–9474 (2020)
14. Lopes, R., Magalhães, J., Semedo, D.: Glória-a generative and open large language model for portuguese. arXiv preprint arXiv:2402.12969 (2024)
15. Ma, H., et al.: Fairness-guided few-shot prompting for large language models. In: Advances in Neural Information Processing Systems, vol. 36 (2024)
16. Marinho, M.C., Di Oliveira, V., Neto, S.A., Weigang, L., Borges, V.R.: Visual analysis of electronic invoices to identify suspicious cases of tax frauds. In: International Conference on Information Technology & Systems, pp. 185–195. Springer (2022)

17. MERCOSUR. Mercosur - consultas à nomenclatura comum e à tarifa externa (2024). https://www.mercosur.int/pt-br/politica-comercial/ncm/. Accessed 4 June 2024
18. MERCOSUR. Mercosur contries (2024). https://www.mercosur.int/en/about-mercosur/mercosur-countries/. Accessed 6 June 2024
19. Meta, A.: Introducing meta LLaMA 3: the most capable openly available LLM to date (2024). https://ai.meta.com/blog/meta-llama-3/. Accessed 3 June 2024
20. Pires, R., Abonizio, H., Almeida, T.S., Nogueira, R.: Sabiá: Portuguese large language models. In: Brazilian Conference on Intelligent Systems, pp. 226–240. Springer (2023)
21. Radosavovic, I., et al.: Humanoid locomotion as next token prediction. arXiv preprint arXiv:2402.19469 (2024)
22. Schulhoff, S., et al.: The prompt report: a systematic survey of prompting techniques. arXiv preprint arXiv:2406.06608 (2024)
23. Schulte, J.P., et al.: ELINAC: autoencoder approach for electronic invoices data clustering. Appl. Sci. **12**(6), 3008 (2022)
24. Souza, F., Nogueira, R., Lotufo, R.: BERTimbau: pretrained BERT models for Brazilian Portuguese. In: Cerri, R., Prati, R.C. (eds.) BRACIS 2020. LNCS (LNAI), vol. 12319, pp. 403–417. Springer, Cham (2020). https://doi.org/10.1007/978-3-030-61377-8_28
25. Touvron, H., et al.: LLaMA: open and efficient foundation language models. arXiv preprint arXiv:2302.13971 (2023)
26. Touvron, H., et al.: LLaMA 2: open foundation and fine-tuned chat models. arXiv preprint arXiv:2307.09288 (2023)
27. Valença, P.R.M., et al.: Essays on foreign trade, labor, innovation and environment. UCB (2023)
28. Van Engelen, J.E., Hoos, H.H.: A survey on semi-supervised learning. Mach. Learn. **109**(2), 373–440 (2020)
29. Vaswani, A., et al.: Attention is all you need. Adv. Neural Inf. Process. Syst. **30** (2017)
30. Warnakulasuriya, S., Hapuarachchi, K.: From knowledge to action: leveraging retrieval augmented fine tuning (raft) to empower quick and confident first-aid decisions in emergencies. Researchgate (Preprint) (2024). http://dx.doi.org/10.13140/RG.2.2.35911.30888
31. WCO. THE HARMONIZED SYSTEM A universal language for international trade. World Customs Organization (2018). https://www.wcoomd.org/-/media/wco/public/global/pdf/topics/nomenclature/activities-and-programmes/30-years-hs/hs-compendium.pdf. Accessed 04 June 2024
32. WCO. List of contracting parties to the HS convention and countries using the HS - world customs organization (2024). https://www.wcoomd.org/en/topics/nomenclature/overview/list-of-contracting-parties-to-the-hs-convention-and-countries-using-the-hs.aspx. Accessed 6 June 2024
33. Weigang, L., Enamoto, L.M., Li, D.L., Rocha Filho, G.P.: New directions for artificial intelligence: human, machine, biological, and quantum intelligence. Front. Inf. Technol. Electron. Eng. **23**(6), 984–990 (2022)
34. Yadav, B.K.: Impact of regulation and conformity assessment procedures on global trade. In: Handbook of Quality System, Accreditation and Conformity Assessment, pp. 1–21. Springer (2023)
35. Zhang, T., et al.: RAFT: adapting language model to domain specific RAG. arXiv preprint arXiv:2403.10131 (2024)

Exploiting Subject and Sender Features for Learning to Predict Email Open Rates

Daniel Vitor de Oliveira Santos and Wladmir Cardoso Brandão(✉)

Pontifical Catholic University of Minas Gerais, Belo Horizonte, Brazil
wladmir@pucminas.br

Abstract. As the volume of daily emails grows steadily, user inboxes have become highly competitive environments where marketers strive to capture attention. This research investigates the pivotal role of subject lines in influencing email open rates, a key performance indicator for marketing success. By applying text mining techniques and machine learning models, we aim to predict open rates based on the combined influence of subject line content and sender information. Our analysis compares eight regression models and employs diverse feature strategies, including morphologic text attributes, operational marketing metrics, and semantic representations generated via TF-IDF, Word2Vec, and OpenAI embeddings. Leveraging historical data from real-world email campaigns, we trained and validated predictive models designed to uncover patterns in user engagement. Among the evaluated models, CatBoost—augmented with operational features and PCA-reduced OpenAI embeddings—demonstrated superior performance, achieving a Root Mean Squared Error (RMSE) of 5.16, Mean Absolute Error (MAE) of 3.60, Coefficient of Determination (R^2) of 77.53%, and Mean Absolute Percentage Error (MAPE) of 14.73%. These findings validate the impact of semantic content and sender reputation on open rates and highlight the effectiveness of integrating advanced embeddings with operational data. By offering actionable insights into email engagement dynamics, this research supports a shift from resource-intensive A/B testing toward predictive, data-driven campaign strategies, equipping practitioners and researchers alike with practical tools to enhance marketing performance.

Keywords: Predictive analytics · Email marketing · Campaign optimization · Text mining · Machine learning

1 Introduction

The digital age has profoundly reshaped how people communicate, both personally and professionally. Among digital communication channels, email remains one of the most influential and efficient, particularly in marketing contexts. As of 2023, the global number of email users was estimated at 4.3 billion and is projected to surpass 4.8 billion by 2027 [2]. Moreover, over 347 billion business and consumer emails were sent and received daily in 2023, expected to exceed 408 billion by 2027.

In this context, email marketing is a key strategy for attracting new customers and maintaining existing relationships, standing out amid the information overload of the

M. Marchiori et al. (Eds.): WEBIST 2024, LNBIP 583, pp. 183–205, 2026.
https://doi.org/10.1007/978-3-032-25534-1_8

digital world. The success of email campaigns depends heavily on the subject line, often the first element a recipient notices. Personalization, emotional appeal, and brevity have been shown to significantly increase open rates compared to generic subject lines [3]. Still, many organizations rely on subjective intuition rather than data-driven methods when creating these essential components.

Industry reports, including Omnisend's 2022 data, highlight email marketing's exceptional return on investment (ROI), reportedly generating approximately $40 for every dollar spent—further emphasizing the need to optimize all facets of email campaigns, particularly subject lines. This impressive ROI is largely due to email's direct and personalized nature, fostering stronger engagement and loyalty. However, these outcomes depend substantially on the effectiveness of subject lines, given their significant influence on whether an email is opened [4].

Despite their impact, crafting compelling subject lines remains challenging, mainly because companies still depend on A/B testing. This technique involves sending multiple email variations to different segments to determine which performs best regarding open and engagement rates. While widely used, this process is time-consuming, costly, and ill-suited for adapting to fast-changing consumer behavior. Frequent iterations and delayed launches increase costs and hinder campaign agility, illustrating the pressing need for more efficient approaches.

To address these limitations, this paper proposes a data-driven solution to enhance the understanding of how subject lines and sender reputation impact open rates. By analyzing extensive datasets from past email campaigns and applying text mining and machine learning techniques, this research develops predictive models that evaluate and improve the effectiveness of subject lines. In addition, an exploratory analysis was conducted to uncover key behavioral patterns and feature relationships, offering strategic insights to guide optimization beyond mere prediction. Together, these models and analyses generate actionable insights, minimizing dependence on traditional A/B testing and improving decision-making in campaign design.

This research evaluates eight regression models—including tree-based methods, ensemble models, kernel-based algorithms, and artificial neural networks—to identify the most effective strategy for assessing email marketing performance. Each model type offers distinct strengths: tree-based models are interpretable, ensemble techniques provide robustness, kernel-based methods handle complex relationships, and neural networks excel at modeling nonlinear patterns in large datasets. The process begins with extracting textual features from subject lines and sender information, then incorporates operational attributes, including contextual and temporal metrics, alongside morphologic features. Ultimately, semantic representations via embeddings—TF-IDF, Word2Vec, and OpenAI's language models—are combined with operational data to assess their overall impact on model accuracy, supporting the central hypothesis that subject line semantics play a key role in influencing open rates.

Historical email campaign data—complete with engagement metrics—were used to build and validate these models. Among them, CatBoost emerged as a standout performer, particularly when operational features were combined with preprocessing methods such as PCA and OpenAI-generated embeddings. This approach significantly improved the analysis and optimization of subject lines, offering valuable insights to enhance the effectiveness of email marketing strategies.

This paper extends our earlier work presented at the WEBIST 2024 conference [1], which introduced the initial version of our predictive framework. In this extended version, we expand the evaluation, provide deeper insights into feature importance, and present new model diagnostics and analysis.

2 Related Work

Research into email subject lines consistently underscores their pivotal role in determining marketing success, particularly in driving user engagement. [8] demonstrated that subject lines which spark curiosity or convey practical value tend to generate higher open rates. This suggests that recipients are more inclined to engage with emails that either intrigue them or promise immediate benefits. Building upon this, [9] revealed that personalization strategies—such as including the recipient's name—can raise open rates from 9.05% to 10.80%, resulting in a 31% increase in sales leads and a 17% reduction in unsubscribe rates, reinforcing the significant appeal of personalized content in email marketing.

The visual presentation of emails also plays an important role. [10] emphasized that design elements significantly affect user engagement, drawing parallels between compelling visual design in direct mail and the impact of concise, visually appealing email subject lines. Simultaneously, the rise of machine learning has provided marketers with powerful tools to enhance campaign effectiveness. For instance, [12] utilized a Random Forest model to predict email open rates, achieving a RMSE of 1.60×10^{-2} and a correlation coefficient of 0.352, thereby illustrating the potential of predictive models to optimize email marketing strategies through data-driven methods.

In the financial industry, [11] applied a Random Forest algorithm to forecast campaign success based on open rates, achieving approximately 82% accuracy. Their model was particularly effective in identifying impactful subject line keywords. Complementing this approach, psychological insights from [13] revealed that emotional cues in subject lines—such as urgency or excitement—can substantially influence user engagement, highlighting the psychological dimensions that shape recipient behavior.

Recent studies by [14] and [15] further emphasize the value of integrating deep learning techniques with traditional machine learning approaches. Joshi's work introduced the Ngram-LSTM model, which excelled in handling sparse datasets, achieving 84% accuracy within a 10% error tolerance range. Meanwhile, Paulo analyzed over 140,000 subject lines and concluded that Random Forest models yielded the best results, with an accuracy of 62.4% and an F1-score of 62.2%. Both studies underscore the importance of combining structural elements and semantic content in subject lines to improve predictive performance. This research builds upon those foundations by adopting a comprehensive strategy that integrates both semantic and morphological features with advanced machine learning models, aiming to deliver higher predictive accuracy and richer insights into email campaign optimization.

3 Background

3.1 Email Marketing Concepts

Optimizing email marketing requires a clear understanding of the key performance indicators that influence campaign success. Metrics such as **Delivered**, which refers to the total number of emails successfully received by recipients, are crucial for assessing the reliability of email delivery systems. The **Open** metric tracks engagement by counting how many of these emails were opened. Critically, the sender's identity (**Sender**) can greatly affect engagement due to factors such as reputation and familiarity. Similarly, the **Subject** line plays a central role in capturing the recipient's attention at first glance. These elements together define the **Open Rate**, a key metric for evaluating campaign effectiveness, calculated as shown in Eq. 1:

$$\text{Open Rate} = \left(\frac{\text{Number of Opens}}{\text{Number of Delivered}} \right) \times 100 \tag{1}$$

The open rate directly reflects how compelling a subject line is and how well the sender resonates with the audience—both critical factors in achieving marketing objectives.

3.2 Dimensionality Reduction with PCA

Principal Component Analysis (PCA) is a widely used technique for reducing the dimensionality of large datasets while preserving most of their variability. It works by transforming the original variables into a new set of uncorrelated variables, called principal components, which are linear combinations of the original features. These components are ranked by the amount of variance they capture. Typically, the first few components retain most of the dataset's variance, allowing for a simplified representation without significant loss of information. PCA is fundamental for analyzing high-dimensional data, as it improves computational efficiency and facilitates clearer insights [18].

3.3 Curse of Dimensionality

The curse of dimensionality, introduced by Bellman [17], refers to challenges encountered when analyzing data in high-dimensional spaces. As the number of dimensions increases, the space grows exponentially, making data points sparse and widely dispersed. This sparsity undermines statistical reliability and complicates pattern detection, reducing the effectiveness of many analytical methods. PCA addresses this challenge by concentrating the data into its most informative components, reducing dimensionality and computational complexity. This not only enhances model performance but also improves the interpretability and accuracy of the analysis.

3.4 Text Embeddings

Text embeddings are essential in natural language processing for converting textual data into numerical form. Like PCA simplifies numerical data, embeddings represent words or phrases as vectors in a high-dimensional space, capturing their meaning based on context. These vectors place semantically similar words close together, allowing models to detect relationships and patterns in language, even when words do not appear together. By learning from large text corpora, embeddings encode semantic similarity and contextual nuance, enabling machine learning models to process language more effectively. This is especially valuable for analyzing elements like email subject lines, where understanding meaning and context directly impacts predictive performance.

4 Exploratory Analysis and Insights

Understanding patterns in email engagement is essential for building accurate predictive models. This section examines key feature relationships and identifies behavioral trends that influence open rates. By analyzing correlations and grouping behaviors, we provide insights that support both feature selection and strategic marketing decisions.

4.1 Feature Correlation Analysis

We begin by investigating the relationships among numerical features to identify correlations that may impact the predictive performance of machine learning models. Understanding these relationships is essential for effective feature engineering and model refinement.

A correlation analysis was conducted to uncover linear relationships among variables, which might influence predictive accuracy and model interpretability.

From this analysis, some notable relationships emerged. The strongest correlation (0.93) was found between *Time of Day Open Rate* and *Hour of Day*, indicating that the time of day significantly influences recipient engagement and emphasizing the importance of strategic email scheduling. Another substantial correlation (0.69) between *Sender Open Rate* and *Open Rate* underscores the critical influence of sender reputation on email engagement, aligning well with the feature importance analysis presented in the results section.

Furthermore, variables such as *Hour Open Rate* and *Time of Day Open Rate* (0.53), as well as *Sender Open Rate* and *Open Rate* (0.69), also showed notable correlations. These findings reinforce the importance of both sender reputation and temporal factors in predicting email open rates.

Table 1 summarizes the pairs of features with strong correlations (more than 0.6):

These insights lay the groundwork for deeper exploratory analyses, particularly in identifying behavioral groupings among campaigns, as explored in the next subsection through cluster analysis.

Table 1. Strongly Correlated Feature Pairs.

Feature 1	Feature 2	Correlation
Time of Day Open Rate	Hour of Day	0.93
Sender Open Rate	Open Rate	0.69

4.2 Cluster Analysis of Email Campaigns

Based on the correlation findings, we performed a cluster analysis to uncover distinct patterns in email campaigns based on key features. Specifically, we applied the K-Means algorithm to features exhibiting strong correlations: *Sender Open Rate*, *Open Rate*, *Hour of Day*, and *Time of Day Open Rate*. This approach allows for segmentation of campaigns into meaningful groups based on shared behavioral traits.

Using the elbow method, we determined the optimal number of clusters to be six, balancing interpretability with analytical depth.

Table 2. Mean Feature Values by Cluster.

Cluster	Sender Open Rate	Open Rate	Hour of Day	Time of Day Open Rate
0	37.53	43.50	19.57	32.60
1	22.01	20.67	7.69	25.47
2	23.47	22.09	18.60	32.60
3	36.24	40.54	13.60	28.42
4	33.13	29.91	7.56	26.00
5	22.59	21.42	14.18	28.54

The cluster analysis in the Table 2 reveals diverse engagement patterns tied to both sender reputation and email dispatch timing. For instance, Cluster 0 features high sender reputation (37.5%) and open rates (43.5%), typically for emails sent in the evening (around 8 PM). In contrast, Cluster 1 shows low sender reputation and early morning sends, aligning with lower engagement. These patterns suggest that temporal factors and sender credibility play a central role in shaping campaign outcomes.

To further interpret these patterns and their strategic implications, the next subsection synthesizes these findings into actionable recommendations for campaign design and optimization.

4.3 Behavioral Patterns and Strategic Recommendations

The behavioral patterns identified through cluster analysis offer valuable strategic insights to guide marketing decisions. When considered alongside the correlation findings, they provide a comprehensive view of how timing and sender reputation influence open rates.

Cluster 0 represents the ideal scenario: emails from highly credible senders, dispatched in the evening, achieved the highest engagement. This aligns with the strong correlation between *Hour of Day* and *Time of Day Open Rate*, reinforcing the importance of precise email scheduling.

In contrast, Clusters 1 and 5 exhibited lower engagement, highlighting the negative impact of low sender credibility and poorly chosen dispatch times. These results suggest that improving the reputation of the sender should be a priority before optimizing the send time.

Cluster 3 reveals an alternative high-engagement window, where reputable senders also performed well. Meanwhile, Clusters 2 and 4, which showed moderate engagement levels, indicate the potential for targeted strategies enhanced by predictive modeling.

Together, these patterns demonstrate the practical value of the predictive model. By inputting key characteristics—such as sender, sender reputation, and intended dispatch time—marketers can forecast open rates, reducing reliance on A/B testing and enabling data-driven decisions. Although subject line content was not analyzed here, the next section incorporates semantic embeddings to further refine the model's predictions.

To validate and complement these behavioral insights, the next subsection presents a performance-based analysis. By comparing high- and low-performing campaigns, we further clarify how timing and sender reputation affect engagement.

4.4 Performance-Based Campaign Analysis

To complement the cluster-based insights, we segmented campaigns by performance tiers, focusing on the top and bottom 10% based on open rates. This comparison highlights operational differences that distinguish high-performing campaigns from underperforming ones.

Table 3. Comparison of Average Feature Values for High and Low-Performance Campaigns

Feature	High Performance	Low Performance
Sender Open Rate	37.50	20.12
Hour of Day	16.09	9.22

As shown in Table 3, high-performing campaigns achieved an average sender open rate of 37.5% and were typically sent around 4 PM. In contrast, low-performing campaigns had a lower sender open rate (20.1%) and were usually dispatched around 9 AM. These results reinforce earlier findings, emphasizing the combined impact of sender credibility and timing on engagement outcomes.

By combining insights from correlation analysis, clustering, and performance comparisons, marketers gain a comprehensive understanding of the factors that drive engagement. This knowledge supports strategic adjustments that can meaningfully improve campaign effectiveness and return on investment.

5 Methodology

The methodological framework adopted in this research is depicted in Fig. 1 and encompasses six key stages designed to structure and guide the predictive modeling process. These stages include: (1) Data Overview, which provides essential context about the dataset and its attributes; (2) Dataset Preparation and Feature Engineering, focusing on data cleaning and the derivation of relevant features; (3) Text Preprocessing and Embedding Generation, aimed at capturing the semantic richness of textual inputs; (4) Modeling Approaches, outlining the strategies used to combine various feature sets for prediction; (5) Predictive Models, detailing the machine learning algorithms evaluated; and (6) Evaluation Metrics and Target Transformation, explaining how model performance is assessed and optimized.

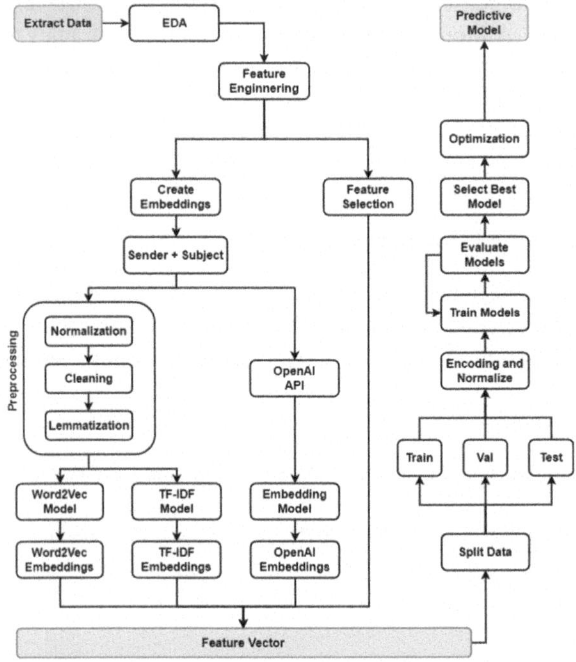

Fig. 1. Flowchart of the methodology (adapted from our previous work [1]).

5.1 Data Overview

The dataset used in this research comprises over 4 billion emails distributed across 4,285 marketing campaigns, supplied by Etus Media Holding [16], a company specializing in email marketing solutions. Spanning from May 2022 to May 2024, the dataset includes Brazilian email campaigns written in Portuguese, featuring key elements such as sender identity, subject lines, delivery statistics, and user engagement indicators.

To preserve client confidentiality and ensure compliance with data privacy policies, the exact data collection mechanisms and sensitive details cannot be disclosed. Nonetheless, the data was obtained through secure queries on Etus's proprietary database, ensuring the integrity and reliability of the information used in this research.

For model development, the dataset was partitioned into training (72%), validation (8%), and testing (20%) subsets. Before modeling, normalization techniques were applied to standardize feature scales, and dimensionality reduction via Principal Component Analysis (PCA) was employed to enhance computational efficiency and improve model performance. These preparatory steps ensure that the dataset is well-suited for the subsequent phases of analysis and predictive modeling.

5.2 Dataset Preparation and Feature Engineering

After preparing the dataset, the next step was to refine the data for accurate analysis and predictive modeling. This process involved two main tasks: ensuring data quality and engineering relevant features to enhance model performance.

Data cleaning began with the removal of entries missing critical information, such as subject lines, sender names, or delivery counts. To improve the reliability of insights, only campaigns with at least 100,000 delivered emails were retained. This threshold was set because smaller campaigns often represent pilot tests or experimental content, which can introduce noise and variability. In contrast, large-scale campaigns tend to be more consistent, offering a stable basis for statistical analysis.

Next, feature engineering was applied to extract informative variables from the cleaned data. Key features included: *sender open rate* (the sender's average open rate across all campaigns), *sender count* (number of campaigns sent by the sender), and *sender sum delivered* (total emails sent by the sender). Temporal features such as *hour of day* and *day of the week* were also extracted to provide context regarding the timing of email dispatches.

Additional email-level metrics were engineered to capture campaign-specific performance, including *email open rate* and *delivered scaled* (normalized delivery volume). These features, combining sender behavior and temporal context, were essential in identifying engagement patterns revealed during exploratory analysis.

To streamline the dataset and focus on the most impactful variables, feature selection was guided by domain knowledge and statistical analysis, prioritizing attributes with strong influence on open rates, as discussed in the previous section. The resulting feature set provided a solid foundation for embedding generation and model training, ensuring the data was both comprehensive and optimized for predictive tasks.

5.3 Embedding Generation

After preparing and enriching the dataset with key operational and contextual features, the next step involved generating textual embeddings to capture the semantic nuances of email subject lines and sender information—two elements that strongly influence recipient engagement.

To accomplish this, three distinct embedding techniques were employed: TF-IDF, Word2Vec, and OpenAI's pre-trained embeddings. Each method offers a unique approach to representing text as numerical vectors, enabling machine learning models to process and interpret language-based data.

The Term Frequency-Inverse Document Frequency (TF-IDF) method quantifies the importance of words in the context of the entire corpus. It highlights terms that are frequent in a specific subject line but rare across the dataset, thus identifying potentially impactful keywords related to higher open rates [5].

The Word2Vec approach, introduced by Mikolov et al. [6], captures the contextual relationships between words based on their co-occurrence patterns. By employing the Continuous Bag-of-Words (CBOW) and Skip-Gram architectures, it generates embeddings that encode semantic similarities, allowing the model to understand the underlying meaning of subject lines beyond surface-level word counts.

In addition to these traditional techniques, this study utilized a pre-trained model from OpenAI [7] to generate embeddings with deeper contextual comprehension. These embeddings, derived from the `text-embedding-3-small` model, benefit from extensive training on large-scale, diverse text data, offering rich and nuanced vector representations that capture both linguistic structure and meaning.

To ensure the embeddings encapsulated both the message content and sender identity, the subject line and sender fields were concatenated and treated as a single text input during embedding generation. This design choice reflects the combined influence of content and sender credibility on recipient behavior, as demonstrated in the earlier exploratory analysis.

By integrating these three embedding strategies, with distinct strengths, the study captured multiple dimensions of textual data, ranging from keyword importance to semantic context. These embeddings, once generated, served as critical inputs for the various modeling strategies developed in subsequent stages.

5.4 Approaches

Based on the extracted features and generated embeddings, several modeling strategies were tested to evaluate different input combinations and determine the most effective method for predicting email open rates. These strategies were grouped into four main approaches, each adding new layers of information and complexity in a progressive manner.

Morphologic. The first approach, called Morphologic, focuses solely on structural characteristics derived from the subject lines. It includes features such as total character count, word count, presence of special characters (e.g., punctuation, numbers, emojis), and ratios such as uppercase letters, vowels, consonants, and named entities. These features aim to quantify the surface-level composition of the subject line, providing insights into how structural design may influence engagement.

Operational. Expanding upon the Morphologic approach, the Operational strategy introduces temporal and campaign-specific features. This includes delivery volume (both absolute and scaled), time-related variables such as hour of the day, day of the week, and aggregated open rate metrics across different time segments (e.g., hourly open rate, weekday open rate, and time of day open rate). By incorporating these elements, the model gains contextual awareness of when emails were sent and how recipients typically respond to such temporal patterns—insights supported by the exploratory analysis results.

Embedding-Based. Before employing embedding models, textual data (i.e., subject and sender fields) underwent preprocessing, including normalization (lowercasing and punctuation removal), cleaning (eliminating numbers and currency symbols), and lemmatization using the SpaCy library. These steps ensured that the text was clean and semantically consistent for embedding generation.

In this third approach, embeddings were used independently of operational or morphologic features. Three types of embeddings were tested:

- TF-IDF to capture keyword relevance.
- Word2Vec to encode contextual word relationships.
- OpenAI embeddings for deep semantic understanding.

This allowed the evaluation of how well text-based features alone could predict open rates, without the influence of campaign context or structural text features.

Combined Approach. Finally, the Combined strategy integrates operational features with the embeddings to leverage both contextual campaign data and semantic text information. Before integration, embeddings were reduced in dimensionality using PCA, condensing them to six principal components—a choice informed by iterative testing to retain maximal information while avoiding the curse of dimensionality.

This approach aimed to test whether the synergy of operational context and textual semantics could enhance predictive performance, building upon patterns identified during the exploratory analysis—such as the influence of sender reputation and dispatch timing. By combining these feature sets, this strategy sought to capture the full spectrum of factors influencing email engagement.

Through these four approaches, this study comprehensively assessed different feature representations, enabling robust evaluation and comparison of model performance in predicting open rates.

5.5 Data Preprocessing

Before model training, several preprocessing steps were undertaken to ensure the dataset was in an optimal format for analysis and predictive modeling. These steps involved both handling categorical and numerical data, as well as transforming the target variable to enhance model performance.

Categorical Data Encoding. Categorical features, particularly the sender identifier, were converted into a machine-readable format using One-Hot Encoding. This method transformed each unique category into a binary feature, preserving the distinct identities of the senders while enabling the models to process this information effectively.

Feature Normalization. To maintain uniformity across numerical inputs, Min-Max Scaling was applied. This technique scaled all numerical features to a [0, 1] range, ensuring that no single feature dominated model learning due to scale differences. Normalization is especially important for algorithms sensitive to feature magnitude, such as gradient-based models and neural networks.

Dimensionality Reduction (PCA). As previously discussed, Principal Component Analysis (PCA) was applied to the embedding vectors generated by TF-IDF, Word2Vec, and OpenAI models. The objective was to reduce dimensionality while preserving the most informative components of these high-dimensional vectors. After testing various configurations, six principal components were selected as the optimal trade-off between retaining variance and improving computational efficiency. These reduced embeddings were then incorporated into the feature set for models using textual data.

Target Transformation with TransformedTargetRegressor. To address the issue of variance instability and skewed distributions in the target variable (open rate), a logarithmic transformation was applied using the TransformedTargetRegressor technique. During model training, the open rate values y were transformed using Eq. 2:

$$y_{\text{transformed}} = \log(y + 1) \tag{2}$$

The following prediction, the original scale was recovered using the inverse transformation in Eq. 3:

$$y_{\text{original}} = \exp(y_{\text{transformed}}) - 1 \tag{3}$$

This transformation stabilized the variance across different scales of open rate values, allowing models to better capture the underlying patterns and reduce the impact of extreme values on learning. By normalizing both input features and transforming the target, the dataset was optimized for accurate and efficient predictive modeling.

5.6 Models

With the dataset fully prepared, the next phase involved selecting and evaluating various regression algorithms to identify the most effective approach for predicting email open rates. The chosen models span diverse families of machine learning techniques, each offering distinct strengths in capturing patterns within complex data.

Tree-Based Algorithms. To achieve both interpretability and robustness, two tree-based models were employed: Decision Tree Regressor and Random Forest Regressor. The Decision Tree model predicts outcomes by learning a series of decision rules from the input features. Random Forest builds upon this approach by combining predictions from multiple decision trees, which helps reduce overfitting and improves overall model stability.

Ensemble Methods. Advanced ensemble algorithms were also evaluated for their effectiveness in handling structured data with high predictive accuracy. The models assessed included Gradient Boosting, LightGBM, XGBoost, and CatBoost. These algorithms are based on ensemble learning strategies—either sequential or parallel—and use gradient-based optimization to iteratively correct errors and improve performance. Among them, CatBoost stood out for its ability to handle categorical variables efficiently and was carefully tuned in this study due to its consistent performance advantages.

Kernel-Based Model. The Support Vector Regressor (SVR) was employed to explore the potential of kernel methods in capturing both linear and non-linear relationships. SVR leverages the kernel trick to transform data into higher dimensions, where linear separation or regression becomes feasible, making it effective for modeling complex feature interactions.

Neural Network. A Multilayer Perceptron (MLP) Regressor, a type of feedforward neural network, was used to model non-linear dependencies across features. Configured with a single hidden layer containing 1024 neurons, this model employed the ReLU activation function and the Adam optimizer with a learning rate of 0.001. These settings were selected to balance training speed and convergence stability, allowing the MLP to learn intricate patterns from both operational and semantic features.

Each of these models was trained and validated using the structured train/validation/test data split established earlier. The evaluation process included both cross-validation and rigorous performance testing across multiple metrics, ensuring each model's generalization capability beyond the training data.

This comprehensive modeling strategy allowed for a robust comparison across traditional, ensemble, and deep learning models, facilitating the selection of the best-performing approach for predicting email open rates in a real-world marketing context.

5.7 Evaluation Metrics

To evaluate the predictive performance of all models, multiple metrics were used, each capturing a distinct aspect of accuracy and error. This approach provided a comprehensive assessment of model effectiveness and enabled consistent comparisons across different modeling strategies.

Mean Absolute Error (MAE). MAE quantifies the average absolute difference between predicted and actual values, offering an intuitive measure of prediction error magnitude without penalizing the direction of the error. It is computed as follows in Eq. 4:

$$MAE = \frac{1}{n}\sum_{i=1}^{n}|y_i - \hat{y}_i| \quad (4)$$

Root Mean Squared Error (RMSE). RMSE is particularly sensitive to larger errors, as it squares the deviations before averaging. This makes it ideal for situations where minimizing large prediction errors is crucial. It is defined by Eq. 5:

$$RMSE = \sqrt{\frac{1}{n}\sum_{i=1}^{n}(y_i - \hat{y}_i)^2} \tag{5}$$

Coefficient of Determination ($\mathbf{R^2}$). R^2 evaluates the proportion of variance in the target variable that is explained by the model. It provides a normalized measure of fit, where values closer to 1 indicate strong explanatory power. We can see by Eq. 6:

$$R^2 = 1 - \frac{\sum_{i=1}^{n}(y_i - \hat{y}_i)^2}{\sum_{i=1}^{n}(y_i - \bar{y})^2} \tag{6}$$

Mean Absolute Percentage Error (MAPE). MAPE expresses the prediction error as a percentage of the actual value using the Eq. 7, offering an interpretable relative measure of accuracy, particularly useful when comparing campaigns of varying scales:

$$MAPE = \frac{100}{n}\sum_{i=1}^{n}\left|\frac{y_i - \hat{y}_i}{y_i}\right| \tag{7}$$

Overall, this rigorous approach to model evaluation ensures that the predictive models developed in this article are effective in theoretical settings and robust and applicable in practical scenarios, providing reliable forecasts that can significantly enhance the efficacy of email marketing campaigns.

6 Results

This section presents a detailed evaluation of the machine learning models developed to predict email open rates, incorporating diverse strategies for feature integration and model optimization. Building on insights from exploratory analysis, which identified the significant role of sender reputation and temporal patterns, this evaluation aims to validate how well different models leverage such patterns for accurate predictions.

6.1 Model Performance Overview

To determine the most effective approach for forecasting email open rates, we conducted a comparative analysis of multiple machine learning models across a range of feature engineering strategies. Each model was evaluated using four key performance metrics—RMSE, MAE, R^2, and MAPE—as visualized in Fig. 2.

In the comparative evaluation, CatBoost and LightGBM consistently delivered the best results, especially when operational features were combined with OpenAI embeddings and reduced via PCA. This configuration mitigated the effects of high dimensionality, as discussed earlier regarding the curse of dimensionality while enhancing the models' ability to capture both semantic and contextual patterns in the data.

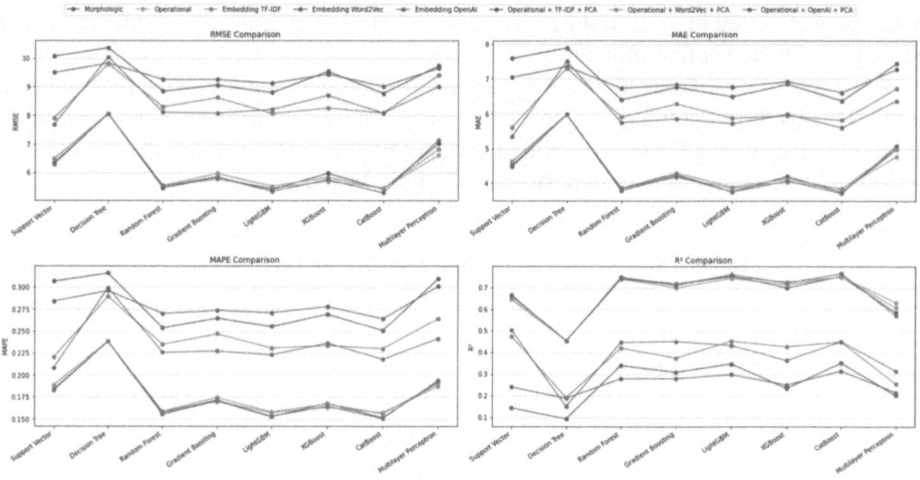

Fig. 2. Comparison of RMSE, MAE, R^2, and MAPE for Different Models and Strategies (reproduced from [1]).

Ensemble models—Random Forest, Gradient Boosting, LightGBM, and CatBoost—performed strongly due to their ability to model complex feature interactions and aggregate multiple learners, which improves accuracy and generalization. In contrast, models relying solely on basic text attributes, such as morphologic features, showed significantly lower performance. This supports the exploratory findings, where semantic and contextual information proved more influential on engagement than structural text features alone.

Notably, models incorporating semantic embeddings consistently outperformed those using only structural or operational data. The integration of embeddings, particularly when combined with operational features and PCA, led to a significant improvement in prediction accuracy. These results underscore the value of combining textual semantics with operational insights to build effective models for predicting email open rates.

6.2 Best Model Selection

Following the model performance comparison, CatBoost and LightGBM consistently achieved the best results, particularly when combined with operational features, OpenAI embeddings, and dimensionality reduction through PCA. This subsection details the methodology used to objectively identify the most effective model and discusses its practical implications for optimizing email marketing strategies.

To rank the models systematically, we employed a comprehensive scoring approach that aggregates their standings across four evaluation metrics: RMSE, MAE, R^2, and MAPE. For RMSE, MAE, and MAPE, lower values indicate better predictive accuracy, while for R^2, higher values denote superior model fit. To ensure consistency, the R^2

scores were inverted in the ranking process, such that a lower rank consistently indicated better performance across all metrics.

Each model's rank per metric was summed to compute a cumulative performance score. This method facilitates a balanced comparison by capturing both the magnitude of prediction errors and the proportion of variance explained by each model—providing a nuanced assessment of overall performance and robustness.

Table 4. Top 5 Best Models Based on Overall Performance.

Type	RMSE	MAE	R^2	MAPE
CatBoost+Operational+Embedding OpenAI+PCA	5.268	3.705	76.6%	15.0%
LightGBM+Operational+Embedding OpenAI+PCA	5.323	3.745	76.1%	15.3%
CatBoost+Operational+Embedding TF-IDF+PCA	5.398	3.732	75.4%	15.1%
LightGBM+Operational+Embedding TF-IDF+PCA	5.392	3.749	75.4%	15.2%
CatBoost+Operational+Embedding Word2Vec+PCA	5.422	3.818	75.2%	15.6%

As shown in Table 4, the CatBoost model—configured with operational features, OpenAI embeddings, and PCA—achieved the best overall performance. It recorded the lowest RMSE and one of the highest R^2 values, reflecting high predictive accuracy and strong generalization across diverse data patterns.

These results highlight the advantage of combining semantic information from embeddings with operational context—a pattern also observed in the exploratory analysis, where sender reputation and timing emerged as key factors influencing engagement. CatBoost's ability to integrate these heterogeneous inputs and model non-linear relationships makes it a highly effective solution for predicting email open rates with precision.

6.3 Model Optimization

After identifying CatBoost as the top-performing model, we carried out a structured hyperparameter tuning process to enhance its predictive accuracy and ensure reliable performance across varied campaign scenarios. This optimization was essential to improve the model's learning efficiency, control the bias-variance trade-off, and minimize the risk of overfitting.

To perform the tuning, we used Grid Search, an exhaustive method for exploring predefined hyperparameter combinations. The focus was on key parameters known to influence performance, including the number of boosting iterations, tree depth, and the evaluation metric applied during training.

As shown in Table 5, the final configuration included 6,000 iterations and a maximum depth of 6, with RMSE as the evaluation metric. A fixed random seed was used to ensure reproducibility, and the use *Best Model* flag was enabled, allowing CatBoost to retain the best iteration based on validation performance.

Table 5. Optimized Hyperparameters for CatBoost (reproduced from [1]).

Hyperparameter	Value
Random Seed	42
Use Best Model	True
Evaluation Metric	RMSE
Iterations	6000
Max Depth	6

These optimized settings were chosen based on their effectiveness in reducing prediction error while maintaining model generalizability, especially important when dealing with real-world datasets that exhibit significant variability, as observed in the exploratory analyses.

Table 6. Performance of Optimized CatBoost Model (reproduced from [1]).

Metric	Value
RMSE	5.164
MAE	3.6097
R^2	77.53%
MAPE	14.73%

Post-optimization, the CatBoost model demonstrated marked improvements across all evaluation metrics (Table 6). Specifically, the RMSE decreased to 5.164 and MAE to 3.6097, while R^2 increased to 77.53%. This uplift confirms the efficacy of the tuning process in enhancing the model's capacity to capture complex interactions between semantic, temporal, and operational factors—a key requirement for accurate email open rate prediction.

These results validate the importance of not only selecting a strong base model but also fine-tuning its parameters to align with the unique characteristics of the dataset. The optimized CatBoost model is well-equipped to support marketers in making data-driven decisions, minimizing reliance on trial-and-error methods like A/B testing.

6.4 Feature Importance Analysis

Beyond its strong predictive performance, the optimized CatBoost model offers valuable interpretability by highlighting the features that most influence its predictions. Understanding these contributions is essential not only for model transparency but also for supporting strategic decisions in email marketing, such as optimizing send times, refining content, and managing sender reputation.

Using CatBoost's built-in feature importance analysis, we evaluated the relative influence of each feature on the model's output. The results closely reflected patterns identified during the exploratory analysis, reinforcing earlier insights and confirming the relevance of both operational and semantic factors in driving engagement.

Table 7. Top 10 Most Important Features in the Optimized CatBoost Model (reproduced from [1]).

Feature	Importance
Sender Open Rate	20.54%
Delivered	9.13%
Delivered Scaled	7.79%
Hour Open Rate	5.94%
Email Open Rate	5.42%
OpenAI PCA 0	4.49%
OpenAI PCA 1	3.63%
OpenAI PCA 2	3.49%
OpenAI PCA 5	3.45%
OpenAI PCA 4	3.29%

As shown in Table 7, *Sender Open Rate* emerged as the most impactful feature, contributing over 20% to the model's predictions. This finding reinforces the critical influence of sender reputation on recipient behavior, consistent with insights from the correlation and cluster analyses.

Other prominent features included delivery-related metrics—*Delivered* and *Delivered Scaled*—which reflect campaign reach, as well as time-sensitive engagement indicators like *Hour Open Rate* and *Email Open Rate*. Together, these features highlight that engagement is shaped not only by who sends the email, but also by when it is sent and the scale of its distribution.

Notably, several principal components derived from OpenAI embeddings also ranked among the top features. This underscores the effectiveness of semantic embeddings in capturing textual subtleties that influence engagement. In particular, components such as *OpenAI PCA 0*, *PCA 1*, and *PCA 2* encapsulated complex patterns present in subject lines and sender names, enhancing the model's ability to make precise predictions.

The combined relevance of operational, temporal, and semantic features underscores the multifaceted nature of email engagement. It also validates the integration of advanced embeddings and dimensionality reduction, as these elements played a direct role in the model's superior performance.

Ultimately, the feature importance analysis not only confirms the strategic value of key campaign attributes but also offers actionable guidance. By focusing on improving sender credibility, optimizing delivery timing, and crafting semantically rich subject lines, marketers can meaningfully increase engagement rates and campaign effectiveness.

6.5 Model Diagnostics

To further assess the effectiveness of the optimized CatBoost model, we conducted diagnostic evaluations to examine the accuracy and distribution of its predictions. These diagnostics provide deeper insight into how well the model generalizes across different data points and whether any systematic errors or biases are present.

Two key visualizations were employed: a histogram of residual errors and a scatter plot of actual versus predicted values. These have been consolidated into a single figure for clarity and space efficiency, as shown in Fig. 3.

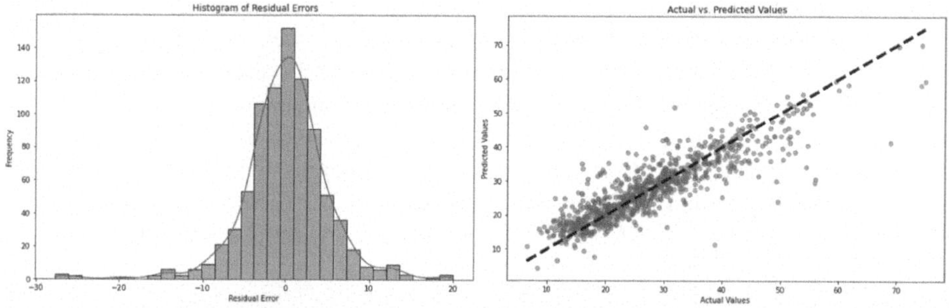

Fig. 3. Histogram of Residual Errors and Actual vs. Predicted Values (reproduced from [1]).

The histogram of residual errors, illustrated on the left, displays the frequency distribution of prediction errors, calculated as the difference between predicted and actual open rates. An ideal model should produce residuals that are symmetrically distributed around zero, indicating no consistent overestimation or underestimation.

In our analysis, the residuals exhibited a near-normal distribution centered around zero, suggesting that the model does not display systematic bias in its predictions. Most residuals are concentrated near zero, indicating high overall accuracy. A few residuals fall in the outer ranges of the distribution, signaling the presence of outliers or harder-to-predict cases, a finding consistent with insights from the feature importance analysis, where complex interactions between features may occasionally challenge the model.

Complementing the residuals analysis, the right side presents a scatter plot comparing actual open rates with those predicted by the model. The closer the points lie to the diagonal line, where predicted values equal actual values, the more accurate the predictions.

The majority of data points are tightly clustered around the diagonal, highlighting that the model maintains strong predictive alignment across a broad range of open rates. This consistency confirms the model's ability to generalize beyond the training data, ensuring reliability in real-world applications. Slight deviations from the diagonal, primarily at extreme values, reinforce the earlier observation of occasional difficulties with outlier cases.

Together, these diagnostic evaluations validate the robustness of the optimized CatBoost model. The balanced residual distribution and close alignment between actual and predicted values support the model's high performance and generalization capacity, as reflected in its RMSE, MAE, R^2, and MAPE scores.

Moreover, these diagnostics suggest that while the model excels under typical campaign conditions, future enhancements could focus on refining predictions for extreme open rate values or atypical campaign characteristics. Strategies such as targeted feature enrichment for edge cases or incorporating additional context-specific variables could help address these scenarios.

6.6 Comparison Across Quartiles

To better understand how the model performs across different levels of email engagement, we segmented the dataset into quartiles based on open rate distribution. This approach allows for a more nuanced evaluation of the model's strengths and limitations when predicting campaigns with low, moderate, or high engagement.

Using the *KBinsDiscretizer*, open rates were divided into five equally sized bins, labeled A through E. Quartile A corresponds to campaigns with the lowest engagement rates, while quartile E includes those with the highest. Table 8 reports the model's performance—measured by RMSE, MAE, and MAPE—within each quartile.

Table 8. Performance Metrics Across Quartiles (reproduced from [1]).

Cut	Min	Max	RMSE	MAE	MAPE
A	6.50	18.07	4.94	3.75	27%
B	18.17	23.73	4.21	2.90	14%
C	23.76	28.84	4.03	3.01	12%
D	28.85	35.84	4.31	3.10	10%
E	35.87	74.85	7.50	5.28	12%

As shown in Table 8, the model performs best in the mid-range quartiles (B, C, and D), where it achieves the lowest error rates. The most significant challenge arises in quartile A (lowest open rates), where MAPE reaches 27%, indicating greater difficulty in accurately predicting underperforming campaigns. Similarly, in quartile E (highest open rates), while MAPE remains low, RMSE and MAE values increase due to the broader range and higher variance of the target variable in this group.

This behavior is further visualized in Fig. 4, which displays the distribution of campaigns across quartiles and associated performance metrics. The figure highlights that the majority of campaigns fall into the mid-range categories, aligning with the model's strongest performance zones.

Overall, quartile-based evaluation provides critical context for model reliability across different engagement levels. The model demonstrates strong predictive capacity for the majority of campaigns, particularly in commonly occurring mid-range open rates. However, the increased error in quartiles A and E suggests that campaigns with extreme open rates—either very low or very high—present additional challenges.

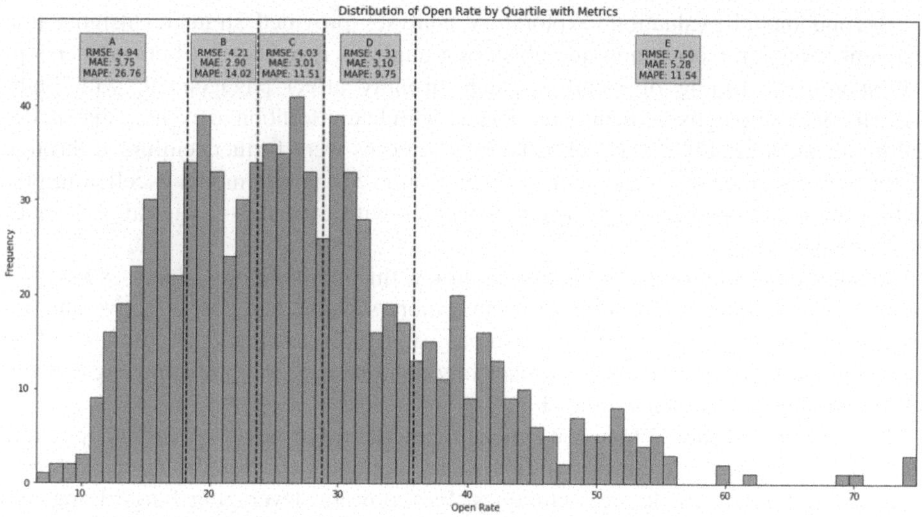

Fig. 4. Distribution of Open Rate by Quartile with Metrics (reproduced from [1]).

These insights underscore potential avenues for future improvement, such as specialized modeling strategies or feature enhancements to better capture the unique characteristics of outlier campaigns. Addressing these extremes can further strengthen model generalization and extend its utility in more diverse marketing scenarios.

7 Conclusion and Future Works

This paper presented a comprehensive and data-driven approach for predicting email open rates by leveraging subject line content, sender information, and contextual campaign features. By integrating text mining techniques and machine learning models, particularly the CatBoost algorithm optimized with operational features and OpenAI-based text embeddings (dimensionally reduced via PCA), the proposed methodology achieved notable predictive performance. The final model reached an RMSE of 5.164, MAE of 3.609, R^2 of 77.53%, and MAPE of 14.73%, underscoring the effectiveness of combining semantic, operational, and temporal features to anticipate recipient engagement.

The findings validated the initial hypothesis that the semantic content of subject lines significantly influences open rates. Furthermore, the analysis highlighted the critical role of sender credibility—quantified through the *Sender Open Rate*—as the most impactful predictor. These conclusions align with prior research emphasizing curiosity, utility [8], and personalization [9] as key drivers of user engagement. However, this study advanced the literature by demonstrating that predictive performance can be substantially enhanced when semantic embeddings are fused with contextual features, enabling the models to capture both linguistic nuances and operational dynamics.

Beyond model evaluation, exploratory analyses provided strategic insights into recipient behavior. Correlation and clustering analyses revealed that both sender reputation and the timing of email dispatch strongly affect engagement, with high-performance campaigns frequently associated with late-afternoon to evening dispatches and high sender credibility. These behavioral patterns were further reinforced through performance segmentation by quartiles, which showed that the model excelled in predicting moderate open rates but faced challenges with extremes—suggesting avenues for refinement.

In addition to improving prediction accuracy, this methodology addresses key limitations of traditional A/B testing, offering a more scalable and cost-effective alternative for optimizing email marketing campaigns. By forecasting open rates based on campaign attributes, marketers can proactively tailor strategies, optimizing engagement while reducing operational overhead.

Future research should focus on enhancing model robustness for extreme open rate predictions, potentially by incorporating more granular behavioral data or exploring advanced non-linear modeling techniques. Furthermore, leveraging Large Language Models (LLMs) for dynamic text embeddings or directly integrating them into regression tasks could significantly boost adaptability and precision. Another promising direction involves developing real-time adaptive models capable of continuous learning from incoming campaign data, enabling rapid, data-driven decision-making without reliance on time-consuming experiments.

Ultimately, this study bridges theoretical advancements in machine learning with practical applications in digital marketing, providing a robust framework for improving email campaign effectiveness. Combining semantic insights, contextual features, and predictive analytics, it contributes to a more strategic, personalized, and economically efficient approach to audience engagement in the evolving landscape of digital communication.

Acknowledgements. The authors thank the Pontifícia Universidade Católica de Minas Gerais – PUC-Minas and Coordenação de Aperfeiçoamento de Pessoal de Nível Superior—CAPES (CAPES – Grant PROAP 88887.842889/2023-00 – PUC/MG, Grant PDPG 88887.708960/2022-00 – PUC/MG - Informática, and Finance Code 001).

References

1. Santos, D.O., Brandão, W.C.: Learning to predict email open rates using subject and sender. In: Proceedings of the 20th International Conference on Web Information Systems and Technologies (WEBIST), pp. 59–70. SciTePress (2024). https://doi.org/10.5220/0012945700003825
2. The Radicati Group, Inc.: Email Statistics Report, 2023–2027. https://www.radicati.com/wp/wp-content/uploads/2023/04/Email-Statistics-Report-2023-2027-Executive-Summary.pdf. Accessed 20 May 2024
3. Stupar-Rutenfrans, S., de Koff, D., van den Elst, J.: The effect of subject lines on open rates of email marketing messages. Adv. Social Sci. Res. J. **6**(7), 181–188 (2019). https://doi.org/10.14738/assrj.67.6749

4. Forbes Advisor: Best Email Marketing Software (2024). https://www.forbes.com/advisor/business/best-email-marketing-software/. Accessed 27 May 2024
5. Salton, G., Buckley, C.: Term-weighting approaches in automatic text retrieval. Inf. Process. Manag. **24**(5), 513–523 (1988)
6. Mikolov, T., Chen, K., Corrado, G., Dean, J.: Efficient estimation of word representations in vector space. In: Proceedings of the International Conference on Learning Representations (ICLR) (2013)
7. OpenAI: OpenAI API (2024). https://platform.openai.com/docs/guides/embeddings
8. Wainer, J., Dabbish, L., Kraut, R.: Should I open this email? In: Proceedings of the SIGCHI Conference on Human Factors in Computing Systems, pp. 343–352. ACM (2011)
9. Sahni, N.S., Wheeler, S.C., Chintagunta, P.K.: Personalization in email marketing: the role of non-informative advertising content. Mark. Sci. **35**(2), 216–233 (2016). https://doi.org/10.1287/mksc.2015.0967
10. Feld, S., Frenzen, H., Krafft, M., Peters, K., Verhoef, P.C.: The effects of mailing design characteristics on direct mail campaign performance. Int. J. Res. Mark. **30**(2), 143–159 (2013). https://doi.org/10.1016/j.ijresmar.2012.07.003
11. Conceição, A.G.: Main Factors Driving the Open Rate of Email Marketing Campaigns. Master's Dissertation, University of Porto, Portugal (2019)
12. Balakrishnan, R., Parekh, R.: Learning to predict subject-line opens for large-scale email marketing. In: IEEE International Conference on Big Data, pp. 579–584. IEEE (2014). https://doi.org/10.1109/BigData.2014.7004277
13. Miller, R., Charles, E.Y.A.: A psychological based analysis of Marketing Email Subject Lines. In: International Conference on Advances in ICT for Emerging Regions (ICTer), pp. 58–65. IEEE (2016). https://doi.org/10.1109/ICTER.2016.7829918
14. Joshi, S., Banerjee, I.: Ngram-LSTM open rate prediction model (NLORPM). Int. J. Dig. Mark. (2023). https://arxiv.org/abs/2302.00651
15. Paulo, M., Miguéis, V.L., Pereira, I.: Leveraging email marketing: using the subject line to anticipate the open rate. Expert Syst. Appl. **207**, 117974 (2022). https://doi.org/10.1016/j.eswa.2022.117974
16. Etus Media Holding: About Etus Media Holding. https://etus.digital. Accessed 30 May 2024
17. Bellman, R.: Adaptive Control Processes: A Guided Tour. Princeton University Press, Princeton (1961)
18. Hastie, T., Tibshirani, R., Friedman, J.: The Elements of Statistical Learning: Data Mining, Inference, and Prediction, 2nd edn. Springer, New York (2009)

Using LLMs for Semi-automatic Handwritten Text Recognition and Elaboration

Angelica Lo Duca(✉)

Institute of Informatics and Telematics, National Research Council, 56124 Pisa, Italy
angelica.loduca@iit.cnr.it

Abstract. Recent advancements in Large Language Models (LLMs) have opened new opportunities for automating complex tasks, including Handwritten Text Recognition (HTR) and named entity extraction from historical manuscripts. This paper presents an approach that leverages LLMs to perform HTR directly on handwritten documents, reducing the reliance on traditional handwriting recognition tools. The system enhances transcription accuracy by incorporating repetitive text patterns and a database of names and surnames. In addition to HTR, the study explores using LLMs for extracting named entities (NEs) from structured and highly repetitive texts, such as historical population registries. The approach evaluates the performance of GPT-3.5 Turbo and GPT-4 in NE extraction tasks, comparing the effects of different levels of instruction detail. For HTR, the impact of integrating an NE database is assessed against a baseline model without additional data support. The results demonstrate that providing LLMs with structured guidance and external NE databases significantly improves both transcription quality and entity recognition accuracy. While GPT-4 achieves the highest precision, GPT-3.5 Turbo presents a cost-effective alternative with a good balance between performance and efficiency. These findings highlight the potential of LLMs as versatile tools for both manuscript transcription and structured data extraction from historical records.

Keywords: Handwritten text recognition · Large Language Models · Named entity recognition · Digital humanities

1 Introduction

Recent advancements in Large Language Models (LLMs) [8] have significantly enhanced information extraction and processing from structured and unstructured texts [13, 15, 38], offering new possibilities for manuscript transcription and text elaboration in different domains. These models can potentially automate complex tasks such as interpreting historical documents, transcribing handwritten records, and structuring textual data for further analysis. Traditional rule-based approaches for text analysis [47] often struggle with the variability and inconsistencies in historical manuscripts, where handwriting styles, abbreviations, and text degradation pose significant challenges [2]. In contrast, LLMs can generalize across different writing conventions, recognize patterns in repetitive texts, and adapt dynamically to diverse document structures, making them a

The original version of the chapter has been revised. The chapter has been corrected. A correction to this chapter can be found at https://doi.org/10.1007/978-3-032-25534-1_18

M. Marchiori et al. (Eds.): WEBIST 2024, LNBIP 583, pp. 206–224, 2026.
https://doi.org/10.1007/978-3-032-25534-1_9

promising tool for digital humanities, archival research, and historical document processing. However, despite their potential, effectively leveraging LLMs requires designing structured prompts, understanding model behavior, and carefully evaluating their outputs [51]. Furthermore, integrating these models into practical workflows raises ethical concerns, particularly regarding biases in training data that could affect decision-making processes [4].

This paper extends a previous study [29, 30] that explored named entity extraction from repetitive texts using LLMs, specifically focusing on population registries. The prior approach demonstrated the feasibility of replacing rule-based methods with LLMs for extracting structured information. The described approach should help reduce the psychophysiological effects of repetitive texts [49]. However, one major limitation remained unaddressed: the reliance on pre-processed digital text, which required external Handwritten Text Recognition (HTR) Tools or manual transcription for converting manuscript images into machine-readable text [36].

The primary contribution of this paper is introducing an LLM-based HTR system, which directly processes handwritten documents, eliminating the dependency on conventional HTR tools for handwritten documents. To achieve this, a new system architecture and a refined workflow are developed, integrating GPT-4 as both an HTR engine and an entity extraction model. The proposed approach enhances recognition accuracy by providing the LLM with structured guidance. This system takes advantage of the fact that LLMs can reason, provided they have a basic context from which to start. Specifically, the LLM is fed with repetitive text patterns and a predefined database of named entities (e.g., names and surnames) to facilitate more precise transcription and entity extraction. A preliminary experiment revealed that HTR performance improves when processing one record at a time rather than full-page scans. To accommodate this, scanned handwritten document images are manually cropped to isolate individual records before feeding them into the system. This preprocessing step significantly improves text recognition accuracy and mitigates errors caused by overlapping or misaligned text.

A secondary contribution of this paper is enhancing the related work section with a review of state-of-the-art techniques of handwritten recognition. This includes an analysis of existing strategies, their effectiveness in manuscript recognition, and their integration with modern language models.

A case study is analyzed to validate this approach, based on the Registry of Births in the Historical Archive of the Jewish Community in Pisa. Although the experiments presented in this paper focus on a specific case study, the techniques and workflow described are designed to be generalizable to other types of repetitive manuscript records. This approach can be adapted to various historical documents featuring structured and recurring patterns, regardless of language or cultural context, making it suitable for broader applications in digital humanities and archival research. Two types of experiments are described. The first experiment involves HTR performance to evaluate the presence of the NE database and determine its effectiveness in direct text transcription. The second experiment refers to Named Entity (NE) extraction from the transcribed text, with a comparison between GPT-3.5 Turbo and GPT-4 across different levels of instruction granularity to assess performance and cost trade-offs.

Finally, this paper improves previous work discussing the challenges and ethical implications of using LLMs for HTR and text elaboration, including bias, transparency, and cultural sensitivity. Section 6 of the paper is dedicated to Ethical Considerations, where these concerns and potential mitigation strategies are discussed in depth.

The remainder of the paper is structured as follows: Sect. 2 reviews related literature, Sect. 3 details the proposed approach, Sect. 4 presents experiments, and Sect. 5 discusses results. Section 6 discusses ethical considerations while using LLMs and possible mitigation strategies. Finally, Sect. 7 provides conclusions and future work.

2 Related Work

The processing of historical and manuscripts is a long-standing challenge that involves two key aspects: *transcription* (converting images into machine-readable text) and *text analysis* (extracting meaningful structured information). The transcription process is typically handled using HTR tools, but historical manuscripts pose unique difficulties, such as degraded text, inconsistent handwriting styles, and non-standard spelling, often resulting in poor HTR accuracy. Once transcribed, the next step is analyzing the text, which may include Named Entity Recognition (NER), relation extraction, and structural parsing. NER plays a crucial role in this pipeline, allowing researchers to identify and classify key entities (e.g., names, locations, dates, and organizations) within the text, facilitating further historical or linguistic analysis. Over time, different NER methodologies have emerged, ranging from rule-based and statistical learning-based approaches to modern deep learning and LLM-based techniques.

The remainder of this section provides an overview of two key areas relevant to this research: approaches to HTR and approaches to NER.

2.1 Approaches to Manuscript Recognition

The recognition of manuscripts has evolved significantly, progressing from traditional machine-learning techniques to modern deep-learning and Transformer-based methods. Early approaches focused on handcrafted feature extraction combined with classic classifiers such as k-nearest neighbors (k-NN), support vector machines (SVMs), and random forests. These systems relied on manually designed features like contours, strokes, and histograms of oriented gradients [2].

Introducing convolutional neural networks (CNNs) marked a turning point in manuscript recognition. CNNs automatically learn hierarchical features from raw image data, outperforming manual feature-based methods in robustness and accuracy. Islam and Iacob demonstrated the effectiveness of a CNN model for recognizing characters in the medieval Beowulf manuscript, achieving accuracies of up to 99%. CNN-based systems became central to handwriting recognition, offering improved handling of cursive and degraded scripts [21].

Despite CNNs success, challenges remained in recognizing sequences of handwritten text. Hybrid architectures that combine CNNs with recurrent neural networks (RNNs), typically using long short-term memory (LSTM) units, became the standard for sequence modeling [18, 41].

More recently, Transformer-based architectures have gained traction in handwritten text recognition. Initially designed for natural language processing, transformers have been adapted for image-based tasks through Vision Transformers (ViT) and encoder-decoder models. Li et al. [27] introduced TrOCR, a Transformer-based model pre-trained on synthetic data and fine-tuned for handwriting recognition. Similarly, Li et al. [28] proposed HTR-VT, a model that leverages Vision Transformers for handwritten text recognition, demonstrating competitive performance on standard benchmarks.

The availability of pre-trained handwritten text recognition (HTR) models and user-friendly toolkits has further accelerated progress in the field. Platforms such as Transkribus [37], Kraken [25], and Calamari [50] have lowered barriers for scholars working with historical manuscripts.

Finally, interactive transcription methods, where users correct system predictions in real-time, can significantly reduce transcription effort while ensuring accuracy [17, 45].

Compared to the existing literature, the approach described in this paper uses general-purpose LLMs, such as OpenAI ChatGPT, adapted with an NEs database to perform HTR. This approach should replace the effort of implementing a specific model with one to build an appropriate NEs database.

2.2 Approaches to NER

There are different approaches to perform NER [16, 20, 39, 40]. Rule-based approaches rely on predefined rules and patterns crafted based on the language's linguistic properties. These rules identify entities based on their grammatical and contextual features. For instance, a previous paper used a rule-based approach to perform the same task as in this paper [31]. Other examples include the research done by Eftimov et al., who presented a rule-based NER method called drNER for extracting evidence-based dietary recommendations from text [12], and MeTAE (Medical Texts Annotation and Exploration), a platform for the annotation of medical entries [5]. Learning-based approaches utilize machine learning algorithms to learn from annotated datasets. These approaches range from traditional machine learning methods to more advanced deep learning techniques. A notable example is the work by Pooja and Jagadeesh, who used a deep learning-based approach using Bidirectional Long Short Term Memory (BiL-STM), Bidirectional Encoder Representations from Transformers (BERT), and Conditional Random Field (CRF) models for biomedical NER [4]. Hybrid approaches combine the strengths of both rule-based and learning-based methods. They often employ machine learning models to capture complex patterns and use rule-based systems to handle well-defined entities. An example of a hybrid approach is presented by Ji et al., who applied a BiLSTM-CRF model with an attention mechanism and post-processing rules for NER in Chinese electronic medical records [23].

While rule-based approaches can be very effective for well-structured entities, learning-based approaches offer greater flexibility and adaptability to diverse and complex entity patterns. Hybrid approaches leverage both advantages to achieve optimal performance on NER tasks. The choice of approach often depends on the task's specific requirements, the text's nature, and the availability of annotated data.

Given the growing interest in LLMs, a thriving literature is also developing around the use of LLMs to perform NER tasks. One way to use LLMs for NER is to transform the sequence labeling task of NER to a generation task that LLMs can quickly adapt to. Wang et al. propose a method to encode the input sentence and the entity type as a single prompt and decode the entity span as the output [48]. They also introduce a self-verification strategy to address the hallucination issue of LLMs [7], where they may generate spurious entities that do not exist in the input sentence. Another way to use LLMs for NER is to leverage their ability to access external knowledge sources, such as Wikipedia or other knowledge bases. Malmasi et al. present a large multilingual dataset for NER that covers three domains (Wiki sentences, questions, and search queries) across 11 languages and multilingual and code-mixing subsets [35]. Some works have also performed NER without labeled data or pre-trained models. For example, Luo et al. propose a fully unsupervised NER model that only relies on pre-trained word embeddings [32]. Another approach uses natural language prompts to guide LLMs to perform NER without fine-tuning or labeling data [3]. Shen et al. propose a simple method that applies an LLM to encode queries and documents into dense vectors and then computes their cosine similarity [42].

Compared to the current literature, this paper describes an empirical study to evaluate the performance of two popular LLMs, without any domain adaptation or other manipulations, to extract named entities from repetitive texts. The objective is to assess if or not LLMs can be used as they are for this type of task without any adaptation.

3 The Proposed Approach

This paper uses two LLM-based applications to transcribe and extract NEs and their relationships from repetitive texts. Figure 1 illustrates the implemented workflow for the task.

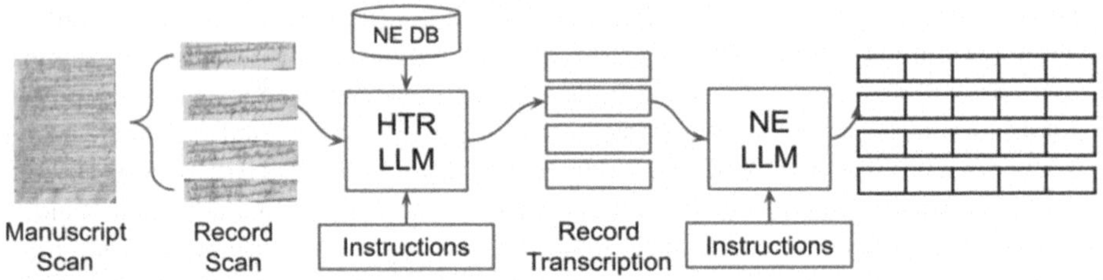

Fig. 1. The implemented workflow transforms the manuscript scan into a structured table.

The workflow starts with a manuscript containing repetitive records, such as population registries, inventories, etc. The manuscript is available as a single PDF file or as a collection of images, one of each page or page pair. Each record in every manuscript page is separated from the others manually using a tool for image editing or screenshot taking and saved as a separate image. Every obtained image is then given as input to an HTR-LLM app, which is used to perform HTR. This app is enriched with information about the NEs in the registry (NE Database, or NE DB for short). For example, if the registry contains a population, the NE DB would contain candidate names and surnames.

If the registry includes an inventory of objects, the NE DB would contain candidate objects. The NE DB is populated using a source external to the manuscript, such as the Web. The HTR-HTR app extracts the transcription associated with each record. Next, each transcribed record and an instructions template containing text describing the task to perform are provided as input to the NE-LLM app. The NE-LLM app extracts NEs from each record and formats them in a tabular format.

3.1 Case Study

The case study considered the Registry of Births of the Historical Archive of the Jewish Community of Pisa [31]. This registry contains 262 records related to the members of the Pisa Jewish community, their date of birth, their sex, and their father's name. The registry also contains some descriptive texts, which this paper has not considered. The birth registry started on October 12, 1749, and ended on November 1809. Each record contains the date of birth, indicated according to the Jewish and Gregorian systems (for a baby born on March 10th, the registry also shows the day of Rosh Chodesh Cheshvan 5510). The original document is written in Italian with some parts in Hebrew, and all the records have more or less the same structure. Figure 2 shows an example of a manuscript page. Each record is separated from the others through a horizontal line.

Fig. 2. An example of a manuscript page in the Registry of Births. Source: The Historical Archives of the Jewish Community in Pisa.

Figure 3 shows a sample record within its original version (the manuscript at the top of the figure), the Italian transcription (in the middle), and the English translation (at the bottom). The figure shows the text translated into English for convenience, although tests have been done using the original Italian language.

Original Text in Italian
5510 Giorno di domenica primo giorno di Rosh Chodesh Cheshvan che corresponde a 12 ottobre 1749.
Naque una figlia al Signore Salamon Sezzi e si pose nome Ribqa bemazal tov

5510 Sunday first day of Rosh Chodesh Cheshvan which corresponds to October 12, 1749. A daughter was born to Lord Salamon Sezzi and she was named Ribqa bemazal tov

Fig. 3. An example of a record in the Registry of Births of the Historical Archive of the Jewish Community of Pisa. Source: Fig. 2 in [29].

The described case study is used to evaluate the performance of the HTR-LLM and NE-LLM apps in the workflow of Fig. 1. In this paper, two sets of metrics are measured, one to assess the performance of the HTR-LLM app and the other to the performance of the NE-LLM app.

For the HTR-LLM app, a single metric is measured:

1. *Average Characters Ratio*: the average ratio between the number of characters correctly identified by the model and the total number of characters in the exact transcription.

For the NE-LLM app, the following metrics are measured:

1. *Father Ratio*: the ratio between the number of entities recognized correctly as a father and the total number of records;
2. *Child Ratio*: the ratio between the number of entities recognized correctly as a child and the total number of records;
3. *Sex Ratio*: the ratio between the number of records where the child's sex is correctly identified and the total number of records;
4. *Date Ratio*: the ratio between the number of records where the child's date of birth is correctly identified and the total number of records.
5. *Total Ratio*: the ratio between the sum of the number of entities recognized correctly as a father, the number of entities recognized correctly as a child, the number of records where the child's sex is correctly identified, the number of records where the child's date of birth is correctly identified and the total number of records multiplied for four.

The current evaluation metrics will be extended in future work with more complex metrics, such as embedding-based semantic similarity scores and weighted edit distance, to better assess the transcriptions' contextual and historical accuracy. Additionally, expert evaluation by historians and domain specialists will be included to ensure the philological reliability of the extracted data.

4 Experiments

Experiments were organized into two sets: one to assess the performance of the HTR-LLM app and the other to assess the performance of the NE-LLM app. This is because the two LLM apps are conceptually separated. The remainder of this section describes the two sets separately.

4.1 HTR-LLM Experiments

The HTR-LLM app was implemented using OpenAI ChatGPT Plus[1] with the GPT-4o model [1]. A preliminary experiment consisted of uploading a scan of an entire manuscript page into ChatGPT. This experiment failed because ChatGPT responded by saying it could not recognize the text. For this reason, individual records were separated manually within each scan. Each image representing a record was uploaded manually in a single ChatGPT conversation using the paperclip button provided by the ChatGPT interface. In total, two experiments were run. The first experiment used the NE database to match names and surnames in the record. The second experiment, instead, did not use any NE database. This second experiment assessed whether the NE database's presence increases the model's performance. Each experiment asked ChatGPT to recognize and transcribe 100 records from the Registry of Births. The results were compared to the manual transcription of the registry performed during previous work [31]. Initially, the idea was to compare the results of the HTR-LLM app with those produced using Transkribus[2], an HTR tool for manuscripts. However, a preliminary experiment using the basic model and the free version did not succeed because the tool did not recognize any records correctly. Thus, Transkribus was not used during the experiments.

Scenario with NE Database. As the first prompt of the conversation with ChatGPT, the following contextual prompt was provided as input:

```
I'll provide you with some manuscripts having the following structure: Giorno
di domenica primo giorno di Rosh Chodesh Cheshvan (ebr.) che corresponde a 12
ottobre 1749. Naque una figlia al Signore Salamon Sezzi e si pose nome Ribqa
bemazal tov (ebr.); Each manuscript is written in Italian and Hebrew. First
transcribe Italian, next transcribe the Hebrew that contains a person name. For
the list of names and surnames, take inspiration from the attached documents.
```

In addition to the prompt, the list of Jewish names and surnames (the NE database) was provided as input. The list of surnames contained 4399 surnames extracted from the Ordre de Saint Andre de Caffa[3], and the list of names contained 100 names extracted

[1] https://openai.com/chatgpt/overview/.

[2] https://www.transkribus.org/it.

[3] http://andreadicaffa02.unblog.fr/2011/10/23/prima-lista-di-cognomi-ebrei-italiani-stranieri-ashkenazi-E-sefardi/.

from Shalom.it[4] and enriched with a list of 29 additional names extracted directly from ChatGPT. ChatGPT provided the following output to the first prompt:

```
I can access the names and surnames list you uploaded. Please upload the
manuscripts, and I will transcribe the Italian text followed by the Hebrew names
while ensuring consistency with the provided name lists.
```

Next, the image of each record was uploaded to ChatGPT using the paperclip button, one each time. ChatGPT answered with the transcription, as shown in Fig. 4.

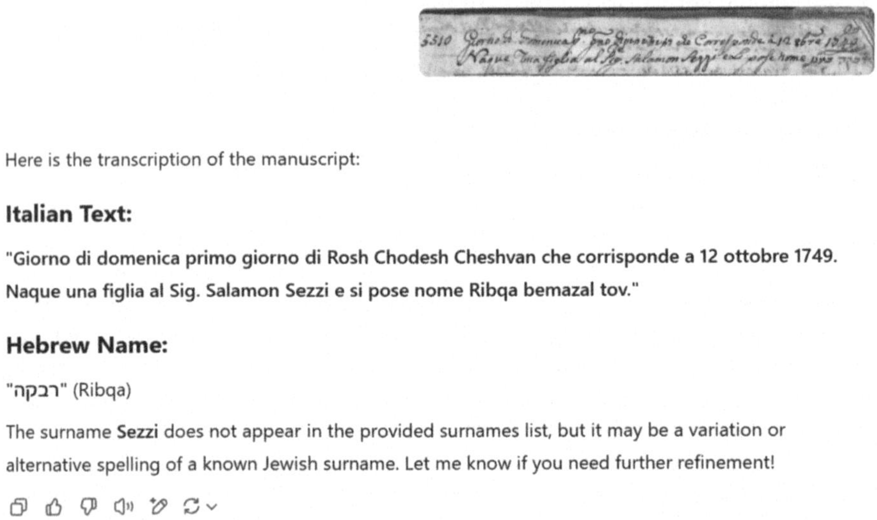

Fig. 4. An example of a conversation with ChatGPT to extract the transcription from the record scan.

Scenario without the NE Database. This experiment followed the same workflow as the previous one, except for the prompt, which was the following:

```
I'll provide you with some manuscripts having the following structure: Giorno
di domenica primo giorno di Rosh Chodesh Cheshvan (ebr.) che corresponde a 12
ottobre 1749. Naque una figlia al Signore Salamon Sezzi e si pose nome Ribqa
bemazal tov (ebr.); Each manuscript is written in Italian and Hebrew. First
transcribe Italian, next transcribe the Hebrew that contains a person name.
Generate a single sentence.
```

Results. Figures 5 and 6 show the Character Ratio for the scenarios with and without the NE database. The Average Character Ratio for the scenario with the NE database was 0.497, and that for the scenario without the NE database was 0.227. The performance increase of the scenario with the NE database was 118.94%.

[4] https://www.shalom.it/israele/i-100-nomi-pia-comuni-nella-storia-da-israele-david-E-noa-in-cima-alla-classifica-b1120081/.

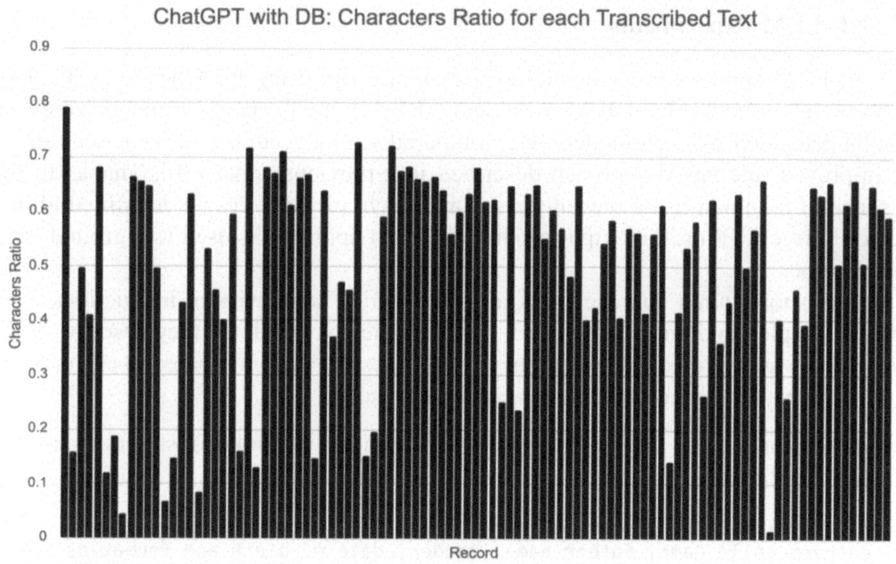

Fig. 5. The Character Ratio using ChatGPT with the NE DB for each analyzed record in the Registry of Births.

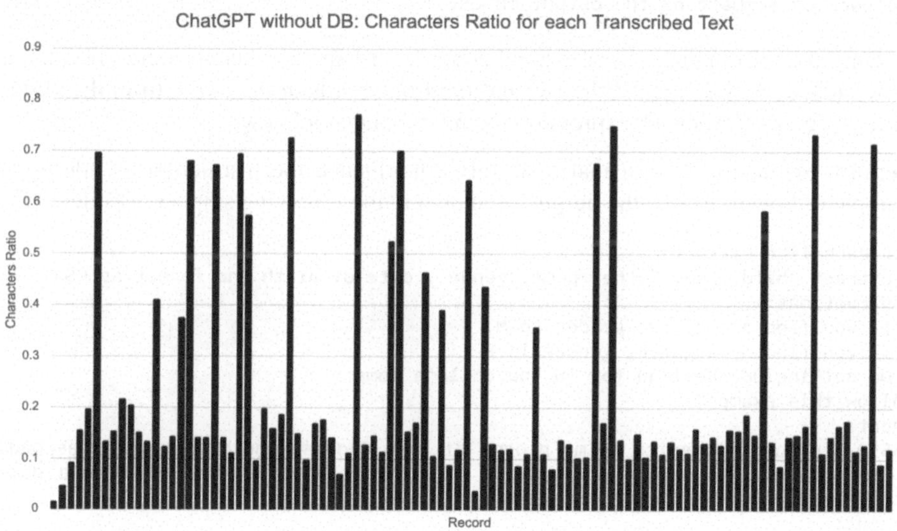

Fig. 6. The character ratio using ChatGPT without the NE DB for each analyzed record in the Registry of Births.

4.2 NE-LLM Experiments

The NE-LLM app was implemented as a Python script using the OpenAI API[5]. Two LLM models were used: GPT-3.5 turbo and GPT-4. In total, six experiments were run. Results generated by each model were compared with a ground truth generated using the improved rule-based approach described in a previous paper [30]. Thanks to the presence of a human using the rule-based approach, previous results identified all the records correctly; thus, the output produced by that approach is used as a ground truth for this paper.

A few-shot prompt approach was followed [33]. Three levels of instructions were defined: simple, medium, and detailed, based on the level of detail they describe. Each instruction was provided as input to the models. Results were compared to evaluate the minimum detail required to achieve satisfactory results.

Simple Scenario. The following snippet of code shows the simple instructions used in this first experiment:

```
For each line extract:
- extract child name, father name, gender, date of birth and format as CSV
Instructions:
- If you find a son, set gender to M
- If you find a daughter, gender is F
- Do not include besiman tov in the child's name
Answer by formatting the output in CSV.
```

Only the information to extract and some record-specific details were provided as input, such as how to extract the sex and omit the words *besiman tov* from the child's name since this is a Jewish expression the model may not know.

Medium Scenario. This scenario slightly complicated the instruction by adding an example of how to format the output, as shown in the following snippet of code:

```
For each line extract:
- extract child name, father name, gender, date of birth and format as CSV
Instructions:
- If you find a son, set gender to M
- If you find a daughter, gender is F
- Do not include besiman tov in the child's name
Follow this example:
Input:
<5510 Giorno di domenica primo giorno di Rosh Chodesh Cheshvan che corresponde
a 12 ottobre 1749. Naque una figlia al Signore Salamon Sezzi e si pose nome
Ribqa bemazal tov>
Output:
Ribqa,Salamon Sezzi,F,1749-10-17

Answer by formatting the output in CSV.
```

This instruction provides an example in angular brackets, defines the desired output, and shows how to format it. For instance, it asks the model to format the date following the yyyy-mm-dd notation.

---

[5] https://openai.com/index/openai-api/.

Detailed Scenario. The detailed scenario complicated the instruction by adding what the model should do if some information is missing, as described in the following piece of code:

```
For each line extract:
- extract child name,father name, gender, date of birth and format as CSV
Instructions:
- If you find a son, set gender to M
- If you find a daughter, gender is F
- Do not include besiman tov in the child's name
- If the child's name is not present, add only a comma
- If the father's name is not present, add only a comma
- If the date of birth is not present, add only a comma
Follow this example:
Input:
<5510 Giorno di domenica primo giorno di Rosh Chodesh Cheshvan che corresponde
a 12 ottobre 1749. Naque una figlia al Signore Salamon Sezzi e si pose nome
Ribqa bemazal tov>
Output:
Ribqa,Salamon Sezzi,F,1749-10-17

Answer by formatting the output in CSV.
```

Results. Figure 7 shows the Father, Child, Sex, and Date ratios for all the experiments. As expected the best model is GPT 4 with detailed instructions. However, the Sex and Date ratios are the same for GPT 4 with medium and detailed instructions. Adding details to the instructions does not improve the model's performance. It is also interesting to notice that GPT 3.5 Turbo with detailed instructions performs better than GPT 4 with simple instructions. This suggests the importance of instructions in obtaining the correct outputs.

		Child Ratio	Father Ratio	Sex Ratio	Date Ratio
GPT 3.5 Turbo	Simple	0.7938931298	0.6832061069	0.893129771	0.6679389313
	Medium	0.8664122137	0.7786259542	0.9465648855	0.9503816794
	Detailed	0.893129771	0.8015267176	0.965648855	0.9503816794
GPT 4	Simple	0.9045801527	0.786259542	0.965648855	0.8358778626
	Medium	0.9236641221	0.8969465649	0.9847328244	0.9961832061
	Detailed	0.9389312977	0.8854961832	0.9847328244	0.9961832061

Legend

0.60-0.69	0.70-0.79	0.80-0.89	0.90-0.95	0.96-1.00

Fig. 7. The Father, Child, Sex, and Date ratios for all the experiments. The darker the cell color, the better the model performance. The father is the most complex entity to extract in all scenarios, while the easiest is the date. This is because the parent entity sometimes has a different structure from the classic one, while the date is almost always in the same format. Source: Fig. 3 in [29].

Only GPT 4 with medium and detailed instructions has a Total Ratio greater than 0.95. The only surprise is given by GPT 3.5 Turbo medium and detailed, which outperforms GPT 4 simple. This confirms the importance of formulating instructions properly.

5 Discussion

The experimental results confirm the effectiveness of integrating LLMs into workflows for transcribing and extracting structured data from historical handwritten documents. Combining LLMs with external Named Entity (NE) databases significantly improved both HTR and NER. Specifically, including an NE database increased the average Character Ratio from 0.227 to 0.497, showing a performance gain of approximately 119%. This demonstrates how LLMs benefit from contextual information, mainly when provided with curated, domain-specific data that helps disambiguate degraded handwriting and repetitive patterns.

An analysis of the errors made by the HTR-LLM app reveals that the most common mistakes concern recognizing entities such as dates, names, and surnames. However, in nearly all cases, the model successfully identifies the overall sentence structure, both with and without the support of the external NE database. In the best-case scenario, the model accurately recognizes most words but introduces minor variations when using the NE database. For example, the term Signor (Lord) is often transcribed as Sig. (an abbreviated form of Signor), and some proper names appear with slight alterations, such as Riqbal instead of Riqba. Without the NE database, the model tends to recognize surnames that are not traditionally Jewish, producing variants like Pallicese, Pallico, and Pallies, which do not correspond to the actual entries in the historical records.

Prompt design also played a crucial role. Detailed instructions led to higher accuracy, with GPT-3.5 Turbo, when given more comprehensive prompts, outperforming GPT-4 under more straightforward instructions. This highlights the importance of prompt engineering in achieving satisfactory results, even with lower-cost models. GPT-4, provided with medium or detailed instructions, consistently exceeded a Total Ratio of 0.95, confirming its reliability when well-guided. For a detailed analysis of costs and the formatting errors generated by each model, refer to previous work [29].

However, the proposed approach presents several limitations. The current workflow requires manual segmentation of individual records from manuscript pages, which, although effective in improving the HTR character ratio, limits scalability and hinders full automation. Another key limitation is the reliance on external NE databases. While these lists help the model improve transcription accuracy, they introduce potential biases if the database is incomplete or non-representative. Overreliance on a predefined NE database may reduce the model's ability to recognize names or entities not included in the list, decreasing generalizability across different datasets, languages, or historical contexts. This can lead to systematic inaccuracies, mainly when processing diverse or less standardized documents.

To address these challenges, careful curation of NE databases is essential, though time-consuming. Future work should explore automated methods for dynamic NE extraction or unsupervised learning techniques to identify new entities on the fly, reducing dependence on external lists and minimizing bias.

Compared to traditional HTR systems like Transkribus, which struggled with the documents used in this study, the LLM-based approach showed greater flexibility in handling inconsistent handwriting and multilingual content. Unlike previously explored rule-based systems [31], this method eliminates the need for predefined extraction rules and extensive post-processing, streamlining the workflow. Nevertheless, LLMs' "black-box" nature raises concerns regarding transparency and verification of results, mainly when dealing with culturally sensitive or historically significant documents.

Lastly, the ethical implications of using LLMs in historical document processing should not be overlooked. Potential biases in both the models and the external data sources require human oversight and validation procedures to ensure accuracy, fairness, and respect for cultural heritage.

6 Ethical Considerations

Integrating LLMs into transcribing and analyzing historical manuscripts introduces several ethical challenges. One of the primary concerns is *bias and misrepresentation*. LLMs trained on vast datasets often reflect the societal and cultural biases in their training data. When applied to historical manuscripts, this can result in distorted representations or omissions, especially when dealing with marginalized communities [11, 24]. To mitigate these risks, curating diverse and representative refinement datasets [19], such as the NE database described in this paper, is essential. Engaging with domain experts and community representatives during the review process can further ensure culturally appropriate interpretations [24]. Integrating bias detection tools into the transcription pipeline can also help identify problematic outputs early [6].

A second major issue is the *lack of transparency and explainability* inherent in LLM systems. These models are often perceived as "black boxes," making it difficult for users to understand the rationale behind specific outputs [34]. This opacity undermines trust, particularly in academic and historical research where accountability and verifiability are essential. To address this, recommended techniques include Explainable AI (XAI) [10], providing explicit metadata distinguishing between AI-generated and human-verified content [26], and maintaining human-in-the-loop oversight [43].

A critical additional concern is *ethical accuracy responsibility*, which ensures that AI-generated transcriptions and analyses accurately reflect historical truth while respecting ethical standards. Mitigation techniques include preventing the AI from generating misleading interpretations or conclusions that could distort historical understanding [6], establishing rigorous quality control protocols [44], and training researchers to critically engage with AI outputs [14].

Finally, *cultural sensitivity, privacy, and respect for communities* must be prioritized. Automated processing of historical records involves data about living descendants or culturally sensitive subjects [9]. Engaging with relevant communities for input and, where applicable, consent is vital to maintaining respect and dignity. Different privacy-preserving practices should be implemented, including data anonymization [4] and established cultural heritage stewardship principles [22].

Table 1 shows the described ethical risks and a possible strategy to mitigate them in the context of manuscript transcription and analysis.

Table 1. Ethical risks associated with LLMs and a potential mitigation strategy.

Ethical Risk	Description	Mitigation
Bias and Misrepresentation	LLMs may produce distorted or incomplete transcriptions due to biases in training data	Curate diverse datasets; involve community experts; use bias detection tools
Lack of Transparency and Explainability	LLMs operate as black boxes, making it difficult to understand how decisions are made	Apply Explainable AI; provide clear metadata; maintain human oversight
Ethical accuracy responsibility	Risk of AI outputs misrepresenting historical facts or generating misleading interpretations	Implement quality control; ensure expert validation; train researchers in critical AI assessment
Cultural Sensitivity, Privacy, and Respect	Processing records may expose sensitive data or disrespect cultural values	Engage communities; anonymize data; follow cultural heritage guidelines

7 Conclusions and Future Work

This study explored the application of Large Language Models (LLMs) for the semi-automatic transcription and structured data extraction from historical handwritten documents. By integrating LLMs into the workflow, the proposed approach enhanced both HTR and NER tasks, particularly when supplemented with external Named Entity (NE) databases and detailed instructional prompts.

The experiments confirm that providing LLMs with structured guidance, repetitive text patterns, and curated lists of candidate entities can substantially improve the accuracy of transcription and data extraction. Notably, GPT-4 consistently achieved the highest performance in scenarios with medium to detailed instructions, although GPT-3.5 Turbo proved to be a cost-effective alternative when properly guided through prompt engineering. These findings highlight the flexibility and adaptability of LLMs, which, unlike traditional rule-based or HTR systems, can dynamically adjust to the complexities of degraded handwriting and varying document structures without requiring extensive pre-training or rule customization.

Future developments should prioritize automating the entire workflow, particularly the segmentation phase. Integrating computer vision techniques, such as image segmentation algorithms [46], could enable the automatic identification and cropping of individual records from manuscript pages, removing manual intervention. Additionally, the dynamic generation and refinement of NE databases through unsupervised or semi-supervised learning techniques could enhance system adaptability and reduce reliance on external data sources.

Expanding the evaluation to include emerging LLMs from other providers, such as Google's Gemini[6], Meta's LLaMA[7], or Anthropic's Claude[8], will be essential to benchmark different architectures' relative performance, cost-efficiency, and domain adaptability. Such comparisons could provide valuable insights into selecting the most appropriate models for specific use cases in digital humanities and archival research.

In addition, exploring more sophisticated prompt engineering methodologies and adaptive instruction generation could help optimize model performance with minimal user intervention. While not addressed in this study, domain-specific fine-tuning remains a promising avenue for further improving accuracy and efficiency, particularly for specialized historical archives or culturally specific datasets.

From a broader perspective, this research contributes to the growing body of literature advocating for the adoption of LLMs in the field of digital humanities. The proposed approach opens new opportunities for historians, archivists, and researchers to access and analyze vast collections of historical documents more efficiently by offering scalable and versatile solutions for document transcription and structured data extraction.

In conclusion, this study demonstrates that LLMs hold substantial potential to improve the transcription and elaboration of historical manuscripts. While several technical and ethical challenges remain, the approach outlined here represents an important step toward developing robust, efficient, and accessible tools for advancing the goals of digital humanities and historical data preservation.

Acknowledgments. This work was partially supported by the IIT-Grant 2022. The author would like to thank Dr. Federico Prosperi and the Jewish Community of Pisa for providing the handwritten documents in the archive.

Disclosure of Interests. The author has no competing interests to declare that are relevant to the content of this article.

References

1. Achiam, J., et al.: GPT-4 technical report. arXiv preprint arXiv:2303.08774 (2023)
2. Alhamad, H.A., et al.: Handwritten recognition techniques: a comprehensive review. Symmetry **16**(6), 681 (2024). https://doi.org/10.3390/sym16060681
3. Ashok, D., Lipton, Z.C.: Promptner: Prompting for named entity recognition. arXiv preprint arXiv:2305.15444 (2023)
4. Bang, J., Lee, B.-T., Park, P.: Examination of ethical principles for LLM-based recommendations in conversational AI. In: 2023 International Conference on Platform Technology and Service (PlatCon), pp. 109–113. IEEE (2023)
5. Ben Abacha, A., Zweigenbaum, P.: Automatic extraction of semantic relations between medical entities: a rule-based approach. J. Biomed. Semant. **2**, 1–11 (2011)
6. Bender, E.M., Gebru, T., McMillan-Major, A., Shmitchell, S.: On the dangers of stochastic parrots: can language models be too big? In: Proceedings of the 2021 ACM Conference on Fairness, Accountability, and Transparency, pp. 610–623. ACM (2021)

[6] https://gemini.google.com/app.

[7] https://www.llama.com/.

[8] https://claude.ai/.

7. Braverman, M., Chen, X., Kakade, S., Narasimhan, K., Zhang, C., Zhang, Y.: Calibration, entropy rates, and memory in language models. In: International Conference on Machine Learning, pp. 1089–1099. PMLR (2020)
8. Brown, T., et al.: Language models are few-shot learners. Adv. Neural. Inf. Process. Syst. **33**, 1877–1901 (2020)
9. Christen, K.: Tribal archives, traditional knowledge, and local contexts: Why the “s” matters. J. Western Arch. **6**(1), 1–19 (2015)
10. Danilevsky, M., Qian, K., Aharonov, R., Katsis, Y., Kawas, B., Sen, P.: A survey of the state of explainable AI for natural language processing. In: Proceedings of the 28th International Conference on Computational Linguistics, pp. 4473–4485 (2020)
11. Deng, C., et al.: Deconstructing the ethics of large language models from long-standing issues to new-emerging dilemmas: a survey. arXiv preprint arXiv:2406.05392 (2024)
12. Eftimov, T., Koroušić Seljak, B., and Korošec, P.: A rule-based named-entity recognition method for knowledge extraction of evidence-based dietary recommendations. PloS One **12**(6), e0179488 (2017)
13. Fani Sani, M., Sroka, M., Burattin, A.: LLMs and process mining: challenges in RPA: task grouping, labeling and connector recommendation. In: International Conference on Process Mining, pp. 379–391. Springer (2023)
14. Floridi, L., et al.: AI4People—an ethical framework for a good AI society: opportunities, risks, principles, and recommendations. Mind. Mach. **28**(4), 689–707 (2018)
15. Gebreab, S.A., Salah, K., Jayaraman, R., ur Rehman, M.H., Ellaham, S.: LLM-based framework for administrative task automation in healthcare. In: 2024 12th International Symposium on Digital Forensics and Security (ISDFS), pp. 1–7. IEEE (2024)
16. Goyal, A., Gupta, V., Kumar, M.: Recent named entity recognition and classification techniques: a systematic review. Comput. Sci. Rev. **29**, 21–43 (2018)
17. Granell, E., Romero, V., Martínez-Hinarejos, C.D.: Multimodality, interactivity, and crowdsourcing for document transcription. Comput. Intell. **34**(2), 398–419 (2018). https://doi.org/10.1111/coin.12169
18. Graves, A., Liwicki, M., Fernández, S., Bertolami, R., Bunke, H., Schmidhuber, J.: A novel connectionist system for unconstrained handwriting recognition. IEEE Trans. Pattern Anal. Mach. Intell. **31**(5), 855–868 (2009). https://doi.org/10.1109/TPAMI.2008.137
19. Guo, Y., et al.: Bias in large language models: origin, evaluation, and mitigation. arXiv preprint arXiv:2411.10915 (2024)
20. Humbel, M., Nyhan, J., Vlachidis, A., Sloan, K., Ortolja-Baird, A.: Named-entity recognition for early modern textual documents: a review of capabilities and challenges with strategies for the future. J. Doc. **77**(6), 1223–1247 (2021)
21. Islam, M.A., Iacob, I.E.: Manuscripts character recognition using machine learning and deep learning. Modelling **4**(2), 168–188 (2023). https://doi.org/10.3390/modelling4020010
22. Jaillant, L.: Introduction to the special issue: using visual AI applied to digital archives. Digit. Humanit. Q. **18**(2) (2024)
23. Ji, B., et al.: A hybrid approach for named entity recognition in Chinese electronic medical record. BMC Med. Inform. Decis. Mak. **19**, 149–158 (2019)
24. Jo, E.S., Gebru, T.: Lessons from archives: strategies for collecting sociocultural data for machine learning. In: Proceedings of the 2020 ACM Conference on Fairness, Accountability, and Transparency, pp. 306–316. ACM (2020)
25. Kiessling, B.: Kraken: an universal text recognizer for the humanities. In: Digital Humanities 2019: Conference Abstracts, pp. 210–213. Alliance of Digital Humanities Organizations, Utrecht (2019)
26. Kirchenbauer, J., Geiping, J., Wen, Y., Katz, J., Miers, I., Goldstein, T.: A watermark for large language models. In: International Conference on Machine Learning, pp. 17061–17084. PMLR (2023)

27. Li, M., et al.: TrOCR: transformer-based optical character recognition with pre-trained models. In: Proceedings of the AAAI Conference on Artificial Intelligence, vol. 37, no. 11, pp. 13094–13102 (2023)
28. Li, Y., Chen, D., Tang, T., Shen, X.: HTR-VT: handwritten text recognition with vision transformer. Pattern Recogn. **158**, 110967 (2025)
29. Lo Duca, A.: An empirical study to use large language models to extract named entities from repetitive texts. In: Proceedings of the 20th International Conference on Web Information Systems and Technologies - WEBIST, pp. 417–424. SciTePress (2024). https://doi.org/10.5220/0013066500003825. ISBN 978-989-758-718-4; ISSN 2184-3252
30. Lo Duca, A., Abrate, M., Marchetti, A., Moretti, M.: Genealogical data-driven visits of historical cemeteries. Informatics **11**(1) (2024)
31. Lo Duca, A., Marchetti, A., Moretti, M., Diana, F., Toniazzi, M., D'Errico, A.: Genealogical data mining from historical archives: the case of the Jewish community in Pisa. Informatics **10**(2) (2023)
32. Luo, Y., Zhao, H., Zhan, J.: Named entity recognition only from word embeddings. arXiv preprint arXiv:1909.00164 (2019)
33. Ma, H., et al.: Fairness-guided few-shot prompting for large language models. Adv. Neural. Inf. Process. Syst. **36**, 43136–43155 (2023)
34. Makhortykh M.: No AI after auschwitz? Bridging AI and memory ethics in the context of information retrieval of genocide-related information. In: Mukherjee, A., Kulshrestha, J., Chakraborty, A., Kumar, S. (eds.) Ethics in Artificial Intelligence: Bias, Fairness and Beyond, pp. 71–85. Springer, Cham (2023). https://doi.org/10.1007/978-981-99-7184-8_4
35. Malmasi, S., Fang, A., Fetahu, B., Kar, S., Rokhlenko, O.: Multiconer: a large-scale multilingual dataset for complex named entity recognition. arXiv preprint arXiv:2208.14536 (2022)
36. Matos, A., Almeida, P., Correia, P.L., Pacheco, O.: IForal: automated handwritten text transcription for historical medieval manuscripts. J. Imaging **11**(2), 36 (2025). https://doi.org/10.3390/jimaging11020036
37. Mühlberger, G., et al.: Transforming scholarship in the archives through handwritten text recognition: Transkribus as a case study. J. Doc. **75**(5), 954–976 (2019). https://doi.org/10.1108/JD-07-2018-0114
38. Olaoye, G., Jonathan, H.: The evolving role of large language models (LLMs) in banking. EasyChair Preprint no. 13367 (2024)
39. Pakhale, K.: Comprehensive overview of named entity recognition: models, domain-specific applications and challenges. arXiv preprint arXiv:2309.14084 (2023)
40. Pooja, H., Jagadeesh, M.P.: A deep learning-based approach for biomedical named entity recognition using multitasking transfer learning with biLSTM, BERT and CRF. SN Comput. Sci. **5**(5), 482 (2024)
41. Puigcerver, J.: Are multidimensional recurrent layers really necessary for handwritten text recognition? In: 14th IAPR International Conference on Document Analysis and Recognition (ICDAR), pp. 67–72. IEEE (2017). https://doi.org/10.1109/ICDAR.2017.20
42. Shen, T., Long, G., Geng, X., Tao, C., Zhou, T., and Jiang, D.: Large language models are strong zero-shot retriever. arXiv preprint arXiv:2304.14233 (2023)
43. Shneiderman, B.: Human-centered artificial intelligence: reliable, safe & trustworthy. Int. J. Hum.–Comput. Interact. **36**(6), 495–504 (2020)
44. Terras, M.: Inviting AI into the archives: The reception of handwritten recognition technology into historical manuscript transcription. In: Jaillant, L. (ed.) Archives, Access and Artificial Intelligence: Working with Born-Digital and Digitized Archival Collections, pp. 179–204. Bielefeld University Press (2022)

45. Toselli, A.H., Romero, V., Pastor, M., Vidal, E.: Multimodal interactive transcription of text images. Pattern Recognit. **43**(5), 1814–1825 (2010). https://doi.org/10.1016/j.patcog.2009.11.013
46. Yuheng, S., Hao, Y.: Image segmentation algorithms overview. arXiv preprint arXiv:1707.02051 (2017)
47. Waltl, B., Bonczek, G., and Matthes, F. (2018). Rule-based information extraction: Advantages, limitations, and perspectives. Jusletter IT **4** (2018)
48. Wang, S., et al.: GPT- ner: named entity recognition via large language models. arXiv preprint arXiv:2304.10428 (2023)
49. Weber, A., Fussler, C., O'hanlon, J., Gierer, R., and Grandjean, E.: Psychophysiological effects of repetitive tasks. Ergonomics **23**(11), 1033–1046 (1980)
50. Wick, C., Reul, C., Puppe, F.: Calamari – a high-performance TensorFlow-based deep learning package for optical character recognition. Digit. Humanit. Q. **14**(2) (2020)
51. Zhang, S., et al.: Instruction tuning for large language models: a survey. arXiv preprint arXiv: 2308.10792 (2023)

Personalized Preferences for Soft Querying JSON Datasets

Paolo Fosci and Giuseppe Psaila(✉)

University of Bergamo - DIGIP, Viale Marconi 5, 24044 Dalmine, BG, Italy
{paolo.fosci,giuseppe.psaila}@unibg.it

Abstract. Soft conditions are a well-established formalism for querying data using linguistic predicates, enabling approximate and preference-based reasoning in big data contexts. This paper builds upon previous work in the field of *Soft Web Intelligence* (SWI) by analyzing the behavior of the logical operators AND and OR when implemented through the Vector p-norm aggregation scheme. The goal is to understand how parameterized logical operators can be tuned to reflect different interpretations of soft conjunction and disjunction.

The investigation is carried out within the *J-CO* Framework, a modular environment designed for acquiring, integrating, and querying *JSON* data collected from heterogeneous web sources. At the core of the framework lies its declarative query language, named *J-CO-QL*$^+$, which allows data scientists and analysts to write high-level scripts combining data extraction, transformation, and fuzzy evaluation. The language natively supports fuzzy sets, soft conditions, and custom-defined logical operators, known as fuzzy evaluators.

This paper shows how the recently introduced concept of user-defined fuzzy evaluator in *J-CO-QL*$^+$ enables the practical implementation of advanced fuzzy aggregation logic; this paper considers the Vector p-norm approach. The behavior of this advanced fuzzy aggregation logic is deeply studied in the paper; a dedicated *J-CO-QL*$^+$ script is developed to systematically apply multiple parameter configurations to a collection of fuzzified documents. The resulting membership degrees are stored and then analyzed through a set of 3-D surface plots.

Through this visual and structural analysis, the paper highlights how different parameterizations influence the behavior of the AND and OR operators. The plots provide useful guidelines for data scientists aiming to calibrate fuzzy queries according to domain-specific interpretations of linguistic predicates, thus enhancing the expressive power and adaptability of soft querying mechanisms in real-world scenarios.

Keywords: Soft web intelligence · User-defined fuzzy evaluators · Novel constructs in J-CO-QL+ · Soft querying on JSON datasets · Preferences among linguistic predicates

---

This study was funded by the European Union - *NextGenerationEU, in the framework of the GRINS - Growing Resilient, INclusive and Sustainable project (GRINS PE00000018 CUP F83C22001720001)*. The views and opinions expressed are solely those of the authors and do not necessarily reflect those of the European Union, nor can the European Union be held responsible for them.

M. Marchiori et al. (Eds.): WEBIST 2024, LNBIP 583, pp. 225–245, 2026.
https://doi.org/10.1007/978-3-032-25534-1_10

1 Introduction

The concept of *Soft Web Intelligence* was introduced in [13, 14] and later refined in [14]: the concept gives a practical interpretation to the general notion of *Web Intelligence*, which was introduced more than two decades ago in [29]. Specifically, the vision behind *Soft Web Intelligence* is to view the World-Wide Web as a giant source of information and datasets to be gathered from web sources, possibly stored within NoSQL (Not Only SQL) data stores, and subsequently integrated and queried; soft querying, based on Fuzzy Sets and Fuzzy Logic (introduced in [30]), a formal approach widely recognized as a key concept in Artificial Intelligence, could be the right tool to deal with imprecise and linguistic conditions to be evaluated on the mass of gathered data.

In the previous works of the authors, such as [13, 14], *Soft Web Intelligence* is performed through the *J-CO* Framework [13, 14], which provides the necessary practical support to formal concepts on which *Soft Web Intelligence* relies. The *J-CO* Framework is under development at the University of Bergamo (Italy): its goal is to provide data scientists and data engineers with a tool capable of gathering, integrating and querying *JSON* datasets [11], possibly through fuzzy sets and soft queries.

In [17], the novel concept of "fuzzy evaluator" was exploited to explore the adoption of a sophisticated approach for specifying preferences in soft querying; specifically, the approach known as "Vector p-Norm" is exploited (see [4, 15]).

The goal of this paper is to deeply study the vector p-norm fuzzy logic scheme, both in the case preferences are not expressed and in the case they are; to achieve this purpose, a collection of dummy *JSON* documents, whose goal is to analyze a progression of membership degrees, and a second collection of *JSON* documents that specify several configurations of Vector p-norm parameters (which determine the behavior of the logical operators AND and OR redefined according to the "Vector p-Norm" semantics), are employed. A dedicated *J-CO-QL*$^+$ script is developed and presented: its goal is to compute membership degrees by aggregating input membership degrees both based on the AND and OR semantics, with different configurations.

The paper studies how the operators AND and OR vary their behavior, on the basis of different configurations of Vector p-norm parameters. The study is conducted through a pool of 3-D plots, in which surfaces depict the aggregated membership degrees. These 3-D plots visualize how the aggregated membership degree varies; furthermore, they could significantly help analysts in understanding how to configure parameters when practically applying logical operators based on the Vector p-norm semantics.

The paper is organized as follows.

Section 2 presents the relevant related work, mostly coming from [17]; in particular, the *J-CO* Framework is briefly presented (in Sect. 2.1) and basic concepts about fuzzy logical aggregators are recalled (in Sect. 2.2). Then, Sect. 3 presents the formal contribution of this paper, i.e., the semantics of the Vector p-norm aggregation scheme (in Sect. 3.1, mostly taken from [17]) and how to implement the logical operators as fuzzy evaluators in the *J-CO-QL*$^+$ language (Sect. 3.2). Section 4 provides the second contribution of this paper, i.e., the behavioral analysis; first of all, the experimental setup is introduced by describing the adopted datasets (Sect. 4.1); second, the *J-CO-QL*$^+$ script that was devised for this purpose is explained (Sect. 4.2); at this point, the behavioral analysis is reported (Sect. 4.3). Finally, Sect. 5 draws the conclusions and highlights possible future work.

2 Previous Work

This paper relies on several previous works. Hereafter, the main ones are discussed. A detailed review of related work on the topic is not reported, because the current proposal is unique and no counterparts are available. Furthermore, readers that are interested in the relation with *Web Intelligence* can refer to [13, 14].

2.1 The J-CO Framework

The *J-CO* Framework is a pool of software tools whose goal is to provide analysts with powerful support for gathering, integrating and querying possibly-large collections of *JSON* datasets. The framework is built around its query language, named *J-CO-QL*$^+$.

The organization of the framework is still the one that was presented in [14]. The reader that is interested in a complete presentation of the framework can refer to [14], as well as to [24] for detailed performance analysis. Nevertheless, to help the full comprehension of this paper, it is worth providing a brief introduction to the main features of *J-CO-QL*$^+$.

- By means of *J-CO-QL*$^+$, users (such as analysts and data scientists) can write scripts that acquire *JSON* datasets from Web sources and *JSON* stores, transform and integrate them, perform soft queries and save results again into *JSON* stores.
- *J-CO-QL*$^+$ instructions are written using declarative statements. Scripts are sequences of statements that receive and generate a "temporary collection", i.e., a pool of *JSON* documents.
- *J-CO-QL*$^+$ natively supports fuzzy sets: for each single *JSON* document, it is possible to evaluate its membership degrees to several fuzzy sets at the same time. This "fuzzification" process is made possible by adding, to each document, a special root-level field, named `~fuzzysets`, holding the membership-degree values to different fuzzy sets. Through membership degrees to fuzzy sets, it is possible to exploit the concept of "linguistic predicate", so as to exploit vague or imprecise conditions.
- *J-CO-QL*$^+$ also supports fuzzy-set models that extend the classical notion provided by Zadeh [30], i.e., "multi-grade models". Such models explicitly manage more than one degree, such as Intuitionistic Fuzzy Sets [2], Pythagorean Fuzzy Sets [28], and Neutrosophic Fuzzy Sets [25]. The language provides constructs for letting the users define their own multi-grade fuzzy-set models and exploit them for advanced soft querying [18].
- *J-CO-QL*$^+$ addresses a large variety of issues related to processing *JSON* documents. Several statements for manipulating and merging documents are provided, even concerning geo-tagging of *JSON* documents (see [23]). Fuzzy sets could be evaluated on the basis of geo-tagging, by fuzzifying specific spatial relationships (see [12]). The language also allows for defining procedural functions through the JavaScript and the Java languages [16].

2.2 Fuzzy Logical Aggregators

When dealing with multiple fuzzy sets, to which an entity can belong, and with a multitude of entities that belong to the same fuzzy set, several interpretations of the concept of "aggregation" can be provided. Indeed, a plethora of proposals can be found in the literature.

T-norm and t-conorm. A family of "t-norm" and "t-conorm" operators, see [10], consider the aggregation of "pairs of fuzzy sets" for the same entity, i.e., an entity belong to two distinct fuzzy sets at the same time.

A typical and well known case of t-norm/t-conorm operators is represented by the classical AND and OR operators in the fuzzy version, where a fuzzy set denotes a linguistic property.

To illustrate, let us consider the linguistic predicate *CheapFlat*: it denotes if a flat belongs to the fuzzy set of "cheap flats". In addition, the linguistic predicate *LargeFlat* denotes if a flat belongs to the fuzzy set of "large flats". Based on the two elementary linguistic predicates, it is possible to build a complex linguistic predicate, as follows:

CheapFlat AND *LargeFlat*

this is a complex linguistic condition that looks for those flats that are "cheap and large". Clearly, the corresponding t-conorm operator is the OR operator. How to obtain the resulting membership degree?

The literature is full of proposals for defining the semantics of t-norm and t-conorm operators; most readers know the simplest one, i.e., for the AND (the t-norm) operator the minimum membership degree is considered[1], where for the OR (the t-conorm) operator the maximum membership degree is considered[2].

Many words can be found in he literature, which address the formal definition of t-norm and t-conomr, such as [3,9].

Groups of Entities. An orthogonal view of the notion of aggregation (studied in [14]), is aggregating entities in groups (or in categories) $G_j = \{x_{j,1}, x_{j,2}, \dots\}$ of items $x_{j,i}$ that belong to the same group G_j because they share some common properties or are samples of the same category of items. Each $x_{j,i}$ may individually belong to a fuzzy set A, thus it is provided with a membership degree $\mu_A(x_{j,i})$. Consequently, the set $\overline{A}$ of groups G_j can be seen as a partition of A: with this vision, since A is a fuzzy set, $\overline{A}$ is a fuzzy set too. As a result, the membership of a group G_j to the fuzzy set $\overline{A}$ should be derived by somehow aggregating memberships degrees $\mu_A(x_{j,i})$, for each single group . Furthermore, $\overline{A}$ can be a fuzzy set even when A is a crisp set, i.e., items $x_{j,i}$ do not have a membership degree; in this case, properties of items $x_{j,i}$ might have to be aggregated to obtain the final membership of the G_j group.

Among the plethora of proposals that are in the literature for group fuzzy aggregators, two are usually considered and are very popular: the first one is the classical "Weighted aggregation" (see [8]); the second one is the "Ordered Weighted Aggregation" (OWA) [19,27].

---

[1] $\mu_{CheapFlat\ \mathrm{AND} LargeFlat} = min(\mu_{CheapFlat}, \mu_{LargeFlat})$.

[2] $\mu_{CheapFlat\ \mathrm{OR} LargeFlat} = max(\mu_{CheapFlat}, \mu_{LargeFlat})$.

3 The Vector p-Norm Approach

This section presents the initial contribution of the paper: first of all, it recaps the definitions of the generalized logical operators on the basis of the approach known as "Vector p-norm" (Sect. 3.1); second, the specifications of two *J-CO-QL*$^+$ fuzzy evaluators are presented, to illustrate how they can be exploited in a practical and declarative way in *J-CO-QL*$^+$ scripts.

3.1 Definitions

In fuzzy logic, t he most common interpretation of the operators AND and OR as t-norm and t-conorm is to interpret them as the minimum (respectively, maximum) membership degree to the input fuzzy sets. An interesting aspect is also the possibility to express preferences over aggregated fuzzy sets (i.e., preferences on linguistic predicates that are represented by fuzzy sets); this issue has been widely investigated in the literature; this paper cites just a few words on the topic, such as [1,7,20], because it is impossible to be exhaustive.

In the literature, the "Vector p-norm" was proposed as an elegant mathematical formalization to cope with this issue (see [5]). Hereafter, the general formulas are reported.

Generalized AND. Given a list $LP = (lp_1, \ldots, lp_n)$ of linguistic predicates lp_k, $\mu_k(x)$ denotes the membership degree of the item x to the fuzzy set associated with lp_k. Consider the list $I = (i_1, \ldots, i_n)$, where i_k is the "importance degree" for the predicate lp_k.

The membership degree computed by the operator AND in the p-norm version is formulated as in Eq. 1:

$$\mu_{\text{AND}}(x) = 1 - \sqrt[p]{\frac{\sum_{k=1}^{n}(i_k)^p \times (1 - \mu_k(x))^p}{\sum_{k=1}^{n}(i_k)^p}} \tag{1}$$

To understand the rationale, in the case of $n = 2$ (bi-dimensional case), all $i_k = 1$ (no preferences) and $p = 2$, the square root represents the Minkowski distance [21] between the point (μ_1, μ_2) and the point $(1, 1)$. Consequently, the final membership degree is maximized when the Minkowski distance [21] between the two above-mentioned points is minimized. In practice, when all $i_k = 1$, the points (μ_1, μ_2) that are equidistant from the point $(1, 1)$ have the same final membership degree ("iso-membership" line), because they are on the same circle that is centered at the point $(1, 1)$ (see, for example, the black solid line in Fig. 1).

Generalized OR. The operator OR is defined as in Eq. 2:

$$\mu_{\text{OR}}(x) = \sqrt[p]{\frac{\sum_{k=1}^{n}(i_k)^p \times \mu_k(x)^p}{\sum_{k=1}^{n}(i_k)^p}} \tag{2}$$

Reasoning for the case $n = 2$, all $i_k = 1$ and $p = 2$, the final membership degree is the Minkowski distance [21] between the point (μ_1, μ_2) and the point $(0, 0)$ (the final

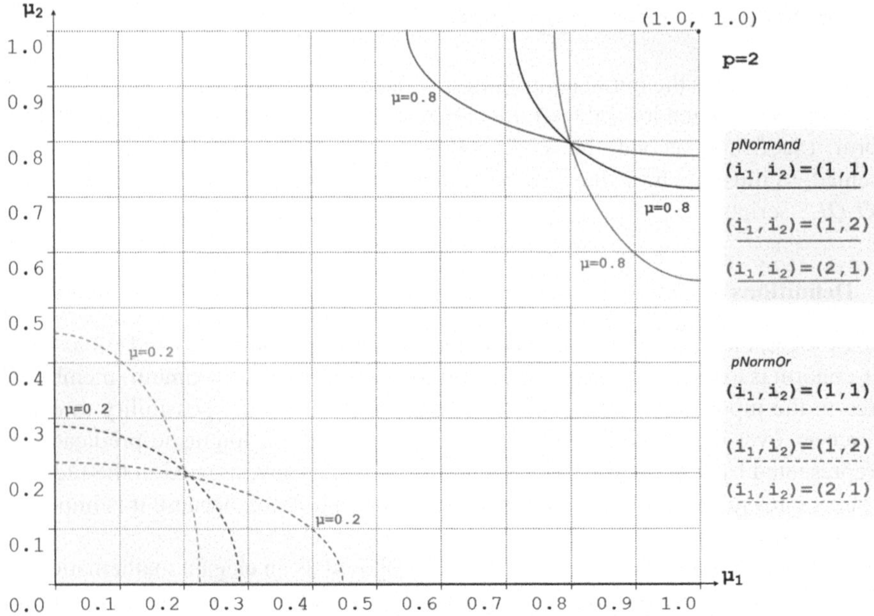

Fig. 1. Iso-membership lines for the AND (solid lines) and the OR (dashed lines) defined as Vector p-norm, with different importance degrees (from [17]).

membership degree is maximized when the Minkowski distance [21] from the point $(0, 0)$ is maximized). Consequently, points on the same circle centered at the point $(0, 0)$ have the same final membership degree (see, for example, the black dashed line in Fig. 1).

Keeping $n = 2$ and varying the importance degrees i_k, circles become ellipses. This effect is shown in Fig. 1.

Looking at solid lines, the blue line is obtained with $(i_1, i_2) = (2, 1)$, i.e., μ_1 is twice as important as μ_2; all the points on this line denote pairs (μ_1, μ_2) giving the same final membership degree $\mu = 0.8$; clearly, a small variation of μ_1 must be compensated by a much greater variation of μ_2, to obtain the same final membership degree. Similarly, the red solid line corresponds to the case $(i_1, i_2) = (1, 2)$, i.e., μ_1 has half the importance of μ_2. Notice that the three solid lines determine the same final membership degree of $\mu = 0.8$; consequently, a point on the main diagonal has the same final membership degree, independently of the importance degrees: as an effect, the three solid lines depicted in Fig. 1 cross on one single point, because they correspond to the same final membership degree.

Similarly, the same happens for the dashed lines in Fig. 1, which correspond to the OR operator: the three dashed lines denote the same final membership degree of $\mu = 0.2$.

Notice that, in the case $i_k = 1$, the limits for p going to infinity of the operators AND and OR are the classical definitions based on min and max, respectively. Conversely, when $p = 1$, AND and OR behave in the same way, i.e., they compute a linear combina-

Listing 1. *J-CO-QL*$^{+}$: Fuzzy Evaluator pNormAnd_FE.

```
CREATE FUZZY EVALUATOR pNormAND_FE
   PARAMETERS
     p               TYPE NUMERIC,
     importances     TYPE ARRAY,
     memberships     TYPE ARRAY
   PRECONDITION      p >= 1
             AND     COUNT(memberships) = COUNT(importances)
   FOR ALL           m IN memberships
     LOCALLY         (1-m)^p                  AS x,
                     importances[POS]^p       AS i
     AGGREGATE       i*x                      AS numerator,
                     i                        AS denominator
   EVALUATE          1 - (numerator/denominator)^(1/p);
```

tion of input membership degrees, possibly weighted by means of importance weights. Indeed, their semantics cannot be distinguished.

The reader can see that the logical operators defined on the basis of the Vector p-norm are a form of fuzzy aggregation: given a vector of membership degrees and a vector of importance degrees, they are aggregated to compute the final membership degree. In this work, the interpretation of t-norm and t-conorm of linguistic predicates is explored; furthermore, the reader can argue that the definitions presented in Eqs. 1 and 2 could be used for determining membership degrees in case of partitions (the authors will investigate this topic in future work).

The above definitions rely on the "Minkowski distance" [21], one of the concepts of the "Minkowski geometry" [26]. These concepts are widely used in Mathematics (see, for example, [6]) and in various applied sciences [22].

3.2 Vector p-Norm Operators in the J-CO Framework

In order to foster the exploitation of soft querying based on the p-norm semantics, a real tool should provide a means to formally and declaratively define the t-norm and t-conorm operators.

In this respect, *J-CO-QL*$^{+}$, the query language provided by the *J-CO* Framework, has been recently extended [17] with statements that support the concept of "fuzzy evaluator", i.e., a standardized way to evaluate membership degrees of *JSON* documents to fuzzy sets, in a declarative and (possibly) very complex way. This section does not present in detail all capabilities of a fuzzy evaluator: the interested reader can refer to [17]; nonetheless, the specific definitions of the fuzzy evaluators that implement the operators AND and OR in the p-norm version are presented in detail.

Operator AND. Listing 1 shows the definition of the fuzzy evaluator pNormAND_FE, which specifies the logical AND operator in the generalized Vector p-norm version. Hereafter, the concept of "fuzzy evaluator" is briefly presented, while explaining Listing 1.

- The concept of "fuzzy evaluator" is the formal tool that *J-CO-QL*$^+$ provides to evaluate membership degrees of *JSON* documents to fuzzy sets. The *J-CO-QL*$^+$ instruction `CREATE FUZZY EVALUATOR`, as reported in Listing 1; once defined, a fuzzy evaluator can be exploited on actual *JSON* documents.
- A fuzzy evaluator is parametric: the clause `PARAMETERS` defines the input parameters of the evaluator.
  Specifically, the fuzzy evaluator named `pNormAND_FE` receives three input parameters: `p` is the p parameter of the Vector p-norm definitions; `importances` is a vector of numerical importance weights; finally, `memberships` is a vector of membership degrees.
- The clause `PRECONDITION` is a logical condition that must be met on the actual parameters; it ensures the validity of the parameters before proceeding with the evaluation.
  Specifically, the precondition checks whether p is no less than 1, while the arrays `importances` and `memberships` must have the same size.
- The clause `FOR ALL` iterates over an input array to compute aggregated values from the array.

  Specifically, the array `memberships` is scanned through the iterator `m`.

  The sub-clause `LOCALLY` computes two local values for each item in the array; these twp local values are the terms multiplied within the p root in Eq. 1; in particular, variable `i` assumes the value of the item in the array `importances` in the same position as the current item in the scanned array; this position is denoted by the built-in variable `POS`.
  The sub-clause `AGGREGATE` computes two aggregated values, named `numerator` and `denominator`: the expressions before the `AS` clause provide the values to be implicitly aggregated through a sum. This way, the numerator and the denominator of Eq. 1 are computed.
- At this point, the clause `EVALUATE` computes the final membership degree, as defined in Eq. 1, i.e., the resulting value will become the membership degree to a fuzzy set of a *JSON* document during the soft query.

Operator OR. Similarly, Listing 2 shows the definition of the complementary fuzzy evaluator `pNormOR_FE`, which corresponds to Eq. 2. The structure of the second fuzzy evaluator is the same as for the previous one; naturally, the expression that evaluates the local variable `x` in the sub-clause `LOCALLY` is different, according to Eq. 2; the same happens in the clause `EVALUATE`.

4 Experimental and Behavioral Analysis

This section provides the second contribution of the paper, i.e., studying the behavior of the Vector p-norm version of the logical operators with preferences, applied within a simple, yet not trivial, *J-CO-QL*$^+$ script.

Listing 2. *J-CO-QL*$^{+}$: Fuzzy Evaluator pNormOR_FE.

```
2. CREATE FUZZY EVALUATOR pNormOR_FE
     PARAMETERS
       p              TYPE NUMERIC,
       importances    TYPE ARRAY,
       memberships    TYPE ARRAY
     PRECONDITION     p >= 1
               AND    COUNT(memberships) = COUNT(importances)
     FOR ALL          m IN memberships
       LOCALLY        m^p                         AS x,
                      importances[POS]^p          AS i
       AGGREGATE      i*x                         AS numerator,
                      i                           AS denominator
     EVALUATE         (numerator/denominator)^(1/p);
```

```
{
    "id"           : 30,
    "name"         : "fuzzysetA:0.7 - fuzzysetB:0.2",
    "~fuzzysets" : {
        "fuzzysetA"   : 0.7,
        "fuzzysetB"   : 0.2
    }
}
```

Fig. 2. Example of document in the collection fuzzyDataCollection.

4.1 Experimental Setup

To analyze the behavior of the Vector p-norm version of the logical operators, two complementary collections of *JSON* documents were designed: the first one contains fuzzified input documents; the second one contains documents that specify parameter configurations. This section introduces the structure and content of these datasets, which serve as the foundation for computing and visualizing the behavior of the operators pNormAND and pNormOR.

Figure 2 shows an example of one of the 121 documents in the collection fuzzyDataCollection, a previously prepared and fuzzified dataset. Each document contains a field name and a field id, which is used for identification purposes; each document reports its membership degrees to two fuzzy sets, which are named fuzzysetA and fuzzysetB. The memberships to fuzzysetA and fuzzysetB are stored within the special root-level field ~fuzzysets, visually highlighted in Fig. 2 by means of a yellow box, for clarity.

Both the memberships to fuzzysetA and fuzzysetB take values in the continuous range $[0, 1]$, discretized using steps of 0.1. This discretization results in 11 possible membership degrees for each fuzzy set, thereby allowing for the systematic representation of all possible input combinations across the two-dimensional space defined by fuzzysetA and fuzzysetB. The complete collection effectively spans the full Cartesian product of the discretized domain of the two input fuzzy sets.

```
{
    "label"          : "p:2 - i1:2 - i2:1",
    "p"              : 2,
    "importances"    : [2, 1]
}
```

Fig. 3. Example of document in the collection `configurations`.

In parallel, Fig. 3 presents a representative document from the collection named `configurations`, which consists of 49 distinct entries. Each document defines a unique combination of the parameters p, i_1, and i_2, as used in Eqs. 1 and 2 to compute fuzzy aggregations; a field `label` summarizes the configuration in a string.

Specifically, the field `p` records the parameter controlling the behavior of the p-norm operator, with integer values ranging from 1 to 7. The importance weights i_1 and i_2 are stored as an array in the field `importances` and can independently take values from the integer range $[1, 3]$. However, to reduce redundancy in the analysis, the symmetric pairs $(2, 2)$ and $(3, 3)$ are omitted from the configuration space, as they yield results equivalent to the baseline case $(1, 1)$. As a result, the configuration dataset spans 7 distinct importance weights combinations for each value of p, leading to a controlled but comprehensive exploration of parameter influence. As a result, the total number of configurations is 49.

4.2 Experiment

The primary objective of this experiment is to conduct a comprehensive analysis of the behavior of the fuzzy logical operators *p-Norm AND* and *p-Norm OR* under various parameter configurations. This is achieved through the use of a dedicated *J-CO-QL*$^+$ script, which systematically applies each configuration from the `configurations` collection to all documents in the `fuzzyDataCollection` dataset.

The script employed for this process integrates the fuzzy evaluators that were defined in Listings 1 and 2, which implement the fuzzy evaluators `pNormAND_FE` and `pNormOR_FE`, respectively. The script that actually acquires datasets, joins them and evaluates membership degrees is reported in Listing 3. The structure and functionality of the *J-CO-QL*$^+$ script are described in detail hereafter.

- *Database Connection.* Line 3 of Listing 3 establishes the connection to the database `WebistBook2025`, managed by a *MongoDB* server. This database contains both the collections`fuzzyDataCollection` and `configurations`, as well as the output collection that will store the results.
- *Data Processing.* The key processing logic begins with the `JOIN OF COLLECTIONS` instruction on Line 4. This operation combines each document d from the `fuzzyDataCollection` dataset with every document c from the `configurations` dataset, resulting in a Cartesian product of all possible data-configuration pairs. The main goal is to evaluate the combined document with the corresponding fuzzy evaluators and store the output in a structured form.

Listing 3. *J-CO-QL*$^{+}$: script.

```
3. USE DB WebistBook2025
     ON SERVER MongoDB 'http://127.0.0.1:27017';

4. JOIN OF COLLECTIONS
       fuzzyDataCollection@WebistBook2025   AS d,
       configurations@WebistBook2025        AS c
     SET FUZZY SETS KEEP LEFT
     CASE WHERE
         KNOWN FUZZY SETS fuzzysetA, fuzzysetB
       GENERATE
         CHECK FOR
           FUZZY SET pNormAND
             USING pNormAND_FE (.c.p, .c.importances,
               MEMBERSHIP_ARRAY([fuzzysetA, fuzzysetB]))
           FUZZY SET pNormOR
             USING pNormOR_FE (.c.p, .c.importances,
               MEMBERSHIP_ARRAY([fuzzysetA, fuzzysetB]))
         BUILD {
           .docName        : .d.name,
           .configuration  : .c.label     };

5. SAVE AS resultCollection@WebistBook2025;
```

The `JOIN OF COLLECTIONS` instruction performs the following steps:

1. **Document Pairing:** For each pair (d, c), where d is a document from `fuzzyDataCollection` and c is a configuration document from `configurations`, a new document is created containing two root-level fields named `d` and `c`. These fields embed the original data and configuration documents, respectively.
2. **Fuzzification Setup:** The clause `SET FUZZY SETS` ensures that the new document is properly fuzzified. The `KEEP LEFT` option specifies that the fuzzy sets defined in d (i.e., `fuzzysetA` and `fuzzysetB`) are retained and assigned to the special root field `~fuzzysets`. Figure 4 shows an example of such a document after fuzzification. Note that the fields `d` and `c` remain intact, and the blue box highlights the inserted fuzzy membership values.
3. **Selection Clause:** The condition `CASE WHERE` filters out documents that do not belong to the fuzzy sets `fuzzysetA` and `fuzzysetB`. This step ensures that only meaningful combinations are considered for further processing.
4. **Evaluation and Transformation:** The block `GENERATE` applies both the fuzzy evaluators `pNormAND` and `pNormOR`, and restructures the output document as follows:
   - The first `CHECK FOR FUZZY SET` branch invokes the evaluator `pNormAND_FE`. It aggregates memberships to `fuzzysetA` and `fuzzysetB` by using the configuration parameters that are provided by the sub-document`c` in the current document. The evaluator receives:

```
{
    "c"              : {
        "label"        : "p:2 - i1:2 - i2:1",
        "p"            : 2,
        "importances" : [2, 1]
    },
    "d"              : {
        "id"           : 30,
        "name"         : "fuzzysetA:0.7 -fuzzysetB:0.2",
        "~fuzzysets"  : {
            "fuzzysetA"   : 0.7,
            "fuzzysetB"   : 0.2
        }
    },
    "~fuzzysets" : {
        "fuzzysetA"   : 0.7,
        "fuzzysetB"   : 0.2,
    }
}
```

Fig. 4. Example of document generated by the `JOIN OF COLLECTIONS` instruction after the clause `SET FUZZY SETS`, and before applying `CASE WHERE`.

- the value of p from `c.p`,
- the importances i_1 and i_2 from `c.importances`, and
- the membership values to the fuzzy sets `fuzzysetA` and `fuzzysetB`, passed via the built-in *J-CO-QL*$^+$ function `MEMBERSHIP_ARRAY`.

The result is stored as a new fuzzy set named `pNormAND` in the special field `~fuzzysets`.

- The second `CHECK FOR FUZZY SET` branch evaluates the membership of the document to the fuzzy set `pNormOR` by using the evaluator `pNormOR_FE`, following the same rationale as for fuzzy set `pNormAND`. Similarly to the previous case, the field `pNormOR` is added to the special field `~fuzzysets`.
- The `BUILD` block restructures the output document. It flattens the document, creating:
  - a new root-level field `docName`, copied from `d.name`,
  - a new root-level field `configuration`, copied from `c.label`.

  The original nested sub-documents `d` and `c` are removed to streamline the output. The special field `~fuzzysets`, now containing the four fuzzy sets, remains unchanged.

Figure 5 displays a sample document from the output collection. At the root level, the fields `docName` and `configuration` identify the input fuzzy memberships and the applied configuration, respectively. The yellow-highlighted `~fuzzysets`

```
{
    "docName"          : "fuzzysetA:0.7 - fuzzysetB:0.2",
    "configuration"    : "p:2 - i1:2 - i2:1",
    "~fuzzysets"       : {
        "fuzzysetA"      : 0.7,
        "fuzzysetB"      : 0.2,
        "pNormAND"       : 0.552786404500042,
        "pNormOR"        : 0.632455532033676
    }
}
```

Fig. 5. Example of document in the collection `resultCollection`.

field includes the membership degrees for `fuzzysetA`, `fuzzysetB`, `pNormAND`, and `pNormOR`.

– *Saving the Results.* The final output consists of $121 \times 49 = 5929$ documents, each storing the computed fuzzy memberships for a specific input-configuration pair. These documents are saved into the *MongoDB* database `WebistBook2025` under the collection name `resultCollection`, as indicated in Line 5 of Listing 3. This structured output serves as the basis for subsequent surface generation and visualization tasks, which are described in the remainder of the paper.

4.3 Analysis

This section provides a detailed visual analysis of the behavior of the fuzzy logical operators `AND` and `OR` in the Vector p-norm version. Charts are obtained by plotting the membership values for the fuzzy sets `pNormAND` and `pNormOR` obtained for documents in resulting collection generated by the *J-CO-QL*$^+$ script presented in Listing 3.

The behavior of the operators is examined by varying the parameter p and the relative importance weights assigned to the input fuzzy sets. A set of 3-D plots illustrates the resulting membership surfaces under different configurations. These visual representations highlight the influence of both parameterization and weighting on the shape and properties of the operators.

Figures 6 and 7 present a series of 3-D plots that illustrate the surfaces that depict how the membership degree varies, based on the variations of memberships to the input fuzzy sets `fuzzysetA` and `fuzzysetB`; different charts are obtained for different parameter configurations. In the following, the reading of the charts is explained.

– Meaning of the axes:
    - the x-axis represents the membership degree to `fuzzysetA`;
    - the y-axis represents the membership degree to `fuzzysetB`;
    - the vertical z-axis, together with the colored surface, represents the resulting membership degree to `pNormAND`.

- Each figure is labeled to indicate the specific configuration of the parameter p and the pair of importance weights (i_1, i_2) used to generate the plot. For example, `p=2, i`$_1$`=1, i`$_2$`=2` indicates that the computation of the membership to `pNormAND` is performed with $p = 2$ and importance weights vector $[1, 2]$.
- For the sake of space and clarity, not all considered parameter configurations are depicted; therefore, only values of the parameter p in the set $\{1, 2, 7\}$ are considered for Figs. 6 and 7. Specifically, the first line in both figures depicts results for $p = 1$; the second line depicts results for $p = 2$; the third line depicts results for $p = 7$. This way, it is observable how surfaces change by varying p and by maintaining the same importance weights looking at the same column from the top to the bottom. Values of p in the range $2 < p < 7$ generate surfaces that are intermediate between those shown for $p = 2$ and $p = 7$.
- As previously discussed, plots in the same column share the same importance weights. Specifically, in Fig. 6, plots in the left column share the importance vector $[1, 1]$, while plots in the right column share the importance vector $[1, 2]$. In Fig. 7, plots in the left column share the importance vector $[1, 3]$, while plots in the right column share the importance vector $[2, 3]$.
- Due to symmetry reasons, certain importance pairs are omitted. In particular, the pairs $(2, 1)$, $(3, 1)$, and $(3, 2)$ are not shown, because the corresponding $(1, 2)$, $(1, 3)$, and $(2, 3)$ are depicted and generate a symmetric surface.

Behavioral Analysis. At this point, it is possible to look at the different shapes of surface, to understand how the Vector p-norm AND changes its behavior, based on different values for each single parameter. Indeed, a closer examination of the plots reveals several noteworthy patterns.

- For $p = 1$, as illustrated in Figs. 6.a, 6.d, 7.a, and 7.d:
  - the resulting surface is a plane; this fact highlights that when $p = 1$, the AND nature of the operator is lost (as argued in Sect. 3.1) and the operator behaves as a pure linear combination of the input membership degrees. This latter consideration is confirmed by the slope of the plane, which is exactly 45° when the importance weights are equal (Fig. 6.a).
  - The slope increases when the difference $i_2 - i_1$ increases, giving a prize to the membership degrees to `fuzzysetB`, to which more importance is given.
  - The plots in Figs. 6.d and 7.d denotes that the planes are not coincident with each other, even though the difference $i_2 - i_1$ is the same, because the actual impact is determined by the ratio $(i_2 - i_1)/i_2$; indeed, the slope of the plane in Figure Figs. 6.d is slightly greater than the slope of the plane in Fig. 7.d.
- Values $p > 1$ give rise to a different behavior of the operator: the surfaces become concave and their shapes become more complex.
  - First of all, let us consider the cases of equal importance weights, depicted in Figs. 6.a, 6.b, 6.c. The lower border of the curves become lower and lower, for increasing values of p; specifically, they tend to the minimum membership degree, as the fuzzy logical operator AND is usually defined; indeed, this is what

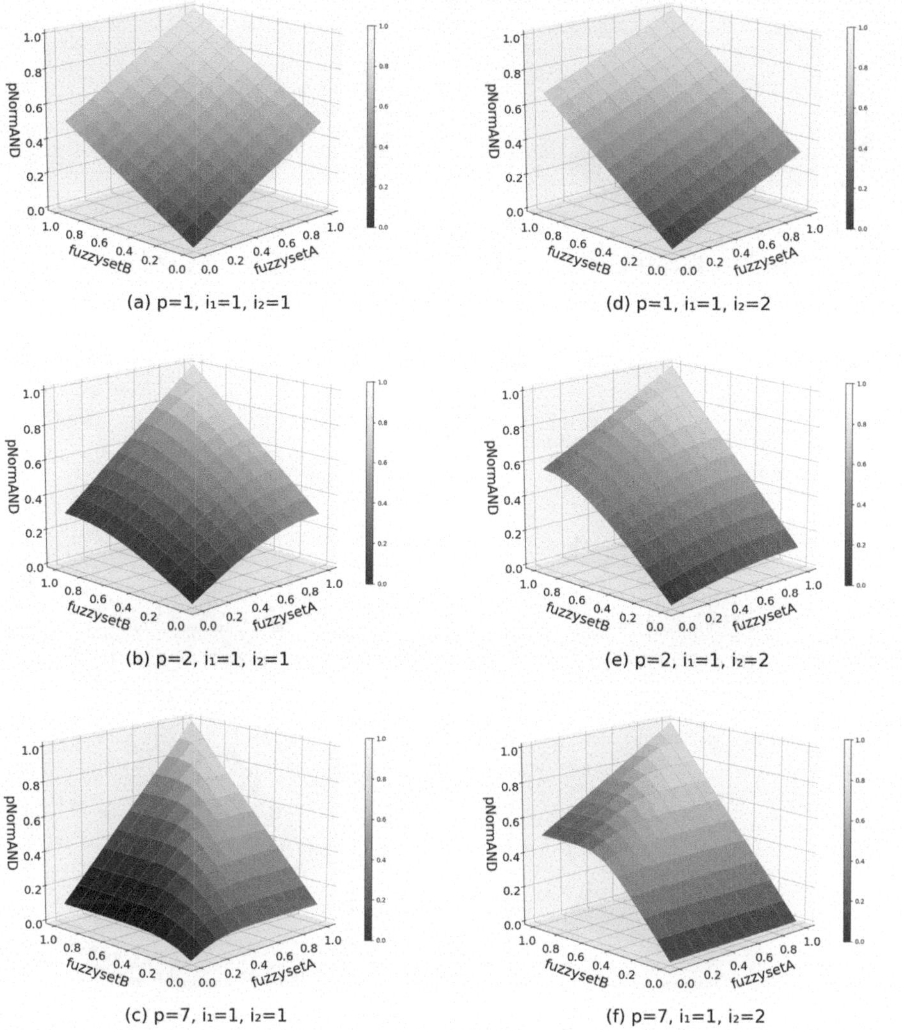

Fig. 6. p-Norm AND with importance weighs $(1, 1)$ and $(1, 2)$.

happens when $p \to \infty$. The reader can notice how the shape of the surface tends to become a pyramid, with the diagonal edge corresponding to the combinations with equal membership degrees.

- The cases with unequal importance weights are plotted in Figs. 6.d, 6.e, 6.f and in Fig. 7. The reader can notice how the pyramidal shape of curves still remains, but it is stretched, due to the different importance weights.
  In particular, it is observable that the base corner that is parallel to the y-axis, which corresponds to the membership degree with higher importance weight, moves up, giving a significant prize to the contribution of the degree with higher

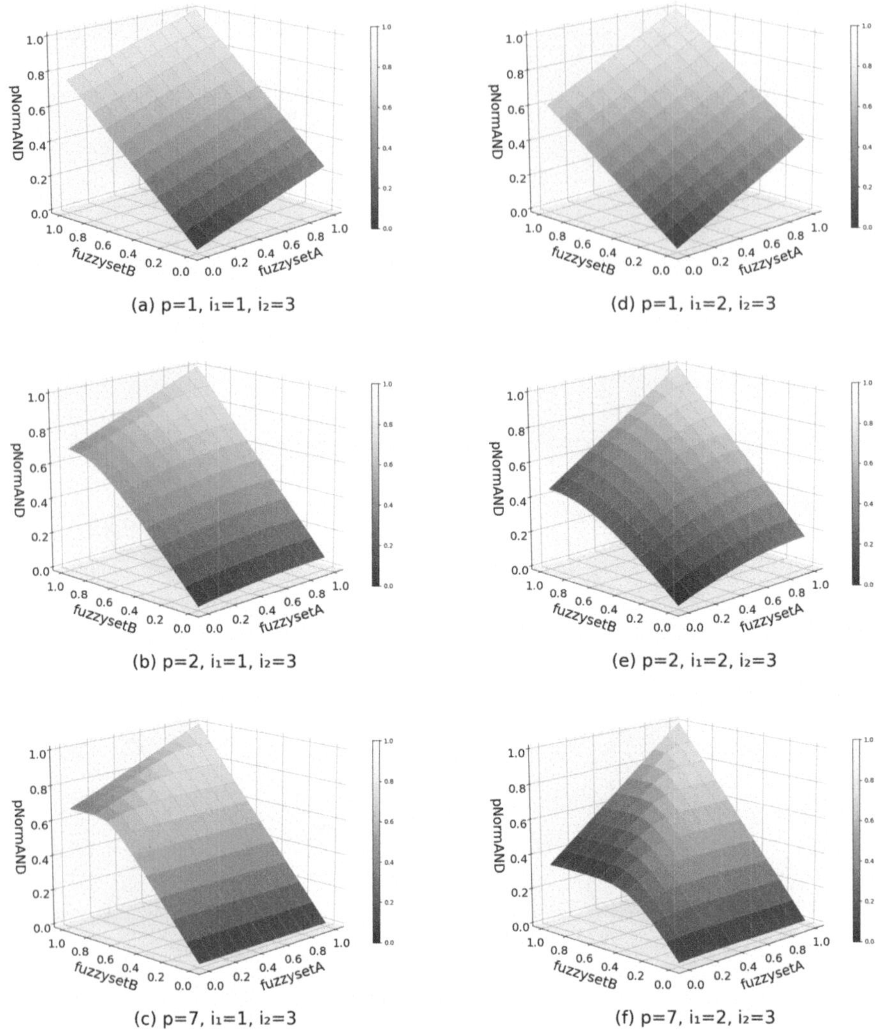

Fig. 7. p-Norm AND with importance weights $(1, 3)$ and $(2, 3)$.

importance weight. This effect is particularly evident in Figs. 7.c, which depicts the case for $p = 7$ and importance vector $[1, 3]$.

- Similar to the case $p = 1$, from Figs. 6.f, 7.c and 7.f, it is possible to see that ratio $(i_2 - i_1)/i_2$ actually determines how much the surface is stretched: the greater the ratio, the higher the stretching.

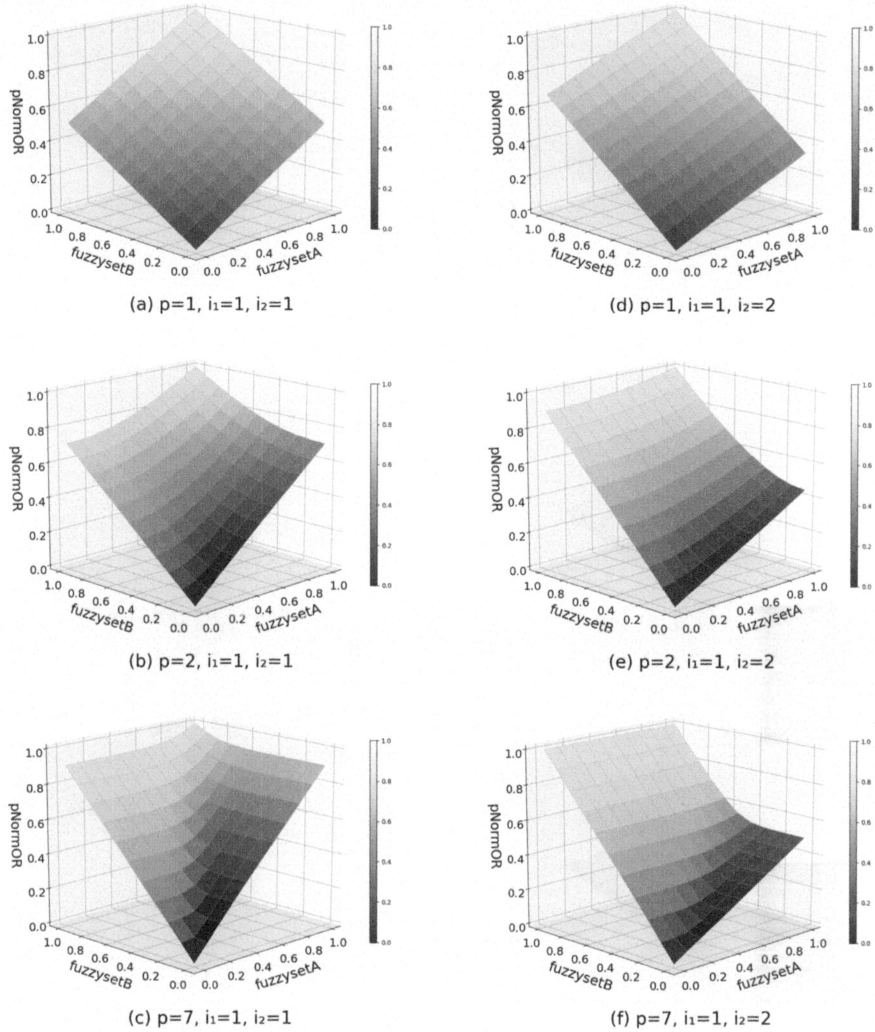

Fig. 8. p-Norm OR with importance weights $(1, 1)$ and $(1, 2)$.

Behavioral Analysis for the OR Operator. Figures 8 and 9 depict the corresponding 3-D plots for the fuzzy set `pNormOR`; they allow for understanding the behavior of the Vector p-norm `OR` operator.

Figures 8 and 9 are organized in a similar way to Figs. 6 and 7. Specifically, the left column of Fig. 8 depicts the case of equal importance weights, with increasing values of the parameter p; the right column of Fig. 8 depicts the surfaces for the importance vector $[1, 2]$. Similarly, the left column of Fig. 9 depicts the surfaces for the importance vector $[1, 3]$, while the right column depicts the surfaces for the importance vector $[2, 3]$.

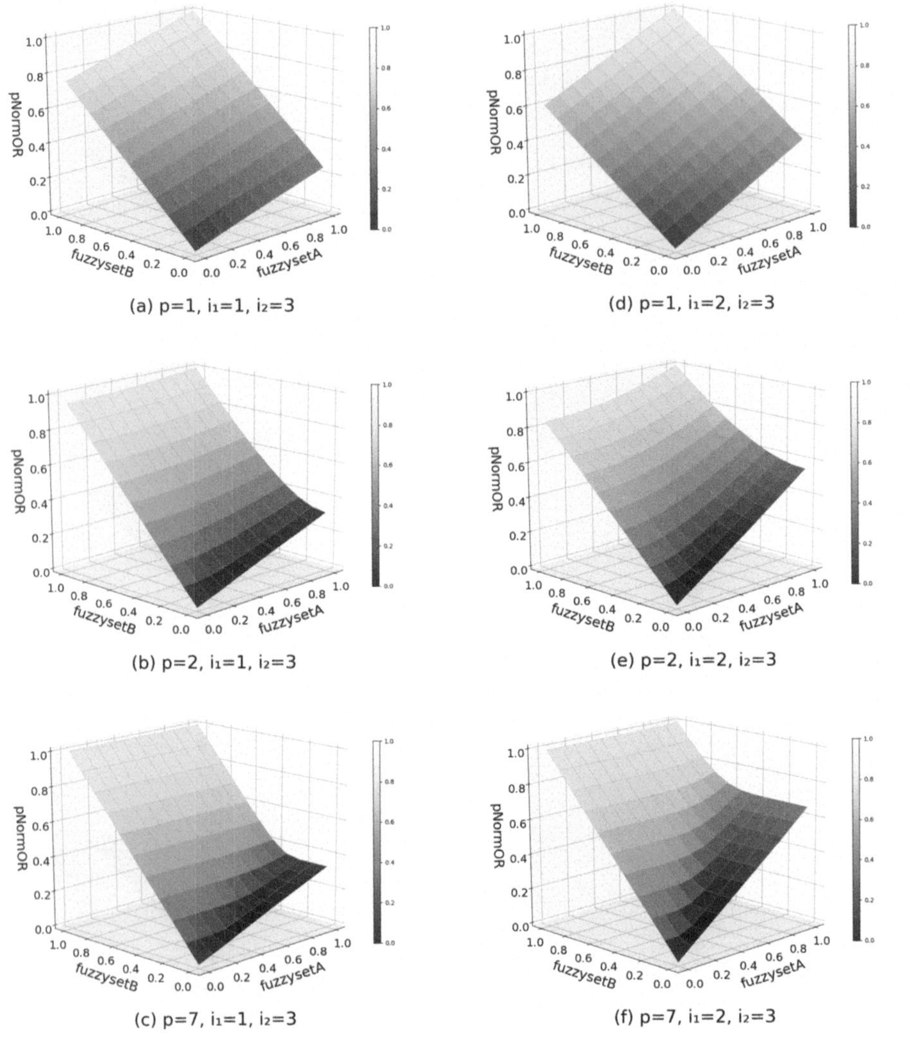

Fig. 9. p-Norm OR with importance weights $(1, 3)$ and $(2, 3)$.

- First of all, let us consider the cases $p = 1$, that are depicted in Figs. 8.a, 8.d, 9.a and 9.d. The reader can notice that not only they are again planes, but they are exactly the same planes that are obtained for the corresponding cases of the AND operator. This is a further confirmation of what was argued in Sect. 3.1: with $p = 1$, both the operators lose their distinctive AND/OR nature and their behavior actually coincide. Indeed, they become a unique aggregation operator that computes a linear combination of the input membership degrees.
- For values $p > 1$, the OR nature emerges. Let us consider again the case of equal importance weights, looking at Fig. 7.c (with $p = 7$). The first thing to notice is that

now the surface has the concavity upwards (i.e., the surface is convex): this is not surprising, because the maximum input membership degree prevails.
In comparison with the corresponding AND case (see Fig. 6.c), the two surfaces share the diagonal line corresponding to two equal input membership degrees; thus, the AND surface is below this diagonal, while the OR surface is above this diagonal.

- Moving to the cases of unequal importance weights, the shape of surfaces is stretched as in the AND case. However, in the OR case the dilatation is performed in the opposite way. Indeed, the surface is stretched downward-right in the OR case, and upward-left in the AND case.
- The reader can make the following qualitative observation about the shapes of surfaces for two corresponding configurations: the surface of a OR configuration could be more or less obtained by reversing the surface for the corresponding AND configuration. Clearly, this is only a qualitative evaluation, which anyway highlights the complementary nature of the AND and OR operators in fuzzy logic, even in the case of the Vector p-norm semantics.

The ultimate usefulness of surfaces depicted in Figs. 6, 7, 8, and 9 is to help the interested reader to visualize the different behaviors. In practical applications, this visualization could significantly aid in understanding how to choose appropriate values for the parameter p and the importance weights.

5 Conclusions

This paper provides a systematic study of the behavior of parameterized fuzzy logical operators, defined according to the Vector p-norm aggregation scheme, within the context of *Soft Web Intelligence*. The investigation is carried out through the *J-CO* Framework, an integrated environment for soft querying over heterogeneous *JSON* datasets. In particular, the paper demonstrates how user-defined fuzzy evaluators, as supported by the *J-CO-QL*$^+$ query language, can be effectively employed to implement flexible and expressive logical aggregation strategies.

The core contribution of this work is twofold. First, the paper formally presents the definitions of the Vector p-norm AND and OR operators, which allow for the tuning of fuzzy logic behavior through two parameters: the parameter p, and a vector of importance weights assigned to the input membership degrees. Second, a behavioral analysis is conducted by executing a dedicated *J-CO-QL*$^+$ script, which applies a wide range of parameter configurations to a representative set of fuzzified documents.

The empirical evaluation is supported by the generation of 3-D surface plots, depicting the resulting membership degrees computed by the operators AND and OR in the Vector p-norm version. These visualizations highlight how the parameter p controls the degree of strictness in the aggregation: low values of p correspond to lenient, averaged behavior, while high values approximate traditional fuzzy logic semantics based on minimum and maximum. Furthermore, the role of importance weights is shown to produce asymmetric distortions on the surfaces, thus providing a clear visual indication of how preferences among linguistic predicates can be integrated into the aggregation process.

An interesting outcome of the analysis is that, for $p = 1$, both AND and OR operators behave identically, reducing to a linear combination of the input membership degrees. This confirms that the distinction between conjunctive and disjunctive semantics is effectively lost in this configuration. On the other hand, when p increases, the operators recover their logical interpretation: the AND operator becomes more conservative and converges to the *min* function, while the OR operator becomes more generous and tends to the *max* function.

The visual and structural analysis provided by this paper can support data scientists and analysts in selecting appropriate parameter configurations for their specific application domains. The presented 3-D plots serve as a practical reference for calibrating soft querying logic when dealing with linguistic predicates and vague conditions.

Future work will consider the application of this aggregation model, within the *J-CO* Framework, to more complex scenarios, including the adoption of multi-grade fuzzy set models and the incorporation of spatial dimensions within fuzzy evaluations.

The *J-CO* Framework is available on a GitHub page[3].

Acknowledgments. This study was funded by the European Union - *NextGenerationEU, in the framework of the GRINS - Growing Resilient, INclusive and Sustainable project (GRINS PE00000018 CUP F83C22001720001).* The views and opinions expressed are solely those of the authors and do not necessarily reflect those of the European Union, nor can the European Union be held responsible for them.

References

1. Abir, B.K., Amel, G.T.: Towards fuzzy querying of NOSQL document-oriented databases. DBKDA **2015**, 163 (2015)
2. Atanassov, K.T., Stoeva, S.: Intuitionistic fuzzy sets. Fuzzy Sets Syst. **20**(1), 87–96 (1986)
3. Boixader, D., Recasens, J.: Vague and fuzzy t-norms and t-conorms. Fuzzy Sets Syst. **433**, 156–175 (2022)
4. Bordogna, G., Psaila, G.: Modeling soft conditions with unequal importance in fuzzy databases based on the vector p-norm. In: Proceedings of the IPMU, Malaga (2008)
5. Bordogna, G., Psaila, G.: Soft aggregation in flexible databases querying based on the vector p-norm. Int. J. Uncertainty Fuzz. Knowl.-Based Syst. **17**(supp01), 25–40 (2009)
6. Crasta, G., Malusa, A.: The distance function from the boundary in a Minkowski space. Trans. Am. Math. Soc. **359**(12), 5725–5759 (2007)
7. Deb, N., Sarkar, A., Biswas, A.: Linguistic q-rung orthopair fuzzy prioritized aggregation operators based on hamacher t-norm and t-conorm and their applications to multicriteria group decision making. In: Archives of Control Sciences, pp. 451–484 (2022)
8. Dombi, J., Jónás, T.: Weighted aggregation systems and an expectation level-based weighting and scoring procedure. Eur. J. Oper. Res. **299**(2), 580–588 (2022)
9. Dong, H., Ali, Z., Mahmood, T., Liu, P.: Power aggregation operators based on hamacher t-norm and t-conorm for complex intuitionistic fuzzy information and their application in decision-making problems. J. Intell. Fuzzy Syst. **45**(5), 8383–8403 (2023)

[3] GitHub repository of the *J-CO* Framework: https://github.com/JcoProjectTeam/JcoProjectPage.

10. Farahbod, F., Eftekhari, M.: Comparison of different t-norm operators in classification problems. arXiv preprint arXiv:1208.1955 (2012)
11. Fosci, P., Psaila, G.: *J-CO*, a framework for fuzzy querying collections of *JSON* documents (demo). In: Andreasen, T., De Tré, G., Kacprzyk, J., Legind Larsen, H., Bordogna, G., Zadrożny, S. (eds.) FQAS 2021. LNCS (LNAI), vol. 12871, pp. 142–153. Springer, Cham (2021). https://doi.org/10.1007/978-3-030-86967-0_11
12. Fosci, P., Psaila, G.: Soft integration of geo-tagged data sets in j-co-ql+. ISPRS Int. J. Geo Inf. **11**(9), 484 (2022)
13. Fosci, P., Psaila, G.: Towards soft web intelligence by collecting and processing json data sets from web sources. In: Proceedings of the 18th International Conference on Web Information Systems and Technologies (2022)
14. Fosci, P., Psaila, G.: Enhancing soft web intelligence with user-defined fuzzy aggregators. In: WEBIST 2023, pp. 258–267 (2023)
15. Fosci, P., Psaila, G.: Fuzzy aggregators in practice: meta-model and implementation. In: International Conference on Soft Computing Models in Industrial and Environmental Applications, pp. 56–68. Springer, Cham (2023). https://doi.org/10.1007/978-3-031-42529-5_6
16. Fosci, P., Psaila, G.: Soft querying powered by user-defined functions in j-co-ql+. Neurocomputing **546**, 126311 (2023)
17. Fosci, P., Psaila, G.: Soft querying json datasets with personalized preferences and aggregations. In: WEBIST 2024, pp. 153–164 (2024)
18. Fosci, P., Psaila, G.: A unified view of multi-grade fuzzy-set models in j-co-ql+. Neurocomputing **565**, 126968 (2024)
19. Li, H., Yen, V.C.: Fuzzy Sets and Fuzzy Decision-Making. CRC press, Boca Raton (1995)
20. Liu, P., Ali, Z., Mahmood, T., Geng, Y.: Prioritized aggregation operators for complex intuitionistic fuzzy sets based on aczel-alsina t-norm and t-conorm and their applications in decision-making. Int. J. Fuzzy Syst. **25**(7), 2590–2608 (2023)
21. Martini, H., Swanepoel, K.J., Weiß, G.: The geometry of minkowski spaces—a survey. Part i. Expositiones mathematicae **19**(2), 97–142 (2001)
22. Merigó, J.M., Gil-Lafuente, A.M.: Using the owa operator in the minkowski distance. Int. J. Econ. Manag. Eng. **2**(9), 1032–1040 (2008)
23. Psaila, G.: A database model for heterogeneous spatial collections: definition and algebra. In: 2011 International Conference on Data and Knowledge Engineering (ICDKE), pp. 30–35. IEEE (2011)
24. Psaila, G., Fosci, P.: J-co: a platform-independent framework for managing geo-referenced json data sets. Electronics **10**(5), 621 (2021)
25. Smarandache, F.: A unifying field in logics: neutrosophic logic. In: Philosophy, pp. 1–141. American Research Press (1999)
26. Thompson, A.C.: Minkowski Geometry. Cambridge University Press, Cambridge (1996)
27. Yager, R.R.: On ordered weighted averaging aggregation operators in multicriteria decision making. IEEE Trans. Syst. Man Cybern. **18**(1), 183–190 (1988)
28. Yager, R.R.: Pythagorean fuzzy subsets. In: 2013 Joint IFSA World Congress and NAFIPS Annual Meeting (IFSA/NAFIPS), pp. 57–61. IEEE (2013)
29. Yao, Y.Y., Zhong, N., Liu, J., Ohsuga, S.: Web Intelligence (WI) research challenges and trends in the new information age. In: Zhong, N., Yao, Y., Liu, J., Ohsuga, S. (eds.) WI 2001. LNCS (LNAI), vol. 2198, pp. 1–17. Springer, Heidelberg (2001). https://doi.org/10.1007/3-540-45490-X_1
30. Zadeh, L.A.: Fuzzy sets. Inf. Control **8**(3), 338–353 (1965)

An Ontology-Driven Framework for Adaptive and Transparent AI-Assisted Student Assessment

Asma Hadyaoui(✉) and Lilia Cheniti-Belcadhi

Sousse University, ISITC, PRINCE Research Laboratory, Hammam Sousse, Tunisia
asmahadyaoui@gmail.com, lilia.cheniti@isitc.u-sousse.tn

Abstract. Artificial Intelligence (AI) has transformed educational assessment through real-time feedback, adaptive learning, and automated evaluation mechanisms. However, existing AI-driven assessment models primarily focus on correctness-based grading, failing to capture cognitive engagement, problem-solving strategies, and AI-assisted modifications. This study introduces IntelliFrame, an ontology-based AI-driven framework designed to improve accuracy, adaptability, and transparency in AI-assisted assessments across multiple disciplines. Unlike traditional models, IntelliFrame systematically evaluates student interactions with AI tools, tracking decision-making processes and iterative learning behaviors to enable process-oriented assessment. A controlled study with 312 undergraduate students demonstrated significant cognitive improvements, including a 32% increase in structured problem-solving ($p < 0.01$, Cohen's $d = 0.78$), an 18% gain in independent critical reasoning ($p < 0.05$, Cohen's $d = 0.62$), and a 27% enhancement in task refinement ability ($p < 0.01$, Cohen's $d = 0.71$). Additionally, 81% of students found IntelliFrame's adaptive feedback mechanisms beneficial, while 74% improved their ability to assess AI-generated content critically. Faculty members observed a 42% reduced grading workload, highlighting IntelliFrame's impact on assessment efficiency and real-time progress tracking. Designed for scalability and cross-disciplinary application, IntelliFrame extends beyond programming education to business analytics, legal studies, and medical education. It integrates seamlessly with Intelligent Tutoring Systems (ITS) and AI-driven peer assessment models, further enhancing personalized learning pathways. While IntelliFrame improves adaptive assessment accuracy, challenges remain in bias mitigation, explainability of AI-generated feedback, and optimizing task complexity. Future research should refine bias-detection algorithms, enhance interoperability with learning analytics platforms, and develop scaffolding techniques for AI-assisted learning. IntelliFrame provides a transparent, adaptable, and process-driven assessment framework, ensuring fairness, cognitive engagement, and discipline-specific adaptability in AI-enhanced education.

Keywords: AI-Driven Assessment · Generative AI · Adaptive Learning · Ontology-Based Assessment · Cognitive Engagement · Real-Time Feedback · Explainable AI (XAI)

M. Marchiori et al. (Eds.): WEBIST 2024, LNBIP 583, pp. 246–267, 2026.
https://doi.org/10.1007/978-3-032-25534-1_11

1 Introduction

Artificial intelligence (AI) continues to transform education, introducing intelligent tutoring systems, automated grading, and adaptive learning environments. These technologies offer new possibilities for personalized learning, yet they also introduce significant challenges in assessment. Traditional evaluation methods emphasize correctness and summative grading but fail to capture the cognitive processes students employ when engaging with AI-generated content [1]. The growing use of generative AI tools raises concerns regarding academic integrity and the authenticity of student work [2]. As students increasingly integrate AI assistance into their learning processes, assessment frameworks must evolve to differentiate genuine student effort from AI-generated contributions.

Current AI-driven assessment frameworks often apply rigid evaluation criteria, prioritizing output accuracy while overlooking reasoning and creativity [3]. Many of these systems lack adaptability and fail to provide feedback aligned with students' evolving skills. Without mechanisms to track how students interact with AI, assessments risk misrepresenting learning outcomes by either ignoring AI dependency or unfairly penalizing students who engage AI tools as a means of exploration and refinement [4]. Addressing these challenges requires a process-oriented assessment model that evaluates learning trajectories rather than solely measuring final outcomes.

Ontology-based assessment models provide a structured approach to capturing student-AI interactions. These models establish relationships between knowledge domains, cognitive processes, and engagement patterns, enabling a more precise evaluation of learning behaviors. Unlike conventional AI-based assessments that rely on static evaluation metrics, ontology-driven systems adjust dynamically based on real-time student activity [5]. This adaptability ensures a balanced assessment approach that considers both the learning process and the final output, allowing for a more transparent and accurate representation of student performance.

This study introduces IntelliFrame, an ontology-based AI-driven assessment framework that enhances evaluation accuracy, adaptability, and fairness in AI-assisted learning environments. IntelliFrame incorporates real-time formative feedback, cognitive engagement tracking, and process-oriented evaluation to assess students based on their reasoning and decision-making rather than correctness alone. The framework applies beyond programming education to fields such as business analytics and research writing, where AI-generated content increasingly influences academic work.

This study investigates the following questions:

1. How does IntelliFrame enhance the accuracy and adaptability of AI-assisted assessments?
2. What effect does real-time AI-driven feedback have on students' problem-solving and critical thinking skills?
3. How can IntelliFrame be applied across disciplines beyond programming education to support broader academic applications?

This paper presents IntelliFrame as an AI-driven, ontology-based adaptive assessment framework that improves AI-integrated education by:

- Designing an ontology-driven assessment model that differentiates between AI-assisted and student-generated responses while tracking cognitive engagement.
- Implementing an adaptive assessment engine that provides real-time, personalized feedback to support student learning progression.
- Demonstrating cross-disciplinary applicability by validating IntelliFrame in programming education, business analytics, and research writing.
- Incorporating AI ethics-aware assessment mechanisms to reduce AI bias, prevent over-reliance on automated feedback, and enhance transparency in AI-assisted learning.

These contributions position IntelliFrame as a framework that enhances student learning by promoting engagement, critical thinking, and originality in AI-powered educational environments. This research advances AI-driven assessment methodologies, ensuring that AI supports student learning while preserving cognitive effort and academic integrity.

2 Literature Review

2.1 AI and the Evolution of Assessment in Education

AI has introduced new opportunities for personalized learning, adaptive instruction, and automated evaluation. However, traditional assessment methodologies remain largely static and outcome-focused, failing to account for cognitive engagement and problem-solving strategies [6]. Standardized tests and multiple-choice exams primarily assess correctness but overlook students' reasoning and iterative learning processes.

The increasing integration of AI tools in education requires a shift in assessment models to distinguish between genuine student effort and AI-assisted responses [4]. Conventional grading systems emphasize final outputs but lack mechanisms to evaluate how students interact with AI to refine their work. The absence of structured models to analyze AI-assisted problem-solving poses a risk of misrepresenting learning outcomes and academic integrity.

AI usage in education varies widely across disciplines [7]. Some students engage AI to enhance understanding and improve analytical skills, while others passively replicate AI-generated solutions. Studies suggest that tracking student interactions with AI can reveal critical thinking patterns and self-regulated learning behaviors [8]. However, existing AI-based assessments focus primarily on correctness rather than capturing adaptive learning behaviors [9]. The need for a process-oriented assessment framework has emerged, enabling the evaluation of the learning process alongside the final output. IntelliFrame introduces an ontology-based model that systematically analyzes cognitive engagement and decision-making, ensuring that AI enhances learning without replacing student reasoning.

2.2 Theoretical Foundations of AI-Driven Assessments

AI-driven assessments must align with established learning theories to ensure pedagogical effectiveness. Traditional evaluations often prioritize final scores over cognitive processes, overlooking how students construct and refine knowledge. Cognitive

Load Theory (CLT), Self-Regulated Learning (SRL), and Process-Oriented Assessment Models provide a strong foundation for designing adaptive and transparent AI-assisted assessments.

Cognitive Load Theory (CLT). CLT [10] explains how cognitive resources affect learning efficiency. Effective AI-enhanced assessments must regulate task complexity to prevent overload while promoting meaningful problem-solving [11]. Many AI-driven assessments either oversimplify tasks or introduce excessive difficulty, lacking dynamic adaptation mechanisms. A well-structured adaptive framework continuously adjusts task difficulty based on student engagement.

Self-Regulated Learning (SRL). SRL [12] highlights the importance of metacognition, motivation, and strategic learning. AI-based assessments should evaluate knowledge acquisition while also fostering students' ability to reflect on problem-solving approaches. Research indicates that AI-generated formative feedback supports SRL by providing real-time guidance for iterative learning [13]. Despite these benefits, many AI-based tools remain static, limiting their effectiveness in fostering deeper engagement.

Process-Oriented Assessment Models. Assessment frameworks in technical disciplines, such as computer science, emphasize efficiency and accuracy, often neglecting creativity and problem-solving depth [14]. Process-oriented evaluation metrics must be integrated into AI-driven assessments to track how students refine responses, engage with AI-generated feedback, and apply adaptive reasoning skills. AI-driven frameworks that incorporate CLT, SRL, and process-oriented assessment principles more effectively evaluate student learning in dynamic, real-world contexts. IntelliFrame applies these theories to ensure that assessment models reflect critical thinking, problem-solving depth, and cognitive flexibility in AI-enhanced learning environments.

2.3 Current Approaches to AI-Driven Student Assessment

Assessment methods in computer science education traditionally rely on coding assignments, projects, and exams to evaluate students' ability to apply theoretical knowledge in practical contexts [15]. These assessments measure correctness and efficiency but often overlook cognitive processes, problem-solving strategies, and creative reasoning [3]. The increasing presence of AI-assisted learning environments further complicates evaluation, as conventional assessments struggle to differentiate between human-generated and AI-augmented responses.

Automated Grading Systems. Natural Language Processing (NLP) and Machine Learning (ML)-based automated grading systems have improved assessment efficiency in large-scale education. AI-driven grading systems achieve high reliability in assessing correctness [9], but fail to evaluate conceptual depth, originality, and iterative problem-solving [16].

AI-Based Formative Assessment Tools. AI-powered formative assessments offer real-time feedback to assist students in iteratively refining their work [17]. Research shows that AI-generated feedback enhances problem-solving and analytical reasoning [18]. Despite these advantages, most AI-driven formative assessment systems remain rigid, making it difficult to accommodate diverse student interactions with generative AI tools.

Many existing models fail to assess creativity and decision-making pathways. AI should enhance student cognition, yet numerous systems lack transparency in evaluation criteria. A shift toward assessment frameworks capable of evaluating both the final output and the decision-making trajectory leading to it is necessary.

2.4 Need for Adaptive AI-Driven Assessment Frameworks

Despite advancements in AI-assisted learning, current assessment models remain limited in their ability to evaluate reasoning, problem-solving, and engagement with AI tools. Many existing frameworks focus on final outputs without accounting for cognitive processes. Limited adaptability in these models prevents assessments from dynamically adjusting to individual proficiency levels or capturing how students interact with AI-generated feedback.

A structured ontology-driven approach provides a solution by systematically modeling student interactions, learning trajectories, and AI engagement patterns. Unlike rigid rule-based assessments, ontology-based frameworks establish relationships between cognitive processes, learning tasks, and adaptive feedback mechanisms. These relationships allow for a more precise evaluation of student reasoning while maintaining flexibility.

The IntelliFrame framework addresses these challenges by implementing an ontology-based AI-driven assessment model designed to evaluate:

- Cognitive engagement,
- Problem-solving strategies, and
- Creative decision-making.

Cognitive load regulation, self-regulated learning principles, and process-oriented assessment methodologies enable real-time adaptive evaluations while ensuring fairness and transparency in AI-assisted education. The following section details its architecture, key components, and implementation.

3 IntelliFrame Framework Design

3.1 Overview of Intelliframe

IntelliFrame is an AI-driven assessment framework designed to evaluate student learning in environments where AI tools play an active role. Traditional AI-based assessments rely on static evaluation metrics, often emphasizing correctness without considering cognitive engagement or decision-making strategies. IntelliFrame introduces a process-oriented approach, integrating student effort, reasoning, and AI interactions into assessment outcomes. The framework adapts dynamically to student progress and learning needs, providing real-time, personalized feedback that fosters deeper engagement and conceptual understanding.

At the core of IntelliFrame is an ontology-driven architecture that models cognitive processes, problem-solving approaches, and AI-generated content usage. This structure enables the framework to analyze student interactions with AI tools, assess how they refine their work, and evaluate their problem-solving strategies. Initially designed for computer science education, IntelliFrame extends to disciplines such as business analytics and scientific research, where AI supports data interpretation, decision-making, and predictive analysis.

4 Modular IntelliFrame Architecture

IntelliFrame comprises six interconnected layers, each responsible for specific functionalities that ensure AI-driven assessment remains adaptive, scalable, and applicable across disciplines. The updated modular architecture, depicted in Fig. 1, refines data exchange, real-time feedback loops, and adaptive learning pathways.

4.1 User Interface Layer

This layer facilitates seamless student-instructor interaction through an intuitive design that supports AI-assisted learning and assessment.

- **Student Interface Module:** Provides access to tasks, AI-generated feedback, and interactive assessments.
- **Instructor Interface Module:** Enables real-time tracking of student performance, assessment adjustments, and AI behavior analysis.

4.2 AI Tools Integration Layer

This layer ensures smooth interoperability between IntelliFrame and AI-driven assessment tools.

- **LMS Integration Module**: Enables task submission, structured feedback delivery, and interaction with platforms such as Moodle.
- **AI Chatbot Module**: Provides domain-specific guidance, real-time hints, and adaptive learning support based on student needs.

4.3 Domain-Specific Adaptation Layer

IntelliFrame accommodates discipline-specific assessment requirements, enhancing its applicability beyond programming to diverse academic fields.

- **Programming Module**: Evaluates coding efficiency, debugging approaches, and algorithmic problem-solving.
- **Business Analytics Module**: Supports financial modeling, risk analysis, and data-driven decision-making.
- **Legal Studies Module**: Assists with legal case interpretation, contract analysis, and argumentation assessment.

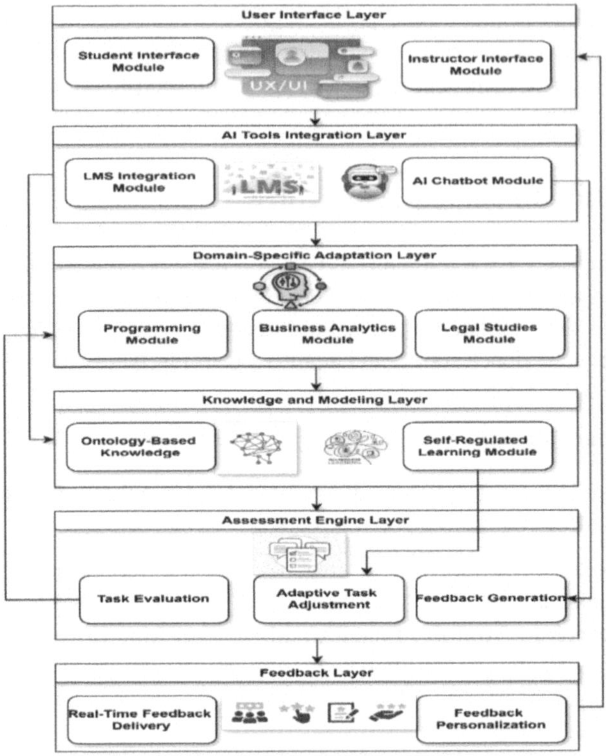

Fig. 1. Modular Architecture of IntelliFrame.

4.4 Knowledge and Modeling Layer

This layer structures AI-student interactions to ensure cognitive engagement tracking and adaptive AI-assisted learning.

- Ontology-based knowledge Module: Maps decision-making processes, engagement levels, and AI interaction patterns to improve assessment transparency.
- SRL Module: Monitors iterative learning, reflective thinking, and independent problem-solving, ensuring AI enhances—rather than replaces—student cognition.

4.5 Assessment Engine Layer

Responsible for real-time evaluation, adaptive learning pathways, and task complexity management, this layer optimizes AI-driven assessments.

- Task Evaluation Module: Analyzes correctness, conceptual depth, and reasoning quality in student responses.
- Adaptive Task Adjustment Module: Dynamically modifies difficulty based on student engagement and progress, ensuring personalized skill development.
- Feedback Generation Module: Produces AI-driven formative feedback to guide students toward deeper understanding and iterative refinement.

4.6 Feedback Layer

Ensuring personalized, real-time feedback delivery, this layer enhances learning outcomes by aligning assessment insights with student needs.

- **Real-Time Feedback Delivery Module**: Provides immediate feedback during tasks, fostering continuous improvement through iterative cycles.
- **Feedback Personalization Module**: Adjusts content complexity and instructional guidance based on student behavior and instructor preferences, ensuring adaptive learning support.

5 Ontological Model for AI-Assisted Assessment

The revised IntelliFrame ontology enhances the Ontology-Based Knowledge Model by incorporating additional cognitive engagement tracking, expanding interaction types, and improving adaptability across disciplines. The update systematically models AI-student interactions, enabling real-time feedback generation, adaptive assessment, and multi-domain academic applications. Compared to its earlier version [19] The extended ontology refines assessment granularity while integrating ethical AI principles and domain-specific needs.

5.1 Ontology Structure and Core Classes

The IntelliFrame ontology consists of five core classes, illustrated in Fig. 2, each modeling AI-assisted learning behaviors, student engagement, and discipline-specific applications. Table 1 presents the existing ontology components, newly introduced elements, and their justifications.

Fig. 2. IntelliFrame's Ontological Model.

5.2 Advancements in Ethical and Adaptive AI-Driven Assessment

The IntelliFrame ontology incorporates bias detection, explainability, and academic integrity tracking to enhance fairness, transparency, and adaptability in AI-driven assessments.

Bias Mitigation: Enhancing Fairness in AI-Based Assessment. To ensure equitable evaluation, IntelliFrame applies statistical debiasing techniques and real-time fairness checks.

- The AI Bias Detection Panel actively monitors student engagement patterns, identifying inconsistencies in AI-generated assessments.
- Empirical findings indicate that students who made minimal modifications to AI-generated responses exhibited higher assessment inconsistencies, emphasizing the need for refined bias mitigation models.
- Future enhancements should integrate adaptive bias correction mechanisms, allowing IntelliFrame to dynamically adjust fairness metrics based on real-time engagement data.

Table 1. Ontology Structure and Justification for New Components.

Ontology Class	Existing Components	Newly Introduced Components	Justification & Impact
Content Generation	TextOutput (explanations, summaries) CodeOutput (programming snippets) CreativeMediaOutput (graphs, visualizations)	LegalTextOutput	Extends IntelliFrame's applicability to legal education, enabling AI-assisted legal case analysis and contract clause evaluation. Supports text-heavy reasoning disciplines
Cognitive Process	Understanding (basic comprehension) Evaluation (critical assessment) Modification (refining AI outputs)	StrategicReasoning	Enhances decision-making assessment in business analytics and legal studies, where students must evaluate multiple AI-generated outputs before making informed judgments. Strengthens higher-order thinking evaluation
Interaction Type	DirectQuery (basic AI queries) IterativeRefinement (step-by-step AI modifications) FeedbackResponse (engagement with AI-generated feedback)	SelfEvaluation, CollaborativeAIUse	SelfEvaluation tracks students' ability to critically assess AI-generated suggestions, improving reflective learning. CollaborativeAIUse formalizes peer-supported AI learning, essential for group-based AI assessments

(*continued*)

Table 1. (*continued*)

Ontology Class	Existing Components	Newly Introduced Components	Justification & Impact
Knowledge Domain	ProgrammingConcepts (coding principles, debugging) SubjectMatterTopics (broad academic content)	FinancialModeling, CaseAnalysis	FinancialModeling enables AI-assisted economic forecasting, risk analysis, and business decision-making. CaseAnalysis allows legal reasoning assessment, tracking how students construct arguments using AI-generated insights
Feedback Mechanism	RealTimeFeedback (instant feedback) FormativeFeedback (iterative learning insights) SummativeFeedback (final evaluations)	AIInstructorFeedback	Introduces human-AI hybrid assessment, allowing instructors to modify AI-generated feedback, monitor engagement, and provide personalized interventions, ensuring pedagogical oversight

AI Explainability: Improving Transparency in AI-Based Evaluation. IntelliFrame ensures assessment interpretability through the Explainable AI (XAI) Justification Panel. This panel enables students and instructors to:

- Interpret confidence scores, indicating assessment certainty.
- Visualize decision pathways, mapping how IntelliFrame processes student inputs.
- Receive natural language explanations, making AI-generated feedback more accessible and actionable.

Although IntelliFrame's XAI features were implemented, the study did not explicitly measure student engagement with explainability tools. Future research should evaluate how effectively students utilize these features and whether they contribute to improved AI literacy and SRL.

The IntelliFrame ontology integrates bias detection, explainability, and assessment integrity to enhance transparency and fairness in AI-assisted evaluation.

5.3 Interoperability and Scalability

This refined ontology aligns with educational technology standards, supporting:

- **xAPI (Experience API)**: Tracks AI-student interactions for learning analytics.

- **LTI (Learning Tools Interoperability)**: Enables seamless integration with LMS platforms (Moodle, Canvas).
- **OWL 2-DL Compliance**: Supports semantic web technologies for structured knowledge representation.

The updated ontology enhances structure, improves domain-specific adaptability, and resolves AI-driven assessment challenges. These advancements establish IntelliFrame as a framework that ensures equitable, scalable, and transparent AI-assisted learning environments.

6 Use Case: AI-Driven Financial Risk Analysis

AI-driven assessment frameworks are increasingly applied beyond programming education. In business analytics, financial decision-making relies on predictive modeling, risk assessment, and adaptive learning. This use case demonstrates how IntelliFrame supports AI-assisted financial forecasting, ensuring students engage in methodological refinement, bias detection, and ethical AI considerations rather than relying passively on AI-generated outputs.

6.1 Task Overview and AI-Assisted Model Refinement

Rayan, a graduate student in financial data science, engages with IntelliFrame to forecast stock market volatility. The system structures the process into distinct phases, guiding him through exploratory data analysis, predictive modeling, and model refinement. The Financial Risk Analysis Interface (Fig. 3) allows Rayan to integrate real-world datasets, including historical stock prices, macroeconomic indicators, and Bloomberg market trends.

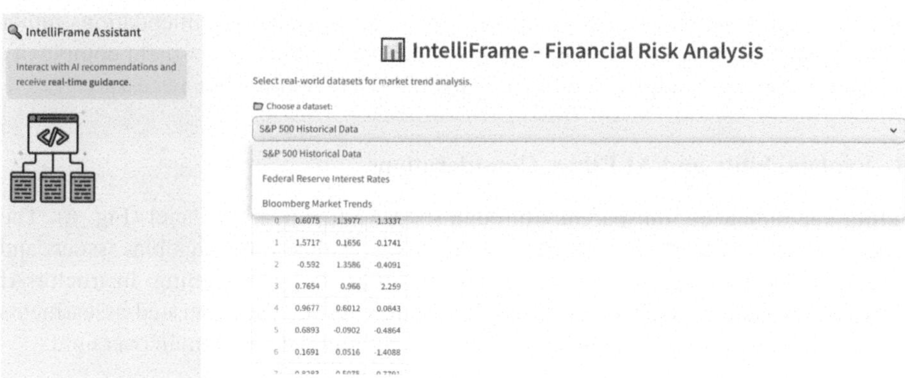

Fig. 3. IntelliFrame Data Integration and AI-Assisted Market Analysis Interface.

The Model Adjustments Panel enables Rayan to refine his approach by experimenting with regression models, incorporating economic fluctuations, and testing feature engineering techniques. IntelliFrame provides real-time AI-generated feedback, ensuring transparent and data-driven model optimization.

6.2 AI-Assisted Model Development and Refinement

Financial risk assessments often contain biases that distort predictions. The AI Bias Detection Panel (Fig. 4) identifies key risks, including over-reliance on historical data without stress testing, algorithmic imbalances affecting small-cap stocks, and the omission of external risk factors such as inflation and geopolitical instability. IntelliFrame prompts Rayan to apply bias mitigation strategies, such as integrating crisis-period data, adjusting model weightings, and expanding feature selection to improve model fairness and robustness.

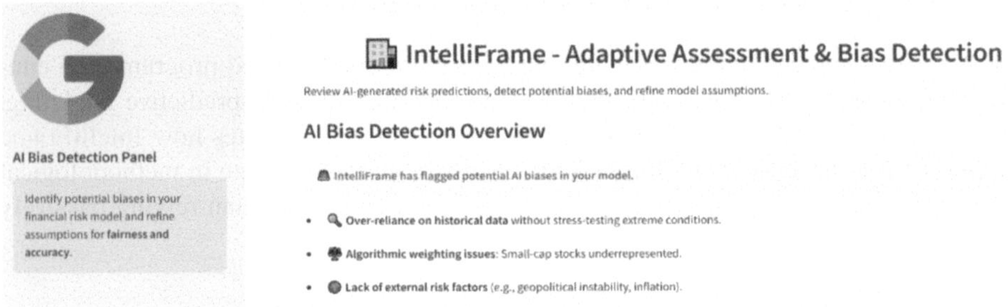

Fig. 4. AI Bias Detection and Assessment Panel.

6.3 Performance Tracking and Instructor Oversight

Student engagement patterns and iterative learning behaviors are tracked through IntelliFrame's Performance Dashboard and Student Engagement Heatmap (Fig. 5). The system captures modifications in AI-generated feedback, error corrections, and adaptive assessment responses. Faculty members monitor these trends using the Instructor Review Panel, ensuring students critically engage with AI-generated recommendations rather than accepting them passively. Based on observed interactions, assessment complexity levels are dynamically adjusted, allowing targeted intervention when necessary.

6.4 Explainability and AI Ethics Considerations

IntelliFrame enhances transparency through its XAI Justification Panel (Fig. 6). The system outlines risk factors considered in AI-driven evaluations, flags bias issues, and ensures fairness by tracking potential distortions in predictive modeling. Instructor-AI collaborative grading mechanisms allow faculty to override AI-generated assessments when inconsistencies emerge, ensuring balanced automation and human oversight.

6.5 Final Outcome

Rayan's completed assessment includes:

- A predictive model that integrates AI insights with structured financial reasoning.
- A bias detection and explainability report addressing model fairness and transparency.
- A self-assessment reflection on ethical AI considerations in financial risk modeling.

IntelliFrame structures financial assessments to reinforce methodological rigor, transparency, and fairness. The system fosters student engagement with AI-generated insights while ensuring accountability through real-time monitoring and instructor oversight.

7 Experimental Validation of IntelliFrame

The effectiveness of IntelliFrame was evaluated through an empirical study incorporating pre/post-tests, student feedback, instructor perspectives, and interaction analysis. This validation aimed to assess IntelliFrame's impact on learning outcomes, adaptive assessment, and AI-driven evaluation transparency.

7.1 Study Design and Participants

The study involved 312 undergraduate students from computer science and business analytics courses over eight weeks. Participants engaged in AI-assisted tasks to measure problem-solving skills, cognitive engagement, and response refinement. Faculty members provided qualitative insights into IntelliFrame's assessment mechanisms.

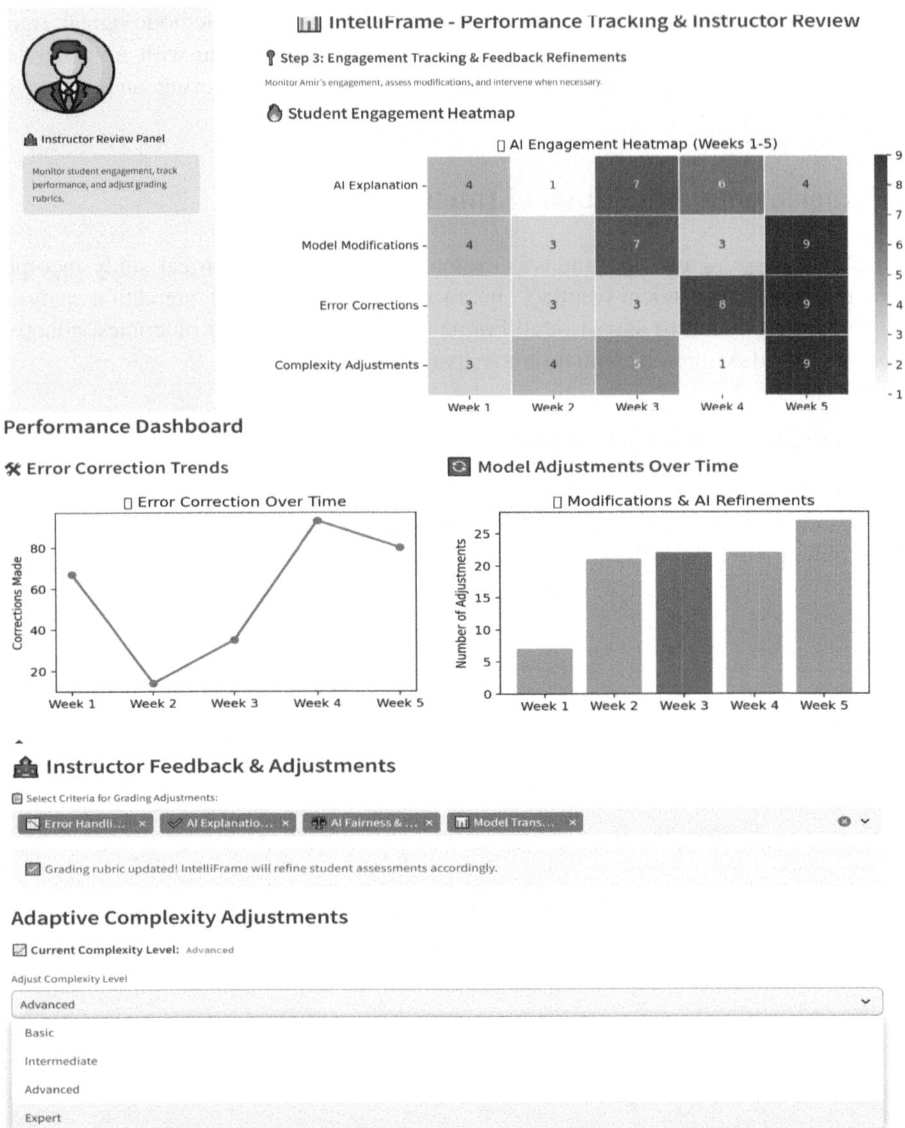

Fig. 5. IntelliFrame's Adaptive Assessment & AI Bias Detection Interface.

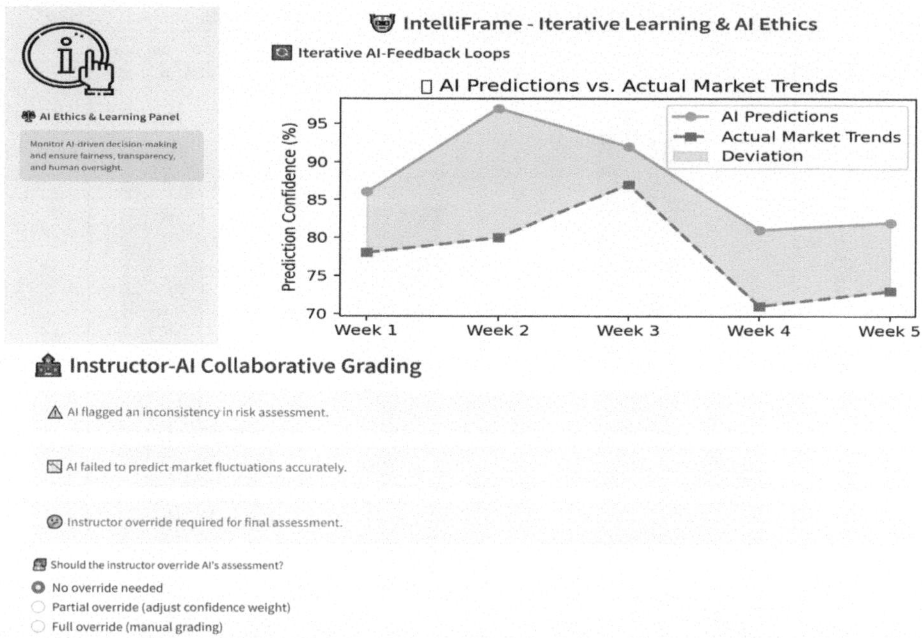

Fig. 6. Iterative Learning and AI Ethics in Financial Risk Assessment.

7.2 Pre/Post-Test Analysis

A controlled pre/post-test experiment measured learning gains in problem-solving, reasoning, and task refinement, as described in Table 2.

Table 2. Impact of IntelliFrame on Cognitive Skill Development.

Cognitive Skill	Improvement (%)	Effect Size (Cohen's d)	Statistical Significance
Structured problem-solving	32%	0.78 (moderate-large)	$p < 0.01$
Independent critical reasoning	18%	0.62 (moderate)	$p < 0.05$
Task refinement ability	27%	0.71 (moderate-large)	$p < 0.01$

Figure 7 presents the cognitive improvements observed after IntelliFrame integration.

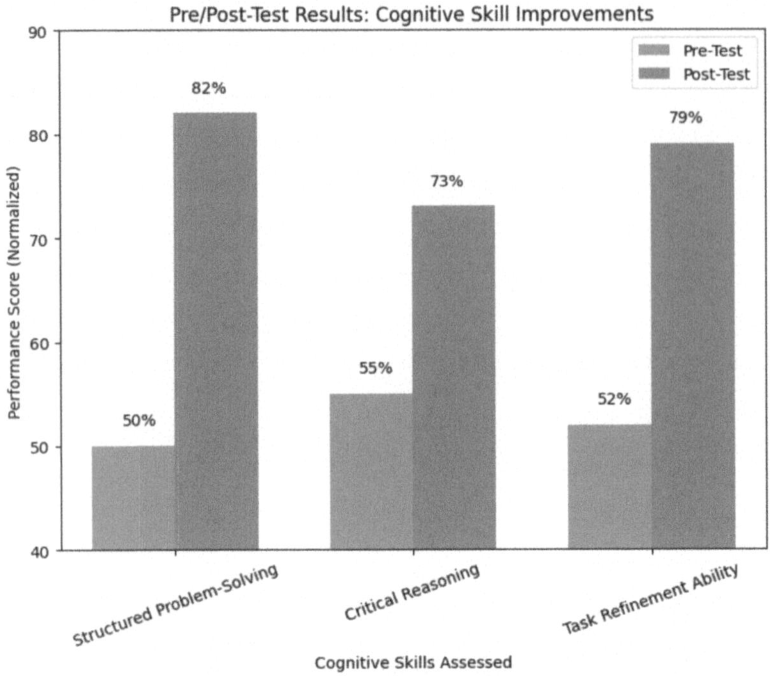

Fig. 7. Cognitive Skill Improvements: Pre/Post-Test Performance with IntelliFrame.

7.3 Student Feedback and Engagement

A post-study survey evaluated student perceptions of IntelliFrame's effectiveness:

- 81% found adaptive feedback useful for refining work.
- 74% reported an improved ability to critically assess AI-generated suggestions.
- 68% indicated that IntelliFrame enhanced decision-making through iterative learning.

Some students faced challenges in interpreting AI feedback, emphasizing the need for scaffolded guidance in modifying AI-generated outputs.

7.4 Student-AI Interaction Analysis

The heatmap visualization (Fig. 8) reveals patterns in student engagement with AI-driven assessments, focusing on feedback modifications, time spent analyzing AI-generated explanations, and interactions with adaptive assessments. These trends highlight differences in cognitive engagement, adaptability, and AI reliance, identifying areas for refinement in AI-assisted learning environments.

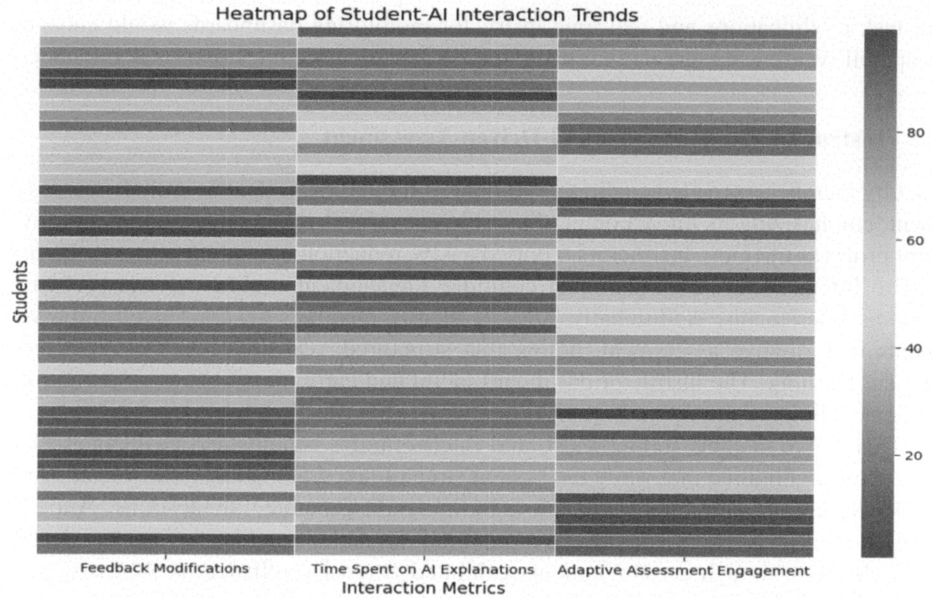

Fig. 8. Heatmap of Student-AI Interaction Patterns in Adaptive Learning.

Patterns in Feedback Modifications. Engagement levels in modifying AI-generated feedback varied widely. Students who actively refined AI suggestions demonstrated iterative learning and critical thinking, whereas others made minimal modifications, often accepting AI-generated responses without deeper evaluation. Limited engagement in feedback adjustments suggests difficulty interpreting AI-generated insights or a lack of confidence in making independent revisions. Addressing these challenges requires adaptive feedback scaffolding that encourages students to critically assess AI-generated content rather than passively accepting it.

Time Spent Analyzing AI-Generated Explanations. Students displayed varying levels of engagement when reviewing AI-generated explanations. Some carefully analyzed feedback, cross-referencing AI insights with existing knowledge before modifying responses. Others skimmed past explanations without meaningful interaction, indicating either cognitive overload due to complex AI feedback or a superficial reliance on AI outputs. Refining IntelliFrame's feedback mechanisms by integrating natural language justifications and confidence scores would enhance clarity, ensuring students can contextualize AI-generated suggestions effectively.

Engagement with Adaptive Assessment Features. The heatmap further illustrates how students interacted with IntelliFrame's adaptive assessments. Highly engaged students frequently adjusted AI-generated feedback and responded actively to dynamic task modifications, demonstrating proactive learning behaviors. Conversely, lower engagement levels in response to changing task complexity suggest hesitation in adapting to AI-driven assessment adjustments. Some students may have struggled with shifting difficulty levels or experienced cognitive strain. Introducing structured explanations for task modifications and real-time instructor monitoring dashboards would enhance adaptability, allowing targeted interventions for students needing additional guidance.

7.5 Instructor Perspectives on AI-Driven Assessment

Faculty members provided qualitative feedback on IntelliFrame's role in student assessment, emphasizing its impact on grading efficiency, feedback personalization, and student progress tracking. Instructors reported a 42% reduction in grading time, attributing this to IntelliFrame's automation of cognitive engagement evaluations and problem-solving assessments. Additionally, 88% of faculty members acknowledged improvements in formative assessment, noting that structured, real-time feedback enhanced student learning. The instructor dashboard facilitated early identification of struggling students, allowing timely interventions and targeted instructional support.

Qualitative insights further illustrated IntelliFrame's benefits and challenges. One instructor highlighted that while the system streamlined grading and assessment, some students needed additional guidance in refining AI-generated suggestions. Another instructor observed that IntelliFrame provided valuable insights into student learning behaviors, though certain students exhibited excessive reliance on AI assistance, necessitating tailored instructional strategies to foster independent problem-solving.

7.6 Error Analysis in AI-Assisted Assessment

The study also examined limitations in AI-driven evaluation, focusing on bias detection and assessment reliability. Although IntelliFrame's automated scoring aligned with instructor grading 87% of the time, inconsistencies emerged, particularly among students who engaged minimally with AI-generated feedback. These discrepancies underscored the need for bias-mitigation techniques tailored to lower-engagement learners.

Analysis revealed that students with limited AI proficiency faced greater challenges in interpreting AI-generated feedback, reinforcing the necessity of adaptive feedback strategies that accommodate diverse learner profiles. Additionally, edge cases requiring manual intervention arose when IntelliFrame misinterpreted nuanced student modifications as errors, highlighting areas for refinement in AI-driven assessment frameworks.

8 Discussion

This study demonstrates IntelliFrame's effectiveness in enhancing AI-assisted assessments by fostering structured problem-solving, critical reasoning, and iterative learning. Empirical validation confirms that students using IntelliFrame showed a 32% improvement in structured problem-solving, an 18% increase in critical reasoning, and a 27% enhancement in task refinement ability. Unlike AI-based grading systems that primarily assess correctness [20, 21], IntelliFrame employs ontology-driven cognitive tracking to ensure a process-oriented evaluation, capturing reasoning, engagement, and learning progression rather than focusing solely on accuracy.

A key advantage of IntelliFrame is its scalability and adaptability across disciplines, extending its application beyond programming education to fields such as business analytics, medical education, and legal studies. The framework dynamically adjusts task complexity based on student performance and engagement, fostering personalized learning and deeper cognitive engagement [22]. The AI-driven financial risk analysis use case illustrates its ability to track student engagement, refine models through adaptive assessment, and ensure ethical AI integration by identifying biases in AI-generated predictions. These features establish IntelliFrame as a data-driven assessment system that balances AI automation with human oversight, ensuring transparency and fairness in evaluation processes.

Unlike fully automated AI grading systems, IntelliFrame integrates instructor oversight, allowing faculty to monitor student-AI interactions in real time and adjust assessment complexity to align with students' demonstrated proficiency levels. Through the Instructor Review Panel and Analytics Dashboard, faculty can track student engagement, ensuring that students critically evaluate AI-generated insights rather than passively accepting automated suggestions. This intervention enhances assessment reliability and accountability, reinforcing the importance of balancing AI-driven automation with human judgment.

Bias detection and mitigation remain integral to IntelliFrame's design. The AI Bias Detection Panel and Bias Breakdown Visualization effectively flag algorithmic biases, such as over-reliance on historical data, weighting imbalances, and exclusion of external risk factors. While these tools improve fairness in AI-driven evaluations, further refinements are necessary to enhance bias correction strategies, particularly for students from diverse learning backgrounds. Additionally, assessment explainability remains critical. The XAI Justification Panel enhances transparency, but expanding student-facing explanations—such as natural language justifications and confidence scores—would further support students in contextualizing AI-generated feedback.

Although IntelliFrame incorporates adaptive AI feedback loops, iterative learning mechanisms, and instructor intervention, further research is needed to assess its long-term impact on student learning outcomes. Current findings primarily reflect short-term improvements, making it essential to evaluate whether cognitive gains persist over multiple semesters. Additionally, integrating learning analytics dashboards (e.g., xAPI-based platforms) could strengthen data-driven insights for educators, enabling a deeper understanding of student learning patterns. Refining faculty intervention mechanisms will also be crucial to ensure real-time adjustments to AI-generated feedback, aligning assessments with discipline-specific criteria while maintaining fairness and transparency.

9 Conclusion

IntelliFrame presents a scalable, process-oriented AI-driven assessment framework that ensures fair, transparent, and adaptive evaluations. The empirical findings confirm its effectiveness in fostering structured problem-solving, critical reasoning, and student engagement, distinguishing it from conventional AI-based grading systems. Moving forward, refining bias mitigation strategies, improving explainability mechanisms, and enhancing adaptive assessment models will be essential for advancing AI-integrated learning environments. Further research should explore scalable fairness-aware AI models, improved instructor intervention dashboards, and dynamic student-facing feedback enhancements to optimize IntelliFrame's ability to support personalized, transparent, and pedagogically sound assessments.

As AI continues reshaping education, frameworks like IntelliFrame will bridge the gap between AI-generated content and authentic student learning, ensuring that assessments remain transparent, personalized, and aligned with pedagogical best practices.

Disclosure of Interests. The authors have no competing interests to declare that are relevant to the content of this article.

References

1. Nguyen, T., Tran, H., Nguyen, M.: Empowering Education: Exploring the Potential of Artificial Intelligence, Chapter 9 - Artificial Intelligence (AI) in Teaching and Learning: A Comprehensive Review, 2023
2. Feuerriegel, S., Hartmann, J., Janiesch, C., Zschech, P.: Generative AI. Bus. Inf. Syst. Eng. **66**(1), 111–126 (2024). https://doi.org/10.1007/s12599-023-00834-7
3. Paiva, J., Leal, J., Figueira, Á.: Automated assessment in computer science education: a state-of-the-art review. ACM Trans. Comput. Educ. **22** (2022). https://doi.org/10.1145/3513140
4. Smolansky, A., et al.: Educator and student perspectives on the impact of generative AI on assessments in higher education. In: Proceedings of the 10th ACM Conference on Learning @ Scale, ACM, New York, NY, USA, pp. 378–382, 2023. https://doi.org/10.1145/3573051.3596191
5. Hadyaoui, A., Cheniti-Belcadhi, L.: Towards an ontology-based recommender system for assessment in a collaborative eLearning environment. In: Proceedings of the International Conference on Web Information Systems and Technologies (WEBIST), pp. 294–301, 2022. https://doi.org/10.5220/0011543500003318
6. Mulder, R., Baik, C., Ryan, T.: Rethinking Assessment in Response to AI, University of Melbourne, July 2023
7. Labadze, L., Grigolia, M., Machaidze, L.: Role of AI Chatbots in education: systematic literature review. Int. J. Educ. Technol. High. Educ. **20** (2023). https://doi.org/10.1186/s41239-023-00426-1
8. Hadyaoui, A., Cheniti-Belcadhi, L.: Ontology-based group assessment analytics framework for performance prediction in project-based collaborative learning. Smart Learn. Environ. **10**(1) (2023). https://doi.org/10.1186/s40561-023-00262-w
9. Mizumoto, A., Eguchi, M.: Exploring the potential of using an AI language model for automated essay scoring. Res. Methods Appl. Linguist. **2**(2), 100050 (2023). https://doi.org/10.1016/j.rmal.2023.100050
10. Sweller, J.: Cognitive load during problem solving: effects on learning. Cogn. Sci. **12**(2), 257–285 (1988). https://doi.org/10.1207/s15516709cog1202_4
11. Kirschner, F., Paas, F., Kirschner, P.: Task complexity as a driver for collaborative learning efficiency: the collective working-memory effect. Appl. Cogn. Psychol. **25**, 615–624 (2011). https://doi.org/10.1002/acp.1730
12. Zimmerman, B.: Becoming a self-regulated learner: an overview. Theory Pract. **41**, 64–70 (2002). https://doi.org/10.1207/s15430421tip4102_2

13. Hooda, M., et al.: Artificial intelligence for assessment and feedback to enhance student success in higher education. Math. Probl. Eng. **2022**, 5215722 (2022). https://doi.org/10.1155/2022/5215722
14. Long, H., et al.: A critical review of assessments of creativity in education. Rev. Res. Educ. **46**, 288–323 (2022). https://doi.org/10.3102/0091732X221084326
15. D. Of, P. In, and C. Science, "A Framework for Competence-Based e-Assessment," Computer Science Education, 2017
16. Rubab, I., Imran, A.: A comparative analysis of traditional and online assessments: perceptions and performance of undergraduate students. Int. J. Learn. Dev. **11**(2), 1352–1358 (2023)
17. Gikandi, J.W.: Enhancing e-learning through integration of online formative assessment and teaching presence. Int. J. Online Pedagog. Course Des. **11**(2), 48–61 (2021). https://doi.org/10.4018/IJOPCD.2021040104
18. Bulut, O., et al.: Standing on the shoulders of giants: online formative assessments as the foundation for predictive learning analytics models. Br. J. Edu. Technol. **54**(1), 19–39 (2023). https://doi.org/10.1111/bjet.13276
19. Hadyaoui, A., Cheniti-Belcadhi, L.: IntelliFrame: a framework for AI-driven, adaptive, and process-oriented student assessments. In: Proceedings of the 20th International Conference on Web Information Systems and Technologies (WEBIST 2024), Porto, Portugal, Nov. 17–19, 2024, SCITEPRESS, pp. 441–448, 2024. https://doi.org/10.5220/0013070800003825
20. Suresh, V., et al.: AI-based automated essay grading system using NLP. In: Proceedings of the 7th International Conference on Intelligent Computing and Control Systems (ICICCS 2023), pp. 547–552, 2023. https://doi.org/10.1109/ICICCS56967.2023.10142822
21. Bernard, J., et al.: Automated grading of anatomical objective structured practical examinations using decision trees: an artificial intelligence approach. Anat. Sci. Educ. (2023).https://doi.org/10.1002/ase.2305
22. Contrino, M.F., et al.: Using an adaptive learning tool to improve student performance and satisfaction in online and face-to-face education. Smart Learn. Environ. **11**(1), 6 (2024). https://doi.org/10.1186/s40561-024-00292-y

Social Network Analytics

Beyond Employee Turnover Prediction: Generalized Data Spatial Dependencies

Sandra Maria Pereira[1(✉)], Alice Pereira de Aguilar Penido[1], Alessandro Garcia Vieira[2], and Wladmir Cardoso Brandão[1]

[1] Institute of Exact Sciences and Informatics, Pontifical Catholic University of Minas Gerais, Dom Jose Gaspar Street, 500, Belo Horizonte, Brazil
sandra.pereira@sga.pucminas.br
[2] Sólides S.A., Tomé de Souza Street, 845, Belo Horizonte, Brazil
https://solides.com.br/
https://www.pucminas.br/

Abstract. Machine learning techniques have been widely applied to human resource challenges, particularly in predicting employee turnover, which represents the likelihood of an employee leaving a company. Since employee turnover directly impacts knowledge retention and business continuity, its management requires multidisciplinary approaches. In previous studies [13], employee turnover prediction served as the foundation for assessing the impact of spatial dependencies in predictive modeling. This study expands that approach by proposing a generalized methodology to evaluate whether prediction problems exhibit spatial dependence, demonstrating the applicability of spatial models beyond workforce analytics. To validate this methodology, we used the California Housing Dataset and applied linear regression models to compare georeferenced and non-georeferenced data. Experimental results reveal significant performance differences when considering geographical positioning. These findings highlight the broader applicability of spatial modeling techniques, reinforcing the importance of integrating geographic attributes into predictive analytics across diverse domains. The experimental results showed that there are consistent differences between distinct geographic points, highlighting a strong influence of spatial position on the metrics, reinforcing the importance of considering geographic location and scale in data modeling and interpretation to avoid biases.

Keywords: Predictive analytics · Spatial models · Spatial dependence · Machine learning · Spatial analysis

1 Introduction

In contemporary times, the emergence of uniquely complex problems has increased the difficulty of understanding and solving them using conventional methods, data scarcity [2] on certain topics and the uniqueness of the phenomena are examples of barrier creating problems [2]. It becomes essential to deepen the understanding of complexity to solve these problems and to determine the appropriate theories.

M. Marchiori et al. (Eds.): WEBIST 2024, LNBIP 583, pp. 271–289, 2026.
https://doi.org/10.1007/978-3-032-25534-1_12

Complex phenomena often exhibit non trivial behavior patterns, testing our ability to predict them. Predictive analytics based on machine learning has been widely used to address complex problems in various domains, including human resources and the real estate market. Predictive modeling, when combined with spatial information, can reveal patterns and dependencies not captured by traditional approaches, significantly enhancing model accuracy.

In previous studies, [13] have demonstrated that incorporating spatial attributes into employee turnover prediction substantially improves model performance, highlighting the importance of spatial dependence in such problems. In prior research, a methodology was proposed to assess the existence of spatial dependencies in predictive problems using linear regression models applied to georeferenced and non-georeferenced data extracted from public government databases. These datasets contained records of employee admissions and terminations in Brazil between 2018 and 2021. Experimental results indicated significant improvements in prediction accuracy when considering the spatial structure of the data.

In this work, the approach is expanded to reinforce the methodological analysis of spatial dependence by employing a new dataset focused on predicting housing prices in California [16]. This context allows for a detailed evaluation of the proposed methodology, as real estate pricing is highly influenced by geospatial factors such as location, urban infrastructure, and regional socioeconomic characteristics. Furthermore, using a well-studied dataset in the literature enables a clearer comparison of the impacts of spatial modeling on predictive performance.

The proposed methodology will be applied to both conventional linear regression models and spatially adjusted models, incorporating spatial dependence metrics such as Moran's I and spatial weight matrices. The impact of including spatial variables will be evaluated through standard error metrics, such as MAE (Mean Absolute Error), RMSE (Root Mean Squared Error), and MAPE (Mean Absolute Percentage Error), allowing for a quantitative comparison of model performance.

With this approach, the aim is to strengthen the understanding of the effects of spatial dependence in predictive problems and establish the methodology as an essential tool for modeling data where geographic location plays a crucial role, allowing for the determination of whether a problem possesses the characteristics of a spatial problem or not.

The remainder of this article of this article is organized as follows: in Sect. 2 one presents the background, in Sect. 3 one presents the dataset description, in Sect. 4 one presents methodology, in Sect. 5 one presents experimental setup, in Sect. 6 one presents experimental results, and finally, in Sect. 7 one presents conclusion and future work.

2 Background

2.1 Spatial Data

Spatial Data refers to information that have a location component, which mean that they are associated to a specific position [12]. This data is used to describe the characteristics and relations between objects and events in a physical or abstract space [4]. They might be shown in different forms, such as points, representing specific coordinates, lines, representing routes or limits and polygons, representing regions [5].

Geo Spatial Data. The geospatial data are a subset of spatial data that includes the coordinates of the position of an object or phenomenon on the Earth's surface. These data include, not only, the location: latitude, longitude and altitude, but also attributes that describe the characteristics of objects or geographic events. In sum, while all geospatial data are spatial, not all spatial data is geospatial, since geospatial data requires an explicit reference to their geographical coordinates [1].

Geographical Positioning. Geospatial data are critical in representing and analyzing the physical world, offering precise information about the location and characteristics of various phenomena. These data types include raster data, typically used for images and continuous data fields, and vector data, which consist of points, lines, and polygons. The accurate representation of geospatial data relies on the selection of multiple scales and projections [11], ensuring the fidelity of spatial relationships.

Geographical Positioning. Geospatial data are critical in representing and analyzing the physical world, offering precise information about the location and characteristics of various phenomena [11]. These data types include raster data, typically used for images and continuous data fields, and vector data, which consist of points, lines, and polygons. The accurate representation of geospatial data relies on the selection of multiple scales and projections [11], ensuring the fidelity of spatial relationships.

2.2 Spatial Analisys

Spatial Analysis aims to directly measure properties and relationships, taking into account the spatial positioning of phenomena. Understanding how data from phenomena occurring in space are distributed is a significant challenge for addressing fundamental questions in various fields of knowledge [3].

Spatial Dependency. Spatial Dependency is as key concept on understanding and analyzing spatial phenomena. Spatial dependence refers to the principle that the location of a geographical object or phenomenon influences, and is influenced by, other nearby objects or phenomena. This concept is fundamental to spatial analysis, as it suggests that spatial patterns are not random but are the result of proximity and interaction between geographic elements.

The rationale for examining spatial dependence analysis lies in the fact that datasets with the same values, when considering their positioning, can yield different results, as illustrated by Fig. 1.

Both maps have the same number of observations, however, by examining the spatial distribution of these observations, distinct results can be obtained due to their positioning. This highlights the importance of spatial analysis in revealing patterns and insights that are not apparent through traditional data analysis methods alone [3].

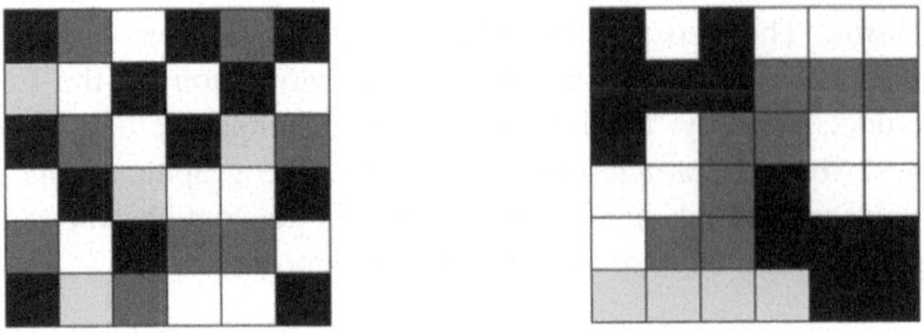

(a) Non spatial. (b) Spatial.

Fig. 1. Feature distributions types [13].

2.3 Spatial Autocorrelation

Spatial autocorrelation is a measure that assesses the degree of similarity or dependence between values of an attribute at different geographical locations. In other words, it indicates how similar the characteristics of a phenomenon at a given location are to the characteristics at nearby locations. If nearby locations have similar values, spatial autocorrelation is positive; if the values differ, autocorrelation is negative. This measure is essential for understanding spatial patterns, as it takes into account the influence that geographical proximity has on the variables under study [14,15].

Measures of Spatial Autocorrelation

- **Weight Matrix:**
  The weight matrix is a mathematical representation, it specifies the degree of proximity and influence that one location has over other locations. Each element W_{ij} in the matrix represents the weight assigned to the relationship between locations *i* and *j*. Specifically:
  - *i* and *j* are indices referring to different locations in the dataset.
  - W_{ij} quantifies the strength or significance of the spatial connection between location *i* and *j*.

- **Moran's I:**
  The Moran's I is a statistical measure used to quantify spatial autocorrelation in a geospatial dataset. It assesses the degree of similarity between values of a variable at geographically close locations and helps identify patterns of spatial aggregation or dispersion. A positive Moran's I value indicates that nearby locations tend to have similar values, whereas a negative value suggests that nearby locations have different values.
  For spatial autocorrelation analysis, this study employed the Moran's I to assess correlation. This statistical measure is crucial for understanding the degree to which a variable is similarly distributed across a geographical space [6].
  Moran's I is defined as:

$$I = \frac{N}{W} \frac{\sum_i \sum_j w_{ij}(x_i - \bar{x})(x_j - \bar{x})}{\sum_i (x_i - \bar{x})^2} \quad (1)$$

where N is the number of spatial units indexed by i and j, x represents the variable of interest, $\bar{x}$ is the mean of x, and w_{ij} is the spatial weight between units i and j. The sum of all spatial weights is denoted as W. When the index value is close to +1, it indicates a strong positive spatial autocorrelation, meaning similar values cluster together in space. A value close to -1 suggests a strong negative spatial autocorrelation, where dissimilar values are spatially clustered. A value around 0 indicates a random spatial pattern with no discernible clustering [7].

2.4 Comparison Metrics

Pearson Correlation

$$r = \frac{n\sum xy - \sum x \sum y}{\sqrt{[n\sum x^2 - (\sum x)^2][n\sum y^2 - (\sum y)^2]}} \tag{2}$$

where r is the Pearson correlation coefficient, n is the number of data points (pairs of scores). x and y are the individual data points for the two variables being compared.

The denominator of the formula contains the product of two square roots. Each square root represents the standard deviations of the respective variables.

ANOVA F-Statistic

$$F = \frac{\text{MSB}}{\text{MSW}} \tag{3}$$

where F is F-statistic in ANOVA, MSB is Mean Square Between (Between-Groups Mean Square), MSW is Mean Square Within (Within-Groups Mean Square).

$$\text{MSB} = \frac{\sum_{i=1}^{k} n_i(\bar{X}_i - \bar{X})^2}{k-1} \tag{4}$$

where n_i is the number of observations in group i, $\bar{X}_i$ is the mean of the observations in group i, $\bar{X}$ is the overall mean of all observations across all groups, k is the number of groups being compared.

$$\text{MSW} = \frac{\sum_{i=1}^{k}\sum_{j=1}^{n_i}(X_{ij} - \bar{X}_i)^2}{N-k} \tag{5}$$

where n_i is the number of observations in group i, X_{ij} is the value of the j-th observation in group i, $\bar{X}_i$ is the mean of the observations in group i, $N - k$ represents the degrees of freedom associated with the within-group variance, where N is the total number of observations and k is the number of groups.

MAPE (Mean Absolute Percentage Error)

$$\text{MAPE} = \frac{1}{n}\sum_{i=1}^{n}\left|\frac{A_i - F_i}{A_i}\right| \times 100\% \tag{6}$$

where MAPE stands for Mean Absolute Percentage Error, n is the number of data points or observations, A_i represents the actual value for the i-th observation, F_i represents the forecasted value for the i-th observation, $\left|\frac{A_i - F_i}{A_i}\right|$ calculates the absolute percentage error for the i-th observation.

MAE (Mean Absolute Error)

$$\text{MAE} = \frac{1}{n}\sum_{i=1}^{n}|A_i - F_i| \tag{7}$$

where MAE stands for Mean Absolute Error, n is the number of data points or observations, A_i represents the actual value for the i-th observation, F_i represents the forecasted value for the i-th observation, $|A_i - F_i|$ calculates the absolute error for the i-th observation.

RMSE (Root Mean Squared Error)

$$\text{RMSE} = \sqrt{\frac{1}{n}\sum_{i=1}^{n}(A_i - F_i)^2} \tag{8}$$

where RMSE stands for Root Mean Squared Error, n is the number of data points or observations, A_i represents the actual value for the i-th observation, F_i represents the forecasted value for the i-th observation, $(A_i - F_i)^2$ calculates the squared error for the i-th observation.

The square root of the mean squared error is taken to return the result to the original units of the data.

3 Dataset Description

The dataset used in this study is the California Housing Prices Dataset [16], which provides a detailed view of real estate pricing across various locations in California. Originally derived from the 1990 U.S. Census data, this dataset has been widely used for benchmarking regression models in predictive analytics. It includes essential housing attributes, such as *median house value, median income, total number of rooms, number of households, population, and geographic coordinates (latitude and longitude)*, making it suitable for analyzing spatial dependencies in housing price prediction.

The dataset consists of 20,640 observations, each representing a block group a small geographic unit defined by the U.S. Census Bureau. The following are the key features available:

- **Median_House_Value:** The target variable, representing the median house price within a block group.
- **Median_Income:** Median household income of residents in the block group.
- **Median_Age:** Median age of the houses in the area.

- **Total_Rooms** and **Total_Bedrooms:** Count of total rooms and bedrooms within the block group.
- **Population** and **Households:** Total population and number of households in the block group.
- **Latitude and Longitude:** Geographical coordinates indicating the location of each block group.

4 Methodology

Figure 2 outlines the proposed methodology to evaluate the impacts of geographical positioning in predictive machine learning models. This methodology provides a comprehensive framework for conducting data analysis, modeling, and result evaluation, enabling a deeper understanding of the problem.

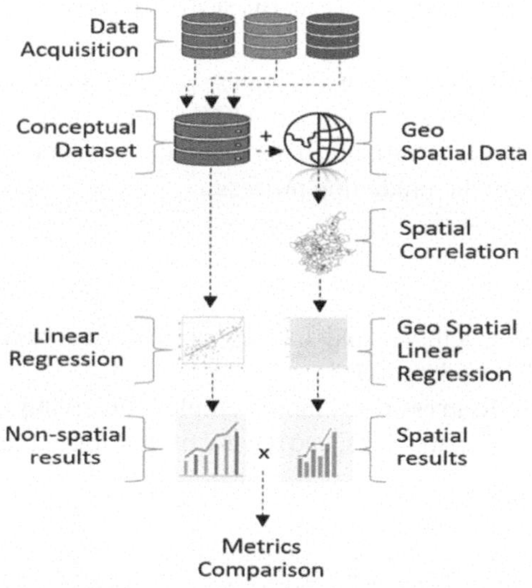

Fig. 2. Guidelines for using a spatial model [13].

Algorithm 1 outlines a method for analyzing the impacts of geographical positioning in machine learning models. This methodology provides a comprehensive framework for conducting data analysis, modeling, and result evaluation, enabling a deeper understanding of the problem.

4.1 Comparison of Methods

Spatial Dependence:

- **Linear Regression** does not consider any spatial relationships or dependencies. It treats each variable independently and performs a simple linear regression using only the selected column.

```
Data: multiple datasets
Result: performance of predictive models
while datasets are available do
    get current dataset;
    extract relevant data for problem solution;
end
execute feature selection algorithms;
georeference the dataset;
execute spatial autocorrelation analysis of features;
if spatial autocorrelation exists then
    apply spatial predictive models;
else
    apply non-spatial predictive models;
end
measure performance;
```

Algorithm 1. Spatial data analysis pipeline.

- **Geo Spatial Linear Regression** incorporates spatial dependency by calculating spatial weights using K-Nearest Neighbors (KNN) and applying a spatial lag to the `Median_House_Value` variable. This method considers the influence of neighboring observations in the prediction process.

Complexity:

- **Linear Regression** is simpler and focuses on a single-variable linear regression without any spatial considerations.
- **Geo Spatial Linear Regression** is more complex, involving the creation of spatial weights, calculation of spatial lags, and the use of multiple variables in the regression model.

Use Cases:

- **Linear Regression** is more appropriate for standard regression tasks where the goal is to understand the linear relationship between individual variables and the target variable, without considering spatial factors.
- **Geo Spatial Linear Regression** is suited for scenarios where spatial relationships are important, such as geospatial data analysis where the location or proximity of data points might influence the outcome.

5 Experimental Setup

This study employs the California Housing Prices Dataset, a publicly available dataset containing real estate price information for properties in California. The primary objective is to evaluate the impact of incorporating spatial variables into price prediction models and assess how geographic positioning influences prediction accuracy.

The dataset, sourced from Kaggle, consists of 20,640 records, with key variables including median house price, median income, number of rooms, latitude, and longitude. To analyze the spatial influence on price predictions, three different regression models were implemented: a Simple Linear Regression as the baseline, a Spatial Linear Regression incorporating spatial weights, and a standard Linear Regression for comparative analysis.

The computational experiments were conducted in a Python 3.9 environment using Pandas, Scikit-learn, GeoPandas, and PySAL libraries. The models were executed on a server equipped with 16 GB RAM and an Intel Core i3 CPU. The dataset was split into 80% for training and 20% for testing, and model performance was evaluated using Mean Absolute Error (MAE), Root Mean Squared Error (RMSE), and Mean Absolute Percentage Error (MAPE). The primary comparison focused on assessing the predictive performance of models with and without spatial variables.

6 Results

The analysis is centered on evaluating how geographic reference influences variations in predictive performance metrics. The regression models were employed solely for demonstration purposes, as the study does not aim to optimize a particular predictive model but rather to explore the extent to which geographic positioning affects prediction outcomes.

The experiment involved observing three geographic sample points while considering two distinct radial distances as reference parameters. These variations were analyzed to determine whether including spatial dependencies could enhance model performance.

Additionally, this study aims to validate the methodology proposed by [13] in a broader context, extending its applicability beyond turnover prediction to explore its potential in other domains, such as real estate price modeling (Table 1).

Table 1. Dataset characteristics.

Houses	
Lines	20,640
Points	12,590
Lower left	(32.54, –124.35)
Upper right	(41.95, –114.31)

The experiment aimed to identify the most influential variables crucial to construct the datasets used in this investigation. Two distinct geographic points were considered for the experiment:

- `POINT1 (-119.01 35.36)`
- `POINT2 (-121.97 37.97)`

6.1 Analysis of the Pearson Correlation

Table 2 presents the Pearson correlation coefficients between the geographic and socioeconomic variables considered in this study, for two distinct points and at two distance scales (30 km and 60 km). The Pearson correlation measures the linear relationship between two variables, ranging from -1 to 1. Positive values indicate a direct correlation, while negative values indicate an inverse correlation.

Table 2. Pearson correlation coefficients for different geographic points and distances.

Feature	POINT1		POINT2	
	30 km	60 km	30 km	60 km
Distance_to_coast	–0.08	–0.02	0.48	–0.17
Distance_to_LA	0.15	–0.11	–0.21	0.06
Distance_to_SanDiego	0.16	-0.11	–0.21	0.05
Distance_to_SanFrancisco	–0.19	0.11	–0.28	–0.40
Distance_to_SanJose	–0.19	0.11	–0.37	–0.18
Households	0.13	0.14	0.02	0.10
Median_Age	–0.43	–0.43	–0.09	0.14
Median_Income	0.84	0.79	0.78	0.61
Population	0.07	0.07	0.04	0.01
Tot_Bedrooms	0.11	0.14	0.00	0.09
Tot_Rooms	0.24	0.26	0.20	0.17

General Trend of Correlations

- **Median_Income** exhibits the highest correlation in all scenarios, ranging from **0.61 to 0.84**, suggesting that median income has a strong relationship with the other variables considered.
- **Median_Age** has a moderately negative correlation in all distances, especially in **POINT (30 km and 60 km: -0.43)**, indicating that areas with higher median ages tend to have an inverse relationship with other variables.
- **Tot_Rooms and Tot_Bedrooms** show weak to moderate positive correlations, suggesting that the number of bedrooms and total rooms has some relationship with geographic and socioeconomic characteristics.

Comparison Between POINT1 and POINT2

- For POINT1, most correlations are low, except for **Median_Income**, which maintains a high value (**0.84 at 30 km and 0.79 at 60 km**).
- In POINT2, there is greater variation in correlations:
  - **Distance_to_coast** exhibits a moderate positive correlation at 30 km (**0.48**) but becomes negative at 60 km (**-0.17**), suggesting that coastal proximity may influence patterns differently depending on the scale of analysis.

- **Distance_to_SanFrancisco** shows the most significant negative variation between distances, ranging from **-0.28 to -0.40**, indicating that as the distance from San Francisco increases, the linear relationship with other variables decreases.

Impact of Distance Scale (30 Km vs. 60 Km)

- Overall, there are minor variations between correlation coefficients at the 30 km and 60 km scales. However, some variables undergo more significant changes, such as:
  - **Distance_to_SanFrancisco** and **Distance_to_SanJose**, which show a greater impact at the 60 km scale.
  - **Distance_to_coast**, which reverses its correlation between scales in POINT2.
- These variations suggest that the spatial dependence of variables may be influenced by the radius of analysis, which could have methodological implications for the study.

Conclusions and Considerations

- **Median Income (Median_Income)** is the most strongly correlated variable, regardless of location or distance, indicating that it is a crucial factor to consider in future analyses.
- **Distance to key geographic locations** (LA, San Diego, San Francisco, and San Jose) presents weak to moderate correlations, suggesting that the relationship with socioeconomic aspects may be non-linear and depend on other factors not captured by simple Pearson correlation.
- **The scale of analysis (30 km vs. 60 km)** affects the strength and direction of some correlations, especially for spatial variables, highlighting the need for further studies to understand spatial effects.

6.2 Analysis of the Feature Scores

Regarding the importance of features, a variation was observed, indicating that different locations have distinct scores for the variables, as shown by Table 3.

Table 3 presents the values of geographic and socioeconomic variables considering two distinct points and two spatial scales (30 km and 60 km). The analysis reveals consistent differences between geographic points, indicating that spatial positioning significantly affects the evaluated metrics.

The results show that distances to major urban centers vary substantially between points, which may impact accessibility and the socioeconomic characteristics of the region. Additionally, variables such as *Median_Income* and *Median_Age* exhibit significant discrepancies, suggesting that demographic and economic aspects are influenced by geographic location.

Table 3. Feature Scores for Different Geographic Points and Distances.

Feature	POINT1		POINT2	
	30 km	60 km	30 km	60 km
Distance_to_coast	1.60	0.08	254.10	90.36
Distance_to_LA	5.70	3.77	37.93	11.53
Distance_to_SanDiego	6.37	3.81	39.56	8.25
Distance_to_SanFrancisco	8.97	4.04	71.32	630.32
Distance_to_SanJose	9.11	4.02	134.74	113.83
Households	4.09	6.01	0.44	29.97
Median_Age	55.41	69.95	7.63	60.27
Median_Income	554.96	519.69	1375.19	1918.91
Population	1.32	1.41	1.26	0.44
Tot_Bedrooms	3.17	5.95	0.02	25.94
Tot_Rooms	15.25	23.07	34.52	90.86

Another relevant aspect is the variation in values between the 30 km and 60 km scales. In some cases, increasing the scale significantly alters the variable means, indicating that the choice of spatial granularity can impact study conclusions.

These findings reinforce the importance of considering geographic positioning and scale of analysis in data modeling and interpretation, as spatial heterogeneity can introduce biases and affect the robustness of inferences.

6.3 Spatial Autocorrelation Analysis

In spatial analysis, the interest is to evaluate whether a feature has a correlation with its neighborhood or if its distribution is random. The analysis consists on verifying the variability of the dependent feature, *Median_House_Value*, across the two geografic points. For the analysis, the Moran's I index was used. Expected Moran's I refers to the expected value of the Moran's I index under the null hypothesis of no spatial autocorrelation. This value is calculated assuming there is no spatial pattern in the data and serves as a comparison base for the observed value of the Moran's I index, regarding Table 4.

The observed Moran's I is the actual calculated value of the Moran's I index derived from the observed data. It quantifies the degree of spatial autocorrelation, indicating how similar or dissimilar values are spatially distributed across the study area. This measure is obtained without assuming any initial hypothesis about the spatial distribution, thus providing an unbiased reflection of the spatial patterns inherent in the data.

The I p-value is the statistical significance value associated with the observed Moran's I. It indicates the probability of observing a Moran's I value equal to or more extreme than the observed one under the null hypothesis, of no spatial autocorrelation. A low p-value, usually less than 0.05, suggests statistically significant evidence of spatial autocorrelation in the data, implying that the observed spatial pattern is unlikely to

Table 4. Spatial Autocorrelation Analysis - Percentage Variation.

Feature	P1(30 km)	P1(60 km)	(%)
Tot_Bedrooms	–0.0063	–0.0065	**–2.33%**
Population	–0.0065	–0.0047	**27.69%**
Households	–0.0060	–0.0037	**37.71%**
Distance_to_coast	–0.0066	–0.0062	**5.69%**
Distance_to_LA	–0.0057	–0.0050	**12.40%**
Distance_to_SanDiego	–0.0090	–0.0062	**30.65%**
Distance_to_SanJose	–0.0082	–0.0010	**88.14%**
Distance_to_SanFrancisco	–0.0054	–0.0046	**14.13%**
Feature	P2(30 km)	P2(60 km)	(%)
Median_House_Value	–0.0015	–0.0007	**49.61%**
Median_Income	–0.0012	–0.0002	**81.64%**
Median_Age	–0.0010	–0.0010	**0.11%**
Tot_Rooms	–0.0020	–0.0012	**40.38%**
Tot_Bedrooms	–0.0028	–0.0005	**82.87%**
Population	–0.0016	–0.0007	**55.36%**
Households	–0.0008	–0.0004	**52.97%**
Distance_to_coast	–0.0028	–0.0019	**32.14%**
Distance_to_LA	–0.0025	–0.0006	**77.50%**
Distance_to_SanDiego	–0.0031	–0.0015	**52.59%**
Distance_to_SanJose	–0.0023	–0.0010	**57.18%**
Distance_to_SanFrancisco	–0.0031	–0.0006	**79.34%**

have occurred by random chance alone. This helps in confirming whether the spatial clustering or dispersion observed in the data is meaningful.

The results presented in Table 4 show that all analyzed variables exhibited statistically significant spatial autocorrelation, with a negative expected Moran's I value and a p-value of 0.001 in all tested scenarios. This indicates that the spatial patterns of these variables do not occur randomly but instead exhibit spatial dependence between observations.

When comparing the results for the analyzed points at different scales (30 km and 60 km), percentage variations in the magnitude of spatial autocorrelation are observed. Some variables, such as Distance_to_SanJose and Median_Income, showed significant reductions in Moran's I values when increasing the analysis scale, suggesting that the intensity of spatial dependence may be influenced by the size of the considered region. On the other hand, variables such as Median_Age and Distance_to_coast maintained smaller percentage variations, indicating a more homogeneous spatial distribution for these characteristics.

Overall, the results confirm that the spatial structure of the data must be considered in statistical modeling and in the interpretation of relationships between the studied variables. The presence of spatial autocorrelation highlights the need for techniques that incorporate this effect, such as spatial models and geostatistical approaches, to avoid bias in predictive analysis results.

6.4 Metrics

This experiment consisted of comparing the MAE (Mean Absolute Error) and RMSE (Root Mean Squared Error) metrics, as well as conducting a detailed study of MAPE (Mean Absolute Percentage Error) [8].

The analysis of the model's performance for Point 1 at two spatial scales (30 km and 60 km) reveals significant differences in model accuracy and error distribution (Tables 5 and 6).

Table 5. Model Performance for Point 1 at 30 km and 60 km.

Metric	30 km	60 km
R^2	34.18%	54.25%
Adjusted R^2	32.84%	53.57%
MAPE	23.62%	27.29%
MAE	26,562.06	26,888.49
RMSE	36,560.03	36,452.97

POINT1

- The coefficient of determination (R^2) increased from 34.18% (30 km) to 54.25% (60 km), indicating that the model explains a larger portion of the data variability when the spatial scale is expanded.
- The adjusted R^2 follows the same trend, increasing from 32.84% to 53.57%, reinforcing the model's improved explanatory power.
- The mean absolute error (MAE) and mean squared error (MSE) showed minimal variation, suggesting that expanding the spatial scale did not significantly impact these error measures.
- The mean absolute percentage error (MAPE) increased from 23.62% to 27.29%, indicating a slight decline in the model's percentage-based accuracy.
- The RMSE remained almost constant between the two models (36,560.03 vs. 36,452.97), showing that the absolute magnitude of the errors did not change significantly.

Table 6. Error Rate Distribution for 30 km and 60 km.

Error Rate Category	30 km	60 km
Very Low	15.69%	13.04%
Low	9.80%	15.94%
Medium	27.45%	20.29%
High	29.41%	27.54%
Very High	17.65%	23.19%

- The Very Low error rate decreased from 15.69% to 13.04%, indicating a reduction in the number of predictions with very low error.
- The Low error rate increased from 9.80% to 15.94%, suggesting that the model is better adjusting some predictions at the larger scale.
- The Medium error rate decreased significantly from 27.45% to 20.29%, indicating a lower occurrence of moderate errors in the 60 km model.
- The Very High error rate increased from 17.65% to 23.19%, highlighting that, although the model's overall explanatory power improved, it still exhibits extreme variations in some cases.

POINT2. Table 7 presents a comparison of model performance at the 30 km and 60 km scales, revealing significant differences in error metrics and explainability.

Table 7. Model Performance Comparison for 30 km and 60 km.

Metric	30 km	60 km
R^2	78.25%	80.63%
Adjusted R^2	77.95%	80.55%
MAPE	23.28%	27.31%
MAE	89,788.28	133,968.63
RMSE	147,759.76	246,183.90

- The R^2 increased from 78.25% (30 km) to 80.63% (60 km), indicating a slight improvement in the model's ability to explain data variability when the spatial scale is expanded.
- The Adjusted R^2 follows the same trend, rising from 77.95% to 80.55%, confirming that the gain in explainability is not merely due to the addition of variables but reflects a better model fit.

- The MAPE (Mean Absolute Percentage Error) increased from 23.28% to 27.31%, suggesting that, despite the model's higher explainability at 60 km, its relative prediction accuracy has slightly deteriorated.
- The MAE (Mean Absolute Error) increased significantly from 89,788.28 to 133,968.63, indicating that absolute errors in predictions are more pronounced in the 60 km model.
- The RMSE (Root Mean Squared Error) grew from 147,759.76 to 246,183.90, suggesting that extreme errors are more prominent when the analysis scale is expanded.

Interpretation of Results

- Although R^2 improved, suggesting a better overall predictive capability of the model at 60 km, absolute and percentage errors increased, indicating that while the model captures broader data patterns, it exhibits greater dispersion in predictions.

- This behavior is consistent with the previous analysis for Point 1, where expanding the spatial scale enhanced global explainability but introduced more extreme errors.
- The variation in MAPE and MAE suggests that the 60 km model may be more susceptible to outliers or regional variations, making its predictions less precise in absolute terms.

Conclusion

- The choice between 30 km and 60 km depends on the study's objective.
  - If the objective is to maximize explainability, the 60 km scale may be preferable due to the increase in R^2.
  - However, if the objective is to minimize absolute errors and improve local precision, the 30 km scale may be more advantageous, as it presents lower MAE and RMSE values.

These results emphasize the importance of careful spatial scale selection in geospatial modeling, as expanding the analysis area can enhance model explainability but also increase uncertainty in individual predictions.

6.5 Comparison of Error Rate Distribution for Dataset 1 (30 Km) and Dataset2 (60 Km)

Table 8. Error Rate Distribution Comparison.

Error Rate Category	Dataset 1	Dataset 2
Very Low	11.79%	16.00%
Low	11.59%	12.00%
Medium	25.00%	20.67%
High	29.47%	36.00%
Very High	22.15%	15.33%

Table 8 presents the comparison between the error rate distributions for models trained with 30 km and 60 km, showing significant differences in predictive performance depending on the spatial scale.

Comparison of Very Low and Low Error Rates. The "Very Low" error rate is higher in the 60 km model (16.00%) compared to the 30 km model (11.79%), indicating that increasing the scale resulted in a slightly larger number of highly accurate predictions. The "Low" error rate also increased in the 60 km model (12.00% vs. 11.59%), though the difference is minor. This suggests that the 60 km model slightly improves accuracy for a specific subset of samples, resulting in more predictions with reduced error.

The "Medium" error rate decreased from 25.00% (30 km) to 20.67% (60 km), indicating that the 60 km model reduced the occurrence of moderate errors. This reduction could mean that, by expanding the analysis scale, the model's predictions became more reliable in certain contexts. However, it may also indicate a redistribution of errors into higher categories.

The "High" error rate significantly increased in the 60 km model (36.00%) compared to the 30 km model (29.47%), suggesting that while some predictions improved, others became less accurate. On the other hand, the "Very High" error rate decreased in the 60 km model (15.33%) compared to the 30 km model (22.15%), indicating that the new model adjustments reduced the occurrence of extreme errors.

Expanding the spatial scale reduced moderate and very high errors but increased the proportion of high errors. The 60 km model exhibited a more balanced performance, with fewer extreme inaccuracies, although it also generated more high-error predictions. The 30 km model had fewer high-error predictions but exhibited more very high errors, suggesting greater instability in some specific regions.

Conclusion. If the goal is to minimize extreme errors, the 60 km model performs better, as it has a lower Very High error rate. However, if the priority is to reduce the overall occurrence of high-error predictions, the 30 km model may be more suitable, as it has a lower High error rate. These results highlight the importance of selecting the spatial scale based on the study objectives, as increasing the scale can improve overall model stability at the cost of increasing high errors in some cases.

The findings suggest that the 60 km model improves accuracy for certain predictions and reduces extreme errors but increases the proportion of high errors, requiring a more detailed analysis to balance precision and model stability. To better understand how errors are classified, we use the following function to categorize the magnitude of the prediction errors:

```
def categorize_error(error):
    if error <= 5:
        return "Very Low"
    elif error <= 10:
        return "Low"
    elif error <= 20:
        return "Medium"
    elif error <= 40:
        return "High"
    else:
        return "Very High"
```

This categorization helps quantify how often errors fall into specific ranges, allowing us to assess how the model's performance varies with different spatial scales.

Considerations

- Expanding the spatial scale from 30 km to 60 km significantly improved the R^2, suggesting that the model captures data variability more effectively at a larger scale.
- However, this change also resulted in a slight increase in MAPE and the Very High error rate, indicating that while predictions became more precise overall, some cases experienced higher extreme errors.

– The error distribution suggests that expanding the scale reduces moderate errors but introduces more extreme error cases.

These findings indicate that spatial scale selection significantly impacts model performance, and the choice between 30 km or 60 km should balance improved explainability (R^2) and control over extreme errors.

7 Conclusion and Future Works

This study proposed a methodology to assess the existence of spatial dependencies in prediction problems. The experiments were essential in validating the hypothesis that the inclusion of geographic attributes can significantly improve the accuracy of predictive models [9].

The experimental results demonstrated differences in the performance of predictive models when comparing georeferenced and non-georeferenced data. In particular, models incorporating spatial variables outperformed those that did not, with improvements ranging from 9.6% to 19.6% in the standard deviation of MAPE, 5.5% to 10.4% in MAE, and 0.99% to 2.9% in RMSE. These findings emphasize the importance of considering the spatial context in predictive modeling, as incorporating geographic variables can lead to significant improvements in prediction accuracy.

Beyond the incorporation of spatial variables, the results also highlight the importance of an efficient feature selection strategy. The excessive inclusion of irrelevant attributes can increase model complexity without necessarily enhancing performance and may negatively impact computational scalability. Feature selection methods, particularly those that combine traditional techniques (such as correlation analysis and statistical filters) with spatial autocorrelation measures (such as Moran's I and spatial weight matrices), prove to be essential for optimizing the performance of spatial models.

For future research, we intend to explore multivariate spatial analyses and investigate more sophisticated spatial models to optimize employee turnover prediction, using geospacial based selection of features to help reach better results, based that static features show variations in the model. Advanced models such as Spatial Autoregressive Models (SAR) and Spatial Error Models (SEM) offer more refined perspectives on spatial interactions that may influence employee tenure [10]. Additionally, the use of Spatial Neural Networks and Hierarchical Bayesian Models can provide deeper and more precise insights by capturing the complexities of spatial dependencies and data heterogeneity.

References

1. Ajjali, W.: Coordinate systems and projections. In: ArcGIS Pro e ArcGIS Online, pp. 103–130. Springer, Cham (2023)
2. Alzubaidi, L., et al.: A survey on deep learning tools dealing with data scarcity: definitions, challenges, solutions, tips, and applications. J. Big Data **10**(1), 46 (2023)
3. Anselin, L.: Spatial models in econometric research. In: Oxford Research Encyclopedia of Economics and Finance (2021)

4. Câmara, G., Monteiro, A.M.V., Paiva, J.A., Gomes, J., Velho, L.: Towards a unified framework for spatial data models. J. Braz. Comput. Soc. **7**, 17–25 (2000)
5. Câmara, G., Monteiro, A.M., Fucks, S.D., Carvalho, M.S.: Spatial analysis and GIS: a primer. Image Processing Division, National Institute for Space Research (INPE), Brasil (2004)
6. Chen, Y.: New approaches for calculating Moran's index of spatial autocorrelation. PLoS ONE **8**(7), e68336 (2013)
7. Chen, Y.: Spatial autocorrelation equation based on Moran's index. Sci. Rep. **13**(1), 19296 (2023)
8. Chicco, D., Warrens, M.J., Jurman, G.: The coefficient of determination R-squared is more informative than SMAPE, MAE, MAPE, MSE and RMSE in regression analysis evaluation. PeerJ Comput. Sci. **7**, e623 (2021)
9. Fatmawati, Saifudin, T., Chamidah, N.: Geographically weighted polynomial regression: selection of the optimal bandwidth and the optimal polynomial degrees and its application to water quality index modelling. In: Proceedings of the International Conference on Mathematics and Islam - ICMIs, pp. 93–100. SciTePress (2020)
10. Garg, P.: Understanding Geospatial Data, pp. 1–14. Your Publisher (2024)
11. Oshan, T.M., Wolf, L.J., Sachdeva, M., et al.: A scoping review on the multiplicity of scale in spatial analysis. J. Geogr. Syst. **24**, 293–324 (2022)
12. Pebesma, E., Bivand, R.: Spatial Data Science: With Applications in R. Chapman and Hall/CRC, Boca Raton (2023)
13. Pereira, S.M., Lima, J.A.A., Vieira, A.G., Brandao, W.C.: Exploiting Data Spatial Dependencies for Employee Turnover Prediction (2024)
14. Rey, S.J., Anselin, L., Li, W.: Handbook of Spatial Analysis in the Social Sciences. Edward Elgar Publishing (2021)
15. Wang, J.F., Zhang, T.L., Fu, B.J.: A measure of spatial stratified heterogeneity. Ecol. Ind. **67**, 250–256 (2016)
16. Nugent, C.: California Housing Prices Dataset (2017). Accessed 18 Mar 2025. https://www.kaggle.com/datasets/camnugent/california-housing-prices

Confidence-Based Filtering for Enhancing Recommendation Quality

Dionisis Margaris[1], Kiriakos Sgardelis[1], Dimitris Spiliotopoulos[2], Costas Vassilakis[2](✉), and Stefanos Ougiaroglou[3]

[1] University of the Peloponnese, 23100 Sparta, Greece
margaris@uop.gr, k.sgardelis@go.uop.gr
[2] University of the Peloponnese, 22131 Tripoli, Greece
{dspiliot,costas}@uop.gr
[3] International Hellenic University, 57400 Sindos, Greece
stoug@ihu.gr

Abstract. In this article, we present an algorithm that leverages rating prediction confidence factors to enhance recommendation quality. More specifically, this algorithm filters candidate recommendation items, by removing those whose rating predictions do not fulfil any rating prediction confidence factor and subsequently proceeds in formulating the recommendation(s) with the remaining candidate items. Under this approach, only rating predictions that have increased accuracy guarantees are utilized, and therefore the quality of the recommendation is enhanced. The presented approach extends previous works, and is proven to maintain high recommendation coverage. At the same time it can be applied to every collaborative filtering dataset, since it is based only on the essential collaborative filtering data (i.e., rating records which include the user id, the item id and the respective rating). To evaluate the proposed extension, datasets commonly used in the recommender systems research field are used. The evaluation results indicate its effectiveness towards recommendation quality, outreaching the performance of state-of-the-art collaborative filtering research works that also consider rating prediction confidence factors. The presented approach can finally be easily combined with collaborative filtering recommendation algorithms that also consider the rating prediction confidence factors.

Keywords: Recommender systems · Collaborative filtering · Recommendation quality · Rating prediction confidence factors · Multi-parameter experimental evaluation

1 Introduction

Collaborative Filtering (CF) is one of the most commonly used techniques for predicting rating values in recommender systems (RecSys). This method relies on the ratings given by users who are closely aligned with the active user (AU), referred to as near neighbors (NNs). Typically, a CF algorithm first generates rating predictions for products the AU has not yet rated. The products with the highest predicted ratings are then recommended

M. Marchiori et al. (Eds.): WEBIST 2024, LNBIP 583, pp. 290–306, 2026.
https://doi.org/10.1007/978-3-032-25534-1_13

to the AU, as they are most likely to be well-received. Therefore, the more accurately these predicted ratings match the actual ratings, the more successful the CF RecSys is proven to be [1–4].

For instance, if two products p_1 and p_2 are candidate for recommendation to an AU u, with rating predictions calculated at $pr_1 = 4.95/5$ and $pr_2 = 4.85/5$, respectively, a typical CF RecSys would firstly select to suggest p_1 to u. This is because its higher predicted rating suggests a greater likelihood of acceptance by u.

However, in the previous example, the information used to calculate rating predictions is not fully considered. Specifically, while a typical CF RecSys computes additional data related to each rating prediction -such as the number of near neighbors (NNs) involved in the rating prediction for each product- this information is not examined during the recommendation process. For instance, if pr_1 is calculated using only 1 of the u's NNs, while pr_2 is based on 25 of the u's NNs, there is a valid reason to suggest product p_2 over p_1. The rationale behind this option is that p_2, besides having a very high prediction value, is also produced from a relatively large number of NNs. This entails higher probability of p_2 recommendation accuracy.

Recent research has explored the concept of rating prediction confidence factors (RPCFs), particularly in relation to the accuracy of rating predictions derived from the CF process [5, 6]. Specifically, these studies have demonstrated that (1) the number of NNs involved in the prediction calculation, (2) the mean rating score of the products, and (3) the mean rating score of the AU, are directly linked to the accuracy of rating predictions generated by the CF process.

These findings point to the direction that the CF RecSys can opt to recommend products with lower rating prediction values but higher prediction confidence and thus improve the overall recommendation quality. In this context, the work in [7] introduces a state-of-the-art algorithm that partitions the set of items in the list of items which are candidate for recommendation (termed as "initial recommendation candidate list"-ICRL) into three subsets depending on their CF prediction values. These three subsets are termed as "Top", "Med" and "Low" and respectively comprise the rating predictions that are believed to be "definitely," "most probably," or "probably" liked by the user. The items within each of these subsets are then sorted in descending order based on the number of RPCFs satisfied, and the items are recommended to the AU, starting from the items in the first class, which are scanned according to their sort order, and then proceeding with the items in the next two classes, in the same fashion.

The present work introduces an extension to the algorithm presented in [7] that leverages RPCFs to further enhance recommendation quality. The proposed extension removes from the ICRL the items whose predictions do not fulfil any confidence factor, irrespectively of their rating prediction values, and subsequently proceeds in formulating the recommendation with the remaining elements of the ICRL. Under this approach, only predictions that have increased accuracy guarantees are utilized, and therefore the quality of the recommendation is enhanced. The proposed algorithm adopts a conservative approach to item removal from the ICRL, achieving the maintenance of high recommendation coverage. At the same time, it can be applied in every CF dataset, since it is based only on the essential CF data (i.e., rating records which include the user id, the item id and the respective rating), and it can be combined with any rating prediction computation method.

A multi-parameter set of experiments is used to thoroughly assess the proposed extension for recommendation quality. This experiment includes (a) 8 CF datasets from various sources, (b) 2 user vicinity measures, (c) 2 NN selection alternatives, and (d) 3 recommendation quality metrics, all of which are commonly employed in CF RecSys research. Based on the results of this evaluation, the inclusion of the presented step to the algorithm presented in [7] has proven to significantly upgrade recommendation quality, while maintaining high coverage levels.

The remainder of the article is structured as follows. In Sect. 2, contemporary related research is summarized. In Sect. 3, we outline the concept of RPCFs, for self-containment of the article. In Sect. 4, we present the proposed approach. In Sect. 5, we display and analyze its evaluation output. Finally, in Sect. 6, we conclude the article and outline future work.

2 Related Work

CF recommendation quality is a subject that numerous works have researched over the last 10 years.

The work in [8] presents a new similarity metric. The mathematical formulation is developed using two main parts. The first is converting intuitive and qualitative conditions that the similarity metric must meet into appropriate equations, including a combination of integral and differential formulas. And the second is solving these formulas to derive the final similarity metric function.

The work in [9] presents a multi-level recommendation strategy designed to assist users in making decisions by providing more accurate recommendations. This approach can be applied to various online platforms that use CF RecSys, improving the overall user experience. Its effectiveness is shown through an extensive experimental evaluation using real-world datasets.

The study in [10] presents a weighted clustering CF RecSys. This system is built to provide effective recommendations with low cost of computations. Unlike traditional incremental methods, the complexity of this approach is not determined by the number of items and users in the rating database. As a result, this CF RecSys is ideal for dynamic environments with large databases, where information changes quickly, such as introduction of new ratings, updating of existing ratings and input of new items and users.

The work in [11] presents Relational CF to utilize the connections between multiple items in RecSys. It highlights the importance of both the relation type and value predicting preferences of users. In order to tackle this issue, this work proposes a two-level hierarchical attention algorithm for modeling user preferences. The first level emphasizes the significance of relation types, while the second level concentrates on specific relation values to evaluate the contributions of items.

The work in [12] introduces a hybrid CF method that integrates semantic with social recommendations. This method incorporates two classification policies to enhance recommendation success. The proposed method applies the incremental K-means technique to the users and then uses the KNN method to handle new users.

The work in [13] presents a hybrid RecSys algorithm that combines CF and content-based filtering. This algorithm takes advantage of the strengths of content filtering while enabling CF for all items, even those that have not been rated. These unrated items can still be filtered and recommended to users, thus addressing the issue of CF cold start. As the number of users and rating increases, the CF rating matrix becomes denser, which reduces sparsity and enhances the accuracy of CF rating predictions. By combining both methods, the CF RecSys performance is improved.

The study in [14] introduces an new CF algorithm that leverages user preference clustering to address the issue of data sparsity. First, user groups are formed to distinguish between users with different preferences. Then, based on the preferences of the AU, the NNs are determined from the relevant user groups. Furthermore, this work proposes a new similarity metric to compute user proximity more accurately, by considering user preferences from both local and global level.

The work in [15] proposes DeepICF, an item-based CF method that accounts for higher-order and nonlinear relations among products. Instead of only considering the similarity between two products, the method incorporates interactions between all product pairs utilizing nonlinear neural networks. This approach enables the method to successfully capture the higher-order relationships between products, uncovering more complex influences on user decision-making.

The work in [16] proposes an algorithm that combines deep interaction modeling and deep learning techniques for RecSys that rely on a rating matrix, namely Hybrid Neural CF algorithm. This approach aggregates ratings from multiple external sources to address the issue of CF cold start. It achieves this by employing a multivariate rating system that aggregated star ratings and sentiment scores. To overcome the identified challenges, the proposed algorithm consists of four main modules, the Hierarchical User and Product and User Attention, the Deep Multivariate Rating, the Deep CF, and the Neural Sentiment Classifier.

The work in [17] presents a deep neural network method that improves CF prediction results. It utilizes the concept of reliability to enhance the quality of predictions by integrating the prediction errors into the deep learning layers. The core idea of this method is to recommend products that both have high rating prediction values and are considered reliable at the same time. The proposed method is organized into three stages: the reliability prediction, the error prediction, and the ratings prediction. Each of these involves a learning procedure and offer a different abstraction level.

The work in [18] proposes a deep learning CF algorithm, namely CbDNCF. Initially, CbDNCF filters the dataset through a preprocessing layer, followed by training the cleaned data using a classification layer. Next, it performs feature extraction and predicts the highest ratings. The incorporation of Chimp functions into the deep neural classification layer allows the model to achieve optimal rating prediction results.

The work in [19] introduces LDCF, a neural location-aware CF technique designed for recommending web services. This technique maps service location features to high-dimensional embedding vectors. Additionally, it incorporates a multilayer neural network to capture nonlinear and high-dimensional attributes, along with a similarity corrector to adjust the predicted QoS characteristics. Therefore, the proposed technique effectively addresses the problem of data sparsity and learns the high-dimensional relationships between web services and users.

The work in [20] proposes a deep learning-based method that integrates CF with textual content in order to produce web services recommendations. The interaction between the functionalities of mashups and services is integrated into a neural network, allowing the method to capture the relationships between mashups and services, using a sparse matrix of interactions.

Still, the inclusion of rating prediction confidence factors in the CF recommendation formulation procedure has not received considerable research attention.

Towards this direction, the work in [21] proposes a CF algorithm that declines products bearing low RPCFs values from becoming recommendations to users. Despite the high recommendation quality enhancement this algorithm accomplished, it suffers from significant coverage reduction, making this algorithm inapplicable to sparse datasets (such as the Ciao dataset, the Epinions dataset and Amazon-sourced ones, used in this work). Since the work in [21] strictly enforces the requirement that a prediction should fulfil all RPCFs to qualify for the recommendation formulation stage, in the rest of this paper, we will refer to the algorithm presented in [21] as Strict RPCF Filtering (S-RCPF-F).

The work in [7] introduces a CF recommendation algorithm that is comprised of 4 steps. In the first step, the RPCFs number satisfied by each rating prediction in the ICRL is calculated. In the second step, the set of products is partitioned into 3 subsets, based on the assumption that the user will "definitely" (subset namely "Top"), "most probably" (subset namely "Med") and "probably" (subset namely "Low") like. The criterion for this partition is solely the CF prediction values of the products ([4.5–5.0], [4.0–4.5), and [3.5–4.0), for the "Top", "Med" and "Low" subsets, respectively). In the third step, the products within each subset are sorted in descending order of their number of the RPCFs number satisfied. Lastly, in the fourth step, the products are recommended to the users, starting from the "Top" dataset, based on the sorting performed in the third step (in case the products in the "Top" subset do not suffice, the products of the "Med", primarily, and "Low", secondarily, subsets are recommended, using the same sorting). Although this algorithm accomplishes zero recommendation coverage reduction, it achieves mediocre recommendation quality upgrade (2–3% both in terms of recommendation precision and real rating value).

The present work introduces an extension to the algorithm presented in [7] that leverages RPCFs to further enhance recommendation quality. The proposed extension removes from the ICRL the items whose predictions do not fulfil any confidence factor, despite their rating prediction values, and subsequently proceeds in formulating the recommendation with the remaining elements of the ICRL, exactly as the algorithm presented in [7] performs (i.e., the second, third, and fourth step of the algorithm presented in [7]). Under this approach, only predictions that have increased accuracy guarantees are utilized, and therefore recommendation quality is enhanced. Contrary to the algorithm presented in [21], it achieves low recommendation coverage reduction, while at the same time it can be applied to every CF dataset, since it is based only on the essential collaborative filtering data (i.e., rating records which include the user id, the item id, and the respective rating).

3 Rating Prediction Confidence Factors in CF

In this Section, the prerequisites of this work, concerning the RPCFs in CF are summarized, for self-containment.

Recent studies have explored the connection between basic rating prediction features and the accuracy of rating predictions in the CF process. It is established that the accuracy of rating predictions can be estimated in advance, with a high degree of certainty. Specifically, the studies in [5, 6] asserted a direct relationship between CF rating prediction accuracy and three key factors (i.e., rating prediction features): (i) the NN number involved in the rating prediction calculation, denoted as NN_{factor}, (ii) the mean value of the AU's ratings, denoted as $AVGU_{factor}$, and (iii) the mean value of the item's ratings, denoted as $AVGI_{factor}$.

In regard to the dense datasets (i.e., density $> 1\%$), it has been found that a rating prediction in CF is regarded as "highly accurate" if:

- $NN_{factor} \geq 15\%$ (i.e., the percentage of the user's NNs that take part in the prediction formulation is $\geq 15\%$),
- $AVGU_{factor} \geq 4.5$ OR $AVGU_{factor} \leq 1.5$ (when using a 5-star rating scale, as happens in the majority of the RecSys datasets), and
- $AVGI_{factor} \geq 4.5$ OR $AVGI_{factor} \leq 1.5$ (again, when using a 5-star rating scale).

On the other hand, as far as sparse datasets are concerned (i.e., datasets with density $< 1\%$) it has been found that a CF rating prediction is considered as "highly accurate" if:

- $NN_{factor} \geq 4$ (i.e., at least 4 of the user's NNs take part in the prediction formulation),
- $AVGU_{factor} \geq 4.5$ OR $AVGU_{factor} \leq 1.5$ (when using a 5-star rating scale), and
- $AVGI_{factor} \geq 4.5$ OR $AVGI_{factor} \leq 1.5$ (again, when using a 5-star rating scale).

Notably, all rules involving rating average thresholds can be generalized for use with any rating scale, by setting the inclusion conditions to comprise users/items whose mean rating value falls within the higher 10% of the rating scale or the lower 10% of the rating scale.

Having this information at hand, in the next Section we present the extension to the algorithm presented in [7] that leverages RPCFs to further enhance recommendation quality. The algorithm in [7] will be denoted as RPCF-S, since it sorts recommendation according to their RCPFs, without performing any filtering.

4 The Proposed Extension

As noted above, the present work introduces an extension to the algorithm presented in [7], that leverages RPCFs to further enhance recommendation quality. The proposed extension removes from the ICRL the items whose predictions do not fulfil any confidence factor, despite their rating prediction values, and subsequently proceeds to formulate the recommendation with the remaining elements of the ICRL.

Practically, the proposed extension inserts a procedure between the first and second step of the RCPF-S algorithm. This procedure considers the RPCFs that each rating prediction fulfills (calculated in the first step of the RPCF-S algorithm) and eliminates predictions that do not fulfill any RPCFs. On the contrary, the rating predictions that fulfill at least one of the RPCFs are forwarded to the second step of the RPCF-S algorithm (i.e., the partitioning into the 3 subsets "Top", "Med", and "Low", and so on), in order to proceed with the recommendation process.

Under this approach, only predictions that have (relatively) increased accuracy guarantees are utilized, and therefore the quality of the recommendations is enhanced. A graphical representation of the proposed algorithm is depicted in Fig. 1.

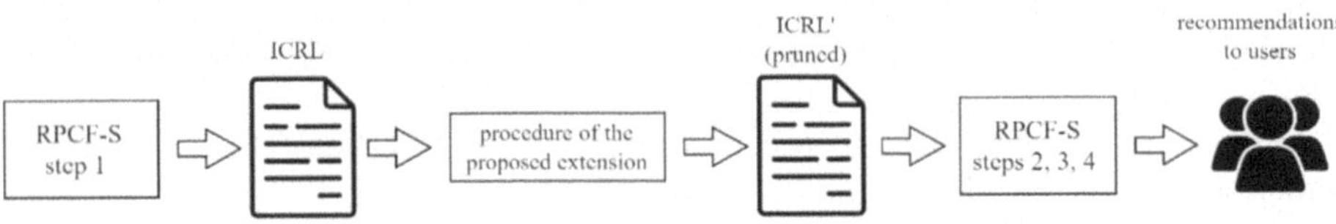

Fig. 1. Activity diagram for the proposed algorithm operation, including the original steps of the RPCF-S algorithm and the proposed extension.

The RPCF-S algorithm, including the proposed extension, achieves upgraded recommendation quality, and maintains high recommendation coverage. Furthermore, this combination can be applied in every CF dataset, since it is based only on the essential CF data (i.e., rating records which include the user id, the item id, and the respective rating).

In the next Section, we experimentally assess the recommendation accuracy of the presented algorithm.

5 Experimental Evaluation

In this section, after presenting the datasets used in the evaluation and the experimental settings (Subsect. 5.1), we detail the results of the experiments. More specifically, in Subsect. 5.2, we report on the results concerning recommendation coverage, demonstrating the viability of the proposed extension. Subsequently, in Subsect. 5.3, we present the experimental outcomes regarding recommendation quality enhancement, substantiating the effectiveness of the algorithm. Lastly, the execution overhead of the presented extension is analyzed in Subsect. 5.4, to confirm its applicability in terms of execution efficiency.

5.1 Experimental Settings

In our experimental evaluation we use eight CF datasets, including sparse, dense, and social datasets, to cover all sparsity levels. These datasets are broadly used in CF research and their characteristics are outlined in Table 1.

Regarding the user similarity metrics, in this work we use the two most commonly used ones in CF research, i.e., the Pearson Correlation (PC) and the Cosine Similarity (COS) metrics [26–29].

Table 1. The characteristics of the datasets used in the experimental evaluation.

Dataset Name	Dataset Type	Dataset Attributes (#ratings, #users, #items, density, rating range)	CF Category
Amazon Videogames [22]	e-commerce	473K, 17.5K, 55K, 0,05%, 1–5	Sparse
Amazon Digital Music [22]	e-commerce	145K, 12K, 17K, 0.07%, 1–5	Sparse
Amazon Musical Instruments [22]	e-commerce	231K, 28K, 11K, 0.08%, 1–5	Sparse
Amazon CDs and Vinyl [22]	e-commerce	1.44M, 112K, 74K, 0.02%, 1–5	Sparse
MovieLens 100K [23]	media consumption	100K, 600, 9.7K, 1.72%, 0.5–5	Dense
MovieLens 1M [23]	media consumption	1M, 6K, 3.7K, 4.5%, 1–5	Dense
CiaoDVD [24]	social-trust network	73K, 17.6K, 16K, 0.03%, 1–5	Sparse, Social
Epinions [25]	social-trust network	665K, 49K, 134K, 0.01%, 1–5	Sparse, Social

Moreover, for the NN selection methods, we use the top-K NN (KNN) and the threshold method (THR). Following the approaches of the works in [7, 21, 30, 31], for the KNN method, we have set K = 200 and K = 500 in our experiments. For the THR method we have set T = 0.0 and T = 0.5.

Afterwards, a 5-fold cross validation process [7, 21] commences, for predicting rating values on the datasets outlined in Table 1, in which the extended algorithm was set to generate 3 and 5 recommendations per user (top-3 and top-5).

The quality of these recommendations was assessed using the following evaluation metrics:

1. the recommendation precision,
2. the mean real arithmetic rating value, and
3. the NDCG (Normalized Discounted Cumulative Gain)

following the works in [7, 21].

Lastly, in order to compute the recommendation precision and NDCG quality metrics, the items having real rating values $\geq 3.5/5$ for the AU are considered as liked/approved by him/her [5, 7, 32–34].

5.2 Evaluating the Applicability of the Proposed Extension

In this subsection we report on our experimental findings for the recommendation coverage achieved by the proposed algorithm, an aspect that is critical to its applicability, since a recommender system must offer personalized recommendations to the widest possible set of its users.

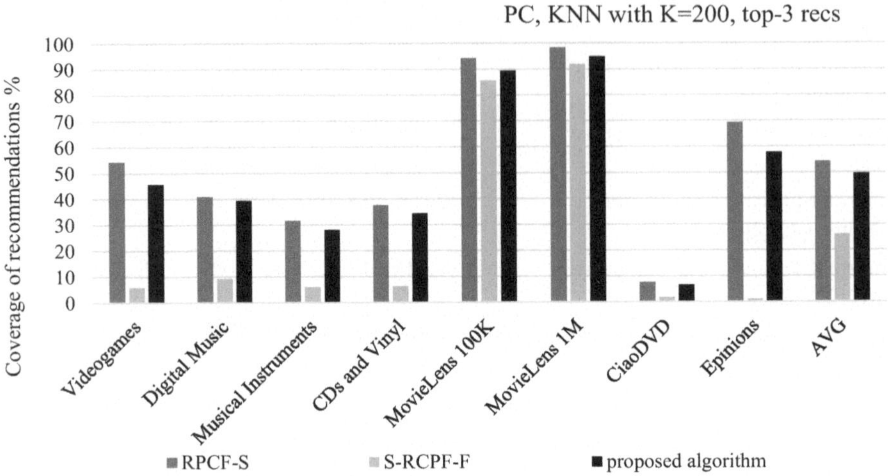

Fig. 2. Recommendation coverage considering the top-3 recommendations, using the PC similarity metric and the KNN selection method.

Figure 2 illustrates the recommendation coverage, when recommending 3 items to each user (top-3 recommendations) and utilizing the PC similarity metric, with the KNN selection method and setting $K = 200$. More specifically, Fig. 2 illustrates the percentage of users where each algorithm is able to generate a complete recommendation (i.e., recommending 3 items) for each user in the dataset. The results obtained for the proposed algorithm are compared against the performance of the RCPF-S algorithm (without the proposed extension), since it achieves no coverage reduction in relation to the plain CF algorithm, and the performance of the S-RCPF-F algorithm [21], which also undertakes a confidence factor-based approach, however performing more aggressive filtering on candidate recommendation items.

We can observe that, contrary to the S-RCPF-F algorithm [21], the RCPF-S algorithm, including the extension proposed in this work, maintains high recommendation coverage. More specifically, while the average recommendation coverage of the algorithm presented in [21] is 26% (corresponding to a reduction equal to 52%, in comparison to the RCPF-S algorithm), the average recommendation coverage of the proposed algorithm is 49.6%, thus sustaining a significantly lower reduction of 8.5%. Regarding the sparse datasets, where the S-RCPF-F algorithm [21] is proven inapplicable, the coverage reduction of the proposed algorithm is less than 17% in each of the datasets tested. A notable case is the Epinions dataset, in which the application of the S-RCPF-F algorithm [21] leads a recommendation coverage decline from 69% to 1%), while the proposed algorithm maintains coverage at the level of 58%.

As depicted in Fig. 3, similar results are observed when the COS similarity metric is used, under the same settings (i.e., KNN selection method, $K = 200$ and recommending

3 items). More specifically, the average coverage reduction is measured at 11.5%, while the respective coverage reduction of the S-RCPF-F [21] is 65%.

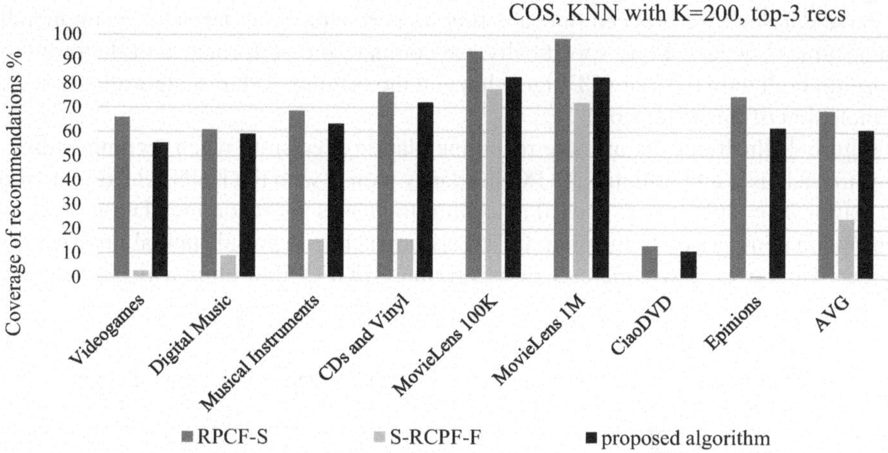

Fig. 3. Recommendation coverage considering the top-3 recommendations, using the COS similarity metric and the KNN selection method.

Similar recommendation coverage results are measured when using the PC similarity metric, with the THR NN selection method with T = 0.0 and recommending 3 items. In this case, the average coverage reduction is measured at 6.8%, while the respective average coverage reduction of the S-RCPF-F algorithm [21] is 51%. Similarly, when the COS similarity metric is used, under the exact same settings, the average coverage reduction is measured at 5%, while the respective coverage reduction of the S-RCPF-F algorithm [21] is 55%.

In our experimental evaluation we have used all the combinations of parameters listed in Subsect. 5.1 (i.e., user similarity computation metric, NN selection method with varying hyperparameters, number of recommended items). All results are in close agreement with the ones reported above and their detailed presentation is omitted for conciseness.

The recommendation coverage results detailed above indicate the applicability of the proposed extension, both in dense and in sparse datasets. Furthermore, considering that the S-RCPF-F algorithm [21] is demonstrated to be inapplicable on sparse datasets, due to excessive recommendation coverage reduction, it will not be considered as a comparison baseline in the experiment results presented in Subsect. 5.3, which aim at assessing the recommendation quality enhancement of the proposed approach. In place of the S-RCPF-F algorithm [21], the plain CF algorithm will be used as a baseline.

5.3 Evaluating the Recommendation Quality Enhancement of the Proposed Extension

After having established the applicability of the proposed extension, both in dense and in sparse datasets, we proceed in evaluating its performance in terms of recommendation accuracy/success. More specifically, we compare the performance of the proposed algorithm both with the plain CF algorithm and the original RPCF-S algorithm (without the inclusion of this extension).

Figure 4 illustrates the average recommendation precision, when recommending 3 items to each user and utilizing the PC similarity metric with the KNN selection method and setting K = 200. The proposed algorithm increases the recommendation precision by 6.7%, in comparison to the plain CF algorithm, achieving a substantial improvement compared to the respective increase of the original RPCF-S algorithm, which is measured at 2.5%.

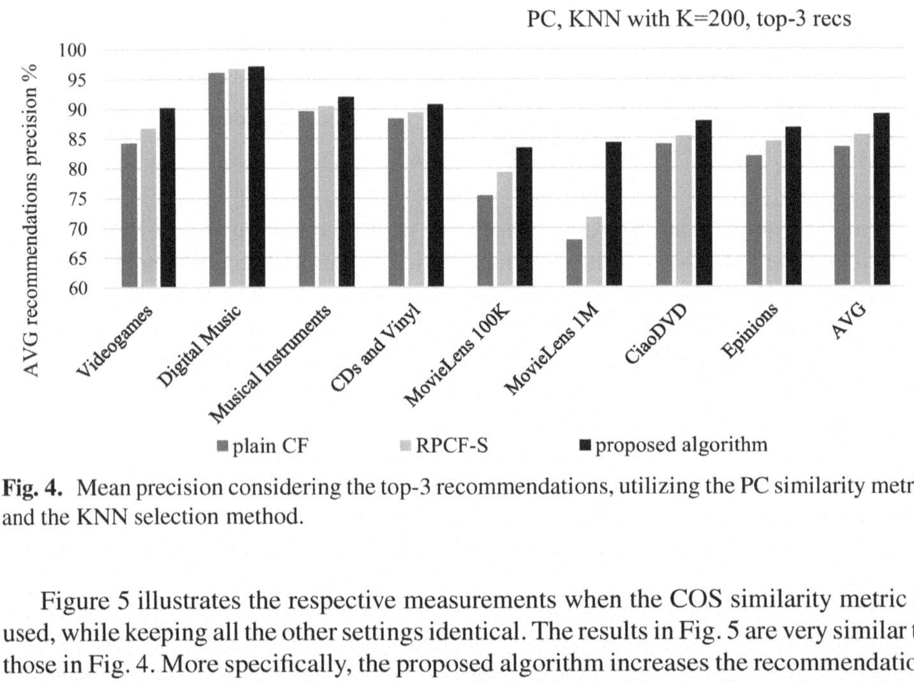

Fig. 4. Mean precision considering the top-3 recommendations, utilizing the PC similarity metric and the KNN selection method.

Figure 5 illustrates the respective measurements when the COS similarity metric is used, while keeping all the other settings identical. The results in Fig. 5 are very similar to those in Fig. 4. More specifically, the proposed algorithm increases the recommendation precision by 7.4%, in comparison to the plain CF algorithm. These gains are considerably higher than the ones achieved by the original RPCF-S algorithm, which are quantified at 2.3%.

Similar results are observed when using the PC similarity metric, with the THR NN selection method with T = 0.0 and recommending 3 items. In this case, the average precision enhancement compared to the plain CF algorithm is measured at 3.1%, while the respective increase of the original RPCF-S algorithm is measured at 1.3%.

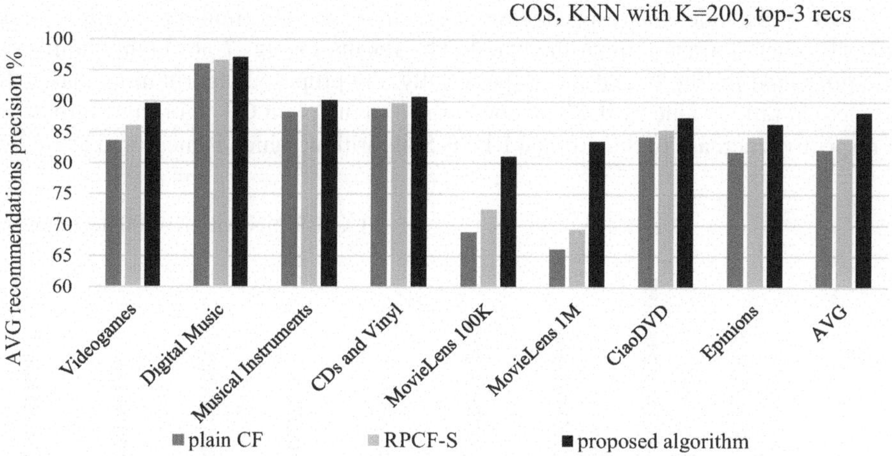

Fig. 5. Mean precision considering the top-3 recommendations, utilizing the COS similarity metric and the KNN selection method.

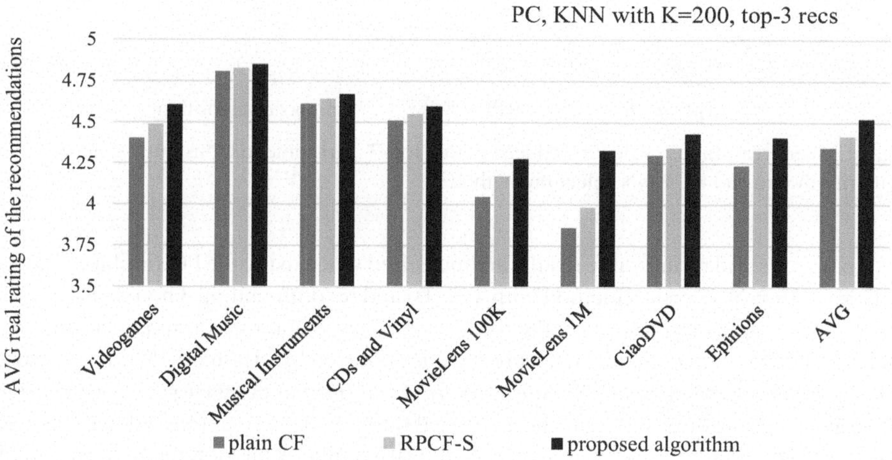

Fig. 6. Mean real rating value considering the top-3 recommendations, utilizing the PC similarity metric and the KNN selection method.

Correspondigly, when the COS similarity metric is used under the exact same settings, the average precision enhancement achieved by the proposed algorithm is measured at 2.5%, while the respective increase of the original RPCF-S algorithm which is measured at 1.3%.

Figure 6 depicts the mean real rating value, when recommending 3 items to each user and utilizing the PC similarity metric and the KNN selection method, setting $K = 200$. The proposed algorithm increases the average real rating value by 4% in comparison to the plain CF algorithm, surpassing the respective increase of the original RPCF-S algorithm, which is measured at 1.6%.

Figure 7 illustrates the respective findings when the COS similarity metric is used, while all other settings remain unaltered. The results in Fig. 7 are highly similar to those presented in Fig. 6, and more specifically, the proposed algorithm increases the average real rating value by 4.4% in comparison to the plain CF algorithm, surpassing the respective increase of the original RPCF-S algorithm, which is measured at 1.5%.

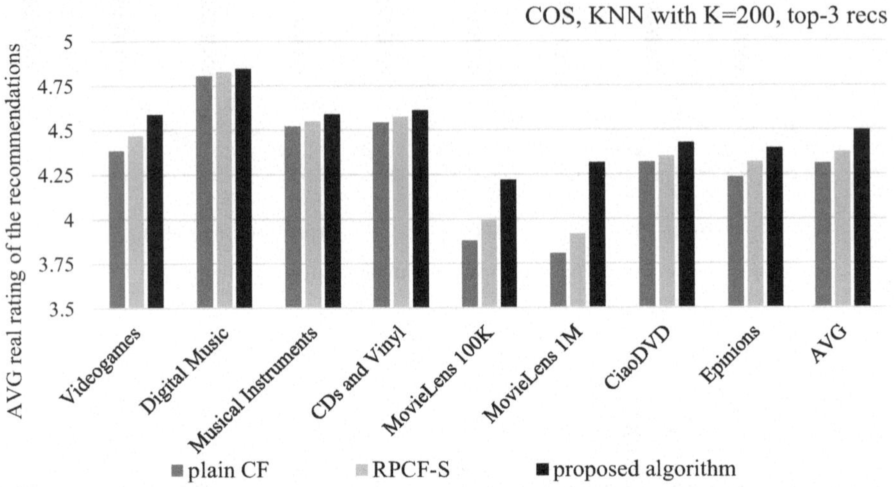

Fig. 7. Mean real rating value considering the top-3 recommendations, utilizing the COS similarity metric and the KNN selection method.

Analogous real rating value results are measured when using the PC similarity metric, with the THR NN selection method with T = 0.0 and recommending 3 items. In this case, the proposed algorithm improves the mean real rating value of recommendations from 4.45/5 to 4.55/5, surpassing the respective value achieved by original RPCF-S, measured at 4.49. Similarly, when the COS similarity metric is used under the exact same settings, the proposed algorithm augments the mean real rating value of recommended items from 4.43 to 4.51/5, while the original RPCF-S algorithm attains an increment up to 4.48/5.

Figure 8 illustrates the average NDCG value of recommendations, when recommending 3 items to each user and utilizing the PC similarity metric with the KNN selection method, setting K = 200. Considering the average of all eight datasets, the proposed algorithm improves the mean NDCG value of recommendations from 0.973 to 0.983, while the RPCF-S algorithm attains an increment up to 0.978.

Figure 9 illustrates the respective output when the COS similarity metric is used, while all the settings remain the same. The results in Fig. 9 are in agreement to those of Fig. 8. More specifically, the proposed algorithm is able to increase the mean NDCG value of recommendations from 0.969 to 0.981, surpassing the respective value achieved by the original RPCF-S algorithm, which is measured at 0.974.

Similar NDCG value results are measured when using the PC similarity metric, with the THR NN selection method with T = 0.0 and recommending 3 items. In this case, the proposed algorithm is able to increase the mean NDCG value of recommendations

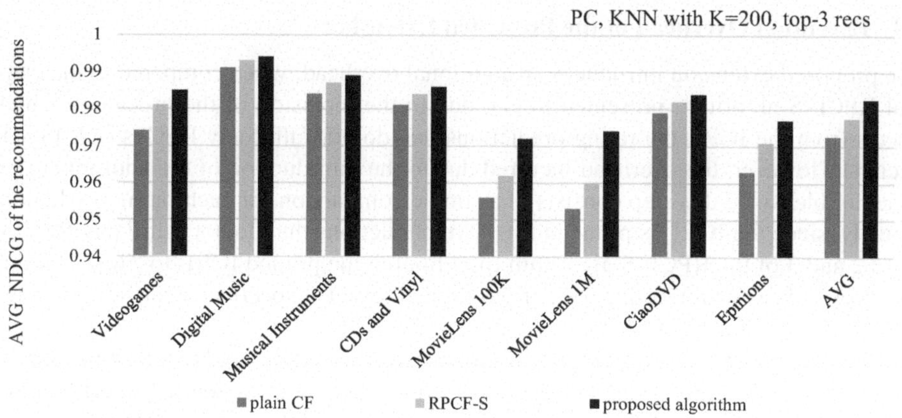

Fig. 8. Mean NDCG considering the top-3 recommendations, utilizing the PC similarity metric and the KNN selection method.

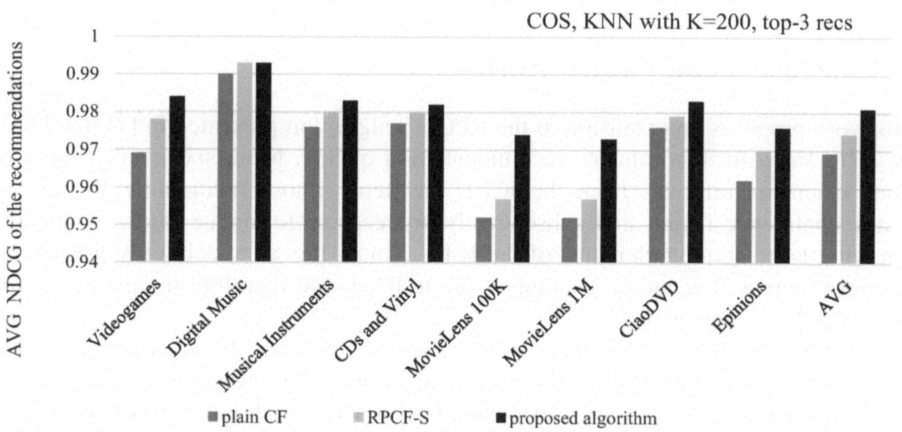

Fig. 9. Mean NDCG considering the top-3 recommendations, utilizing the COS similarity metric and the KNN selection method.

from 0.976 to 0.982, exceeding the respective value achieved by RPCF-S algorithm, which is measured at 0.98. Similarly, when the COS similarity metric is used under the exact same settings, the mean NDCG value is enhanced from 0.974 to 0.980, while the respective value of the original RPCF-S algorithm is measured at 0.978.

All the combinations of parameters listed in Subsect. 5.1 (i.e., user similarity computation metric, NN selection method with varying hyperparameter values, number of recommended items) have been experimentally tested, and the results obtained are in close agreement with the ones reported above. Their detailed presentation is omitted for conciseness.

The findings reported in this subsection substantiate that the proposed algorithm achieves considerable recommendation quality enhancement, both in dense and in sparse datasets.

5.4 Execution Overhead of the Presented Extension

The proposed extension introduces an additional overhead, when compared to the original RPCF-S algorithm presented in [7], due to the inclusion of the procedure which rejects from the ICRL the rating predictions that do not fulfill any RPCFs (c.f. Fig. 1, Sect. 4). However, the overhead incurred due to the introduction of the additional step is negligible, since this step consists of a simple comparison for each rating prediction. Notably, since the ICRL is pruned to remove predictions that do not fulfill any RPCFs, steps 2 and 3 of the RPCF-S algorithm (partitioning the pruned ICRL to "Top", "Med" and "Low" classes, and sorting predictions in each subset, respectively) can be performed in shorter time (due to the decreased length of the ICRL).

The execution time of the proposed algorithm has been measured for all eight datasets used in this work. The obtained measurements indicate that the extended algorithm proposed in this paper exhibits execution time gains from 2% to 15% in comparison to the RPCF-S algorithm (depending on the dataset and the execution settings and effectively mapping to the percentage of ICRL elements which are eliminated). This finding corroborates the applicability of the proposed extension.

6 Conclusion and Future Work

This work proposes an extension to the RPCF-S algorithm presented in [7] that leverages RPCFs to further enhance recommendation quality. More specifically, the proposed extension removes from the ICRL the items whose predictions do not fulfil any confidence factor, and subsequently proceeds to formulate the recommendation with the remaining elements of the ICRL. Under this approach, only predictions that have increased accuracy guarantees are utilized, and therefore the quality of the recommendation is enhanced.

A multi-parameter set of experiments is used to thoroughly assess the proposed extension for both applicability and recommendation quality. Regarding its applicability, the inclusion of the proposed extension (i) maintains high rating recommendation coverage, (ii) reduces the recommendation formulation time, and (iii) it can be applied in every CF dataset, since it is based only on the essential CF data.

Furthermore, the inclusion of the proposed extension has been shown to significantly upgrade the recommendation quality in all datasets and settings (i.e., similarity metrics, NN selection methods and number of recommendations produced per user), based on all three qualitative metrics used, namely (i) recommendation precision, (ii) the real rating of the recommendations, and (iii) NDCG values.

Regarding our future work, we will focus on investigating more CF prediction accuracy-related features and apply them into the recommendation procedure. Furthermore, we are planning to incorporate additional RecSys information sources (e.g., users' social information and demographics, attributes and categories of items, etc.) into the CF rating prediction and recommendation processes.

Acknowledgments. This research received no external funding.

Disclosure of Interests. The authors have no competing interests to declare that are relevant to the content of this article.

References

1. Wu, L., He, X., Wang, X., Zhang, K., Wang, M.: A survey on accuracy-oriented neural recommendation: from collaborative filtering to information-rich recommendation. IEEE Trans. Knowl. Data Eng. 1 (2022) https://doi.org/10.1109/TKDE.2022.3145690
2. Koren, Y., Rendle, S., Bell, R.: Advances in collaborative filtering. In: Ricci, F., Rokach, L., Shapira, B. (eds.) Recommender Systems Handbook, pp. 91–142. Springer US, New York, NY (2022). https://doi.org/10.1007/978-1-0716-2197-4_3
3. Xie, Z., et al.: Neighborhood-based collaborative filtering for conversational recommendation. In: 18th ACM Conference on Recommender Systems, pp. 1045–1050. ACM, Bari Italy (2024). https://doi.org/10.1145/3640457.3688191
4. Papadakis, H., Papagrigoriou, A., Panagiotakis, C., Kosmas, E., Fragopoulou, P.: Collaborative filtering recommender systems taxonomy. Knowl. Inf. Syst. **64**, 35–74 (2022)
5. Margaris, D., Vassilakis, C., Spiliotopoulos, D.: On producing accurate rating predictions in sparse collaborative filtering datasets. Information **13**, 302 (2022)
6. Spiliotopoulos, D., Margaris, D., Vassilakis, C.: On exploiting rating prediction accuracy features in dense collaborative filtering datasets. Information **13**, 428 (2022)
7. Sgardelis, K., Margaris, D., Spiliotopoulos, D., Vassilakis, C., Ougiaroglou, S.: Improving recommendation quality in collaborative filtering by including prediction confidence factors. In: Proceedings of the 20th International Conference on Web Information Systems and Technologies, pp. 372–379. SCITEPRESS - Science and Technology Publications, Porto, Portugal (2024). https://doi.org/10.5220/0013052200003825
8. Gazdar, A., Hidri, L.: A new similarity measure for collaborative filtering based recommender systems. Knowl.-Based Syst. **188**, 105058 (2020)
9. Polatidis, N., Georgiadis, C.K.: A multi-level collaborative filtering method that improves recommendations. Expert Syst. Appl. **48**, 100–110 (2016)
10. Salah, A., Rogovschi, N., Nadif, M.: A dynamic collaborative filtering system via a weighted clustering approach. Neurocomputing **175**, 206–215 (2016)
11. Xin, X., He, X., Zhang, Y., Zhang, Y., Jose, J.: Relational collaborative filtering: modeling multiple item relations for recommendation. In: Proceedings of the 42nd International ACM SIGIR Conference on Research and Development in Information Retrieval, pp. 125–134. ACM, Paris France (2019). https://doi.org/10.1145/3331184.3331188
12. Ramakrishna, M.T., et al.: HCoF: hybrid collaborative filtering using social and semantic suggestions for friend recommendation. Electronics **12**, 1365 (2023)
13. Li, L., Zhang, Z., Zhang, S.: Hybrid algorithm based on content and collaborative filtering in recommendation system optimization and simulation. Sci. Program. **2021**, 1–11 (2021)
14. Zhang, J., Lin, Y., Lin, M., Liu, J.: An effective collaborative filtering algorithm based on user preference clustering. Appl. Intell. **45**, 230–240 (2016)
15. Xue, F., et al.: Deep item-based collaborative filtering for Top-N recommendation. ACM Trans. Inf. Syst. **37**, 1–25 (2019)
16. Ibrahim, M., Bajwa, I.S., Sarwar, N., Hajjej, F., Sakr, H.A.: An intelligent hybrid neural collaborative filtering approach for true recommendations. IEEE Access **11**, 64831–64849 (2023)
17. Bobadilla, J., Alonso, S., Hernando, A.: Deep learning architecture for collaborative filtering recommender systems. Appl. Sci. **10**, 2441 (2020)
18. Mandalapu, S.R., Narayanan, B., Putheti, S.: A hybrid collaborative filtering mechanism for product recommendation system. Multimed. Tools Appl. **83**, 12775–12798 (2023)
19. Zhang, Y., Yin, C., Wu, Q., He, Q., Zhu, H.: Location-aware deep collaborative filtering for service recommendation. IEEE Trans. Syst. Man Cybern. Syst. **51**, 3796–3807 (2021)

20. Xiong, R., Wang, J., Zhang, N., Ma, Y.: Deep hybrid collaborative filtering for Web service recommendation. Expert Syst. Appl. **110**, 191–205 (2018)
21. Margaris, D., Sgardelis, K., Spiliotopoulos, D., Vassilakis, C.: Exploiting rating prediction certainty for recommendation formulation in collaborative filtering. BDCC **8**, 53 (2024)
22. Ni, J., Li, J., McAuley, J.: Justifying recommendations using distantly-labeled reviews and fine-grained aspects. In: Proceedings of the 2019 Conference on Empirical Methods in Natural Language Processing and the 9th International Joint Conference on Natural Language Processing (EMNLP-IJCNLP), pp. 188–197 Association for Computational Linguistics, Hong Kong, China (2019). https://doi.org/10.18653/v1/D19-1018
23. Harper, F.M., Konstan, J.A.: The MovieLens datasets: history and context. ACM Trans. Interact. Intell. Syst. **5**, 1–19 (2016)
24. Guo, G., Zhang, J., Thalmann, D., Yorke-Smith, N.: ETAF: an extended trust antecedents framework for trust prediction. In: 2014 IEEE/ACM International Conference on Advances in Social Networks Analysis and Mining (ASONAM 2014), pp. 540–547. IEEE, China (2014). https://doi.org/10.1109/ASONAM.2014.6921639
25. Ma, N., Lim, E.-P., Nguyen, V.-A., Sun, A. & Liu, H. Trust relationship prediction using online product review data. In: Proceedings of the 1st ACM International Workshop on Complex Networks Meet Information & Knowledge Management, pp. 47–54. ACM, Hong Kong China (2009). https://doi.org/10.1145/1651274.1651284
26. Jain, G., Mahara, T., Tripathi, K.N.: A Survey of similarity measures for collaborative filtering-based recommender system. In: Pant, M., Sharma, T., Verma, O., Singla, R., Sikander, A. (eds.) Soft Computing: Theories and Applications. AISC, vol. 1053, pp. 343–352. Springer, Singapore (2020). https://doi.org/10.1007/978-981-15-0751-9_32
27. Hassanieh, L.A., Jaoudeh, C.A., Abdo, J.B., Demerjian, J.: Similarity measures for collaborative filtering recommender systems. In: 2018 IEEE Middle East and North Africa Communications Conference (MENACOMM), pp. 1–5. IEEE, Jounieh (2018). https://doi.org/10.1109/MENACOMM.2018.8371003
28. Chowdhury, P., Sinha, B.B.: Evaluating the effectiveness of collaborative filtering similarity measures: a comprehensive review. Procedia Comput. Sci. **235**, 2641–2650 (2024)
29. Isnanto, R.R., Warsito, B., Firdaus, N., A'la, F.Y.: Towards the application of artificial intelligence: cosine similarity in recommendation systems based on collaborative filtering. In: 2024 7th International Conference of Computer and Informatics Engineering (IC2IE), pp. 1–5. IEEE, Bali, Indonesia (2024). https://doi.org/10.1109/IC2IE63342.2024.10747946
30. Fkih, F.: Similarity measures for collaborative filtering-based recommender systems: review and experimental comparison. J. King Saud Univ. Comput. Inf. Sci. **34**, 7645–7669 (2022)
31. Wang, D., Yih, Y., Ventresca, M.: Improving neighbor-based collaborative filtering by using a hybrid similarity measurement. Expert Syst. Appl. **160**, 113651 (2020)
32. Trattner, C., Said, A., Boratto, L., Felfernig, A.: Evaluating group recommender systems. In: Felfernig, A., Boratto, L., Stettinger, M. Tkalčič, M. (eds.) Group Recommender Systems, pp. 63–75. Springer, Cham (2024). https://doi.org/10.1007/978-3-031-44943-7_3
33. Margaris, D., Vassilakis, C., Spiliotopoulos, D.: What makes a review a reliable rating in recommender systems? Inf. Process. Manag. **57**, 102304 (2020)
34. Felfernig, A., Boratto, L., Stettinger, M., Tkalčič, M.: Evaluating group recommender systems. In: Group Recommender Systems, pp. 59–71. Springer, Cham (2018). https://doi.org/10.1007/978-3-319-75067-5_3

Data-Driven Discourse Analysis of Autism-Related Reddit Channels

Narges Azizifard(✉), Lidia Pivovarova, and Eetu Mäkelä

University of Helsinki, Unioninkatu 40, Helsinki, Finland
{narges.azizifard,lidia.pivovarova,eetu.makela}@helsinki.fi

Abstract. The Autism Spectrum Disorder (ASD) community comprises individuals with diverse needs, facing unique challenges that affect their well-being. The COVID-19 pandemic has deepened the necessity of understanding and addressing their specific health information needs. Social media platforms, particularly Reddit, provide a space where autistic individuals and their caregivers share experiences and concerns while also enabling broader discussions on ASD-related topics. This study explores ASD-related conversations on Reddit during the COVID-19 lockdowns, aiming to understand the sentiment and thematic patterns within these discussions. Building on our previous work that focused specifically on autism and COVID-19 discussions, this study adopts a broader perspective, analyzing all comments from autism-related subreddits during the lockdown period. Using natural language processing techniques such as topic modeling and sentiment analysis, we examine key themes, sentiment distributions, and engagement patterns across different subreddits. Our findings reveal that, despite the pandemic's impact, direct discussions about COVID-19 were relatively limited, with discourse instead centering on everyday struggles and needs. However, we observed shifts in online engagement, including the growth of certain subreddits and the emergence of new communities. Sentiment analysis showed that discussions on social interactions and employment were often negative, while those on sensory experiences and daily interests tended to be more positive. Although the most prominent topics differed from those in our previous study, we still observed disparities in topic prominence across subreddits, supporting our earlier claim that data-driven analysis is able to reveal viewpoint differences in social media discussions. This analysis provides valuable insights into evolving autism-related online discussions, highlighting how the ASD community navigated the challenges of the pandemic.

Keywords: Autism · Social Media · COVID-19 · Reddit · Discussions

1 Introduction

The Autism Spectrum Disorder (ASD) community includes a diverse range of individuals, each with distinct needs and challenges. Living as an autistic person can be a multifaceted and demanding experience, involving various dimensions of health and well-being [19,23]. Following the COVID-19 pandemic, the need to address the specific health information requirements of this community has become even more critical

M. Marchiori et al. (Eds.): WEBIST 2024, LNBIP 583, pp. 307–320, 2026.
https://doi.org/10.1007/978-3-032-25534-1_14

[18]. In the digital era, they can share their personal experiences online through social media. Simultaneously, diverse perspectives and opinions about these individuals are also expressed on these platforms. As a result, social media facilitates the analysis of multidimensional discussions on specific events and conditions, as well as the identification of communities engaging with similar topics from different viewpoints.

On some social media platforms, discussions are structured into groups and channels, offering an additional dimension for analysis. Reddit, being one of the most widely used online forums, serves as a distinctive platform where autistic individuals and their caregivers openly share their experiences, challenges, and concerns regarding health and well-being [16]. This paper examines ASD-related discussions on Reddit during the COVID-19 outbreak. Our goal is to explore the impact of COVID-19 and lockdowns on individuals with ASD and their close contacts.

In our previous work [5], we focused on Reddit discussions concerning both autism and COVID-19 and identified key themes in these discussions, including challenges in education, employment, and family life, as well as conspiracy theories and propaganda surrounding vaccination. Our findings shed light on the struggles faced by individuals with autism during the lockdown and highlight their coping strategies.

In this paper we take a broader perspective and analyze all comments from autism-related subreddits posted during COVID-19 lockdowns period. By examining the content of these comments, we seek to identify sentiments and patterns, offering insights into autism during the COVID-19 lockdown. Our broader objective is to shed light on the challenges that emerge in such circumstances, often leading to shock and confusion.

We employed several language analysis methods, including topic modeling and sentiment analysis, to identify recurring themes in the discussions and examine how the insights derived from these techniques are spread across different subreddits and topics. Despite the significant impact of the global pandemic on daily life, we found that discussions about COVID-19 and related issues occupy only a small portion of autism-related subreddits, where the focus is primarily on the specific challenges and needs faced by individuals with ASD. At the same time, we noticed certain dynamics in this segment during COVID-19 period, such as the growth of certain autism-related subreddits and organization of new ones.

2 Related Work

Autistic individuals, who rely on routine and predictability, faced significant challenges due to abrupt disruptions caused by lockdowns, school closures, and social distancing measures [13,15]. The pandemic also restricted access to essential support services such as therapy, education, and social engagement, increasing stress and anxiety for both autistic individuals and their families [6,20,29]. The pandemic has had a significant effect on the healthcare system, with hospitals and clinics struggling to manage the surge in COVID-19 cases. This strain redirected attention and resources away from routine medical care and specialized services for autistic individuals [4,6].

The use of social media as a channel for sharing health-related information has attracted significant attention in recent years. These platforms enable users to engage in discussions on health topics and participate in advocacy efforts [27]. Research indicates that social media enables real-time data collection, effectively capturing immediate public reactions and concerns in a way that traditional methods may not [14,21]. A key benefit of utilizing social media for health research is the ability to gather a wide range of unfiltered patient perspectives and experiences [16]. For autistic individuals and their families, social media platforms provide a sense of community, a space to share experiences, and a forum for seeking advice and information [1,28,31].

Each platform offers distinct benefits. Twitter, for instance, is useful for tracking public health trends, such as the spread of infectious diseases like COVID-19, and for monitoring mental health and chronic illnesses [2]. However, its lack of anonymity and character limits can make it less suitable for in-depth or sensitive discussions [8,12].

In contrast, Reddit allows users to engage anonymously in community-driven discussions [22], fostering more open and honest conversations, especially on sensitive health topics like mental health [9] and autism spectrum disorder (ASD) [7]. Additionally, Reddit's "subreddits", or topic-specific forums, enable autistic individuals, caregivers, and healthcare professionals to engage in detailed discussions about their challenges and the health information they seek [16]. Analyzing the conversations in autism-related subreddits provides valuable insights into the health information needs of the autistic community, allowing us to capture diverse perspectives in real time [16].

Reddit, with its accessible and user-driven content, has been less studied compared to larger platforms like Twitter and Facebook [32]. Recent reviews highlight that much of the research on Reddit content relies on computational text analysis, yet there is a growing need for greater contextualization of this data [24].

Qualitative methods are also frequently used to analyze Reddit discussions related to autism. For instance, in [30], the authors employed a qualitative approach to examine how individuals reflect on their experiences of motherhood within a Reddit community dedicated to autistic parents. This method allowed for a deeper understanding of the unique challenges and perspectives associated with parenting as an autistic individual.

Among studies empirically investigating Reddit content related to ASD, authors in [7] explored the representation of applied behavior analysis (ABA) interventions within Reddit discussions through topic modeling. Additionally, researchers analyzed ABA discourse on Reddit using inductive manual coding of contextualized thread content [27]. Other research has examined how Reddit's internal voting system influences community dynamics by promoting content deemed useful or relevant and suppressing content considered irrelevant or misleading [17,25].

In our previous work [5], we performed a data-driven analysis of Reddit comments related to both autism and the COVID-19 outbreak. By combining quantitative analysis with close reading, we showed that language analysis techniques such as topic modeling and sentiment analysis can reveal viewpoint differences in Reddit communities. We identified key themes, including vaccination, family issues, conspiracy theories, and propaganda. Our findings highlighted the complex, multi-dimensional nature of online discussions, where themes and emotional tones interact with user engagement. For example, we found that discussions about autistic individuals and their families during quarantine were more emotional, optimistic, and supportive, receiving fewer downvotes than other topics. In this paper, we present a broader study of all content from autism-related subreddits during the pandemic, regardless of using keywords such as COVID-19.

3 Methodology

3.1 Data Collection and Preprocessing

We collected our data using the Reddit API. We selected autism-related subreddits with a minimum of 50,000 members. These subreddits were identified through a search in Reddit communities and covered all or part of the lockdown periods documented on Wikipedia[1], i.e. from March 2020 to October 2021. Table 1 shows the list of subreddits meeting these criteria together with the number of members and the date on which these subreddits were created.

Table 1. Selected Subreddits.

Subreddit	# Members (thousand)	Date Created
Autism	443	09-04-2008
aspiememes	258	09-01-2018
AutismInWomen	198	16-02-2021
aspergers	169	24-03-2010
aspergirls	96	29-05-2014
AutisticAdults	86	14-12-2013
AutisticWithADHD	69	10-06-2021
Autism_Parenting	60	12-07-2017
AutismTranslated	59	11-04-2019
AutisticPride	54	07-06-2019
autismmemes	52	21-06-2013

Unlike our previous study [5], where we filtered comments using specific keywords, in this study we collected all comments from these subreddits during the COVID-19 lockdown period. To examine the filtered comments, we excluded posts that were not in English. All text was converted to lowercase. We eliminated irrelevant information from the data, such as URLs, special characters (e.g., @, /, ...), and stopwords (e.g., in, the, ...). Since we observed some comments consisting of a few words without any meaningful themes, we considered only those comments that contain at least 10 words. To eliminate comments posted by bots, we filtered out authors with the following characteristics in their usernames:

- Ends with 'bot'
- Starts with 'bot'

[1] https://en.wikipedia.org/wiki/COVID-19_lockdowns.

- Contains ‘GPT’
- Contains ‘auto’ (e.g., AutoModerator)
- Contains ‘assistant’
- Contains ‘helper’
- Long number sequences (e.g., user123456789)

After completing these steps, 844,294 comments from 75,296 users remained for further analysis.

As illustrated in Fig. 1, the number of comments in most subreddits increased compared to the beginning of quarantines. This shows that these communities and the individuals relating to them faced growing challenges during this time. For example, they experienced disruptions to their daily routines, which were already challenging due to their reliance on predictability for navigating society [11]. Furthermore, school closures, canceled therapy sessions, and changes in family routines contributed to heightened anxiety and behavioral difficulties for autistic individuals. The absence of in-person social interactions further hindered communication and the development of social skills, which are core characteristics of ASD [3].

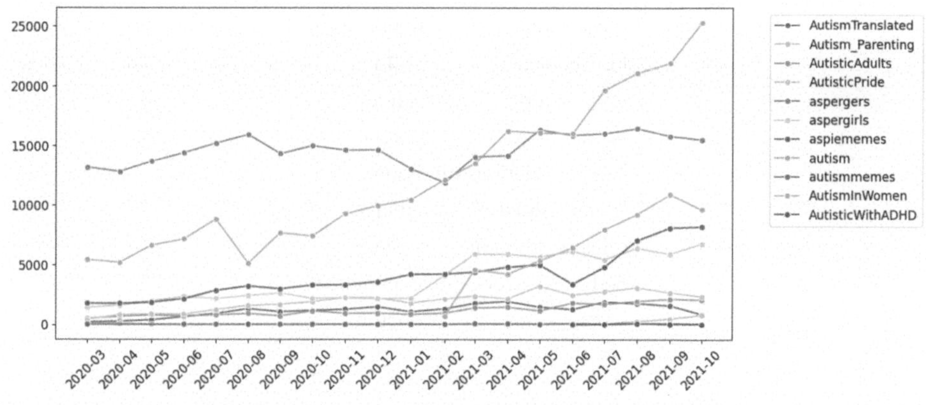

Fig. 1. Temporal distribution of comments in subreddits.

3.2 Methods

We utilized the Multicore implementation of Latent Dirichlet Allocation (LDA) from the Gensim library, which leverages multiple CPU cores to enhance processing speed for large datasets. This approach was used to identify the most frequently discussed topics during the COVID-19 lockdown, particularly those related to the challenges faced by individuals with autism and their supporters. To determine the optimal number of topics, we trained LDA models with topic counts ranging from 2 to 10 and selected the best model based on the coherence metric [26].

To examine variations across topics and users’ responses to the challenges they encounter, we conducted sentiment analyses on the comments associated with each topic separately. For sentiment analysis, we leveraged the transformer-based model RoBERTa[2], which has been pretrained on approximately 58 million tweets and fine-tuned for sentiment classification using the TweetEval benchmark. This model is particularly well-suited for analyzing longer texts.

4 Results

Topic Modeling. After utilizing the LDA Multicore approach, we identified that a model with 3 distinct topics yields the highest coherence score and used this model for further analysis. The topic keywords are presented in Table 2. Roughly, they could be described as topics related to sensory experience and daily interests (Topic 0), social situations (Topic 1) and diagnosis and parental aspects (Topic 2).

Table 2. Top keywords for each topic.

Topic 0	Topic 1	Topic 2
music	friend	autism
game	life	diagnosis
movie	social	child
noise	job	school
hand	hard	parent
hair	relationship	issue
sound	situation	adhd
sensory	problem	woman
body	conversation	experience
issue	issue	doctor

Similar to our previous research [5], we conducted an in-depth analysis of each topic by close reading the comments associated with them, with particular emphasis on the most prominent keywords.

One notable observation from our close reading of the comments, in contrast to previous research [5], is that discussions in autism-related communities did not prominently feature topics such as vaccines, COVID-19, or lockdowns. While a few comments briefly mentioned these issues, the majority of discussions centered around personal experiences and challenges, including:

- Struggling to maintain eye contact in social interactions and finding communication challenging.
- Discussing ordinary aspects of life and interests, such as engaging in personal hobbies like reading books, gaming, and watching television or movies.

[2] https://huggingface.co/cardiffnlp/twitter-roberta-base-sentiment.

- Experiencing sensory overload and processing disorders, particularly related to touch sensitivity and noise.
- Navigating friendships and relationships as an autistic individual.
- Sharing experiences related to self-diagnosis (especially for women) or the diagnosis of their children (e.g., autism, Asperger's, ADHD) and receiving supportive comments or advice from others.
- Discussing feelings of isolation and experiences with bullying in school, either as autistic individuals or as parents of autistic children.
- Expressing frustration with parents who struggle to understand autism.
- Talking about mental health challenges and experiences with therapy.
- Discussing employment challenges and job-seeking experiences as autistic individuals.

As previously mentioned, direct discussions about COVID-19 and lockdowns were scarce. However, many of the problems highlighted by the community are likely to be exacerbated during times of crisis, such as the COVID-19 pandemic, that is why it is important to understand and classify these challenges.

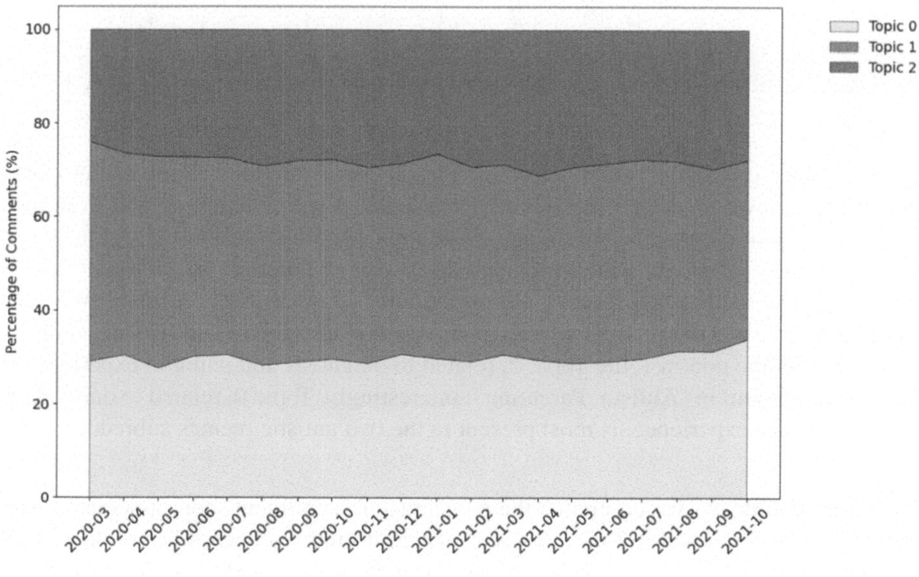

Fig. 2. Percentage of comments related to each topic.

Figure 2 illustrates the percentage of comments associated with each topic across the selected time periods. Notably, Topic 1, which primarily pertains to working situations and difficulties in having conversations and relationships with others, has the highest proportion of comments (42%), followed by Topic 0 (30%) and Topic 2 (28%). However, its prevalence declined as the end of lockdowns approached. In contrast, discussions on Topics 0 and 2 increased during the same period.

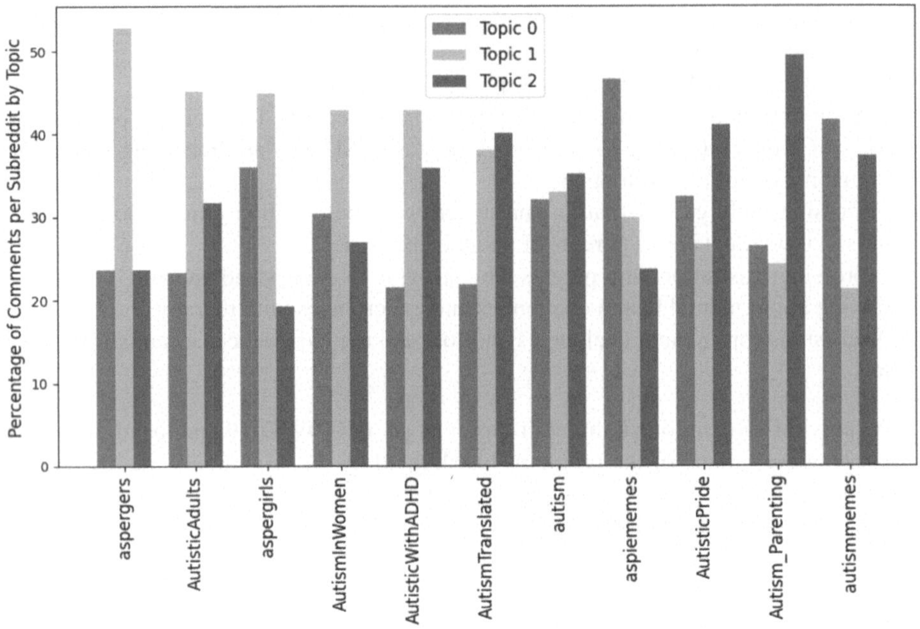

Fig. 3. Distribution of topics per each subreddit, sorted by the prominence of Topic 1.

To enhance our analysis and determine the specific subreddits where each topic is most prevalent, we identified the subreddits associated with each topic and examined the distribution of comments pertaining to each topic. As illustrated in Fig. 3, the largest concentration of Topic 1, which includes discussions related to social situations, is found in the subreddits "aspergers", "AutisticAdults", "aspergirls", "AutismInWomen" and "AutisticWithADHD", all of which can be broadly described as discussing adult life with ADS. On the contrast, the Topic 2, related to diagnosis and parental experience is the most prominent in "Autism_Parenting". Interestingly, Topic 0, related to daily interests and sensory experience, is most present in the two autistic memes subreddits.

Sentiment Analysis. We computed the percentage of sentiment score associated with each topic. As illustrated in Fig. 4, Topic 1, which primarily concerns workplace challenges and difficulties in social interactions and relationships, exhibits the highest proportion of negative sentiments. This is followed by Topic 2, which revolves around diagnosis, schooling, and parental aspects. Topic 0, which is mainly focused on users' interests and sensory experiences has the least number of negative sentiment scores.

Regarding the positive sentiment, Topic 0 has the highest percentage, followed by Topic 1 and Topic 2. In terms of neutral sentiment, Topic 0 again leads, followed by Topic 2 and then Topic 1. Overall, user engagement with Topic 1 appears to be more pronounced than with other topics, as it exhibits the lowest proportion of neutral sentiments and probably most related to lockdowns situations.

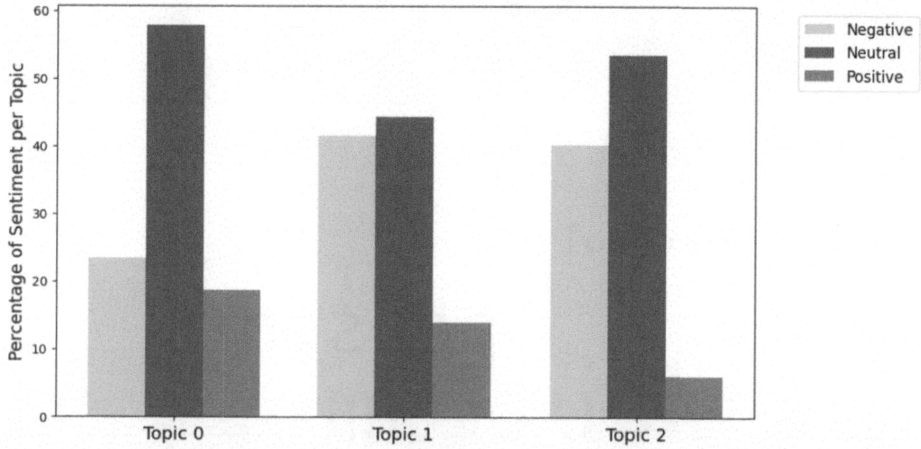

Fig. 4. Sentiment distribution across topics.

Figure 5 displays the 50 most frequently occurring keywords associated with each sentiment. As can be expected, the positive and negative sentiment is associated with evaluative vocabularly-such as ‘great’ or ‘bad’, respectively-though some content words can be found, e.g. prominence of word ‘friend’ in association with positive sentiment.

We also examined the scores (votes) that users assigned to comments across various topics, using the categories established in [10]. In contrast to our previous study [5], we did not observe any significant differences among the three topics, so we have omitted the results from this paper.

(a) Positive

(b) Neutral

(c) Negative

Fig. 5. Top 50 keywords per each sentiment.

5 Conclusion

Our study provides a data-driven analysis of the ASD community's discussions on Reddit during the COVID-19 lockdown period. Through a combination of topic modeling and sentiment analysis, we uncovered several key themes that reveal the unique challenges faced by individuals with ASD during the pandemic. While COVID-19-related discussions were relatively sparse in our data, broader challenges related to daily life, including sensory experiences, social interactions, and concerns about diagnosis, dominated the discourse. These findings highlight the difficulties, many individuals in the ASD community experienced in maintaining routines, managing relationships, and coping with the compounded stress caused by lockdown measures.

Online platforms like Reddit played an essential role for many individuals during the crisis, offering a space for individuals with ASD to share their personal experiences and express their perspectives. These channels allowed for open and anonymous discussions, which proved particularly valuable in fostering honest conversations about sensitive issues. The growth of autism-related subreddits during the lockdown further reflects the increased demand for these spaces, where individuals can discuss their challenges and seek support in an environment that feels more accessible and less stigmatized.

This study builds on our previous research [5] that has demonstrated the potential of Reddit as a valuable resource for revealing complex, multidimensional conversations. Previously we have shown that methods such as topic modeling and sentiment analysis can be used to uncover key themes within Reddit discussions. By extending the scope of our analysis to encompass all autism-related discussions during the pandemic, regardless of direct mentions of COVID-19, we gain a broader and deeper understanding of the struggles faced by the ASD community. This expanded approach offers new insights into the practical challenges individuals with ASD encountered during the pandemic.

Though most prominent topics revealed in the bigger dataset are different, and focused on specific ASD issues as opposed to COVID-related issues in our previous study, we are still observing disparity in topic prominence across subreddits, which confirms our earlier claim that data-driven analysis is able to reveal viewpoint differences in social media discussions.

At the same time, we noticed some differences with our previous observations. In particular, we do not find any significant difference in a number of upvoting and downvoting scores, while in COVID-related discussions some personal comments were met with more compassion and less dowmvote. However, this effect is negligeble in the total mass of ASD-related discussion, as we show in the current study.

Sentiment analysis in our study revealed that discussions about social situations and work-related issues were often associated with negative sentiments, reflecting the heightened stress and isolation many individuals with ASD experienced during lockdowns. Conversely, discussions focused on sensory experiences and users' hobbies, such as changes in routine or sensory sensitivities, tended to evoke more positive sentiments. This contrast in sentiment highlights the multidimensional nature of the challenges faced by the ASD community during the pandemic. Despite significant difficulties, many individuals found solace and connection through shared experiences in these online communities, showing the strength of the support networks that have formed around autism-related subreddits.

Moving forward, our study emphasizes the importance of ensuring that individuals with ASD have access to accurate, tailored information through appropriate online channels, especially in times of crisis such as the COVID-19 pandemic. Health professionals and support organizations must recognize the unique needs of the ASD community and prioritize creating resources that meet these needs. Online spaces, such as Reddit, offer critical opportunities for individuals with ASD to connect, share experiences, and find support. By fostering these communities and ensuring that they are equipped with the right information, we can better address the challenges faced by individuals with ASD, both in times of crisis and beyond.

References

1. Abel, S., Machin, T.M., Brownlow, C.: Support, socialise and advocate: an exploration of the stated purposes of facebook autism groups. In: Research in Autism Spectrum Disorders (2019). https://api.semanticscholar.org/CorpusID:150791650
2. Aiello, A.E., Renson, A., Zivich, P.N.: Social media- and internet-based disease surveillance for public health. In: Annual Review of Public Health (2020). https://api.semanticscholar.org/CorpusID:210042290
3. Al-Beltagi, M., Saeed, N.K., Bediwy, A.S., Alhawamdeh, R., Qaraghuli, S.: Effects of covid-19 on children with autism. World J. Virol. **11**, 411 – 425 (2022). https://api.semanticscholar.org/CorpusID:253863111
4. Amaral, D.G., de Vries, P.J.: Covid-19 and autism research: perspectives from around the globe. Autism Res. **13**, 844 – 869 (2020). https://api.semanticscholar.org/CorpusID:220120529
5. Azizifard, N., Pivovarova, L., Mäkelä, E.: Viewpoint analysis of autism-related comments in reddit during covid-19. In: International Conference on Web Information Systems and Technologies (2024). https://api.semanticscholar.org/CorpusID:274187565
6. Baweja, R., Brown, S.L., Edwards, E.M., Murray, M.J.: Covid-19 pandemic and impact on patients with autism spectrum disorder. J. Autism Dev. Disord. **52**, 473 – 482 (2021). https://api.semanticscholar.org/CorpusID:232169184
7. Bellon-Harn, M.L., Boyd, R.L., Manchaiah, V.: Applied behavior analysis as treatment for autism spectrum disorders: topic modeling and linguistic analysis of reddit posts. Front. Rehabil. Sci. **2**, 1–10 (2022). https://api.semanticscholar.org/CorpusID:245671941
8. Choi, D., Matni, Z., Shah, C.: What social media data should i use in my research?: a comparative analysis of twitter, youtube, reddit, and the New York times comments. In: Proceedings of the Association for Information Science and Technology, vol. 53 (2016). https://api.semanticscholar.org/CorpusID:51952081
9. Choudhury, M.D., De, S.: Mental health discourse on reddit: self-disclosure, social support, and anonymity. In: Proceedings of the International AAAI Conference on Web and Social Media (2014). https://api.semanticscholar.org/CorpusID:1578178
10. Davis, J., Graham, T.: Emotional consequences and attention rewards: the social effects of ratings on reddit. Inf. Commun. Soc. **24**, 1–18 (2021). https://doi.org/10.1080/1369118X.2021.1874476
11. Dekker, L.P., et al.: Impact of the covid-19 pandemic on children and adolescents with autism spectrum disorder and their families: a mixed-methods study protocol. BMJ Open **12** (2022). https://api.semanticscholar.org/CorpusID:246287052
12. Jafar, Z., et al.: Social media for public health: reaping the benefits, mitigating the harms. Health Promot. Perspect. **13**, 105–112 (2023). https://api.semanticscholar.org/CorpusID:260049121

13. Kaku, S.M., et al.: Coping with autism during lockdown period of the covid-19 pandemic: a cross-sectional survey. Indian J. Psychiatry **63**, 568–574 (2021). https://api.semanticscholar.org/CorpusID:245057131
14. Korda, H., Itani, Z.: Harnessing social media for health promotion and behavior change. Health Promot. Pract. **14**, 15–23 (2013). https://api.semanticscholar.org/CorpusID:510123
15. Kreysa, H., et al.: Psychosocial and behavioral effects of the covid-19 pandemic on children and adolescents with autism and their families: overview of the literature and initial data from a multinational online survey. Healthcare **10** (2022). https://api.semanticscholar.org/CorpusID:248164571
16. Larnyo, E., Nutakor, J.A., Addai-Dansoh, S., Nkrumah, E.N.K.: Sentiment analysis of post-COVID-19 health information needs of autism spectrum disorder community: insights from social media discussions. Front. Psychiat. **15** (2024). https://api.semanticscholar.org/CorpusID:273296270
17. Leavitt, A., Robinson, J.: Upvote my news: the practices of peer information aggregation for breaking news on reddit.com. Proc. ACM Hum.-Comput. Interact. **1**, 1–18 (2017). https://doi.org/10.1145/3134700
18. Lee, P., et al.: Digital health COVID-19 impact assessment: lessons learned and compelling needs. NAM Perspect. **2022** (2022). https://api.semanticscholar.org/CorpusID:245980971
19. Lee, S., Yoon, Y.: Mechanistic examination of why caregiver strain undermines quality of life: unravelling the roles of mental health symptoms and social participation. Asia Pac. J. Social Work Dev. (2023). https://api.semanticscholar.org/CorpusID:261919615
20. Lee, V., et al.: The impact of covid-19 on the mental health and wellbeing of caregivers of autistic children and youth: a scoping review. Aut. Res. **14**, 2477–2494 (2021). https://api.semanticscholar.org/CorpusID:238228454
21. Martino, B.D., Bobadilla-Suarez, S., Nouguchi, T., Sharot, T., Love, B.C.: Social information is integrated into value and confidence judgments according to its reliability. J. Neurosci. **37**, 6066–6074 (2017). https://api.semanticscholar.org/CorpusID:3860490
22. Park, A., Conway, M.: Tracking health related discussions on reddit for public health applications. In: AMIA ... Annual Symposium proceedings. AMIA Symposium 2017, pp. 1362–1371 (2017). https://api.semanticscholar.org/CorpusID:33540223
23. Prabavathy, M., Mr, A., Sivaranjani, R.: Integrated social story-based video modelling as a tool to promote air travel skills among youngsters with autism spectrum disorder. J. Re Attach Therapy Dev. Diversit. 592–601 (2023)
24. Proferes, N., Jones, N., Gilbert, S.A., Fiesler, C., Zimmer, M.: Studying reddit: a systematic overview of disciplines, approaches, methods, and ethics. Social Media Soc. **7** (2021). https://api.semanticscholar.org/CorpusID:235724916
25. Richterich, A.: 'karma, precious karma!' karmawhoring on reddit and the front page's econometrisation. J. Peer Prod. **4** (2014)
26. Röder, M., Both, A., Hinneburg, A.: Exploring the space of topic coherence measures. In: Proceedings of the Eighth ACM International Conference on Web Search and Data Mining (2015). https://api.semanticscholar.org/CorpusID:7743332
27. Saar, K.W., Saar, M., Bellon-Harn, M.L., Harn, W.E., Boyd, R.L., Manchaiah, V.: Upvote or downvote aba for autism? Content and support in reddit posts. J. Consumer Health Internet **27**, 119–138 (2023). https://api.semanticscholar.org/CorpusID:258093514
28. Skafle, I., Gabarron, E., Nordahl-Hansen, A.: Social media shaping autism perception and identity. Autism **28**(10), 2489–2502 (2024). https://doi.org/10.1177/13623613241230454
29. Spain, D., Mason, D., Capp, S.J., Stoppelbein, L., White, S.W., Happé, F.: "this may be a really good opportunity to make the world a more autism friendly place": Professionals' perspectives on the effects of covid-19 on autistic individuals. Res. Aut. Spect. Disord. **83**, 101747 – 101747 (2021). https://api.semanticscholar.org/CorpusID:233542589

30. Thom-Jones, S., Melgaard, I., Gordon, C.: Autistic women's experience of motherhood: a qualitative analysis of reddit. J. Aut. Dev. Disord. 1–11 (2024)
31. Wayman, L.: Social media offers benefits for autistic community (2021). https://www.autismspeaks.org/science-news/social-media-offers-benefits-autistic-community
32. Yeung, A.W.K., et al.: Medical and health-related misinformation on social media: bibliometric study of the scientific literature. J. Med. Internet Res. **24** (2021). https://api.semanticscholar.org/CorpusID:245475678

Defining, Understanding, and Detecting Online Toxicity: Challenges and Machine Learning Approaches

Gautam Kishore Shahi[1(✉)] and Tim A. Majchrzak[2,3]

[1] University of Duisburg-Essen, Duisburg, Germany
gautam.shahi@uni-due.de
[2] Center for Advanced Internet Studies (CAIS), Bochum, Germany
[3] University of Bochum, Bochum, Germany

Abstract. Online toxic content has grown into a pervasive phenomenon, intensifying during times of crisis, elections, and social unrest. A significant amount of research has been focused on detecting or analyzing toxic content using machine-learning approaches. The proliferation of toxic content across digital platforms has spurred extensive research into automated detection mechanisms, primarily driven by advances in machine learning and natural language processing. Overall, the present study represents the synthesis of 140 publications on different types of toxic content on digital platforms. We present a comprehensive overview of the datasets used in previous studies focusing on definitions, data sources, challenges, and machine learning approaches employed in detecting online toxicity, such as hate speech, offensive language, and harmful discourse. The dataset encompasses content in 32 languages, covering topics such as elections, spontaneous events, and crises. We examine the possibility of using existing cross-platform data to improve the performance of classification models. We present the recommendations and guidelines for new research on online toxic consent and the use of content moderation for mitigation. Finally, we present some practical guidelines to mitigate toxic content from online platforms.

Keywords: Toxic content · Literature review · Artificial intelligence · Datasets · Content moderation

1 Introduction

With the emergence of Web 2.0, which enables users to produce and consume content on digital platforms such as social media and news media, the Internet has witnessed significant growth in accessibility and user engagement [76]. Simultaneously, the global internet user base expanded rapidly, currently covering more than 68% of the world population.[1] While user-generated content proliferated, the dissemination of toxic content – such as hate speech and cyberbullying – also increased [36]. Subsequently, with the intervention of government regulations (such as the European Union (EU) Digital Service Act (DSA) [102], United Kingdom (UK)'s Online Safety Act [111]) and

[1] https://www.itu.int/itu-d/reports/statistics/2024/11/10/ff24-internet-use/.

M. Marchiori et al. (Eds.): WEBIST 2024, LNBIP 583, pp. 321–340, 2026.
https://doi.org/10.1007/978-3-032-25534-1_15

the enforcement of content moderation policies by social media platforms, efforts were made to regulate and mitigate such content. However, despite these measures, the creation and dissemination of toxic content persist.

Toxic content appears in multiple forms, such as hate speech and offensive speech and in different data formats [118]. One of the commonly occurring toxic content is hate speech, which has become a widespread problem [49]. With easy access to social media platforms, such as Twitter (now *X*), YouTube, and Gab, the amount of toxic content has been increasing [97] over the years. The topic of toxic content is linked to global developments and recent crises, such as hate speech on the Russo-Ukrainian conflict [29], COVID-19 [97], Israel-Hamas Conflict [96] and elections in different countries [95]. Digital platforms enable users to share content in various media formats and languages while requiring them to adhere to platform-specific guidelines. For example, on YouTube, users can post-attack someone or a group by posting videos or commenting on existing videos in multiple languages.

Prior research shows that the majority of studies were done with specific languages, most notably English, and on specific platforms such as Twitter [104], Facebook [27], and YouTube [33]. However, the presence of toxic content is not limited to one platform or language. In the last couple of years, multiple platforms such as TikTok, Reddit, and Bluesky have grown a considerable user base but have not been researched well. Toxic content has been studied using various approaches, including machine learning-based classification and user studies. In particular, researchers have developed models to detect toxic content, which require large-scale, fine-grained annotated datasets for effective training [38]. Gathering such high-quality training data is expensive and time-consuming [99]. Thus, Every research endeavour needs to start from scratch, i.e., data collection, annotation, and building a classification model, which is time-consuming and practically challenging.

Subsequently, a classification model was developed to detect hate speech in YouTube comments, demonstrating that augmenting training data with additional datasets based on definitions and content similarity can significantly enhance model performance [94]. Previous research shared different datasets without providing insightful information such as definitions used and annotation guidelines [4,35,82]. However, datasets vary considerably by social media platform, period of data collection, and linguistic style [4]. Hence, in prior research, it is difficult to identify the similarity of datasets across different platforms. This motivated us to conduct a literature review of existing literature on toxic content, current guidelines and regulations, and the platform's policy and provide a comprehensive understanding based on the topic of research, definitions, and annotation goodliness. It will be helpful in selecting an appropriate dataset as an additional training dataset for the classification model.

Having a unified platform that provides a descriptive view of hate speech will help to do cross-platform studies and cross-topic studies, and to use of an existing dataset for building a classification model. The key contributions of our research are:

- Provide a comprehensive overview of existing research on toxic content across digital platforms.
- Present a detailed analysis of datasets and highlight their key parameters, such as annotation guidelines, definitions of hate speech, and the proportion of toxic content.

- Offer a publicly accessible repository to promote data sharing and enhance dataset reusability.

This article is organized as follows: Sect. 2 discusses the related work on toxic content, followed by the research method in Sect. 3. We then show our experiment and results in Sect. 4 before discussing the findings in Sect. 5. Finally, we discuss the ideas for future work in Sect. 6.

2 Related Work and Background

Toxic content has been studied by experts on different subjects for its detection, patterns, and impact on society. Machine learning is the dominant approach to classification in various domains such as political sentiment analysis [88], detecting incivility and impoliteness in online discussions [109] as well as the classification of political tweets [23]. Especially the state-of-the-art technique BERT (Bidirectional Transformers for Language Understanding) [65] has been used for the detection of toxic contents [2, 62, 91, 123, 124]. Prior research has done predominately on text data, and text classifier aims to train a robust classifier to recognize hate comments globally, i.e., on different platforms and languages. For the identification and training of the models, several studies classify hate speech using deep neural network architectures or standard machine learning algorithms. Wei et al. compare machine learning models on different public datasets [117]. The results indicate that their approach of a convolution neural network outperforms the previous state-of-the-art models in most cases [117]. A recent study used transfer learning [122] to train 37,520 English tweets, showing a trend towards more complex models and better results. Prior studies have analyzed hate speech on YouTube; one study highlights the hate speech on YouTube on Syrian refugees [10]. In another study, hate speech on gender is studied on a small dataset quantitatively [32]. Vidgen & Derczynskivid provides a literature review on abusive languages by highlighting the issue in creating training datasets and possible direction for combining more datasets for helping data-driven research [112].

Previous studies have mainly focused on detecting toxic content in different languages [77] and on comparing different social media platforms [91]. Considering the past studies about toxic content, it is noticeable that many studies only concentrate on one platform or specific language, such as English [115], German [90], Spanish [13] and Italian [27] to train a machine learning model to automatically classify and predict which unseen texts can be considered hate speech. Ousidhoum et al. applied a multilingual and multitasking approach to train a classifier on three languages (English, French, and Arabic) based on Twitter tweets using a comparison of traditional machine learning and deep learning models [77]. In another work, a Twitter-like user interface was built to flag hate speech and it helps in user awareness for hateful content [98].

Previous research uses annotated datasets for the supervised classification model. Beyond the different methods for training the model, different guidelines are used for data annotation. At the same time, [26, 116] opted for a multi-label procedure (*hateful*, *offensive (but not hateful)*, and *neither* [26]; *racist*, *sexist* [116]), the annotation of the data of [90] was collected with a binary labeling schema (hate speech as *yes* or *no*).

However, research is needed to consider the classifiers' performance in multilingual contexts in combination with datasets from social media platforms. Salminen et al. [91] points out that the mono-platform focus in hate speech detection research is problematic, as there are no guarantees that the models developed by researchers will generalize well across platforms. This issue underscores the importance of our research in exploring cross-platform generalization. Fortuna et al. have shown that merging and combining different datasets can enhance the overall performance of classification models [35]. However, a more systematic evaluation is needed to determine the extent of improvement when a classifier is trained on one dataset, and then another is added. This approach could potentially lead to significant advancements in hate speech detection. The role of LLMs such as ChatGPT in generated annotated data without any background truth is still under exploration [60]. Consequently, toxic content detection still depends on gathering human-annotated data to build a classification model.

In the prior work it has been shown that a dataset with similar content and definition helps in improving the performance of a classification model. However, there is a lack of resources which provide the description of hateful words. Datasets on toxic content are created on different platforms, in different languages and with different topics of hate; having a unified platform which provides a descriptive view of toxic content will be helpful for doing a cross-platform study or cross-topic study or for using existing datasets for building classification models. Hence, we conducted a literature review of prior research on toxic content.

3 Research Method

This section explains the process of collecting publications using the PRISMA framework [78]. The eligibility criteria to research work is that they should discuss new datasets for any kind of toxic content regarding people or groups of people, such as hate speech, cyberbullying, interpersonal harassment, toxic language, trolling, aggression, bullying and profanity. The search was covered different languages, topic of datasets, platforms (such as social media, online news source), definition provided, and data extraction processes. We have not included the datasets for countering toxic content or explanation of toxic content because the goal is to have more similar data to enhance the performance of the classification model.

3.1 Sources of Content

Toxic content was discovered from a wide range of bibliography sources as described below:

- Google Scholar is a freely accessible search engine that indexes scholarly literature across various disciplines, including journal articles, conference papers, theses, books, and patents. It covers publication from different sources.
- Springer: Springer offers a wide collection of research articles. Springer covers many conference proceedings.
- AISEL: A central repository for research papers and journals published in the information system community.

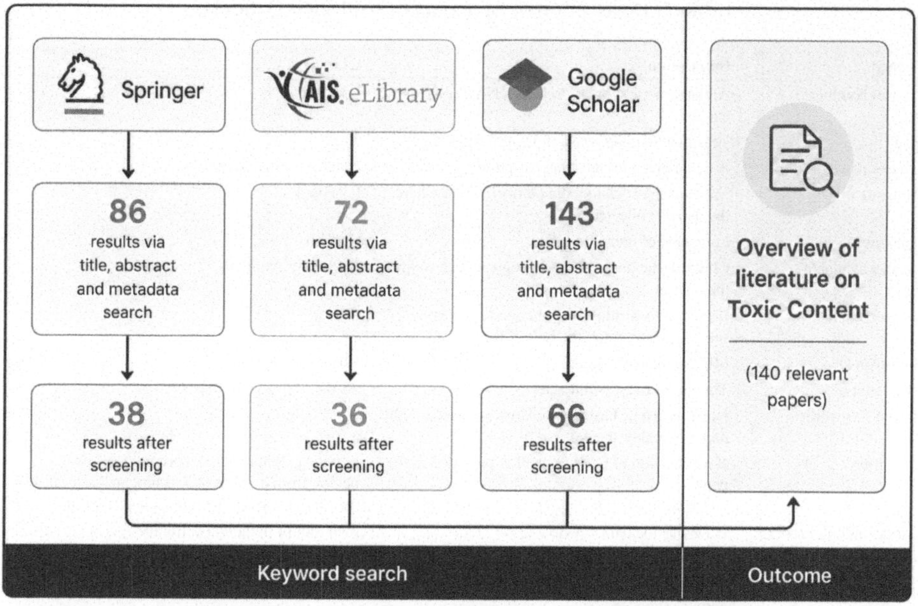

Fig. 1. Overview of Publications During the Literature Search.

3.2 Search

In the initial search, Google Scholar returned 143 results, of which 66 were deemed relevant to this study. AISEL yielded 72 results, 36 of which met our criteria, while Springer provided 86 results, 38 of which were considered appropriate. Two researchers independently screened the titles and abstracts to identify suitable articles. In cases of disagreement, the full text of the article was reviewed collaboratively, and consensus was reached through discussion. Overall, we have got 140 publications for this literature review. An Overview of search process and number of publications obtained is shown in Fig. 1.

4 Description of Datasets

Different metadata elements have been identified for analyzing each publication's dataset, as detailed in the Table 1. First, we defined a unique identifier for the date, then followed with the dataset name (if given by authors), platforms covered, languages, data collection and annotation process, the definition of toxic content and the research method used. Prior research [94] suggests that for datasets having similar definitions, content, and hate words, a combination of these datasets helps to improve the classification performance. In the following, the elaborate on the criteria.

Table 1. Description of Metadata of Collected Datasets.

Element	Description	Example
Dataset Number	Alphanumeric number to uniquely identify the dataset	HS1
Year	Year in which the research is published	2022
Dataset name	A name given to the dataset (optional)	Hateful Memes Dataset
Platform	Name of the social media platform from where the data is collected	Facebook
Language	Language of content in data	English
Dataset available	Check in the paper or do a google search to find the dataset	Publically Available
Dataset available at	If the link is available or obtained from google search then mention the link of the dataset	(Link)*
Data format	Multi-modality of data	Image+text
Evaluated in	Time used to crawl the data	23-04-2020 to 23-06-2020
Search Keywords	Name or list of hashtags or keywords used in the paper to gather the data	–
Definition	If a definition of toxic content is provided in the paper	Language that expresses prejudice against a person from a group or a group, primarily based on ethnicity, religion, or sexual orientation.
Data Crawling Process	How was the data crawled	own tool or python/java library
Topics covered	Topic od analysis of toxic content	racism, sexism, refugee
Size of dataset	Size of data of the crawled dataset that has been annotated/coded	24 582 tweets
Annotation Guidelines	If annotation guidelines is available.	–
Annotation Process	Process of annotating toxic content	Aamazon Mechanical Turk(AMT)
Number of Annotators	Number of annotator used	2
Intercoder measure	Measure to show intercoder agreement	Cohen's kappa
Classification model used	name of classification model used	BERT, LSTM

* https://ai.meta.com/tools/hatefulmemes/

4.1 Language

The collected dataset are dominated by English content [43,44], which appears over a hundred times. Other frequently researched language are Arabic [70,77], Hindi [56, 66], German [90,94], Indonesian [8,48], Russian [17,126] and Spanish [24,42], each appearing multiple times. French [24], Turkish [9] and, Italian [92] are also present.

Languages such as Greek [24], Urdu [87], Bengali [5,89], Vietnamese [64], Czech [47], Croatian [63], Polish [83], Danish [3], Korean [58], and Hingish [18,68] each appear only a couple of times. Some dataset contain multiple languages. The reason for content having in multiple languages could be the dominance of major digital platforms in English language and, presence of an extensive tools and library for Natural Language Processing (NLP) processing such as Natural Language Toolkit (NLTK)[2], spaCy[3].

[2] https://www.nltk.org/.
[3] https://spacy.io/.

4.2 Platforms

Most toxic content studies collected their data from social media platforms, with Twitter serving as the primary source [98], mainly due to ease of access of dataset (prior to becoming *X*). Other frequently mentioned platforms include Facebook [47,56], YouTube [25,94] and Reddit [41]. A few research have been done on the content from Instagram [84], Gab [54], Whisper [105] and Yik Yak [74]. In terms of news media [14], research has been done on the content from Al Jazeera, Fox News [37], SacBee.com [30], and several Turkish newspapers [9]. Notably, some data come from synthetic sources, radio shows [52], gaming platforms (like World of Warcraft and League of Legends [21]), and forums such as Stormfront [43]. Some research also targets community platform such as Wikipedia [1,44,75,118]. Overall, datasets incorporate a diverse range of platforms but are clearly dominated by social media, reflecting its central role in online discourse and toxic content analysis.

For data collection, a wide range of approaches were used from different platforms. For social media, the researcher used APIs to collect data using keywords [11,57,66,85] and accounts [120]. Researchers typically used the official API to gather data from Twitter, Facebook, YouTube, Reddit, and Whisper. Public data dumps like Pushshift.io were also utilized to gather data from Wikipedia talk pages[4] and Gab posts. Twitter data was typiclaly collected from API[5] using keywords, hashtags, or geo-locations. Several studies employed tools like Sifter (in partnership with Gnip), DiscoverText, or custom-built Twitter engines [108] to facilitate efficient data retrieval. Other research used web scraping from comment sections of news websites, crawling blogs from hate directories, and manual capture of platforms like Yik Yak [74] via screenshots. Some studies also collected data *offline* through simulation and role-play exercises involving participants [107]. Once data was collected, researchers used the sampling method for data annotation, and to ensure balanced sampling, some studies adopted random walk algorithms and days-based sampling.

Overall, a combination of automated APIs, keyword-based crawling, manual methods, and existing datasets were used to compile robust corpora for analyzing online discourse and toxic content.

4.3 Topic Covered

For the analysis of toxic content, researchers have focused on different topics for data collections. Researchers covered content related on evolving topics such as refugees [125], immigrants [15], and migrants [77]. In terms of personal attacks, toxic content was analyzed on topics such as LGBTQ+ phobia [59], misogyny [16], and harassment toward individuals with Autism Spectrum Disorder (ASD) [26]. Researchers covered specific events such as the George Tiller shooting [120], the Charlie Hebdo attack [22], and the murder on a Romani family in Olaszliszka [113]. Some studies addressed the dark side of Web such as vulgar and pornographic content [70] and obscene speech [59], often in connection with online harassment or personal attacks.

[4] https://en.wikipedia.org/wiki/Help:Talk_pages.

[5] https://developer.x.com/en/docs/x-api.

Overall, the topics reflect the varied and evolving nature of hate speech and offensive communication in online spaces which are summarized below.

- **Identity-Based Hate and Discrimination**
  - Ethnicity: Racism, anti-Hungarian attacks, race-based hate speech, ethnic discrimination.
  - Religion: Islamophobia, anti-Muslim sentiment, religious intolerance, attacks related to religious identity (e.g., Charlie Hebdo shooting).
  - Gender and Sexism: Misogyny, sexism, feminism-related hate, appearance-based and intellectual/political bias against women.
  - Sexual Orientation and LGBTQ+: Hate towards LGBTQ+ communities, sexuality-related hate, body shaming.
  - Disability: Hate towards individuals with disabilities (e.g., ASD), discrimination based on handicap or health condition.
  - Immigrants and Refugees: Hate toward immigrants, migrants, and refugees; xenophobia; issues around migration policies.
- **Sociopolitical Conflicts and Controversial Events**
  - Violence and Crimes: Murders in Olaszliszka and Tatárszentgyörgy, George Tiller shooting.
  - Geopolitical Conflicts: Israel-Palestinian conflict, attacks on refugees.
  - Political and Ideological Tensions: Political correctness, Islamic leftism, feminist debates, US elections.
  - Anti-fascist Protests: Communication and coordination during protests.
- **Media and Platform-Related Issues**
  - Online Content and Platform Abuse: Malicious Facebook pages, phishing, spam, untrustworthy information, misleading claims.
  - Toxicity and Health Judgements: Evaluations of online content based on perceived toxicity or emotional harm.
  - Controversial Media: Celebrity footage, provocative or offensive media content.
- **Mixed and Unspecified Themes**
  - No Specific Topic: General hate speech without specific targets or categories.
  - Multiple Combined Themes: Entries covering combined aspects (e.g., race, religion, gender).
  - Other Keywords: Knowledge reuse, vulgar speech, emotional responses, controversial humor.

4.4 Definition of Toxic Content

Before proceeding to studying toxic content, the definition of toxic content is important in terms of the development of a code book and performing data annotation. There is a lack of common understanding definition of different toxic content [94]. Each toxic content is defined differently for data annotation; we looked at different sources for providing definitions, such as UNICEF[6] defines cyberbullying as spreading lies or sharing information which harms, abuse or threatens others users. It can happen online or

[6] https://www.unicef.org/end-violence/how-to-stop-cyberbullying.

offline, but is most commonly seen on social media. In 2021, the European Union (EU) formed a law to counter hate crime and hate speech. Peršak defines hate speech as a direct attack on people based on what we call *protected characteristics*: race, ethnicity, national origin, religious affiliation, sexual orientation, caste, sex, gender, gender identity, and serious disease or disability [79]. Nockleby defines hate speech as any communication that disparages a person or a group based on some characteristics such as race, color, ethnicity, gender, sexual orientation, nationality, religion, or other characteristics [73].

However, over the years, the coverage and granularity of toxic content has changed. Both governments and platforms come up with extensive definitions of toxic content. With the implementation of several government regulations such as EU DSA, the UK's Online Safety Act 2023[7], and USA's Kids Online Safety Act [7]. Platforms have adapted their policies and laws in dealing with toxic content. Here, we are listing the platform guidelines provided by very large online platforms (VLOPs) social media platforms under EU DSA. Platforms use both manual and automated methods to detect and remove content. Platforms also allow users to flag or report suspicious content, which is later moderated.

Meta, the parent company of Facebook, Instagram, and WhatsApp, started defining toxic content as bullying and harassment in 2019 and continuously updates this definition regularly [69]. Presently, Meta defines bullying and harassment for public figures and private individuals, giving higher protection to private individuals. Content intended to degrade or shame may be removed or demoted. **Google** (or rather Alphabet), a parent company of YouTube, provides community guidelines for *Violent or dangerous content*, which includes Harmful or dangerous content and Hate speech, and content falling in this category is not allowed on the platform [121]. **X (formerly Twitter)** covers toxic content as abuse and harassment, which include different types of offensive content that is not allowed on the platform. It has removed posts, suspended accounts, and made posts less visible [119]. **TikTok**, a platform platform for video sharing, defines community guidelines for abuse and harassment content and removes and restricts content on the platforms [110]. **LinkedIn** prohibits bullying or harassment, including abusive language, unwanted advances, and encouraging others to harass a member on LinkedIn, and these contents are removed once detected [61]. **Snapchat** provides community guidelines to monitor *Sexual content, thereat, violence, harm, hateful content, harassment and bullying* [106]. **Pinterest** includes harmful, hateful, or violent content or behavior in the community guidelines [80]. Pinterest may take action by removing, restricting, or limiting the reach of such content – as well as the accounts, individuals, groups, or domains responsible for creating or spreading it – depending on the level of harm it presents.

4.5 Annotation Technique

For building classification models for toxic content, often research collected raw data from online platforms. Annotation processes were performed by using a mix of in-house

[7] https://www.legislation.gov.uk/ukpga/2023/50.

and crowdsourcing methods [1,125]. In-house annotation [8,26] includes data annotation using humans as well as automated tools. The common practice of in-house annotation involves researchers, student assistants, volunteers, and native speakers. Crowdsourcing annotation is performed using third-party software or websites; The latter hire annotators from different backgrounds. Crowdsourcing annotation is rather fast, expensive, and commonly offers quality checks. Some of the crowdsourcing platforms widely used are CrowdFlower [70] and Mechanical Turk [85]. Crowdsourcirng annotation is done either independently or in conjunction with in-house annotation to ensure quality and scalability. A few studies adopted a mixed approach, starting with in-house annotation and then validated the results using crowdworkers. However, not all studies specified their annotation procedures.

4.6 Models Used

Once data is collected and annotation is completed, several approaches have been applied for achieving a deeper understanding. For toxic content as a classification problem, traditional models include traditional machine learning classifiers such as Naive Bayes (NB) [26,51], Logistic Regression (LR) [6], Support Vector Machines (SVM) [18,34,40,50], and Random Forests (RF) [8]. Other researchers used Liblinear & Multinomial Naive Bayes (MNB) [114], and Stochastic Gradient Descent Classifier (SGDC) [81] for binary and multi-class classification problems [71]. In terms of features, these models use textual features such as n-grams, TF-IDF [20], and lexicon-based features.

With the development of deep learning, complex models such as Convolutional Neural Networks (CNNs) [12,123], Recurrent Neural Networks (RNNs) [85], Long Short-Term Memory (LSTM) [125], bi-LSTM [37] with attention, Gated Recurrent Unit (GRU) [28], and CNN+GRU hybrids have gained popularity and used for classification. Several researchers used ensemble methods, such as combining CNN with GRU, LSTM, and attention-based models, have been deployed to capture contextual and sequential nuances in language. Transformer-based models such as BERT [94], M-BERT [59], ULMFiT [39], and Bag of Word(BoW) with AutoML [59] enhanced models are also widely used for transfer learning and zero-shot scenarios. Some researchers have applied Graph-based models such as GraphSAGE [46], as well as embedding modeling [31] paragraph2vec and CBOW for capturing feature for classification models. Additionally, some studies used Linguistic Inquiry and Word Count (LIWC) [21], SentiStrength [44], and sentiment analysis [45] for analyzing psycholinguistics approaches [114] of toxic content.

5 Discussion

In previous studies, researchers focused on a variety of topics. Toxic content is not limited to online platforms; it may lead to violence and social unrest, including but not limited to public protest [53] and even to incidents such as mob lynching [100]. Most research focused on Twitter and Facebook; however, collecting data from these platforms is no longer feasible with free APIs [101]. In terms of language, research was dominantly performed in English. However, each country has a public discourse of its own, leading to a variety of languages that need to be studied.

For studying toxic content, collecting datasets is a vital step, which requires choosing the proper platforms and keywords to select relevant posts. For instance, YouTube allows to scrap YouTube videos and comments; however, keywords search leads to a lot of noise with a wide range of videos that do not fit with the criteria. Hence, a manual check of videos is required. Furthermore, based on data requirements adding a dataset from existing research will be helpful in adding a training dataset for classification as proposed by [94]. Data dumps are also available on PushShift and through the Internet Archive. However, such datasets might be only interesting for analyzing user behavior or training data because of the evolving patterns of platforms and content, but the latest datasets are always useful.

For tackling the problem of toxic content, the research community actively organizes workshops and challenges to gather evolving approaches to counter toxic content. Organizers collect data for toxic content and ask participants to make a classification model for the detection of toxic content. One of the events is HASOC [67], which has organized competitions for hate speech, offensive speech, and counter hate speech detection in Hindi, English, and German since 2019. Similar workshops and challenges, such as EVALITA [19], SEMEVAL [11], CONSTRAINTS [103], and PAN@CLEF [86] focus on different aspects of toxic content, including hate speech, offensive content, and online abuse.

Not only research communities but also companies organizes competition on this topic; the Facebook memes challenge [55] was organized with artificial datasets of hateful memes. Jigsaw organized a challenge [51] to detect toxic content using Wikipedia content. These competitions played a crucial role in advancing the field of toxic content detection. Also, they provide crucial datasets to explore research such as the Facebook memes datasets explored by researchers from natural language processing, computer vision, and sociology to analyze computation and human factors by consuming toxic contents. However, the participants fail to make a generalizable and universal model for the detection of toxic contents. With the proliferation of generative AI, particularly Large Language Models (LLMs) have been used for different tasks such as data annotation [93] and data profiling. In the future, data annotation can be performed by LLM, which might reduce cost and time in preparing datasets for studying toxic content. Also, interpretable machine learning models are able to explain results [72,93] to make detection of toxic content transparent.

With the emergence of acts and regulations from different countries asked platforms for content moderation. In the last couple of years, platforms have extensively provided guidelines for the allowed content, and they regularly moderate to mitigate the toxic content. Platforms use both manual and automatic approaches for identifying content. Also, the EU provides an option to demand datasets for research, which might be an interesting way of collecting moderated content from platforms and use for study. This will also help remove the cost of data collection and annotation for studying toxic content.

It needs to be mentioned as an ethical outlook that the same tools and techniques that can be used to remove toxic content could be exploited to *moderate* content that by some criterion is considered undesirable. While there is a understanding in the research community what facilitates toxic content, countries might declare certain opinions, standpoints, ideologies, or even scientific consensuses or facts to be *toxic* and make them, thus, subject to removal. This mandates particular care for the research described in this article, as well as it mandates careful weighing of freedom of speech versus content moderation, ultimately aiming at a pleasant, non-harmful experience for all people being online.

6 Conclusion and Future Work

The rise of toxic content, especially hate speech, across digital platforms has prompted a surge in research focused on its detection and mitigation. This literature review presents findings from prior studies, emphasizing the definitions, data sources, annotation guidelines, and machine learning approaches used in hate speech detection. Findings show that the present studies are mainly focused on English and mono-platform sources. Despite much research, hate speech detection in under-resourced languages, particularly regional languages, is limited. Our review shows that cross-platform and cross-lingual datasets can significantly enhance the performance and robustness of classification models. As a step toward this, we propose practical guidelines for researchers and practitioners planning to create or curate new datasets in this domain.

With the changes in platform policy and monetary demand, data collection from social media platforms such as Facebook, Instagram, and X is challenging, which limits the data collection. However, having limited datasets or dataset from less research platforms such as YouTube, Reddit we might use the existing datasets based on definitions and topics to increase the training size of dataset for machine learning models.

With the emergence of government guidelines such as the EU DSA, platforms are actively monitoring contents. They have extensive guidelines for moderation of toxic content in the platforms, which might help in mitigating toxic content.

Overall, our work serves as a foundation for future research and development efforts aimed at mitigating online toxicity in a more holistic, inclusive, and scalable manner.

Data Sharing

The papers collected in the present study will be provided on GitHub[8], allowing researchers to use it based on different criteria. GitHub repository includes detailed annotations and metadata, enabling reproducibility and further analysis across various research contexts.

References

1. Abderrouaf, C., Oussalah, M.: On online hate speech detection. effects of negated data construction. In: 2019 IEEE International Conference on Big Data (Big Data), pp. 5595–5602 (2019). https://doi.org/10.1109/BigData47090.2019.9006336

[8] https://github.com/Gautamshahi/ToxicContent

2. Aggarwal, P., Horsmann, T., Wojatzki, M., Zesch, T.: LTL-UDE at SemEval-2019 task 6: BERT and two-vote classification for categorizing offensiveness. In: Proceedings of the 13th International Workshop on Semantic Evaluation, pp. 678–682 (2019)
3. Ajvazi, A., Hardmeier, C.: A dataset of offensive language in kosovo social media. In: Proceedings of the Thirteenth Language Resources and Evaluation Conference, pp. 1860–1869 (2022)
4. Al-Hassan, A., Al-Dossari, H.: Detection of hate speech in social networks: a survey on multilingual corpus. In: 6th International Conference on Computer Science and Information Technology (2019)
5. Al Maruf, A., et al.: Hate speech detection in the Bengali language: a comprehensive survey. J. Big Data **11**(1), 97 (2024)
6. Albadi, N., Kurdi, M., Mishra, S.: Are they our brothers? Analysis and detection of religious hate speech in the arabic twittersphere. In: 2018 IEEE/ACM International Conference on Advances in Social Networks Analysis and Mining (ASONAM), pp. 69–76. IEEE (2018)
7. Alemi, F., et al.: Support for the kids online safety act (KOSA), with caution. Qual. Manag. Healthc. **32**(4), 278–280 (2023)
8. Alfina, I., Mulia, R., Fanany, M.I., Ekanata, Y.: Hate speech detection in the Indonesian language: a dataset and preliminary study. In: 2017 International Conference on Advanced Computer Science and Information Systems (ICACSIS), pp. 233–238 (2017). https://doi.org/10.1109/ICACSIS.2017.8355039
9. Arcan, H.E.: Interrupted social peace: hate speech in Turkish media. IAFOR J. Media Commun. Film **1**(1), 43–56 (2013)
10. Aslan, A.: Online hate discourse: a study on hatred speech directed against Syrian refugees on Youtube. J. Media Critiques **3**(12), 227–256 (2017)
11. Basile, V., et al.: Semeval-2019 task 5: multilingual detection of hate speech against immigrants and women in twitter. In: Proceedings of the 13th International Workshop on Semantic Evaluation, pp. 54–63 (2019)
12. Baziotis, C., Pelekis, N., Doulkeridis, C.: Datastories at semeval-2017 task 4: deep LSTM with attention for message-level and topic-based sentiment analysis. In: Proceedings of the 11th International Workshop on Semantic Evaluation (SemEval-2017), pp. 747–754. Association for Computational Linguistics, Vancouver, Canada (2017)
13. Ben-David, A., Matamoros-Fernández, A.: Hate speech and covert discrimination on social media: monitoring the Facebook pages of extreme-right political parties in Spain. Int. J. Commun. **10**, 1167–1193 (2016)
14. Benček, D., Strasheim, J.: Refugees welcome? A dataset on anti-refugee violence in Germany. Res. Polit. **3**(4), 2053168016679590 (2016)
15. Berglind, T., Pelzer, B., Kaati, L.: Levels of hate in online environments. In: Proceedings of the 2019 IEEE/ACM International Conference on Advances in Social Networks Analysis and Mining (ASONAM), pp. 842–847. Association for Computing Machinery (2019). https://doi.org/10.1145/3341161.3343521
16. Bhattacharya, S., et al.: Developing a multilingual annotated corpus of misogyny and aggression. In: Kumar, R., et al. (eds.) Proceedings of the Second Workshop on Trolling, Aggression and Cyberbullying, pp. 158–168. European Language Resources Association (ELRA), Marseille, France (2020)
17. Bodrunova, S.S., Litvinenko, A.A., Gavra, D.P., Yakunin, A.V.: Twitter-based discourse on migrants in Russia: the case of 2013 bashings in biryulyovo. Int. Rev. Manag. Mark. **6**(1), 97–104 (2015)
18. Bohra, A., Vijay, D., Singh, V., Akhtar, S.S., Shrivastava, M.: A dataset of Hindi-English code-mixed social media text for hate speech detection. In: Proceedings of the Second Workshop on Computational Modeling of People's Opinions, Personality, and Emotions in Social Media, pp. 36–41 (2018)

19. Bosco, C., Dell'Orletta, F., Poletto, F., Sanguinetti, M., Tesconi, M., et al.: Overview of the evalita 2018 hate speech detection task. In: CEUR Workshop Proceedings, vol. 2263, pp. 1–9. CEUR (2018)
20. Bretschneider, U.: Detektion von Directed Hate Speech, Online Harassment und Cyberbullying in Online Communities. Ph.D. thesis, Universitäts-und Landesbibliothek Sachsen-Anhalt (2017)
21. Bretschneider, U., Peters, R.: Detecting offensive statements towards foreigners in social media. In: Proceedings of the 50th Hawaii International Conference on System Sciences (2017)
22. Bretschneider, U., Wöhner, T., Peters, R.: Detecting online harassment in social networks. In: Proceedings of the 35th International Conference on Information Systems (ICIS) (2014)
23. Charalampakis, B., Spathis, D., Kouslis, E., Kermanidis, K.: A comparison between semi-supervised and supervised text mining techniques on detecting irony in Greek political tweets. Eng. Appl. Artif. Intell. **51**, 50–57 (2016)
24. Charitidis, P., Doropoulos, S., Vologiannidis, S., Papastergiou, I., Karakeva, S.: Towards countering hate speech against journalists on social media. Online Soc. Netw. Media **17**, 100071 (2020)
25. Chowdhury, S.A., Mubarak, H., Abdelali, A., Jung, S.G., Jansen, B.J., Salminen, J.: A multi-platform Arabic news comment dataset for offensive language detection. In: Proceedings of the International Conference on Language Resources and Evaluation (LREC'20) (2020)
26. Davidson, T., Warmsley, D., Macy, M., Weber, I.: Automated hate speech detection and the problem of offensive language. In: Proceedings of the International AAAI Conference on Web and Social Media, vol. 11, no. 1, pp. 512–515 (2017). https://doi.org/10.1609/icwsm.v11i1.14955
27. Del Vigna, F., Cimino, A., Dell'Orletta, F., Petrocchi, M., Tesconi, M.: Hate me, hate me not: hate speech detection on Facebook. In: Proceedings of the First Italian Conference on Cybersecurity (ITASEC17), Venice, Italy (2017)
28. Dey, R., Salem, F.M.: Gate-variants of gated recurrent unit (GRU) neural networks. In: 2017 IEEE 60th International Midwest Symposium on Circuits and Systems (MWSCAS), pp. 1597–1600. IEEE (2017)
29. Di Fátima, B., et al.: Hate Speech on Social Media: A Global Approach. Pontificia Universidad Católica del Ecuador (2023)
30. Diakopoulos, N., Naaman, M.: Towards quality discourse in online news comments. In: Proceedings of the ACM 2011 Conference on Computer Supported Cooperative Work, pp. 133–142 (2011)
31. Djuric, N., Zhou, J., Morris, R., Grbovic, M., Radosavljevic, V., Bhamidipati, N.: Hate speech detection with comment embeddings. In: Proceedings of the 24th International Conference on World Wide Web Companion, pp. 29–30. Association for Computing Machinery (2015). https://doi.org/10.1145/2740908.2742760
32. Döring, N., Mohseni, M.R.: Fail videos and related video comments on Youtube: a case of sexualization of women and gendered hate speech? Commun. Res. Rep. **36**(3), 254–264 (2019)
33. Döring, N., Mohseni, M.R.: Gendered hate speech in Youtube and Younow comments: results of two content analyses. SCM Stud. Commun. Media **9**(1), 62–88 (2020)
34. Fersini, E., Rosso, P., Anzovino, M., et al.: Overview of the task on automatic misogyny identification at ibereval 2018. Ibereval@ sepln **2150**, 214–228 (2018)
35. Fortuna, P., Nunes, S.: A survey on automatic detection of hate speech in text. ACM Comput. Surv. (CSUR) **51**(4), 85 (2018)

36. Fulantelli, G., Taibi, D., Scifo, L., Schwarze, V., Eimler, S.C.: Cyberbullying and cyberhate as two interlinked instances of cyber-aggression in adolescence: a systematic review. Front. Psychol. **13**, 909299 (2022)
37. Gao, L., Huang, R.: Detecting online hate speech using context aware models. In: Proceedings of the International Conference Recent Advances in Natural Language Processing, RANLP 2017, pp. 260–266 (2017)
38. Garg, T., Masud, S., Suresh, T., Chakraborty, T.: Handling bias in toxic speech detection: a survey. ACM Comput. Surv. **55**(13s), 1–32 (2023)
39. Gertner, A.S., Henderson, J., Merkhofer, E., Marsh, A., Wellner, B., Zarrella, G.: Mitre at semeval-2019 task 5: transfer learning for multilingual hate speech detection. In: Proceedings of the 13th International Workshop on Semantic Evaluation, pp. 453–459 (2019)
40. de Gibert, O., Perez, N., García-Pablos, A., Cuadros, M.: Hate speech dataset from a white supremacy forum. In: Fišer, D., Huang, R., Prabhakaran, V., Voigt, R., Waseem, Z., Wernimont, J. (eds.) Proceedings of the 2nd Workshop on Abusive Language Online (ALW2), pp. 11–20. Association for Computational Linguistics, Brussels, Belgium (2018). https://doi.org/10.18653/v1/W18-5102
41. Gibson, A.: Safe spaces & free speech: effects of moderation policy on structures of online forum discussions. In: Proceedings of the 50th Hawaii International Conference on System Sciences (2017)
42. Giglietto, F., Lee, Y.: To be or not to be Charlie: Twitter hashtags as a discourse and counter-discourse in the aftermath of the 2015 Charlie Hebdo shooting in France. In: Proceedings of the 5th Workshop on Making Sense of Microposts Co-located with the 24th International World Wide Web Conference, vol. 1395, pp. 33–37. CEUR (2015)
43. Gitari, N.D., Zuping, Z., Damien, H., Long, J.: A lexicon-based approach for hate speech detection. Int. J. Multimedia Ubiquitous Eng. **10**(4), 215–230 (2015)
44. Grigore, M., Rosenkranz, C.: Increasing the willingness to collaborate online: an analysis of sentiment-driven interactions in peer content production. In: Proceedings of the 32nd International Conference on Information Systems (ICIS 2011), Shanghai, China (2011)
45. Grigore, M., Rosenkranz, C., Sutanto, J.: The impact of sentiment-driven feedback on knowledge reuse in online communities. AIS Trans. Hum.-Comput. Interact. **7**(4), 212–232 (2015)
46. Horta Ribeiro, M., Calais, P., Santos, Y., Almeida, V., Meira Jr, W.: Characterizing and detecting hateful users on twitter. In: Proceedings of the International AAAI Conference on Web and Social Media (2018)
47. Hrdina, M.: Identity, activism and hatred: Hate speech against migrants on Facebook in the Czech Republic in 2015. Naše společnost **14**(1), 38–47 (2016)
48. Ibrohim, M.O., Budi, I.: Multi-label hate speech and abusive language detection in Indonesian twitter. In: Proceedings of the Third Workshop on Abusive Language Online, pp. 46–57 (2019)
49. Jahan, M.S., Oussalah, M.: A systematic review of hate speech automatic detection using natural language processing. Neurocomputing 126232 (2023)
50. Jha, A., Mamidi, R.: When does a compliment become sexist? Analysis and classification of ambivalent sexism using twitter data. In: Proceedings of the Second Workshop on NLP and Computational Social Science, pp. 7–16 (2017)
51. Jigsaw: Jigsaw toxic comment classification challenge (2018). https://www.kaggle.com/competitions/jigsaw-toxic-comment-classification-challenge. Kaggle Competition
52. Josey, C.S.: Hate speech and identity: an analysis of neo racism and the indexing of identity. Discourse Soc. **21**(1), 27–39 (2010)
53. Jung, A.K., Shahi, G.K., Fromm, J., Røysland, K.A., Gronert, K.H.: Multi-platform framing analysis: a case study of kristiansand quran burning. In: Disinformation in Open Online Media, pp. 101–130. Springer, Cham (2024)

54. Kennedy, B., et al.: Introducing the gab hate corpus: defining and applying hate-based rhetoric to social media posts at scale. Lang. Resour. Eval. 1–30 (2022)
55. Kiela, D., Firooz, H., Mohan, A., Goswami, V., et al.: The hateful memes challenge: detecting hate speech in multimodal memes. In: Proceedings of the 34th Conference on Neural Information Processing Systems (NeurIPS 2020) (2020)
56. Kumar, R., Reganti, A.N., Bhatia, A., Maheshwari, T.: Aggression-annotated corpus of Hindi-English code-mixed data. In: Proceedings of the Eleventh International Conference on Language Resources and Evaluation (LREC 2018) (2018)
57. Kwok, I., Wang, Y.: Locate the hate: detecting tweets against blacks. In: Twenty-Seventh AAAI Conference on Artificial Intelligence (2013)
58. Lee, J., et al.: K-MHaS: a multi-label hate speech detection dataset in Korean online news comment. In: Proceedings of the 29th International Conference on Computational Linguistics, pp. 3530–3538 (2022)
59. Leite, J.A., Silva, D., Bontcheva, K., Scarton, C.: Toxic language detection in social media for Brazilian Portuguese: new dataset and multilingual analysis. In: Wong, K.F., Knight, K., Wu, H. (eds.) Proceedings of the 1st Conference of the Asia-Pacific Chapter of the Association for Computational Linguistics and the 10th International Joint Conference on Natural Language Processing, pp. 914–924. Association for Computational Linguistics, Suzhou, China (2020). https://doi.org/10.18653/v1/2020.aacl-main.91
60. Li, L., Fan, L., Atreja, S., Hemphill, L.: "hot" chatgpt: the promise of chatgpt in detecting and discriminating hateful, offensive, and toxic comments on social media. ACM Trans. Web **18**(2), 1–36 (2024)
61. LinkedIn: Linkedin ads settings. https://www.linkedin.com/help/linkedin/answer/a1342443. Accessed 02 May 2025
62. Liu, P., Li, W., Zou, L.: NULI at semeval-2019 task 6: transfer learning for offensive language detection using bidirectional transformers. In: Proceedings of the 13th International Workshop on Semantic Evaluation, pp. 87–91 (2019)
63. Ljubešić, N., Erjavec, T., Fišer, D.: Datasets of Slovene and Croatian moderated news comments. In: Proceedings of the 2nd Workshop on Abusive Language Online (ALW2), pp. 124–131 (2018)
64. Luu, S.T., Nguyen, H.P., Van Nguyen, K., Nguyen, N.L.T.: Comparison between traditional machine learning models and neural network models for Vietnamese hate speech detection. In: 2020 RIVF International Conference on Computing and Communication Technologies (RIVF), pp. 1–6. IEEE (2020)
65. Malmasi, S., Zampieri, M.: Detecting hate speech in social media. In: Proceedings of the International Conference Recent Advances in Natural Language Processing, RANLP 2017, pp. 467–472 (2017)
66. Mandl, T., et al.: Overview of the HASOC track at fire 2020: hate speech and offensive content identification in Indo-European languages. In: CEUR Workshop Proceedings, vol. 2826, pp. 87–111. CEUR Workshop Proceedings (2020)
67. Mandl, T., et al.: Overview of the HASOC track at fire 2019: hate speech and offensive content identification in Indo-European languages. In: Proceedings of the 11th Forum for Information Retrieval Evaluation, pp. 14–17 (2019)
68. Mathur, P., Sawhney, R., Ayyar, M., Shah, R.: Did you offend me? Classification of offensive tweets in hinglish language. In: Proceedings of the 2nd Workshop on Abusive Language Online (ALW2), pp. 138–148 (2018)
69. Meta: Bullying and harassment. https://transparency.meta.com/en-gb/policies/community-standards/bullying-harassment/. Accessed 02 May 2025
70. Mubarak, H., Darwish, K., Magdy, W.: Abusive language detection on Arabic social media. In: First Workshop on Abusive Language Online 2017, pp. 52–56. Association for Computational Linguistics (ACL) (2017)

71. Mulki, H., Haddad, H., Ali, C.B., Alshabani, H.: L-HSAB: a levantine twitter dataset for hate speech and abusive language. In: Proceedings of the Third Workshop on Abusive Language Online, pp. 111–118 (2019)
72. Nandini, D., Schmid, U.: Explaining hate speech classification with model-agnostic methods. In: Koert, D., Minor, M. (eds.) Joint Proceedings of Workshops, Tutorials and Doctoral Consortium co-located with the 45th German Conference on Artificial Intelligence (KI 2022). CEUR Workshop Proceedings, vol. 3457. CEUR-WS.org, Trier, Germany (2022). https://ceur-ws.org/Vol-3457/, accepted paper from Text Mining Workshop at KI 2022
73. Nockleby, J.T.: Hate speech. In: Encyclopedia of the American Constitution, vol. 3, pp. 1277–1279 (2000)
74. Northcut, K.M.: Dark side or insight? Yik yak and culture on campus. In: 2015 IEEE International Professional Communication Conference (IPCC), pp. 1–5 (2015). https://doi.org/10.1109/IPCC.2015.7235779
75. Oak, R.: Poster: adversarial examples for hate speech classifiers. In: Proceedings of the 2019 ACM SIGSAC Conference on Computer and Communications Security, pp. 2621–2623 (2019)
76. O'reilly, T.: What is web 2.0: design patterns and business models for the next generation of software. Commun. Strat. **1** (2007)
77. Ousidhoum, N., Lin, Z., Zhang, H., Song, Y., Yeung, D.Y.: Multilingual and multi-aspect hate speech analysis. In: Proceedings of the 2019 Conference on Empirical Methods in Natural Language Processing and the 9th International Joint Conference on Natural Language Processing (EMNLP-IJCNLP), pp. 4675–4684 (2019)
78. Page, M.J., et al.: The PRISMA 2020 statement: an updated guideline for reporting systematic reviews. BMJ **372** (2021)
79. Peršak, N.: Criminalising hate crime and hate speech at EU level: extending the list of Eurocrimes under article 83(1) TFEU. Crim. Law Forum **33**(2), 85–119 (2022). https://doi.org/10.1007/s10609-022-09440-w
80. Pinterest: Community guidelines. https://policy.pinterest.com/en/community-guidelines. Accessed 02 May 2025
81. Pitenis, Z., Zampieri, M., Ranasinghe, T.: Offensive language identification in Greek. In: Proceedings of the Twelfth Language Resources and Evaluation Conference, pp. 5113–5119 (2020)
82. Poletto, F., Basile, V., Sanguinetti, M., Bosco, C., Patti, V.: Resources and benchmark corpora for hate speech detection: a systematic review. Lang. Resour. Eval. **55**, 477–523 (2021)
83. Ptaszynski, M., Pieciukiewicz, A., Dybała, P.: Results of the poleval 2019 shared task 6: first dataset and open shared task for automatic cyberbullying detection in polish twitter. In: Proceedings of the PolEval 2019 Workshop (2019)
84. Putra, I.G.M., Nurjanah, D.: Hate speech detection in Indonesian language Instagram. In: 2020 International Conference on Advanced Computer Science and Information Systems (ICACSIS), pp. 413–420. IEEE (2020)
85. Qian, J., Bethke, A., Liu, Y., Belding, E., Wang, W.Y.: A benchmark dataset for learning to intervene in online hate speech. In: Inui, K., Jiang, J., Ng, V., Wan, X. (eds.) Proceedings of the 2019 Conference on Empirical Methods in Natural Language Processing and the 9th International Joint Conference on Natural Language Processing (EMNLP-IJCNLP), pp. 4755–4764. Association for Computational Linguistics, Hong Kong, China (2019). https://doi.org/10.18653/v1/D19-1482. https://aclanthology.org/D19-1482/
86. Rangel, F., Rosso, P., Sarracén, G.L.D.L.P., Fersini, E., Chulvi, B.: Profiling hate speech spreaders on twitter task at PAN 2021. In: Faggioli, G., Ferro, N., Joly, A., Maistro, M., Piroi, F. (eds.) CLEF 2021 Labs and Workshops, Notebook Papers. CEUR-WS.org (2021)

87. Rizwan, H., Shakeel, M.H., Karim, A.: Hate-speech and offensive language detection in roman Urdu. In: Proceedings of the 2020 Conference on Empirical Methods in Natural Language Processing (EMNLP), pp. 2512–2522 (2020)
88. Röchert, D., Neubaum, G., Ross, B., Brachten, F., Stieglitz, S.: Opinion-based homogeneity on Youtube. Comput. Commun. Res. **2**(1), 81–108 (2020)
89. Romim, N., Ahmed, M., Talukder, H., Saiful Islam, M.: Hate speech detection in the Bengali language: a dataset and its baseline evaluation. In: Proceedings of International Joint Conference on Advances in Computational Intelligence: IJCACI 2020, pp. 457–468. Springer (2021)
90. Ross, B., Rist, M., Carbonell, G., Cabrera, B., Kurowsky, N., Wojatzki, M.: Measuring the reliability of hate speech annotations: the case of the European refugee crisis. In: Proceedings of NLP4CMC III: 3rd Workshop on Natural Language Processing for Computer-Mediated Communication. Bochumer Linguistische Arbeitsberichte, vol. 17, pp. 6–9. Bochum (2016)
91. Salminen, J., Hopf, M., Chowdhury, S.A., Jung, S.G., Almerekhi, H., Jansen, B.J.: Developing an online hate classifier for multiple social media platforms. Hum.-Centric Comput. Inf. Sci. **10**(1), 1 (2020)
92. Sanguinetti, M., Poletto, F., Bosco, C., Patti, V., Stranisci, M.: An Italian twitter corpus of hate speech against immigrants. In: Proceedings of the 11th Conference on Language Resources and Evaluation (LREC2018), May 2018, Miyazaki, Japan, pp. 2798–2895 (2018)
93. Shahi, G., Hummel, O.: On the effectiveness of large language models in automating categorization of scientific texts. In: Proceedings of the 27th International Conference on Enterprise Information Systems - Volume 1: ICEIS, pp. 544–554. INSTICC, SciTePress (2025). https://doi.org/10.5220/0013299100003929
94. Shahi, G., Majchrzak, T.: Hate speech detection using cross-platform social media data in English and German language. In: Proceedings of the 20th International Conference on Web Information Systems and Technologies - WEBIST, pp. 131–140. INSTICC, SciTePress (2024). https://doi.org/10.5220/0013070000003825
95. Shahi, G.K., Basyurt, A.S., Stieglitz, S., Neuberger, C.: Agenda formation and prediction of voting tendencies for European parliament election using textual, social and network features. Inf. Syst. Front. 1–19 (2024)
96. Shahi, G.K., Jaiswal, A.K., Mandl, T.: Fakeclaim: a multiple platform-driven dataset for identification of fake news on 2023 Israel-Hamas war. In: European Conference on Information Retrieval, pp. 66–74. Springer (2024)
97. Shahi, G.K., Kana Tsoplefack, W.: Mitigating harmful content on social media using an interactive user interface. In: Social Informatics: 13th International Conference, SocInfo 2022, Glasgow, UK, Proceedings, pp. 490–505. Springer (2022)
98. Shahi, G.K., Kana Tsoplefack, W.: Mitigating harmful content on social media using an interactive user interface. In: Hopfgartner, F., Jaidka, K., Mayr, P., Jose, J., Breitsohl, J. (eds.) Social Informatics, pp. 490–505. Springer, Cham (2022)
99. Shahi, G.K., Majchrzak, T.A.: Amused: an annotation framework of multimodal social media data. In: Intelligent Technologies and Applications: 4th International Conference, INTAP 2021, Grimstad, Norway, 11–13 October 2021, Revised Selected Papers, pp. 287–299. Springer (2022)
100. Shahi, G.K., Majchrzak, T.A.: An exploratory study and prevention measures of mob lynchings: a case study of India. In: Maślankowski, J., Marcinkowski, B., Rupino da Cunha, P. (eds.) Digital Transformation, pp. 103–118. Springer, Cham (2023)
101. Shahi, G.K., Mejova, Y.: Too little, too late: moderation of misinformation around the Russo-Ukrainian conflict. In: Proceedings of the 17th ACM Web Science Conference, Web-

Sci 2025. Association for Computing Machinery, New York, NY, USA (2025). https://doi.org/10.1145/3717867.3717876

102. Shahi, G.K., Tessa, B., Trujillo, A., Cresci, S.: A year of the DSA transparency database: what it (does not) reveal about platform moderation during the 2024 European parliament election. arXiv preprint arXiv:2504.06976 (2025)
103. Sharma, S., et al.: Findings of the constraint 2022 shared task on detecting the hero, the villain, and the victim in memes. In: Proceedings of the Workshop on Combating Online Hostile Posts in Regional (2022)
104. Siegel, A.A.: Online hate speech. Social media and democracy: The state of the field, prospects for reform, pp. 56–88 (2020)
105. Silva, L., Mondal, M., Correa, D., Benevenuto, F., Weber, I.: Analyzing the targets of hate in online social media. In: Proceedings of the International AAAI Conference on Web and Social Media, vol. 10, no. 1, pp. 687–690 (2016)
106. Snap Inc.: Community guidelines. https://values.snap.com/policy/policy-community-guidelines. Accessed 02 May 2025
107. Sprugnoli, R., Menini, S., Tonelli, S., Oncini, F., Piras, E.: Creating a whatsapp dataset to study pre-teen cyberbullying. In: Proceedings of the 2nd Workshop on Abusive Language Online (ALW2), pp. 51–59 (2018)
108. Stieglitz, S., Basyurt, A.S., Mirbabaie, M.: Smart-portal: a data tracking tool for research purposes from social media and news websites. In: HICSS, pp. 1–10 (2022)
109. Stoll, A., Ziegele, M., Quiring, O.: Detecting incivility and impoliteness in online discussions. Comput. Commun. Res. **2**(1), 109–134 (2020)
110. TikTok: Community guidelines. https://www.tiktok.com/community-guidelines. Accessed 02 May 2025
111. UK Parliament: Online safety act 2023 (2023). https://www.legislation.gov.uk/ukpga/2023/50/enacted. Accessed 02 May 2025
112. Vidgen, B., Derczynski, L.: Directions in abusive language training data, a systematic review: garbage in, garbage out. PLoS ONE **15**(12), e0243300 (2020)
113. Vidra, Z., Fox, J.: The rise of the extreme right in Hungary and the Roma question: the radicalization of media discourse. Technical Report 2012/13, European University Institute (2012), funded by the European Commission under the Seventh Framework Programme (FP7/2007-2013), Grant Agreement no: 243837
114. Wang, W., Chen, L., Thirunarayan, K., Sheth, A.P.: Harnessing twitter "big data" for automatic emotion identification. In: 2012 International Conference on Privacy, Security, Risk and Trust and 2012 International Conference on Social Computing, pp. 587–592 (2012). https://doi.org/10.1109/SocialCom-PASSAT.2012.119
115. Waseem, Z.: Are you a racist or am i seeing things? Annotator influence on hate speech detection on twitter. In: Proceedings of the First Workshop on NLP and Computational Social Science, pp. 138–142 (2016)
116. Waseem, Z., Hovy, D.: Hateful symbols or hateful people? Predictive features for hate speech detection on twitter. In: Proceedings of the NAACL Student Research Workshop, pp. 88–93 (2016)
117. Wei, X., Lin, H., Yang, L., Yu, Y.: A convolution-LSTM-based deep neural network for cross-domain MOOC forum post classification. Information **8**(3), 92 (2017)
118. Wulczyn, E., Thain, N., Dixon, L.: Ex machina: personal attacks seen at scale. In: Proceedings of the 26th International Conference on World Wide Web, pp. 1391–1399 (2017)
119. X: Abuse and harassment. https://help.x.com/en/rules-and-policies/abusive-behavior. Accessed 02 May 2025
120. Yardi, S., Boyd, D.: Dynamic debates: an analysis of group polarization over time on twitter. Bull. Sci. Technol. Soc. **30**(5), 316–327 (2010). https://doi.org/10.1177/0270467610380011

121. YouTube: Youtube's community guidelines. https://support.google.com/youtube/answer/9288567. Accessed 02 May 2025
122. Yuan, L., Wang, T., Ferraro, G., Suominen, H., Rizoiu, M.A.: Transfer learning for hate speech detection in social media. J. Comput. Soc. Sci. **6**(2), 1081–1101 (2023)
123. Zampieri, M., Malmasi, S., Nakov, P., Rosenthal, S., Farra, N., Kumar, R.: Semeval-2019 task 6: identifying and categorizing offensive language in social media (offenseval). In: Proceedings of the 13th International Workshop on Semantic Evaluation, pp. 75–86 (2019)
124. Zhang, J., Wu, Q., Xu, Y., Cao, C., Du, Z., Psounis, K.: Efficient toxic content detection by bootstrapping and distilling large language models. In: Proceedings of the AAAI Conference on Artificial Intelligence, vol. 38, no. 19, pp. 21779–21787 (2024)
125. Zhang, Z., Robinson, D., Tepper, J.: Detecting hate speech on twitter using a convolution-GRU based deep neural network. In: The Semantic Web: 15th International Conference, ESWC 2018, Heraklion, Crete, Greece, 3–7 June 2018, Proceedings. Lecture Notes in Computer Science, vol. 10843, pp. 745–760. Springer (2018). https://doi.org/10.1007/978-3-319-93417-4_48
126. Zueva, N., Kabirova, M., Kalaidin, P.: Reducing unintended identity bias in Russian hate speech detection. In: Proceedings of the Fourth Workshop on Online Abuse and Harms, pp. 65–69 (2020)

HCI in Mobile Systems and Web Interfaces

On the Measurement of Learner Experience in Online Tutorials

Martin Schrepp[1(✉)], Harry Budi Santoso[2], and Jörg Thomaschewski[3]

[1] SAP SE, Hasso-Plattner-Ring 7, 69190 Walldorf, Germany
martin.schrepp@sap.com

[2] Fakultas Ilmu Komputer, Universitas Indonesia, Depok, Indonesia
harrybs@cs.ui.ac.id

[3] University of Applied Sciences Emden/Leer, Emden, Germany
joerg.thomaschewski@hs-emden-leer.de

Abstract. Online tutorials are effective tools to enable knowledge transfer and learning. They can be easily shared with a large audience by embedding links on websites or uploads to video platforms. In commercial settings, tutorials can help to manage service demands, serve as a substitute for product documentation, or enable customers to explore more complex products over free trials. In educational settings, online tutorials can efficiently support knowledge transfer and learning by providing accessible, interactive, and engaging resources for students to learn at their own pace. But to reach these goals tutorials must meet the demands of learners. Therefore, it is crucial to be able to assess learner satisfaction with a tutorial, especially in commercial settings. We describe in this paper first steps to define a modular framework to efficiently set up questionnaires that measure learner satisfaction with several types of tutorials. As a result of two studies we present first suggestions on how to measure learner experience for two types of tutorials.

Keywords: Online tutorials · Learner experience · Measurement · Modular questionnaire · User Experience (UX)

1 Introduction

Online tutorials are an efficient and attractive method of knowledge transfer. It is easy and cost effective to make them available to large audiences by placing links on websites or uploading the tutorial to video platforms. For this reason, online tutorials are frequently used [20].

Manufactures of technical devices often use tutorials to explain how to operate, maintain or even repair the device. For example, how to operate a remote control of a TV or how to change the SIM card of a smartphone. Software providers use online tutorials to help customers to get started with their products or to explain how to fix typical issues. Tutorials are also frequently used in educational settings. A classical example are the tutorials concerning web development that are offered on platforms like SelfHTML. Such tutorials support skill acquisition by providing interactive and

M. Marchiori et al. (Eds.): WEBIST 2024, LNBIP 583, pp. 343–359, 2026.
https://doi.org/10.1007/978-3-032-25534-1_16

engaging resources that enable students in schools or universities to learn at their own pace and convenience.

The use of online tutorials for learning is, for example, investigated in a handbook edited by Mayer [19] and a study conducted by Mautone and Mayer [18]. Using tutorials in websites or applications is relevant for one of the usability components (i.e., learnability) [23] and can enhance the user experience by following a human-centered design approach [11].

What exactly do we mean by the term "tutorial"? Unfortunately, this term is used differently in various contexts. In this paper, we define a tutorial as instructional materials that teach learners specific skills or explains how to perform specific tasks with products in a sequence of steps, without the assistance of an instructor or the ability to ask questions in a community. Larger online courses covering general topics or concepts, as well as pure documentation, are not considered tutorials in this paper, although distinguishing such approaches from tutorials in our sense can sometimes be challenging. We do not restrict our discussion to a certain presentation technology. Thus, video tutorials, step-by-step explanations in a web-page (which are often supported by illustrations or even interactive elements to try out certain aspects) or other mechanisms are all in scope.

Similar to the concept of user experience different learners will have different opinions about the quality of a tutorial [29]. Thus, learner experience is a purely subjective impression. To get a clear picture on this perception of learners requires thus to gather feedback from larger samples. This makes surveys a promising tool for this purpose. Such surveys can be placed at the end of a tutorial or triggered when a learner reaches a certain point in the tutorial.

Online tutorials have a variety of interesting use cases. However, a tutorial can only be successful if it meets the expectations and needs of the learners. Thus, tutorials must be well-designed, engaging, and easy to understand. If this is not the case, then a tutorial may even have a negative impact on learner satisfaction. This is especially problematic in commercial contexts, since bad tutorials can negatively impact the market success and business goals for a product.

Certain detailed quality aspects of tutorials are discussed in research papers. If the step-by-step explanations in a tutorial does not work as expected learners are quickly lost and frustrated [21]. Such a mismatch between explanation and real behavior in a product can result, for example, from missing or poorly written instructions, or the fact that the tutorial is simply outdated. Especially for longer tutorials it is important that they are interesting and motivating to follow. This can be supported by using different presentation techniques, for examples videos, interactive diagrams, or executable code snippets [8]. Tutorials should consider learners' prior knowledge and should clearly state what knowledge level they require [13]. Practice, interactive exercises and sufficient feedback also helps learners to follow interactive tutorials [13]. In addition, the length of a tutorial [15] plays an important role. Long and complex tutorials can cause a high cognitive load to learners. It usually makes sense to split long tutorial into several less complex and shorter parts [32].

Our goal is to construct items and scales that can be used to measure learner experience for tutorials. However, tutorials can have quite divers application areas, goals or complexity. Thus, it is questionable if a single questionnaire will work for all types of tutorials. Thus, we follow a modular approach. Our goal is to define several scales that measure single aspects of learner experience and that can be combined to meet the needs of different tutorial types. This idea is similar to the basic idea of the UEQ+ [27], which is a modular framework for the construction of UX questionnaires.

A first questionnaire to measure learner experience for simple tutorials that explain with a step-by-step description how to perform tasks in applications was described in a study conducted by Schrepp and Santoso [30]. This paper extends these results by presenting a second study concerning learner experience for tutorials that have a more educational character and introduce some conceptual information to learners. Results of the second study clearly show that the type of tutorial has, as expected, some impact on the scales and items that should be used for the measurement of learner experience.

2 Application Scenarios for Online Tutorials

In this section we will investigate some typical application scenarios of online tutorials in more detail.

Providing online tutorials offers several benefits for companies. The availability of such tutorials empowers customers to troubleshoot many issues with products on their own, and this will naturally reduce calls to customer support [10]. Thus, providing suitable online tutorials can save resources and costs. If tutorials for the most frequent issues with a product are available, this can have a massive impact.

Tutorials are also a highly cost-efficient way to train customers on how to use a product [20] and this can increase customer satisfaction and loyalty. For example, the Microsoft support page contains a huge number of short and engaging tutorials (in most cases a short video accompanied with a step-by-step textual description) that demonstrate features of Microsoft Office products.

However, tutorials must be well-designed to be successful in such use cases to reach the goals associated with their production. A tutorial that misses customer expectations and needs can cause quite negative emotions towards a product or vendor. As a consequence, a bad learner experience in a tutorial can negatively impact the willingness to use or purchase a product [1,33]. For example, in a study concerning mobile online games tutorial quality had an impact to user adoption [34].

Well-designed tutorials provide learners with easy to follow step-by-step instructions. They use visual aids such as videos, images, and interactive elements to illustrate the content. Such tutorials can provide the feeling of an active participation in the learning process and also provide interactive feedback to the learning success. Thus, well-designed online tutorials are often more attractive than traditional documentation. But such tutorials are often hard to adjust to changes, for example if they contain videos, and have thus a higher risk to be outdated. Tutorials can also be perceived by users as disruptive and are often skipped and forgotten [16].

Many commercial software providers offer free cloud-based demo systems or time-limited free downloads to support sales. For more complex products, for example business software packages or development tools, granting free access may not be sufficient, since users need some deeper understanding to fully explore the capabilities of the product. Tutorials can be used to address this issue and showcasing the product's potential functionalities. Tutorials serve in this use case as a valuable marketing tool. A prominent example are cloud platforms, for example *Amazon Web Services*, *IBM Cloud Platform*, *Microsoft Azure* or *SAP Business Technology Platform*. These platforms offer web developers free trial accounts and support learning by many tutorials that help to explore product features. Since users decide based on such explorations if the cloud platform is a suitable choice for their projects the quality of these tutorials is very important for product success.

Some studies examine the evaluation of tutorial quality in certain domains using surveys with some ad hoc formulated questions, for example, a research conducted by Brill and Park explores the role of just-in-time online tutorials in supporting university stakeholders for learning and skill development [2]. Of course, tutorials differ massively concerning their use cases and complexity. Thus, we can not expect that a single questionnaire will be sufficient to accurately measure learner experience for all types of tutorials. The goal of our research is to develop a framework that contains some standardized scales that can be combined to create questionnaires for different tutorials and some recommendations which scales should be used for each type of tutorial.

From the use cases described above we can derive one basic requirement concerning questionnaires that measure tutorial quality. Tutorials are often rather short, since complex topics are usually split into several shorter tutorials. Thus, the time spent to provide feedback on learner experience must be somehow proportional to the duration of the tutorial. In addition, tutorials are typically only visited once. Thus, learners expect no benefit from giving feedback. This is different to UX feedback for products that are used frequently, since in this case users expect that their feedback contributes to product improvements in the near future. Therefore, the motivation to provide feedback to a tutorial will be lower than filling out a traditional UX questionnaire for a product.

For these reasons, questionnaires measuring learner experience must be short to avoid high dropout rates [31]. Long questionnaires will reduce the number of completed questionnaires and will impact a massive bias, since mainly very satisfied or dissatisfied learners will be sufficiently motivated to submit feedback. Thus, with respect to the creation of the intended framework, we need to make sure that the provided scales contain not too many items.

3 Construction of Candidate Items

As a first step of the construction of a measurement framework we create a set of candidate items for a tutorial questionnaire. These candidate items represent typical quality aspects of tutorials. We will reduce these candidates items by some empirical studies to suitable subsets that represent scales of the new questionnaire.

This is an established procedure to construct UX questionnaires [29] that is, for example, used to develop well-known instruments like SUMI [14], AttrakDiff2 [7], UEQ [17] or VISAWI [22]. The overall process looks like this:

1. Select a large set of potential items in a common format that represent positive aspects of tutorial quality.

2. Collect data sets from several studies. Per study a larger sample of participants rate several tutorials with all potential items.
3. Get deeper insights in the structure of the collected data by principal components analysis (PCA) [9,25]. This analysis will determine the number of components required to explain the variance in the data sufficiently.
4. Choose the most relevant components as scales and per scale determine the items with the highest loadings on the underlying component as items for the questionnaire.

As a first step in the identification of potential items existing research papers that deal with learner experience were analyzed.

There are several free resources that explain how to create successful tutorials. Several blog posts or even "tutorials on how to write a good software tutorial" are available in the web. We did an extensive research for such resources. We collected quality aspects of "good" tutorials and condensed them into statements (in English). The list of statements was reviewed, potential duplicates were removed and the remaining statements were aligned concerning their formulations. This resulted in the following list of candidate items:

- Q1: The content of the tutorial fits my needs.
- Q2: The tutorial contains only relevant information.
- Q3: I am satisfied with the duration of the tutorial.
- Q4: In my opinion the tutorial is well-structured.
- Q5: The content of the tutorial is easy to understand.
- Q6: The duration and preconditions of the tutorial are as expected.
- Q7: It is interesting to work through the tutorial.
- Q8: The tutorial motivates me to learn more about this topic.
- Q9: The language used in the tutorial is simple and free of jargon.
- Q10: Technical terms are adequately explained.
- Q11: The tutorial is divided into manageable steps that form a logical sequence.
- Q12: It is clearly stated at the beginning of the tutorial what learners will achieve.
- Q13: The tutorial includes practical examples and demonstrations.
- Q14: Visuals like images, diagrams, and videos are used to explain complex concepts.
- Q15: The content of the tutorial is up to date.
- Q16: The tutorial explains not just how to do something, but why it's done that way.
- Q17: All steps in the tutorial worked exactly as described.
- Q18: Required prerequisites for the tutorial are explained at the start of the tutorial.
- Q19: The tutorial is easy to follow.
- Q20: The examples given in the tutorial are practically relevant.
- Q21: The tutorial covers all the features I am interested in.
- Q22: The pace of the tutorial is appropriate.

4 The First Study: Indonesian Learners' Experience with Seven Online Tutorials

The first study was done with Indonesian participants. Therefore, the candidate items were carefully translated into Indonesian language. Translations were reviewed independently by several native speakers and some adjustments were performed in an iterative process until an agreed translation was reached. The translated items can be found in the Appendix.

4.1 Participants

As participants we recruited undergraduate students from various faculties of science and engineering. Participants came from a number of universities spread across several provinces in Indonesia including Jakarta, West Java, and Bengkulu. Around 300 participants were contacted over email and 117 (61 male, 55 female, 1 unknown, average age: 21.23 years, standard deviation 3.97 years) responded and filled out the questionnaire. Participation in the study was entirely voluntary.

4.2 Rated Tutorials

The participants could select one of seven different tutorials. All tutorials represent simple step-by-step explanations that describe how to perform some important tasks in popular applications. Thus, all tutorials fall into a special class of tutorials. This restriction was done intentionally to concentrate first on the simplest class of tutorials. Tutorials for the following applications were presented:

- *SATUSEHAT:* A mobile application that provides comprehensive health services and information, ensuring a continuum of care for Indonesia's citizens.
- *DJP Online:* A service managed by Indonesia's Directorate General of Taxation (Direktorat Jenderal Pajak Republik Indonesia), offering a range of tax-related applications and services for tax filers.
- *Shopee:* A well-known e-commerce platform in Indonesia, where shoppers can conveniently find a wide range of products, including clothes, electronics and other products. This platform can be accessed both as a website and a mobile app.
- *Gojek:* An app providing a range of on-demand services including transportation and food delivery, where tutorials on how to use Gojek are generally accessible. The products of Gojek consist of transport and logistics, payments, food and shopping as well as business.
- *Bukalapak:* Another widely used e-commerce platform in Indonesia, allowing users to purchase or sell both new and second-hand items via this application. Anyone in Indonesia has the opportunity to sell their products on Bukalapak by establishing an economical online storefront, which accommodates both single item and wholesale shopping systems.
- *Tokopedia:* A digital shopping application providing a wide range of products from various categories, with extensive Tokopedia instruction guides readily accessible. Tokopedia's online marketplace delivers products through various channels.

- *Traveloka:* A platform designed for booking flights, hotels, buses and travels, train tickets and other services. Traveloka offers comprehensive tutorials to assist users in planning their trips more effectively.

The corresponding products are very popular among the target group and we could therefore assume that the students we contacted knew at least one of these products and had watched a corresponding tutorial.

4.3 Survey

The participants receive an email that contains a short motivational text and a link to open the survey. The survey starts with a short instruction, followed by two questions concerning age and gender of the participant. Below these fields the participants could select the tutorial they want to rate from a selection field showing all the 7 alternatives. Below this selection the 22 candidate items were shown. Each item had a 7-point response scale with the endpoints *Fully Disagree* and *Fully Agree*. After the last item a button to submit the response was shown. The survey can be completed within five to ten minutes.

4.4 Analysis of the Data

To get a closer picture concerning the structure of the data we applied a Principal Component Analysis (PCA) with varimax rotation. Figure 1 shows the eigenvalues of the potential components. Higher eigenvalues (they are shown in order from largest to smallest) indicate a higher predictive value of a component.

Accordingly, to the scree-test [3] (determine the point after which eigenvalues differ only slightly) two components could be identified. The Kaiser-Gutmann criterion [6] (remove components with eigenvalues smaller than one) would in this case provide the same result.

These two components represent 73% of the variance in the data. A commonly used decision rule is to retain enough components to explain more than 70% of the variance in the data [12]. Thus, our two component solution seems to be a reasonable choice.

To create a semantic interpretation we analyze the items with the highest loadings on each component (see Table 1). A common heuristic considers component loadings greater than 0.4 as generally acceptable, see [4]. The loadings of the items that are in the following selected to semantically represent a component are all above 0.7, and can be thus considered as good representations.

The four items with the highest loading on the first component and low loadings on the second component were Q4, Q5, Q11 and Q19. These items are shown below (we show the English version):

- In my opinion the tutorial is well-structured.
- The content of the tutorial is easy to understand.
- The tutorial is divided into manageable steps that form a logical sequence.
- The tutorial is easy to follow.

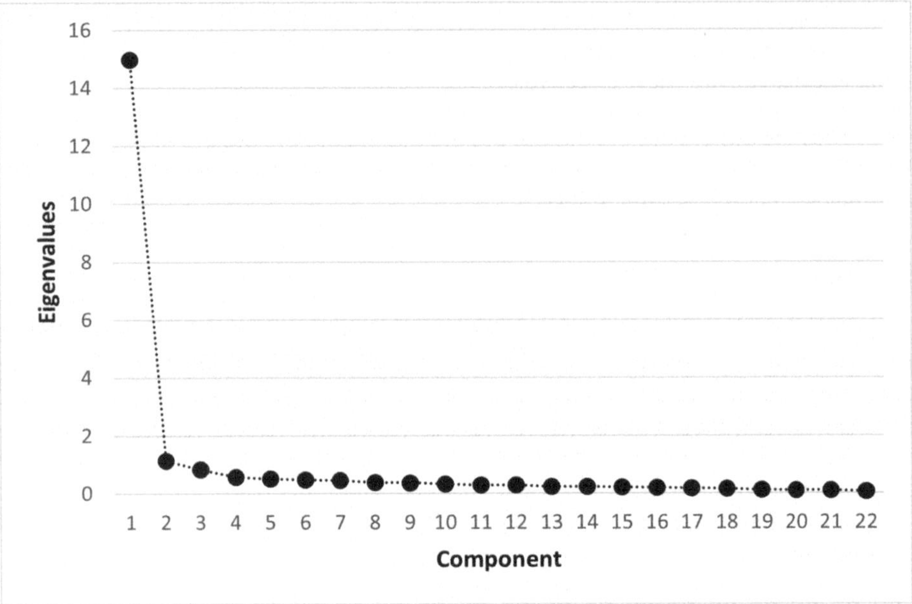

Fig. 1. Scree plot of the eigenvalues for the first study as already described in [30].

The common meaning of these items is that a tutorial is well-structured in a logical sequence that is easy to follow and understand. We name this scale therefore *Structural Clarity*.

The items with the highest loadings on the second component and low loadings on the first component are Q12, Q13, Q16, and Q18. These items are shown below:

- It is clearly stated at the beginning of the tutorial what learners will achieve.
- The tutorial includes practical examples and demonstrations.
- The tutorial explains not just how to do something, but why it's done that way.
- Required prerequisites for the tutorial are explained at the start of the tutorial.

These items refer to the way the tutorial communicates the underlying learning goals, prerequisites, and concepts and how they can be applied to practice. Thus, they describe that the tutorial makes its purpose transparent to the learner. Therefore, we call this scale *Transparency*.

Table 1. Loadings of the items to the components in Study 1 as already described in [30].

Item	Component 1	Component 2
Q1	0.771	0.331
Q2	0.750	0.319
Q3	0.762	0.421
Q4	0.821	0.345
Q5	0.872	0.280
Q6	0.752	0.428
Q7	0.636	0.518
Q8	0.457	0.589
Q9	0.560	0.517
Q10	0.686	0.606
Q11	0.816	0.410
Q12	0.457	0.702
Q13	0.301	0.853
Q14	0.608	0.529
Q15	0.586	0.594
Q16	0.297	0.801
Q17	0.594	0.658
Q18	0.280	0.796
Q19	0.793	0.451
Q20	0.630	0.633
Q21	0.622	0.531
Q22	0.558	0.636

5 The Second Study: German Learners' Experience with Six Online Tutorials

The second study was performed with German participants. Again the items were carefully translated to German language following the same process as used for the Indonesian translation. The translated items can be found in the Appendix.

5.1 Participants

As participants we recruited 46 students (21 male, 24 female, 1 no answer, average age 31 years with a standard deviation of 6.7 years) of the University Emden/Leer. All students participated in an informatics course and received some course credits for their participation. Each student rated two tutorials, thus we have 92 completed surveys.

5.2 Rated Tutorials

The participants could select one of six tutorials. For the second study a different type of tutorials was selected. The offered tutorials explain more complex concepts or usage scenarios. The intention of these tutorials is not just to show how something works in a step-by-step guidance, but to explain concepts or ideas. The following tutorials were available:

- *Microsoft Co-Pilot*: A short tutorial that explains typical use cases of Microsoft Co-Pilot. The usage of Co-Pilot for email creation and planning of meetings are explained.
- *Prompt Engineering*: A video tutorial that explains how to create effective prompts that get the best results from ChatGPT or other chatbots.
- *MKDOCS*: A longer video tutorial that explains how the material theme of MkDocs (a documentation framework for software projects) can be used to efficiently create and publish documentation.
- *Balsamic*: A video tutorial that demonstrate how Balsamic (a tool to create UI mock-ups) can be used to efficiently create wireframes. The tutorial explains possibilities and limitations of the tool.
- *Descriptive Statistics*: A video tutorial that gives a short introduction into basic concepts of descriptive statistics. It explains the definition and interpretation of mean, median and standard deviation.
- *PhD Project*: A video that explains in a funny format typical phases of a dissertation project. The goal is to inform potential PhD candidates on the long time development and typical hurdles of such a long running project.

5.3 Survey

The participants were recruited from an informatics course. The survey was available inside the learning platform used to share course materials and information. The corresponding area contained a short instruction and links to all 6 tutorials. Participants were instructed to open a tutorial and to complete it. Afterwards they could directly open the survey by a link that was also contained in the learning platform. The structure of the survey was identical to the survey used for Study 1, of course with a bit a different introduction due to the different type of tutorials and using German language. Participants were instructed to rate two of the six offered tutorials.

5.4 Analysis of the Data

Again we used PCA with varimax rotation to analyse the structure of the data. Figure 2 shows the eigenvalues of the extracted components.

The Kaiser-Gutmann criterion suggests a solution with 5 components. The interpretation of the scree-test would allow solutions with 4 or 5 components.

After a closer look into the loadings of the items we decided for a 5 component solution, since it allows a more convincing interpretation. These five components represent 68,5% of the variance in the data. Thus, the fit of the solution is not as good as

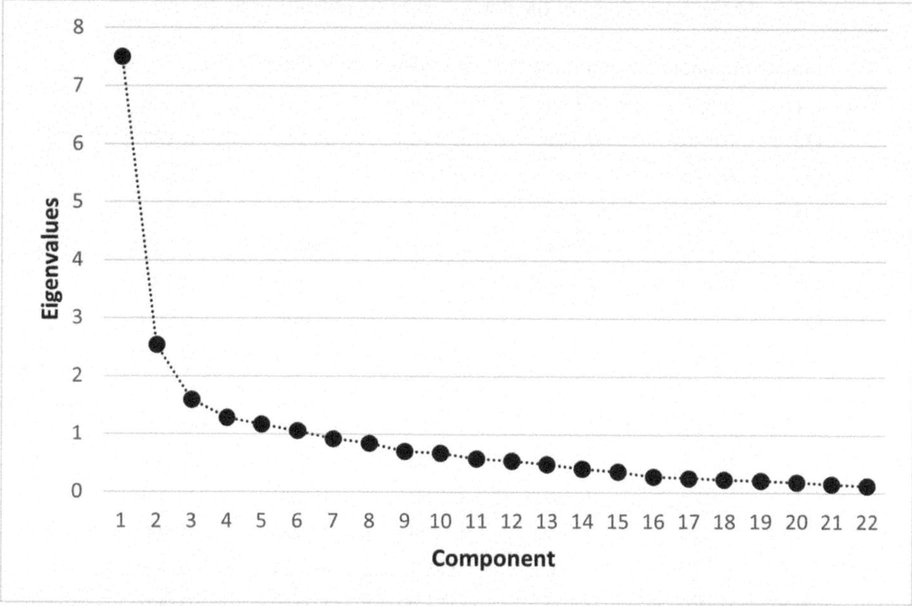

Fig. 2. Scree plot of the eigenvalues for the second study.

in the first study, but still close enough to the usual 70% border to be considered as reasonable. The loadings of the items on the 5 components are shown in Table 2.

To interpret the semantic meaning of the components we again determine the items that load highest on a component and low on other components.

For Component 1 we select Q3, Q4 and Q11:

- I am satisfied with the duration of the tutorial.
- In my opinion the tutorial is well-structured.
- The tutorial is divided into manageable steps that form a logical sequence.

This is semantically similar to the first component from Study 1. Thus, we refer to this component as *Structural Clarity*.

For Component 2 we select Q7 and Q8:

- It is interesting to work through the tutorial.
- The tutorial motivates me to learn more about this topic.

These items both focus on the motivational aspects of the tutorial. We name the component *Stimulation*.

For Component 3 we select Q5, Q9 and Q19:

- The content of the tutorial is easy to understand.
- The language used in the tutorial is simple and free of jargon.
- The tutorial is easy to follow.

Table 2. Loadings of the items to the components in Study 2.

Item	Component 1	Component 2	Component 3	Component 4	Component 5
Q1	0.559	0.605	0.186	0.135	0.000
Q2	0.630	0.344	0.399	0.122	0.127
Q3	0.686	0.142	0.160	0.190	0.000
Q4	0.733	0.224	0.128	0.000	0.372
Q5	0.172	0.257	0.771	0.000	0.345
Q6	0.561	0.307	0.417	0.000	0.377
Q7	0.366	0.724	0.247	0.000	0.000
Q8	0.151	0.850	0.141	0.177	0.000
Q9	0.000	0.000	0.753	0.000	0.318
Q10	0.322	0.214	0.371	0.268	0.368
Q11	0.670	0.113	0.000	0.000	0.431
Q12	0.285	0.000	0.200	0.000	0.674
Q13	0.000	−0.146	0.000	0.804	0.000
Q14	0.212	0.140	0.294	0.718	−0.190
Q15	0.106	0.495	−0.170	0.672	0.000
Q16	0.101	0.458	0.000	0.177	0.681
Q17	0.000	0.433	0.199	0.328	0.437
Q18	0.156	0.000	0.305	−0.141	0.723
Q19	0.337	0.139	0.799	0.142	0.000
Q20	0.155	0.345	0.000	0.774	0.227
Q21	0.489	0.395	−0.172	0.465	0.109
Q22	0.659	0.000	0.281	0.146	0.134

These three items all refer to the fact that the content is well-prepared and easy to understand. We name this component therefore *Understandability*.
For Component 4 we select Q13, Q14 and Q20:

- The tutorial includes practical examples and demonstrations.
- Visuals like images, diagrams, and videos are used to explain complex concepts.
- The examples given in the tutorial are practically relevant.

These items refer the quality and relevance of examples and illustrations. We name the component *Content Quality*.
For Component 5 we select Q12, Q16 and Q18:

- It is clearly stated at the beginning of the tutorial what learners will achieve.
- The tutorial explains not just how to do something, but why it's done that way.
- Required prerequisites for the tutorial are explained at the start of the tutorial.

This is highly similar to second component from the first study and we thus name this component *Transparency*.

Two of the components are similar to the two extracted components of the first study. The other three components were not visible in the first study. This can be easily explained by the differences of the rated tutorials. The first study contained only tutorials that represent simple step-by-step explanations (click-through) that describe how to perform tasks in popular applications. Aspects like *Stimulation*, *Content Quality* and *Understandability* obviously play no role for such tutorials. The tutorial just explains click by click what must be done to perform a task and that is all the learner is interested in. Thus, there are no concepts to understand, the user is only interested how to do something and there is not motivational aspect and since the content is simply a sequence of steps, there is no additional material required.

6 Potential Scales for Tutorial Questionnaires

In our two studies we investigated two types of tutorials. The results showed that different aspects are important to explain the structure of the data in the two studies.

As mentioned above, it is important that a questionnaire that tries to measure learner experience in tutorials is short, since the willingness to provide feedback will be relatively low. Therefore, we select two items per scale. Based on our results we propose the following scales and items:

- *Structural Clarity*: Items Q4 and Q11.
- *Transparency*: Items Q12 and Q18.
- *Stimulation*: Items Q7 and Q8.
- *Content Quality*: Items Q13 and Q14.
- *Understandability*: Items Q5 and Q9.

The items can be answered on a 7-point response scale with the endpoints *Fully disagree* and *Fully agree*. The responses are scored from -3 (Fully disagree) to +3 (Fully agree). Per scale the mean over all items in the scale and all participants that filled the questionnaire is reported as scale score. In addition, an overall score that represents the overall satisfaction with the tutorial is calculated as mean over all items used in a study and all participants.

Table 3 shows the Cronbach-Alpha [5] values for the scales in both studies. This coefficient represents the reliability of scales. Often scores above 0.7 are interpreted as a sign of sufficient reliability [24], but such rules of thumb are not really supported by statistical arguments and smaller values can be accepted for UX questionnaires [28]. Overall, the Alpha scores for our scales are all above or at least close to the 0.7 border, so reliability seems to be not a problem.

As described in the introduction our approach is modular. Thus, for different types of tutorials different combinations of scales should be used. Our results indicate that for simple tutorials that explain just the steps required to complete a task in an application only the two scales *Structural Clarity* and *Transparency* should be used. Thus, such a survey would only consist of 4 items. For tutorials that explain concepts all five scales described above are important. A survey for such a tutorial would thus contain 10 items.

Table 3. Cronbach-Alpha values for the scales in both studies.

Scale	Study 1	Study 2
Structural Clarity	0.87	0.86
Transparency	0.83	0.67
Stimulation	0.86	0.86
Content Quality	0.79	0.64
Understandability	0.79	0.80

7 Summary

Based on an extensive research for relevant quality aspects and two empirical studies we described a first version of a modular framework that can be used to define questionnaires to measure learner experience in tutorials. We have described 5 scales that represent different aspects of learner experience. These scales can be combined to form questionnaires adapted to the tutorial that should be investigated.

For two types of tutorials we can already propose which scales should be used for their measurement.

Of course, this is just a first step. There are many different types of tutorials available and more studies are required to clarify which scales are required and which of the already available scales should be used. In addition, the already constructed scales need of course further validations in more studies.

Participants in both studies are students, thus younger persons with a high educational level. Another open issue that must be further investigated is if the items are easy to understand by participants from different age groups and with different educational backgrounds. More specifically, students' knowledge and skills in using information technology may influence their ability to engage with online applications, including online tutorials. Science, Technology, Engineering, and Mathematics (STEM) students, in particular, may have more relevant expertise in this area.

Another point that requires further research is the impact of cultural differences on the expectations of learners. We already addressed this by doing research in Germany and Indonesia. For UX quality aspects it is known that the cultural background of users has only a small impact on their subjective importance [26]. Thus, it is unlikely that this is much different for quality aspects of tutorials.

The presented results are a promising starting point for the creation of a modular framework that can be used to measure learner experience in many different usage domains of tutorials.

Appendix

Indonesian Translation

The following list shows the translations for the English items into Indonesian language. These translations were used for data collection in Study 1.

- Q1: Materi tutorial sesuai dengan kebutuhan saya.
- Q2: Tutorial hanya memuat informasi yang relevan.
- Q3: Saya puas dengan durasi tutorial.
- Q4: Tutorial telah disusun dengan baik.
- Q5: Materi tutorial mudah dipahami.
- Q6: Durasi dan prasyarat yang diperlukan sesuai ekspektasi.
- Q7: Tutorial menarik untuk diikuti.
- Q8: Tutorial memotivasi saya untuk mempelajari lebih banyak hal/materi mengenai topik ini.
- Q9: Bahasa yang digunakan dalam tutorial sederhana dan bebas dari jargon.
- Q10: Istilah teknis dijelaskan dengan cukup memadai.
- Q11: Tutorial disusun dengan tahapan yang logis.
- Q12: Apa yang akan dicapai pengguna aplikasi disampaikan secara jelas di awal tutorial.
- Q13: Tutorial memuat contoh-contoh penerapan dan demonstrasi.
- Q14: Visualisasi seperti gambar, diagram, dan video digunakan untuk menjelaskan konsep yang kompleks.
- Q15: Tutorial memuat konten terkini.
- Q16: Tutorial menjelaskan 'bagaimana' dan 'mengapa' sesuatu perlu dilakukan.
- Q17: Semua tahapan dalam tutorial berjalan sebagaimana yang dijelaskan.
- Q18: Prasyarat yang diperlukan untuk tutorial dijelaskan di awal tutorial.
- Q19: Tutorial mudah diikuti.
- Q20: Contoh-contoh yang diberikan dalam tutorial bersifat praktis dan relevan.
- Q21: Tutorial mencakup semua fitur yang menarik bagi saya.
- Q22: Tutorial dijelaskan dengan tempo yang sesuai.

German Translation

The following list shows the translations for the English items into German language. These translations were used for data collection in Study 2.

- Q1: Der Inhalt des Tutorials entspricht meinen Bedürfnissen.
- Q2: Das Tutorial enthält nur relevante Informationen.
- Q3: Ich bin mit der Länge des Tutorials zufrieden.
- Q4: Meiner Meinung nach ist das Tutorial gut strukturiert.
- Q5: Der Inhalt des Tutorials ist leicht zu verstehen.
- Q6: Beschriebene Dauer und Voraussetzungen des Tutorials entsprechen den Erwartungen.
- Q7: Es ist interessant, das Tutorial durchzuarbeiten.
- Q8: Das Tutorial motiviert mich, mehr über dieses Thema zu lernen.
- Q9: Die im Tutorial verwendete Sprache ist einfach und frei von speziellen Fachbegriffen.
- Q10: Technische Begriffe werden angemessen erklärt.
- Q11: Das Tutorial ist in überschaubare Schritte unterteilt, die eine logische Reihenfolge bilden.

- Q12: Zu Beginn des Tutorials wird deutlich angegeben, was die Lernenden erreichen werden.
- Q13: Das Tutorial enthält praktische Beispiele und Demonstrationen.
- Q14: Visuelle Hilfsmittel wie Bilder, Diagramme und Videos werden verwendet, um komplexe Konzepte zu erklären.
- Q15: Der Inhalt des Tutorials ist aktuell.
- Q16: Das Tutorial erklärt nicht nur, wie etwas gemacht wird, sondern auch, warum es auf diese Weise gemacht wird.
- Q17: Alle Schritte im Tutorial haben genau so funktioniert, wie beschrieben.
- Q18: Benötigte Voraussetzungen für das Tutorial werden zu Beginn des Tutorials erklärt.
- Q19: as Tutorial ist leicht zu verfolgen.
- Q20: Die im Tutorial gegebenen Beispiele sind praxisrelevant.
- Q21: Das Tutorial deckt alle Funktionen ab, die mich interessieren.
- Q22: Das Tempo des Tutorials ist angemessen.

References

1. Beaudry, A., Pinsonneault, A.: Understanding user responses to information technology: a coping model of user adaptation. MIS Q. 493–524 (2005)
2. Brill, J., Park, Y.: Evaluating online tutorials for university faculty, staff, and students: the contribution of just-in-time online resources to learning and performance. Int. J. E-Learn. **10**(1), 5–26 (2011)
3. Cattell, R.B.: The scree test for the number of factors. Multivar. Behav. Res. **1**(2), 245–276 (1966)
4. Comrey, A.L., Lee, H.B.: A First Course in Factor Analysis. Psychology Press (2013)
5. Cronbach, L.J.: Coefficient alpha and the internal structure of tests. Psychometrika **16**(3), 297–334 (1951)
6. Guttman, L.: Some necessary conditions for common-factor analysis. Psychometrika **19**(2), 149–161 (1954)
7. Hassenzahl, M., Burmester, M., Koller, F.: AttrakDiff: Ein Fragebogen zur Messung wahrgenommener hedonischer und pragmatischer Qualität. Mensch & Computer 2003: Interaktion in Bewegung, pp. 187–196 (2003)
8. Head, A., Jiang, J., Smith, J., Hearst, M.A., Hartmann, B.: Composing flexibly-organized step-by-step tutorials from linked source code, snippets, and outputs. In: Proceedings of the 2020 CHI Conference on Human Factors in Computing Systems, pp. 1–12 (2020)
9. Hotelling, H.: Analysis of a complex of statistical variables into principal components. J. Educ. Psychol. **24**(6), 417–441 (1933)
10. Hsieh, C.: Implementing self-service technology to gain competitive advantages. Commun. IIMA **5**(1), 77–83 (2005)
11. Husseniy, N., Abdellatif, T., Nakhil, R.: Improving the websites user experience (UX) through the human-centered design approach (an analytical study targeting universities websites in Egypt). J. Des. Sci. Appl. Arts **2**(2), 24–31 (2021)
12. Jolliffe, I.T., Cadima, J.: Principal component analysis: a review and recent developments. Philos. Trans. Roy. Soc. A Math. Phys. Eng. Sci. **374**(2065) (2016)
13. Kim, A.S., Ko, A.J.: A pedagogical analysis of online coding tutorials. In: Proceedings of the 2017 ACM SIGCSE Technical Symposium on Computer Science Education, pp. 321–326 (2017)

14. Kirakowski, J., Corbett, M.: The software usability measurement inventory. Br. J. Edu. Technol. **24**(3), 210–212 (1993)
15. Lamontagne, C., Sénécal, S., Fredette, M., Labonté-LeMoyne, E., Léger, P.M.: The effect of the segmentation of video tutorials on User's training experience and performance. Comput. Hum. Behav. Rep. **3** (2021)
16. Laubheimer, P.: Onboarding Tutorials vs. Contextual Help. https://www.nngroupcom/articles/onboarding-tutorials/. Accessed 9 Apr 2024
17. Laugwitz, B., Held, T., Schrepp, M.: Construction and evaluation of a user experience questionnaire. In: HCI and Usability for Education and Work: 4th Symposium of the Workgroup Human-Computer Interaction and Usability Engineering of the Austrian Computer Society, USAB 2008, Graz, Austria, November 20-21 (2008)
18. Mautone, P.D., Mayer, R.E.: Signaling as a cognitive guide in multimedia learning. J. Educ. Psychol. **93**(2), 377–389 (2001)
19. Mayer, R.E.: The Cambridge Handbook of Multimedia Learning. Cambridge University Press (2005)
20. Van der Meij, H., van der Meij, J.: Eight guidelines for the design of instructional videos for software training. Tech. Commun. **60**, 205–228 (2013)
21. Mirhosseini, S., Parnin, C.: Docable: evaluating the executability of software tutorials. In: Proceedings of the 28th ACM Joint Meeting on European Software Engineering Conference and Symposium on the Foundations of Software Engineering, pp. 375–385 (2020)
22. Moshagen, M., Thielsch, M.: Facets of visual aesthetics. Int. J. Hum. Comput. Stud. **68**(10), 689–709 (2010)
23. Nielsen, J.: Usability 101: Introduction to Usability. https://www.nngroup.com/articles/usability-101-introduction-to-usability/. Accessed 9 Apr 2024
24. Nunnally, J.C.: Psychometric Theory, 2nd edn. McGraw-Hill (1978)
25. Pearson, K.: On lines and planes of closest fit to systems of points in space. London Edinburgh Dublin Philos. Mag. J. Sci. **2**(11), 559–572 (1901)
26. Santoso, H.B., Schrepp, M.: The impact of culture and product on the subjective importance of user experience aspects. Helion **5** (2019)
27. Schrepp, M., Thomaschewski, J.: Design and validation of a framework for the creation of user experience questionnaires. Int. J. Interact. Multimedia Artif. Intell. **5**(7), 88–95 (2019)
28. Schrepp, M.: On the usage of Cronbach's Alpha to measure reliability of UX scales. J. Usability Stud. **15**(4) (2020)
29. Schrepp, M.: User Experience Questionnaires: How to use questionnaires to measure the user experience of your products? KDP ISBN-13: 979-8736459766 (2021)
30. Schrepp, M., Santoso, H.B.: Construction of a questionnaire to measure the learner experience in online tutorials. In Proceedings of the 20th International Conference on Web Information Systems and Technologies, pp. 315–322 (2024)
31. Schrepp, M.: Designing and analyzing questionnaires and surveys. In: User Experience Methods and Tools in Human-Computer Interaction, pp. 121–169. CRC Press (2024)
32. Spanjers, I., Wouters, P., Van Gog, T., Van Merrienboer, J.: An expertise reversal effect of segmentation in learning from animated worked-out examples. Comput. Hum. Behav. **27**(1), 46–52 (2011)
33. Venkatesh, V., Morris, M., Davis, G.B., Davis, F.D.: User acceptance of information technology: toward a unified view. MIS Q. 425–478 (2003)
34. Zhiyong, X., Jiani, W., Lijun, J.: How game tutorials in mobile online games affect user adoption. In: 2021 10th International Conference on Educational and Information Technology (ICEIT), pp. 264–268 (2021)

EEG-Based Engagement Prediction in e-Learning Environments Using Machine Learning Techniques

Elias Dritsas, Maria Trigka, and Phivos Mylonas(✉)

Department of Informatics and Computer Engineering, University of West Attica, Aigaleo, Greece
{idritsas,mtrigka,mylonasf}@uniwa.gr

Abstract. Accurately assessing learner engagement in e-learning environments is crucial for enhancing educational outcomes and optimizing personalized learning experiences. This study presents a machine learning (ML) framework for electroencephalogram (EEG)–based engagement prediction, leveraging multichannel EEG recordings to capture cognitive responses during learning sessions. A well-defined methodology was implemented, including EEG signals preprocessing, feature extraction based on Power Spectral Density (PSD), and three techniques for feature ranking and selection to identify the most relevant neural features for engagement classification. By evaluating several ML models, including Logistic Regression (LR), Support Vector Machines (SVM), Random Forest (RF), Gradient Boosting Machines (GBM), Neural Networks (NNs), Convolutional NNs (CNNs), and Hybrid Ensemble approach, we demonstrate that feature selection significantly enhances classification performance. The Hybrid Ensemble model achieved the highest accuracy (92.7%) and the area under the ROC curve (AUC) (95.1%) when trained on a highly refined set of 14 features, improving interpretability while reducing computational complexity. The selected features, primarily from temporal, occipital, and parietal EEG channels, align with established neural mechanisms underlying memory processing, sensory integration, and attentional regulation. The results reinforce the potential of EEG-based analytics for real-time engagement monitoring, supporting adaptive e-learning systems that personalize content based on cognitive states.

Keywords: E-learning · EEG · Machine learning · Classification

1 Introduction

The advent of e-learning has significantly transformed the educational landscape, offering unprecedented opportunities for flexible and accessible learning experiences. However, this paradigm shift has brought about new challenges, especially in maintaining learner concentration on a task. Engagement is a critical factor in educational success, influencing both the retention of information and the overall learning experience. Traditional methods of assessing engagement, such as questionnaires, self-reports and behavioural observations, are often subjective and prone to biases. They constitute a

M. Marchiori et al. (Eds.): WEBIST 2024, LNBIP 583, pp. 360–383, 2026.
https://doi.org/10.1007/978-3-032-25534-1_17

simple method to collect initial information about a subject, but the acquired model about the learner's profile isn't dynamically updated/adapted using feedback from the objects in the interaction environment. Consequently, there is a growing interest in leveraging objective physiological measures to gain deeper insights into learner engagement [15,21].

In Human-Computer Interaction (HCI), there has been a rising tendency to design systems able to detect internal physiological changes, process the acquired raw data, and recognize and respond to users' cognitive states. The term "cognitive state" indicates the human cognitive processes and resources such as perception, attention, cognitive effort, engagement, working memory, arousal, stress and fatigue. A major goal in interaction design is to decrease the cognitive load for users [13]. In recent years, the scientific community has been increasing their efforts for the joint application of advanced signal processing, machine/deep learning (DL) and cognitive computing techniques to develop reliable systems predicting human cognition status [16].

In this context, EEG, a neuroimaging technique that records human brain activity, has emerged as a promising tool. EEG can provide real-time knowledge of cognitive and emotional states by capturing brainwave patterns across different frequency bands. These patterns can indicate various cognitive and mental states [20,32], including attention, relaxation, and cognitive load, which are all relevant to engagement in learning activities. By analyzing EEG data, researchers can obtain a more accurate and dynamic understanding of how learners interact with online materials [6,36].

Recent advancements in EEG technology combined with ML have significantly improved the interpretation of cognitive and physiological states. EEG signals have been effectively utilized in diverse areas, such as eye-state classification for clinical diagnostics, neuroscience research, and brain-computer interfaces (BCIs). Additionally, ML techniques like ensemble algorithms, often coupled with class imbalance handling methods such as Synthetic Minority Over-sampling Technique (SMOTE), have consistently improved the accuracy and robustness of EEG-based models [33,34].

In educational contexts, EEG-based ML methods offer promising approaches to accurately detect and enhance learner engagement, leveraging adaptive learning and immersive technologies, including Augmented Reality and Virtual Reality. However, practical implementation poses challenges such as addressing the digital divide, ensuring data privacy, and creating scalable, equitable solutions. Consequently, robust methodological frameworks are required to maximize the educational benefits of EEG analytics in adaptive e-learning environments [9,35].

Engagement is a fundamental factor in e-learning, directly impacting learning retention, comprehension, and overall academic performance. EEG-based engagement prediction offers a more objective and responsive approach by capturing neural activity associated with cognitive states during learning. However, effectively leveraging EEG data requires advanced preprocessing, feature selection, and ML techniques to enhance accuracy while minimizing computational complexity.

At this point, it should be noted that the current study represents an extended version of [10] detailing and further enhancing the methodology and findings presented in the original study. More specifically, the key contributions of this work are four-fold:

- A structured methodology consisting of EEG signals collection, preprocessing, feature extraction and selection, and ML models training and testing for engagement classification.
- Feature extraction was performed through power spectrum analysis, focusing on specific frequency bands, including alpha, low and high beta, theta, and gamma.
- Estimated Pearson Correlation Coefficients (CCs), Information Gain (IG), and Gain Ratio (GR) to identify the most relevant EEG features, improving classification accuracy and interpretability.
- Evaluated multiple ML models (LR, SVM, RF, GBM, NN, CNN, and Hybrid Ensemble), demonstrating that feature selection enhances predictive performance.

The rest of this paper is organized as follows. Section 2 presents related works for the subject under consideration. In Sect. 3, the methodological framework for EEG-based engagement prediction is outlined, while Sect. 4 provides data analysis. Next, Sect. 5 offers a performance evaluation of the engagement models. Finally, Sect. 6, summarizes the findings of this study.

2 Related Works

Capturing attention in educational settings has seen significant advancements with the application of EEG-based BCI systems [31]. Numerous studies have explored various computational methods and classification approaches to effectively monitor and enhance student engagement in both traditional and e-learning environments.

Firstly, in [23], a novel approach was presented for real-time emotion classification leveraging EEG data streams. The proposed system called the "Real-time Emotion Classification System" (RECS), employed LR and trained online with the Stochastic Gradient Descent (SGD) algorithm. The research used the DEAP dataset for validation, demonstrating that RECS could classify emotional states more effectively in real-time compared to existing offline and online classifiers, including Hoeffding Tree (HT), Adaptive RF (ARF), and others. The system was designed for practical applications, particularly in e-learning environments, where real-time emotional feedback can enhance learning. The authors in [32] introduced an ML methodology by comparing various classifiers trained and tested on EEG data, specifically focusing on band power, attention, and mediation features collected by the MindSet device. The goal was to effectively differentiate between "Confused" and "Not-Confused" individuals. Notably, the J48 model emerged as the most effective, achieving optimal performance with accuracy, precision, and recall rates of 99.9%, and an AUC of 1.

Moreover, [4] proposed a BCI system to enhance the quality of distance education by using EEG signals to detect students' attention during online classes. The study extracted PSD features from a public dataset and calculated various attention indexes using the fast Fourier transform (FFT). K-nearest neighbours (KNN), SVM, and RF models were employed to assess their performance in recognizing students' attentive states. The results showed that the RF classifier achieved the highest accuracy of 96%, indicating its effectiveness in distinguishing attention states in online learning environments.

In [27], a novel solution that employed real-time EEG data collected from individuals wearing EEG headsets during online courses was presented. This method focuses on a CNN model, which efficiently classifies these EEG signals with an accuracy rate of 70%. The performance highlighted the speed of processing and accuracy of the developed models, offering a promising solution to current e-learning validation challenges. Research work [26] introduced DL model to address the limitations of existing ones in ML, which rely on manual feature extraction and training with limited data. Real-time e-learning data was gathered from students wearing EEG headsets during online classes. This approach overcame the challenges associated with traditional ML models and historical data. The proposed CNN model classified students into different grade levels, aiding in the creation of an automated system to monitor student learning progress and provide recommendations to enhance e-learning course materials.

Also, [8] presented a novel approach utilizing Probability-Based Features (PBF) derived from RF and GBM models to enhance the performance of ML classifiers for detecting confusion in students during online learning sessions. The study evaluated various classifiers, including RF, GBM, LR, SVC, and Extra Trees Classifier (ETC), achieving an accuracy, precision, recall, and f1-score of 100%, with the proposed PBF approach. Additionally, the approach was validated using a separate EEG dataset, demonstrating superior performance compared to existing methodologies. The best-performing model numerically was the proposed PBF using RF and GBM features, achieving consistent top scores across all evaluation metrics. Moreover, [29] proposes an e-learning system that enhances learning by adapting content based on users' emotional states detected through EEG signals. Using the Neurosky Brainwave detector and the RF classification method, the study demonstrates how brainwave analysis can predict learners' attention levels and trigger personalized content adjustments. The system provides alerts for low concentration and recommends suitable videos, ultimately aiming to improve knowledge retention and engagement.

Finally, [2] evaluated learners' attention levels in MOOC (Massive Open Online Courses) environments and compared them with traditional classroom settings using brain signals. The proposed approach involved capturing EEG frequency bands from various subjects during short lectures in both e-learning and classroom environments. An SVM model was employed to classify students' mental states as either attentive or non-attentive. Additionally, [18] develops a classification system based on EEG signals to detect mental effort in MOOCs. Using different normalization techniques and supervised learning algorithms, the study shows that EEG data can be processed effectively to classify cognitive load levels with high accuracy, precision, and recall. This approach facilitates self-awareness of mental effort among learners and enables automated feedback mechanisms to enhance learning experiences in online education.

Unlike previous studies summarized in Table 1 that primarily relied on either raw EEG signals or spectral features, the present work integrates both spatial (electrode-based) and spectral (PSD) features, ensuring a comprehensive representation of engagement-related neural activity. In contrast to approaches that employ large, unfiltered feature sets, our study applies a rigorous feature selection process using Pearson CCs, IG, and GR, refining the feature space to retain only the most relevant 14 features. This targeted selection not only enhances interpretability but also improves classification accuracy and computational efficiency. Additionally, while prior research has often focused on individual ML models, this work conducts an extensive comparative evaluation of various classifiers, including LR, SVM, RF, GBM, Neural NNs, CNN, and a Hybrid Ensemble model, demonstrating that feature selection improves predictive performance across all models. Furthermore, our findings align with established neuroscientific evidence by emphasizing engagement-related cortical regions, particularly in the temporal, occipital, and frontal lobes, reinforcing the validity of EEG-based engagement monitoring. By systematically optimizing feature selection and evaluating model performance, this study advances the field by providing a structured, scalable, and interpretable framework for EEG-based engagement prediction in e-learning environments.

Table 1. Summary of EEG-Based Learning Related Works.

Ref.	Objective	Method	Best Performance
[23]	Real-time emotion classification using EEG	LR, DEAP dataset validation	Accuracy = 99.9%, AUC=1
[32]	Distinguish 'Confused' vs. 'Not-Confused' using EEG features	J48 Decision Tree model, EEG band power features	Accuracy = 99.9%, AUC=1
[4]	Detect attention in distance learning using EEG	KNN, SVM, RF applied to EEG spectral features	RF achieved highest accuracy of 96%
[27]	Use CNN for EEG classification in e-learning	CNN for EEG signals	CNN classification accuracy = 70%
[26]	DL model to classify student engagement	DL-based classification of engagement levels	CNN model effectively classified student levels
[8]	Enhance ML classifiers for confusion detection in students	RF, GBM, LR, SVC, ETC	Accuracy = 100% using PBF with RF and GBM
[29]	Adapt learning content using EEG-based emotion detection	Neurosky Brainwave detector with RF	Personalized attention tracking using EEG
[2]	Analyze learner attention in MOOCs vs. classrooms	SVM for EEG frequency bands	SVM effectively classified attentive vs. non-attentive states
[18]	Detect cognitive load and mental effort in MOOCs	Supervised learning algorithms with normalization techniques	High accuracy in detecting cognitive load levels

3 Methodological Framework for EEG-Based Engagement Prediction

The EEG-based learner engagement prediction framework follows a structured, multi-stage approach designed to capture, process, and analyze neural responses during e-learning sessions. EEG data are initially collected using wearable EEG devices in controlled learning environments, allowing for real-time monitoring of cognitive activity while learners engage with digital educational content.

To ensure signal integrity, the raw EEG recordings undergo rigorous preprocessing, including noise reduction, artifact removal, and normalization, thereby mitigating inter-individual variability. Subsequently, a comprehensive feature extraction process is applied to derive meaningful characteristics that serve as additional indicators of learner engagement. The methodological framework consists of five key stages

- **Data Acquisition and Preprocessing** – Capturing EEG signals and ensuring data quality through filtering, artifact removal, and normalization.

- **Feature Extraction** – Computing spectral features (besides raw data) to quantify engagement levels.
- **Feature Selection and Dimensionality Reduction** – Identifying the most relevant features while reducing complexity and improving computational efficiency.
- **Classification** – Applying advanced ML models, including DL architectures, to predict engagement state.
- **Evaluation** – Assessing model performance using stratified cross-validation and statistical metrics to ensure robustness and reliability.

Figure 1 illustrates the EEG-based data acquisition framework using the EMOTIV Epoc-X headset, detailing the entire processing pipeline, from raw EEG signal collection to engagement classification. The figure highlights the placement of the 14 EEG electrodes strategically positioned to capture cognitive, sensory, and motor-related brain activity. It also outlines the sequential data processing steps, including noise filtering, artifact removal, and normalization, followed by feature extraction and selection to refine the most informative EEG characteristics. The extracted features serve as inputs for ML models, enabling the classification of learner engagement [37]. The structured approach depicted in Fig. 1 ensures a robust methodology for interpreting cognitive states in e-learning environments while maintaining data reliability and model accuracy.

3.1 Data Acquisition

The EEG data acquisition process employs the EMOTIV Epoc-X [7], a high-resolution, wireless 14-channel EEG headset designed for real-time cognitive monitoring in controlled e-learning environments. This non-invasive device captures neural activity, providing valuable insights into learner engagement, cognitive workload, and attentional focus.

Following the 10–20 international electrode placement system, the Emotiv Epoc-X ensures comprehensive brain region coverage. The frontal electrodes (AF3, AF4, F3, F4, F7, F8) monitor cognitive processing and attention regulation, while T7 and T8, positioned over the temporal lobes, capture activity related to memory formation and language comprehension. Electrodes in the parietal region (P7, P8) track spatial processing and sensory integration, whereas O1 and O2, located in the occipital lobe, record visual perception and processing. Additionally, FC5 and FC6, near the prefrontal cortex, play a key role in executive functions, motor planning, and decision-making. The letters in the electrode names indicate the lobe locations: F (frontal), P (parietal), T (temporal), O (occipital), and C (central). Odd numbers correspond to the right hemisphere, and even numbers correspond to the left hemisphere.

Table 2 outlines the functional significance of each EEG channel, detailing the specific brain activity recorded and its corresponding brain region. The precise placement of these electrodes facilitates a comprehensive assessment of learner engagement, allowing for targeted analysis of cognitive states, attentional fluctuations, and neural responses during e-learning sessions [30].

The EEG signals are recorded at a sampling rate of 128 Hz with a 16-bit resolution, ensuring high temporal precision suitable for cognitive state analysis. Bluetooth

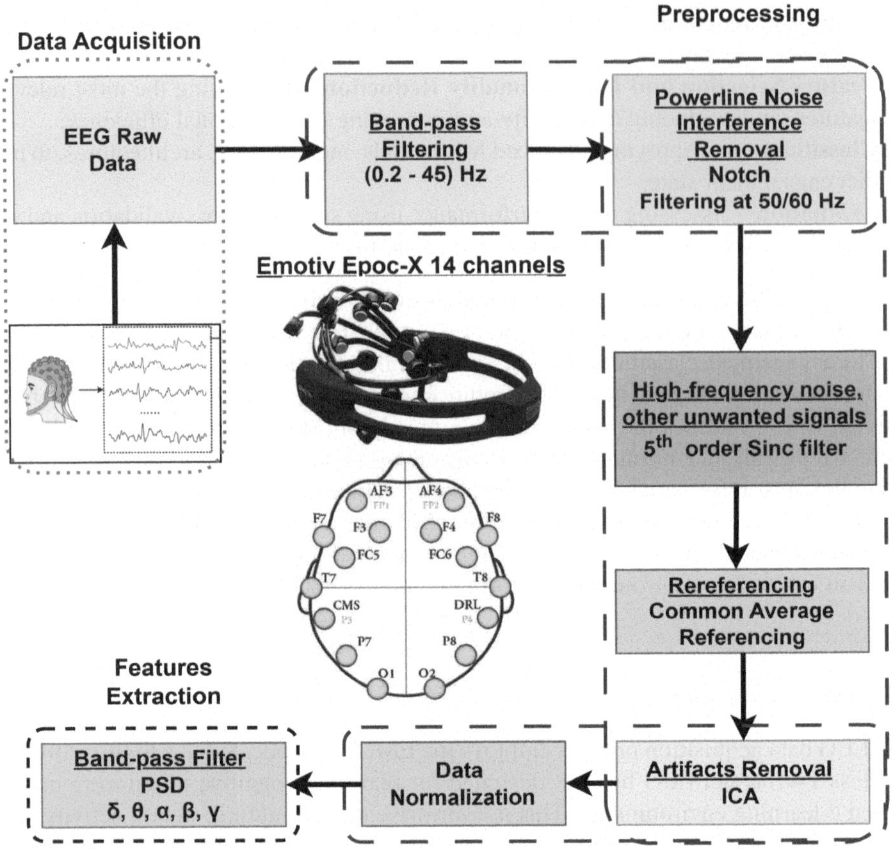

Fig. 1. EEG-based processing pipeline in multi-channel Emotiv Epoc-X device [10].

low-energy connectivity facilitates seamless data transmission, enabling real-time monitoring without restricting participant mobility. The hydrophilic polymer sensors use a saline-based gel, ensuring optimal impedance levels for high-quality signal acquisition while maintaining participant comfort. A built-in signal quality indicator continuously monitors electrode connectivity, ensuring data reliability throughout the recording session.

During e-learning sessions, EEG signals are continuously recorded while participants engage with digital learning materials. The data collection process is synchronized with instructional content, capturing fluctuations in cognitive engagement levels as learners interact with the educational material. After data recording, engagement levels are annotated using self-reported questionnaires and behavioral markers, enabling the creation of labeled datasets for training predictive models.

In the following paragraphs, we will focus on the collected signals preprocessing (noise removal), feature extraction, and selection to enhance interpretability before being used for ML-based engagement prediction.

Table 2. Description of EEG Channels in Emotiv Epoc-X.

Channel	Activity Captured	Brain Lobe/Region
AF3	Attention, executive functions, working memory	Frontal Cortex (Left)
AF4	Attention, executive functions, working memory	Frontal Cortex (Right)
F3	Logical processing, decision making, cognitive workload	Frontal Lobe (Left)
F4	Logical processing, decision making, cognitive workload	Frontal Lobe (Right)
F7	Verbal expression, language processing, analytical tasks	Frontal/Temporal Lobe (Left)
F8	Emotional expression, social interaction, creative tasks	Frontal/Temporal Lobe (Right)
FC5	Verbal fluency, speech production, cognitive control	Frontal/Central Region (Left)
FC6	Emotional regulation, attentional control	Frontal/Central Region (Right)
T7	Auditory processing, language comprehension, memory retrieval	Temporal Lobe (Left)
T8	Auditory processing, emotional memory, sensory integration	Temporal Lobe (Right)
P7	Visual-spatial processing, object recognition	Parietal/Occipital Lobe (Left)
P8	Visual-spatial processing, facial and emotional recognition	Parietal/Occipital Lobe (Right)
O1	Primary visual processing, visual perception	Occipital Lobe (Left)
O2	Primary visual processing, visual perception	Occipital Lobe (Right)

3.2 Preprocessing

Effective preprocessing of EEG data is crucial for ensuring accurate and reliable analysis. Raw EEG signals often contain noise and artifacts that obscure the underlying neural activity associated with engagement. To address these challenges, a multi-step preprocessing pipeline is employed to enhance signal quality and optimize the data for ML analysis.

The Emotiv Epoc-X incorporates dedicated digital filtering mechanisms to preprocess raw EEG signals. Band-pass filtering is first applied to retain frequencies between 0.2 and 45 Hz, which encompass the key spectral components relevant to cognitive and emotional state analysis. This step effectively removes low-frequency drifts and high-frequency noise, preserving only the frequencies that contribute to engagement detection. Additionally, the device integrates built-in digital notch filters at 50 Hz and 60 Hz, eliminating power line interference that could otherwise distort the signal and impact the accuracy of PSD calculations. In EEG-based ML models, unwanted power line noise could introduce false correlations in feature selection. Hence, notch filtering ensures that only meaningful neural activity is used for engagement prediction. A 5th-order Sinc filter is also utilized, providing a sharp cutoff to suppress high-frequency noise and aliasing artifacts, further refining the EEG data for analysis.

Independent Component Analysis (ICA) is applied to remove physiological artifacts, isolating and eliminating noise sources such as eye blinks, muscle movements (EMG), and cardiac activity (ECG), thereby preserving the integrity of engagement-related neural signals. Following artifact removal, Z-score normalization is performed on each EEG channel to reduce inter-subject variability and prevent features with larger magnitudes from dominating the learning process. This transformation standardizes the data to have a zero mean and unit variance, ensuring that extracted features remain comparable across participants and improving the robustness of ML models. The Z-score normalization is computed as

$$X' = \frac{X - \mu}{\sigma}, \tag{1}$$

where X represents the original feature value, μ is the mean of the feature, and σ is its standard deviation. This transformation enhances model stability and improves the effectiveness of ML algorithms in engagement classification.

By implementing this structured preprocessing approach, the EEG data are effectively denoised, standardized, and optimized for subsequent feature extraction and classification, ensuring a reliable foundation for engagement prediction [11].

3.3 Feature Extraction

Following normalization, band-pass filtering was applied to isolate relevant frequency components of the EEG signals, ensuring accurate estimation of PSD. The PSD serves as the primary feature extraction method, quantifying the distribution of signal power across different frequency bands. These bands are closely linked to cognitive processes, including attention, relaxation, and cognitive load, making them essential for engagement assessment.

The PSD was computed using the Fast Fourier Transformation (FFT), which decomposes the EEG signal into its constituent frequencies. The PSD at frequency f is estimated as

$$PSD(f) = \frac{1}{N} \sum_{n=1}^{N} |X(n,f)|^2, \tag{2}$$

where $X(n, f)$ represents the Discrete Fourier Transform (DFT) of the EEG signal at frequency f, and N is the total number of frequency components. This method provides a spectral representation of neural activity, enabling the identification of engagement-related patterns in different frequency bands.

By analyzing the PSD across established EEG frequency bands, including θ (4–8 Hz), α (8–12 Hz), low β (13–20 Hz), high β (20–30 Hz), γ (30–45 Hz), meaningful neural signatures associated with cognitive engagement are extracted. These spectral features serve as inputs for subsequent classification, forming the basis of EEG-based engagement prediction [3].

3.4 Feature Ranking and Selection

To enhance model interpretability and reduce computational complexity, feature selection is applied using three key ranking methods: Pearson CCs, IG, and GR. These techniques identify the most relevant EEG features for engagement prediction by assessing their relationship with the target variable.

Pearson CCs. measures the linear relationship between feature X and target variable Y. It is computed as

$$r_{X,Y} = \frac{\sum_{i=1}^{N}(X_i - \bar{X})(Y_i - \bar{Y})}{\sqrt{\sum_{i=1}^{N}(X_i - \bar{X})^2}\sqrt{\sum_{i=1}^{N}(Y_i - \bar{Y})^2}}, \tag{3}$$

where $\bar{X}$ and $\bar{Y}$ are the mean values of feature X and Y, respectively, and N is the number of samples. X_i, Y_i are the values of two specific features for the i-th sample in the dataset. A higher absolute correlation value ($|r_{X,Y}|$) indicates a stronger linear dependency between the feature and engagement level [38].

IG. evaluates the reduction in uncertainty about the target variable Y when knowing a feature X. It is defined as

$$IG(X) = H(Y) - H(Y|X), \tag{4}$$

where $H(Y)$ is the entropy of Y, given by $H(Y) = -\sum_{i=1}^{2} P(Y_i)\log_2 P(Y_i)$ and $H(Y|X) = -\sum_{j=1}^{m} P(X_j)\sum_{i=1}^{2} P(Y_i|X_j)\log_2 P(Y_i|X_j)$ is the conditional entropy with $P(Y_i)$ being the probability of class Y_i, and $P(Y_i|X_j)$ is the conditional probability of Y_i given feature value X_j. A higher IG value indicates a more informative feature [24].

GR. is an extension of IG that normalizes the feature importance by considering its intrinsic entropy, thereby mitigating bias toward attributes with many unique values. It is given by

$$GR(X) = \frac{IG(X)}{H(X)}, \tag{5}$$

where $H(X) = -\sum_{j=1}^{m} P(X_j)\log_2 P(X_j)$ is the intrinsic entropy of feature X. A higher GR indicates a feature that provides high discriminative power while maintaining generalization.

After ranking the EEG features using the three aforementioned methods, the most informative subset is selected based on their scores. Features exhibiting strong correlation, high IG, or a high GR are retained for classification. This ensures that the feature set maximally contributes to engagement prediction while reducing redundancy and improving model efficiency [17].

3.5 Machine Learning Models

We assume a training set consisting of M EEG data instances and a test set comprising N instances, each labelled with a categorical variable Y, representing learner engagement. Under the defined problem, this class variable is binary taking two possible values: Y = "Engaged" (denoted as "1") or Y = "Not Engaged" (denoted as "0"). Each EEG instance i is represented by a feature vector $f_i = (f_{i1}, f_{i2}, \ldots, f_{iF})$ of size F, containing multiple extracted features capturing distinct EEG signal characteristics relevant to cognitive states.

Subsequently, the selected EEG features serve as inputs for training classical and advanced supervised ML models. The selection of appropriate ML models is critical to successfully predicting e-learning engagement using EEG data. This study investigated several ML models with distinct strengths and capabilities, to determine the most effective approach for this task. The models evaluated include LR, SVM, RF, GBM, NNs, CNN, and a hybrid ensemble model.

The primary goal is to achieve high predictive accuracy and reliability, specifically emphasizing recall or sensitivity (correct identification of engaged learners) and the AUC, to ensure accurate (real-time) identification of learner engagement. All models are rigorously validated using stratified k-fold cross-validation, which preserves class proportions in training and testing datasets, ensuring representative evaluation, robust predictive generalization, and minimized selection bias. The following analysis provides a detailed description of each model and the rationale behind their selection.

LR [19] model is based on the logistic function (a special case of sigmoid function), which maps any real-valued number to a value between 0 and 1. This function is particularly useful for binary classification tasks. The LR equation can be expressed as follows: $P(y = 1 \mid X) = \sigma(z) = \frac{1}{1+e^{-z}}$, where $P(y = 1 \mid X)$ is the probability that the output y is 1 (engaged) given the input features X. Also, z is defined as $z = \beta_0 + \beta_1 X_1 + \beta_2 X_2 + \ldots + \beta_n X_n$, where $\sigma(z)$ is the logistic function, $(\beta_0, \beta_1, \beta_2, \ldots, \beta_n)$ are the coefficients of the model and $(X_1, X_2, \ldots, X_n)$ are the input features. Putting it all together, the LR model can be written as $P(y = 1 \mid X) = \frac{1}{1+e^{-(\beta_0+\beta_1 X_1+\beta_2 X_2+\ldots+\beta_n X_n)}}$. This equation calculates the probability that the input X belongs to class 1 "engaged". The predicted class label can be determined by applying a threshold (typically 0.5) to this probability.

SVM [28] with a radial basis function (RBF) kernel, mainly aims to find the optimal hyperplane that separates the classes with the maximum margin. The mathematical formulation involves solving a quadratic optimization problem. The decision function for SVM is given by: $f(X) = \text{sign}\left(\sum_{i=1}^{n} \alpha_i y_i K(X_i, X) + b\right)$, where α_i are the Lagrange multipliers, y_i are the class labels, $K(X_i, X)$ is the kernel function and b is the bias term.

Our focus here is on the RBF kernel whose function K is defined as: $K(X_i, X) = \exp\left(-\gamma \|X_i - X\|^2\right)$, where γ is a parameter that determines the spread of the kernel. Summarizing these together, the decision function with the RBF kernel is $f(X) = \text{sign}\left(\sum_{i=1}^{n} \alpha_i y_i \exp\left(-\gamma \|X_i - X\|^2\right) + b\right)$.

RF [12] is an ensemble learning method that combines multiple decision trees to improve the robustness and generalizability of the model. The overall prediction of the RF model is obtained by aggregating the predictions of individual trees, often by taking the mode (majority vote) in classification tasks. Here's the mathematical formulation for RFs:

1. **Individual Decision Tree Prediction**-Let $h_m(X)$ be the prediction of the m-th decision tree in the forest for input X.
2. **RF Prediction**-The final prediction $H(X)$ of the RF is obtained by taking the majority vote of all M trees' predictions:

$$H(X) = \text{mode}\{h_1(X), h_2(X), \ldots, h_M(X)\}$$

GBM [5] is an ensemble learning technique that builds models sequentially, with each new model correcting errors made by the previous ones. The goal is to optimize the overall prediction by minimizing the loss function. Here's the mathematical formulation for GBMs:

1. **Model Initialization** $F_0(X) = \arg\min_\gamma \sum_{i=1}^{n} L(y_i, \gamma)$, where L is the loss function, and y_i are the actual target values.
2. **Additive Model**-The model is built in a stage-wise manner. At each stage m, a new model $h_m(X)$ is added to minimize the loss: $F_m(X) = F_{m-1}(X) + \eta h_m(X)$, where η is the learning rate, and $h_m(X)$ is the new model fitted to the residuals of the previous model.
3. **Residual Calculation** - For each stage m, compute the residuals $r_{im} = -\frac{\partial L(y_i, F(X_i))}{\partial F(X_i)}\Big|_{F(X_i)=F_{m-1}(X_i)}$
4. **Fit New Model** $h_m(X)$ to the residuals:

$$h_m(X) = \arg\min_h \sum_{i=1}^{n} (r_{im} - h(X_i))^2$$

5. **Update the Model** with the new fitted model $F_m(X) = F_{m-1}(X) + \eta h_m(X)$.

NNs [14] are DL models that use multiple layers of neurons to capture intricate patterns in data. In a feedforward neural network, the data flows from the input layer through multiple hidden layers to the output layer. Each neuron computes a weighted sum of its inputs, applies an activation function, and passes the result to the next layer. The training process involves backpropagation to adjust the weights. The mathematical formulation for a feedforward neural network is as follows:

1. **Weighted Sum and Activation for a Single Neuron**-For each neuron in layer l, the output $a_i^{(l)}$ is computed as: $z_i^{(l)} = \sum_{j=1}^{n^{(l-1)}} w_{ij}^{(l)} a_j^{(l-1)} + b_i^{(l)}, a_i^{(l)} = \sigma(z_i^{(l)})$, where $z_i^{(l)}$ is the weighted sum of inputs to the i-th neuron in layer l, $w_{ij}^{(l)}$ are the weights from neuron j in layer $l-1$ to neuron i in layer l, $b_i^{(l)}$ is the bias term for the i-th neuron in layer l, σ is the activation function (e.g., ReLU, sigmoid, tanh), and $a_j^{(l-1)}$ is the activation of the j-th neuron in the previous layer.
2. **Output Layer**, the process is similar: $z_k^{(L)} = \sum_{j=1}^{n^{(L-1)}} w_{jk}^{(L)} a_j^{(L-1)} + b_k^{(L)}, \hat{y}_k = \sigma(z_k^{(L)})$, where L is the final layer, and $\hat{y}_k$ is the predicted output.
3. **Loss Function** L measures the difference between the predicted outputs $\hat{y}$ and the true targets y. For example, using Mean Squared Error (MSE) $L = \frac{1}{N}\sum_{i=1}^{N}(y_i - \hat{y}_i)^2$, where N is the number of training examples.
4. **Backpropagation:** During this step, gradients of the loss with respect to the weights and biases are computed and used to update the parameters. For weights $w_{ij}^{(l)}$: $w_{ij}^{(l)} \leftarrow w_{ij}^{(l)} - \eta \frac{\partial L}{\partial w_{ij}^{(l)}}$, where η is the learning rate.

CNNs [25] are DL architectures particularly effective at modeling data that exhibit spatial-temporal relationships. EEG signals inherently contain both spatial information (due to electrode positions) and temporal dynamics (signal variations over time), making CNNs highly suitable for EEG-based predictive tasks. In this study, EEG data were reshaped into spatial-temporal feature maps, enabling convolutional filters to learn discriminative patterns related to learner engagement. Each convolutional layer applied multiple filters (kernels) across EEG signals, capturing localized spatial-temporal features indicative of engagement. Convolution operations are mathematically represented as

$$X_{conv}^{(l)} = \sigma\left(\text{conv}(X^{(l-1)}, W^{(l)}) + b^{(l)}\right),$$

where $X^{(l-1)}$ denotes the input from the previous layer, $W^{(l)}$ represents convolutional kernel weights, $b^{(l)}$ is the bias vector, and σ is the Rectified Linear Unit (ReLU) activation function. Following convolutional layers, pooling layers reduced feature-map dimensionality and computational complexity by summarizing feature representations. Extracted features were then flattened and passed to dense layers, culminating in a sigmoid activation function for binary classification

$$\hat{y} = \sigma\left(\sum_{i=1}^{m} w_i a_i + b\right).$$

The CNN was trained using the Adam optimizer to minimize binary cross-entropy loss, ensuring efficient convergence and robust predictive accuracy.

Hybrid Ensemble Model combines multiple individual classifiers to enhance predictive accuracy by leveraging the strengths of diverse modeling approaches. In this research, the hybrid ensemble integrates three powerful algorithms: GBM, RF, and NNs, combined through stacking. In this stacking approach, each base model independently predicts probabilities of learner engagement. These predictions serve as inputs—meta-features—for a LR meta-classifier, which makes the final prediction. Mathematically, the base-model predictions $P_{GBM}(X)$, $P_{RF}(X)$, and $P_{NN}(X)$ are combined into a final prediction given by the LR meta-model:

$$\hat{y}_{ensemble} = \sigma\left(\beta_0 + \beta_1 P_{GBM}(X) + \beta_2 P_{RF}(X) + \beta_3 P_{NN}(X)\right).$$

The GBM model contributes iterative error minimization, the RF model adds robustness through ensemble-based decision-making, and the NN captures complex nonlinear EEG data patterns.

3.6 Evaluation Metrics

Several metrics were used to evaluate the performance of the ML models, accuracy, precision, recall, F1-score, and AUC [22]. These metrics provide insights into models' performance, ensuring a robust assessment of their predictive capabilities. It should be noted that the ultimate value in each metric was derived by averaging the outcomes of both classes from all folds. The definition of these metrics is based on the confusion matrix consisting of the elements true-positive (Tp), true-negative (Tn), false-positive (Fp) and false-negative (Fn). Below is a brief description of each metric:

- **Accuracy** is the proportion of correctly predicted instances out of the total instances. It is a straightforward metric indicating the overall correctness of the model. Accuracy $= \frac{\text{Tp+Tn}}{\text{Total Instances}}$.

- **Precision** is the ratio of correctly predicted positive observations to the total predicted positives. It reflects the accuracy of the positive predictions made by the model. Precision $= \frac{\text{Tp}}{\text{Tp}+\text{Fp}}$.
- **Recall** is the ratio of correctly predicted positive observations to all the observations in the actual class. It measures the model's ability to capture all relevant instances. Recall $= \frac{\text{Tp}}{\text{Tp}+\text{Fn}}$.
- **F1-score** is the harmonic mean of Precision and Recall. It provides a single metric that balances the trade-off between Precision and Recall, especially useful when the class distribution is imbalanced: F1-Score $= 2 \times \frac{\text{Precision} \times \text{Recall}}{\text{Precision}+\text{Recall}}$.
- **AUC** measures the ability of the model to distinguish between classes. It represents the degree of separability achieved by the model. An AUC of 1 indicates a perfect model, while an AUC of 0.5 suggests no discriminative power.

These metrics provided a comprehensive view of the model performance, enabling the identification of the most effective model for predicting e-learning engagement based on EEG data.

4 Data Analysis

The dataset used in this study comprised EEG recordings collected from participants engaged in an e-learning activity. More specifically, 8 students, with varying levels of education (High school, Middle school, Undergraduate) were invited to watch 11 online video lectures (e.g., Quantum Physics, Statistics, String Theory, Photosynthesis, Linear Algebra, Biology, Numbers and Operations, Computational Geometry, Mythology). During these lectures, the students' EEG brain waves were recorded using the Emotiv Epoc X 14-channel headset, a multi-channel EEG system.

The dataset contained preprocessed data from the channels AF3, F7, F3, FC5, T7, P7, O1, O2, P8, T8, FC6, F4, F8, and AF4, as shown in Fig. 1. The target class captures whether a student understood the lecture or not. In total, the dataset consists of 85 features, 54370 samples in class "Engaged" and 14461 samples in class "Not-Engaged".

4.1 Statistical Measures

An exploratory data analysis was conducted to gain a deeper understanding of the dataset. Figure 2 summarizes, across all participants, the statistical measures of PSD, namely, mean, minimum, maximum and standard deviation values across different frequency bands per engagement class, allowing for easy comparison.

In the following, such an analysis is presented.

1. **Theta band:** In the engaged group, theta activity remains relatively low, indicating efficient cognitive processing with minimal unnecessary effort. Conversely, the non-engaged group exhibits elevated theta activity, which may suggest increased cognitive effort without effective comprehension, potentially reflecting mind-wandering or cognitive overload.

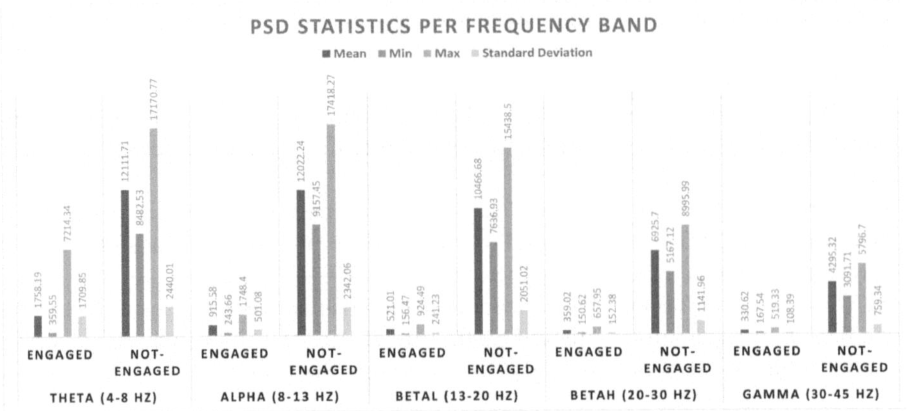

Fig. 2. Statistics of PSD per frequency band and engagement state [10].

2. **Alpha band:** Engaged learners demonstrate lower alpha activity, which aligns with focused attention and active information processing. In contrast, the non-engaged group shows higher alpha power, often associated with inattentiveness or relaxation, suggesting that these individuals may be disengaged from the learning process.
3. **Low Beta band:** Engaged learners display moderate beta activity, which corresponds to active cognitive engagement and problem-solving. However, the non-engaged group shows excessively high beta activity, indicating cognitive effort without effective learning, possibly reflecting stress or inefficient cognitive strategies.
4. **High Beta band:** The engaged group maintains consistent high beta activity, which is typically linked to sustained focus and cognitive effort. In contrast, the non-engaged group exhibits greater fluctuations, suggesting unstable concentration and inefficient mental resource allocation.
5. **Gamma band:** Gamma activity is associated with information processing and integration. In the engaged group, gamma levels are regulated, reflecting effective learning and comprehension. However, in the non-engaged group, gamma activity is elevated but inconsistent, suggesting that while some information is being processed, it may not be meaningfully integrated into learning.

The engaged group exhibits stable, well-regulated EEG activity, corresponding to focused attention, efficient cognitive processing, and active learning. Meanwhile, the non-engaged group demonstrates excessive but unstable neural activity, indicating cognitive effort without effective comprehension, potentially due to mind-wandering, stress, or disengagement. These findings highlight the importance of monitoring EEG patterns to understand better and enhance learner engagement in educational settings.

4.2 Feature Ranking and Selection

Figure 3 presents the Pearson correlation heatmap for EEG-based learner engagement features. The heatmap visually represents the CCs between different EEG channels recorded during e-learning sessions, illustrating the degree of linear relationship between each pair of features. Darker red colors indicate a stronger positive correlation, whereas cooler colors (closer to light blue) signify weaker or negative correlations. Key observations highlight that AF3 exhibits the strongest overall associations with other channels, reinforcing its role in attention regulation and cognitive workload processing in the prefrontal cortex. Additionally, the correlation between the "Class" variable (learner engagement) and EEG features reveals that T8, O1, P8, T7 and O2 have the highest correlations, indicating their importance in engagement classification. In contrast, AF4 and FC6 show weak or slightly negative correlations, suggesting they may contribute less significantly to engagement prediction. These findings underscore the importance of selecting relevant EEG features for improving model accuracy while minimizing redundant or weakly related signals.

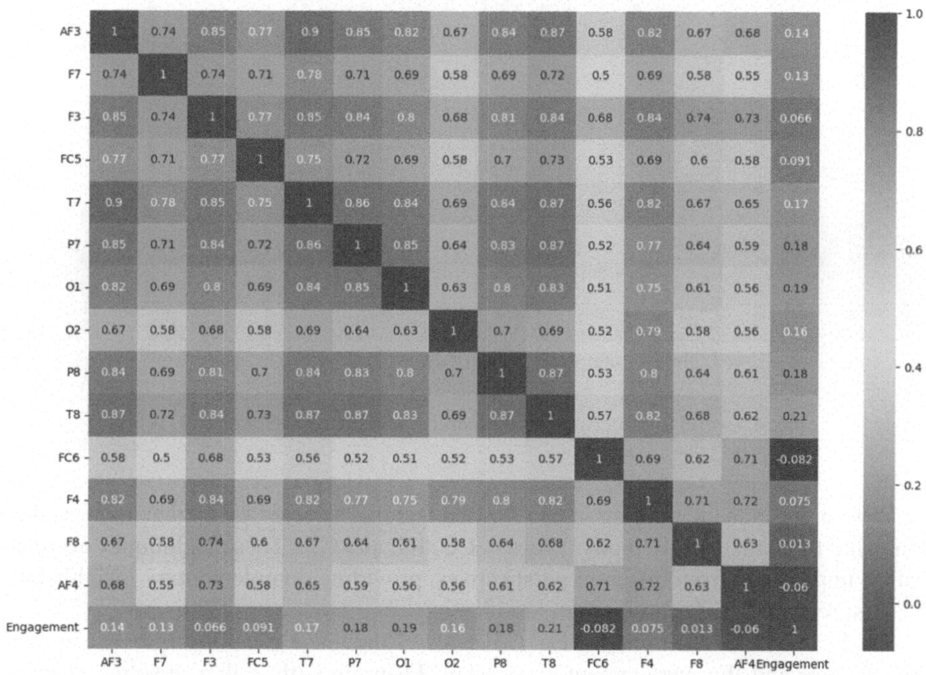

Fig. 3. Pearson Correlation Matrix among the 14 EEG Channels.

Additionally, Fig. 4 depicts the correlation between PSD-based features including engagement class (engaged, non-engaged) using a heatmap. This visualization helps identify which frequency bands are most closely associated with the engagement class.

It was observed that power-based features are highly linearly dependent on one another, but according to the Pearson CCs in the blue area of the heatmap, their importance in improving the predictive performance of the ML models is low. Hence, further and extensive analysis should be conducted to understand the features' importance and apply proper selection techniques to indicate the most important ones that raise the model's performance while reducing complexity.

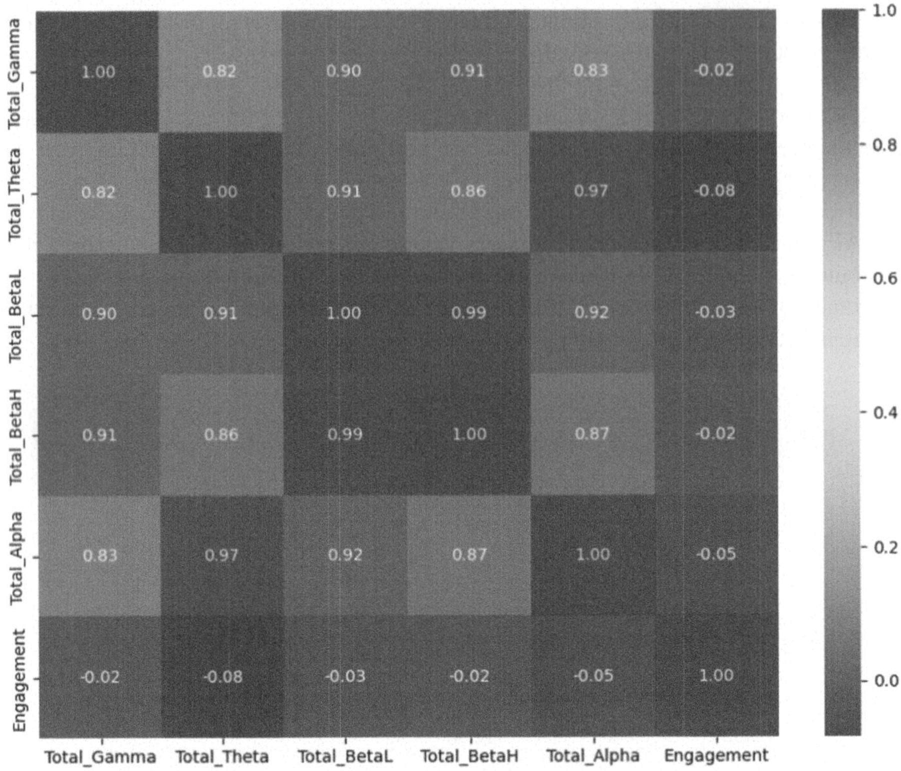

Fig. 4. Correlation between PSD features and engagement class [10].

Table 3 presents the ranking of EEG-based features selected for engagement prediction using three distinct methods: Pearson CC, IG, and GR. These techniques evaluate feature importance from different perspectives, providing complementary insights into the most relevant EEG features for classification.

The Pearson CC, as defined in Eq. (3), assesses the linear relationship between each EEG feature and the engagement class label. Features with higher absolute correlation values indicate stronger associations with engagement levels. Notably, EEG.T8, EEG.O1, and EEG.P8 exhibit the highest correlation values, suggesting that neural activity in the temporal and occipital regions plays a significant role in engagement prediction.

In contrast, IG, computed using Eq. (4), quantifies the reduction in uncertainty about the engagement state when a given feature is known. Features with higher IG scores provide more discriminative information for classification. The rankings in Table 3 highlight EEG.T7, EEG.O1, and EEG.T8 as the most informative raw EEG channels, while power spectral features such as POW.F7.Theta and POW.FC5.Theta also achieve high scores, indicating that spectral characteristics contribute meaningfully to engagement differentiation.

The GR, derived from Eq. (5), refines IG by normalizing it with the intrinsic entropy of each feature, reducing bias toward attributes with a high number of unique values. The rankings in Table 3 demonstrate that spectral features such as POW.F7.Theta, POW.F7.Alpha, and POW.FC5.Theta outperform some raw EEG signals, reinforcing the relevance of frequency-based features in engagement classification.

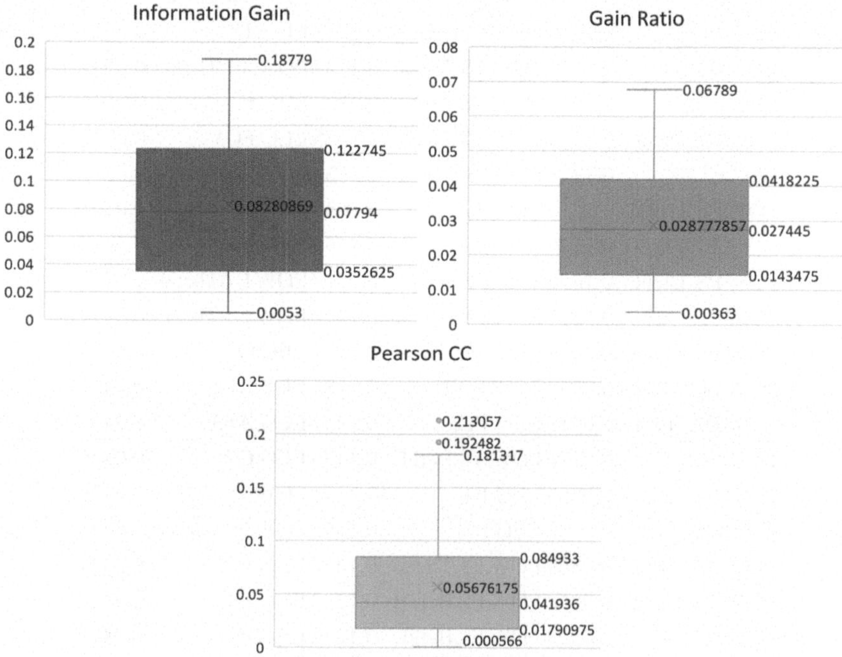

Fig. 5. Statistics for 3 feature selection techniques assuming the whole (84) feature set.

The statistics of the ranking scores are captured in Fig. 5, providing an overview of the distribution of feature importance across the three feature selection techniques: Pearson CC, IG, and GR. This visualization offers insight into the variability in feature relevance depending on the selection criteria. While Table 3 presents a subset of the most relevant features, Fig. 5 ensures a comprehensive representation of the entire feature set, allowing for a comparative evaluation of ranking consistency and the influence of specific EEG channels and spectral power components. This combined approach justifies the selection of the final reduced feature set by demonstrating the statistical patterns in feature importance, ensuring that only the most discriminative and informative features are retained for engagement classification.

Feature selection was performed to enhance model interpretability and improve classification performance by reducing redundancy while retaining the most informative EEG features for engagement prediction. The selection process integrated Pearson CC, IG, and GR as ranking criteria. Features were chosen based on their consistently

Table 3. Feature Importance based on the score estimated by Pearson CCs, IG and GR.

Feature	CC	Feature	IG	Feature	GR
EEG.T8	0.2131	EEG.T7	0.1878	POW.F7.Theta	0.0679
EEG.O1	0.1925	EEG.O1	0.1808	POW.F7.Alpha	0.0615
EEG.P8	0.1813	EEG.T8	0.1794	POW.FC5.Theta	0.0614
EEG.P7	0.1799	POW.F7.Theta	0.1761	POW.T8.Theta	0.0578
EEG.T7	0.1670	POW.FC5.Theta	0.1733	EEG.T8	0.0554
EEG.O2	0.1575	POW.T8.Theta	0.1733	POW.T7.Theta	0.0542
EEG.AF3	0.1395	POW.T8.Alpha	0.1728	EEG.F3	0.0536
POW.F7.Theta	0.1293	POW.T7.Theta	0.1645	EEG.FC5	0.0527
EEG.F7	0.1278	EEG.F3	0.1634	POW.T8.Alpha	0.0516
POW.F8.Theta	0.1230	EEG.P8	0.1634	EEG.P8	0.0503
POW.T7.Theta	0.1136	EEG.O2	0.1550	EEG.T7	0.0484
POW.P8.Theta	0.1095	EEG.P7	0.1512	POW.P7.Theta	0.0479
POW.F3.Theta	0.1087	POW.F8.Alpha	0.1497	POW.F3.Theta	0.0479
POW.F8.Alpha	0.1083	EEG.AF3	0.1491	EEG.O1	0.0478
POW.FC5.Theta	0.0958	POW.P7.Theta	0.1481	EEG.AF4	0.0471
POW.P7.Theta	0.0911	EEG.FC5	0.1451	EEG.AF3	0.0467
EEG.FC5	0.0910	POW.T8.BetaL	0.1430	EEG.O2	0.0458
POW.F4.Theta	0.0906	EEG.F4	0.1411	POW.T8.BetaL	0.0436
POW.O2.Theta	0.0882	EEG.F7	0.1353	POW.F8.Alpha	0.0433
POW.AF3.Theta	0.0869	POW.F3.Theta	0.1312	EEG.FC6	0.0431
POW.T8.Theta	0.0858	POW.F8.BetaH	0.1232	EEG.F4	0.0419
EEG.FC6	0.0822	POW.F8.BetaL	0.1213	EEG.P7	0.0417
POW.F3.Alpha	0.0794	POW.O2.Theta	0.1162	POW.F4.Theta	0.0413

high rankings across these methods, ensuring a balance between raw EEG electrode signals and spectral PSD features.

The final selection of 14 features was made by prioritizing attributes that contributed unique and non-redundant information while discarding those with overlapping or low-importance scores. This approach ensures that the retained features effectively capture engagement-related brain activity without excessive dimensionality, which could introduce noise and reduce model efficiency. The selected features include EEG.O1, EEG.T8, EEG.T7, EEG.AF3, EEG.FC5, EEG.F7, EEG.F4, POW.FC5.Theta, POW.P8.Theta, POW.F3.Alpha, POW.F4 .Theta, POW.O2.Theta, POW.AF3.Theta, and POW.T8.Theta. These features provide a comprehensive representation of frontal, temporal, and occipital lobe activity, as well as frequency-specific engagement markers, ensuring an optimal trade-off between performance and interpretability.

5 Performance Evaluation of Engagement Models

The ML models' evaluation was carried out using WEKA [1], a free software suite offering a range of tools for data preprocessing, classification, regression, clustering, and visualization. The experiments were executed on an Apple MacBook Pro with a 13.3" Retina Display, equipped with an M2 chip, 16 GB of RAM, and a 256 GB SSD.

Each model was trained on the preprocessed EEG dataset using a stratified 10-fold cross-validation to ensure robust performance evaluation. Hyperparameter tuning was performed using grid search to identify the optimal parameter settings for each model as shown in Table 4.

Table 4. Optimal Hyperparameter Tuning for ML Models.

Traditional ML Models		
Model	**Hyperparameter**	**Optimal Value**
LR	Regularization (C)	1.0
SVM	Kernel Type	RBF
	Kernel Coefficient (γ)	0.01
	Regularization (C)	10
RF	Number of Trees	100
	Maximum Depth	None (unlimited)
	Minimum Samples Split	2
GBM	Number of Estimators	200
	Learning Rate	0.1
	Maximum Depth	3
NN	Number of Layers	3
	Neurons per Layer	[64, 128, 64]
	Activation Function	ReLU
	Learning Rate	0.001
	Batch Size	32
	Epochs	150

DL and Hybrid Models		
Model	**Hyperparameter**	**Optimal Value**
CNN	Convolutional Layers	3
	Kernels per Layer	[32, 64, 128]
	Pooling Method	MaxPooling
	Fully Connected Layers	[128, 64]
	Activation Function	ReLU
	Optimizer	Adam
	Learning Rate	0.001
	Batch Size	32
	Epochs	150
Hybrid Ensemble	Base Learners	GBM, RF, NN
	GBM Estimators	200
	RF Estimators	100
	NN Layers	[64, 128, 64]
	Meta-classifier	LR (C = 1.0)

The performance results, presented in Table 5, highlight the impact of feature selection on EEG-based engagement prediction. Our methodology follows two distinct approaches: i) leveraging the full feature set and ii) incorporating feature selection (as analyzed in Sect. 4.2). Feature selection plays a crucial role in EEG-based engagement prediction by reducing feature space dimensionality, and enhancing model interpretability and classification performance. The selected features in this study include EEG.T8, EEG.O1, EEG.P8, EEG.T7, EEG.AF3, EEG.FC5, EEG.F7, EEG.F4, POW.FC5.Theta, POW.P8.Theta, POW.F3 .Alpha, POW.F4.Theta, POW.O2.Theta, and POW.AF3.Theta, and align with neuroscientific findings and prior research in EEG-based engagement prediction for e-learning. It has been consistently shown that engagement-related cognitive activity is reflected in distinct cortical regions and frequency bands, particularly those associated with attention, memory, sensory integration, and cognitive load regulation.

The temporal and occipital electrodes (e.g., EEG.T8, EEG.O1, EEG.P8) correspond to memory retrieval and visual processing functions, which are fundamental to learning engagement. Also, right temporal lobe activation (EEG.T8) has been linked to active listening and information retention, indicating its strong association with engagement intensity in auditory learning tasks. Similarly, occipital electrodes (EEG.O1, O2) play a critical role in visual attention and cognitive load regulation, particularly in multimedia-based learning environments, where visual engagement determines comprehension and retention.

Additionally, the parietal electrode P8, selected as a key feature, is supported by studies highlighting its role in sensorimotor integration and attentional control. Sustained engagement in e-learning has been shown to correlate with increased parietal cortex activation, reflecting cognitive processing, attentional shifts, and sensory integration. The inclusion of POW.F7.Theta and POW.FC5.Theta reinforces the neuroscientific basis of engagement prediction, as theta power in frontal and fronto-central regions has been associated with working memory load, sustained attention, and cognitive focus.

The impact of feature selection on model performance is evident in the results. By retaining only the most relevant features, classification models exhibited higher accuracy, precision, recall, and AUC scores compared to models trained on all features. The Hybrid Ensemble model, integrating GBMs, RF, and NN, achieved the highest performance, with an accuracy of 92.7% and an AUC of 95.1% when trained on the selected 14 features. This finding suggests that eliminating less informative features not only reduces computational complexity but also enhances model generalization. Similarly, the CNN model, leveraging spatial and temporal dependencies in EEG signals, demonstrated superior classification performance with feature selection, indicating that a refined feature set improves DL models' ability to capture engagement-related patterns.

These findings are consistent with prior EEG-based engagement prediction studies, which emphasize that targeted feature selection eliminates redundant data while preserving only the most discriminative neural signatures of engagement. Research in EEG-driven learning analytics has demonstrated that optimized feature sets, particularly those based on PSD and spatial cortical activations, contribute to higher classification accuracy and model efficiency. The feature selection methodology applied in this study ensures that models are not overwhelmed by noise or irrelevant variability, thereby improving the robustness, interpretability, and reliability of engagement prediction.

The results also reinforce the scientific validity of EEG-based engagement classification in e-learning. By aligning feature selection outcomes with established neurophysiological evidence, this study underscores the importance of strategic feature selection in optimizing engagement prediction models for real-world applications.

Table 5. Performance Comparison of Models with All Features vs. Selected Features.

Model	All Features (84)					Selected Features (14)				
	Accuracy	Precision	Recall	F1-Score	AUC	Accuracy	Precision	Recall	F1-Score	AUC
LR	78.0%	75.0%	76.0%	75.5%	80.0%	79.1%	76.5%	77.3%	76.9%	81.5%
SVM	82.0%	80.0%	81.0%	80.5%	84.0%	83.2%	81.5%	82.3%	81.9%	85.7%
RF	85.0%	83.0%	84.0%	83.5%	87.0%	86.1%	84.5%	85.2%	84.8%	88.6%
GBM	87.0%	85.0%	86.0%	85.5%	89.0%	88.0%	86.4%	87.1%	86.8%	90.5%
NN	90.0%	88.0%	89.0%	88.5%	92.0%	91.2%	89.8%	90.5%	90.1%	93.0%
CNN	89.0%	87.5%	88.2%	87.8%	91.5%	90.3%	89.0%	89.7%	89.3%	92.8%
Hybrid Ensemble	91.5%	90.2%	91.0%	90.5%	93.7%	92.7%	91.5%	92.0%	91.8%	95.1%

6 Conclusions

This study explored EEG-based engagement prediction in e-learning environments using ML models. By leveraging EEG signals recorded from learners during online educational sessions, we developed a robust framework for feature extraction, selection, and classification to assess engagement levels. The results demonstrated that integrating feature selection techniques significantly enhances model interpretability and performance by reducing redundancy and preserving the most informative neural features.

The evaluation of multiple ML-based engagement models, including traditional classifiers (LR, SVM, RF, GBM, Hybrid Ensemble) and DL architectures (NNs and CNNs), revealed that feature selection leads to improved classification performance. The Hybrid Ensemble model achieved the highest accuracy (92.7%) and AUC (95.1%) when trained on the selected 14 features, demonstrating the effectiveness of a refined feature set in optimizing engagement prediction. Furthermore, the CNN model, designed to capture spatial and temporal dependencies in EEG signals, also exhibited strong performance, reinforcing the importance of DL approaches in EEG-based learning analytics.

The selected features related to EEG channels T7, T8, O1, P8, AF3, FC5, F4, F7, the PSD of F4, AF3, FC5, P8, and O2 at θ band, and the PSD of F3 at α band, align with neuroscientific evidence linking engagement-related cognitive processes to specific cortical regions and frequency bands. The temporal, occipital, and parietal electrodes capture critical aspects of memory retrieval, sensory integration, and attentional focus, while spectral power features provide insights into cognitive load and sustained attention.

By systematically refining the EEG feature space, this study highlights the advantages of targeted feature selection in improving computational efficiency while maintaining high classification accuracy. Our findings support the broader adoption of EEG-based engagement monitoring systems in adaptive e-learning environments, enabling real-time adjustments to instructional content based on learners' cognitive states.

Future research should explore the integration of real-time EEG-based adaptive learning systems that dynamically adjust content delivery based on engagement levels. Additionally, expanding the study with a larger and more diverse participant pool would further validate the generalizability of the proposed approach. The intersection of EEG analytics and ML holds immense potential for revolutionizing personalized e-learning by providing objective, data-driven insights into learner engagement, ultimately enhancing educational outcomes.

References

1. Weka. https://www.weka.io/. Accessed 17 July 2024
2. Aggarwal, S., Lamba, M., Verma, K., Khuttan, S., Gautam, H.: A preliminary investigation for assessing attention levels for massive online open courses learning environment using EEG signals: an experimental study. Hum. Behav. Emerg. Technol. **3**(5), 933–941 (2021)
3. Al-Fahoum, A.S., Al-Fraihat, A.A.: Methods of EEG signal features extraction using linear analysis in frequency and time-frequency domains. Int. Sch. Res. Not. **2014**(1), 730218 (2014)

4. Al-Nafjan, A., Aldayel, M.: Predict students' attention in online learning using EEG data. Sustainability **14**(11), 6553 (2022)
5. Ayyadevara, V.K., Ayyadevara, V.K.: Gradient boosting machine. In: Pro Machine Learning Algorithms: A Hands-On Approach to Implementing Algorithms in Python and R, pp. 117–134 (2018)
6. Chrysanthakopoulou, A., Dritsas, E., Trigka, M., Mylonas, P.: An EEG-based application for real-time mental state recognition in adaptive e-learning environment. In: 2023 18th International Workshop on Semantic and Social Media Adaptation & Personalization (SMAP) 18th International Workshop on Semantic and Social Media Adaptation & Personalization (SMAP 2023), pp. 1–6. IEEE (2023)
7. Dadebayev, D., Goh, W.W., Tan, E.X.: EEG-based emotion recognition: review of commercial EEG devices and machine learning techniques. J. King Saud Univ.-Comput. Inf. Sci. **34**(7), 4385–4401 (2022)
8. Daghriri, T., Rustam, F., Aljedaani, W., Bashiri, A.H., Ashraf, I.: Electroencephalogram signals for detecting confused students in online education platforms with probability-based features. Electronics **11**(18), 2855 (2022)
9. Dritsas, E., Trigka, M.: Methodological and technological advancements in e-learning. Information **16**(1), 56 (2025)
10. Dritsas, E., Trigka, M., Mylonas, P.: Application of machine learning models to predict e-learning engagement using EEG data. In: Proceedings of the 20th International Conference on Web Information Systems and Technologies - Volume 1: WEBIST, pp. 323–330. INSTICC, SciTePress (2024). https://doi.org/10.5220/0013016000003825
11. Fei, N., Gao, Y., Lu, Z., Xiang, T.: Z-score normalization, hubness, and few-shot learning. In: Proceedings of the IEEE/CVF International Conference on Computer Vision, pp. 142–151 (2021)
12. Genuer, R., Poggi, J.M., Genuer, R., Poggi, J.M.: Random Forests. Springer (2020)
13. Gupta, J., Ahuja, M., Garg, N.: A review on human-computer interaction (HCI). In: 2022 2nd International Conference on Innovative Sustainable Computational Technologies (CISCT), pp. 1–6. IEEE (2022)
14. Gurney, K.: An Introduction to Neural Networks. CRC Press (2018)
15. Herbig, N., et al.: Investigating multi-modal measures for cognitive load detection in e-learning. In: Proceedings of the 28th ACM Conference on User Modeling, Adaptation and Personalization, pp. 88–97 (2020)
16. Kaluarachchi, T., Reis, A., Nanayakkara, S.: A review of recent deep learning approaches in human-centered machine learning. Sensors **21**(7), 2514 (2021)
17. Karegowda, A.G., Manjunath, A., Jayaram, M.: Comparative study of attribute selection using gain ratio and correlation based feature selection. Int. J. Inf. Technol. Knowl. Manag. **2**(2), 271–277 (2010)
18. Lin, F.R., Kao, C.M.: Mental effort detection using EEG data in e-learning contexts. Comput. Educ. **122**, 63–79 (2018)
19. Lu, W., Wang, Y.: Logistic regression. In: Textbook of Medical Statistics: For Medical Students, pp. 181–189. Springer (2024)
20. Maimaiti, B., et al.: An overview of EEG-based machine learning methods in seizure prediction and opportunities for neurologists in this field. Neuroscience **481**, 197–218 (2022)
21. Mejbri, N., Essalmi, F., Jemni, M., Alyoubi, B.A.: Trends in the use of affective computing in e-learning environments. Educ. Inf. Technol. 1–23 (2022)
22. Naidu, G., Zuva, T., Sibanda, E.M.: A review of evaluation metrics in machine learning algorithms. In: Computer Science On-line Conference, pp. 15–25. Springer (2023)
23. Nandi, A., Xhafa, F., Subirats, L., Fort, S.: Real-time emotion classification using EEG data stream in e-learning contexts. Sensors **21**(5), 1589 (2021)

24. Nelson, J.D.: Finding useful questions: on Bayesian diagnosticity, probability, impact, and information gain. Psychol. Rev. **112**(4), 979 (2005)
25. O'shea, K., Nash, R.: An introduction to convolutional neural networks. arXiv preprint arXiv:1511.08458 (2015)
26. Pathak, D., Kashyap, R.: Electroencephalogram-based deep learning framework for the proposed solution of e-learning challenges and limitations. Int. J. Intell. Inf. Database Syst. **15**(3), 295–310 (2022)
27. Pathak, D., Kashyap, R.: Evaluating e-learning engagement through EEG signal analysis with convolutional neural networks. In: International Conference on Computer & Communication Technologies, pp. 225–239. Springer (2023)
28. Pisner, D.A., Schnyer, D.M.: Support vector machine. In: Machine Learning, pp. 101–121. Elsevier (2020)
29. Tambe, N.R., Khachane, A.: Mood based e-learning using EEG. In: 2016 International Conference on Computing Communication Control and Automation (ICCUBEA), pp. 1–4. IEEE (2016)
30. Thwe, Y., Maneetham, D., Crisnapati, P.N.: Review of applications in wheelchair control using emotiv insight and emotiv epoc headsets. In: 2024 6th International Conference on Cybernetics and Intelligent System (ICORIS), pp. 1–6. IEEE (2024)
31. Trigka, M., Dritsas, E., Fidas, C.: A survey on signal processing methods for EEG-based brain computer interface systems. In: Proceedings of the 26th Pan-Hellenic Conference on Informatics, pp. 213–218 (2022)
32. Trigka, M., Dritsas, E., Mylonas, P.: Mental confusion prediction in e-learning contexts with EEG and machine learning. In: Novel & Intelligent Digital Systems Conferences, pp. 195–200. Springer (2023)
33. Trigka, M., Dritsas, E., Mylonas, P.: Driver sleepiness detection using machine learning models on EEG data. In: Proceedings of the 13th Hellenic Conference on Artificial Intelligence, pp. 1–4 (2024)
34. Trigka, M., Dritsas, E., Mylonas, P.: Eye state classification using ensemble machine learning models and smote on EEG data. In: 2024 9th South-East Europe Design Automation, Computer Engineering, Computer Networks and Social Media Conference (SEEDA-CECNSM), pp. 168–173. IEEE (2024)
35. Trigka, M., Dritsas, E., Mylonas, P.: New perspectives in e-learning: EEG-based modelling of human cognition individual differences. In: IFIP International Conference on Artificial Intelligence Applications and Innovations, pp. 290–299. Springer (2024)
36. Trigka, M., Papadoulis, G., Dritsas, E., Fidas, C.: Influences of cognitive styles on EEG-based activity: an empirical study on visual content comprehension. In: IFIP Conference on Human-Computer Interaction, pp. 496–500. Springer (2023)
37. Wong, A., Walishetti, A., Yang, Y.: Evaluating home-based EEG systems for public health telemonitoring: a scoping review. 2024 IEEE Healthcare Innovations and Point of Care Technologies (HI-POCT), pp. 5–8 (2024)
38. Xu, G., Wang, Z., Xu, T., Zhou, T., Hu, H.: Engagement recognition using a multi-domain feature extraction method based on correlation-based common spatial patterns. Appl. Sci. **13**(21), 11924 (2023)

Correction to: Using LLMs for Semi-automatic Handwritten Text Recognition and Elaboration

Angelica Lo Duca

Correction to: Chapter 9 in: M. Marchiori et al. (Eds.): *Web Information Systems and Technologies*, LNBIP 583, https://doi.org/10.1007/978-3-032-25534-1_9

The title of chapter 09 has been updated from "Using LLMs for Semi-automatic Handwritten Text Recognition and Elaborationns" to "Using LLMs for Semi-automatic Handwritten Text Recognition and Elaboration".

The updated version of this chapter can be found at https://doi.org/10.1007/978-3-032-25534-1_9

M. Marchiori et al. (Eds.): WEBIST 2024, LNBIP 583, p. C1, 2026.
https://doi.org/10.1007/978-3-032-25534-1_18

Author Index

M. Marchiori et al. (Eds.): WEBIST 2024, LNBIP 583, pp. 385–386, 2026.
https://doi.org/10.1007/978-3-032-25534-1